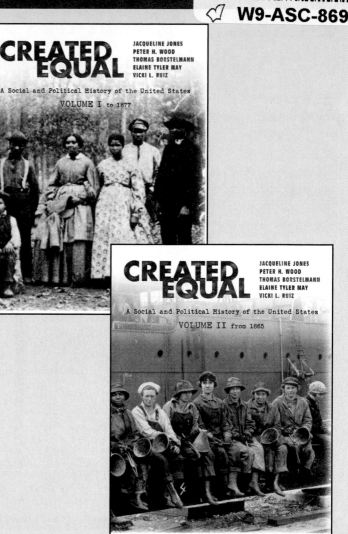

Jacqueline Jones, *Brandeis University*
Peter H. Wood, *Duke University*
Thomas Borstelmann, *Cornell University*
Elaine Tyler May, *University of Minnesota*
Vicki L. Ruiz, *University of California, Irvine*

With its sweeping inclusive view of American history, *Created Equal* emphasizes social history — including the lives and labors of women, immigrants, working people, and persons of color in all regions of the country — in the context of political and economic history. This new text from Longman Publishers acknowledges and reflects the diversity of class, race, culture, region, and gender that has always been part of the American story, and pays unique attention to the large middle class that has been central to the development of American society.

SVE • ©2003 • 1168 pages • Hardcover • ISBN 0-321-05296-X
Volume I • ©2003 • 656 pages • Paper • ISBN 0-321-05298-6
Volume II • ©2003 • 640 pages • Paper • ISBN 0-321-05300-1

Outstanding Features in *Created Equal*

▶ **Part Openers and Timelines.**
Part Openers preview the key issues and the political, cultural, ethnic, and regional diversity characteristic of the distinctive historical period covered in each three-chapter part. **Illustrated timelines** highlight significant events and trends and serve as a convenient preview/review for students. Each part covers approximately the era of a single generation of Americans.

1900	U.S. troops sent to China to crush Boxer Rebellion
1901	McKinley is assassinated; Vice President Theodore Roosevelt becomes President
1902	Newlands Act spurs dam building and irrigation in the Southwest
1903	First motorized flight by Orville and Wilbur Wright Henry Ford founds Ford Motor Company
1904	Roosevelt Corollary to the Monroe Doctrine
1905	Industrial Workers of the World founded Japan defeats Russia
1906	San Francisco Earthquake Sinclair Lewis, The Jungle Pure Food and Drug Act Indiana becomes first state to pass compulsory sterilization law
1907	"Gentlemen's Agreement" with Japan Oklahoma (former Indian Territory) becomes a state
1908	Muller v. Oregon upholds maximum hours for working women
1909	New York City garment workers' "Uprising of the 20,000" Peary/Henson Expedition reaches North Pole with four Greenland Inuit
1910	Mexican Revolution begins National Association for the Advancement of Colored People (NAACP) founded
1911	Triangle Shirtwaist fire, New York City Society of American Indians founded
1912	Theodore Roosevelt helps form Progressive Party
1913	Federal Reserve Act Sixteenth Amendment (federal personal

PART SEVEN

Reform at Home, Revolution Abroad, 1900-1929

MANY AMERICANS GREETED THE FIRST YEARS OF THE TWENTIETH century with optimism. Developments at home and abroad seemed to promise a new era of prosperity and progress. The mass manufacturing of automobiles proved a boon to the economy and transformed patterns of travel, leisure, and consumption. The beginning of commercial air flights heralded a revolution in communication and transportation. Moving pictures and new musical forms such as jazz delighted millions.

Focused on the new challenges of urbanization and industrialization, Progressive reformers sought to use science to solve a wide range of problems related to public health and welfare. Some advocated overhauling the system of public education; others pressed for legislation affecting the sale and distribution of alcohol. Some lobbied for worker health and safety legislation, while still others sought to exercise social control through eugenics and state-mandated sterilization.

A variety of social groups challenged white men's exclusive claim to civil rights. African Americans took the national stage to argue for equality under the law and for freedom from state-sanctioned violence in the form of lynching and debt peonage. Beginning with the "Great Migration" of World War I, southern blacks abandoned the southern cotton fields to seek jobs in northern cities.

The changing roles of women bolstered the women's suffrage movement. Growing numbers of women were becoming labor organizers, reformers, and college professors. Rising divorce rates and the emergence of birth control as a political as well as medical issue signaled challenges

---

CONNECTING HISTORY

Systems of Unfree Labor

The controversy over slavery ultimately precipitated the Civil War, the bloodiest conflict in the nation's history. Yet the abolition of slavery (with the ratification of the Thirteenth Amendment in 1865) did not eradicate forms of coerced labor. Indeed, systems of unfree labor—in which individuals are forced to work without compensation and for the benefit of someone else—have characterized the whole sweep of American history.

In the seventeenth century, most tobacco field workers in the Chesapeake region were indentured servants. These young men and women received passage from Europe to the colonies. In return, they bound themselves to a master for a stipulated amount of time (usually 7 years). Apprentices, children and young people, labored for a master artisan until they reached age 21.

Beginning in the late seventeenth century, the institution of slavery spread throughout the colonies. This system, which depended on the labor of Africans and their descendants, differed in crucial ways from indentured servitude and apprenticeship. Slaves remained slaves for life, and they had no rights under law. Children took the status of their enslaved mother.

States outside the South had emancipated their slaves by the mid-

Shackled inmates work to clear brush along a highway near Prattville, Alabama. A 1996 settlement prevented the state from shackling prisoners together on a "chain gang" but shackling of individual convict laborers was still permissible.

such as growing crops, spinning thread, weaving cloth, and producing handicrafts. In some cases, ship captains kidnapped sailors and forced them to work for no pay on long voyages. Indian and African American children remained at risk as labor-hungry whites forcibly "apprenticed" them with the aid of the courts.

By the late nineteenth century, peonage characterized the southern staple crop economy as well as the rural extractive sector (logging, sawmills, turpentine production, and

men) into the rough and dangerous work of building roads through swamps and digging coal out of the earth. Convict labor officials often demonstrated a reckless disregard for human life. Unlike slave owners, prison officials and the private individuals who leased convicts had few incentives to treat these workers in a humane way.

In the early twenty-first century, coerced labor persists. Some illegal immigrants continue to indenture themselves to smugglers and remain indebted to these smugglers for many

▶ **"Connecting History"** features demonstrate the relationship between the ways we experience and the ways we remember history. These short essays examine a specific topic related to the chapter content tracing it both forward and backward in time, showing students how the issues and concerns relevant to one period of American history reverberate in other eras.

Martin Luther King, Jr., and the Vietnam War

Most Americans approved of the war in Vietnam until at least 1968. Appreciative of Lyndon Johnson's commitment to reduce poverty and end racial discrimination at home, African Americans generally supported the president's policies in Southeast Asia. However, younger, more radical civil rights workers were among those who opposed the first insertion of U.S. combat troops in 1965. Within 2 years, the nation's most prominent black leader, Martin Luther King, Jr., decided that he could no longer keep quiet about his growing unease with the American war effort. A storm of criticism greeted his public denunciation of the war, most of it suggesting that he should limit himself to domestic civil rights work. But King no longer believed that events at home and abroad could be separated. The following excerpt is from his speech at Riverside Church, New York City, April 4, 1967:

A few years ago there was a shining moment in that struggle [against poverty and discrimination]. It seemed as if there was a real promise of hope for the poor—both black and white—through the Poverty Program. There were experiments, hopes, new beginnings. Then came the build-up in Vietnam and I watched the program broken and eviscerated as if it were some idle political plaything of a society gone mad on war. . . . I was increasingly compelled to see the war as an enemy of the poor and to attack it as such....

We were taking the black young men who had been crippled by our society and sending them 8,000 miles away to guarantee liberties in Southeast Asia which they had not found in Southwest Georgia and East Harlem. So we have been repeatedly faced with the cruel irony of watching Negro and white boys on TV screens as they kill and die together for a nation that has been unable to seat them together in the same schools....

As I have walked among the desperate, rejected and angry young men [in the ghettos of the North the last three summers] I have told them that Molotov cocktails and rifles would not solve their problems. I have tried to offer them my deepest compassion while maintaining my convictions that social change comes most meaningfully through non-violent action. But they asked—and rightly so—what about Vietnam? They asked if our own nation wasn't using massive doses of violence to solve its problems, to bring about the changes it wanted. Their questions hit home, and I knew that I would never again raise my voice against the violence of the oppressed in the ghettos without having first spoken clearly to the greatest purveyor of violence in the world today—my own government....

[Our troops in Vietnam] must know after a short period there that none of the things we claim to be fighting for [such as freedom, justice, and peace] are really involved. Before long they must know that their government has sent them into a struggle among Vietnamese, and the more sophisticated surely realize that we are on the side of the wealthy and the secure while we create a hell for the poor. ■

His birthday now a national holiday, Martin Luther King, Jr., has become widely accepted as a heroic figure in the American past. But in the last few years of his life, King's increasingly sharp criticisms of injustice in American society disturbed many fellow citizens.

"Interpreting History" features help students critically analyze source documents related to the issues discussed in each chapter. Providing students with the opportunity to "do history" on their own, these boxes encourage readers to examine primary documents in their socio-historical context to see how people — both famous and obscure — have reflected on and interpreted the historical developments of their time and their particular role in history.

Sites to Visit

Secession Era Editorial Project
history.furman.edu/~benson/docs/
Furman University is digitizing editorials about the secession crisis and already includes scores of them on this site.

John Brown trial links
www.law.umkc/edu/faculty/projecs/ftrials/Brown.html
For information about the John Brown trial, this site provides a list of excellent links.

Abraham Lincoln and Slavery
odur.let.nl/~usa/H/1990/ch5_p6.html
This site discusses Lincoln's views and actions concerning slavery, especially the Lincoln–Douglas debate.

The Compromise of 1850 and the Fugitive Slave Act
www.pbs.org/wgbh/aia/part4
From the series on Africans in America, an analysis of the Compromise of 1850 and the effect of the Fugitive Slave Act on black Americans.

The 1850s: An Increasingly Divided Union
nac.gmu/mmts/50proto.html
A tutorial skill development site of the Multi-Media Thinking Skills project that focuses on events in the 1850s leading to the Civil War.

Words and Deeds in American History
leweb2.loc.gov/ammem/mcchtml/corhome.html
A Library of Congress site containing links to Frederick Douglass; the Compromise of 1850; speeches by John C. Calhoun, Daniel Webster, and Henry Clay; and other topics from the Civil War era.

Harriet Beecher Stowe and Uncle Tom's Cabin
xroads.virginia.edu/~HYPER/STOWE/stowe.html
This site provides both text and descriptions of Stowe's important books and information about the author's life.

For Further Reading

General Works

Foner, Eric. *Free Labor, Free Soil, Free Men: The Ideology of the Republican Party Before the Civil War*. 1970.
Freehling, William W. *The Road to Disunion*. 1990.
Hine, Robert V. and John Mack Faragher. *The American West: A New Interpretive History*. 2000.
Horton, James Oliver and Lois E. Horton. *In Hope of Liberty: Culture, Community and Protest Among Northern Free Blacks, 1700–1860*. 1997.
Isenberg, Nancy. *Sex and Citizenship in Antebellum America*. 1998.

Regional Economies and Conflicts

Montejano, David. *Anglos and Mexicans in the Making of Texas, 1836–1986*. 1987.

Shifting Collective Identities

Almaguer, Tomás. *Racial Faultlines: The Historical Origins of White Supremacy in California*. 1994.
Anderson, Bonnie S. *Joyous Greetings: The First International Women's Movement, 1830–1860*. 2000.
Blewett, Mary H. *Men, Women, and Work: Class, Gender, and Protest in the New England Shoe Industry, 1780–1910*. 1988.
Chen, Yong. *Chinese San Francisco, 1850–1943: A Trans-Pacific Community*. 2000.
Levine, Frances. *Our Prayers Are in This Place: Pecos Pueblo Identity over the Centuries*. 1999.

"Sites to Visit" at the end of each chapter list both actual historical sites and Web sites with URLs relevant to the chapter content.

Supplements

For Qualified Adopters:

Instructor's Resource Manual

Yvonne Johnson, *Central Missouri State University* • Jason Tetzloff, *University of Wisconsin – Eau Claire*
0-321-10856-6

Each chapter contains a chapter outline, significant themes, learning objectives, lesson enrichment ideas, discussion suggestions, and questions for discussing the primary source document in the text.

Test Bank

D. Niler Pyeatt, *Wayland Baptist University*
0-321-10840-X

This supplement contains over 1200 multiple-choice, true/false, and essay questions. Multiple-choice and true-false questions are referenced by topic and text page number.

TestGen EQ Computerized Testing System

0-321-10736-5

This flexible, easy-to-master computerized test bank on a dual-platform CD includes all of the items in the printed test bank and allows instructors to select specific questions, edit existing questions and add their own items to create exams. Tests can be printed in several different fonts and formats and can include figures, such as graphs and tables.

Companion Website for Created Equal

Download the Instructor's Manual, maps and figures from the book, and the *Created Equal* PowerPoint™ Presentations
Website address: http://www.ablongman.com/jonescreatedequal

CourseCompass

www.ablongman.com/coursecompass

Combines the strength of the content from *Created Equal* with state-of-the-art eLearning tools. CourseCompass is an easy-to-use online course management system that allows professors to tailor content and functionality to meet individual course needs. Every CourseCompass course includes a range of pre-loaded content — all designed to help students master core course objectives. Organized by era, CourseCompass allows you to access maps, map exercises, and primary sources from several of our best-selling supplements. The course can also be quickly and easily customized to include the test questions from the printed test bank, interactive quizzes from the companion website, or other book specific resources.

BlackBoard and WebCT

The American history course in CourseCompass is also available in BlackBoard and WebCT.

Visual Aids:

Comprehensive American History Transparency Set

0-673-97211-9

This collection includes more than 200 four-color American history map transparencies on subjects ranging from the first Native Americans to the end of the Cold War, covering wars, social trends, elections, immigration, and demographics.

Discovering American History Through Maps and Views Transparency Set

0-673-53766-8

Created by Gerald Danzer, the recipient of AHA's James Harvey Robinson Prize for his work in using maps — including primary source maps — to teach American history, this set of 140 four-color acetates is a unique instructional tool. The collection includes cartographic and pictorial maps, views and photos, urban plans, building diagrams, and works of art.

Text-specific Transparency Set

0-321-10855-8

A set of four-color transparency acetates showing maps, graphs, and charts from the text selected to complement our other general American history transparencies sets.

For Students:

Multimedia Edition CD-ROM
0-321-11246-6

This electronic version of *Created Equal* contains the entire text with hundreds of images, maps, interactive maps, and audio/video clips integrated throughout. Electronic versions of the Study Guide and numerous supplementary books as well as links to interactive review quizzes for each chapter are also included. *Free when bundled.*

Study Guide
William Pelz, *Elgin Community College*
Volume I: 0-321-10838-8; Volume 2: 0-321-10839-6

This two-volume supplement for students contains activities and study aids for every chapter in the text. Each chapter includes a thorough summary; learning objectives; identification, completion, multiple-choice, and thought questions; and critical thinking questions based on primary source documents included in the text.

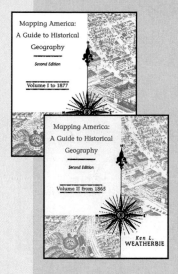

Companion Website for Created Equal

Popular features of the Website include interactive practice tests, summaries, flash cards, and web links for every chapter of the book. The site also includes a comprehensive glossary and an online appendix.
Website address: http://www.ablongman.com/jonescreatedequal

Mapping American History
Gerald A. Danzer
0-673-53768-4

A workbook created for use in conjunction with *Discovering American History Through Maps and Views* and designed to teach students to interpret and analyze cartographic materials as historical documents. *Free when bundled.*

Mapping America: A Guide to Historical Geography, 2/e
Ken L. Weatherbie, *Del Mar College*
Volume I: 0-321-00487-6; Volume II: 0-321-00488-4

A two-volume workbook that presents the basic geography of the United States and helps students place the history of the United States into spatial perspective.
Free when bundled.

Longman American History Atlas
0-321-00486-8

A four-color reference tool and visual guide to American history that includes almost 100 maps and covers the full scope of history. Atlas overhead transparencies available to adopters.
$3.00 when bundled.

iSearch Guide for History (with ContentSelect)
0-321-14282-9

The most practical, indispensible guide to the Internet available. This guide book contains exercises and tips specific to using the Internet for the study of history. It also includes access to the History ContentSelect Research Database. The database is a customized, searchable collection of 25,000+ discipline-specific articles from top-tier academic publications and journals. *Free when bundled.*

America Through the Eyes of Its People
0-673-97738-2

A comprehensive anthology that makes primary sources widely available in an inexpensive format, balancing social and political history and providing up-to-date narrative material.
Free when bundled.

The partnership between Penguin-Putnam USA and Longman Publishers offers your students a discount on the titles below when you bundle them with any Longman survey.

Available titles

Horatio Alger, *Ragged Dick & Struggling Upward*

Louis Auchincloss, *Woodrow Wilson*

Edward Bellamy, *Looking Backward*

Willa Cather, *O Pioneers!*

Alexis De Tocqueville, *Democracy in America*

Frederick Douglass, *Narrative of the Life of Frederick Douglass*

Gordon Hutner, *Immigrant Voices*

Martin Luther King, Jr., *Why We Can't Wait*

L. Jesse Lemisch (Editor), *Benjamin Franklin: The Autobiography & Other Writings*

Sinclair Lewis, *Babbitt*

Wendy Martin (Editor), *Colonial American Travel Narratives*

Tony Morrison, *Beloved*

Thomas Paine, *Common Sense*

Clinton Rossiter (Editor), *The Federalist Papers*

Upton Sinclair, *The Jungle*

Harriet Beecher Stowe, *Uncle Tom's Cabin*

Mark Twain, *Adventures of Huckleberry Finn*

U.S. History Readers

Historical Viewpoints, 9/e

John A. Garraty

Volume One — ISBN 0-321-10299-1
Volume Two — ISBN 0-321-10211-8

This collection of secondary source readings features articles adapted from the popular magazine *American Heritage*. Accessible, interesting, and significant, *Historical Viewpoints*, introduces students to a broad spectrum of historical issues and opinions from many of the world's foremost historians.

The Social Fabric, 9/e

Thomas L. Hartshorne
Robert A. Wheeler
John H. Cary
Julius Weinberg

Volume One — ISBN 0-321-10139-1
Volume Two — ISBN 0-321-10140-5

An engaging collection of secondary sources oriented to social history, this reader leads students to consider the role of women, ethnic groups, and laboring Americans in the weaving of the nation's social fabric.

Retracing the Past, 5/e

Gary B. Nash
Ronald Schultz

Volume One — ISBN 0-321-10137-5
Volume Two — ISBN 0-321-10138-3

This anthology of readings — both secondary and primary ("Past Traces") — describes the lives of ordinary Americans and examines the diversity of the American people, from the earliest settlement of America to the present day.

U.S. History Readers continued

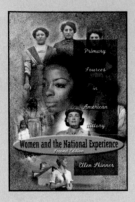

Women and the National Experience, 2/e

Ellen Skinner, *Pace University*

ISBN 0-321-00555-4

This brief, affordable primary source reader contains over one hundred different sources that describe the history of women in the United States. Combining classic and unusual sources, this anthology explores the private voices and public lives of women throughout U.S. history.

20th Century U.S. Foreign Policy

Gary A. Donaldson, *Xavier University*

ISBN 0-321-10506-0

With full-length primary source documents, including several contemporary opposing viewpoints, this collection is intended as a supplement to a U.S. Foreign Policy course that covers the 20th Century.

American History in a Box

Julie Roy Jeffrey, *Goucher College*
Peter J. Frederick, *Wabash College*

Volume One — ©2002 • Boxed Set • 12 folders • ISBN 0-321-03005-2
Volume Two — ©2002 • Boxed Set • 13 folders • ISBN 0-321-03006-0

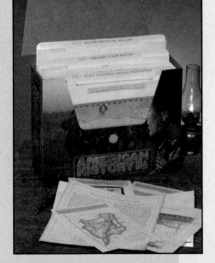

American History in a Box takes your students on a fascinating journey through our nation's past. Containing a wealth of facsimiles of original documents – poems, photographs, speeches, cartoons, advertisements, sheet music, letters, and much more – these two volumes allow your students to learn first-hand what history is and what historians actually do.

CREATED
EQUAL

CREATED EQUAL

A SOCIAL AND POLITICAL HISTORY OF THE UNITED STATES

VOLUME I ▪ TO 1877

Jacqueline Jones

Brandeis University

Peter H. Wood

Duke University

Elaine Tyler May

University of Minnesota

Thomas Borstelmann

Cornell University

Vicki L. Ruiz

University of California, Irvine

Longman

New York San Francisco Boston
London Toronto Sydney Tokyo Singapore Madrid
Mexico City Munich Paris Cape Town Hong Kong Montreal

Vice President and Publisher: Priscilla McGeehon
Acquisitions Editor: Ashley Dodge
Director of Development: Lisa Pinto
Development Manager: Betty Slack
Executive Marketing Manager: Sue Westmoreland
Media Editor: Patrick McCarthy
Supplements Editor: Kristi Olson
Director of Market Research: Laura Coaty
Production Manager: Ellen MacElree
Project Coordination, Electronic Page Makeup, and Cartography: Electronic Publishing Services Inc., NYC
Interior Design: Pearson Education Development
Cover Designer/Manager: Wendy Ann Fredericks
Photo Researcher: Photosearch, Inc.
Manufacturing Buyer: Lucy Hebard
Printer and Binder: Webcrafters
Cover Printer: Phoenix Color Corps.
Cover/Frontispiece Photo: Group of freed slaves who worked as laborers and servants with the 13th Massachusetts Infantry
  Regiment during the American Civil War, 1862 © Corbis

Credits for literary selections, selected maps and figures, and timeline photos appear on pages C-1–C-2.

Library of Congress Cataloging-in-Publication Data
Created equal : a social and political history of the United States / Jacqueline Jones ... [et al.].
    p. cm.
  Includes bibliographical references and index.
  ISBN 0-321-05296-X
  1. United States—History. 2. United States—Social conditions. 3. United States—Politics
and government. 4. Pluralism (Social sciences)—United States—History. 5.
Minorities—United States—History. 6. Pluralism (Social sciences)—United
States—History—Sources. 7. Minorities—United States—History—Sources. I. Jones,
Jacqueline, 1948–
E178 .C86 2003
973—dc21

                                                                        2002069476

Please visit our website at www.ablongman.com

ISBN: 0-321-05296-X (Complete Edition)
ISBN: 0-321-05298-6 (Volume I)
ISBN: 0-321-05300-1 (Volume II)

2 3 4 5 6 7 8 9 10—WC—05 04 03

To our own teachers, who helped set us on the historian's path, and to our students, who help keep us there. You have touched our intellects, our hearts, and our lives.

A nuestros propios maestros, quienes nos ayudaron a seguir en el sendero de historiador, y a nuestros estudiantes que ayudan a mantenernos alli. Usted ha tocado nuestros intelectos, nuestros corazones, y nuestras vidas.

Brief Contents

Detailed Contents

■ INTERPRETING HISTORY
"These Gods That We Worship Give Us Everything We Need" 31

■ CONNECTING HISTORY
Lost at Sea 39

List of Maps

List of Figures and Tables

Figures

Tables

List of Features

Connecting History

Interpreting History

Preface

> *"We hold these truths to be self-evident: That all men are created equal; that they are endowed by their Creator with certain unalienable rights; that among these are life, liberty, and the pursuit of happiness...."*

Ever since the Continental Congress approved the Declaration of Independence on July 4, 1776, the noble sentiments expressed in the document have inspired people in the United States and around the world. The Founding Fathers conceived of the new nation in what we today would consider narrow terms—as a political community of white men of property. Gradually, as the generations unfolded, diverse racial and ethnic groups, as well as women of all backgrounds, cited the Declaration in their struggle to achieve a more inclusive definition of American citizenship. American history is the story of various groups of men and women, all "created equal" in their common humanity, claiming an American identity for themselves.

In fact American history consists of many stories—the story of territorial growth and expansion, the story of the rise of the middle class, the story of technological innovation and economic development, and the story of U.S. engagement with the wider world. *Created Equal* incorporates these traditional narratives into a new and fresh interpretation of American history, one that includes the stories of diverse groups of people and explores expanding notions of American identity.

The book's basic framework focuses on the political events and economic structures discussed in most American history textbooks. *Created Equal* aims not to overturn the familiar chronology of American history, but to incorporate into it a variety of groups and individuals whose stories help us to provide an accurate, comprehensive, and compelling view of the past.

Four Themes

We have chosen to highlight four significant themes that run throughout American history.

- **Diversity.** In considering the theme of diversity, we acknowledge that the formation of social identity is a central element of the American story. We examine how individual Americans have understood and identified themselves by gender, religion, region, income, race, and ethnicity, among other factors. Native Americans, African Americans, Spanish-speaking inhabitants of the Southwest, Chinese immigrants, members of the laboring classes, women of all groups—all of these people have played a major role in defining what it means to be an American. At the same time, diverse forms of identity are by no means fixed or static. For example, in the early twentieth century, a Russian immigrant garment worker on New York's Lower East Side might think of herself in any number of ways—as a Jew, an employee, a union member, a single woman, a resident of a thriving city—and these forms of identity might change over time, depending on the woman's circumstances.

- **Class and systems of power.** These have also shaped American society in profound ways and an understanding of them is fundamental to understanding events in American history. Those systems take many forms. The institution of slavery denied people of African descent basic human freedoms. Class differences based on income and formal education mocked broader ideals of social equality. Some groups used the law to deny other groups the right to participate in the political system. Popular ideas related to alleged social differences and innate inferiority served to justify the treatment of certain groups as second-class citizens. U.S. military leaders launched military campaigns against vulnerable peoples within and outside the nation's borders. By the end of the nineteenth century, the United States boasted the largest and most comfortable middle class in the world—and yet the most substantial political and economic power was distributed among a relatively small contingent of white men. During the twentieth century, Americans dismantled the legal system of inequality that reduced blacks, women, and other groups to second-class citizenship. Nevertheless, a growing gap between the rich and poor continued to mock the notion of true equality.

- **Environment.** The role of the environment in American history has been significant. The physical landscape has profoundly shaped American society, and has in turn been shaped by it. The theme of the environment is key to understanding cultural, political, and economic developments. Many Native American groups shared a sense of oneness with the land; for them, the material and spiritual worlds were intimately related. In contrast, many European Americans saw the land as a means of making a living or making money, or as the source of valuable raw materials—in other words, as a thing to be bought, sold, and used. The vast richness of the American landscape has provoked violent conflict over the years, even as it has formed a key component in American wealth and power. We examine regional differences in all geographic areas—not just the eastern seaboard.

- **Globalization.** Finally, the increasing globalization of the United States' economy and society in recent decades reminds us of how deeply the country has always been engaged with the rest of the world. Since the earliest days of colonial settlement, Americans have traded goods, cultural practices, and ideas with peoples outside their borders. As an immigrant nation and the modern world's superpower, America's foreign and domestic relations have always been intertwined. After World War II, Americans' fears of Communism and the Soviet Union exerted a profound effect upon the country's politics and society. In the wake of the attacks of September 11, 2001, all Americans were forced to confront the role of the United States in the larger world, with all the opportunities and dangers that role entailed.

These four themes serve as the lenses through which we view the traditional narrative framework of American history. Readers of *Created Equal* will understand the major political developments that shaped the country's past, as well as the role of diverse groups in initiating and reacting to those developments. Chapter 13, for example, which focuses on the 1850s, includes a detailed account of the effects of the slavery crisis on Congress and the political party system, as well as a discussion of shifting group identities affecting Indians, Latinos, northern women, and enslaved and free blacks. Chapter 18, focusing on the 1890s, covers the rise of the Populist Party and stirrings of American imperialism, as well as a discussion of barriers to a U.S. workers' political party and challenges to traditional gender roles. Thus *Created Equal* builds upon the basic history that forms the foundation of most major textbooks and offers a rich and comprehensive look at the past by including the stories of all Americans, in addition.

Chronological Organization

One of the challenges in writing *Created Equal* has been to emphasize the way in which the four major themes come together and influence each other, affecting specific generations of Americans. Thus, the text is organized into ten parts, most of these covering a generation. Many textbooks organize discussions of immigrants, cities, the West, and foreign diplomacy (to name a few topics) into separate chapters that cover large time periods. In contrast, *Created Equal* integrates material related to a variety of topics within individual chapters. Although the text adheres to a chronological organization, it stresses coherent discussions of specific topics within that framework. This provides students with a richer understanding of events. Chapter 15, for example, which covers the dozen or so years after the end of the Civil War, deals with Reconstruction in the South, Indian wars on the High Plains, and the rise of the women's and labor movements, stressing the relationships among all these developments. To cite another example: Many texts devote a chapter exclusively to America's post–World War II rise to global power; *Created Equal* integrates material related to that development in a series of six chapters that cover the period of 1945 to 2000. Each of these chapters illustrates the effects of dramatic world developments on American social relations and domestic policy on a decade-by-decade basis. This approach allows readers to appreciate the rich complexity of any particular time period and to understand that major events occur not in a vacuum, but in a larger social context.

Special Features

The book includes a number of features designed to make American history clear and engaging to the reader, and to encourage students to "do" history on their own. These features include:

- **Parts and timelines.** *Created Equal* consists of ten parts covering three chapters each. An opening section that lays out the basic themes of the period introduces each part. Each part opener also includes an illustrated timeline highlighting major events covered in the three chapters that follow.

- **Chapter introductory vignettes and conclusions.** Each chapter begins with a story that introduces the reader to groups and individuals representative of the themes developed in the chapter. Among the chapter introductory vignettes are the stories of a Norwegian immigrant woman in Wisconsin (Chapter 12), a group of runaway slaves accused of treason by Confederate authorities in wartime (Chapter 14), Spanish-speaking inhabitants of Northern New Mexico struggling to retain their culture in the face of an onslaught of European American settlers (Chapter 17), and a Sioux Indian boy at a government boarding school (Chapter 18). At the end of each chapter, a concluding section sums up the chapter's themes and points the reader toward the next chapter.

- **"Connecting History."** *Created Equal* encourages students to think outside the boundaries of specific periods by including in each chapter a boxed feature called "Connecting History." A topic is examined at two different periods, or as it evolved over time. Several of these mini-essays span the entire sweep of American history. Topics include the history of naval navigation, civil liberties, education, advertising, the Ku Klux Klan, and the Internet.

- **"Interpreting History."** This feature consists of a primary document on a topic relevant to the chapter's themes. Through this feature we hear the voices of a variety of Americans—a seventeenth-century slave, a sail maker in post-Revolutionary New York City, a Mexican lawyer visiting New Mexico in the early nineteenth century, a group of Cherokee women in early nineteenth-century Georgia, an antebellum southern professor, industrial titan Andrew Carnegie, and the environmental activist Rachel Carson. The "Interpreting History" feature takes many different forms—letters, sermons, court decisions, labor contracts, Congressional hearings, and songs. Students thus have an opportunity to analyze primary documents and to better appreciate the historian's task—to read materials critically and to place them in their larger socio-historical context.

- **Maps, charts, pullout quotes, and artifacts.** Illustrations—photographs, tables, pictures of objects from the time period, and figures—enhance the narrative. Large maps offer greater geographical detail and invite students to see the relationship between geography and history. Highlighted quotes help the reader grasp the chapter's major themes.

- **"Sites to Visit" and "For Further Reading."** At the end of each chapter is a list of "Sites to Visit," identifying sites on the World Wide Web relevant to the chapter and occasionally listing the location of important historical sites and landmarks as well. There is also a list of suggested works related to each section of the chapter. These features encourage students to follow up on major topics on their own—either on the computer or in the library.

Created Equal introduces students to recent scholarship in social history as well as providing a firm grounding in the traditional political narrative. In recent decades social identity has emerged as a central theme of American history. However, exclusive attention to cultural and social diversity can overshadow the political and economic structures of American society. Students should gain an understanding of our nation's social diversity but also learn about the power relations that have shaped that past—which groups have had influence and how they have maintained and wielded that influence. Placing these issues at the forefront, *Created Equal* tells the dramatic, evolving story of America in all its complexity—a story of a diverse people "created equal" yet struggling to achieve equality.

The Authors

Meet the Authors

Jacqueline Jones was born in Christiana, Delaware, a small town of 400 people in the northern part of the state. The local public school was desegregated in 1955, when she was a third grader. That event, combined with the peculiar social etiquette of relations between blacks and whites in the town, sparked her interest in American history. She attended the University of Delaware in nearby Newark and went on to graduate school at the University of Wisconsin, Madison, where she received her Ph.D. in history. Her scholarly interests have evolved over time, focusing on American labor, and women's, African American, and southern history.

One of her biggest challenges has been to balance her responsibilities as teacher, historian, wife, and mother (of two daughters). One of her proudest achievements is the fact that she has been able to teach full-time and still pick up her daughters at school every day at 2:30 in the afternoon (thanks to a flexible professor's schedule). She is the author of several books, including *Soldiers of Light and Love: Northern Teachers and Georgia Blacks* (1980); *Labor of Love, Labor of Sorrow: Black Women, Work, and Family Since Slavery* (1985), which won the Bancroft Prize and was a finalist for a Pulitzer Prize; *The Dispossessed: America's Underclasses Since the Civil War* (1992); and *American Work: Four Centuries of Black and White Labor* (1998). In 2001, she completed a memoir that recounts her childhood in Christiana: *Creek Walking: Growing Up in Delaware in the 1950s.*

She teaches American history at Brandeis University, where she is Harry S. Truman Professor. In 1999, she received a MacArthur Fellowship.

Peter H. Wood was born in St. Louis (before the famous arch was built). He recalls seeing Jackie Robinson play against the Cardinals, visiting the courthouse where the Dred Scott case originated, and traveling up the Mississippi to Hannibal, birthplace of Mark Twain. Summer work on the northern Great Lakes aroused his interest in Native American cultures, past and present. He studied at Harvard (B.A., 1964; Ph.D., 1972) and at Oxford, where he was a Rhodes Scholar (1964–1966). His pioneering book, *Black Majority* (1974), concerning slavery in colonial South Carolina, won the Beveridge Prize of the American Historical Association. Since 1975, he has taught early American history at Duke University, where he also coached the women's lacrosse club for three years. The topics of his articles range from the French explorer LaSalle to Gerald Ford's pardon of Richard Nixon. He coauthored *Winslow Homer's Images of Blacks,* and he has written *Strange New Land,* a book about early African Americans. In 1989 he coedited *Powhatan's Mantle: Indians in the Colonial Southeast.* His demographic essay in that volume provided the first clear picture of population change in the eighteenth-century South. Dr. Wood has served on the boards of the Highlander Center, Harvard University, Houston's Rothko Chapel, the Menil Foundation, and the Institute of Early American History and Culture in Williamsburg. He is married to colonial historian Elizabeth Fenn; his varied interests include archaeology, documentary film, and growing gourds. He keeps a baseball bat used by Ted Williams beside his desk.

Thomas Borstelmann, the son of a university psychologist, has taught at the elementary, high school, and college levels. He taught second-grade physical education, taught and coached high school lacrosse, soccer, and basketball, and since 1991 has taught American history at Cornell University. In addition to his teaching experience, he also served as "Head Maid" of a conference center near Lake Tahoe. He lives with his wife and two sons in Syracuse, New York, where his greatest challenge—and delight—is doing the bulk of childcare while commuting 60 miles to Cornell. An avid bicyclist, runner, and cross-country skier, he earned his B.A. from Stanford University in 1980 and Ph.D. from Duke University in 1990.

He became a historian to figure out the Cold War and American race relations, in part because he had grown up in the South. His first book, concerning American relations with southern Africa in the mid-twentieth century, won the Stuart L. Bernath Book Prize of the Society for Historians of Foreign Relations. His second book, *The Cold War and the Color Line*, appeared in 2002. His commitment to the classroom remains clear at Cornell University, where he has won a major teaching award: the Robert and Helen Appel Fellowship. He found writing *Created Equal* a natural complement to what he does in the classroom, trying to provide both telling details of the American past and the broad picture of how the United States has developed as it has. A specialist in U.S. foreign relations, he is equally fascinated with domestic politics and social change. He is currently working on a book about the 1970s.

Elaine Tyler May grew up in the shadow of Hollywood, performing in neighborhood circuses with her friends. She went to high school before girls could play on sports teams, so she spent her after-school hours as a cheerleader and her summer days as a bodysurfing beach bum. Her passion for American history developed in college when she spent her junior year in Japan. The year was 1968. The Vietnam War was raging, along with turmoil at home. As an American in Asia, often called on to explain her nation's actions, she yearned for a deeper understanding of America's past and its place in the world. She returned home to study history at UCLA, where she earned her B.A., M.A., and Ph.D. She has taught at Princeton and Harvard Universities and since 1978 at the University of Minnesota. She has written four books examining the relationship between politics, public policy, and private life. Her widely acclaimed *Homeward Bound: American Families in the Cold War Era* was the first study to link the baby boom and suburbia to the politics of the Cold War. The *Chronicle of Higher Education* featured *Barren in the Promised Land: Childless Americans and the Pursuit of Happiness* as a pioneering study of the history of reproduction. *Lingua Franca* named her coedited volume *Here, There, and Everywhere: The Foreign Politics of American Popular Culture* a "Breakthrough Book." She served as president of the American Studies Association in 1996 and as Distinguished Fulbright Professor of American History in Dublin, Ireland, in 1997. She is married to historian Lary May and has three children who have inherited their parents' passion for history.

Vicki L. Ruiz is a professor of history and Chicano/Latino studies at the University of California, Irvine. For her, history remains a grand adventure, one that she began at the kitchen table listening to the stories of her mother and grandmother and continued with the help of the local bookmobile. She read constantly as she sat on the dock catching small fish ("grunts") to be used as bait on her father's fishing boat. As she grew older, she was promoted to working with her mother selling tickets for the *Blue Sea II.* The first in her family to receive an advanced degree, she graduated from Gulf Coast Community College and Florida State University, then went on to earn a Ph.D. in history at Stanford in 1982, the fourth Mexican American woman to receive a doctorate in history. Her first book, *Cannery Women, Cannery Lives,* received an award from the National Women's Political Caucus, and her second, *From Out of the Shadows: Mexican Women in 20th-Century America,* was named a *Choice* Outstanding Academic Book of 1998 by the American Library Association. She is coeditor with Ellen Carol Dubois of *Unequal Sisters: A Multicultural Reader in U.S. Women's History.* She and Virginia Sánchez Korrol coedit *Latinas in the United States: A Historical Encyclopedia,* and both were recognized by *Latina Magazine* as Latinas of the Year in Education for 2000. Active in student mentorship projects, summer institutes for teachers, and public humanities programs, Dr. Ruiz served as an appointee to the National Council of the Humanities. She has also served on the national governing bodies of the American Historical Association, the Organization of American Histories, and the American Studies Association. The mother of two grown sons, she is married to Victor Becerra, urban planner and gourmet cook extraordinaire.

A Conversation with the Authors

> Created Equal *tells stories across generations, regions, and cultures, integrating the lives of individuals within the economic, political, cultural, global, and environmental vectors shaping their lives. These tales of simple courage breathe life into history, bringing an immediacy and vibrancy to the past. We cherish the telling of stories for it is within these tales that we remember the* ánimo y sueños *(spirit and dreams) of the American people.*
>
> VICKI RUIZ

How Did This Project Begin?

PETER: It started with a videocassette. The Longman history editor taped a lively conversation with a dozen exceptional history teachers from very different backgrounds. They were all energized about teaching U.S. history in new ways, but they felt frustrated by their current texts. Then Longman sent the video to me. The video was not great cinematography, just talking heads. But their voices were so articulate, and I shared so many of their concerns. I remember watching the cassette on a Sunday night, and it set my mind spinning. I couldn't get much sleep. Here were real teachers like me who wanted a dramatically different text. And here was a major publisher, Longman, saying, "What do you think?"

At the time, I was teaching one of those special classes, a group of history majors that really clicked. Four of the best students had parents from other countries—South Africa, Mexico, Haiti, Vietnam—and all four were fascinated by American history. I remember thinking, "I'd love to be part of a team of historians who developed a text that would excite Darlene Aquino from Texas and Minh-Thu Pham from North Carolina." I called Longman and said, "Let's find a way to do it."

How Did You Come to the Decision to Write This Book?

JACKIE: I thought that writing a new kind of text would be a real intellectual challenge. We have the opportunity to rethink and reconfigure the traditional American history narrative, and that's exciting.

PETER: I was not eager to write a "feel good" text. American history has not been a big happy rainbow. I was convinced that we could be much more open and inclusive than most current texts. We could also be more direct and matter-of-fact in many areas. It is important to be frank about differences and contradictions in the American story in a way that actually helps explain things.

THOMAS: Writing a textbook was attractive because it's so complementary to what I do in the classroom, particularly teaching the introductory American history survey. Having the chance to try to tell the entire story of the American past was exciting as a balance to the other work we do.

How Did the Author Team Come Together, Work Together?

PETER: The Longman videotape circulated. Eventually, we had a team of people who felt that they could answer, collectively, the challenge presented by those articulate teachers. Obviously, no one could do it alone, but the right combination might be able to pull it off.

Having watched the Duke basketball team for two decades, I know what five very different people can do if they pay attention to each other, and if they all have the same goal in mind. An author team is like a basketball team: The players have to complement one another. (Sometimes we *compliment* each other, too!) And each person gets better and contributes more through practice and hard work. This team works hard.

VICKI: I joined the *Created Equal* team out of the profound respect I have for the scholarship of my colleagues. I had met Elaine and Jackie previously at conferences and knew Peter and Thomas only from their scholarship. The first brainstorming meeting I attended in New York City was intellectual magic, pure and simple. From the first hour onward, we exchanged our separate visions and expectations, debated periodization and conceptual frames, and began the process of intellectual coalescence that marks this truly collaborative enterprise. I left New York exhilarated and exhausted.

> *I joined the* Created Equal *team out of the profound respect I have for the scholarship of my colleagues.*
>
> — VICKI RUIZ

ELAINE: I joined this project because I was excited about the challenge of writing a textbook that would convey the drama and excitement of the nation's history. It offered an opportunity to work with a team of scholars who I have long admired, and it has been a joy and a privilege to collaborate with them. We have become a close group of friends and colleagues, and our text reflects the lively exchanges, debates, and brainstorming sessions we've had over email, phone calls, and gatherings when we have come together to work on the project.

Tell Us About the Title—*Created Equal.*

JACKIE: The title reflects our commitment to be inclusive in our coverage of different groups and the part they played in shaping American history. Of course, we are invoking the Declaration of Independence: "We hold these truths to be self-evident, that all men are created equal." That document, and those words, have inspired countless individuals, groups, and nations around the world.

PETER: We all recognize the phrase, "Created Equal" from the Declaration of Independence, but we rarely ponder it. For me, it represents an affirmation of humanity, the family of mankind. But it also raises the deepest American theme—the endless struggles over defining whose equality will be recognized. I suppose you could say that there is equality in birth and death, but a great deal of inequality in between.

Many of those inequities—and their partial removal—drive the story of American History. Tom Paine understood this in 1776 when he published *Common Sense*. Months before the Declaration of Independence appeared, Paine put it this way: "Mankind being originally equal in the order of creation, the equality could only be destroyed by some subsequent circumstance."

How and Why Did You Choose the Themes that Structure the Text?

THOMAS: The themes that we chose to highlight in *Created Equal* reflect what we see as the current and future state of the field of U.S. history, as well as the needs of future generations of students.

The prominence of multiculturalism in recent decades made clear that identity remains a central piece of the American story: how individual Americans understand and identify themselves (by religion, class, region, sex, race, ethnicity, etc.). But too much attention to cultural issues has often led to a discounting of the political and economic structure of American society: Who has material wealth and power, and how they use it, is fundamental for determining the course of the past and present. The increasing globalization of the U.S. economy and American society (e.g., through rising immigration) in recent decades has reminded us of how deeply the United States has always been engaged with the rest of the world—as an immigrant nation and the modern world's superpower, America's foreign and domestic affairs have always been intertwined. And the deepening awareness in recent decades of the fragility of the earth's environment has stimulated a whole subfield of American environmental history, which we try to tap into—in a sense, the environment represents the clearest example of the interconnectedness of American and international history.

JACKIE: It was time to integrate recent scholarship related to the many different groups that have been part of the American story, and to open up that story to include all geographical areas (and not just the eastern seaboard). The theme of the environment is key to understanding American history; we explore the ways American cultural, political, and economic developments influence and are shaped by the nation's natural resources and landscape. The theme of power relations helps students to understand that differences of class, and differences in political and material resources, are significant aspects of the country's history. We balance this perspective by showing how America emerged as a uniquely open and middle-class nation—one that has attracted immigrants from all over the world throughout its history.

ELAINE: *Created Equal* brings together aspects of the nation's story that are usually examined separately. It demonstrates that the people who make change are not only those in major positions of power—they are also ordinary Americans from all backgrounds. We illuminate ways that ordinary Americans have seized opportunities to improve their lives and their nation. In *Created Equal*, the land itself is a major player in the story—the environment, the different regions, and the ways in which people, businesses, public policies, and the forces of nature have shaped it. We also address the ongoing interaction between the United States and the rest of the world, examining the nation in a truly global context.

> Created Equal *brings together aspects of the nation's story that are usually examined separately.*
>
> ELAINE TYLER MAY

How Is the Book Organized?

PETER: History is the study of change over time, so chronology becomes extremely important. We wanted to emphasize central themes, but we wanted to explore and explain how they related to one another at any given moment. So we made a conscious decision to be more chronological than many recent texts in our presentation. It makes for less confusion, less jumping back and forth in time, than when broad themes are played out separately. After all, this is the way we lead our own lives—sequentially.

JACKIE: Most of the 10 separate parts in the book each cover about a generation. The parts give students a sense of the big picture over a longer period—the way our themes fit together and the impact of major developments on a particular generation of Americans. The chronological organization of the book forces us to understand the "wholeness" of any particular period—to consider links among political, social, economic, and cultural developments. By maintaining a strictly chronological focus, we hope to show students how the events and developments of any one period are intertwined with each other. For example, for coverage of the period after the end of the Civil War, it is important to show links between the Indian wars in the West and the process of Reconstruction in the South. In most texts, those regional perspectives are separated into different chapters, but, in *Created Equal*, these connections are presented together in Chapter 15.

Each of the Chapters Has Two Feature Essays: "Interpreting History" and "Connecting History." What are the Benefits of These Features?

JACKIE: The "Interpreting History" feature provides students with an opportunity to "do history" on their own. These are brief primary documents related to the issues presented in a particular chapter. We have chosen documents that are particularly rich in terms of providing material for discussion and analysis. By working with this material, students will learn how to balance the close reading of a text with an understanding of the larger historical context of the document.

The "Connecting History" feature follows a particular subject backward and forward in time, suggesting ways that a topic discussed in a particular chapter has evolved through American history. These mini-essays encourage students to consider change over long periods of time.

What Did You Enjoy Most About Writing this Text?

JACKIE: The intellectual stimulation and the opportunity to work with a wonderful group of people.

PETER: Three things. My teammates and their different energies, for sure. Also, the staff at Longman. I had never worked on a big collective effort like this, and I still marvel at the intricacies and coordination of the whole operation.

But most of all, writing this text has reinforced my sense of the intense relevance of history. We were hard at work when the World Trade Center attack occurred, and our editor lived only a few blocks from the destruction. I saw the hole in the Pentagon first-hand. Suddenly, our entire society was on a new footing. A culture oriented to the present and the future had to re-examine the past, both locally and globally, recent and distant. In reconnecting to our history in new ways—examining it openly and fearlessly and critically—we find a story that is more relevant than most of us imagined. It is complex, dramatic, sobering, and uplifting all at once. . .like life itself.

> *Writing this text has reinforced my sense of the intense relevance of history.*
>
> PETER WOOD

THOMAS: It's been a pleasure to work as a team. When I first joined the project in its early phases, I was lured by the prospect of working with Peter—and then I got that much more excited as the rest of the team was filled in. I've been deeply impressed by how well we communicate, especially the combination of serious intellectual challenges to each other and our great personal support for each other. I simply learn a lot every time we communicate, and I'm grateful for the friendships that have emerged out of our joint endeavor.

What Do You Hope Students Will Get Out of the Book?

PETER: I want readers to connect. As a child, you connect to your family, your neighbors, your schoolmates. As you get older, that circle expands; you begin to relate to people in other places and other times. In a good history class, or a strong history book, that relationship becomes close. You start to care about, argue with, and connect to the persons you are studying. Pretty soon, their tough choices and surprising experiences in life start to resemble our own in ways we never expected, even though their worlds are dramatically different from ours.

JACKIE: By presenting an inclusive view of the past, we give students a more accurate account of American history. Many texts only pay lip service to diversity. Non-elite groups are tacked on, marginalized, or segregated from the "real" story of America. In contrast, we believe that the history of all groups constitutes the real story of America.

Acknowledgments

As authors, we could not have completed this project without the loving support of our families. We wish to thank Jeffrey Abramson, Lil Fenn, Lynn Borstelmann, Lary May, and Victor Becerra for their interest, forbearance, and encouragement over the course of many drafts. Our children, now ranging in age from 6 to 32, have been a source of inspiration, as have our many students, past and present. We are grateful to scores of colleagues and friends who have helped shape this book, both directly and indirectly, in more ways than they know.

Special thanks are due to Pam Gordon for pulling this team together and launching the project, to Dan Usner and Jay O'Callaghan for their useful involvement in the early stages, and to Steve Fraser for his insightful midcourse corrections, which came at a crucial time in the process. Along the way, Matt Basso, Chad Cover, Eben Miller, Andrea Sachs, Mary Strunk, and Melissa Williams provided useful research and administrative assistance; their help was invaluable. Louis Balizet provided careful reading of several chapter drafts. Thanks to Deborah Anderson for a stellar job in locating images, and to Jennifer Mazurkie for all her terrific work in overseeing the layout.

Our friends at Longman have shown their belief in this project from the beginning. They supported an invaluable two-day retreat at Truro, on Cape Cod, and they worked hard to smooth out numerous bumps along this long road. We thank all the creative people at Longman (and there are many) who have had a hand in bringing this book to life. We are especially grateful to Priscilla McGeehon, Lisa Pinto, Betty Slack, and Sue Westmoreland for their enthusiastic devotion to this project and their expertise and friendship from start to finish. Ashley Dodge, joining the Longman team recently, has embraced *Created Equal* and given it her full and timely support.

From the beginning, we knew that we wanted a unique and distinctive look for this book. For their comments and feedback on sample design material, we thank the following reviewers:

Scott Barton
East Central University

Constance M. McGovern
Frostburg State University

Keith Pacholl
California State University–Fullerton

Robert E. Rook
Fort Hays State University

Rachel Standish
Foothill College

Michael M. Topp
University of Texas–El Paso

Finally, we wish to express our deep gratitude to the following people who read and commented on the manuscript as it went through its several drafts. Collectively, they pushed us hard with their high standards, tough questions, and shrewd advice. The thoughtful criticisms and generous suggestions from these colleagues have helped improve the book.

Ken Adderley
Upper Iowa University

Leslie Alexander
Ohio State University

John Andrew
Franklin and Marshall College

Abel Bartley
University of Akron

Donald Scott Barton
Central Carolina Technical College

Mia Bay
Rutgers University

Chris Bierwith
Treasure Valley Community College

Charles Bolton
University of Arkansas at Little Rock

Susan Burch
Gallaudet University

Tommy Bynum
Georgia Perimeter College

Robert B. Carey
Empire State College–SUNY

Todd Carney
Southern Oregon University

Kathleen Carter
Highpoint University

Jonathan Chu
University of Massachusetts

Amy E. Davis
University of California–Los Angeles

Judy DeMark
Northern Michigan University

James A. Denton
University of Colorado

Joseph A. Devine
Stephen F. Austin University

Margaret Dwight
*North Carolina Agricultural
    and Technical University*

Nancy Gabin
Purdue University

Lori Ginzberg
Pennsylvania State University

Gregory Goodwin
Bakersfield College

Amy S. Greenberg
Pennsylvania State University

Nadine Isitani Hata
El Camino College

James Hedtke
Cabrini College

Fred Hoxie
University of Illinois

Tera Hunter
Carnegie Mellon University

David Jaffe
City College of New York

Jeremy Johnson
Northwest College

Yvonne Johnson
Central Missouri State University

Kurt Keichtle
University of Wisconsin

Anne Klejment
University of St. Thomas

Dennis Kortheuer
California State University–Long Beach

Joel Kunze
Upper Iowa University

Joseph Laythe
Edinboro College of Pennsylvania

Chana Kai Lee
Indiana University

Dan Letwin
Pennsylvania State University

Gaylen Lewis
Bakersfield College

Kenneth Lipartito
Florida International University

Kyle Longley
Arizona State University

Edith L. Macdonald
University of Central Florida

Lorie Maltby
Henderson Community College

Sandra Mathews-Lamb
Nebraska Wesleyan University

Constance M. McGovern
Frostburg State University

Henry McKiven
University of South Alabama

James H. Merrell
Vassar College

Earl Mulderink
Southern Utah State University

Steven Noll
University of Florida

Jim Norris
North Dakota State University

Elsa Nystrom
Kennesaw State University

Keith Pacholl
California State University–Fullerton

William Pelz
Elgin Community College

Melanie Perrault
University of Central Arkansas

Delores D. Petersen
Foothill College

Robert Pierce
Foothill College

Louis Potts
University of Missouri–Kansas City

Sarah Purcell
Central Michigan University

Niler Pyeatt
Wayland Baptist University

Steven Reschly
Truman State University

Arthur Robinson
Santa Rosa Junior College

Robert E. Rook
Fort Hays State University

Steven Ruggles
University of Minnesota

Christine Sears
University of Delaware

Rebecca Shoemaker
Indiana State University

Howard Shore
Columbia River High School

James Sidbury
University of Texas

Arwin D. Smallwood
Bradley University

Margaret Spratt
California University of Pennsylvania

Rachel Standish
Foothill College

Jon Stauff
St. Ambrose University

David Steigerwald
Ohio State University–Marion

Kay Stockbridge
Central Carolina Technical College

Daniel Thorp
Virginia Tech University

Michael M. Topp
University of Texas–El Paso

Clifford Trafzer
University of California–Riverside

Deborah Gray White
Rutgers University

Scott Wong
Williams College

Bill Woodward
Seattle Pacific University

Nancy Zens
Central Oregon Community College

David Zonderman
North Carolina State University

CREATED EQUAL

25,000 to 11,000 years ago
Low ocean levels expose land bridge linking Siberia to Alaska.

14,000 years ago
Early Paleo-Indians in Florida and Pennsylvania regions, and also in Monte Verde, Chile.

13,900 to 12,900 years ago
Clovis hunters spread across North America.

10,000 to 3000 years ago
Archaic Indians flourish in diverse settings.

4200 to 2700 years ago
Poverty Point culture existing in Louisiana.

300 to 900 A.D.
Mayan culture flourishes in Mesoamerica.

400 Polynesian explorers reach the Hawaiian Islands.

500 to 600
Teotihuacan in central Mexico becomes one of the world's largest cities.

900 to 1100
Anasazi culture centered in Chaco Canyon in Southwest.

1000 Norse explorers establish a Vinland colony in Newfoundland.

1100 Cahokia in Illinois becomes one focus of Mississippian culture.

1250 to 1400
Mississippian culture reflected at Moundville in Alabama.

1400 Aztecs build capital at Tenochtitlán (site of modern Mexico City).

1405 to 1433
Chinese fleet of Admiral Zheng He reaches Indian Ocean and Africa's east coast.

1420 to 1460
Prince Henry of Portugal sends ships to explore Africa's west coast.

1492 First voyage of Columbus.

1494 Treaty of Tordesillas arranges division between overseas claims of Spain and Portugal.

1497 to 1499
Vasco da Gama completes trading voyage from Portugal to India.

1517 Martin Luther launches Protestant Reformation.

1519 Cortés invades Mexico.

2

P A R T   O N E

North American Founders

W E SOMETIMES CALL THE FRAMERS OF THE U.S. CONSTITUTION America's Founding Fathers, using capital letters for emphasis. The men who met in Philadelphia in 1787 were indeed founders in a political sense, having drafted our enduring frame of government. But the 1780s seem recent in relation to most of North America's long human history. We must explore far back in time, long before the eighteenth century, to find the varied men and women who were the continent's first founders.

Two kinds of foundation builders emerge: the distant ancestors of today's Native Americans and newcomers from abroad who colonized North America in the sixteenth and seventeenth centuries.

Our earliest human ancestors evolved in Africa and then spread across the landmass of Eurasia. In the Southern Hemisphere, they managed to cross to Australia some 40,000 years ago, but evidence suggests that they reached the Americas from Asia much later, probably less than 20,000 years ago. These first human arrivals took advantage of the land bridge that joined Siberia to Alaska when Ice Age glaciers prompted a dramatic decline in sea levels. Roughly 14,000 years ago, these hunters apparently bypassed melting glaciers to reach the North American interior. They came on foot, but additional newcomers may have skirted the Pacific coast in small boats or even drifted across the South Pacific.

We still understand very little about these earliest Americans. What we do know is that they spread rapidly across North America over the next thousand years, and they continued to hunt mammoths and other large animals until these ancient species became extinct. Later, their descendants adapted to a wide range of different environments, learning to fish, hunt for smaller game, and gather berries. It has been 10,000 years since the extinction of the mammoths and 3000 years since the early signs of agriculture in the Americas. By 500 A.D. complex societies were beginning to appear in equatorial America, and a succession of diverse and rich societies had arisen in the Americas by the time a second set of founders appeared around 1500 A.D.

Although Vikings from Scandinavia had preceded Christopher Columbus by five centuries, their small outpost on the coast of Newfoundland lasted only a few years. In contrast, when Columbus reached the West Indies and returned to Spain in 1492, his voyage launched a human and biological exchange between the Eastern and Western Hemispheres that has never ceased. Spanish and Portuguese ships initiated this exchange, but they were soon followed by vessels from England, France, and Holland. Half a century after Columbus's first voyage, Spanish overland expeditions had already pushed from Florida to Arkansas and from Mexico to Kansas. French explorers, hoping to find a Northwest Passage to Asia, had penetrated far up the St. Lawrence River in Canada.

Europeans brought new materials such as iron and new animals such as horses, cattle, and pigs. They also brought deadly diseases previously unknown in the Americas, such as measles and smallpox, which had a catastrophic impact on Native American societies. By 1565 Europeans had established their first lasting outpost in the North American continent, the town of St. Augustine in Spanish Florida. Two decades later the English tried, unsuccessfully, to plant a similar colony at Roanoke Island along the coast of what is now North Carolina.

In the first decades of the seventeenth century, permanent European settlements took hold at Quebec on the St. Lawrence River and at Santa Fe near the Rio Grande. A trans-Atlantic outpost of English society appeared at Jamestown on Chesapeake Bay in 1607. Farther north, behind the sheltering hook of Cape Cod, other settlers formed additional coastal outposts and renamed the region New England.

Numbers were small at first, but these communities and others endured and expanded, often with crucial help from Native Americans who knew the keys to survival in their own domains. The gradual success of these European footholds prompted imitation and competition; colonizers clashed with each other and with long-time Indian inhabitants over control of the land and its resources. Disappointed in their early searches for easy mineral wealth, the new arrivals made do in various ways: cutting timber, catching fish, raising tobacco, or trading for furs. The French in particular, with aid once again from Native Americans, explored the interior of the continent. By 1700, they had laid claim to the entire Mississippi River valley and established a colony on the Gulf of Mexico.

Each new colonizing enterprise in the seventeenth century took on a distinctive life of its own—or, rather, numerous lives. First of all, there was the internal life of the community: Who would be allowed to take part, how would participants govern themselves, and how would they subsist? In each instance, relations with the region's native inhabitants constituted a second unfolding story. Complicated ties to Europe—economic, religious, social, and political—made a third crucial narrative. Furthermore, relations between colonies and between the distant European powers that backed them had a determining influence, as when England took over the Dutch colony at New Netherland in the third quarter of the seventeenth century. Finally, there was the compelling drama of the newcomers' relationship to the environment itself. These founding generations labored to understand—or to subdue and exploit without fully understanding—the continent they had started to colonize.

1519 to 1522
Magellan's ship circumnavigates the globe and returns to Spain.

1533 Pizarro overthrows Inca Empire in Peru.

1534 to 1543
Expeditions of Cartier (Canada), De Soto (Southeast), and Coronado (Southwest) probe North America.

1565 Spanish establish St. Augustine.

1577 to 1580
Voyage of Drake challenges Spanish dominance in the Pacific.

1585 to 1590
English attempt to establish Roanoke colony fails.

1588 Spanish Armada fails in an effort to invade England.

1599 Spanish colonize New Mexico.

1607 England's Virginia Company launches colony at Jamestown.

1620 *Mayflower* passengers establish Plymouth Colony.

1630 English Puritans found Massachusetts Bay Colony.

1637 Pequot War in New England.

1660 Restoration of monarchy in England under Charles II.

1664 Charles II grants a charter to his brother James, Duke of York, sanctioning the takeover of the Dutch New Netherland colony and the creation of New York.

1675 to 1676
Metacom's War in New England.

1676 Bacon's Rebellion in Virginia.

1680 Pueblo Revolt in New Mexico.

1681 Quaker William Penn receives charter for Pennsylvania.

1682 La Salle explores the Mississippi River and claims Louisiana for France.

1689 Dutch leader William of Orange and his wife Mary become joint English sovereigns in the Glorious Revolution, replacing King James II.

1691 Witchcraft trials in Salem, Massachusetts.

1699 Iberville begins colony in French Louisiana.

1711 to 1715
Tuscarora Indians in North Carolina, and then the Yamasee in South Carolina, resist English colonial expansion.

CHAPTER

1

First Founders

Georgia Department of Natural Resources. Photograph ©1985 The Detroit Institute of Arts

■ Carved stone figures created nearly 1000 years ago at Etowah in Georgia.

ONE DAY IN 1908, A COWBOY NAMED GEORGE MCJUNKIN WAS CHECKING FENCES ON A cattle ranch near Folsom, New Mexico, when something strange caught his eye. McJunkin noticed several large bones protruding from the earth. Dismounting from his horse, he also spotted an old arrowhead, something common in these parts. But it was the bones beside it that seemed unusual. They were larger than cattle bones and buried under layers of dirt, so McJunkin decided to show them to others. Nearly 20 years later, ancient-bones expert Jesse Figgins came to Folsom after seeing McJunkin's evidence. Soon Figgins unearthed an extensive bone bed containing the remains of 23 large Ice Age bison of a species that had been extinct for 10,000 years. He also uncovered a spear point, clearly fashioned by human hands, embedded between two bison ribs. Figgins's finds confirmed McJunkin's earlier discovery. The objects stirred first disbelief and then excitement, for they proved that human hunters had existed in North America 7000 years earlier than scientists had supposed. The discovery of the thin projectile tips, named Folsom points after the site, sparked a revolution in North American archaeology.

In 1908, the year of McJunkin's discovery, the nation still had a great deal to learn about the oldest chapters in American history. The United States had just commemorated the 300th anniversary of England's Jamestown settlement in Virginia, and across the country, U.S. citizens memorialized Anglo-American beginnings. They expected newly arrived immigrants to learn English quickly and leave their Old World cultures behind. Textbooks of the era shared in the celebration of English colonization. They paid scant attention to the earlier Spanish and French arrivals in North America and none at all to the Native American inhabitants who had preceded them by thousands of years. *The Beginner's American History,* like most popular texts of the time, opened by relating the voyages of Christopher Columbus, the Italian explorer who encountered America while sailing for the Indies in 1492.

In 1908 a discovery by African American cowboy George McJunkin started a revolution in American archaeology.

Even as far back as the sixteenth century, European newcomers to North America showed only occasional interest in the origins of the people who already lived there. Columbus, thinking he had reached the Asian islands close to India and China ("the Indies"), mistakenly lumped America's peoples together as "Indians." Europeans who were curious about Native Americans had little but the Bible to guide their inquiries. Christians speculated that North America's original residents were descendants of the Lost Tribe of Israel who had somehow wandered to these lands in Old Testament times. Whatever their origin, these inhabitants could hardly have been here more than 3000 years, the Europeans reasoned, for the world itself was thought to be scarcely 6000 years old.

Such views had changed little by the nineteenth century when American settlers swarmed westward in search of farmsteads. The newcomers speculated on the origin of mysterious burial mounds they saw throughout much of the Mississippi valley. Impressed by the size of these structures but convinced that Indians could not have built them, these new settlers suggested that the hills had to be the work of another race. Perhaps the ancient builders were European in origin and had somehow fallen victim to ancestors of the Native Americans. By 1890, as decades of Indian wars on the Great Plains drew to a close, only a few scientists took an interest in who the earliest North Americans really were, where they came from, when they arrived on the continent, and how they lived.

In the century since George McJunkin picked up a prehistoric bison bone, all of that has changed. Scholars who explore and debate the long history of early North America have steadily learned more about the continent's first inhabitants. An expanding American history now stretches back in time far before the Jamestown settlement and reaches broadly from coast to coast. Its earliest roots lie with the indigenous inhabitants of the continent over many millennia. In addition, the foreigners who suddenly intruded into portions of the Native American world in the sixteenth century—speaking Spanish, French, and occasionally English—also represent a significant beginning. All these people now number, in different ways, among America's first founders.

Ancient America

The discoveries at Folsom more than doubled archaeologists' estimates of the time span that humans had lived in North America. Clearly, they had resided on the continent for at least 10,000 years. After the Folsom find, collectors immediately began combing the Southwest for additional evidence. They soon found it at nearby Clovis, New Mexico, 170 miles south of Folsom and close to the Texas border.

In 1929 a teenager reported spotting large, well-chipped spear heads near Clovis. Three years later, amateur collectors located more in the same vicinity, this time beside the tooth of an extinct mammoth. These so-called Clovis points lay beneath a soil layer containing Folsom points, so they were clearly older than McJunkin's and Figgins's finds. Ever since, scientists have unearthed Clovis-like points throughout much of North America. According to the latest calculations, humans started creating these weapons roughly 13,900 years ago and ceased about 12,900 years ago. This means that people were hunting widely on the continent nearly 14,000 years ago. Archaeologists continue to push back and refine the estimated date for the appearance of the first people in the Americas. Recently, they have unearthed evidence suggesting the possible presence of pre-Clovis inhabitants.

The Question of Origins

Like all other peoples, the Indian societies whose ancestors have lived in America for at least 14,000 years retain rich and varied accounts of their own origins. No amount of scientific data can diminish or replace the powerful creation stories, in the Americas or elsewhere throughout the world, that have been passed down from distant ancestors and continue to serve an important cultural purpose. Nevertheless, modern researchers continue to compile evidence about the origin and migration of humans, very recent newcomers on a planet estimated to be 4.5 billion years old.

Scientists have determined that multicelled organisms began to evolve less than 600 million years ago. The higher primates who were humans' direct ancestors (that is, in the genus *Homo*, like today's humans) first emerged in Africa some 2.5 million years ago. Some ancient members of the *Homo* family tree may have migrated out of Africa as far as the Black Sea region by 1.7 million years ago. But it was scarcely 70,000 years ago when the most recent

Polar view shows that glaciers blocked movement from Beringia (B) into North America (A) 20,000 years ago. By 14,000 years ago (large map) melting had created an access corridor.

■ MAP 1.1

THE EARLIEST AMERICANS The Ice Age ancestors of Native Americans crossed from Siberia when a land bridge linked Asia and Alaska. Some probably migrated south along an ice-free corridor 14,000 years ago. Others may have followed a Pacific coastal route, moving rapidly down the shores of North and South America by boat, with frequent stops along an ancient coastline that is now submerged.

ancestors of modern humans moved from Africa to spread across the Eurasian landmass, the area comprising Europe and Asia. These more recent forebears possessed well-developed language capacities and hunting skills.

By 40,000 years ago some of these Stone Age hunter–gatherers had already reached Australia, somehow crossing more than 40 miles of water. Others lived on the steppes of Central Asia and the frozen tundra of Siberia. They had perfected the tools they needed to survive in a cold climate: flint spear points for killing mammoths, reindeer, and the woolly rhinoceros; and bone needles to sew warm, waterproof clothes out of animal skin.

Over thousands of years, bands of these northern hunters migrated east across Siberia in search of game. Eventually they arrived at the region where the Bering Strait now separates Russia from Alaska. The geography of this area has fluctuated over time because of dramatic changes in global weather. Between 25,000 and 11,000 years ago, cold conditions expanded arctic ice caps, trapping vast quantities of the earth's water in the form of huge glaciers. As a result, ocean levels sank by 300 feet—enough to expose a bridge of land 600 miles wide between Asia and America.

The Bering Land Bridge formed part of a frigid, windswept region known as Beringia. Small groups of people could have subsisted in this cold landscape by hunting mammoths and musk oxen. As the climate warmed and the ocean rose again, some might have headed farther east onto higher ground in Alaska. If so, these newcomers would have been cut off permanently from Siberia as water once more submerged the land bridge. But the same warming process also eventually opened a pathway through the glaciers blanketing northern America. This opening could account for the sudden appearance of Clovis hunters across much of North America nearly 14,000 years ago.

Geologists have shown that as Ice Age glaciers receded about 14,000 years ago, an ice-free corridor opened along the eastern slope of the Rocky Mountains. For decades, scholars have conjectured that small bands of people probably moved south from Alaska through that route. Presumably these hunters, armed with razor-sharp Clovis points, spread rapidly across the continent, destroying successive herds of large animals that had never faced human predators before. Perhaps, according to this theory, generations of hunters moved swiftly south as local game supplies dwindled. They would have migrated as far as the tip of South America within several thousand years.

The Newest Approaches

In recent decades, intriguing developments have complicated the picture. At Cactus Hill, Virginia, and Topper, South Carolina, archaeologists have uncovered artifacts suggesting the presence of immediate predecessors to the Clovis people. At Florida's Aucilla River, divers have recovered a 14,000-year-old cache of ivory and bone tools. Other pre-Clovis objects have surfaced at the Meadowcroft site southwest of Pittsburgh. The most provocative new discovery has come from South America. In an ancient campsite at Monte Verde, Chile, experts found knotted cords, and even a footprint, dating back more than 14,000 years.

Scholars agree that early inhabitants of North and South America—whether they arrived by land or sea—came primarily from distant Asian ancestry.

We know that travelers in the Paleolithic era reached Australia from the Asian landmass by water. Could other small groups have used a coastal route around the North Pacific rim to reach the Americas? If so, bands of so-called Paleo-Indians may have migrated in boats down the Northwest Coast, pausing to fish or gather food. Such seaborne journeys, stretching over generations, could help explain the rapid diffusion of humans into South America. Most of their campsites beside the Pacific would now be several hundred feet under water, for the rising oceans have since covered America's ancient coastlines. Perhaps Monte Verde, located on higher ground and preserved by a layer of peat moss, represents a revealing exception.

Meanwhile, genetic comparisons of different peoples, present and past, are yielding increasingly specific, if controversial, details about ancient migrations and interactions. Advances in understanding DNA—the genetic material that determines our physical make-up and transmits it to our offspring—may someday sharpen or change our awareness regarding Native American origins. To date, they have confirmed one basic conclusion of the physical anthropologists who have examined blood types, dental formation, and other evidence for years. Scholars agree that early inhabitants of North and South America—whether they arrived by land or sea—came primarily from distant Asian ancestry.

The Archaic World

Some 10,000 years ago, the Paleo-Indian era in North America gradually gave way to the Archaic era, which lasted for roughly 7000 years. Changes in wildlife played a large part in the transition. As the continent warmed further and the great glaciers receded north, more than 100 of America's largest species disappeared. These included mammoths, mastodons, horses, camels, and the great long-horned bison. Researchers debate whether these large animals were hunted to extinction, wiped out by disease, or destroyed by climate change.

Whatever the causes—and probably there were many—human groups had to adapt to the shifting conditions. They developed new methods of survival. Inhabitants turned to the smaller bison, similar to modern-day ones, that had managed to survive and flourish on the northern plains. Hunters learned to drive herds over cliffs and use the remains for food, clothing, and tools. One such bison jump is located in eastern Colorado. Another mass kill site, known as Head-Smashed-In, is in western Alberta; native peoples used it for 7000 years.

Kenneth Garrett/National Geographic Society

■ Archaeologists digging at Cactus Hill, Virginia, and several other sites have unearthed artifacts that suggest human habitation before the arrival of hunters using Clovis points. The foreground objects are laid out clockwise by apparent age, with the most recent at the top. Clovis-like spearheads appear in the second group. The third and fourth groups, taken from lower layers of soil, are thought to be older items, some reaching back well beyond 14,000 years. With the most primitive tools, it becomes difficult to separate implements made by humans from natural rock fragments.

A weighted spear-throwing device, called an atlatl, let hunters bring down medium-sized game. Archaic peoples also devised nets, hooks, and snares for catching birds, fish, and small animals. By 4000 years ago, they were even using duck decoys in the Great Basin of Utah and Nevada.

Though genetically similar, these far-flung bands of Archaic Indians developed diverse cultures as they adapted to very different landscapes and environments. Nothing illustrates this diversity more clearly than speech. A few early languages branched into numerous language families, then divided further into hundreds of separate languages. The Algonkian family of North American languages, which includes Wampanoag in the east and Cheyenne in the west, in turn has links to Choctaw, Chickasaw, and other southeastern languages of the Muskogean family. Similar cultural variations emerged in everything from diet and shelter to folklore and spiritual beliefs.

All of these variations reflected local conditions, and each represented an experiment that might potentially lead to more elaborate social arrangements. Among hunting and gathering societies, subsistence was a way of life, and people lived in small and widely dispersed groups, moving regularly to take advantage of seasonal food sources. As a result, their social structure remained very simple. Eventually in the Americas, as elsewhere, the cultivation of domesticated plants led to settled horticultural societies. A more stable food supply allowed the creation of surpluses, prompting larger permanent villages, wider trade, and a greater accumulation of goods. With this settled lifestyle came greater social stratification and the emergence of hereditary chiefdoms.

Frequently, a class of priests appeared near the top of the expanding hierarchy, mediating between the people and a god or gods who were intimately involved in human affairs. And slaves, unknown in hunting and gathering societies, appeared at the bottom of the hierarchy, since captives could be put to work for their conquerors, and an expanded population meant an increased labor force, not only to produce more food but also to create the public works that demonstrated, and enhanced, the power of the chiefs and priests. As the social structures became more complex, greater specialization ensued, allowing the development of more extensive communities with more elaborate political and religious activities and greater concentrations of power. But such developments were slow and uneven, depending on local conditions.

The Rise of Maize Agriculture

One condition remained common to all the various Archaic American groups, despite their emerging regional differences: they all shared a lack of domesticated animals. Diverse peoples living in the Eurasian landmass had managed to domesticate five important species—sheep, goats, pigs, cows, and horses—by 6000 years ago, leading to the creation of stable pastoral societies. But none of these mammals existed in the Americas, nor did camels, donkeys, or water buffalo. Archaic Indians, like their Asian forebears, did possess dogs, and settlers in the Andes domesticated the llama over 5000 years ago. Herds of buffalo and deer could be followed, and even managed and exploited in various ways. But no mammal remaining in the Americas could readily be made to provide humans with milk, meat, hides, and hauling power.

Although their prospects for domesticating animals were severely limited, early Americans had many more options when it came to the domestication of plants. Humans managed to domesticate plants independently in five different areas around the world, and three of those regions were located in the Americas. First, across parts of South America, inhabitants learned to cultivate root crops of potatoes and manioc (also known as cassava, which yields a nutritious starch). Second, in Mesoamerica (modern-day Mexico and Central America), people gradually brought squash, beans, and maize (corn) under cultivation—three foods that complement one another effectively in dietary terms.

Maize agriculture became a crucial ingredient for the growth of complex societies in the Americas, but its development and diffusion took time. Unlike wheat, the Eurasian cereal crop which offered a high yield from the start, maize took thousands of years of cultivation in the Americas to evolve into an extremely productive food source. Moreover, most of Eurasia stretches east-west through a temperate climate that fosters the spread of similar agriculture. Because of this similarity of climate, a crop that succeeds in one place can readily be grown in another. The western hemisphere, in contrast, lies on a north-south axis; the Americas stretch through numerous different climate zones. Some experts speculate that this geographical fact of life made crop diffusion more difficult. For example, the differences between Mesoamerica and North America proved substantial when it came to mastering maize agriculture. Southwestern Indians in North America began growing thumb-sized ears of maize only about three thousand years ago (at a time of increasing rainfall), well after the crop had taken hold in Mesoamerica. More than a thousand years later, maize reached eastern North America, where it adapted slowly to the cooler climate and shorter growing season.

Southwestern Indians in North America began growing thumb-sized ears of maize only about three thousand years ago.

In the east, a different agriculture had already taken hold, centered on other once-wild plants. This was the third zone where the independent domestication of plants occurred in the Americas. As early as 4000 years ago, eastern Indians at dozens of Archaic sites were cultivating domesticated squash and sunflowers. The latter yielded edible seeds, as did several less familiar plants. Sumpweed, or marsh elder, flourished near lakes and rivers and produced an oily seed. Goosefoot, knotweed, and maygrass all produced starchy seeds that have been found near Archaic sites in Kentucky, Illinois, and elsewhere. These domesticated plants provided supplemental food sources for eastern communities that continued to subsist primarily by hunting and gathering until the arrival introduction of maize agriculture into the eastern woodlands during the first millennium A.D.

About 3000 years ago, as maize cultivation began in the Southwest and gardens of squash and sunflowers appeared in the Northeast, the first of several powerful Mesoamerican cultures—the Olmecs—emerged in the lowlands along the southwestern edge of the Gulf of Mexico. Their name meant "those who live in the land of rubber," for they had learned how to turn the milky juice of several plants into an unusual elastic substance. The Olmecs grew maize and manioc in abundance, and their surplus of food supported a hierarchical society. Its leaders built large burial mounds and pyramids, and they erected distinctive stone monuments—huge heads standing five to nine feet high. The Olmecs, who revered the jaguar in their religion, developed a complex calendar and played a distinctive game with a large ball of solid rubber. Since they traded widely with people across Mesoamerica, they passed on these cultural traits, which reappeared later in other societies in the region.

Olmec traders, traveling by coastal canoe, may even have encountered and influenced the Poverty Point culture that existed near the lower Mississippi River 4,200 to 2,700 years ago. Numerous late Archaic locations near the Gulf Coast shed light on Poverty Point culture. It takes its name from the largest of these sites—a 500-acre complex in northeast Louisiana first rediscovered through aerial photography in the mid-twentieth century. Since then, archaeologists have determined that workers constructed Poverty Point between 3,500 and 2,700 years ago. This religious and political center consists of a vast semicircle of six concentric earthen ridges that span four-fifths of a mile. Researchers estimate that the complex required three million worker-hours to build. Each ridge, more than 80 feet wide and 8 feet high, may have served to raise human dwellings above the flood plain.

The Poverty Point culture, with its trade network on the lower Mississippi and its tributaries, stands as a mysterious precursor to the mound-building societies of the Mississippi Valley that emerged much later. (In a similar way, the Olmecs prefigured the later Mayan, Toltec, and Aztec cultures in Mesoamerica.) Remnants of these more extensive Mississippian cultures still existed when newcomers from Europe arrived to stay, around A.D. 1500. But in many parts of North America, smaller and less stratified Archaic cultures, that combined hunting for a variety of animals with gathering and processing local plant foods, remained intact well into the era of European colonization.

A Thousand Years of Change: A.D. 500 to 1500

The millennium stretching from the fifth century to the explorations of Columbus in the fifteenth century witnessed dramatic and far-reaching changes in the separate world of the Americas. In the warm and temperate regions on both sides of the equator, empires rose and fell as maize agriculture and elaborate irrigation systems provided food surpluses, allowing the creation of cities and the emergence of hierarchical societies.

On the coast of Peru, for example, the Moche people excelled in delicate gold work, intricate pottery, and bright weavings made from domesticated cotton. The Moches built huge pyramids to honor the sun, and their realm prospered for centuries. But around A.D. 800 it collapsed suddenly, perhaps a victim of the periodic disturbance in Pacific weather known as El Niño.

In the 1400s, centuries after the Moches and their neighbors disappeared, the expansive Inca empire emerged in their place. Inca emperors, ruling from the capital at Cuzco, prompted the construction of a vast road system throughout the Peruvian Andes. Stonemasons built large storage facilities at provincial centers to hold food for garrisons of soldiers and to store tribute items such as gold and feathers destined for the capital. Until the empire's fall in the 1530s, officials leading pack trains of llamas ferried goods to and from Cuzco along mountainous roadways.

Similarly, Mesoamerica also saw a series of impressive civilizations—from the Mayans to the Aztecs—in the millennium spanning A.D. 500 to 1500 in the western calendar. Developments in North America in the same millennium were very different but bear enough resemblance to patterns in Mesoamerica to raise intriguing and still unanswerable questions. Did significant migrations northward from Mesoamerica ever take place? And if not, were there substantial trade links at times, allowing distinctive materials, techniques, ideas, and seeds to reach North American peoples? Or did the continent's distinctive societies, such as the Anasazi in the Southwest and the Cahokia mound builders on the Mississippi River, develop almost entirely independently? Not surprisingly, North American archaeologists continue to debate the extent of possible links to Mesoamerica in the centuries before Columbus.

Valleys of the Sun: The Mesoamerican Empires

In Mesoamerica, the Mayans and the Aztecs established rich empires where worship of the sun was central to their religious beliefs. Mayan culture flourished between A.D. 300 and 900. The Mayans controlled a domain stretching from the lowlands of the Yucatan peninsula to the highlands of what is now southern Mexico, Guatemala, Honduras, and El Salvador—an area half the size of Texas. They derived their elaborate calendar—a 52-year cycle made up of 20-day months—and many other aspects of their culture from the earlier Olmecs, but they devised their own distinctive civilization.

The Mayan people built huge stone temples and held ritual bloodletting ceremonies to appease their gods. They also constructed narrow courts for a ball game—which some Mexicans still play—where opposing players hit a rubber ball with their hips. Recently, researchers have deciphered the complex glyphs that appear throughout Mayan art. These pictographs are yielding detailed information and precise dates for individual rulers. The Mayans, like the Moches in Peru, declined mysteriously, and dominance in Mesoamerica moved farther west, where great cities arose in the highlands of Central Mexico, first at Teotihuacan and then nearby at Tenochtitlán, the capital of the powerful but short-lived Aztec empire.

The people who constructed the metropolis of Teotihuacan in the Mexican highlands remain an enigma. They appear to have traded with the Mayans and perhaps with the Olmecs before that. They laid out their immense city in a grid, dominated by the 200-foot Pyramid of the Sun. By A.D. 500, the city held more than 100,000 inhabitants, making it one of the largest in the world. But Teotihuacan's society declined fast, for unknown reasons, succeeded first by the Toltecs and then by the Aztecs.

Eager to expand their empire and to extend their rule, the Aztecs launched fierce wars against neighboring lands.

The Aztecs (or Mexicas) had migrated to the central Valley of Mexico from the north in the twelfth century. Looked down upon at first by the local people, they swiftly rose to power through strategic alliances and military skill. According to legend, the Aztecs' war god instructed their priests to locate the place where a great eagle perched on a cactus. They found such a spot, on a swampy island in Lake Texcoco. By the 1400s the Aztecs had transformed the island into Tenochtitlán, an imposing urban center, located on the site of modern Mexico City.

The impressive city of Tenochtitlán, surrounded by Lake Texcoco and linked to shore by causeways, became the Aztec capital. Its architecture imitated the ruined temple city of Teotihuacan, which lay 35 miles to the north, and exceeded it in grandeur. The Aztecs also adopted many other features of the cultures they had displaced. They used the cyclical 52-year Mesoamerican calendar, and they worshipped the great god Quetzalcoatl, the plumed serpent associated with wind and revered by the Toltecs, their predecessors in the Valley of Mexico.

Schooled in hardship, pessimism, and violence, the Aztecs saw themselves as living in the World of the Fifth Sun, a final human era destined to end in cataclysm just as earlier epochs had. Eager to expand their empire and to extend their rule as long as possible, they launched fierce wars against neighboring lands. But their primary objective was not to kill enemies or gain more territory. Instead, Aztec warriors demanded tribute and took prisoners from the people they subdued. They then sacrificed numerous captives at pyramid temples to placate the gods. These deities, they believed, would in turn protect them as they conducted further wars of capture, leading to more tribute and sacrifices.

The Aztecs' grim cycle of conflict helped them ward off deep fears of extended drought and lasting destruction. But it also weakened their expanding realm. Like the Incas of Peru, the Aztecs imposed harsh treatment on the peoples they conquered, extracting heavy annual tributes. This harsh policy alienated the provinces from the Aztecs and made their centralized empire vulnerable to external attack. When a foreign assault prompted their downfall in the early sixteenth century, it came from a direction the Aztec priests and generals could not predict.

The Anasazi: Chaco Canyon and Mesa Verde

The great urban centers of Peru and Mesoamerica had no counterparts farther north. The peoples inhabiting North America in the millennium before Columbus never developed the levels of social stratification, urban dynamism, architectural grandeur, astronomical study, or intensive corn agriculture that characterized the Mayans, Incas, or Aztecs. Yet elements of all these traits appeared in North America, especially in the Southwest and the Mississippi valley, with the emergence of increasingly settled societies and widening circles of exchange.

Modern scholars wonder whether the maize, squash, and bean agriculture, sun worship, and astronomical knowledge found among North America's southwestern peoples had roots farther south. After all, the Aztecs' ancestors had apparently migrated down from this dry region to the interior of Mexico after A.D. 1100. Could other north–south movements back and forth have occurred, earlier or later, between Central Mexico and the American Southwest? Links of migration or trade would help to explain the dozens of ancient ball courts, similar to those in Mesoamerica, that archaeologists have excavated in Arizona. Recently, researchers have identified a north–south traffic in turquoise, highly prized in both Mexico and the Southwest.

Three identifiably different cultures were already well established in the North American Southwest by A.D. 500. The Mogollons occupied the dry, mountainous regions of eastern Arizona and southern New Mexico. Mogollon women were expert potters who crafted delicate bowls from the fine clay of the Mimbres River. Families lived in sunken pit houses that were cool in summer and warm in winter. The Hohokams, their neighbors to the west in south-central Arizona, did the same. The Hohokams also constructed extensive canal and floodgate systems to irrigate their fields from the Gila and Salt rivers. According to their Native American successors, who still dwell in the Phoenix area, the name *Hohokam* means "those who have gone."

Farther north, in what is now the Four Corners Region, where Utah and Colorado meet Arizona and New Mexico, lived the people remembered as the Anasazi, or "ancient ones." By A.D. 750 the Anasazi inhabited aboveground houses clustered around a central ceremonial room dug into the earth. They entered this circular space by descending a ladder through the roof. The climb back up from this sunken chamber, known as a kiva, symbolized the initial ascent of humans into the Upper World from below. European explorers used the Spanish word for town, *pueblo,* to describe the Anasazis' multiroom and multistory dwellings of masonry or adobe.

Beginning in the 850s, Chaco Canyon in the San Juan River basin of northwest New Mexico emerged as the hub of the Anasazi world. Wide, straight roads radiating out from Chaco let builders haul hundreds of thousands of logs for use as roof beams in the nine great pueblos that still dot the canyon. The largest of them, Pueblo Bonito, rises five stories high in places and has 600 rooms arranged in a vast semicircle. Yet the canyon's population remained small,

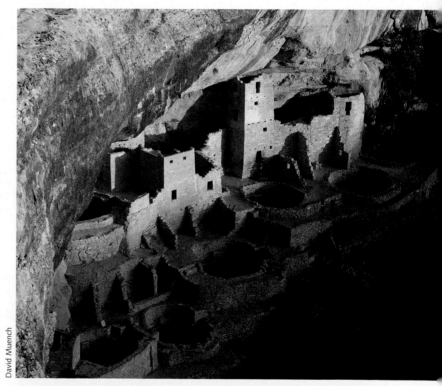

David Muench

■ Cliff Palace, at Mesa Verde National Park in southwest Colorado, was created 900 years ago, when the Anasazi left the mesa tops and moved into more secure and inaccessible cliff dwellings. Facing southwest, the building gained heat from the rays of the low afternoon sun in winter, and overhanging rock protected the structure from rain, snow, and the hot midday summer sun. The numerous round kivas, each covered with a flat roof originally, suggest that Cliff Palace may have had a ceremonial importance.

■ MAP 1.2

AMERICA IN THE MILLENNIUM BEFORE COLUMBUS, A.D. 500–1500 A number of distinctive cultures emerged in the Americas during the ten centuries before 1500. Most learned from their predecessors—Mississippians from Hopewells and Aztecs from Mayans, for example—but debate continues over the full extent of trade and travel networks at any given time.

perhaps dominated by priestly rulers who used violence to extract labor, food, and tribute from the region's inhabitants.

Violence and warfare played a significant part in Anasazi life, as they did in the Mesoamerican world of the same era. But in the end, environmental change exerted the greatest destructive force. Tree rings show that after 1130, a drought gripped the Colorado Plateau for half a century. The turquoise workshops of Chaco Canyon fell silent. Most of the inhabitants moved away. Some no doubt headed north, where dozens of Anasazi communities with access to better farming conditions dotted the landscape. Earlier, they had resided atop mesas (from the Spanish word meaning "table," for the region's distinctive hills with steep sides and level tops). But gradually—with populations growing, the climate worsening, and competition for resources stiffening—they moved into sheltered cliff dwellings built into the mesa walls. Cliff Palace at Mesa Verde in southwestern Colorado, with its 220 rooms and 23 kivas, remains the most famous today because of its ready access and careful preservation. Yet other sites were even larger. Reached only by ladders and steep trails, these pueblos offered protection from enemies and shelter from the scorching summer sun. Still, another prolonged drought (1276–1299) forced the Anasazi to move once again by 1300. Survivors dispersed south into lands later occupied by the Hopi, Zuni, and Rio Grande peoples.

The Mississippians: Cahokia and Moundville

Earlier, in the Mississippi Valley, the Hopewell people had prospered for half a millennium before A.D. 500 (in the era of the Roman Empire in Europe). The Hopewell lived primarily in southern Ohio and western Illinois. But their network of trade extended over much of the continent. Archaeologists excavating ornate Hopewell burial sites have found a wide array of objects, including pipestone and flint from the Missouri River Valley, copper and silver from Lake Superior, mica and quartz from Appalachia, sea shells and shark teeth from Florida, and artwork made from Rocky Mountain obsidian and grizzly-bear teeth. Hopewell trading laid the groundwork for larger mound-building societies, known as the Mississippian cultures that emerged in the Mississippi Valley and the Southeast in roughly the same centuries as the great Mesoamerican civilizations and the Anasazi in the Southwest.

The more elaborate and widespread Mississippian tradition developed gradually after A.D. 500. Then after A.D. 900, it flourished broadly for six centuries. Shifts in technology and agriculture facilitated the rise of the Mississippians.

Bows and arrows, long used in arctic regions of North America but little known elsewhere, began to see widespread use in the eastern woodlands around A.D. 700. At the same time, maize underwent a transformation from a marginal oddity to a central staple crop. Growers as far east as northern Florida were producing it by the eighth century, and it soon appeared farther north with the spread of a more hardy variety. By 1300, maize and bean agriculture reached all the way to the Iroquoian peoples around Lake Ontario and in the St. Lawrence River valley. Across the east, food supplies expanded as Native American communities planted corn in the rich bottomland soil along the region's many rivers. More and more people began settling in these fertile areas. Maize agriculture also spurred bureaucracy and hierarchy. With greater productivity, commercial and religious elites asserted greater control over farmers to take advantage of the community's expanding resources.

The largest mound at Cahokia—indeed, the largest ancient earthwork in North America—rises 100 feet in four separate levels.

The extent of contacts, rivalries, and exchanges between separate Mississippian mound-building centers remains uncertain. Mississippian sites have been found as far apart as Spiro, in eastern Oklahoma, and Etowah, in northern Georgia. The largest complex was at Cahokia in American Bottom, the 25-mile floodplain below where the Illinois and Missouri rivers flow into the Mississippi. We will never know Cahokia's full extent, for city planners expanding St. Louis in the nineteenth century flattened more than two dozen mounds on the Mississippi's west bank, leaving little record of their work. Across the river, builders in East St. Louis, Illinois, and farmers eager to increase their acreage leveled more mounds. But nearby, on Cahokia Creek, dozens of rectangular, flat-topped temple mounds still remain after almost a thousand years. The largest mound at Cahokia—indeed, the largest ancient earthwork in North America—rises 100 feet in four separate levels, covering 16 acres and using nearly 22 million cubic feet of earth. A log palisade with gates and watchtowers once enclosed this temple mound and its adjacent plaza in a 200-acre central compound. In a separate construction nearby, residents used engineering and astronomy skills to erect 48 posts in a huge circle, 410 feet in diameter. This creation, now called Woodhenge after England's Stonehenge, functioned as a calendar to mark the daily progression of the sun throughout each year.

Richard A. Cooke/CORBIS

■ The most striking Mississippian earthwork to survive is the enigmatic Serpent Mound, built in the eleventh century by the Fort Ancient people in southern Ohio. The snake (holding an egg in its mouth) has links to astronomy because its curves are aligned toward key positions of the sun. The serpent may even represent Halley's Comet, which blazed in the heavens in A.D. 1066. Completely uncoiled, the earthwork would measure more than a quarter mile in length.

Cahokia's mounds rose quickly in the decades after A.D. 1050, as the local population expanded beyond 10,000. A succession of powerful leaders reorganized the vicinity's small, isolated villages into a strong regional chiefdom that controlled towns on both sides of the river. These towns provided the chiefdom's centralized elite with food, labor, and goods for trading. The elaborate religious rituals and the wealth and power of the leaders are seen in a burial site opened by archaeologists in the 1970s. The body of one prominent figure, presumably a chief, was laid out on a surface of 20,000 shell beads. Near him lay six young adults who must have been relatives or servants sacrificed at the ruler's funeral. They were supplied with hundreds of stone arrowheads—finely chipped and neatly sorted—plus antler projectile points, a rolled tube of sheet copper, bushels of glistening mica (a transparent mineral crystallized into very thin sheets), and 15 stone disks used in the popular spear-throwing game known as chunkey. Archaeologists found further evidence of sacrifice nearby. They uncovered the remains of four men, whose heads and hands had been cut off, and a pit filled with nearly four dozen young women who apparently had been strangled.

The population of Cahokia perhaps exceeded 15,000 people around A.D. 1100. It then waned steadily over the next two centuries as the unstable hierarchy lost its sway over nearby villages. As Cahokia declined, other regional chiefdoms rose along other rivers. The most notable appeared at Moundville in west-central Alabama, 15 miles south of modern Tuscaloosa. A century of archaeological work at this site has revealed clear phases of development after A.D. 900. First, the inhabitants adopted corn agriculture. This in turn allowed them to intensify craft production, and a budding elite emerged. Before long, the leaders directed the creation of mounds in several small villages. Shortly before 1250, workers laid out an 80-acre rectangular plaza at the Moundville site. They began construction on more than 20 flat-topped mounds (some larger than football fields), which provided dwelling sites and burial locations for the small ruling class. Excavated burial objects—ceremonial axes, beads carved from conch shells, and distinctive copper spools worn as giant earrings—reveal evidence of long-distance trade and elaborate rituals. But by 1400, Moundville had started to lose its grip as a dominant ceremonial center. The causes of this decline remain unclear, but once again small villages became the norm.

Linking the Continents

Estimates vary widely, but probably around one-sixth of the world's population—as many as 60 to 70 million people—resided in the Americas when Columbus arrived in 1492. Most of them lived near the equator, where their ancient ancestors had developed efficient forms of tropical agriculture. But roughly one-tenth of the hemisphere's population (6 to 7 million people) was spread across North America from coast to coast.

We cannot rule out the appearance in America of ancient ocean travelers on occasion. Around A.D. 400, Polynesian mariners sailed their double-hulled canoes from the Marquesas Islands in the South Pacific to the Hawaiian archipelago. Conceivably, in the millennium before 1500, one or two boats from Africa, Ireland, Polynesia, China, or Japan sailed—or were blown—to the American mainland. But any survivors of such a journey would have had little genetic or cultural impact, for no sustained back-and-forth contact between the societies occurred. Even the seafaring Norse from Scandinavia, known as Vikings, whose brief settlement on Canadian soil a thousand years ago is now well documented, remained for only a few years and never established a lasting colony. Native American societies, therefore, knew nothing of the people, plants, animals, and viruses of the Eastern Hemisphere.

America's near isolation ended dramatically, beginning in the late fifteenth century, after innovations in deep-sea sailing opened the world's oceans as a new frontier for human exploration. Chinese sailors in the North Pacific or Portuguese mariners in the South Atlantic could well have been the first outsiders to establish ongoing contact with the peoples of the Western Hemisphere. But instead, it was Christopher Columbus, an Italian navigator in the service of Spain, who became the agent of this sweeping change. He encountered the Americas by accident and misinterpreted what he had found. But his chance encounter with a separate realm would spark new patterns of human migration, cultural transfer, and ecological exchange, which would reshape the modern world.

The Vikings Reach Newfoundland and Beyond

Scandinavian settlers had colonized Ireland in the 830s and Iceland in the 870s. A century later, these Norse seafarers—led by Erik the Red—reached Greenland in the 980s. When Erik's son, Leif, learned that Vikings blown off course had sighted land farther west, he sailed from Greenland to the North American coast. Here he explored a region near the Gulf of St. Lawrence that he named Vinland. Around A.D. 1000, Leif Eriksson's relatives directed several return voyages to Vinland, where the Vikings built an outpost called Straumfjord. The tiny colony of 160 people, including women and children, lived and grazed livestock in Vinland for several years until native peoples drove them away.

For centuries, this Norse contact was known only through epic Icelandic tales called the Vinland Sagas—medieval transcriptions of oral traditions. But in the 1960s archaeologists found Viking artifacts at L'Anse aux Meadows, a coastal site in northern Newfoundland. Perhaps this secure base, today reconstructed with Viking-style sod houses, was Straumfjord. Researchers believe that Norsemen returned occasionally to cut timber and that they traded with inhabitants of northeastern Canada for generations.

For three centuries, the Viking community in Greenland endured. The Norse settlers shipped walrus tusks and hunting falcons to Europe in return for farm tools and livestock. But trade slumped in Europe after the plague known as the Black Death swept away a third of the continent's population around 1350. Other factors made the settlement less viable as well. Climate changes brought colder, wetter weather, and conflict increased with Inuit natives. Soil erosion, caused by tree-cutting and overgrazing of sheep, goats, and cattle, also took a toll. By 1450 Viking settlements in Greenland had died out completely. Whether sailors elsewhere in Europe knew much about Norse exploits in the North Atlantic remains shrouded in mystery.

Oceanic Travel and the Beginnings of Globalization

What Europeans did know, vaguely, was the existence of the distant Chinese Empire. They called the realm Cathay, a term used by Italian merchant Marco Polo, who journeyed from Venice across Asia along the fabled Silk Road in the 1270s. Polo returned to Italy in 1292 to publish his *Travels*, an account of adventures in China during the reign of Kublai Khan. He told of many things unknown to Europeans, including rocks that burned like wood (coal) and spices that preserved meat. Lacking winter fodder for their herds, Europe's farmers regularly slaughtered numerous cattle in the fall and pickled or salted the beef to preserve it. Asian spices such as nutmeg, cinnamon, pepper, ginger, and cloves, if they could be obtained, would offer new preservatives. When renewed Islamic power in the Middle East cut off the Silk Road to Cathay, Europeans searched for other ways to reach that far-off region.

The desire to obtain oriental spices at their source fueled European oceanic exploration, leading eventually to the transformation of the Americas, yet it was China, not Europe, that first mastered ocean sailing. In 1281, during Marco Polo's sojourn in Beijing, Kublai Khan's formidable navy sailed with 4500 ships to invade Japan, only to fall victim to a huge typhoon en route. Still, China increased its deep-sea commerce with Southeast Asia, India, and the Persian Gulf. Chinese strength in overseas exploration and trade reached its height in the early fifteenth century under Admiral Zheng He (pronounced "Jung Huh"). Between 1405 and 1433, this brilliant officer led seven large fleets to the Indian Ocean, sailing as far as east Africa. His squadron included immense treasure ships 400 feet long and equipped with 24 cannon.

Then, abruptly, China turned away from the sea, losing its opportunity to become the first global maritime power and to play a leading role in shaping oceanic trade and the destiny of North America. Within a century of Zheng He's accomplishments, the empire grew dismissive of foreign trade and turned inward. Chinese officials destroyed the log books of earlier voyages and curtailed production of oceangoing vessels. Instead of powerful China on the Pacific, it was tiny Portugal, overlooking the Atlantic from the Iberian peninsula, that emerged as the leader in maritime innovation and exploration in the fifteenth century.

Geography and religious zeal helped to spur Portugal's unlikely rise to world prominence. The tiny country faced the sea at the crossroads between Mediterranean commerce and the coastal traffic of Northern Europe. This strategic location also exposed Portugal to the ongoing conflict between Christianity and Islam. The religion founded by Muhammad (born at Mecca in 570) had spread rapidly across North Africa from Arabia. By the eighth century, followers of Islam (known as Muslims, Moslems, or Moors) had crossed the Straits of Gibraltar to establish a kingdom in southern Spain. Centuries later, Spanish and Portuguese Christians rallied to force Islam out of the Iberian peninsula—a campaign that concluded in 1492—and to join other militant Europeans in fighting against Islamic power in the Middle East.

When Christian crusades to the holy land failed to defeat Islam and reopen overland trade routes to China, European strategists dreamed of skirting Africa by sea to reach Asia. The Portuguese were well positioned to lead this flanking movement around Islam. And if no such oceanic route to Asia existed, some speculated that Portuguese exploration south beyond the Sahara Desert, along the coast of sub-Saharan Africa, still might yield contact with strong Chris-

Courtesy, Algarve Tourism Board

■ Prince Henry of Portugal rarely went to sea himself. Instead, he established a base at Sagres, overlooking the Atlantic Ocean. From here, beginning in 1418, he sent mariners south along the African coast. They quickly laid claim to the islands of the eastern Atlantic, and by the 1440s they had initiated trade along the west African coast, carrying gold and slaves back to Portugal.

tian allies. For generations, Europeans had fostered legends of a wealthy kingdom somewhere in Africa, said to be ruled by a black Christian known as Prester John. Even if Prester John's imaginary realm could not be found, probes south from the Iberian Peninsula in ships might explore the full extent of Islamic influence in Africa and seek out fresh converts to Christianity.

Intellectual and economic motives also existed for these ventures. Such journeys could boost European knowledge of the unknown, based upon observations of the real world, and they might well open new markets for trade if technical difficulties could be overcome. The Portuguese had fished and traded in Atlantic coastal waters and the Mediterranean for ages, but long voyages far from land presented new challenges in shipbuilding and navigation. The first step involved an investment of leadership and resources, before early efforts could bear fruit and give the exploration process a momentum of it own.

Prince Henry of Portugal (1394–1460) provided these initial ingredients. The young prince— later honored as "Henry the Navigator"—had been appointed by the pope to head Portugal's military Order of Christ, an elite and wealthy organization of knights committed to the campaign against Islam. In 1415, at age 22, he crossed the Straits of Gibraltar to fight Muslims at Ceuta in North Africa. For the next 45 years, Henry waged a religiously inspired crusade-at-sea. He built his headquarters at Sagres in southwest Portugal. The center overlooked the ocean near Cape St. Vincent, the western tip of Europe. From there, his sailors launched a far-reaching revolution in human communication and trade, perhaps the most momentous single step in a globalization process that continues to the present day.

Henry's small ships, known as caravels, pushed south along the African coast. Innovative in design, caravels boasted narrow hulls, deep keels, and high gunwales for ocean sailing. Most importantly, they used triangular lateen sails, an idea that Mediterranean sailors had borrowed from Arab boats on the Red Sea. The lateen sail let a vessel travel into the breeze, tacking back and forth on a zigzag course against a prevailing wind; traditional square sails could not do this. Henry's experts at Sagres also drew on the work of Jewish cartographers from the island of Majorca to develop state-of-the-art charts, astronomical tables, and navigational instruments. His captains mastered the winds and currents off western Africa, but when he died in 1460, they

Topkapi Serail-Museum/AKG Photo

■ This Atlantic chart illustrates key aspects of Portuguese success in overseas exploration. Cape St. Vincent (A) where Prince Henry built his headquarters at Sagres, lies near the Strait of Gibraltar (B), the narrow entrance to the Mediterranean Sea. As Henry's mariners explored along the African coast for a sea passage to Asia, they also looked for possible allies such as Prester John, a mythical black king (C). They used the island groups of the eastern Atlantic to check their position: Azores (D), Madeiras (E), Canaries (F). Their small caravels (G) adopted the triangular lateen sail seen on traditional Arab boats in the Red Sea. Larger square-rigged ships that later sailed from Portugal to India (H) also incorporated lateen sails on a mast at the stern (I). A skilled Turkish navigator—who had never sailed on the Atlantic—made this unusual map in 1513. Piri Re'is used charts captured from a Christian ship in the Mediterranean; his inscriptions (J) are in Turkish.

had only sailed as far as what is now Sierra Leone. While skeptics wondered when the expensive ventures would see a tangible payoff, optimists noted that the African coast near Sierra Leone trended to the east and might eventually lead to Asia, despite the teaching of ancient scholars that no such route existed.

The early voyages during Henry's lifetime launched two developments that would have a lasting impact on the world. First, the Portuguese pioneered the course of European overseas colonization that would continue unabated for centuries. The harsh process began with the European discovery of three island groups off Northwest Africa—the Canaries, the Madeiras, and the Azores. Settlers sent to these islands from Portugal killed the native peoples; introduced crops such as sugar for export; and imported thousands of laborers to plant and process the sugar cane.

Second, in the 1440s Portuguese mariners initiated the Atlantic slave trade. They began by seizing people who lived on the coast of West Africa and deporting them to the new Atlantic sugar islands. Portuguese captains also carried slaves back to Europe and sold them there to supplement the growing sub-Saharan trade in ivory and gold. Africans themselves already had their own domestic slave trade. But this new Atlantic traffic, which grew relentlessly, eventually proved far more elaborate and devastating.

Looking for the Indies: da Gama and Columbus

During the 1480s, following a war with Spain, the Portuguese continued their African designs. In 1482 they erected a trading fort called Elmina Castle on the Gold Coast (modern Ghana) to guard against Spanish competition and to support exploration toward the east. But they soon encountered a new obstacle: Africa's long coastline turned abruptly south and continued in that direction for a vast distance. This led Portuguese captains below the equator, where they observed strange new constellations of stars in the night sky. Rather than sailing directly east toward China, as they had hoped, they had entered the unfamiliar Southern Hemisphere for the first time. Several years later, they reached the vast Congo River.

Finally, in 1487, Bartolomeu Dias rounded the southernmost tip of Africa, around the Cape of Good Hope, proving that a link existed between the Atlantic and Indian oceans. The Portuguese rejoiced: It now seemed possible to sail from Lisbon to India and tap into the rich spice trade flowing from the islands of Southeast Asia that Europeans vaguely called the Indies. Success came a decade later with the voyage of Vasco da Gama (1497–1499). When his ship returned to Portugal from India laden with pepper and cinnamon, Europeans realized they had finally opened a southeastern sea route to the silk and spice markets of the East.

Meanwhile, the rulers of rival Spain, who were reconquering their realm from Muslim control at great expense, gambled on finding a profitable *westward* route to the Indies. In 1492, King Ferdinand and Queen Isabella finally succeeded in driving Islam from their realm by military means. The monarchs imposed Christian orthodoxy and forced Jews into exile. That same year, they agreed to sponsor an Atlantic voyage by Christopher Columbus. Leaving Spain with 90 men aboard three small vessels, the Italian-born navigator headed for the Canary Islands, eluding Portuguese caravels sent to stop him. From the Canaries, he sailed due west on September 6. After a voyage of three or four weeks, he expected to encounter the island of Cipangu (Japan), which Marco Polo had mentioned, or to reach the coast of Asia. After weeks without sight of any land, his crewmen worried that they might not have enough supplies for the long return home. So Columbus gave out a false, reduced estimate of each day's headway, leading his sailors to believe they were still close to Europe. He recorded the much longer, more accurate distance in his own private log.

Early on October 12, the distressed seamen finally sighted a small island, naming it San Salvador after their Christian savior. The inhabitants proved welcoming, and Columbus recorded pleasure over the "gold which they wear hanging from their noses. But I wish to go and see if I can find the island of Cipangu." Within several weeks he located an impressively large island and found reason to hope that the mainland of the Great Khan was only "a 10 days' journey" further west. He claimed a nearby island as La Isla Española, the Spanish island, or Hispaniola (current-day Haiti and the Domican Republic). He noted stories of hostile islanders further south called Caribs, or Caniba, who were said to devour their enemies. "I repeat," he asserted, "the Caniba are no other than the people of the Grand Khan." (Upon hearing of these fierce Caribs, Europeans soon fashioned the word *cannibal* and named the region the Caribbean.)

Bolstered by these encounters, the explorers returned hastily across the Atlantic on a more northerly route. They weathered a horrendous winter storm to reach Spain in March 1493. Columbus told the Spanish court that he had reached the Indies off the Asian coast, and he displayed several natives he called "Indians" to prove it. His three later voyages did not shake this belief, which he clung to until his death in 1506. But in fact San Salvador, the tiny islet where Europeans had waded ashore on October 12, 1492, was not close to Asia but rather a

Zvi Richard Dor-Ner

■ Two weeks after his initial landfall in the Bahamas, Columbus approached the island of Cuba. "I have never seen anything so beautiful," he wrote in his diary. "There are many birds of all sizes that sing very sweetly, and there are many palms different from those in Guinea or Spain." The Indians he brought with him from the Bahamas told him the huge island contained many rivers and rich gold mines and that other lands lay farther west.

On Cuba's northeast coast, Columbus noted these "two very round mountains," one of them shaped "like a beautiful little mosque."

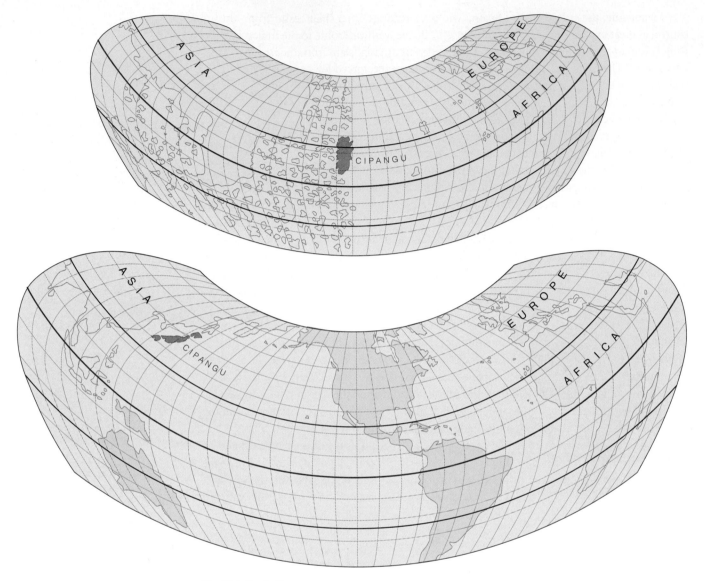

THE EXPECTATIONS OF CHRISTOPHER COLUMBUS   The globe as Columbus understood it (upper map) was decidedly smaller than the actual earth (lower map). He also believed Asia to be wider than it is, and he imagined Japan, or Cipangu, too far east and south from the Asian coastline. He was unaware of the Western Hemisphere. Therefore, when he sailed west and encountered Cuba, he thought it was Japan. He believed the adjacent Caribbean islands were the spice-rich Asian Indies.

part of the Bahamas (now called Watling's Island). Columbus's island of Hispaniola was half a world away from Cathay. The people who inhabited the region, Tainos and Caribs, were not subjects of the Great Khan. Nor was Cuba the land of Cipangu (Japan), which Marco Polo had mentioned.

Why these huge misunderstandings? The mariner made several crucial mistakes. Columbus, born in Genoa, had grown up in a European generation eager to find access to the East. Like others, he knew the world was round, not flat. He also accepted the idea of ancient geographer Ptolemy that by using north–south lines, one could divide the globe into 360 degrees of longitude. But he questioned Ptolemy's estimate that each degree measures 50 nautical miles at the equator. (Each actually measures 60 miles.) Instead, Columbus accepted an alternative figure of 45 miles, which made the circumference of his theoretical globe 25 percent smaller than the real distance around the earth. Although he underestimated the world's circumference, he also compounded his error by overestimating two other crucial distances: the breadth of the Eurasian landmass and the extent of Japan's separation from China. The first distance is actually 130 degrees of longitude, and the second is 20. Columbus used authorities who suggested 225 and 30 degrees, respectively. His estimates placed Japan 105 degrees closer to Europe, at the longitude that runs through eastern Lake Superior and western Cuba.

Columbus's errors came from relying on obscure passages in Christian scripture and dwelling on conflicting ancient geography treatises. But the navigator had practical familiarity with the Atlantic world. He visited the Madeiras, West Africa (Guinea), and perhaps even Iceland. He also benefited from the knowledge of his brother Bartolomew, a mapmaker. Both men heard stories from English and Portuguese fishermen about islands, real and imagined, that dotted the Atlantic. And they presented their unusual ideas in Portugal, England, and France before finding support. It was Columbus's experience and knowledge that gained him the trust of Spain's king and queen. The captain, one observer wrote in 1493, "has sailed. . ., as he believes, to the very shores of India, . . .even though the size of the earth's sphere seems to indicate otherwise." Columbus had not reached the lands he sought, but his exploits would have immediate and extraordinary consequences.

In the Wake of Columbus: Competition and Exchange

Within months of Columbus's return, the pope in Rome issued a papal bull, or decree. This pronouncement, titled *Inter Caetera*, viewed the world as the rightful inheritance of Christianity, ignoring the rights of non-Christians in all lands, whether known or unknown to Europeans. It brashly divided the entire world between two Christian powers, Spain and Portugal, by drawing a line down through the western Atlantic Ocean from the North Pole to the South Pole. For 180 degrees west of the line, the Spanish alone could continue to seek access to Asia. East of the line, on the other half of the globe, Portugal would have a monopoly in developing the route that Dias had opened around the Cape of Good Hope.

The two Iberian powers affirmed this division of the earth in the Treaty of Tordesillas (1494), which put the line 370 leagues west of the Cape Verde Islands. Within years, both parties realized that this agreement placed Brazil on the Portuguese side of the demarcation line, so Portugal quickly claimed the region. But by then, the Portuguese had already focused their attention on the African route to Asia, following da Gama's successful voyage to India in 1497. Despite their new foothold in the Americas, they left further Atlantic exploration to other European countries.

Spain and England acted swiftly. In 1494, Columbus led a huge venture back to Hispaniola, taking 1200 men aboard 17 ships. By employing only men at first to launch Spain's overseas empire, the expedition initiated a pattern of warfare against native Caribbean men and intermarriage with indigenous women. A mestizo, or mixed-race, population emerged swiftly in Spanish settlements there. On his third Atlantic crossing (1498), Columbus glimpsed the wide mouth of Venezuela's Orinoco River. Given the huge volume of fresh water entering the sea, he knew he had reached a large landmass, perhaps a part of Asia. When Amerigo Vespucci, another Italian in the service

Courtesy, Bancroft Library, University of California, Berkeley (SF309 G7 M25 1769 pl.20)

■ Horses, absent from the Americas for nearly 10,000 years, returned aboard Spanish ships. They awed Native Americans at first and played a crucial role in European conquests. "After God," the Spanish wrote, "we owe victory to the horses."

PACIFIC
OCEAN

NORTH
AMERICA

ATLANTIC
OCEAN

Columbus
(first voyage)

CUBA

Line created
by Treaty of
Tordesillas
(1494)

Orinoco R.

SOUTH
AMERICA

Magellan

The largest Chinese vessels of Zheng He (400ft.) were
nearly five times larger than Columbus's flagship (85ft.).

Strait of Magellan

Major expeditions

- - - Marco Polo: from Venice (1271) to China along the Silk Road
―――― Zheng He: from China to East Africa with a fleet of huge ships (1420s)
―――― Prince Henry's ships: from Portugal as far as Sierra Leone (1420–1460)
―――― Columbus: first voyage west from Spain via Canary Islands (1492–1493)
―――― Da Gama: from Portugal to India via Cape of Good Hope (1497–1499)
―――― Magellan's circumnavigation, completed by his crew (1519–1522)

■ **MAP 1.4**

OPENING NEW OCEAN PATHWAYS AROUND THE GLOBE, 1420–1520   In the 1420s, ships from
Portugal and China explored opposite coasts of Africa. But China withdrew from oceanic trade, and
European mariners competed to explore the earth by sea. Within a century, Magellan's ship had circled
the globe for Spain. The colonization in North America is a chapter in this larger saga of exploration.

of Spain, saw the same continent in 1499, he described it as a *Mundus Novus,* or New World.
European geographers wrote his name, *America,* across their maps.

Meanwhile, a third Italian navigator—John Cabot (or Caboto)—obtained a license from
the English king, Henry VII, to probe the North Atlantic for access to Cathay. Cabot knew
that English mariners from the port of Bristol had been fishing in the waters off Newfoundland for decades. In 1497, Cabot sailed west from Bristol across the Atlantic to Newfoundland and perhaps Nova Scotia, thinking he was viewing the coast of Asia. When Cabot died
at sea during a follow-up voyage the next year, Henry VII, the founder of England's new
Tudor monarchy, lacked the resources to pursue the explorer's claims. Nevertheless, the ventures of Columbus had sparked widespread excitement and curiosity in European ports about
what lay to the west. Within a generation, navigators and cartographers began to compre-
hend the geographic reality that Columbus had so thoroughly misunderstood. Their increasing knowledge fueled greater contact.

After thousands of years, the long separation of the hemispheres had been broken. The
destinies of the world's most divergent continents swiftly became linked. Those links fostered
human migrations of an unprecedented scale. With European ships came transfers of seeds and
viruses, bugs and birds, plants and animals that forever reshaped the world. Scholars call this
phenomenon the Columbian Exchange. The term also underscores the two-way nature of
the flow. West across the Atlantic went horses, cows, sheep, pigs, chickens, and honeybees

and important foods such as sugar cane, coffee, bananas, peaches, lemons, and oranges. But Europeans' westbound ships also carried devastating diseases unknown in the Americas such as smallpox, measles, malaria, and whooping cough. East in the opposite direction traveled corn, potatoes, pumpkins, chili peppers, tobacco, cacao, pineapples, sunflowers, turkeys—and perhaps syphilis. The planet and all its inhabitants would never be the same again.

Spain Enters the Americas

Throughout the sixteenth century, European mariners, inspired by the feats of Columbus and da Gama, risked ocean voyaging in hopes of scoring similar successes. Those who survived brought back novelties for consumers, information for geographers, and profits for ship owners. New wealth prompted further investment in exploration, and expanding knowledge awakened cultural changes for both explorers and the people they met. The dynamic European era known as the Renaissance owed much to overseas exploration. Returning mariners brought reports of suprising places and people. Their experiences challenged the inherited wisdom of traditional authorities and put a new premium on rational thought, scientific calculation, and careful observation of the natural world.

In turn, Europe's Renaissance, or rebirth, stimulated ever wider exploration as breakthroughs in technology and navigation yielded practical results. Sailing south around Africa and then east, Portuguese caravels reached China by 1514 and Japan by 1543. Sailing west, Spanish vessels learned first that the Caribbean did not offer a passage to Asia and then later—through the voyage of Magellan (1519–1522)—that the ocean beyond America was enormous. In the West Indies, and then elsewhere in the Western Hemisphere, Native Americans began to pay dearly for the exchange that ships from Spain had initiated.

Syphilis

■ FIGURE 1.1
THE COLUMBIAN EXCHANGE The voyages of Columbus 500 years ago initiated a dramatic interchange between once-isolated continents. The so-called Columbian Exchange involved the movement of numerous plants and animals to and from the Americas, including those shown here. Seeds and microorganisms have been a crucial part of this process, which continues at an ever-increasing rate.

The Devastation of the Indies

Spanish arrival in the West Indies in 1492 triggered widespread ecological and human disaster within decades. Well-armed and eager for quick wealth, the early colonizers brought havoc to the Taino Indians and Caribs who inhabited the islands. The strange newcomers killed and enslaved native peoples and extracted tribute from the survivors in the form of gold panned from streams. Spanish livestock trampled or consumed native gardens, prompting severe food shortages. Worse, European diseases ravaged countless villages. The West Indian population plummeted as island societies totaling more than 1 million lost 19 of every 20 people within a generation.

This near-extinction had three consequences. First, devout Catholics back in Spain protested the loss of potential American converts. When Dominican friars reached Cuba in

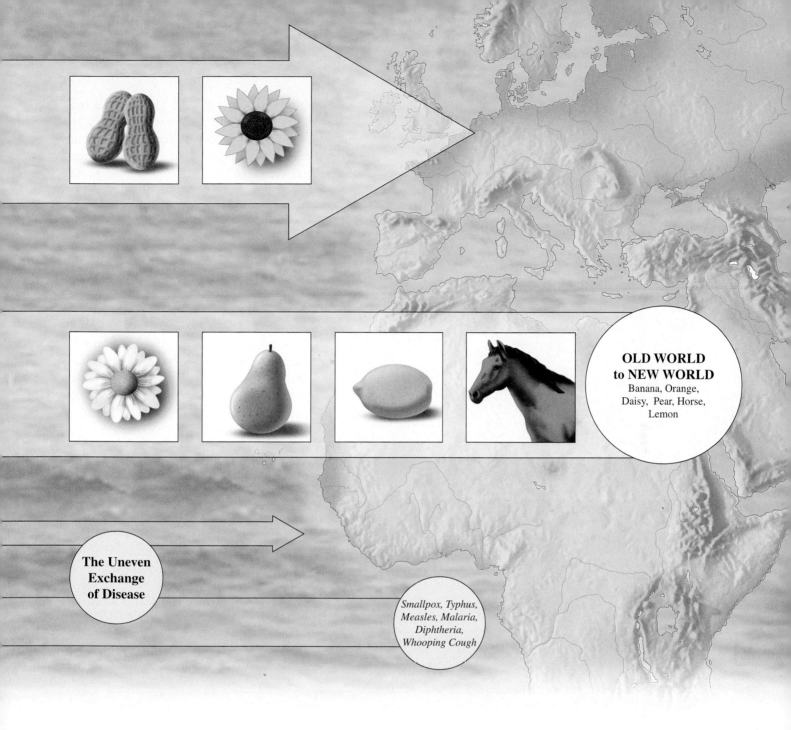

OLD WORLD
to NEW WORLD
Banana, Orange,
Daisy, Pear, Horse,
Lemon

The Uneven
Exchange
of Disease

Smallpox, Typhus,
Measles, Malaria,
Diphtheria,
Whooping Cough

1510, they denounced Spanish brutality as sinful. The Indians, they argued, possessed souls that only Christian baptism could save. A Spanish soldier named Bartholomé de Las Casas, who repented and joined the Dominican order, led the outcry for reform. He published a scathing exposé titled *The Devastation of the Indies*.

Second, in response to the steep drop in population, Spanish colonizers began importing slaves from Africa to replace the decimated Indian workforce. The same Christians who bemoaned Native American enslavement (including Las Casas) justified this initiative and overlooked the contradictions. The first importation of Africans came in 1502, following the Portuguese precedent in the Azores. Over the coming centuries, the African slave trade to the Americas slowly evolved into an enormous system of human exploitation.

Third, decimation in the islands prompted the Spanish to intensify their explorations. They sought new sources of Indian labor close at hand, fresh lands to exploit, and easy

The Pierpont Morgan Library/Art Resource, NY

■ As the Indian population of the Caribbean plummeted in the face of new diseases and exploitation, the Spanish began importing Africans to the New World as slaves. Many were put to work mining precious metals. Here men are forced to dig for gold nuggets beside a mountain stream, then wash them in a tub and dry them over a fire, before handing them to their Spanish master to weigh in his hand-held scale.

passageways to the Pacific. They pushed out from the Caribbean in several directions. In 1510, they established a mainland outpost at Darien on the Atlantic coast of Panama. From there, Vasco Núñez de Balboa pressed south over the mountainous isthmus to glimpse the Pacific in 1513. That same year, Juan Ponce de León sailed northwest from Puerto Rico, where he had amassed a fortune as governor. Despite later tales that he sought a fountain of youth, he actually hoped the nearby land would yield new gold and slaves. "He named it Florida, because he discovered it on the Feast of the Resurrection, which is called *Pasqua Florida*" in Latin, explained Peter Martyr, an Italian humanist of the day who chronicled early European explorations of America in *Decades of the New World*. "They got a bad reception," Martyr reported, for the peninsula's Indians already were familiar with Spanish raiders. The Ais people near Cape Canaveral and the Calusas on Florida's west coast turned Ponce de León away after he claimed the region for Spain.

The Spanish Conquest of the Aztecs

By 1519, the Spanish had determined that the Gulf of Mexico offered no easy passage to Asia. They needed fresh alternatives. In Spain, crown officials sought someone to sail southwest, around the South American continent that Columbus and Vespucci had encountered. For this perilous task, they recruited a Portuguese navigator named Ferdinand Magellan, who had sailed in the Indian Ocean. On his epic voyage (1519–1522), Magellan located a difficult passage through the tip of South America—now called the Strait of Magellan. But the journey also revealed the vast width of the Pacific. The crew nearly starved crossing its enormous expanse, which covers one-third of the earth's surface. Warring factions in the Philippines killed Magellan and 27 of his men shortly after they reached the islands. However, one of his ships, the *Victoria,* made it back to Spain via Africa's Cape of Good Hope, becoming the first vessel to circumnavigate the globe.

If the western route to Asia was far longer than Columbus had estimated, the New World itself soon proved more enticing than Europeans had first imagined. As news of Magellan's voyage raced through Spain in 1522, word also arrived that a Spanish soldier, or *conquistador,* named Hernán Cortés had toppled the gold-rich empire of the Aztecs in Central Mexico. Like other ambitious conquistadores, Cortés had followed Columbus to the Caribbean. In 1519, hoping to march overland to the Pacific as Balboa had done, Cortés sailed along Mexico's east coast and established a base camp at Vera Cruz. He quickly realized he had reached the edge of a powerful empire.

At Tenochtitlán the Aztec emperor, Moctezuma, reacted with uncertainty to news that bearded strangers aboard "floating islands" had appeared off his coast. Ominous signs—shooting stars, fierce storms, unknown birds—had foretold an extraordinary arrival. If the newcomers' leader was the returning god Quetzalcoatl, the court had to welcome him with the utmost care. The emperor sent basketloads of precious objects encrusted with gold to Cortés's camp. But the elaborate gifts only alerted Cortés and his men to the Aztecs' wealth.

Although the Spanish numbered scarcely 600, they had several key advantages over the Aztecs. Their guns and horses, unknown in America, terrified the Indians. So did their ruthless European style of warfare, for the Spanish gained victory by killing enemies, whereas the Aztecs measured military success by taking captives. If European war making surprised the Aztecs, the Indians' rituals of human sacrifice shocked the Spanish. The Europeans could now add moral indignation to their lust for gold as reasons to vanquish the Aztecs. When Cortés found coastal peoples staggering under heavy Aztec taxes, he recruited them as willing allies. Where Aztec leadership proved weak and divided, Cortés acted aggressively. He marched directly to the capital and seized Moctezuma as his hostage. An Indian woman (christened Doña Marina, or La Malinche) acted as his translator and companion.

To be sure, the Spanish still faced daunting obstacles. But sickness worked decisively to their advantage. Smallpox was a disease the Aztecs had never encountered before, so they lacked any immunity. The European illness reached the mainland with the invading army, and a crushing epidemic swept the Aztec capital in 1521. The disaster let Cortés conquer Tenochtitlán (which he renamed Mexico City) and claim the entire region as New Spain. He expanded his control by introducing the encomienda system, which became central to Spanish colonization. Cortés granted encomiendas to his restless lieutenants, expanding their power and control. Each grant "commended" a group of villages to an officer. The newcomers received payments of tribute and

The Newberry Library, Chicago

■ Cortés enclosed this map of Tenochtitlán in a letter to King Charles V (the Holy Roman Emperor and grandson of Ferdinand and Isabella). The map remained secret in Spain, but it was published in a 1524 Nuremberg edition of the letter, giving many Europeans their first glimpse of the defeated Aztec capital that was later rebuilt as Mexico City. The city plan shows the causeways over Lake Texcoco and the central square, with high temples where Aztec priests conducted human sacrifices. The flag with the double-headed eagle of Charles V's Hapsburg dynasty may mark Cortés's headquarters.

labor similar to those the Aztec overlords once demanded. In return, the Spanish agreed, at least in theory, to protect their villagers and convert them to Christianty. More often they exploited them as workers.

Magellan and Cortés Prompt New Searches

Cortés's conquest of Mexico raised Spain's hopes of additional windfalls in the Americas. Moreover, the length of Magellan's voyage spurred European interest in finding a shorter route to Asia. By 1524, the Spanish controlled the Pacific coast of Mexico, Guatemala, and the Isthmus of Panama, and they were building ships for further expansion. They explored the Pacific coastline north and south, and in 1531 Spanish raiders under Francisco Pizarro set sail from Panama for Peru, with plans to overthrow the Inca empire.

Pizarro had limited resources (180 men and 37 horses), but smallpox assisted him, as it had helped Cortés, and his invaders accomplished their mission. Marching overland to Cuzco in 1533, they killed the emperor, Atahualpa, and sacked the mountain capital for the gold it contained. The Spanish also pressed west across the Pacific, emboldened by Magellan's success. One of three ships dispatched by Cortés from Mexico for the Philippines actually reached its destination. Still, not until the 1560s did Spanish cargo ships, known as galleons, accomplish the arduous round trip from Acapulco to the Philippines and back across the Pacific.

In 1524, Italian navigator Giovanni da Verrazzano, sailing for the French, reached North America near modern Cape Fear, North Carolina, later cruising north to enter New York harbor and explore further along the coast. In 1526, Lucas Vásquez de Ayllón led 500 men and women from the Spanish Caribbean to the Santee River region (near present-day Georgetown, South Carolina) to settle and explore. But Ayllón fell sick and died, and the colony proved short-lived. Two years later, Pánfilo de Narváez directed an even greater disaster.

A rival of both Cortés and Ayllón, Narváez launched his expedition from Cuba in 1528. He landed near Florida's Tampa Bay, intending to bring wealth and glory to his 400 soldiers. But disease, hunger, and Indian hostilities plagued the party's journey along the Gulf Coast. Only four men—three Spanish and one north African black named Esteban—survived to make an extended trek on foot across the Southwest from Galveston Bay to Mexico City. Their leader, Álvar Núñez Cabeza de Vaca, wrote about the odyssey after he returned to Spain in 1537. Scholars now recognize Cabeza de Vaca's *Relation* (1542) as an early classic in North American literature.

Three New Views of North America

Even before Cabeza de Vaca published his narrative, Europeans initiated three more expeditions into North America. Each probed from a different direction, hoping to gauge the land's dimensions, assess its peoples, and claim its resources. Competing with one another, the three parties entered separate regions of the continent. But together, the enterprises led by Jacques Cartier, Hernando de Soto, and Francisco Vásquez de Coronado made the brief span between 1534 and 1543 the most extraordinary decade in the early European exploration of North America, for Native Americans and newcomers alike.

In the Northeast, Frenchman Jacques Cartier visited the Gulf of St. Lawrence in 1534 and bartered for furs with the Micmac Indians. He returned the next year and penetrated southwest up the St. Lawrence River into Canada. (The name comes from *kanata*, the Huron–Iroquois word for "village.") After a friendly reception at the large Indian town of Hochelaga near modern Montreal, the French returned downriver to camp at Stadacona, the future site of Quebec. Following a hard winter, in which he lost 25 men to scurvy, the explorer and his remaining crew sailed for France.

Cartier came back to Quebec in 1541, seeking precious minerals and signs of a water passage farther west to the Pacific Ocean. He found neither. When he returned to France,

"These Gods That We Worship Give Us Everything We Need"

Three years after the army of Cortés captured the city of Tenochtitlán, a dozen missionaries from the Franciscan Order arrived in Mexico to preach Christianity to the conquered Aztecs. In several meetings with principal elders and priests from the city, they explained their beliefs and laid out their plans through a translator. Similar talks would take place throughout America in later generations.

No transcript of the 1524 conversations exists, but another Franciscan, the famous preserver of Aztec culture Bernardino de Sahagún, gathered recollections of the encounter from both sides and reconstructed the dialogue. He published his version in 1564, creating parallel texts in Spanish and Nahuatl, the Aztec language. "Having understood the reasoning and speech of the twelve," Sahagún reports, the city leaders "became greatly agitated and fell into a great sadness and fear, offering no response." The next morning, they requested a complete repetition of the unsettling message. "Having heard this, one of the principal lords arose, asked the indulgence of the twelve, . . . and made the following long speech."

Our lords, leading personages of much esteem, you are very welcome to our lands and towns. . . . We have heard the words that you have brought us of the One who gives us life and being. And we have heard with admiration the words of the Lord of the World which he has sent here for love of us, and also you have brought us the book of celestial and divine words.

You have told us that we do not know the One who gives us life and being, who is Lord of the heavens and of the earth. You also say

The Bibliothèque Nationale, Paris

that those we worship are not gods. This way of speaking is entirely new to us, and very scandalous. We are frightened by this way of speaking because our forebears who engendered and governed us never said anything like this.

On the contrary, they left us this our custom of worshiping our gods. . . . They taught us how to honor them. And they taught us all the ceremonies and sacrifices that we make. They told us that . . . we were beholden to them, to be theirs and to serve countless centuries before the sun began to shine and before there was daytime. They said that these gods that we worship give us everything we need for our physical existence: maize, beans, chia seeds, etc. We appeal to them for the rain to make the things of the earth grow.

These our gods are the source of great riches and delights, all of which belong to them. . . . They live in very delightful places where there are always flowers, vegetation, and great freshness, a place . . . where there is never hunger, poverty, or illness. . . . There has never been a time remembered when they were not worshiped, honored, and esteemed. . . .

It would be a fickle, foolish thing for us to destroy the most ancient laws and customs left by the first inhabitants of this land. . . . We are accustomed to them and we have them impressed on our hearts. . . . How could you leave the poor elderly among us bereft of that in which they have been raised throughout their lives? Watch out that we do not incur the wrath of our gods. Watch out that the common people do not rise up against us if we were to tell them that the gods they have always understood to be such are not gods at all.

It is best, our lords, to act on this matter very slowly, with great deliberation. We are not satisfied or convinced by what you have told us, nor do we understand or give credit to what has been said of our gods. . . . All of us together feel that it is enough to have lost, enough that the power and royal jurisdiction have been taken from us. As for our gods, we will die before giving up serving and worshiping them. This is our determination; do what you will. ■

Source: Kenneth Mills and William B. Taylor, Colonial Spanish America: A Documentary History (Wilmington: Scholarly Resources, 1998), 21–22.

Parisians ridiculed his rock crystals as "Canada diamonds." In Cartier's wake came a colonizing party of several hundred in 1542, led by a nobleman named Roberval. This was the first French expedition to include women. But again, scurvy and cold took a heavy toll at the Quebec campsite, and the weakening colony withdrew after a single winter. Despite a decade of effort, the French still had not established a beachhead in the New World. Nevertheless, they had demonstrated their resolve to challenge Spain's exclusive claim to American lands, sanctioned by the pope 50 years earlier.

In the Southeast, news of Pizarro's 1533 triumph over the Incas in Peru renewed the Spanish search for wealthy kingdoms to conquer. In 1537, Emperor Charles V of Spain granted one hardened veteran of the Peruvian campaign—Hernando de Soto—the right to explore and conquer in Florida. De Soto could divide all gold and jewels with the crown while establishing a hereditary domain for himself and his descendants. The conquistador spent most of his fortune assembling a force of more than 600 soldiers that reached Tampa Bay in 1539. The enterprise included several women and priests, along with scores of servants and African

■ In 1547, a mapmaker prepared this elegant chart of North America's Atlantic coast to document the early explorations and claims of France. (South is at the top; Florida is at the upper right.) It shows the men and women of Roberval's short-lived colonizing expedition as they disembarked in Canada in 1542, watched by Native Americans.

slaves, plus 200 horses. De Soto had also brought along a herd of 300 pigs that multiplied rapidly and provided food during the long march through the interior.

During the next four years, de Soto's party traversed a wide region, eventually traveling through ten modern southern states. They hoped to find a city as wealthy as Cuzco in Peru or Tenochtitlán in Mexico. Instead, they found scattered towns inhabited by surprised and frightened villagers. At Cofitachequi, in what is now central South Carolina, the invaders also found something else: evidence of Ayllón's coastal visit in the form of Spanish axeheads, Catholic rosaries, and villages decimated by disease. Cofitachequi's woman leader welcomed de Soto warmly but then watched in horror as the Spanish pillaged her town for pearls. Settlements that refused to provide the intruders with porters or guides met with brutal reprisals that included the use of attack dogs. After passing through Cherokee Indian country in the southern mountains, de Soto's army descended into lands once dominated by Mississippian chiefdoms.

Here, tensions between the foreigners and the North American inhabitants intensified. Violence escalated. On October 18, 1540, a native leader named Tuscaluza attacked the Spanish at the village of Mabila near modern-day Selma, Alabama. Tuscaluza's bowmen proved no match for the mounted, armored riders brandishing swords and lances. Spanish accounts put Indian deaths at 2500 and de Soto's losses at only 22 men. Still, the conquistador's elaborate enterprise slowly unraveled as frustrations grew stemming from the difficult terrain, stiff Indian resistance, and failure to find riches. Exhausted and depressed, de Soto died of a fever in 1542 after exploring beyond the Mississippi River. His disheartened followers escaped downstream to the Gulf of Mexico the next year, leaving epidemic sickness in their wake.

At the same time, an equally complex encounter was unfolding in the Southwest. By 1539, Spanish sailors voyaging up Mexico's West Coast had explored the Gulf of California and skirted the Baja Peninsula. Over the next four years, similar expeditions cruised the coast of California and southern Oregon. Once again, they found no signs of a passage linking the Pacific and Atlantic oceans. In Mexico, speculation about gold in the north intensified with the return of Cabeza de Vaca. His African companion, Esteban, guided a reconnaissance party north in 1539. Esteban was killed by the Zuni Indians, but exaggerated accounts of the region's pueblos prompted rumors about the seven golden cities known as Cibola.

The next year, aspiring conquistador Francisco Vásquez de Coronado set out from northern Mexico to reach these wealthy towns before de Soto could. He left his post as a frontier governor to lead a huge expedition. Only 30 years old, Coronado assembled more than 300 Spanish adventurers and a thousand Indian allies. However, his grandiose expectations were quickly dashed. The pueblos of the Zunis, he reported, "are very good houses, three and four and five stories high," but the fabled "Seven Cities are seven little villages." Hoping to gauge his distance from the Pacific, Coronado sent explorers northwest. They returned after reaching the impassable Grand Canyon and realizing they could go no farther.

The presence of Spanish forces soon imposed a heavy burden on the Pueblo Indians, as the newcomers demanded food and burned helpless towns. Desperate to get rid of Coronado, the Pueblos told him stories of a far-off, wealthy land called Quivira. They secretly recruited a Plains Indian to lead the Spaniards to some place where men and horses "would starve to death." In the spring of 1541, Coronado's seemingly earnest guide led his party far out onto the Great Plains, repeating tantalizing tales of gold and silver. Coronado's soldiers became the first Europeans to see this rolling ocean of grass and its endless herds of buffalo. But when Quivira proved to be a Wichita Indian village in what is now central Kansas, the Spanish strangled their deceitful guide and made their way back south to New Spain. They left several Indians and Africans behind in the Rio Grande valley. At one point, as they crossed northern Texas, they even came within 300 miles of de Soto's ill-fated party in eastern Arkansas. But neither de Soto nor Coronado—nor Cartier in the north—ever discovered the wealthy cities or the passage to the Far East that had seemed such real and alluring possibilities.

Desperate to get rid of Coronado, the Pueblos told him stories of a far-off, wealthy land called Quivira.

■ European mapmakers learned quickly about the expeditions into the North American interior led by Cartier, de Soto, and Coronado. This 1566 Italian chart places New France, or Canada, in the North, and shows the Indian town of "Ochelaga" visited by Cartier. "La Florida," labeled twice, includes not only the crudely drawn peninsula but also all of the Southeast explored by de Soto. The imagined regions of Cibola and Quivira, sought by Coronado, appear in the Southwest. European hope of a Northwest Passage from the Atlantic to Asia continues, and the size of the North Pacific remains uncertain, so Japan (Giapan) is shown near the coast of California.

The Protestant Reformation Plays Out in America

In 1520, while Cortés vied with the Aztecs for control in Mexico and Magellan maneuvered around South America, the pope excommunicated a German monk named Martin Luther. Three years earlier, Luther had nailed to Wittenberg's cathedral door a list of 95 theses, statements challenging long-standing church practices and papal authority. Luther's followers questioned lavish church spending—construction of the ornate St. Peter's Basilica was under way in Rome at the time—and the practice of selling religious pardons to raise money. They also rejected the church's elaborate hierarchy and criticized its refusal to translate the Latin Bible into modern languages. Luther's reform movement triggered sharp doctrinal disputes and the division of western Christianity into competing faiths. For their written protestations against the papacy, Luther and his fellow insurgents received the enduring name *Protestants*. Their movement became known broadly as the Reformation. Those who opposed it, siding with Rome, launched a Counter-Reformation to defend and revitalize the Roman Catholic church.

For the first time in history, a controversy in Europe made waves that washed onto American shores. Throughout the remainder of the sixteenth century, European national and religious conflict played out in part overseas, a pattern that repeated itself in future centuries. France and Spain, competing in Europe, wrestled to claim control of Florida. And England, an upstart island nation with a rising population and an expanding navy, seized control of Ireland and launched its first attempt to plant a colony in North America.

Reformation and Counter-Reformation in Europe

As zeal for Luther's religious reforms spread across Europe, it split communities and even sparked armed conflict. In Switzerland, a priest named Ulrich Zwingli led the revolt. He abolished the practice of confession, condemned the church calendar full of fasts and saints' days, and defied the tradition of a celibate clergy by marrying. Zwingli was killed in battle in 1531, but the Swiss Reformation soon found a new leader in John Calvin. A French Protestant, Calvin settled in Geneva and ruled the city as a church-centered state for more than two decades (1541–1564).

Calvin imposed his own strict interpretation on Lutheranism and drew dedicated followers to his church. Offended by expensive vestments and elaborate rituals, he donned a simple black "Geneva" robe. He argued that faith alone, not "good works," would lead Christians to be saved. Salvation, he preached, was determined by God, not bought by giving tithes to the church. Only a select few people, Calvin explained, were destined to be members of God's chosen elect. Moreover, only an informed clergy and the careful study of scripture could reveal signs of a person's status. Soon Calvinist doctrine helped shape Protestant communities across northern Europe: Huguenots in France, Puritans in England, Presbyterians in Scotland, and the Dutch Reformed Church in the Netherlands.

The Protestant Reformation that Luther had ignited coincided roughly with another important change in Europe, the emergence of the modern nation-state. Kings and queens gradually expanded court bureaucracies and asserted greater control over their subjects and economies. They strengthened their armies, gaining a near-monopoly on the use of force, and they took full advantage of the new medium of printing. Monarchs also surveyed the boundaries of their kingdoms, claiming control over persons because they inhabited a particular territory, rather than because they held an established relationship to the ruler. As religious ferment spread and local allegiances gave way to a broader sense of national identity, strong sovereigns moved to distance themselves from papal authority in Rome.

In 1542, Catholic authorities established a new religious-judicial proceeding, known as the Inquisition, to help resist the spread of Protestantism.

The emergence of England as a nation-state under the Tudor dynasty (founded by Henry VII in 1485) illustrates this shift in power away from Rome. In 1533, when the pope refused to grant Henry VIII an annulment of his first marriage, the king wrested control of the English church from papal hands and had Parliament approve his divorce and remarriage. The new Church of England, or Anglican Church, continued to follow much of the Catholic Church's doctrine. However, its "Protector and only Supreme Head" would now be the English monarch. During her long reign from 1558 to 1603, Henry VIII's daughter Queen Elizabeth I managed to steer the Church of England on a middle course between advocates of Catholicism and extreme Protestants.

Throughout Europe, as zealous believers on both sides of the debate staked out their positions, attempts to heal religious divisions gave way to confrontation. Challenges to the pope in Rome, whether from Christian parishes or powerful monarchs, met with stiff resistance as Catholic leaders mobilized opposition. Their followers rallied to defend Roman Catholicism in a variety of ways. Taken together, these efforts are known as the Counter-Reformation.

One dimension of the Counter-Reformation is represented in the Jesuit order, founded by Ignatius Loyola. This Spanish soldier had studied alongside Calvin at a Paris college in the 1530s, but he took an opposite path from that of the Geneva preacher. By 1540, Loyola had organized a militant new Catholic religious community called the Society of Jesus, or the Jesuits. Willing to give their lives for their beliefs, these dedicated missionaries and teachers helped to reenergize the Catholic faith and spread it to distant parts of the world.

Another institution, the Inquisition, reflects a different side of the Counter-Reformation. In 1542, Catholic authorities established a new religious-judicial proceeding, known as the

Inquisition, to help resist the spread of Protestantism. Heretics—persons accused of denying or defying church doctrine—were brought before the Inquisition's religious courts. Anyone who refused to renounce heretical beliefs suffered severe punishment. These heresy trials made clear to Inquisition leaders that the advent of printing was helping to spread the works of Luther and his Protestant allies. In 1557, therefore, the Vatican issued an "Index" of prohibited books.

Royalty also played a part in the Counter-Reformation. In France, where religious wars raged until the end of the century, struggles for control between competing dynasties became entwined with disputes over church doctrine. In Spain, King Philip II, who ruled from 1556 to 1598, led an Inquisition to root out Protestant heresy. His harsh policies sparked a lengthy revolt in the Spanish Netherlands that resulted in the creation of the United Provinces, Europe's first Protestant republic. Philip expanded Spain's power in 1581, when he acquired Portugal. The move combined Europe's two great overseas empires until their separation in 1640.

The Spanish monarch came close to acquiring England as well. In 1588 he sent a fleet of warships—the Spanish Armada—to England in hopes of reconquering it for the Catholic church. A timely storm and hasty mobilization by the island nation foiled the Spanish king's invasion. But Philip II's confrontation with the navy of Queen Elizabeth epitomized the sharp new division between Catholic and Protestant power in Europe. This deepened antagonism—religious, ideological, and economic—shaped events overseas in the second half of the sixteenth century. The struggle became especially clear in Florida, the vague region claimed by Spain that encompassed Indian lands from Chesapeake Bay to the Gulf of Mexico.

Competing Powers Lay Claim to Florida

As Spain used force to obtain the dazzling wealth of New World societies, its European rivals looked on jealously. As early as 1523, French sea raiders had captured Spanish ships returning from Mexico with Cortés's Aztec bounty: coffers of jewels and pearls, ingots of silver, and bags filled with 500 pounds of gold dust. Ten years later, French pirates made a similar haul. To protect the flow of riches from America, the Spanish soon initiated a well-armed annual convoy to escort their wealth from Havana to Seville. Each year, Spain's huge West Indies treasure fleet made an enticing target as it followed the Gulf Stream along the Florida coast. "Thus it is a matter of great moment in the preservation of the Indies, and for its trade and commerce," Spanish officials realized, "that Florida remain Spanish and be strongly guarded."

Each year, Spain's huge West Indies treasure fleet made an enticing target as it followed the Gulf Stream along the Florida coast.

But France had its own designs, furthered by the special concerns of French Huguenots. Unsure of their future in a religiously divided country, these Protestants took a leading role in the colonization efforts of France. When Gaspard de Coligny became admiral of the French Navy in 1552, he saw a way to help fellow Huguenots and the realm by encouraging the formation of anti-Catholic colonies in the New World. French Huguenots established a settlement in Brazil in 1555. But after the Portuguese uprooted it, Coligny turned his attention to the Florida region. In 1562 he supported a Protestant colony at Port Royal Sound (Parris Island, South Carolina), close to the route of Spain's annual treasure fleet. The effort lasted only two years and aroused Spanish suspicions of "Lutheran" intruders.

Undaunted, Admiral Coligny backed a larger colonizing effort to Florida in 1564. French Protestants erected Fort Caroline on the St. John's River at present-day Jacksonville. This time, the Spanish crown took swift action against the Huguenots. In 1565 Philip II sent 300 soldiers and 700 colonists under Pedro Menéndez de Avilés to oust the French and secure Florida. Menéndez carried out his assignment with zeal. He captured Fort Caroline and massacred hundreds of French settlers. The heretics, he feared, might attack the treasure fleet, forge alliances with Florida's Indians, or provoke revolt among slaves in the Spanish Caribbean.

The New York Public Library

■ In 1562, French Protestants established a short-lived colony at Port Royal Sound on the South Carolina coast. "The commander, on landing with some soldiers, found the country very beautiful, as it was well wooded with oak, cedar, and other trees. As they went through the woods, they saw Indian peacocks, or turkeys, flying past, and deer going by." Traveling upstream beyond Parris Island, they surprised an encampment of Indians, "who, on perceiving the boats, immediately took flight," leaving behind the meat "they were roasting."

To prevent further French incursions on Florida's Atlantic coast, Menéndez established a new outpost at nearby St. Augustine. He also laid out ambitious plans to discover precious resources from Chesapeake Bay to the Mississippi. As part of this design, explorer Juan Pardo led several parties inland from the Carolina coast in the 1560s, establishing a post far up the Savannah River and crossing the southern Appalachian Mountains, as de Soto had done, but to no avail. Because the Spanish did not yet understand the magnitude of the distance between Florida and New Spain, they even discussed building a road for transporting silver from mines in northern Mexico to their posts on the Atlantic shoreline.

With French threats defeated, the Spanish at St. Augustine attempted to plant strategic missions farther north to convert Native Americans to Christianity and secure Spain's land claims. In 1570, eight missionaries from Loyola's Society of Jesus sailed north from Florida to Chesapeake Bay. There, the Jesuits established a mission to convert local Indians and looked for "an entrance into the mountains and on to China." But the friars' rules and beliefs antagonized the Native Americans. All the missionaries had been killed by the time Menéndez visited the region in 1572. Spain's failure to secure a foothold on Chesapeake Bay soon proved costly as a new European rival appeared on the scene. Almost

■ MAP 1.5

THE EXTENT OF NORTH AMERICAN EXPLORATION BY 1592 A century after the initial voyage of Columbus, European explorers and colonists had touched the edges of North America, and a few had ventured far inland. But they had not found riches or a passageway to the Pacific, and only the Spanish had managed to establish a lasting foothold along the Florida Coast.

overnight, Protestant England emerged as a contending force in the Atlantic world. Now English adventurers began challenging Spanish dominance in the Caribbean and along North America's southeastern coast.

The Background of English Expansion

The voyages of John Cabot and the visits of Bristol fishing vessels to Newfoundland's Grand Banks had stimulated an early English interest in the Atlantic. But for several reasons this curiosity intensified after 1550. Henry VIII had used his power, plus the wealth he had seized from the Catholic Church, to begin a fleet that would one day dominate the world's oceans. Inheriting a navy of only 5 ships in 1509, the monarch added 85 vessels before he died in 1547. The merchant fleet grew as well, carrying English wool and cloth to Antwerp and other European ports. In addition, the English population, which had declined in the previous 150 years, grew steadily after 1500. Overall numbers more than doubled during the sixteenth century, cre-

Lost at Sea

Lost at sea? Nowadays you can hold in your palm a marine global positioning system (GPS) receiver. It lets you know exactly where you are, which direction you are heading, what course you have traveled, and how fast you are moving. To increase your confidence, one maker of GPS devices uses the name of one of the world's greatest navigators: Magellan.

Thanks to GPS, we are getting used to knowing our precise location on the globe at any moment. Originally developed and operated by the U.S. Department of Defense for military purposes, GPS uses signals from satellites to determine an object's latitude and longitude within a matter of inches. But it hasn't always been that way.

Before the 1400s, countless generations of sailors navigated only within sight of land, where they could take their bearings from familiar landmarks such as mountains and rivers. Captains on the Mediterranean Sea carried charts listing the visible guideposts along every coast. If fog surrounded them, a piece of lead lowered over the bow until it touched bottom told them whether they were in dangerously shallow water. Norse seafarers in the Atlantic and some ancient mariners in the Pacific learned to read ocean swells and follow the stars well enough to undertake long ocean voyages. But most Europeans avoided sailing out of sight of land until the fifteenth century.

It took centuries for navigators to experience, and overcome, the numerous dilemmas associated with deep sea sailing. For one thing, a compass needle does not point to true north but to a slightly different magnetic north. And that difference varies from one place to another. Also, winds and currents imperceptibly nudge a boat off course, making it harder to estimate exact location. Position is relative and concerns relationships to known places. So it was important for mariners at sea to have a grid on which to fix their position. Ancient geographer Ptolemy had suggested that horizontal lines of latitude running parallel to the equator and meridians of longitude circling the earth vertically could provide that grid.

Locating your position on such a grid proved simple in one way and impossibly hard in another. Latitude was the easy part, finding one's north–south location between the pole and the equator. Sailors in the Northern Hemisphere could determine their latitude by measuring the angle of the North Star (or Pole Star) above the horizon at night. By keeping the Pole Star at the same height in the sky, they could steer along the same latitude, parallel to the equator.

Magellan Handheld Marine GPS Receiver

Columbus used this technique in sailing due west across the Atlantic from the Canary Islands.

But finding east–west location, or longitude, at sea was a more difficult matter. Mariners had to guess at longitude, and often over the years those guesses proved fatal. A notorious example occurred in October 1707 when fog enveloped a British fleet returning home. Officers estimated that they were a safe distance west of the English coast. They were wrong, and nearly 2000 men drowned when the ships crashed ashore at night. The British Parliament responded in 1714 by offering a huge reward to anyone who could finally solve the vexing "longitude problem." The solution came half a century later from English clockmaker John Harrison. He revolutionized navigation by creating a clock (using a spring instead of a pendulum) that could keep time at sea.

From the late eighteenth century to the late twentieth century, timepieces grew increasingly portable, durable, and accurate, helping sailors determine their positions. Now GPS has created yet another revolution, bringing a new technology to bear on the mariner's ancient question: "Where am I?" Ferdinand Magellan would be amazed. ■

ating pressure for limited resources, especially land. Adding to the squeeze, property owners, eager to enclose pastures for sheep grazing, pushed tenants off their land. This "enclosure movement" set even more people adrift to seek work in towns and cities. London's population soared from 50,000 in 1500 to 200,000 a century later. And when Europe's saturated woolen textile market collapsed suddenly, English cloth exports fell 35 percent in 1551. Merchants searched hastily for new avenues of foreign commerce.

Starting in the 1550s, therefore, England's overseas exploration pushed in all directions. Investors in the new Muscovy Company sent ships north around Scandinavia through the Arctic Ocean as far as Archangel on the White Sea. They established contact with Czar Ivan the Terrible in Moscow and opened trade with Russia, but they failed to find a northeastern route above the Asian landmass to China. Other English vessels sailed south to Morocco and the Gold Coast, challenging the Portuguese monopoly of the African trade. English mariner John Hawkins conducted three voyages to west Africa during the 1560s. Horning in on the growing transatlantic slave traffic, he purchased Africans and then sold them in Caribbean ports to Spanish buyers. In doing so, he marked out a grim "triangular trade" linking England, west Africa, and the Americas. In later centuries this inhuman trade yielded untold profits for the owners and investors who funded thousands of slaving voyages.

Philip II, having driven the French out of Florida, had had enough of Protestant interlopers. A Spanish fleet forced Hawkins and his young kinsman Francis Drake out of Mexican waters in 1568. But thereafter, English sea rovers stepped up their challenges to Spain on the high seas, with quiet support from Queen Elizabeth. Drake proved the most wideranging and successful. On a voyage to the Pacific (1577–1580) he plundered Spanish ports in Peru and landed near San Francisco Bay. He claimed California for England as New Albion and then sailed around the globe. In the 1580s, Drake continued, in his words, "to singe the Spaniard's beard." He sacked ports in the West Indies, encouraged slave uprisings against the Spanish, and attacked the settlement at St. Augustine. He also captured numerous treasure ships, sank two dozen enemy vessels in their home port at Cadiz, and helped to defeat Philip's Spanish Armada in 1588.

England's anti-Catholic propagandists made Drake a national hero. Moreover, they painted Spanish cruelties toward Indians in the New World in the worst possible terms. To bolster their case, they translated the vivid writings of Las Casas into English. But the English were not blameless themselves. In their brutal conquest of Ireland, they established their own pattern of violence during the Elizabethan years. Sir Humphrey Gilbert and others who played leading roles in this bloody takeover came to view a colony in America as the next logical step in England's aggressive overseas expansion.

In 1576 Gilbert published his *Discourse for a Discovery for a New Passage to Cathay*. In it, he speculated on a short northwestern route to China. Martin Frobisher, another veteran of the Irish campaign, undertook voyages to locate such a route. He mistakenly thought he had found the passage, or strait, to Asia. As evidence, he brought back an Eskimo family he believed to be Chinese, and English artist John White drew their pictures. The next year, writing an essay on "How Her Majesty May Annoy the King of Spain," Gilbert proposed a colony in Newfoundland. The queen granted him a patent—a license giving him exclusive rights—for such a project. But the venture failed because of shipwrecks and desertions. When Gilbert died at sea on the homeward voyage, his half-brother, Walter Raleigh, obtained a similar patent to plant a colony in North American lands "not actually possessed by any Christian prince."

Lost Colony: The Roanoke Experience

In 1584 Raleigh sent explorers to the Outer Banks, the string of barrier islands below Chesapeake Bay that Verrazzano had glimpsed 60 years earlier. The men visited Roanoke Island and then returned to England in September. They brought back positive reports about the land and two Indian informants. The next month, Richard Hakluyt, England's foremost advocate and chronicler of overseas expansion, handed Queen Elizabeth an advisory paper entitled "Western Planting." The document called for the establishment of a strategic outpost on the North American coast, where the English could launch attacks against Spanish shipping, hunt for useful commodities, and convert Indians to Protestant Christianity.

Raleigh's three efforts to establish such an outpost failed in rapid succession. In 1585, he first sent Ralph Lane, a hardened veteran of the Irish campaigns, to build a fort at Roanoke Island. Like other Europeans who had preceded him to America, Lane anticipated "the discovery of a good mine, or a passage to the South Sea." But storms at sea scattered his ships, and most of Lane's initial force never arrived. Those who did, including artist John White, fared badly because of scarce food, bad discipline, and hostile relations with the Indians. Francis Drake, arriving in 1586 after harassing the Spanish in the West Indies and Florida, expected to find a thriving enterprise. Instead, he carried the disheartened soldiers back to England. They had paid a price, Hakluyt commented, "for the cruelty and outrages committed by some of them against the native inhabitants of that country." A second expedition diverted to the Caribbean to prey on enemy shipping, after leaving a few men at Roanoke, who did not survive.

In May 1587 John White led a third English venture to America, with 110 people, including women and children. They planned to settle on Chesapeake Bay, but a contentious captain refused to carry them farther north after an initial stop at Roanoke Island. So the settlers remained huddled at Roanoke, unseen by a Spanish ship from Florida sent north to check on rumors of English activity. In August they agreed to send White back to England for more supplies and to leave a message for him if they moved. When he finally returned in 1590—delayed by England's clash with the Spanish Armada—he found the site deserted. The word *Croatoan* carved on a post suggested that survivors had joined the nearby Croatan Indians, but the Lost Colony's fate remains a source of endless speculation. The Spanish, worried by the English foray, drew up plans for a fortification at Chesapeake Bay, but warfare between Spain and England kept both countries preoccupied elsewhere until Philip II and Elizabeth I had died.

The British Museum

■ John White took part in several voyages to Roanoke Island in the 1580s. A skilled artist, the Englishman made valuable first-hand drawings of Native Americans living in what is now coastal North Carolina, including the wife and daughter of a local leader. The woman kept her "haire trussed opp in a knott," had tattoos on her arms, wore "a chaine of great pearles," and often carried "a gourde full of some kinde of pleasant liquor." The girl holds an English doll, for Indian children "are greatly Deligted with puppetts . . . brought oute of England."

Conclusion

Over approximately 150 centuries, people of distant Asian ancestry had explored and settled the bountiful Western Hemisphere. In every region of North America, from the arctic North to the semitropical Florida Keys, they had adapted and prospered over countless generations. Then suddenly, in a single century, unprecedented intrusions brought newcomers from foreign lands to the coasts of the Americas, in wooden castles that floated on the sea. Their numbers only increased with time. In the next century, the contest for European control of the Atlantic seaboard began in earnest.

Sites to Visit

Cahokia Mounds State Historic Site

Covering 2200 acres just south of Highway 40 near Collinsville, in East St. Louis, Illinois, Mississippian earthworks dot this World Heritage Site. The Cahokia Mounds Museum Society conducts an archaeological field school each summer.

Chaco Culture National Historical Park

The most striking structure in this park is Pueblo Bonito, the largest building in North America until 1882. Lying in Chaco Canyon northwest of Albuquerque, New Mexico, these Anasazi ruins can be reached by driving south from Aztec (where there are several important museums) or north from Thoreau.

Makah Cultural and Research Center

This site, in Neah Bay, Washington, at the tip of Olympic Peninsula, houses thousands of artifacts from an ancestral Macah Indian village, at nearby Ozette, that was covered in a mudslide shortly before European contact and revealed by a 1970 winter storm.

Mesa Verde National Park

Located near Cortez, Colorado, this is the oldest archaeological national park in the United States. It covers 80 square miles in southwest Colorado, adjoining the Ute Mountain Indian Reservation. The park contains impressive Anasazi ruins, the most famous of which is Cliff Palace.

Moundville Archaeological Park

Located half a mile west of State Route 69, on the Black Warrior River outside Moundville, Alabama, just south of Tuscaloosa, this well-preserved Mississippian mound complex also contains an archaeological museum.

Poverty Point State Commemorative Area

A visitors' center is located near the center of the geometric earthworks from the late Archaic era on this 400-acre site on State Route 577 near Epps, Louisiana.

Pueblo Grande Museum

This downtown Phoenix, Arizona, museum, just off State Route 143, contains artifacts of the Hohokam culture. A large platform mound, a ball court, and ancient irrigation canals are preserved within the park.

Fort Raleigh National Historical Site

This site is on Route 64 at the north end of Roanoke Island, in eastern North Carolina. A reconstructed Elizabethan ship at nearby Manteo suggests the experience of England's sixteenth-century "lost colony." A drive or walk on the sandy Outer Banks (Route 12) recalls the coastline seen by Verrazzano in 1524.

Serpent Mound State Memorial

Four miles northwest of Locust Grove, Ohio, on State Route 73, this site includes a small museum and a viewing tower that allows visitors to look down on the winding effigy mound, now thought to be roughly 1000 years old.

L'Anse aux Meadows National Historic Site

parkscanada.pch.gc.ca/parks/newfoundland/anse_meadows/anse_meadows_e.htm

Take a tour of the reconstructed Viking settlement at this Web site.

www.acs.ucalgary.ca/applied_history/tutor/eurvoya/index.html

The University of Calgary has developed a course around this Web site titled "The European Voyages of Exploration: The Fifteenth and Sixteenth Centuries."

www.pbs.org/weta/thewest/resources/archives/one/cabeza.htm

Read the narrative by Cabeza de Vaca of his journey across the Southwest in the 1530s.

www.win.tue.nl/cs/fm/engels/discovery/

See the "Discoverers Web" for numerous links concerning the era of European exploration.

For Further Reading

General

John Logan Allen, *North American Exploration, Volume 1, A New World Disclosed* (1997).

Alfred W. Crosby, *Ecological Imperialism: The Biological Expansion of Europe, 900–1900* (1986; Canto edition, 1993).

Jared Diamond, *Guns, Germs, and Steel: The Fates of Human Societies* (1997).

Henry F. Dobyns, *Their Number Become Thinned: Native American Population Dynamics in Eastern North America* (1983).

Brian M. Fagan, *Ancient North America* 3rd ed. (2000).

William H. Goetzmann and Glyndwr Williams, *The Atlas of North American Exploration: From the Norse Voyages to the Race to the Pole* (1992).

J.C.H. King, *First Peoples, First Contacts: Native Peoples of North America* (1999).

David B. Quinn, *North America from Earliest Discovery to First Settlements: The Norse Voyages to 1612* (1977).

David Hurst Thomas, *Exploring Native North America* (2000).

Ancient America

Brian M. Fagan, *The Great Journey: The Peopling of Ancient America* (1987).

Brian M. Fagan, *The Journey from Eden: the Peopling of Our World* (1990).

Stuart J. Fiedel, *Prehistory of the Americas* (1987).

Francis Jennings, *The Founders of America* (1993).

Helen Roney Sattler, *The Earliest Americans* (1993).

Robert Silverberg, *Mound Builders of Ancient America: The Archaeology of a Myth* (1968).

A Thousand Years of Change: A.D. 500 to 1500

Sally A. Kitt Chappell, *Cahokia: Mirror of the Cosmos* (2002).

Brian M. Fagan, *Kingdoms of Gold, Kingdoms of Jade: The Americas Before Columbus* (1991).

Alvin M. Josephy, Jr., ed., *America in 1492: The World of the Indian Peoples Before the Arrival of Columbus* (1992).

Thomas C. Patterson, *The Inca Empire: The Formation and Disintegration of a Pre-Capitalist State* (1991).

Linda Schele and David Freidel, *A Forest of Kings: The Untold Story of the Ancient Maya* (1990).

David Hurst Thomas, *Exploring Native North America* (2000).

Linking the Continents

Alfred W. Crosby, Jr., *The Columbian Exchange: Biological and Cultural Consequences of 1492* (1972).

Zvi Dor-Ner, *Columbus and the Age of Discovery* (1991).

William W. Fitzhugh and Elisabeth I. Ward, eds., *Vikings: The North Atlantic Saga* (2000).

Louise Levathes, *When China Ruled the Sea: The Treasure Fleet of the Dragon Throne* (1994).

Samuel Eliot Morison, *The European Discovery of America: The Northern Voyages, A.D. 500–1600* (1971).

J. H. Parry, *The Age of Reconnaissance: Discovery, Exploration, and Settlement, 1450–1650* (1963).

Peter Russell, *Prince Henry "The Navigator": A Life* (2000).

Carl Ortwin Sauer, *The Early Spanish Main* (1969).

Spain Enters the Americas

Herbert E. Bolton, *Coronado: Knight of Pueblos and Plains* (1990).

Hernán Cortés, *Letters from Mexico,* translated and edited by Anthony Pagden (1986).

Cyclone Covey, trans. and ed., *Cabeza de Vaca's Adventures in the Unknown Interior of America* (1961).

W. J. Eccles, *France in America* (1972).

Charles Hudson, *Knights of Spain, Warriors of the Sun: Hernando de Soto and the South's Ancient Kingdoms* (1997).

Miguel Leon-Portilla, *The Broken Spears: The Aztec Account of the Conquest of Mexico* (1962).

Jerald T. Milanich, *Florida Indians and the Invasion from Europe* (1995).

The Protestant Reformation Plays Out in America

Karen Ordahl Kupperman, *Roanoke: The Abandoned Colony* (1984).

Eugene Lyon, *The Enterprise of Florida: Pedro Menéndez de Avilés and the Spanish Conquest of 1565–1568* (1976).

John T. McGrath, *The French in Early Florida: In the Eye of the Hurricane* (2000).

David Beers Quinn, *Raleigh and the British Empire* (1962).

David Beers Quinn, *England and the Discovery of America, 1481–1620* (1974).

Carl Ortwin Sauer, *Sixteenth Century America: The Land and the People as Seen by the Europeans* (1971).

Online Practice Test

Test your understanding of this chapter with interactive review quizzes at

www.ablongman.com/jonescreatedequal/chapter1

CHAPTER 2

European Footholds on the Fringes of North America, 1600–1660

Unknown Artist, *Mrs. William Pollard*, 1721. Courtesy of the Massachusetts Historical Society, MHS #1495

■ Mrs. William Pollard, 1721. Anne Pollard migrated to New England as a young woman.

IN THE SUMMER OF 1621, AN ENGLISHMAN AND AN INDIAN LEFT PLYMOUTH VILLAGE ON foot to visit a Native American leader named Massasoit. Stephen Hopkins and Squanto had a threefold purpose: to "view the country," to assess Massasoit's military strength, and to secure his support for the struggling English colony. During their 40-mile journey, the two men saw numerous signs of a wave of disease that had swept the New England coast four years earlier, killing thousands of Indians. Weakened survivors had lacked the energy to bury the dead, whose skulls and bones still lay aboveground in many places.

The two men who encountered these grim scenes had come together from strikingly different backgrounds. Back in 1609, Hopkins had boarded the *Sea Adventure* and left England in a fleet of nine vessels, all heading for Jamestown in Virginia. When a storm wrecked his ship on the uncharted island of Bermuda, Hopkins and others rebelled against their official leader. They refused to go further under his command. Accused of mutiny and sentenced to hang, Hopkins pleaded his case and narrowly escaped the noose. When the rest of the company finally managed to build two small boats and sail safely to Virginia, he went along. Soon after that, he managed to return to England and start a family, but he could not shake off the lure of America.

A Mayflower replica is now part of the restored Plymouth Colony site.

In 1620 Hopkins decided to return. At the English port of Plymouth, Hopkins, his pregnant wife, Elizabeth, and several children and servants boarded another vessel: the *Mayflower*. Headed for Virginia, the *Mayflower* had been chartered to carry a group of English Protestants to America from their exile in Holland. Paying passengers such as the Hopkins family also joined the journey. Tensions mounted when a midpassage decision changed the *Mayflower*'s destination from Virginia to New England. Hopkins, remembering his experiences in Bermuda, was among those who muttered "mutinous speeches" and argued that "when they came ashore, they should use their own libertie, for none had power to command them." But after Elizabeth gave birth, Hopkins joined the other 40 men aboard in signing the *Mayflower* Compact. The agreement bound all the passengers together in a "Civil Body Politic" to be governed by laws "most meet and convenient for the general good." They reached New England in early winter, and Hopkins and others laid out the village of Plymouth in the snow. There, the newcomers met Squanto, a Native American with a command of English who helped them negotiate with local Indians.

Squanto had also endured great hardship and Atlantic travel. He remembered the first French and English fishing vessels, which had appeared when he was a small boy. The sailors mapped the coast, traded with local tribes for beaver pelts or corn, and occasionally took Indian hostages back to Europe. In 1614 Squanto was among 27 Indians seized by an Englishman departing with a cargo of fish for the Mediterranean port of Malaga. Rescued from certain slavery by Spanish friars, Squanto somehow reached England, voyaged to Newfoundland, and returned to his homeland in 1619, only to find his entire village swept away by disease.

■ As a boy, Squanto probably saw Samuel de Champlain's vessel enter this bay in July 1605. The French dropped anchor (A) and took soundings until they ran aground (G). Champlain climbed a sand dune (D) to sketch this map, noting numerous Indian dwellings and gardens (F). These settlements had been devastated by disease when the *Mayflower* colonists arrived in December 1620. They renamed the harbor Plymouth and spent their first night ashore on Clark's Island (C).

The *Mayflower* pilgrims, arriving a year after Squanto's return, would also suffer heavy losses. Of the 102 settlers who had begun the voyage, half of them died in Plymouth colony by the next spring. But in New England, as elsewhere in America, death seemed to play favorites in the following years. As colonization continued, recurrent epidemics took a particularly heavy toll on Native Americans, who lacked immunity when exposed to foreign diseases for the first time. In 1622 Squanto fell sick and died of a fever, leaving no relatives behind. In contrast, Stephen and Elizabeth Hopkins lived on to see numerous children and grandchildren thrive.

By the middle of the seventeenth century, English settlements had taken root in both Virginia and Massachusetts. The success of these colonies would exert a lasting influence on the future direction of American society. But their stories unfolded as part of a far wider North American drama. It embraced both the Atlantic and the Pacific shores, and it included a diversity of European groups besides the English settlements near Cape Cod and Chesapeake Bay. The French founded towns at Quebec and Montreal, while the Spanish held onto St. Augustine and established Santa Fe in the Southwest. Dutch traders built New Amsterdam on Manhattan Island, overlooking the Hudson River, and Swedish colonists erected a fort near the mouth of the Delaware.

Nor was the drama confined to the tiny colonies, struggling against steep odds to establish lasting footholds on the fringes of the continent. In each outpost the lives of the new arrivals remained linked to the broad religious struggles, economic ambitions, and imperial contests that absorbed the Atlantic powers in far-off Europe. And closer at hand, the wellbeing of Indian groups, near and far, proved to be linked with the lives of colonists such as the Hopkins family. As the story of Squanto illustrates, Native American communities faced their own set of new challenges that altered traditional ways of living and threatened their very survival.

Spain's Ocean-Spanning Reach

In 1580 Spain's Philip II had laid claim to the throne of Portugal. This consolidation, (which endured until 1640) unified Europe's two great richest seaborne empires, for Spain and Portugal had each been sanctioned by the pope nearly a century earlier to explore opposite sides of the globe.

Both kingdoms had had remarkable success in these overseas endeavors. The Portuguese had established trade with India and Southeast Asia, and their traders and Catholic missionaries had even created a foothold in Japan. The Spanish, sailing in the opposite direction, had staked out huge claims in the Americas and had founded Manila in the Philippines as a Pacific port of trade. By the turn of the century, however, Spain faced two fresh problems. First, combining with Portugal put huge additional burdens on the overstretched Spanish bureaucracy. Second, the global success of the combined Iberian empires invited challenges from envious rivals in northern Europe. The new international competition came from the French, the Dutch, and the English. Each of these realms constituted an aspiring naval power with imperial ambitions of its own.

In 1598, for example, ten Dutch ships found their way to the Pacific, defying Spanish claims for control of that ocean. One of these vessels, piloted by Englishman Will Adams, ended up in Japan, where the new Tokugawa dynasty (1600–1868) was consolidating its control. Adams visited Edo—the rising military town that would grow into modern Tokyo. He even built a ship for the *shogun* (ruler) and trained Japanese carpenters to become shipwrights. Adams's experience in Japan serves as a reminder that in the decades before the *Mayflower* sailed the Atlantic, the issue of who would dominate Pacific sea lanes to America was anything but clear.

Vizcaíno in California and Japan

In April 1607, a letter from the king of Spain reached Mexico City. The king commanded his viceroy in charge of affairs in Mexico (New Spain) to create an outpost on California's Monterey Bay in order to aid Spanish galleons crossing the Pacific from Manila. The logical person to execute the plan for the viceroy was Sebastián Vizcaíno, a seasoned navigator who had already explored Monterey Bay on the California coast four years earlier.

Vizcaíno understood the Pacific trade, having sailed between Acapulco on Mexico's west coast and the new Spanish stronghold at Manila. His ships had carried American chocolate to the Philippines and brought back silks and spices from Asia. Vizcaíno knew that galleons returning through the North Pacific to the west coast of Mexico desperately needed a haven along the route, after crossing the immense ocean. As he had seen, Monterey Bay was well supplied with water, food, and timber. The sheltering harbor would provide a perfect way station, where ships could take on supplies and make repairs before heading south. The royal plan directed Vizcaíno to sail to Manila and then establish a new colony at Monterey during his return voyage.

But the viceroy in Mexico City had other ideas. He diverted the necessary funds into a search for the fabled North Pacific isles of Rica de Oro ("Rich in Gold") and Rica de Plata ("Rich in Silver"). In 1611, the viceroy authorized Vizcaíno to search for the mysterious islands. The venture took Vizcaíno to Japan. When he finally returned east in 1613 aboard a vessel built

Spanish exploration by land and sea

▪ Spanish territory, 1610
— Juan de Oñate, 1598–1601
— Juan de Oñate, 1604–1605
— Sebastián Vizcaíno, 1602–1603
— Sebastián Vizcaíno, 1611–1613
Present state boundaries provided for orientation

■ **MAP 2.1**
THE SPANISH SOUTHWEST IN THE EARLY SEVENTEENTH CENTURY

in Japan, he brought 180 Japanese with him to Mexico. This unique delegation was bound for Spain and Italy to open doors between East and West. However, the Tokugawas soon began to persecute the European traders and Christian missionaries who had been allowed in the Japanese islands for a generation. Because of this persecution, the frail link between Europe and Japan through Mexico never developed further.

Tokugawa officials, it seems, feared that tolerating foreigners in Japan's ports might foster the spread of Christianity and undermine their supremacy. Moreover, developing Japanese fleets might bring guns to warlords and disrupt hard-won peace. So Japan passed up an opportunity for naval expansion, just as Ming China had done two centuries earlier after the voyages of Cheng Ho. Instead, the new dynasty adopted a policy of commercial and cultural isolation that would last for more than two hundred years. Had Japanese society followed another route, co-opting Western technologies and aggressively exploring and colonizing the Pacific, the subsequent history of North America and the world would almost certainly have taken a very different path.

■ Acoma, often called Sky City, sits atop a high sandstone mesa west of Albuquerque, New Mexico. The name means "place that always was," and the pueblo has been continuously inhabited for roughly 1000 years. Acoma's Native American community survived a devastating attack by Spanish colonizers in 1599.

For the Spanish, Vizcaíno's Pacific adventure also failed to open new prospects. His fruitless search for gold and silver consumed crucial funds, and the possibility of a Spanish settlement at Monterey quickly disappeared. Spanish mariners knew California's rugged coastline only from the sea, and the steep cliffs discouraged them from approaching the mainland too closely. Moreover, fresh probes by ships sailing to the north along California's coast might reveal the "Straits of Anian"—the mythic Northwest Passage from the Atlantic to the Pacific that Spain's rivals had been seeking. Concerned that their empire had already become overextended, Spanish officials postponed plans to colonize California's coast. In addition, Spain wondered whether to maintain its existing North American colony in Florida and its newest frontier province: New Mexico.

Oñate Creates a Spanish Foothold in the Southwest

In 1598 Juan de Oñate renewed the northern efforts of Coronado's expedition several generations earlier. Setting out from New Spain, he led 500 men, women, and children north into the upper Rio Grande valley to create the province of New Mexico. Oñate was a wealthy man—his father had discovered a major silver mine at Zacatecas—and he had bold ambitions. Aided by Franciscan friars (organized followers of St. Francis loyal to the Roman Catholic pope), Oñate and his colonists expected to convert the Indians to Christianity. (The newcomers called these local inhabitants the Pueblo people, using the Spanish word for *town*, since they lived in compact apartment-like villages.) Expanding outward from the native towns, or pueblos, the intruders hoped to open a vast new colonial realm. It would be a "new world," they proclaimed, "greater than New Spain."

But Oñate drastically underestimated the difficulties. When embittered Indians at Acoma pueblo killed 11 of his soldiers in 1599, he retaliated by bombarding the mesa-top citadel, killing 800 inhabitants and enslaving nearly 600 others. Hearing of the brutal repression of the residents of Acoma, neighboring pueblos reluctantly submitted to Spanish demands for labor and food. Oñate had expended his entire personal fortune to establish a fragile toehold in the region. But reinforcements arriving in 1600 were dismayed by the harsh conditions; Oñate needed new discoveries if the colony were to prosper. In 1601, he launched an expedition east onto the Great Plains, mistakenly believing that the Atlantic Ocean was not far away. The venture proved as futile as Coronado's earlier march had been.

To make matters worse, 1601 proved to be a year of drought. When Oñate returned to the Rio Grande, he found that two-thirds of his tiny colony—including many of the recent reinforcements—had given up and departed. Instead of silver, they had found sand. The disillusioned settlers returned to Mexico in a pitiful condition. Asked why they had deserted the colony, they said that the region lacked woods, pastures, water, and suitable land.

Foiled on the east and weakened along the Rio Grande, Oñate next pressed west to seek a link to the Pacific. When he reached the Gulf of California in 1605, he mistook it for the great ocean. He even inscribed a notice of his feat (still visible) on the great sandstone rock, El Morro, between Acoma and Zuni pueblos. But his new "Mexico" remained isolated and impoverished, with the remaining colonists strapped for clothing and food. The newcomers, desperate to survive, pressed hard on the native peoples they had harried into submission. They demanded tribute in the form of cotton blankets, buffalo hides, and baskets of scarce maize. In winter, ill-equipped Spanish soldiers stripped warm robes off the backs of shivering women and children; in summer, they scoured each pueblo for corn. Sometimes they tortured residents to find out where food was hidden.

Meanwhile, a few hundred Pueblo Indians—intimidated by the Spanish, desperate for a share of the food they had grown, and fearful of attacks by neighboring Apaches—began to accept Christian baptism and seek Spanish protection. By 1608, when the crown threatened to withdraw support from the struggling province, the colony's Franciscan missionaries appealed that their converts had grown too numerous to resettle and too dependent to abandon. Their argument may have been exaggerated, but it caught the attention of authorities.

Besides, England and France were launching new colonies in Virginia and Canada. Since mapmakers still could not accurately calculate longitude (east-west distance on the globe), no one was sure whether these bases created by international rivals posed a threat that was dangerously close at hand. England's failed Roanoke colony, after all, had the same latitude (or north-south position) as Santa Fe, and many Europeans still estimated the two points were not far apart. Worried Spanish officials finally agreed with the Franciscan friars that New Mexico must carry on. But, they replaced Oñate with a new governor and asserted royal control over the few dozen settlers who remained in the colony.

New Mexico Survives: New Flocks Among Old Pueblos

The Spanish decision to hold on in New Mexico reshaped life for everyone in the region. At least 60,000 Indians living in nearly separate pueblos found their world transformed and their survival threatened over the next half-century. In 1610 the new governor, ruling over scarcely 50 colonists, created a capital at the village of Sante Fe. Every three years, a government supply train of 30 wagons made the long trip to the new capital from Mexico City. Within two decades, roughly 750 colonists inhabited the remote province, including Spanish, Mexican Indians, Africans, and mixed-race children.

The racial and ethnic diversity of New Mexico repeated the colonial pattern established in New Spain. Similarly, labor practices and

■ The Spanish made Santa Fe the capital of their New Mexico colony in 1610 and built the church of San Miguel there in 1626. Though destroyed in the Pueblo Revolt of 1680, it was rebuilt and has remained in use. "The floor is bare earth," wrote an eighteenth-century observer, "the usual floor throughout these regions."

religious changes also followed models established after the conquest of the Aztecs in Mexico. As in New Spain, certain privileged people in the new colony received *encomiendas*; such grants entitled the holders (known as an *encomenderos*), to the labor of a set number of Native American workers. With labor in short supply throughout the Spanish colonies, other settlers led occasional raids against nomadic Plains Indians, keeping some captives and shipping others south to toil as slaves in the Mexican silver mines.

Meanwhile, the number of missionaries rose rapidly, just as it had throughout Spain's American empire. By the 1630s, 46 Franciscan friars staffed missions in 35 pueblos. They preached a mix of Christian religion and Hispanic cultural values. They forbade traditional Pueblo celebrations, known as kachina dances, and destroyed sacred kachina masks. Their combination of intense zeal and harsh punishments prompted many Indians to learn Spanish and become obedient converts. However, it also drove the Indians' own religious practices underground—literally, into the hidden, circular kivas that had long been a focal point for Native American spiritual activities in the region. There, people kept their traditional faith alive in secret and passed sacred rituals along to the next generation.

The Spanish brought more than Christianity to New Mexico. The newcomers also transferred novel crops (wheat, onions, chilies, peas) and planted new fruits (peaches, plums, cherries). Settlers introduced metal hoes and axes to the area as well, along with donkeys, chickens, and other domesticated animals previously unknown to the native inhabitants. Horses and cattle, led north from New Spain in small herds, eventually revolutionized life across the North American West. But Spanish sheep, well suited to the semi-desert conditions, exerted the most immediate impact. Each friar soon possessed a flock of several thousand. Pueblo artisans, skilled at spinning cotton, now wove woolen cloth for their own use and for export.

But the Pueblo world, like Squanto's world, was eroding under the onslaught of new European diseases. The large Pueblo population, cut in half in the 60 years after Coronado's appearance, still numbered more than 60,000 in 1600, after the arrival of Oñate's colonizing expedition. Yet sickness, along with warfare and famine, cut this number in half again by 1650 and in half once more by 1680.

Conversion and Rebellion in Spanish Florida

The flat, lush environment of the Florida peninsula contrasts sharply with the dry, rugged landscape of New Mexico. Yet by 1600, Spain's Florida colony had also disappointed imperial officials. Dreams of gold-filled kingdoms and a strategic passage from the Southeast to the Orient had never materialized. The 500 needy soldiers, settlers, and slaves who resided in thatched huts at St. Augustine struck Spanish officials at home as an undue burden. The government planned to disband the colony and end its annual subsidy. But Franciscan missionaries won the day, as in New Mexico. They argued that scores of Indian towns appeared ready to receive Christianity. By 1608, the crown had decided to let the colony continue. A handful of missionaries fanned out among the Indians of northern Florida, erecting small churches, celebrating mass, and explaining the rudiments of the Catholic faith.

Florida Division of Historical Resources

■ The Spanish found that glass beads, colorful and easy to transport, made fine gifts and trade items in their contacts with Florida Indians. Chiefs often received special quartz crystal beads and pendants to retain their loyalty.

However, the Franciscans soon realized that literacy itself held a more powerful appeal among Florida Indians than the Christian word. The friars therefore set up schools "for imprinting the Christian discipline and doctrine in those hearts and lands with letters." At missions (known as *doctrinas*), where a resident friar taught church doctrine, they recruited Indian students aggressively without regard to age or sex. In 1612 Francisco de Pareja published an illustrated, bilingual confessional in Castilian and Timucuan, the earliest text in any North American Indian language. The book enabled wary friars to ask villagers, "Have you said suggestive words?" and "Have you desired to do some lewd act with some man or woman or kin?"

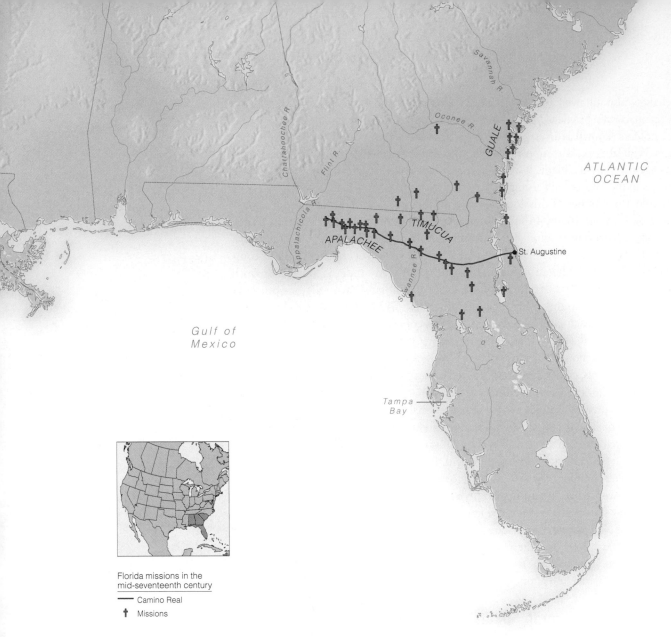

Florida missions in the
mid-seventeenth century

—— Camino Real

✝ Missions

■ **MAP 2.2**
SITES OF CATHOLIC MISSIONS IN SPANISH FLORIDA IN THE MID-SEVENTEENTH CENTURY

Contact with Christian beliefs and books came at a steep price, for each inland village was expected to help feed the colonial garrison at St. Augustine. Local women neglected their own household crops to grow additional maize and grind it into meal. Annually, the crown requisitioned the labor of Indian men from each village. Spanish officials compelled them to transport the cornmeal overland to the Atlantic coast and return to the mission bringing supplies back to the Franciscans. Imported candles, communion wine, and mission bells all had to be hauled inland from St. Augustine. The trip to and from the coast took several weeks, and each bearer shouldered a 75-pound load. When missions appeared in the western province of Apalachee (around modern-day Tallahassee) after 1633, the treks from the coast needed to cover even greater distances.

Friars and Indian bearers traveling to the interior also carried sicknesses from St. Augustine. Epidemics of measles, bubonic plague, malaria, typhus, smallpox, and influenza took a devastating toll on the Native Americans. Harsh work conditions and poor diets lowered people's resistance to illness. Indians expired more rapidly than the Spanish could convert them, and friars hastened to baptize the dying and claim their souls for Christ. In a letter to the Spanish king in 1617, a Franciscan reported that the local population had been cut in half in the five years since his arrival "on account of the great plagues and contagious diseases that the Indians have suffered." But he reassured his majesty that "a very rich harvest of souls for heaven has been made in the midst of great numbers of deaths."

Even though the small cadre of friars grew, reaching a high of 70 after midcentury, the region's overall population plummeted. A report from 1635, shortly after Spanish expansion into Apalachee, claimed 30,000 baptisms at 44 missions. But within a generation, the number of native Floridians, whether baptized or not, had plunged by nearly half. In 1655 the governor noted "high mortality" throughout Timucua caused by a "series of small-pox plagues which have affected the country for the last ten months" and by "the trials and hunger which these unfortunate people have suffered." Two years later, he reported that the people of Timucua and Guale had been almost "wiped out with the sickness of the plague and small-pox which has overtaken them."

As whole villages disappeared, Spanish entrepreneurs began to expand cattle ranching across the newly vacated lands of northern Florida. Faced with encroaching farms, crushing labor demands, and frightful mortality, local native leaders saw their power reduced and their communities depleted. When the Spanish established a cattle ranch in Apalachee in 1645, a local chief protested that they drew in "all the men and the women, boys and girls," to provide labor, and "what we gained from all this work was solely fatigue and nothing else."

Two years later, in 1647, Indians at Apalachee staged a revolt. They burned down seven of the area's mission compounds, killing three friars, the deputy governor and his family, and a number of recent converts. But the garrison at St. Augustine reacted quickly, and when its soldiers arrived, they tried and executed 12 of the rebel leaders. In 1656 a wider Native American uprising shook Timucua in north central Florida. The rebellion occurred because the governor of Florida feared a possible attack by English ships on the garrison at St. Augustine. He therefore requisitioned 500 Indian warriors from the Timucua region to help fend off the rumored invasion, and he required each man to bring along 75 pounds of corn for the campaign. Insulted by the demand, Timucuan leaders staged a revolt that took months to suppress.

In the end, the English threat to Spanish Florida did not materialize, but the rumor in 1656 underscored how much had changed in the preceding half-century. Two generations earlier, in 1600, no European power besides Spain had possessed a solid foothold in any portion of the Americas.

Even Portuguese Brazil had recently come under the rule of Spain. But over the next six decades, France, Holland, and England all asserted claims on the American mainland. These rivals challenged Spain not only in the Atlantic but in the Pacific as well.

France and Holland: Overseas Competition for Spain

At the turn of the seventeenth century, interlopers from Holland had challenged Spanish colonizers in the Philippines and Portuguese traders in Japan. These Dutch efforts illustrated the growing competition between European powers for control of the world's oceans. In London, commercial leaders received a royal charter to create the English East India Company in 1600, and merchants in Amsterdam took a similar step. Hoping to capture Portugal's lucrative Asian trade, they established the Dutch East India Company in 1602. Four years later, Dutchman Willem Jansz became the first European to glimpse Australia. Within a generation (as the Ming dynasty ended in China during the 1640s), Dutch sailors expanded their Asian reach still farther. They took Malacca (near Singapore) from the Portuguese in 1641, reached Tasmania and New Zealand in 1642, and charted the coast of northern Japan in 1643. By 1652 they had also founded a Dutch colony at Cape Town, on the southern tip of Africa.

The united powers of Spain and Portugal proved even more vulnerable in the Atlantic. To be sure, Spanish convoys continued to transport Mexican gold and silver to Europe annually, along with Asian silks and spices shipped to Mexico via the Pacific trade. Portuguese vessels carried Africans to the New World at a profit. But ships from rival European nations preyed on these seaborne cargoes with increasing success. Defiantly, they also laid claim to numerous islands in the Caribbean.

By 1660, the English had taken control of Barbados, Providence Island, Antigua, and Jamaica; the Dutch had acquired St. Maarten, St. Eustacius, Saba, and Curaçao; and the French had claimed Guadeloupe, Martinique, Grenada, and St. Lucia. For France, however, the most promising Atlantic prospects lay farther north in Canada. There, Spanish power was absent, hopes for a Northwest Passage persisted, and French imperial claims stretched back generations.

The Founding of New France

Since the time of Jacques Cartier, fishing boats from the coast of France had crisscrossed New-foundland's Grand Banks. One old French salt claimed to have made the voyage for 42 consecutive years. The trade increased after 1580 as crews built seasonal stations along the American coast for drying codfish. These stations brought them into greater contact with Indians; soon both parties were exchanging metal goods for furs on terms that pleased all. A Native American could trade a worn-out robe made from beaver skins for a highly valued iron kettle. For a European, the older the robe the better, for its Indian owner wore it with the fur side in. Steady wear rubbed away the long guard hairs and left the soft underlayer of fur. Back home in Europe, workers removed these greasy short hairs and matted them into felt for the manufacture of beaver hats. (They used mercury in the process, not knowing that its poison made some of them insane, hence the phrase "mad as a hatter.") The finished product proved warm, waterproof, and fashionable. Because one robe yielded felt for six to eight hats (each worth a steep three pounds), its high sale price let dealers purchase scores of kettles and knives for the next year's exchange.

As North Atlantic fishing and trading expanded, the domestic situation in France improved after 1600. In 1598, a generation of religious war between Catholics and Protestants in France ended when King Henry IV issued the Edict of Nantes. The decree granted political rights and limited toleration to French Protestants, or Huguenots. With peace restored, the king could now afford to look favorably on new colonization initiatives in America. An experienced French soldier and sailor named Samuel de Champlain emerged as a key leader in this effort. Between 1599 and 1601, Champlain scouted Spain's New World empire and brought back suggestions to Paris for overseas advancement of French interests. He even offered a proposal to create a canal across the Isthmus of Panama. But from 1602 until his death in 1635, Champlain devoted

himself to the St. Lawrence River region, where Acadia on the Atlantic coast and Canada along the extensive river valley made up the anticipated realm of New France.

Year-round French settlements in Acadia could support the Atlantic fisheries, extend the fur trade, and preempt the English, who were eyeing the same coast. Spurred by rumors of precious metals and western passages to Asia, Champlain explored and mapped the coast from Cape Breton to Cape Cod. But settlement efforts came to nothing, so the French directed their attention inland. In 1608 Champlain and several dozen other men established the outpost of Quebec at a narrow spot in the St. Lawrence River, where Cartier and Rober-val had wintered generations earlier.

In June 1609 Champlain joined a band of Algonquin and Huron Indians in a raid on the Iroquois. They journeyed south to a large lake in modern New York, which he proudly renamed as Lake Champlain. When they engaged their Iroquois enemies in battle, Champlain fired his gun to kill several war chiefs. A novelty in the region, the gun sparked a rout. For the powerful Iroquois League south of the St. Lawrence (the Five Nation confederation composed of the Seneca, Cayuga, Onondaga, Oneida, and Mohawk Indians), the defeat spawned lasting bitterness. But the victory sealed good relations for the French with the Algonquins and Hurons, ensuring the survival of Quebec and spurring unprecedented commerce. Within 15 years, Native Americans were trading 12,000 to 15,000 beaver pelts annually via the St. Lawrence River valley.

By permission of the Houghton Library, Harvard University

■ Champlain's drawing of the battle on Lake Champlain, 1609

In 1627, the powerful first minister in France, Cardinal Richelieu, pressed for greater French settlement in Canada through a new private company. He banned Huguenots from participating and pushed to make sure that only Roman Catholics were allowed to migrate to Canada. But his expansive policies alarmed England, which began aggressive efforts to force out the French colonists. In 1628 English privateers (privately owned ships commissioned to seize enemy vessels for profit) captured an arriving convoy of 400 French Catholic settlers. The next year, they forced the surrender of Quebec. When restored to French control several years later, the tiny outpost contained fewer than a hundred people. In an effort to expand the meager settlement and populate the fertile valley upriver from Quebec, French authorities began granting narrow strips of land with river frontage to any Catholic lord who would take up residence there and bring French tenants to his estate.

Competing for the Beaver Trade

Cardinal Richelieu's power in France epitomized the ongoing Counter-Reformation. Indeed, the effects of this outpouring of Catholic zeal reached as far as North America. In 1635 Jesuits from the Society of Jesus, created a century earlier by Ignatius Loyola to defend and spread the Catholic faith, founded a college in Quebec to educate the sons of colonists, and in 1639 six nuns arrived to begin a school and a hospital for Indian girls. Other religious workers established a station farther west in 1641. Their outpost where the Ottawa River joined the St. Lawrence, in territory recently dominated by the Iroquois, marked the beginnings of Montreal. This move upstream had strategic as well as religious significance. The French wanted to control the beaver trade as it expanded west. They also hoped to prevent the Iroquois League from diverting furs south to Holland's new colony on the Hudson River.

But the desperate Iroquois nations, facing collapse, took a stand. Increasing contact with Europeans and their contagious diseases had brought catastrophic epidemics to the Iroquois homelands below Lake Ontario. Beginning in 1633, sicknesses that were new to the region swept away some 10,000 people and cut the Five Nations' population in half within a decade. The Mohawks—farthest east and most exposed to French, Dutch, and English newcomers—suffered the most, losing as many as three out of four people from the distinctive longhouses

■ MAP 2.3

EUROPEAN AND NATIVE AMERICAN CONTACT IN THE NORTHEAST, 1600–1660 French and English colonization efforts brought devastating diseases to the Five Nations of the Iroquois League. Eager to take captives and profit from the growing trade in furs, the Iroquois ranged north and west to make war on the French and their Huron Indian allies.

that made up Iroquois villages. According to Iroquois tradition, survivors must replace deceased individuals swiftly with captives to maintain the community's strength and continuity. Pressed by grieving families, Iroquois warriors initiated a generation of violent campaigns intended to capture and absorb neighboring groups. These so-called mourning wars are also remembered as the Beaver Wars because they included a clear economic as well as cultural motive. Besides captives, the Iroquois aggressors sought furs. If they could seize pelts before the valuable items reached the French, they could trade them to the Dutch for guns and powder. Well armed, they could then engage in further wars for captives and furs.

This spiral of aggression put the Iroquois on a collision course with the Hurons and their Catholic allies, a small band of Jesuit missionaries from France. These members of the militant Society of Jesus were willing to risk martyrdom to win converts in New France. But the seasonal mobility of most local Indians frustrated them. According to one discouraged priest, "Not much ought to be hoped for from the savages as long as they are wanderers." Eager to find "a stable nation" for potential converts, the Jesuits focused their attention on Huronia, the region east of Lake Huron and Georgian Bay. There, 30,000 Huron Indians lived in large, settled villages. The Jesuits erected chapels at four of these towns. And in 1639, they constructed a central base at St. Marie on the Wye River, part fort and part mission. Having volunteered for hardship, they witnessed far more of it than they ever imagined.

First came the same foreign epidemics that had wasted the Iroquois; smallpox cut down roughly two-thirds of the Huron population, or 20,000 people, between 1635 and 1640. Then came the Iroquois themselves, bent on capturing Huron women and children to revitalize their longhouses, swept empty by disease in the 1630s. Armed by Dutch traders eager for furs, 1000 warriors descended on the weakened Hurons in March 1649. They burned villages, secured captives, tortured several priests to death, and seized large stocks of pelts. Some lucky survivors dispersed to neighboring tribes, and the 500 who remained behind took refuge near Quebec. The Iroquois then launched raids on the St. Lawrence valley, disrupting the fur trade and frightening the several thousand French inhabitants. By 1660, it seemed that New France—thinly settled, weakly defended, and poorly supplied—might face the same extinction that the much older and larger Huronia community had suffered.

A Dutch Colony on the Hudson River

The Dutch traders who supplied firearms to the Iroquois in exchange for furs owed their start to English-born navigator and arctic explorer Henry Hudson. In 1608 the Dutch East India Company, eager to locate a northeastern route to China, hired Hudson and his crew to probe above Scandinavia. But when snowstorms blocked their way, Hudson sailed his vessel, the *Half Moon,* across the Atlantic in search of a western passage to the Orient. During the summer of 1609, the *Half Moon* visited Chesapeake Bay and Delaware Bay, then rediscovered modern-day New York harbor, the bay that Verrazzano had entered in 1524. Flying the Dutch flag, Hudson sailed north up the broad river that now bears his name. Along the way, he obtained food and furs from Algonkian Indians in exchange for knives and beads. He noted that saltwater and ocean tides pushed 60 miles upstream—Indians called the river "the water that flows two ways." But no channel to the Pacific materialized.

The Dutch moved quickly to gain a foothold in the region. Ships from Amsterdam soon appeared far up the Hudson, exchanging metal goods for beaver pelts and occasionally leaving men behind to engage in trading with the Indians. One Dutch captain arriving in 1613 encountered Juan Rodrigues, a mulatto from the West Indies who had jumped ship the previous year with 80 hatchets and other trade goods. The captain, in turn, left behind a young Amsterdam clerk and took away two sons of the principal Indian leader, or *sachem.* Soon the Dutch clerk had established a year-round trading post at Fort Orange (near present-day Albany). Mohawk traditions recall how the Indians "Planted the Tree of Good Understanding" with the Dutch newcomers, whom they called *Kristoni,* for "I am a metal maker."

In 1621, responsibility for New Netherland—the region claimed between the Delaware and Connecticut rivers—fell to the newly chartered Dutch West India Company (DWIC).

Collection of The New-York Historical Society, Neg. #1049

■ **New Amsterdam Fort on Manhattan Island**

Modeled on the Dutch East India Company, this enterprise made Holland a formidable force in the Atlantic, especially after the spectacular Dutch capture of the Spanish silver fleet off Cuba in 1628. The DWIC concentrated on piecing together an empire in the South Atlantic. Dutch ships seized part of sugar-rich Brazil (1632), the island of Curaçao near Venezuela (1634), and Portugal's African outpost at Elmina, on the coast of modern-day Ghana (1637). But the DWIC also laid plans for a North American colony.

To begin, company officials recruited a group of Walloon refugees, French-speaking Belgians who had hoped to found a community in English Virginia. They transported these people to New Netherland in 1624. To secure the boundaries of the province, they deposited farm families far up the Hudson at Fort Orange and along the Connecticut and Delaware rivers. However, Peter Minuit, the colony's director from 1626 to 1631, saw danger in this dispersal. He worried that the widely scattered newcomers lacked defenses, trade, and community ties. To consolidate Dutch settlement, he purchased Manhattan Island at the mouth of the Hudson from the local Indians. By 1630, the village of New Amsterdam boasted 270 settlers clustered in cottages around a waterfront fort at the southern tip of Manhattan. (When the inhabitants built a wall around the village to protect against Indian attacks, the road inside this palisade became known as Wall Street.)

Next, the DWIC began granting land along the Hudson to wealthy *patroons* (patrons), similar to the French seigneurs along the St. Lawrence. Hoping that private investment would strengthen their colony, the company gave a huge tract with 18 miles of river frontage to any wealthy investor who could send 50 people to farm there as tenants. An Amsterdam merchant named Kiliaen van Rensselaer formed the first and most lucrative of these patroonships near Fort Orange. But this effort to promote migration faltered, and new conflicts began to appear on several fronts.

Mrs. Lazare Bayard, 1636. Collection of The New-York Historical Society (Acc. #1915.6)

■ When Judith Bayard Stuyvesant arrived in New Amsterdam with her husband in 1647, she carried this portrait of her mother, Judith de Vos Bayard, painted in Holland in 1636. Dutch painting flourished at the time, led by Rembrandt and Hals.

When the company threw open the Indian trade to others besides its own agents, the careless and greedy actions of unregulated traders sparked a series of violent wars with coastal tribes. Settlers also squabbled with neighboring English settlers over fur-trading rights and other matters. The small colony of New Sweden, which materialized on the west side of the Delaware River in 1637, posed yet another problem. That short-lived venture was sponsored partly by Dutch capital, and Peter Minuit was put in charge. But the settlers who actually built Fort Christina (now Wilmington, Delaware) were Swedes and Finns hoping to establish their own trade with the Indians. But in 1655, these several hundred Scandinavian settlers were obliged to surrender to Dutch power.

"All Sorts of Nationalities": Diverse New Amsterdam

The symbol of Dutch power in the region, and the commander of the fleet that seized New Sweden, was Peter Stuyvesant. He ruled New Netherland aggressively for several decades before England seized the colony in 1664. His career reveals the close ties among the DWIC's Atlantic ventures. Stuyvesant had served as governor of Dutch Curaçao (losing his right leg in an attack on the Spanish at St. Maarten). His next commission made him director general of several DWIC dependencies, including New Netherland and Curaçao. He married Judith Bayard in Holland, and the couple sailed from Amsterdam for New Netherland in 1647.

Stuyvesant, age 37, moved swiftly to assert control. He limited beer and rum sales, fined settlers for promiscuity and knife fighting, and established a nine-member night watch. If disobeyed, he turned to whippings. "He proceeds no longer by words or writings," a resident complained in 1651, "but by arrests and stripes." When a group of English Quakers, members of the newly formed Society of Friends, arrived aboard a trading vessel in 1657, he attempted to expel the radical Protestants and fine any who gave them shelter. However, Dutch residents of Flushing, on Long Island, defied his ban and signed a public letter of objection stressing religious toleration. "Whether Presbyterian, Independent, Baptist or Quaker," they protested, "let every man stand and fall to his own."

To address the colony's chronic labor shortage, Stuyvesant endorsed trade in African slaves, by now a mainstay in Holland's South Atlantic commerce. He also used his Caribbean connections to expand this traffic. When the Portuguese forced Holland out of Brazil in 1654 and closed that sugar colony to Dutch slave vessels, some of the ships brought their cargoes to New Amsterdam instead. Like the Dutch-speaking blacks who already lived in the colony, most of these newcomers were enslaved for life. But the DWIC, the largest importer and owner of slaves in New Netherland, granted "half-freedom" to some people whom it could not employ year-round. These people, in return for an annual fee, could travel and marry freely, acquire property, and hire out their labor. By 1664, African arrivals made up more than 10 percent of New Netherland's population, and at least half of them lived in Lower Manhattan. These 375 black New Amsterdam residents—most enslaved, some half-free, and at least 75 entirely free—made up 20 percent of the town's populace.

> *Compared with New France, New Netherland seemed far more populous, prosperous, and ethnically diverse.*

New Amsterdam, home to fewer than 2000 people, also had a small Jewish contingent, the first in mainland North America. In 1654, 23 Sephardic Jews (forced out of Brazil when the Portuguese took over) reached New Amsterdam aboard the French frigate *Sainte Catherine*. But Stuyvesant promptly asked the DWIC for permission to expel the refugees. Strident in his anti-Semitism, he claimed such "blasphemers of the name of Christ" would "infect and trouble this new colony." The DWIC, which included Jewish stockholders and was eager for newcomers of all kinds, overruled the governor's request. In the end, colony officials authorized a Jewish ghetto, or segregated neighborhood. They instructed the newcomers to build homes "close together in a convenient place on one or the other side of New Amsterdam." Here, they could pray together freely in private. At first, however, they were not allowed to construct a synagogue for public worship.

In the early 1660s, the colony continued to grow, "slowly peopled by the scrapings of all sorts of nationalities," as Stuyvesant complained. Huguenots occupied New Paltz near the Hudson; farther north, other newcomers founded Schenectady in 1661. Swedes and Finns continued to prosper along the Delaware, and numerous English had settled on Long Island. Compared with New France, New Netherland seemed far more populous, prosperous, and ethnically diverse. But whereas the French colony to the north endured for another century, the Dutch enterprise soon was absorbed by England. For, despite a slow start and innumerable setbacks, the English managed to outdistance all their European rivals and establish thriving North American colonies in the first half of the seventeenth century.

English Beginnings on the Atlantic Coast

When Queen Elizabeth I passed away in 1603, several important elements were already in place to help England compete for colonial outposts. The so-called enclosure movement, where large landholders had fenced in their fields and turned to raising sheep, had pushed thousands of tenants off rural farms. These people, who roamed the countryside and flocked to urban centers in search of work, formed a restless supply of potential colonists. Also, the country had an expanding fleet of English-built ships, sailed by experienced mariners who had accumulated extensive knowledge of the North Atlantic. In addition, England had a group of seasoned and ambitious leaders. A generation of soldiers (many of them younger sons of the property-holding elite known as the gentry) had participated in the brutal colonization of Ireland or sailed as privateers in the conflict with Spain. Some, including John Smith, who later became a leader of the Jamestown Colony, had skipped school and fought Spanish forces in the Netherlands. Smith himself had even survived battles and enslavement in Hungary, Turkey, and Russia.

Because Elizabeth died without heirs, the king of Scotland, James Stuart, succeeded her as ruler. During the reigns of James I (1603–1625) and his son Charles I (1625–1649), religious and economic forces in England prompted an increasing number of people to consider migrating overseas. With the expansion of the country's Protestant Reformation, religious strife escalated toward civil war, which erupted in 1642. During the tumultuous 1630s, English public officials were glad to transplant Puritans and Catholics alike to foreign shores. In turn, many ardent believers—weary of conflict or losing hope for their cause at home—welcomed the prospect of a safe haven abroad. Others, eager to support their faith, saw an opportunity to spread their beliefs more widely. Economically, the development of joint stock organizations enabled merchants to raise capital and spread the high risk of colonial ventures by selling numerous shares to small investors. At the same time, the fluctuating domestic economy prompted many people to consider seeking their fortunes elsewhere.

Nor had English geographers given up on finding a sea route somewhere in the Northern Hemisphere leading to the riches of Asia. Perhaps Virginia would prove no wider than the Isthmus of Panama, or a short passage to China would reveal itself farther north. With this latter prospect in mind, England pressed Henry Hudson into service in 1610, shortly after his promising voyage for the Dutch. The experienced explorer ventured far to the northwest, navigating the strait and bay in northern Canada that still bear his name. Mutinous crewmen set the captain adrift in a small boat—resulting in his death—and returned to England claiming they had found the Northwest Passage. But efforts to discover a northern "Passage into the South Sea" proved futile, and English attention moved elsewhere.

The Virginia Company and Jamestown

For Richard Hakluyt, England's leading publicist for overseas expansion, the proper focus seemed clear: "There is under our noses," he wrote in 1599, "the great & ample countery of Virginia." Great and ample, indeed, especially before the rival Dutch established New Netherland. On paper, the enormous zone that England claimed as Virginia stretched north to south from the top of modern-day Vermont to Cape Fear on Carolina's Outer Banks. From east to west, it spanned North America from the Atlantic to the Pacific, however narrow or wide the continent might prove to be.

In 1606 James I chartered the Virginia Company as a two-pronged operation to exploit the sweeping Virginia claim. Under the charter, a group of London-based merchants took responsibility for colonizing the Chesapeake Bay region. Meanwhile, merchants from England's West Country, based in the seaports of Plymouth, Exeter, and Bristol, took charge of developing the northern latitudes of the American coast. In 1607, two ships from Plymouth deposited roughly a hundred colonists at the Sagadahoc (Kennebec) River in Maine. The Sagadahoc settlers erected a fort and buildings; they even constructed a small sailing vessel called the *Virginia*, the first of hundreds of ships that the English built from American forests. But frostbite, scurvy, and dwindling supplies prompted a retreat home in 1608, two decades after the Roanoke failures.

A parallel effort by the Londoners proved more enduring—but just barely. In April 1607, three ships from the Thames sailed into Chesapeake Bay carrying 105 men. They disembarked on what appeared to be a secluded island near a broad river. In fact, they had entered the territory of a large Indian confederation. The confederacy numbered more than 13,000 people living in dozens of villages spread across the Tidewater area. The paramount chief, Powhatan, had been steadily expanding his power in the region. Initially, his councilors wondered whether to view the new arrivals as dangerous intruders or as potential trading partners, military allies, and members of the confederacy. The isolated English proved equally unsure whether to offer friendship or defiance. Within months, these subjects of James I had named the waterway the James River and established a fortified village beside it called Jamestown. In June, hoping for quick rewards, they shipped to London various stones that they thought contained precious gems and gold ore.

When the rocks proved worthless, the colonists' dreams of easy wealth evaporated. So did ideas about pushing west beyond the watershed. During the outpost's first winter, a fire destroyed the tiny settlement, and death from hunger, exposure, and sickness cut the garrison's population in half. The governor and council appointed by the Virginia Company to oversee the enterprise bickered among themselves, providing poor leadership in the face of hardship. Fully one-third of the early arrivals claimed to be gentlemen, from England's leisure class—a proportion six times higher than in England—and most proved unaccustomed to hard manual labor. Moreover, all the colonists were employees of the company, so any profits from their labor went to repay London investors.

Despite the unsuitable make-up of the garrison and the stiff rules governing work, conditions improved briefly with the emergence of John Smith as an artful and vigorous leader who dealt forcefully with the Indians. (Later, he claimed to have been assisted and protected by Powhatan's young daughter, Pocahontas.) Fears of Spanish attacks on the infant outpost came to nothing. Still, the poorly supported enterprise limped along.

With hopes of a swift bonanza dashed, the London merchants decided to alter their strategy. They would salvage the venture by attracting fresh capital; then they would recoup their high initial costs by recruiting new settlers who could produce staple products suited for export—perhaps grapes, sugar, cotton, or tobacco. In 1609, amid much fanfare, the company began to sell seven-year joint stock options to the English public. Subscribers could invest money or, as "adventurers of person," they could sign on for service in Virginia according to their needed skills. Company officials promised them at least a hundred acres of land when their investment matured in 1616. Surprising numbers responded, including Stephen Hopkins. In June 1609, he joined another 500 men and 100 women departing for the Chesapeake.

"Starving Time" and the Lure of Tobacco

In retrospect, Hopkins and the other passengers of the *Sea Adventure* who were shipwrecked on Bermuda appear to have been the lucky ones. When the fleet's remaining vessels arrived at Jamestown, they found insufficient supplies to feed the hundreds of additional colonists. Moreover, the first round of settlers had failed to discover a profitable staple crop. Even the local tobacco proved "poor and weake, and of a byting tast." The settlers, now numbering 500, depended heavily on the Native Americans for food, and Powhatan's Confederacy proved increasingly unwilling and unable to supply it. As one Indian told them, "We know that you cannot live" without "our harvest" and the "reliefe we bring you." Indeed, most of the settlers did not live. In a grim "starving time," caused in large part by drought conditions, the ill-equipped newcomers scavenged for berries and bark. Extreme hunger drove a few to cannibalize the dead before dying themselves. By the spring of 1610, seven of every eight people had died; scarcely 60 remained alive.

In June, these survivors abandoned their ghost town altogether. But they had scarcely set sail for England when they encountered three long-overdue ships entering Chesapeake Bay with fresh supplies and 300 new settlers. Reluctantly, they agreed to try again. More years of harsh discipline, Indian warfare, and scarce resources followed. The beleaguered colony continued to face mismanagement and factionalism, underfunding and misinformation, inexperience, and poor communication. But another force—a severe dry spell—also conspired against the hapless newcomers. Indian and English crops alike shriveled from 1607 through 1612.

Relief came from an unexpected quarter: *Nicotiana tabacum,* or Orinoco tobacco, a variety of tobacco grown in parts of the West Indies and South America. John Rolfe and his pregnant wife had endured the wreck of the *Sea Adventure* with Stephen Hopkins in 1609. Their child died in infancy, and Mrs. Rolfe perished shortly after reaching Jamestown in 1610. But her husband survived and promptly joined in the colonists' search for a viable staple. He found

National Geographic Society ©1998 Photo by Steve Rawls

■ Inexperience prompted initial English difficulties at Roanoke and Jamestown, but so did poor weather. Scientists studying the region's bald cypress trees have recently shown (from certain narrow rings) that terrible droughts struck the coastal area in the late 1580s and again from 1606 through 1612. These two sequences of narrow annual rings are visible under the magnifying glass.

that local Indians cultivated an indigenous tobacco plant, *Nicotiana rustica*. Rolfe, a smoker himself, wondered whether better-tasting varieties might also prosper in Virginia soil.

Within a year, Rolfe had somehow managed to obtain seeds for the sweet-flavored Orinoco tobacco. This "bewitching vegetable" had captured English taste in the previous generation. Sales of this New World product in England sent profits to the Spanish crown and prompted James I to launch a vigorous antismoking campaign in 1604. In his tract titled *Counterblaste to Tobacco,* the king condemned inhaling the noxious weed as a dangerous, sinful, and enfeebling custom, "lothsome to the eye, hatefull to the Nose, harmefull to the braine, daungerous to the Lungs." But by 1612, Rolfe's patch of West Indian tobacco was flourishing. The next year, he grew a sample for export. Desperate settlers and impatient London investors were delighted by Rolfe's successful experiment with tobacco. Production of the leaf soared at Jamestown, to the neglect of all other pursuits.

The colony's tobacco exports rose exponentially from 2000 pounds in 1615 to 20,000 in 1617, 40,000 in 1620, 60,000 in 1622, 500,000 in 1626, and an astounding 1,500,000 pounds in 1629. That year, saturated markets and stiff taxes led to slumping prices. Profits declined in ensuing decades. A dubious luxury good rather than a crucial resource, tobacco nevertheless could yield a profit. Thus authorities in England began to regulate its sale to raise customs revenues and reduce foreign competition. The island of Bermuda also became a tobacco colony after 1613. A decade later, the crown gave Virginia and Bermuda a virtual monopoly on English tobacco sales, lowering import duties for the two colonies when they shipped tobacco to England and aiding them further by imposing limits on the same product from Spanish America.

> *The Virginia Company went out of its way to assure its colonists access to established English freedoms.*

During Virginia's initial tobacco boom, recently starving settlers saw handsome profits within reach. Because land was plentiful at first (a novelty for the English), the only limitations to riches were the scarcity of workers and the related high cost of labor. Any farmer who could hire half a dozen field hands could increase his profits fivefold, quickly earning enough to obtain more land and import more servants. The company transported several shiploads of apprentices, servants, and London street children to the labor-hungry colony. When a Dutch captain delivered 20 enslaved blacks in 1619, settlers eagerly purchased these first Africans to arrive in English Virginia. They also bid on the 100 women who disembarked the same year, shipped from England by the company to be sold as wives and workers. Still, men continued to outnumber women more than three to one for decades to come.

To encourage English migration further, the Virginia Company offered transportation and 50 acres to tenants, promising them ownership of the land after seven years of work. Men who paid their own way received 50 acres and an additional "headright" of 50 acres for each household member or laborer they transported. The Virginia Company went out of its way to assure its colonists access to such established English freedoms as the right to trial by jury and to a representative form of government. The company established civil courts controlled by English common law. It also instructed its appointed governor to summon an annual assembly of elected burgesses—the earliest representative legislature in North America. First convened in 1619, the House of Burgesses wasted no time in affirming its commitment to fundamental English rights. The governor, the house said, could no longer impose taxes without the assembly's consent.

Launching the Plymouth Colony

To attract additional capital and people, the Virginia Company also began awarding patents (legal charters) to private groups of adventurers "to erect and build a town and settle and plant dyvers inhabitants there for the advancement of the general plantation of the country." The newcomers would live independently on a large tract, with only minimal control from the governor and his council. Between 1619 and 1623, the company granted more than 40 such patents, with the exact location of each settlement to be determined on the colonists' arrival. Two such small colonies originated among English Protestants who were living in exile in Holland because their separatist beliefs did not allow them to profess loyalty to the Church of England. The first group of 180, based in Amsterdam, obtained a patent late in 1618 and departed for America on a crowded ship. Winter storms, sickness, and a shortage of fresh water destroyed the venture; scarcely 50 survivors straggled ashore in Virginia.

A second group of English Separatists, residing in the smaller Dutch city of Leiden, fared better. Most had migrated to Holland from northeast England in 1608, led by William Brewster, who had often hosted their prayer meetings at his home in Nottinghamshire. This group openly opposed the hierarchy, pomp, and inclusiveness of the Church of England. Instead, they wanted to return to early Christianity, where small groups of worthy (and often persecuted) believers formed their own communities of worship. After a decade in Holland, many of them had wearied of the foreign culture. Dismayed by the effect of worldly Leiden on their children, they also sensed, correctly, that warfare would soon break out in Europe. A few families pushed for a further removal to America, despite the obvious dangers of such a journey.

Possible destinations ranged from Guiana in South America to the Gulf of St. Lawrence in Canada. Dutch entrepreneurs suggested the Hudson River. But in the end, still loyal to England, the Separatists decided to use a patent granted by the Virginia Company to a group of English capitalists. On the negative side, they had to work for these investors for seven years. They also had to take along outsiders who did not share their beliefs: paying passengers, as well as artisans assigned to the venture. On the positive side, they received financial support from backers who paid to rent a ship. Moreover, instead of having their daily affairs controlled from London, they could elect their own leader and establish civil authority as they saw fit. In short, they had the power to govern themselves.

In September 1620, after costly delays, 35 members of the Leiden congregation and additional Separatists from England departed from Plymouth, along with other passengers (including the family of Stephen and Elizabeth Hopkins). They were crowded aboard the *Mayflower,* a 160-ton vessel converted from the wine trade, and bound for Virginia. But a stormy two-month crossing brought them to Cape Cod, in modern-day Massachusetts, no longer considered part of the Virginia Company's jurisdiction. Already sickly from their long journey, they feared pressing south with winter closing in. They decided to disembark and establish their Plymouth Plantation, having signed a compact aboard the *Mayflower* binding them together in a civil community.

William Bradford, the chronicler and longtime governor of the Plymouth Colony, later recalled their plight:

> They had now no friends to welcome them nor inns to entertain or refresh their weatherbeaten bodies; no houses or much less towns to repair to. . . . And for the season it was winter, and they that know the winters of that country know them to be sharp and violent. . . . Besides, what could they see but a hideous and desolate wilderness. . . . If they looked behind them, there was the mighty ocean which they had passed and was now as a main bar and gulf to separate them from all the civil parts of the world. . . . What could now sustain them but the Spirit of God and His grace?

Bradford could scarcely exaggerate the challenge. His own wife drowned (an apparent suicide) shortly after the *Mayflower* dropped anchor. And by the time the ship departed for its return voyage in April, an illness had swept away half the colonists. When those remaining planted barley and peas, the English seeds failed to take hold. But settlers had abundant fish and wildlife, along with ample Indian corn, and soon reinforcements arrived from England bringing needed supplies. The newcomers also brought a legal patent for the Plymouth colony's land. With Squanto's aid, the settlers secured peaceful relations with Massasoit's villages. When survival for another winter seemed assured, they invited Massasoit and his followers to join in a three-day celebration of thanksgiving so that, according to one account, all might "rejoice together after we had gathered the fruit of our labors."

Colonization Then and Now

You may not be set to blast off yet, but lots of people are ready. Before the first space shuttle lifted off a generation ago, a Tucson engineer named Keith Henson had formed the L–5 Society for people eager to live beyond the earth. By 2000 the Hilton Hotel chain was beginning to plan stays in space. Scientists talk hopefully of launching settlers on an eight-month voyage to Mars by October 2007, when Earth comes closest to the Red Planet's orbit. A private advocacy group called the Mars Society is already conducting practice expeditions in the Arctic.

Space attracts Americans in part because colonization played such a large part in our own beginnings. The "ships" look different, but basic issues remain the same. Motivation, for instance, may spring from scientific fascination, social necessity, or a desire for material success. "It's raining gold," Henson observed about space opportunities back in 1978, "and we're trying to figure out how to get a bucket." And what of saving souls? Because strange encounters between human beings proved a crucial aspect of earth-bound colonization, our *Star Trek* imaginings often turn on confrontations with life forms like our own. Will we be the colonizers or the colonized? Will we save the extraterrestrials or be saved by them?

Financing remains crucial too. European governments once debated the proper mix of public and private funds to support colonization and argued the costs and benefits of each successive venture. They also developed new ways, such as joint stock companies, for mobilizing the capital to cover huge start-up costs and to spread enormous risks. U.S.–Russian competition fueled the initial space race, but resources dried up with the end of the Cold War. An elaborate 1989 proposal to put Americans on Mars fell through because the 30-year price tag approached half a trillion dollars. Hoping to spread costs, 16 nations are now cooperating to complete the International Space Station by 2006.

But will the first space colonies orbit close to Earth, inhabit the nearby moon, or travel much further to Mars, a planet with its own atmosphere? Bret Drake, head of mission studies at the Johnson Space Center in Houston, believes that by 2025, "we could have human exploration of Mars being conducted routinely." In the twenty-first century, as in the seventeenth, the progression from initial landings to lasting colonization has a logic, a timetable, and a price tag of its own. And no one can predict the outcome in advance. Last time, successful colonies more than paid for themselves by providing crucial resources for their mother country—at least until they sought independence.

Space colonies, like the overseas colonies, may well become self-sufficient. After much costly trial and error, they may even send vital supplies of minerals and food back to Earth. A quarter century ago, planetary scientist

The Puritan Experiment

After more than a generation of costly colonization attempts, England still had little to show for its efforts when Charles I inherited the throne in 1625. Then two forces prompted rapid change: positive publicity about America and negative developments at home. John Smith, long a key promoter of overseas settlement, drew inspiration from the early efforts at Jamestown, Plymouth, and Bermuda. His book *The Generall Historie of Virginia, New-England and the Summer Isles* (1624) predicted future success for these regions. Smith's volume heralding overseas adventures went through six printings in eight years. Ironically, however, its popularity depended in large measure on a combination of worsening conditions in England—religious, political, and economic—that suddenly gave such literature a broad appeal.

Formation of the Massachusetts Bay Company

European Christianity had taken a number of different forms since the religious upheaval sparked by Luther a century earlier. The first Protestants had demanded a reformation of the Roman Catholic church and had questioned papal authority over Christians. Now many non-Catholic English worshippers doubted whether the Church of England (also known as the Anglican Church) had gone far enough toward rejecting the beliefs and practices of Rome. They lamented what they saw as the church's bureaucratic hierarchy, ornate rituals, and fail-

A quarter century ago, this sketch of life inside a vast space colony graced the dust jacket of T. A. Hoppenheimer's book, *Colonies in Space*, with an introduction by science fiction writer Ray Bradbury. Space colonization, like Earth colonization, no doubt will involve imagination as well as money and navigational skills.

is entirely reasonable to plan to grow grain in the space farm at a rate of 850 pounds per acre *per day*."

Heppenheimer may well be exaggerating, to make the challenge of launching a colony appear more plausible. In 1600 English propagandist Richard Hakluyt was doing the same thing. To most seventeenth-century Europeans, overseas settlement sounded quite unreasonable—intriguing to fantasize and debate about, but dangerous to undertake. Still, for thousands of people, overseas settlement became their life.

Some argue that colonization may happen again, sooner than we think. If so, who will go into space and under what conditions? Will we depart voluntarily or be forced to move? Will we go with our family and like-minded friends, or will we leave them behind and migrate with strangers? Will some economic or military elite lead the way, or will misfits and dissenters be the first aboard? Will we stay in close touch and plan to return, or will we endure in remote isolation, telling stories of the old country to our children? ■

T. A. Heppenheimer wrote *Colonies in Space: A Factual and Comprehensive Account of the Prospect for Human Colonization of Space* (1977). He predicted that in the weightless, sun-filled environment of an orbiting colony, "It

ure to enforce strict observance of the Christian Sabbath each Sunday. They scoffed at the gaudy vestments of Anglican bishops, elaborate church music, and other trappings of worship unjustified by biblical Scripture. Instead, they praised the stark simplicity that John Calvin had brought to his church in Geneva.

As English Calvinists grew in number, their objections to the Church of England increased. They protested that the Anglican Church, like the Catholic Church, remained inclusive in membership rather than selective. They argued for limiting participation to the devout rather than assuming general access for all. They accused the Church of England of corruption and argued that it should be independent and self-governing rather than tied to the monarchy. This keen desire for further cleansing and purity, so common to reformers, spurred the movement known as Puritanism. Some of the most radical members of this broad religious coalition (including Bradford and the Plymouth pilgrims) became known as Separatists because they were committed to an extreme position: complete separation from what they saw as the corrupt Church of England. But many more Puritans (including most of the reformers who migrated to Massachusetts Bay) resisted separation. They hoped to stay technically within the Anglican fold while taking increased control of their own congregations—a practice known as congregationalism. Unwilling to conform to practices that offended them, these nonseparating Congregationalists remained determined to save the Anglican Church through righteous example, even if it meant migrating abroad for a time to escape persecution and demonstrate the proper ways of a purified Protestant church.

A Catalogue of such needefull things as every Planter doth or ought to provide to go to New-England

as namely for one man, which being doubled, may serve for as many as you please, viz.

Victuals for a whole yeere for a man, and so after the rate for more.

8 Bushels of meale.	1 Gallon of Oyle.
2 Bushels of pease.	2 Gallons of Vinegar.
2 Bushels of Otemeale.	1 Firkin of Butter.
1 Gallon of Aquavitæ.	

Apparel.

1 Monmoth Cap.	3 Paire of Stockings.
3 Falling bands.	4 Paire of Shooes.
3 Shirts.	2 Paire of Sheets.
1 Wast-coat.	7 Ells of Canvas to
1 Suit of Canvase.	make bed and boulster.
1 Suit of Frize.	1 Paire of Blankets
1 Suit of Cloth.	1 Course Rug.

Armes.

1 Armor compleat.	1 Bandilier.
1 Long peece.	20 Pound of Powder.
1 Sword.	60 Pound of Lead.
1 Belt.	1 Pistoll and Goose shot.

Tooles.

1 Broad Howe.	1 Broad Axe.
1 Narrow Howe .	1 Felling Axe.
1 Steel Handsawe.	1 Gimblet.
1 Whipsawe.	1 Hatchet.
1 Hammer.	2 Frowes.
1 Shovell.	1 Hand-Bill.
1 Spade.	1 Grindstone.
2 Augres.	1 Pickaxe.
4 Chissels.	Nayles of all sorts.
2 Percers stocked.	

Household Implements.

1 Iron pot.	1 Spit.
1 Kettle.	Wooden Platters.
1 Frying Pan.	Dishes.
1 Gridiron.	Spoones.
2 Skellets.	Trenchers.

Spices.

Sugar.	Cinnamon.
Pepper.	Nutmegs.
Cloves.	Fruit.
Mace.	

Also there are divers other things necessary to bee taken over to this Plantation, as Bookes, Nets, Hookes and Lines, Cheese, Bacon, Kine, Goats, &c.

■ FIGURE 2.1
A 1630 LIST OF ITEMS NEEDED BY EACH ADULT FOR MIGRATION TO NEW ENGLAND

An emphasis on instructive preaching by informed leaders lay at the heart of the Puritan movement. Translation of scripture from Latin and its publication into everyday languages the people spoke or read, using the newly invented printing press, had been a central theme of the Reformation. An improved English translation of the Bible in 1611, known as the King James version, provided further access to scripture for all who could read or listen. But James and his bishops, realizing that a "priesthood of all believers" threatened their power, moved to control who could preach and what they could say. A 1626 law prohibited preaching or writing on controversial religious topics such as the conduct of the clergy, the nature of church hierarchy, and the interpretation of Scripture. "There should be more praying and less preaching," wrote one royal supporter, "for much preaching breeds faction, but much praying causes devotion."

Such laws and sentiments only strengthened Puritans' arguments that the religious and political establishment had no interest in allowing people full access to God's word. Why else would the elite encourage sports and recreation on the Sabbath rather than restricting the Lord's Day to religious study and devotion? Puritans believed that the sermon, not the communion sacrament (in which bread and wine signify the presence of the crucified Christ), should form the center of the Christian worship service. Their churches resembled lecture halls, emphasizing the pulpit more than the altar. In preaching, Puritans stressed a "plain style" that all listeners could understand. Moreover, they urged listeners to play an active role in their faith—to master reading and engage in regular study and discussion of scripture. In response to mounting public interest in these practices, Puritan ministers intensified their preaching and published their sermons. In effect, they dared authorities to silence them.

Reprisals came swiftly, led by William Laud, bishop of London, whom Charles I elevated to Archbishop of Canterbury in 1633. Laud instructed all preachers to focus their remarks on biblical passages and avoid writing or speaking about controversial religious matters. The bishop's persecution of Puritan leaders who appeared to disobey these orders only broadened their movement at a time when the king himself was arousing Protestant suspicions. In 1625 Charles I had married Henrietta Maria, Catholic sister of the French king, and had granted freedom of worship to English Catholics, disturbing a wide array of Protestants in the realm. When the House of Commons refused to approve finances for his policies, he arrested its leaders and disbanded Parliament in 1629. He governed on his own for 11 years by levying taxes without parliamentary approval.

As England's church grew more rigid and its monarchy more controlling, the nation's economy also took a turn for the worse. Rents and food costs had risen more rapidly than wages, and workers paid dearly. Jobs grew more scarce after 1625, and several years later, unemployed workers staged local revolts. In 1629 entrepreneurs who viewed New England as a potential opportunity teamed up with disaffected Puritans to obtain a charter for a new entity: the Massachusetts Bay Company. Through a generation of costly trial-and-error experiments, the English had amassed great expertise in colonization. And given the worsening conditions at home, especially among the Puritan faithful, proposals for overseas settlement attracted widespread attention.

"We Shall Be As a City upon a Hill"

During the next dozen years, more than 70,000 people left England for the New World. Two-thirds of them sailed to the West Indies, attracted by the prospect of a warmer climate and a longer growing season. But a large contingent of Puritans (many from the eastern counties of Norfolk, Suffolk, and Essex) embarked from England for the new Massachusetts Bay colony, adjacent to the Plymouth settlement. A loophole in the king's grant permitted them to take the actual charter with them and to hold their company meetings in America. This maneuver took them out from under the usual control of London investors and let them turn the familiar joint stock structure into the framework for a self-governing colony. In 1629 five vessels anchored at Salem. Three years earlier, an advance party had established a post there "for such as upon the account of religion would be willing to begin a foreign plantation."

In England, meanwhile, a Suffolk squire named John Winthrop, whose Puritan commitment had cost him his government post, assumed leadership of the Massachusetts Bay Company. "God will bring some heavy Affliction upon this lande," he predicted to his wife, but the Lord "will provide a shelter & a hidinge place for us and others." In exchange, God would expect great things from these chosen people, as from the Old Testament Israelites. "We are entered into covenant with him for this work," Winthrop told his companions aboard the *Arbella* en route to America in 1630.

Winthrop laid out this higher Calvinist standard in a memorable shipboard sermon titled "A Model of Christian Charity." The values that others merely profess, he explained, "we must bring into familiar and constant practice," sharing burdens, extending aid, and demonstrating patience. "For this end, we must be knit together in this work as one," regardless of social rank. If we fail, he warned, "the Lord will surely break out in wrath against us, and make us know the price of the breach of such a covenant." Far from hiding in obscurity, dedicated Puritans must set a visible example for the rest of the world. Winthrop's listeners understood the biblical reference to Jesus and the Sermon on the Mount (Matthew 5:14) when he concluded, "We shall be as a city upon a hill."

The *Arbella* was one of 17 ships that brought more than 1000 English people to New England in 1630. Choosing Winthrop as governor, the newcomers established Boston and laid out counties with names recalling their homeland: Essex, Norfolk, and Suffolk. By 1634, English arrivals totaled 4000. By the time civil war erupted in England eight years later, nearly 20,000 people had made the journey, eager to escape the religious persecution and denial of parliamentary rights that inflamed partisans against the Royalist forces of Charles I. Whole congregations migrated with their ministers; other people (more than 20 percent) crossed as servants. But most came as independent families with young children. On average, of every 100 newcomers, roughly half

Worcester Art Museum, Worcester, Massachusetts. Gift of Mr. and Mrs. Albert W. Rice

■ Port records for 1635 show that groups leaving London varied markedly, depending on their colonial destination. Young children were common aboard ships heading for New England, as were women and girls. Among passengers for New England, 8 of every 20 were female. In contrast, females made up only 3 in 20 of those going to Virginia and 1 in 20 among people heading for Barbados.

were adults (30 men to 20 women); the other half were all below age 18, divided about evenly between boys and girls.

Earlier settlers traded food, lodging, and building materials to fresh arrivals in exchange for textiles, tools, money, and labor. When new groups of church members wanted to establish a village, they applied for land to the General Court, a legislature made up of representatives elected from existing towns. By 1640, English settlements dotted the coast and had cropped up inland along the Connecticut River, where smallpox had decimated the Indians in 1633. There, English outposts rose at Hartford and Springfield, where English traders hoped to attract furs away from the French and Dutch.

The sheer number of land-hungry settlers drove this rapid expansion. So did friction among newcomers, who competed for scarce resources and complained about price controls and other economic constraints intended to impose civic order. In his initial call to "work as one," Winthrop had worried that migrants would neglect the duties of spiritual regeneration. However, the sharpest dissents came from zealous people who feared that the religious experiment had not gone far enough. Challenging authority lay at the heart of radical Protestantism, for its practitioners stressed inner conviction and personal belief over outward conformity and deference to wealth and status. The more seriously New England's believers took their "errand into the wilderness," the more contentious they became about the proper ways to fulfill God's covenant.

Dissenters: Roger Williams and Anne Hutchinson

Like the biblical Hebrews before them, the Puritans—self-appointed saints—believed that God had chosen them for a special mission in the world. The Almighty, they believed, would watch carefully, punish harshly, and reward mightily. Inevitably, some devout people, raised to question careless ministers or excessive hierarchy, continued to advocate dissenting beliefs in New England. Not everyone accepted the idea that Puritans should dominate Indians or that women should defer to men. Roger Williams, a recent graduate of Cambridge University, and Anne Hutchinson, the talented eldest daughter of an English minister, stand out as two of the earliest and most effective challengers to leadership in the Massachusetts Bay colony.

When Williams arrived in Boston, his Separatist leanings angered Bay Colony authorities, who still hoped to reform the Anglican Church rather than renounce it. But Williams's other contentions proved equally distressing. The young minister argued that civil authorities, inevitably corrupt, had no right to judge religious matters. He even pushed for an unprecedented separation of church and state—to protect the church. He also contended that the colony's land patent from the king had no validity. The settlers, he said, had to purchase occupancy rights from the Native Americans. Unable to silence him, irate magistrates banished Williams from Massachusetts Bay in the winter of 1635. Moving south, he took up residence among the Narragansett Indians and built a refuge for other dissenters, which he named Providence. Still subject to arrest in Boston, he sailed home from New Amsterdam in 1643. Once back in London, he persuaded leaders of England's rising Puritan Revolution to grant a charter (1644) to his independent colony of Rhode Island.

A more explosive popular challenge centered on Anne Hutchinson, who had grown up in England with a strong will, a solid theological education, and a thirst for spiritual perfection. She married a Lincolnshire textile merchant and took an active part in religious discussions while also bearing 15 children. When her Puritan minister, John Cotton, departed for New England, Hutchinson claimed that God, in a private revelation, had instructed her to follow. In 1634 the family migrated to Boston, where Hutchinson attended Cotton's church and hosted religious discussions in her home. The popularity of these weekly meetings troubled authorities, as did her argument that the "Holy Spirit illumines the heart of every true believer." Hutchinson downplayed outward conformity—modest dress or regular church attendance—

Anne Bradstreet: "The Tenth Muse, Lately Sprung Up in America"

The Puritans who migrated to America stressed literacy and education as part of their faith. They wrote down a great deal, and they left extensive records for posterity. But most of their sermons, diaries, and chronicles were drafted by men; few documents about the thoughts and experiences of New England's early migrants come from the pens of women. The poems and reflections of Anne Bradstreet provide a notable exception. "Here you may find," she reminded her children shortly before her death in 1672, "what was your living mother's mind."

The lifelong poet was born Anne Dudley in Lincolnshire, England, in 1612. She already "found much comfort in reading the Scriptures" by age seven. "But as I grew to be about 14 or 15," she recalled, "I found my heart more carnal, and . . . the follies of youth took hold of me. About 16, the Lord . . . smote me with the smallpox . . . and again restored me." That same year, she married Simon Bradstreet, the son of a minister. Two years later, despite a frail constitution, she sailed for Massachusetts Bay with her husband and her father (both future governors of the colony) aboard the Arbella.

Having left England at age 18, Anne Bradstreet was alert to all that seemed strange and different in America. When I "came into this country," she related, "I found a new world and new manners." The young couple set up housekeeping in the town of Cambridge, on the Charles River, but life was difficult at first. Anne suffered from "a lingering sickness like a consumption." Moreover, "It pleased God to keep me a long time without a child, which was a great grief to me and cost me

Cambridge looked something like this in the 1660s. The large building in the foreground is Harvard College, founded in 1636, and the smaller brick building beside it is the Indian College, built in 1655. The village was even smaller when Anne Bradstreet resided there briefly after her arrival in Massachusetts Bay.

Courtesy, Dartmouth University Library

many prayers and tears." Finally, she bore a son in 1633, and seven more children followed.

As the family grew and moved about, "Mistress Bradstreet" wrote poems and meditations, although detractors hinted that she should put down her quill pen and take up a sewing needle. "If what I do prove well, it won't advance," she lamented in rhyme; "They'l say it's stol'n, or else it was by chance." Nevertheless, a book of her poems was published in England in 1650, hailing her as "The Tenth Muse, Lately Sprung Up in America."

As a writer, Anne Bradstreet was more interested in spiritual improvement than literary grace. "Many speak well," she observed, "but few can do well." Throughout life, she followed a simple creed: "There is no object that we see; no action that we do; no good

that we enjoy; no evil that we feel or fear, but we may make some spiritual advantage" of it. Nothing epitomizes this belief more clearly than "some verses upon the burning of our house, July 10th, 1666." Bradstreet composed the lines on an unburned scrap of paper as she groped to make sense of the calamity. The poem helped her to mourn her loss, take stock of her blessings, and renew her faith. In part, it reads,

In silent night when rest I took,
For sorrow neer I did not look,
I waken'd was with thundring nois
And Piteous shreiks of dreadfull
voice. . . .

I, starting up, the light did spye,
And to my God my heart did
cry. . . .
Then coming out beheld a space
The flame consume my dwelling
place.

And, when I could no longer look,
I blest his Name that gave and took,
That layd my goods now in the
dust:
Yea so it was, and so 'twas just. . . .

When by the Ruines oft I past,
My sorrowing eyes aside did cast,
And here and there the places spye
Where oft I sate, and long did lye.

Here stood that Trunk, and there
that chest;
There lay that store I counted best:
My pleasant things in ashes lye,
And them behold no more
shall I. . . .

Then streight I gin my heart to
chide,
And did thy wealth on earth
abide?
Didst fix thy hope on mouldring
dust,
The arm of flesh didst make thy
trust?. . . .

Thou hast a house on high erect
Fram'd by that mighty Architect. . . .
The world no longer let me Love,
My hope and Treasure lyes Above. ∎

as a route to salvation. Instead, she stressed direct communication with God's inner presence as the key to individual forgiveness.

Most Puritans sought a delicate balance in their lives between respected outer works and inner personal grace. Hutchinson tipped that balance dangerously toward the latter. To the colony's magistrates, especially Winthrop, such teaching pointed toward dangerous anarchy—more dangerous when it came from a woman. These officials labeled Hutchinson and her followers as Antinomians (from *anti*, "against," and *nomos*, "law"). But the vehement faction grew, attracting merchants who chafed under economic restrictions, women who questioned men's domination of the church, and young adults who resented the strict authority of their elders. By 1636, this religious and political coalition had gained enough supporters to turn Winthrop out as governor.

Facing complete overthrow, members of the Puritan establishment fought back. They divided the opposition to win reelection for Winthrop, they established Harvard College to educate ministers who would not stray from the fold, they staged a flurry of trials for contempt and sedition (inciting resistance to lawful authority), and they made a special example of Hutchinson herself. After a two-day hearing in which she defended herself admirably, Winthrop sentenced his antagonist to banishment as "a woman not fit for our society." Forced into exile, Hutchinson moved first to Rhode Island and later to the vicinity of Dutch settlements near the Hudson. There she and most of her family were killed by Indians in 1643. A river and a parkway in Bronx, New York, still bear her name.

Expansion and Violence: The Pequot War

Immigration to New England slowed during the 1640s because of religious and political upheaval at home. In England, Puritans and supporters of Parliament formed an army and openly challenged royal authority during the English Civil War. After seizing power, these revolutionaries beheaded Charles I in 1649, abolished monarchy, and proclaimed England a republican Commonwealth. The dramatic struggle preoccupied Puritans in England. Those across the ocean also took heart when they heard news of events at home favorable to their cause.

Nevertheless, word that English Puritans had established a revolutionary commonwealth in their absence shook the settlers' faith that their venture remained at the center of God's plan. They struggled to square such sweeping developments in England with Winthrop's earlier assurance that the eyes of God and humankind would be fixed on New England. Making matters worse, religious and economic controversies intensified as the next generation quickly came of age. Needing new farmland and intellectual breathing room, fresh congregations began to "hive off" from the original settlements like swarms of bees. By 1640, New Hampshire, Rhode Island, and Connecticut each had at least four new towns that would provide the beginnings for independent colonies.

The New York Public Library, Astor, Lenox and Tilden Foundations

■ **Captain John Underhill, who directed the dawn raid on a Pequot village in 1637, depicted the massacre in his account the next year. Placing their Indian allies behind them, the English surrounded the palisade and entered the town, firing on unarmed Indians and shooting those who tried to fight their way out.**

But the northeastern forest was not an empty wilderness, any more than the Chesapeake tidewater, the Florida interior, or the mesas of New Mexico had been. As the Hutchinsons discovered, newcomers who pushed inland were co-opting the land of longtime residents. Pressure on New England's Native Americans erupted in armed conflict in the Pequot War of 1637, at the height of the Antinomian Crisis. The neighboring Pequot Indians near the mouth of the Connecticut River had been English allies for several years, and a recent smallpox epidemic had weakened them dramatically. But Winthrop, whose son was leading a settlement effort in the area, fanned fears that the Pequots "would cause all the Indians in the country to join to root out all the English."

Recruiting Narragansett and Mohegan Indians to the English side, the colonists unleashed all-out war against the Pequots. The campaign culminated in a dawn raid on a stockaded Pequot town that sheltered noncombatants. The invaders torched the village (at Mystic, Connecticut) and shot or put to the sword almost all who tried to escape. Some 400 Indian men, women, and children died. The Puritans' Indian allies, accustomed to campaigns of capture, adoption, and ritual torture, were shocked by the wholesale carnage. English warfare, they protested, "is too furious, and slaies too many men." Chastened by this intimidating display of terror and weakened by recurrent epidemics, the tribes of southern New England negotiated away much of their land over the next generation, trading furs to the expanding colonists and seeking to understand their perplexing ways.

■ Title page from John Eliot's Indian Bible, 1663

Having gained the upper hand, the Bible-reading English made gestures to convert their Native American neighbors. Whether the Indians were descended from the Lost Tribe of Israel, as scholars suggested, Puritans believed that "saving the heathen" would almost certainly help them raise funds in London. It would also demonstrate England's zeal to compete with the Catholic Spanish and French in converting souls to Christ. Enthusiastic about these possibilities, the Massachusetts General Court took steps to encourage missionary work. It forbade the worship of Indian gods, mandated the religious and social conversion of local tribes, and set aside land for "praying towns" to encourage "the Indians to live in an orderly way amongst us." On the island of Martha's Vineyard, Reverend Thomas Mayhew, Jr., converted a man named Hiacoomes, who in turn converted several Wampanoag sachems during a 1645 epidemic. In Roxbury, another minister, John Eliot, created a 1200-page Indian Bible. And in Cambridge, officials at Harvard, committed by their charter to the "education of the English and Indian youth of this Country," erected a well-publicized Indian College.

The Chesapeake Bay Colonies

On Chesapeake Bay, settlers' relations with the Indians remained strained at best during the first half of the seventeenth century. In 1608, in an effort to secure the support of Indian leadership, the English performed an elaborate ceremony granting a scarlet cloak and a copper crown to Chief Powhatan. But two years later, suspicious that he was harboring runaway colonists, the English burned the nearest Indian villages and unthinkingly destroyed much-needed corn. One Indian woman leader, taken as a captive, watched English soldiers throwing her children in the river and shooting them in the head before she herself was stabbed to death.

John Carter Brown Library, Brown University

■ Captain John Smith boasted that in 1608 he intimidated Opechancanough with his pistol to disarm the Indians and obtain their corn. Decades later, the Pamunkey leader launched two major attacks on the Jamestown colony. This image of the early incident appeared in Smith's popular *Generall Historie* of 1624.

For both sides, hopes of reconciliation rose briefly in 1614 with the match between Pocahontas, daughter of Powhatan, and John Rolfe, the prominent widower who had introduced tobacco. But the marriage proved brief; Pocahontas died in England three years later, after bearing one child. If leaders intended the wedding alliance as a diplomatic gesture toward peace, it did little to curtail the settlers' bitterness over their lingering dependence on Indian supplies. For their part, the Native Americans resented the encroaching tobacco fields and belligerent tactics of their arrogant neighbors.

The Demise of the Virginia Company

Powhatan's death in 1618 brought to power his more militant younger brother, Opechancanough, the leader of the Pamunkey tribe. His encounters with the English had been frequent and unfriendly. John Smith had even taken him captive at gunpoint to extort food supplies. By 1618, the English tobacco crop was booming, and more newcomers were arriving annually. Over the next three years, 42 ships brought 3500 people to the Chesapeake colony. The influx disheartened the Indians, and Opechancanough and his followers in the Powhatan Confederacy sought ways to end the mounting intrusion.

Briefly, disease seemed to work in the Indians' favor. Immigrants who made the long sea voyage with poor provisions often fell ill in the swampy and unhealthy environment of Jamestown. By 1622, the colony's inhabitants were dying almost as rapidly as newcomers arrived. Sickness had carried off 3000 residents in the course of only three years.

Opechancanough sensed a chance to deliver the finishing blow. He planned a sudden and coordinated offensive against all the settler communities stretched out along the lower James River. On March 22, 1622, his forces attacked the English, surprising the outlying settlements and sparing no one. Of the 1240 colonists, nearly 350 lost their lives. Warned by an Indian, Jamestown survived the uprising, but hope for peaceful relations ended. The attack of 1622 launched a ten-year war in which the Indians showed their versatility by capturing muskets and using them as well as or better than the English.

In London, tales of the disaster fueled opposition to the Virginia Company among disgruntled investors. In 1624 King James annulled the company's charter, making Virginia a royal colony controlled by the crown. In the colony's first 17 years, more than 8500 people, almost all of them young, had embarked for the Chesapeake. By 1624, only 15 of every 100 remained alive.

The colonists placed a bounty on Opechancanough's head, but attempts to ambush or poison him failed. The Indian leader lived on, nursing his distrust of the English. In 1644 he inaugurated a second uprising that killed some 500 colonists. But the English settlement had grown too large to eradicate. By this time old age forced the "Great General" to be carried on a litter. When the English finally captured him and brought him to Jamestown in 1646, Opechancanough was too old to walk unassisted. Still, he remained defiant until shot in the back by one of the Englishmen guarding him.

After two years of brutal warfare, the Pamunkeys and their allies in the Powhatan Confederacy conceded defeat and submitted to English authority. From then on, they would pay a token annual tribute for the privilege to remain on lands that had once belonged to them.

The Pull to Settle in America
1. Word-of-mouth information about America
2. Effective work and writing by recruiters
3. Appeal of land and economic opportunities
4. Desire to join earlier migrants to America
5. Safe pursuit of personal religious beliefs
6. Hope of educating and converting Indians

The Push to Leave Home in Europe
1. Escape from direct religious persecution
2. Fear regarding the religious future at home
3. Anxiety about political change in Europe
4. Dismay over economy; need for farmland
5. Relief from joblessness or personal adversity
6. Restlessness and desire for adventure

■ **FIGURE 2.2**
THE TOUGH CHOICE TO START OVER

With the way cleared for expansion, land-hungry English settlers appeared in ever-increasing numbers in Virginia and neighboring Maryland. By 1660, roughly 25,000 colonists lived near the shores of Chesapeake Bay.

Maryland: The Catholic Refuge

Maryland, the smaller and the younger of the two English colonies on the Chesapeake, owed its beginnings to George Calvert. In a Protestant country, Calvert rose to become a respected Catholic member of England's government. He was named the first Baron of Baltimore, in Ireland, in 1625. Calvert had a keen interest in colonization, and he established a short-lived colony of his own in Newfoundland, welcoming all religious groups. But when attacks by the French defeated that scheme, he sought a safer location.

Calvert (now Lord Baltimore) had followed events in the Chesapeake, and in 1632 he petitioned Charles I for land there. The king granted him 10 million acres adjacent to Virginia, to be named Maryland in honor of the Catholic queen, Henrietta Maria. The Maryland charter, like the one that had governed the Newfoundland colony, gave the proprietor and his heirs unprecedented personal power, especially in the granting of lands to colonists without limitations based on religious belief.

Because Calvert died before the royal charter took effect, his eldest son, the second Lord Baltimore, took charge of the settlement effort. In 1634, the *Ark* and the *Dove* carried more than 200 settlers—both Protestants and Catholics—to the new colony. There, they established a capital at St. Mary's, near the mouth of the Potomac River. With the execution of the king in 1649 and the creation of an anti-Catholic commonwealth in England, the Calvert family provided a haven in Maryland for their coreligionists. However, Catholics never became a majority in the Chesapeake colony.

In 1649, Maryland's assembly passed an Act Concerning Religion, guaranteeing toleration for all settlers who professed a belief in Jesus Christ. This assertion of religious toleration, though limited, proved too broad for many to stomach. In the 1650s supporters of the English Puritan cause seized power in Maryland, repealed the act, and briefly ended the Calverts' proprietorship. But by 1660, with the restoration of the Stuart monarchy in England, proprietary rule returned to the prosperous farming colony.

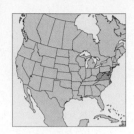

The Chesapeake Region, 1600–1660

Powhatan Confederacy in 1607

English settlement by 1650

New Sweden, 1637–1655

— Maryland boundary in 1632

— Current state boundaries

■ **MAP 2.4**
CULTURES MEET ON THE CHESAPEAKE
When the English founded Jamestown in 1607, the numerous tribes of the Powhatan Confederacy controlled a wide region south of the Potomac River. In 1632, King Charles I granted all of Virginia north of the Potomac River to Lord Baltimore for his Maryland colony. This domain, with its capital at St. Mary's, stretched from the headwaters of the Potomac to the Delaware River. It reached north to 40 degrees (above the current boundary of Maryland), and it included the settlement of New Sweden on the Delaware (1637–1655). By midcentury, European settlement remained confined along main waterways.

Conclusion

During half a century, the French, Dutch, and English had all moved to challenge Spanish claims in North America. By 1660, all four of these maritime powers of western Europe had taken aggressive steps to establish permanent footholds on the fringes of the enormous continent. In each instance, the European colonizers benefited first from the presence of knowledgeable Native Americans and then from the sharp decline of those same people through warfare and the onslaught of new diseases.

Granted, warfare with foreign invaders and death from unknown diseases had become a part of Native American history in the preceding century. One need only think of the destruction that followed in the path of Hernando de Soto's expedition through the Southeast. But for the most part, the sixteenth century was an era of intermittent European exploration that was as tentative as it was sweeping. In contrast, the first half of the seventeenth century saw Europeans move from occasional forays to persistent attempts at permanent colonization. As these foreign intruders competed with one another, their tenacious efforts began to yield lasting results.

■ By the mid-seventeenth century, most English still had only a vague view of North America. In a 1650 sketch of the Atlantic coast, shown here, John Farrer struggled to piece together the region's geography and recent history. His map, later made into a print, mixed fact and fiction from 70 years of exploring and settlement. Starting in the South (left) Farrer showed the Barrier Islands and the 1584 effort to settle Roanoke Island in "Ould Virginia, now Carolana." In "New Virginia" he drew the James and Potomac Rivers flowing into Chesapeake Bay and noted the founding of Maryland in the 1630s. He correctly placed Swedes along the Delaware River and Dutch on "Hudsons River," doing "a great trade of furs." New England remains vague beyond the hook of "Cape Codd," but "1606" suggests the brief Sagadahoc colony on the coast of Maine.

The most dramatic speculation is in the upper (western) part of the map, beyond the well-defined Appalachian mountains. In 1577, Sir Francis Drake had entered the "West Sea" (Pacific Ocean) and sailed to 37 degrees north latitude, claiming the region around San Francisco Bay as New Albion. Farrer knew that Virginia was in the same latitude and that geographers had speculated about narrow portions of the continent ever since the explorations of Verrazzano. So he repeated the persistent idea that New Albion "was just opposite the backe of James River." Moreover, a Northwest Passage to the Pacific might yet be found if the Hudson and Saint Lawrence Rivers reached the Great Lakes rumored to exist in the interior.

Except for several small pockets on the edges of the continent, Native American societies still held the upper hand. Most had not seen the alien newcomers, learning about them only indirectly, if at all. But on the fringes, stark confrontations had started to occur—small in number but huge in their implications. They involved vastly different languages, lifeways, and beliefs about the world.

Confrontations had also begun among the invaders themselves. After all, they represented rival nations and competing versions of the Christian faith. Although it was clear by 1660 that none would withdraw from North America without a fight, it was also clear that no single nation had decisively obtained the upper hand as yet. Spain, France, Holland, and England each had formidable assets in Europe and on the high seas. All had sponsored colonial settlements that had endured for several generations, and each had begun to taste the seductive fruits of empire in America and elsewhere.

The English, slowest to become involved in overseas colonization, had caught up with their competitors by 1660. Among European countries, England had proven the most aggressive in forming expansive family-based colonies rather than military garrisons or trading outposts. Elizabeth Hopkins and Anne Hutchinson, embarking from England with their husbands and families, exemplified a migration pattern that included thousands of women. Their presence led to the formation of stable households, especially in New England, where the balance of women and men was most even. Women took an immediate role in crucial aspects of domestic manufacture and production, and their numerous children provided additional hands where labor was in short supply. As a result, by 1660 the population of England's fledgling North American colonies had already outstripped that of its rivals, and it was growing at an increasing rate. This emerging superiority in numbers was advantageous in the imperial clashes that lay ahead.

Sites to Visit

Acoma Pueblo

Located near Highway 40 west of Albuquerque, New Mexico, within the Acoma Indian Reservation, the Acoma Pueblo Visitors' Center offers guided tours of "Sky City" that leave in vans from the center. Once on top of the 420-foot mesa, visitors can walk the streets of one of the oldest continuously inhabited sites in North America.

Mission San Luis Park

After the state of Florida acquired 50 acres in northwest Tallahassee in 1983, archaeologists excavated the Apalachee Indian town and Spanish mission that existed there in the seventeenth century. Mission San Luis Park, between Rt. 10 and Rt. 90, contains an outdoor museum with reconstructed buildings, exhibits, and guided tours.

Sainte-Marie Among the Hurons Museum

Overlooking the Wye River near Midland, Ontario, 80 miles north of Toronto on Canada's Georgian Bay, this reconstructed seventeenth-century Jesuit mission site offers canoe trips and candlelight tours in the summer.

The New Netherland Museum and Half Moon Visitor Center

Located in Albany, New York, the museum maintains a full-scale replica of Henry Hudson's ship, the *Half Moon,* which is usually docked at Albany and open for visitors. For information, contact the Main Office at 518-443-1609.

Plimoth Plantation

www.plimoth.org

This living history museum of seventeenth-century Plymouth is located off Route 3 along the coast south of Boston, Massachusetts. It recreates the pilgrim village as it appeared

in 1627, with a Wampanoag Indian site nearby. Visit the *Mayflower II* at State Pier on Water Street. Take a virtual tour of the site at www.plimoth.org.

Historic Jamestown

www.history.org/nche/

www.ngdc.noaa.gov/paleo/drought/drght_james.html

At Historic Jamestown you can tour ruins, visit a glass-blowing exhibition, and see excavations of the original fort. Nearby, the Jamestown–Yorktown Foundation runs Jamestown Settlement, with reconstructed ships, fortifications, and Indian dwellings. These sites are seven miles from Williamsburg on Virginia's Colonial Parkway; they can also be approached by ferry across the James River. All are gearing up for the 400th anniversary in 2007. The link to "Virtual Jamestown" is http://www.history.org/nche/. For recent evidence on the severe seven-year Jamestown drought (1606–1612), visit www.ngdc.noaa.gov/paleo/drought/drght_james.html.

Wolstenholme Towne

Archaeologists have excavated this palisaded village, located near Jamestown, which was destroyed in the 1622 Indian attack. The site is located at Carter's Grove Plantation, near Williamsburg. The Winthrop Rockefeller Archaeology Museum next door contains impressive exhibits on English settlement in Virginia.

Historic St. Mary's City

The site of Maryland's first capital lies off Route 5, near the mouth of the Potomac River, in southern Maryland, several hours' drive from Baltimore, Annapolis, and Washington, D.C. Since 1971, an annual summer archaeology field school has worked to excavate additional elements of the town.

For Further Reading

General

Bernard Bailyn, *The Peopling of British North America: An Introduction* (1985).

David Hackett Fischer, *Albion's Seed: Four British Folkways in America* (1989).

Mary Beth Norton, *Founding Mothers and Fathers: Gendered Power and the Forming of American Society* (1996).

Alan Taylor, *American Colonies* (2001).

David J. Weber, *The Spanish Frontier in North America* (1992).

Spain's Ocean-Spanning Reach

Amy Turner Bushnell, *Situado and Sabana: Spain's Support System of the Presidio and Mission Provinces of Florida* (1994).

Ramón A. Gutiérrez, *When Jesus Came, the Corn Mothers Went Away: Marriage, Sexuality, and Power in New Mexico, 1500–1846* (1991).

John H. Hann, *A History of the Timucua Indians and Missions* (1996).

W. Michael Mathes, *Vizcaíno and Spanish Expansion in the Pacific Ocean* (1968).

Jerald T. Milanich, *Laboring in the Fields of the Lord: Spanish Missions and Southeastern Indians* (1999).

France and Holland: Overseas Competition for Spain

Denys Delâge, *Bitter Feast: Amerindians and Europeans in Northeastern North America, 1600–1664* (1993).

W. J. Eccles, *France in America* (1972).

Michael Kammen, *Colonial New York: A History* (1975).

Oliver A. Rink, *Holland on the Hudson: An Economic and Social History of Dutch New York* (1986).

Bruce G. Trigger, *Natives and Newcomers: Canada's "Heroic Age" Reconsidered* (1985).

English Beginnings on the Atlantic Coast

John Demos, *A Little Commonwealth: Family Life in Plymouth Colony* (1970).

Karen Ordahl Kupperman, *Indians and English: Facing Off in Early America* (2000).

Ivor Noël Hume, *The Virginia Adventure: Roanoke to James Towne, An Archaeological and Historical Odyssey* (1994).

Neal Salisbury, *Manitou and Providence: Indians, Europeans, and the Making of New England, 1500–1643* (1982).

Alden T. Vaughan, *American Genesis: Captain John Smith and the Founding of Virginia* (1975).

The Puritan Experiment

David Cressy, *Coming Over: Migration and Communication Between England and New England in the Seventeenth Century* (1987).

William Cronon, *Changes in the Land: Indians, Colonists, and the Ecology of New England* (1983).

Alison Games, *Migration and the Origins of the English Atlantic World* (1999).

Philip F. Gura, *A Glimpse of Sion's Glory: Puritan Radicalism in New England, 1620–1660* (1984).

Alan Heimert and Andrew Delbanco, eds., *The Puritans in America: A Narrative Anthology* (1985).

Edmund S. Morgan, *The Puritan Dilemma: The Story of John Winthrop* (1958).

The Chesapeake Bay Colonies

Wesley Frank Craven, *The Southern Colonies in the Seventeenth Century, 1607–1689* (1949).

James Horn, *Adapting to a New World: English Society in the Seventeenth-Century Chesapeake* (1994).

Edmund S. Morgan, *American Slavery, American Freedom: The Ordeal of Colonial Virginia* (1975).

James R. Perry, *The Formation of a Society on Virginia's Eastern Shore, 1615–1655* (1990).

Helen C. Rountree, *The Powhatan Indians of Virginia* (1989).

Online Practice Test

Test your understanding of this chapter with interactive review quizzes at

www.ablongman.com/jonescreatedequal/chapter2

CHAPTER 3

Controlling the Edges of the Continent, 1660–1715

Laurie Platt Winfrey, Inc.

■ Seventeenth-century Spanish frontier guard wearing an arrow-resistant vest.

MARGUERITE MESSIER MADE AN IMPRESSIVE FIGURE ON THE MONTREAL WATERFRONT in April 1704 as she loaded a large canoe. Surrounded by her five children, she worked with her brother, Jean-Michel, to stow food and belongings for their strenuous journey to meet her husband at a new French outpost on the Gulf of Mexico. They were assisted by the guide they had hired to carry them on this daunting wilderness expedition.

At 28, Messier had already been married half her life, having wed explorer–trader Pierre-Charles Le Sueur in 1690 when he was 34 and she was only 14. While her husband traveled often and far, she raised their boy and four girls. She was deeply involved, through family ties, in the dramatic changes taking place throughout the vast North American hinterland claimed by France.

Messier's cousin, an adventurous Canadian named Pierre Le Moyne d'Iberville, had established the French colony of Louisiana near the mouth of the Mississippi River in 1699, and three years later Iberville and his younger brother (Bienville) had started the village of Mobile (near present-day Mobile, Alabama) to serve as the first capital. Messier's husband had long been active in Canada's far-flung western fur trade with the Ojibwe and Sioux Indians living near the Great Lakes. In 1700 he had ascended the Mississippi to the Blue Earth River in what is now Minnesota. Two years later he paddled down the Mississippi with minerals and furs and made his way to the new outpost at Mobile. There he constructed a house for his family; then he accompanied Iberville back to France.

Le fort Louis

French fort at Mobile, 1705

In 1704, confident about the future success of the Louisiana venture, Le Sueur sent word to his wife in Montreal to attempt the inland journey of nearly 2000 miles to Mobile. He himself departed from France aboard the *Pelican* for the same destination, hoping to reunite with his family. With the ice gone from the St. Lawrence, Messier and her party set out from Montreal on April 30, 1704, making their way up river and passing through Lake Ontario and Lake Erie. A year later, they reached the outpost at Kaskaskia in southern Illinois. Heat and sickness took their toll as they descended the Mississippi River. Messier's brother, Jean-Michel, and a daughter, Louise-Marguerite, died in June, two months before the party got to its destination. More bad news awaited them when they finally reached Mobile in August 1705, having covered nearly 2000 miles in 16 months.

The voyage of the *Pelican* had met with disaster. Pierre-Charles Le Sueur had boarded the ship in France, joining missionaries, soldiers, and potential brides recruited to go to Mobile. But at a stopover in Cuba, he had caught yellow fever and died before the ship left Havana. Sixty other passengers also fell ill, and several more died before the immigrants reached Mobile. The town—home to just 160 men and a dozen women—hardly had enough food and shelter for the sickly newcomers, and yellow fever spread quickly. The epidemic swept away 40 residents in two months and decimated nearby Indian villages.

Still, life at the outpost persisted. Townsmen welcomed the *Pelican*'s eligible young women, ages 14 to 18, and priests celebrated 13 marriages within the first three weeks. By 1705, when Marguerite Messier arrived from Montreal, new children were being born. Moving into the house her late husband had built, Messier determined to stay on and help the colony endure. She sent instructions back to Canada for friends to sell her property and forward the proceeds to her. Meanwhile, she managed a storehouse for her cousins, Iberville and Bienville who had survived the ordeal of the *Pelican,* she made a fresh start in the Louisiana colony.

Many of the changes that took place in North America during Marguerite Messier's lifetime occurred within a broad international context. During the second half of the seventeenth century, the English, Dutch, French, Spanish, and Portuguese were caught up in a race to expand and protect their overseas empires, and they were waging the contest on a global scale. Backed by growing economic and military strength at home, the French planted their flag in the West Indies, West Africa, Madagascar, India, and Ceylon. The Dutch, meanwhile, established a settlement at Cape Town in South Africa in 1652 that helped them challenge Portuguese power in the Indian Ocean and the Spice Islands of the East Indies. But expansion in one region often coincided with contraction somewhere else. By the 1670s, Dutch authorities had been forced to withdraw entirely from North America, leaving that arena of commercial and military competition to their rivals.

With the departure of the Dutch from North America, the three remaining European powers intensified their competition to control the fringes of the continent. In the East, England expanded the number and size of its coastal colonies, and English port towns multiplied along the Atlantic seaboard. On Chesapeake Bay, Anne Arundel (later Annapolis), became Maryland's port of entry in 1668. English newcomers also pressed inland along numerous rivers to found trading towns at the "fall line," the point where falls and rapids provided water power to run grist mills. In the 1670s, a London goldsmith's son named William Byrd established one such town at the falls of the James River on a site that grew to become Richmond, Virginia.

Pushing up from the south, meanwhile, Spain struggled to retain its foothold in Florida and New Mexico and to lay claim to parts of Arizona and Texas as well. New Spanish towns appeared at Albuquerque, El Paso, and Pensacola. Of the three competing powers only France, pressing in from the St. Lawrence Valley, managed to penetrate the interior of the continent extensively. Its government created a string of forts from the Great Lakes to the Gulf of Mexico: Detroit, Peoria, and Mobile all came into being under the French flag.

But the clash between empires would not be the only dynamic at work throughout the continent in these years. The religious strife among Christians that had marked the previous century in Europe continued in North America. Catholic missionaries labored diligently to recruit Native American converts in Canada, Florida, New Mexico, and numerous points in between. Opposed to such activities, Protestants in the English-speaking colonies remained on the alert for any threat—external or internal, real or imagined—that they could decry as a "popish plot". It was a term they used frequently to express their continuing hostility toward the Catholic Church and its leader, the pope in Rome.

Behind all these tensions, one fundamental question recurred in numerous places during the decades after 1660: Who has the right to govern? The structures of control were tenuous almost everywhere, and dissenters and rebels who felt jealous, excluded, or exploited could openly question the legitimacy of those in charge. In congregations, towns, and whole colonies, challenges to authority arose repeatedly, and often they could only be settled by resort to arms. Disruptions, violence, and sudden death were familiar experiences for thousands of people inhabiting North America during these years.

France and the American Interior

For decades before Marguerite Messier traveled from Montreal to Mobile with her family, the potential wealth of the North American interior had intrigued government ministers in France. If French fur traders based in Canada (known as *voyageurs*) could explore and map this vast domain, discovering its resources and befriending its Indian inhabitants, France might control some of the continent's most fertile farmland and keep its extensive natural assets out of the hands of European rivals. If the French could recruit enough Native Americans as loyal allies, they might even threaten the rich mines of the Spanish empire in Mexico and challenge the growing English colonies lying to the east of the Appalachian mountains. But for France to realize such wide ambitions, the French king, Louis XIV, would need to make North American colonization a national priority, and the extent of his commitment remained uncertain.

The Rise of the Sun King

King Louis XIV stood at the center of France's expanding imperial sphere. Indeed, so much seemed to revolve around him that he became known as the "Sun King." He had inherited the French throne in 1643, as a child of five, and in 1661, at age 22, he assumed personal control of a realm of 20 million people. During most of his long rule—from 1661 to his death in 1715 at age 77—Louis dominated European affairs. Always a builder of monuments, he expanded the Louvre in Paris and then dazzled the French nobility and clergy with his opulent new palace at Versailles.

In religion, the Sun King challenged the authority of the Catholic pope on one hand and suppressed the dissent of French Protestants (known as Huguenots) on the other. In politics, he centralized the monarchy's power as never before. His administration consolidated the laws of France, strengthened the armed forces, and expanded commerce. As the government ministries grew in strength, they foreshadowed the modern nation-state, regulating industry, promoting road building, and imposing tariffs and taxes.

Portrait of Louis XIV

Throughout Louis XIV's reign, his officials followed a set of policies known as mercantilism. According to this general system, a government stressed economic self-sufficiency and the importance of a favorable balance of trade. By avoiding foreign debts and drawing in precious metals and other resources from its competitors and its own colonies, a state could pay for wars abroad and costly projects at home. The French mercantilist strategy was to exploit labor efficiently and import raw materials cheaply, while exporting expensive manufactured products, such as glassware, wine, silk, and tapestries, in exchange for foreign gold and silver. France's colonies, like those of Spain and England, were expected to generate much-needed natural resources and to provide eager consumers for the mother country's manufactured goods.

In Paris, finance minister Jean-Baptiste Colbert emerged as the chief architect of this strategy of aggressive mercantilism. At home he taxed foreign imports, removed domestic trade barriers, and improved internal transportation. Moreover, he reduced worker holidays and outlawed strikes. With an eye toward colonial expansion, Colbert improved France's ports and created a code to regulate maritime shipping. He expanded the naval fleet and pressed French sailors into its service. Pushing still harder, he organized overseas trading companies and provided insurance for their expensive ventures. In addition, he sanctioned France's involvement in the African slave trade. Colbert yearned to acquire new territory to increase the empire's self-sufficiency and keep overseas resources out of enemy hands. To that end, he and his successors encouraged French exploration of North America on an unprecedented scale.

The government of Louis XIV assumed direct control over New France (Canada and neighboring Acadia on the Atlantic coast) from a private company in 1663. Colbert hoped to diversify production away from the fur trade and limit settlers from dispersing widely. Therefore, he shipped livestock and tools to help build up the colony's tenuous agricultural base. To establish the power of the king, Colbert dispatched a military governor general to Quebec, along with shiploads of artisans and indentured servants. To promote domestic life and population growth, the government also transported young single women and announced cash incentives for early marriages and large families. Many of the soldiers sent to protect New France from Iroquois and English threats stayed on to establish farms.

On balance, however, Colbert's plans for a prosperous, well-populated colony failed. The small population of New France—ten thousand by 1680—never grew as rapidly as French imperial strategists desired. The harsh winters and short growing seasons hindered the expansion of agriculture. Also, concerns on the part of the king and his ministers played a role in limiting growth. Colbert worried that too much emigration to Canada could depopulate and thereby weaken France at home. In addition, he tried to make sure that the few whom he sent abroad had "suitable" backgrounds as pious and loyal Catholics. "In the establishment of a country," he declared, it was important "to plant good seed."

In contrast to the English, the French did not elect to use their overseas colonies as useful havens for social outcasts, political troublemakers, and religious dissidents. This became clear in 1685, when Louis XIV revoked the Edict of Nantes, which had granted French Protestants their legal rights for nearly a century. The king explicitly forbade these dissenters from traveling to France's colonies. Faced with rising persecution at home, more than 150,000 Huguenots migrated abroad by the early eighteenth century. Several thousand of them found refuge in the new English colonies on America's Atlantic seaboard.

Exploring the Mississippi Valley

Encouraged by the government of Louis XIV, French Canadian explorers probed steadily across the Great Lakes and down the Mississippi River. (They mastered the interior waterways by learning to handle Native American canoes, just as Indian hunters soon learned to ride European horses on the Great Plains.) As early as 1634, some 70 years before Marguerite Messier and her family journeyed through the continental interior, Champlain had sent explorer Jean Nicolet west across Lake Huron to find a route to China. Thinking that Asia might be close at hand, Nicolet even carried a letter of introduction to the Chinese emperor as he paddled through the Straits of Mackinac with his Huron Indian companions. Instead of finding the salt water of the Pacific, they came upon the fresh water of Lake Michigan. They ended up near modern-day Green Bay, Wisconsin. There, Winnebego Indians (today's Ho-Chunk Nation) told of a river called the "Messisipi." When they claimed that the mighty waterway led to a distant sea, Nicolet wondered whether it might flow southwest into the Pacific Ocean.

Rumors of this river circulated among the French on the Great Lakes for a generation. Finally, in 1673, trader Louis Joliet and his associate Jacques Marquette, a Jesuit priest from the St. Ignace mission near Mackinac, entered the upper Mississippi via the Wisconsin River. The two men embarked on what Father Marquette described as a "voyage toward New Mexico." They descended the great stream to the mouth of the Arkansas River, far enough south to suspect that the waterway flowed into the Gulf of Mexico. If it was not an outlet to the Pacific, perhaps the river could still prompt a viable "southern strategy." That is, it might give France a path to the wealth of New Spain and provide French settlers with access to a warm-water port. "The worst thing about Canada," Colbert observed from France, is that the St. Lawrence, "being so far to the north, allows ships to enter only during four, five or six months of the year."

The new governor general in Quebec, Comte de Frontenac, moved to exploit these western prospects, making effective use of an experienced young adventurer: René-Robert Cavelier, Sieur de La Salle. In 1673, to secure control of the growing fur trade on the Great Lakes, La Salle erected Fort Frontenac at the eastern end of Lake Ontario. From there, inspired by word of Joliet's exploits, he and his men pushed west through the Great Lakes to southern Lake

■ **MAP 3.1** FRANCE IN THE AMERICAN INTERIOR, 1670–1720

Michigan. After carrying their canoes overland to the Illinois River, they erected several forts on that tributary of the Mississippi. These outposts strengthened French trading ties with local Indians and provided a launching point for more exploration. In 1680 one party dispatched by La Salle traveled down the Illinois River to the Mississippi, which the French called the Colbert. Then turning north, they paddled 500 miles against the Mississippi's strong current all the way to the Falls of St. Anthony: modern-day Minneapolis.

Two years later La Salle himself led a contingent of French and Indians south from the Illinois to explore the lower Mississippi. He returned to confirm that the great river indeed emptied into the Gulf of Mexico. He claimed the rich land drained by all its tributaries for Louis XIV, naming the entire river basin "Louisiana" after his king. Hindered by poor maps and crude navigational instruments, La Salle miscalculated the location of the mouth of the Mississippi.

■ When La Salle's colonizing expedition landed on the Texas coast in 1685, one supply ship, the *Belle*, sank in Matagorda Bay during the unloading process. Lost and discouraged, the French colony faded away within two years. In 1995, archaeologists found the *Belle* in shallow water and salvaged its remains.

The Granger Collection, New York

Therefore, when he tried to return by sea, sailing from France with four ships and several hundred colonists, he disembarked on the Texas coast early in 1685, mistakenly believing that he was close to the entrance to the river. Slowly, the entire colonization plan unraveled. When one ship sank near shore, the hapless settlers lost valuable supplies and any hope of relocating. Jealous French lieutenants eventually killed La Salle before he could discern the nature of his mistake and locate the whereabouts of the Mississippi River. Most of the colonists he had brought perished in the Texas wilderness, lost like the English settlers at Roanoke a century before.

King William's War in the Northeast

The French colonizers had overreached themselves. They had failed to find a route to the Pacific, to challenge Spanish power in Mexico, or to establish a southern port. Spread thin by the widening fur trade, French Canadians were in a weak position to repel renewed Iroquois attacks along the St. Lawrence River in the 1680s. Moreover, a strengthened Protestant regime emerged in London with the ascent of William III to the English throne in 1689. This transition set in motion more than 100 years of bitter struggle between Protestant England and Catholic France. In North America, the ideological and military contest of these two superpowers stretched out over several generations.

The American conflict began in the Northeast with the outbreak of King William's War in 1689. In that year the Iroquois, well supplied with English arms, launched raids on the French near Montreal. Governor Frontenac struck back against the Iroquois' allies, sending separate forces south to terrorize the English frontier. In February 1690, a force of French and Indians traveling on snowshoes attacked the snowbound village of Schenectady, New York. Farther east, other French joined local Abenaki Indians in setting fire to outposts in northern New England. At Fort Loyal (modern Portland, Maine) raiders butchered 100 English men, women, and children after they surrendered and took others captive. Leaving their dead unburied, the survivors fled south toward Salem and Boston in Massachusetts. Many who experienced the attack viewed it as part of a wider design to undo the Reformation and expand the authority of the Catholic Church, led by the pope in Rome. One wrote fearfully, that there must be "a popish design against the Protestant interest in New England as in other parts of the world."

As the frontier war raged on, bitter New Englanders tried unsuccessfully to seize Quebec. In turn, the French Canadians and their Huron allies conducted punishing raids against Iroquois villages. After eight years of bloodshed, King William's War ended in a stalemate in 1697. The Iroquois realized that staying out of European conflicts would improve their lot. In 1701, therefore, the Iroquois League promised to remain neutral during any future colonial wars between France and England, a pledge they generally honored for more than half a century. The French, having strengthened their position in Canada, could now revive the "southern strategy" of colonization that had so intrigued Colbert and obsessed the adventurer La Salle.

As King William's War closed, a turn in European events opened the door for renewed French efforts in the American heartland. King Carlos II of Spain fell ill without an immediate heir, and the royal courts of Europe competed to determine his successor. Louis XIV, eager to acquire Spain's European realm and American dominions for France, proposed that his grandson, Philip of Anjou, receive the Spanish crown. But England supported an opposing candidate, so the War of Spanish Succession (1701–1714) broke out soon after Carlos died.

Founding the Louisiana Colony

Even before new hostilities erupted in Europe in 1701, Louis XIV and his ministers took steps to secure French claims in the Gulf of Mexico. Given Spain's naval dominance throughout the area, the gulf had long been considered a "Spanish Sea" among the rival colonial powers. By renewing La Salle's plan to create a Louisiana colony, France could strengthen its hand in the impending war over succession to the Spanish throne. A colony on the Gulf of Mexico would provide much more than a southern outlet for the French fur trade; it could serve as a strategic outpost as well. The Spanish had just built a permanent Gulf Coast fortification at Pensacola in western Florida. The French realized that a settlement farther west along the same coast would help them hold onto any new territories in New Spain or the West Indies that might suddenly fall to France through a royal inheritance or a military conquest.

Caught up in the same competition, England also saw advantages to establishing a base on the lower Mississippi. Such a post could challenge Spanish and French claims to the gulf region and increase English trade with the Chickasaws and other southern Indians. In 1698 a London promoter quietly made plans to transport a group of Huguenot refugees to the mouth of the Mississippi. Catching wind of this scheme, the French naval minister, Comte de Pontchartrain, organized his own secret expedition to the Gulf of Mexico under an aspiring Canadian officer, Pierre Le Moyne d'Iberville.

The Newberry Library, Chicago

■ Le Boutaux, *View of the Camp on the Concession of Monseigneur Law at New Biloxi on the Louisiana Coast,* 1720. When the French constructed a new settlement on Biloxi Bay in 1720, colonists still faced crude living conditions along the Gulf Coast. Rats eat our food supplies, one newcomer complained, and "no greens can be raised" in the sandy soil.

During King William's War, Iberville had led the winter raid on Schenectady in 1690 and had later opposed the English at Hudson's Bay and Newfoundland. Coming from a large and well-connected Montreal family, the Le Moynes, Iberville quickly drew several siblings into the gulf colonization plan, including his teenage brother, Bienville. Iberville and his party sailed for the Gulf of Mexico from the French port of Brest in 1699. Their ship entered the mouth of the Mississippi in time to repel the English expedition at a site on the river still known as English Turn. They also managed to build a fort at nearby Biloxi Bay before returning to France.

The two brothers were now well on their way to creating the gulf coast colony that La Salle and his followers had failed to establish. A second voyage let Iberville conduct further reconnaissance of the lower Mississippi. On a third trip, in 1702, he established Fort Louis, near Mobile Bay, giving French traders access to the Choctaw Indians. Young Bienville, placed in charge of Fort Louis, labored to sustain the tiny outpost at Mobile (where the *Pelican* would arrive in 1704). Iberville himself left to pursue other schemes and died an early death in 1706.

Enmeshed at home in the lengthy War of Spanish Succession, France largely ignored its new gulf colony. Epidemics took a heavy toll on the newcomers and an even heavier toll on their Indian neighbors. Sharp divisions separated settlers drawn from Canada and other colonists sent from France. The former had prior wilderness experience, maintained close ties with local Native Americans, and resented the incompetence and haughtiness of newcomers from across the Atlantic. The latter missed the comforts of life in France, complained about the poor living conditions, and looked down on their Canadian counterparts as lacking in education and religious training. However, despite social friction and a chronic lack of supplies from France, the small community at Mobile survived.

North of Mobile, additional French posts began to dot the American interior. They reinforced the territorial claims of France and offered increased trade and protection to neighboring Indians. French traders built the village of Peoria on the Illinois River in 1691. Not far away, Catholic missions sprang up at Cahokia (1697) and Kaskaskia (1703). Between these two missions, the French would later erect Fort de Chartres (1719) overlooking the Mississippi in southern Illinois. Further north, the French established two strategic posts at opposite ends of Lake Huron. In 1689, they laid out a garrison where Lake Huron joins Lake Michigan, expanding their foothold there in 1715 with the construction of Fort Michilimackinac. In 1701, they also created a lasting town on the strait (*le détroit* in French) connecting Lake Erie to Lake Huron. The founder of this outpost—called Detroit—was a Monsieur Cadillac, who foresaw a prosperous future for the village. The powerful Iroquois had pledged their neutrality in 1701, and the new trading post, Cadillac wrote, lay open "to the most distant tribes which surround these vast sweet water seas."

> *Over two generations, the French had established a solid claim on the American interior.*

In 1712 the French crown, its resources depleted by a decade of warfare in Europe granted control over Louisiana to a powerful Paris merchant, Antoine Crozat. Drawing Cadillac from Detroit to the Gulf of Mexico to serve as Louisiana's governor general, Crozat hoped to develop connections to mineral-rich Mexico and to discover precious metals in the Mississippi watershed. But probes on the upper Mississippi, the Missouri, and the Red rivers yielded no easy bonanza. Instead, explorers established three new trading posts among the Indians: Natchitoches on the Red River, Fort Rosalie on the Mississippi (at Natchez), and Fort Toulouse (near modern Montgomery, Alabama) where two streams join to form the Alabama River, flowing southwest to Mobile.

When Louis XIV died in 1715, the colonial population of Louisiana stood at scarcely 300 people. But over two generations, the French had established a solid claim on the American interior. Their position was an ongoing challenge to English and Spanish competitors, for the crescent of wilderness outposts arcing north and then east from the Gulf Coast offered a useful network for additional exploration, Indian trade, and military conquest. French control of the Mississippi Valley remained a real possibility until the era of Thomas Jefferson and Napoleon Bonaparte nearly a century later.

The Spanish Empire on the Defensive

Whereas France's power expanded during Louis XIV's reign, Spain's overextended empire continued to weaken. This decline opened the door for Louis (leader of the House of Bourbon) to maneuver his own grandson onto the Spanish throne in 1700 as Philip V. Eventually, the resulting new line of Bourbon monarchs brought much-needed changes to the administration of Spain's overseas empire. However, these so-called Bourbon reforms took several generations to devise and implement. Meanwhile, Spanish colonizers struggled to defend vast territorial claims that spread—on paper—from the Gulf of California to the Florida peninsula.

In its remote colonies of New Mexico and Florida, Spain had weak imperial oversight at best. Local administration often proved corrupt, and communication with officials in Spain remained slow and cumbersome. For several generations, the Indian majority had resented the harsh treatment and strange diseases that came with colonial contact. Now, cultural disruptions and pressures from hostile Indian neighbors fanned the flames of discontent. In the late seventeenth century, a wave of Native American rebellions swept the northern frontier of New Spain.

La V. M. Maria de Iesus de Agreda. Predicando à los Chichimecos del Nuebo-mexico. *Nettie Lee Benson Latin American Collection, University of Texas, Austin*

■ In the 1630s, missionaries on the Southwest asserted that a nun living in Spain had miraculously appeared to Native American converts. But a generation later, when Indians questioned claims of Christian miracles and European superiority, it resulted in the Pueblo Revolt of 1680.

The Pueblo Revolt in New Mexico

The largest and most successful revolt took place along the upper Rio Grande. There, Pueblo Indians from dozens of separate communities (or pueblos) united in a major upheaval in August 1680. They murdered 21 of the 40 friars serving in New Mexico, ransacked their churches, and killed more than 350 settlers. After laying siege to Santa Fe, the rebels drove the remaining Spanish colonists and their Christian Indian allies south out of the province and kept them away for more than a decade. Several thousand refugees ended up at El Paso del Norte, a crossing point on the Rio Grande where the Franciscans had constructed a mission in 1659. These stunned survivors, at what is now El Paso, soon began questioning Indian informants to find an explanation for the fearsome rebellion they had just endured.

No single answer existed for the rebellion's source since diverse pressures combined to ignite the Pueblo Revolt of 1680. In retrospect, several factors, stretching back over decades, stand out clearly as providing fuel for the fire. First, a severe drought beginning in 1666 had inflicted a five-year famine with long-lasting effects on the peoples of New Mexico. Second, around the same time, neighboring Apaches and Navajos stepped up their hostilities against the small colonial population and the numerous Pueblo Indians who had been linked with the Spanish over several generations. The attackers were embittered by the continuing Spanish slave raids that took Indian captives to work in the Mexican silver mines. In retaliation these raiding parties, riding stolen Spanish horses, killed livestock and seized scarce food. When Spanish soldiers proved unable to fend off the hit-and-run attacks, their credibility among the Pueblo Indians living alongside the colonists weakened.

Third, a smoldering controversy over religion flared during the 1670s. The mystique surrounding Christianity was damaged when an epidemic struck in 1671 and Spanish missionaries could not stem the sickness through prayer. In response, traditionalist Indian priests regained favor, and they fostered a revival of age-old Pueblo religious customs. Horrified, the Spanish friars and government officials united to punish what they saw as backsliding within a Pueblo population that seemed to have accepted key elements of the Catholic faith. At Santa Fe in 1675, they hanged three Indian leaders for idolatry and whipped and imprisoned 43 others. The Spanish intended to sell the offenders—including a militant leader from San Juan pueblo named Popé—into slavery. However, armed Indians confronted the New Mexico governor and successfully demanded the release of Popé and the other prisoners.

NAVAJO

HOPI

Pojoaque — Taos
San Ildefonso — Picuris
Santa Fe — San Juan
Cochiti — Nambe
Zia — Jemez — Cuyamongue
Santa Ana — Tesuque
Halona — Sandia — Alameda
Acoma
Isleta — Chilili
Quarai — Tajique
Abo
Socorro
Senecu — Gran Quivira
San Marcial

ARIZONA

NEW MEXICO

YUMA

PACIFIC
OCEAN

Gulf of California

Colorado R.

San Xavier
del Bac
Mission

El Paso

Rio Grande

Chihuahua

Santa Barbara

Mazatlán

Southwest in the era of the Pueblo Revolt

- Spanish colonization up to 1680
- Pueblo Revolt, 1680
- Navajo settlements, 1600
- Navajo settlements, 1800
— Fr. Kino's missionary travels, 1681–1711
— Navajo Reservation boundaries, 2000
▫ Indian pueblos
● Spanish towns
✝ Mission at San Xavier del Bac

Present state names and boundaries are provided for orientation,
and Navajo Indian relocation is shown over 400 years

■ **MAP 3.2**   **CHANGES IN THE SOUTHWEST**
The 1680 Pueblo Revolt (green) overwhelmed Spain's small New
Mexico colony. In the next three decades, Father Kino and other Jesuits
moved the mission frontier north into what is now Arizona. Over time, the
Navajo relocated their homelands; they remain an important presence in the region.

This confrontation over religion only deepened the divisions within local Indian communities and families. Over several generations, thousands of Pueblo people had converted to
the Christian faith and the Spanish way of life. They had accepted the colonizers' promises of
heavenly rewards, and they feared the reprisals that had followed previous acts of resistance. But
many others felt embittered, especially against the despised encomienda system that granted
control over Native American labor to Spanish newcomers who backed up their claims by force.
These Pueblo malcontents believed that the time for successful opposition was slipping away.

Popé himself, banned from San Juan for disturbing the peace, withdrew to Taos, the north-
ernmost pueblo in New Mexico. From there, he negotiated secretly with like-minded factions

in other pueblos, unifying resistance to Spanish domination. He invoked the spirits of the Pueblo deities, especially the powerful sun spirit known as Po he yemu. He also killed those who threatened to reveal his plot, including his own brother. Popé's militant resolve helped him build an underground movement. In part, he built support around widespread resentment of the encomienda system, used by the Spanish to require Indian communities to supply labor or pay tribute. But two other long-term issues contributed to his success as well. One involved sex and gender; the other combined race and class.

From their earliest encounters, nothing divided the Spanish and Indians more sharply than their contrasting notions of sexuality. For example, Native Americans, like members of most societies around the world, accepted homosexuality. But many Christians considered it an abomination deserving death. More generally, whereas the Pueblos viewed sexuality as a crucial ingredient in social and spiritual life, Christians saw it as a source of sin and embarrassment. Indeed, Franciscans forbade traditional Indian religious ceremonies in part because they included erotic symbols and acts. The ban threatened the very essence of life for the Pueblos, who believed that sexual intercourse yielded not only human children but also bountiful crops, prompting male rains to join with female corn seeds to produce sustenance. Who were these friars who professed celibacy and punished themselves and others with whips for their natural sexual desires? The Pueblos had learned from experience that the same people who prohibited open displays of Indian sexuality occasionally practiced and condoned private acts of rape and molestation. The Indian women whom Spanish priests or soldiers had abused took Popé's side in this cultural clash, covertly supporting his militant design.

The movement also received secret support from numerous *mestizos* and mulattos, mixed-race people whose dark skin and lack of "pure" Spanish blood cost them any chance to rise in the colonial hierarchy. Members of this class included the elderly Pedro Naranjo, son of an Indian woman and a mulatto former slave who had received his freedom in return for joining an early expedition of colonists to New Mexico. At 80 years of age, the bilingual Naranjo could still sign his name in Spanish. He or some other family member may well have worked with Popé behind the scenes to plot the 1680 uprising. Historians have noted a "common report among all the Indians" about an inspirational letter written by a "very tall" and "black" Indian—likely Naranjo. This person was considered a "lieutenant" of the sun spirit, Po he yemu. His letter ordered that "all of them in general should rebel" and threatened destruction on "any pueblo that would not agree to it."

Along with such threats, Popé and his organizers sent runners to each conspiring pueblo in the summer of 1680. The runners delivered knotted ropes so all would know (by untying one knot each day) that the date for the rebellion was August 11. When several messengers were captured on August 9, Popé moved the revolt ahead one day, and his Pueblo warriors swiftly routed their adversaries. Unified in triumph, the zealous victors smeared excrement on Christian altars and bathed themselves to remove the stigma of baptism.

But initial cohesion soon gave way to friction. The successful rebels soon quarreled over who should hold power and how best to return to ancient ways. Kivas would replace churches, and the cross would give way to the kachina. But what other parts of the imported culture should the Indians abandon after eight decades of intermingling with the newcomers? Various Pueblo groups could not agree on which Spanish words, tools, and customs to discard or on which foreign crops and animals they would retain.

In 1681, the Pueblos fended off a Spanish attempt at reconquest. But they remained divided among themselves and more vulnerable than ever to Apache raids. Within a decade, rival factions had deposed Popé, and another Spanish army, under Governor Diego de Vargas, had entered New Mexico. It took the new governor several years to subdue the province, and the Pueblos managed another full-scale rebellion in 1696. But Vargas anticipated the revolt and crushed the opposition with overwhelming force, just as Oñate had done a century earlier. In 1706, several soldiers and their families established the town of Albuquerque on its present site. Learning from previous mistakes, Spanish officials did not reimpose the hated encomienda, with its demand for Native

■ Horses and sheep arrived in the Southwest with the Spanish, and both became central to the Navajo (or Diné) culture in northern Arizona and New Mexico. Navajo women continue to herd sheep and weave their wool into rugs and blankets, as they have done for more than three centuries.

Harald Sund/Getty Images

American labor or tribute. A new generation of Franciscan missionaries tolerated indigenous Pueblo traditions as long as the Indians also attended Catholic mass.

Navajos and Spanish on the Southwestern Frontier

The repercussions of rebellion and reconquest along the upper Rio Grande echoed throughout the Southwest. To the north, the Navajos benefited from Pueblo refugees who joined their communities. The Pueblo newcomers had valuable experience as corn farmers. Already known to the Navajos, corn now became an increasingly important food and sacred symbol for them. Moreover, the new arrivals had learned from the Spanish how to plant peach orchards and raise sheep. Pueblo men, long skilled at weaving textiles on stationary looms, showed their Navajo neighbors how to shear sheep, then how to wash the fleece, dye it, card it, and spin it into woolen yarn. Long before the arrival of sheep, Navajo women had always been the weavers in their society. Soon, therefore, women owned the expanding flocks and created wool blankets on their traditional portable looms. The Pueblos also brought more Spanish horses, a key asset that let the Navajos spread their domain west into fine grazing country in what is now northeast Arizona. Farther north, the Utes and Comanches also acquired horses after the Pueblo Revolt. After 1700, the Comanches pressed southeast onto the plains of present-day Texas and honed new skills as mounted buffalo hunters.

The Pueblo Revolt also brought reprcussions for the Spanish, since they had clearly overextended themselves along New Spain's wide northern frontier. Most worried officials agreed that the remote colony of New Mexico needed protection from further upheavals. So, despite their limited resources, authorities in Mexico City sent a few missionary-explorers north near the Gulf of California to spread Christianity and pacify hostile Indians. If possible, they were to extend Spain's geographic knowledge and discover new sources of wealth. In addition, they were to warn of any moves by imperial rivals, for hostile French ships had appeared in the Gulf of California in 1689.

Year by year, these friar–explorers edged north toward what is now southern Arizona until they reached the cactus-studded landscape of the Sonoran Desert in the 1690s. Eusebio Kino, a tireless Jesuit missionary born in Italy and educated in Germany, spearheaded the early exploration of the Arizona region. In 1701, this padre on horseback established a mission at San Xavier del Bac, near the Santa Cruz River below modern Tucson, Arizona. But his incessant travels continued, and the mission fell into disuse after his death in 1711.

During one of his extended explorations, Father Kino visited the Yuma Indians, where the Gila River meets the lower Colorado. He noticed blue seashells that he knew had to have come via overland trade from coastal California. From this he reasoned that California was not an island, as European mapmakers had long supposed. Rather, it was a part of the continent that might be reached by traveling west across the desert above the Gulf of California. Hearing this news, Philip V ordered an outpost to be established on California's upper coast beyond the Baja peninsula. It was the very charge that Sebastián Vizcaíno had failed to complete a century earlier, and once again it went unfulfilled. The Spanish did not take advantage of their improved understanding of the coastal geography until the 1760s.

Meanwhile, Kino's missions languished after his death in 1711. Warfare and sickness eroded the local population of Pima Indians, and attacks by Apache raiders destabilized the entire frontier region. The Spanish finally reinstalled priests at San Xavier del Bac and other missions along the Santa Cruz River in 1732. Four years later, a silver strike at "Arizonac," near present-day Nogales on the U.S.–Mexican border, provided a new name for the region, which would eventually become the state called Arizona.

Borderland Conflict in Texas and Florida

The encounters on Spain's other North American borderland frontiers took different forms, in part because European rivals appeared on the scene. Conflict with the French led the Spanish to found missions in Texas, a land they named after the local Tejas Indians. Still farther east, Indian resentments and war with the English weakened Spanish missions in Florida.

After 1685, Spanish expeditions probed the Gulf Coast region, eager to find and destroy La Salle's French colony. But Indians had already burned the short-lived outpost when the Spanish discovered its whereabouts. (Modern archaeologists have recently rediscovered the site.) In 1693, with any immediate European competition removed, the Spanish postponed attempts to establish a mission in Texas. They renewed their wholehearted commitment to the effort two decades later, when Louisiana's Governor Cadillac (the founder of Detroit) proved eager to open a trade across Texas with the Spanish frontier.

Governor Cadillac sent the Frenchman Louis Saint-Denis from Louisiana to forge ties with Spanish communities south of the Rio Grande. Saint-Denis and two dozen men set out from Natchitoches on the Red River and crossed East Texas, reaching the longtime Spanish outpost at San Juan Bautista, below the modern U.S.-Mexican border, in 1714. Surprised by this intrusion, Spanish authorities swiftly dusted off their plans for colonizing Texas. By 1717 they had established half a dozen small missions on both sides of the Sabine River, the boundary between modern Texas and Louisiana.

The next year, the Spanish took steps to expand their missionary activities and secure the supply route from San Juan Bautista to their distant outposts in east Texas. They built a second cluster of settlements at a midpoint in the trail beside the San Antonio River. Within two decades, a string of missions stretched along the river. Indian converts tended herds of cattle and sheep and constructed aqueducts to irrigate new fields of wheat and corn. The earliest mission, San Antonio de Valero (1718), provided a nucleus for the town of San Antonio. It also strengthened Spanish claims to Texas against the threat of French intrusion. (The same mission, converted into a military post known as the Alamo, became known far and wide for the battle fought there in 1836, when Anglo-Texans pushed for independence from Mexican rule.)

During the second half of the seventeenth century, the Indians of Florida, like the Pueblos in New Mexico, debated whether to reject generations of Spanish rule. The Columbian Exchange had altered their lives in dramatic ways. They ate new foods such as figs, oranges, peas, cabbages, and cucumbers. They used Spanish words such as *azúcar* (sugar), *botija* (jar), and *caballo* (horse). The acquisition of metal hoes allowed them to produce more corn than ever before. But expanding contact with missionaries had major drawbacks as well. By 1660 devastating epidemics had whittled away at Native American towns. The Indians still outnumbered the newcomers more than ten to one, but they had to expend enormous energy raising, processing, and hauling food for the Spanish. When colonists at St. Augustine grew fearful of French and English attacks after 1670, they forced hundreds of Indians to perform even more grueling labor: constructing the stone fortress of San Marcos.

Nothing proved more troubling to Florida's Indians than the spread of livestock farming. St. Augustine's elite had established profitable cattle ranches on the depopulated savannas of Timucua, near present-day Gainesville in north central Florida. These entrepreneurs could ship hides to Havana from both Florida coasts. They ignored the colony's requirements to keep cows away from unfenced Indian gardens, and they enforced harsh laws to protect their stock. Any Florida Indian who killed cattle faced four months of servitude; people caught raiding Spanish herds had their ears cut off.

> *Any Florida Indian who killed cattle faced four months of servitude; people caught raiding Spanish herds had their ears cut off.*

Resentment grew among the converts living in Florida's scattered mission villages. Restless Indians wondered whether the English, who had founded their Carolina colony on the Ashley River near modern Charleston in 1670, might make viable allies. The English, less committed to establishing missions than their Spanish rivals, seemed eager to trade for deerskins. In return, they offered the Native Americans a steadier supply of desirable goods than the Spanish could provide. Several Indian communities moved closer to Carolina to test this new alternative for trade. But disillusionment soon set in. When France and Spain joined forces against the English after 1700, Florida's Indians suddenly found themselves caught up in a struggle far larger than they had bargained for.

Ever since the days of Francis Drake, the English had schemed to oust the Spanish from St. Augustine. In 1702 English raiders from Carolina, under Governor James Moore, rampaged through the town. Yet the new stone fortress of San Marcos held firm, protecting the inhabitants. Two years later, Moore devised a more profitable way to disrupt the Spanish colony. With native allies, he invaded Apalachee (near modern Tallahassee). His troops crushed the mission towns, killing hundreds and carrying away more than 4000 Indian captives. Most of them were women and children, whom the English sold as slaves in Carolina and the Caribbean. By 1706 the Spanish settlement at St. Augustine endured, but numerous mission villages in Apalachee and Timucua lay in ruins. "In all these extensive dominions," wrote a troubled Spanish official from St. Augustine, "the law of God and the preaching of the Holy Gospel have now ceased."

England's American Empire Takes Shape

In 1660, as Louis XIV began his long reign in France and Spanish missionaries labored in obscurity in New Mexico and Florida, England experienced a counterrevolutionary upheaval that influenced American colonial affairs dramatically. In the 1640s, amid violent civil war, rebels supporting Puritans and the Parliament had overthrown the ruling Stuart family, beheaded Charles I, and abolished hereditary monarchy altogether.

For a brief period, England became a republican commonwealth without a king. But Oliver Cromwell, the movement's dictatorial leader and self-styled Lord Protector, died in 1658. Pressures quickly mounted to undo the radical Puritan Revolution and return to monarchical government. In May 1660, a strong coalition of conservative interests welcomed the late king's son back from exile and "restored" him to the throne as King Charles II. For this reason, the last three decades of the Stuart dynasty (1660–1688) are remembered in English politics and culture as the Restoration Era.

England's efforts in North America after the restoration of the Stuart monarchy differed sharply from the strivings of France and Spain. Europe's two Catholic powers emphasized geographic exploration and religious conversion. They stretched their claims across vast areas but had less success planting self-sustaining colonial populations. The English, in contrast, focused on precisely this goal along the Atlantic coast.

Monarchy Restored and Navigation Controlled

The shift in London's political winds could hardly have been more sudden, and Charles II moved quickly in 1660 to underscore the end of England's Puritan experiment. He ordered his hangman to burn the revolutionary constitution and parliamentary acts of the preceding government. He also commanded the execution of those responsible for beheading his father in 1649. Several of these individuals (known as regicides) escaped to find sanctuary in Puritan New England, and many who had served the "Good Old Cause" by fighting to end monarchy and strengthen parliament likewise sought refuge across the Atlantic.

The American colonies grew with the arrival of people whose religious and political beliefs had suddenly fallen out of favor at home. But other elements of colonial demographics—early marriage, high birth rates, and a low level of mortality in most places—did even more to prompt expansion up and down the Atlantic coast. Because most colonists still lived within 50 miles of the shoreline, this increase in people steadily broadened the opportunities for seaborne trade. Growing ship traffic, in turn, sparked government desires to regulate colonial navigation to bring mercantilist advantages to the realm.

In 1660 Parliament passed a major Navigation Act designed to promote British shipping and trade. The new law laid out important conditions that shaped England's colonial commerce for generations. First, merchants could not conduct trade to or from the English colonies in foreign-owned ships. Second, key non-English products imported from foreign lands—salt, wine, oil, and naval stores (the tar, pitch, masts, and other materials used to build boats)— had to be carried in English ships or in ships with mostly English crews. Third, the law contained a list of "enumerated articles" produced overseas. The items listed—tobacco, cotton, sugar, ginger, indigo, and dyewoods—could no longer be sent directly from a colony to a foreign European port. Instead, merchants had to ship them to England first and then reexport them, a step that directly boosted England's domestic economy. Another Navigation Act, in 1663, required that goods from the European continent to England's overseas colonies also needed to pass through the island. Moreover, they had to arrive and depart on English ships.

Ten years later, yet another navigation measure—the Plantation Duty Act of 1673— tried to close loopholes regarding enumerated articles. The new act required captains to pay a "plantation duty" before they sailed between colonial ports with enumerated goods. Otherwise, colonial vessels carrying such goods had to post bond before leaving harbor to ensure that they would sail directly to England. To enforce these rules, the government sent customs officers to the colonies for the first time. These officials' income depended on the fees they collected and goods they confiscated. Not surprisingly, colonists resented these new intruders as meddling parasites. But almost a century passed before fights over imperial customs collection finally helped spark a revolution.

Backed by the Navigation Acts, English shipbuilding prospered at home and in the tree-rich North American colonies. England's naval and merchant fleets burgeoned. A report to the king claimed that Chesapeake tobacco produced more revenue for the crown "than the East Indies four times over" and boasted that England's growing colonies in America "are his majesty's Indies," for "without charge to him" they had been "raised and supported by the English subjects, who employ above two hundred sail of good ships every year, breed abundance of mariners, and begin to grow into commodities of great value and esteem." Colonial trade, with all its related activities, became a major sector in England's economy.

Multituds flying from London by water in boats & barges.

Flying by land.

Burying the dead with a bell before them.   Searchers.

Carts full of dead to bury.

The Pepys Library, Magdalene College, Cambridge

■ **Images of the Great Plague in London.**

Even the Great Plague, which swept England in 1665, could not blunt this mercantile growth. And when a catastrophic fire destroyed most of London the next year, the huge loss also provided an opportunity. Planners redesigned the city with the broad streets and impressive buildings that suited the prosperous hub of an expanding empire. The fashionable coffee shops that sprang up as a novelty in late-seventeenth-century London became common meeting places for exchanging news and views about England's increasingly wide and profitable activities overseas. Much of what transpired in English North America was hashed out here, over pipes filled with Virginia tobacco.

Fierce Anglo–Dutch Competition

At the beginning of his reign, Charles II knew he had to build loyalty and strengthen an economy weakened by civil war. The king, with expensive tastes and an impoverished treasury, found that he could reward loyal family members and supporters, at no cost to the crown, by granting them control over pieces of England's North American domain. With this prospect in hand, he and his ministers sought to bolster foreign trade, strengthen the royal navy, and outstrip England's commercial rivals, focusing first on the Dutch.

As London stepped up its search for new profits, English officials moved to strengthen control over existing colonies and establish (or seize) new ones wherever possible. The Navigation Acts cut sharply into the Dutch carrying trade and spurred a decade of renewed warfare between England and Holland. For the most part, these intermittent Anglo–Dutch Wars ended in stalemate. But at the final Peace of Westminster in 1674, the English emerged with two gains in Africa and America that quickly took on huge and lasting significance.

In west Africa, the English captured and held several key coastal outposts: an island at the mouth of the river Gambia (renamed James Fort for the Duke of York) and Cape Coast Castle on the Gold Coast (near Elmina, the African headquarters of the Dutch West India Company). This encroachment challenged Dutch dominance of commerce with Africa for gold and ivory. It also gave England the footholds it needed to force its way into the Atlantic slave trade. Charles II moved quickly to take advantage of the situation. He granted a monopoly to the Royal Adventurers into Africa (1663) and then the Royal Africa Company (1672) to exploit the grim but highly profitable slave traffic. Within several generations, this ruthless initiative reshaped England's American colonies at enormous human cost.

Across the Atlantic, the English had seized the Dutch colony of New Netherland and its poorly defended port of New Amsterdam. Charles II claimed that the land had belonged to England from the time his grandfather endorsed the Virginia Company in 1606. In 1664, the king used his royal prerogative to regain control of this domain. He issued a charter putting the entire region between the Delaware and Connecticut rivers under the personal control of his brother James, Duke of York. That same year, James sent a fleet to claim his prize. When Governor Peter Stuyvesant surrendered the Dutch colony without a fight, both the province and its capital on Manhattan Island each received the name *New York*. Fort Orange on the Hudson became Albany because England's traditional name was *Albion*.

James now controlled an enormous domain that included the Dutch and English settlements on Long Island. He wielded nearly absolute powers over his new dukedom. He never visited New York. But as proprietor, he chose the colony's governor. That official ruled with an appointed council and enforced "the Duke's Laws" without constraint by any assembly. English newcomers to the colony resented the absence of an elected legislature, and the governor finally authorized an elected body in 1683. But the new assemblymen promptly approved a Charter of Liberties, in which they endorsed government by consent of the governed, so the Duke of York disallowed the legislature.

Married women living in the New York colony lost ground in the transition to English rule. Dutch law codes had ensured their full legal status, whereas English common law assigned wives to an inferior status (known as *coverture* or *feme covert*). They could not own property or keep control over money they earned, and they lacked any independent standing before the law.

As the English asserted political control over New York, the Dutch presence remained evident everywhere. Many English married into Dutch families and worshipped in the Dutch Reformed Church. The village of Harlem built a proper road to lower Manhattan in 1669, but an effort to change the town's Dutch name to Lancaster failed. English-speaking New Yorkers borrowed such Dutch words as *waffle, cookie, coleslaw,* and *baas* (boss). Anyone who was bilingual, such as Albany merchant Robert Livingston, had a special advantage. Livingston, an immigrant from Scotland, had learned to speak Dutch in Holland in his youth. His marriage in Albany linked him to powerful Dutch families in the Hudson Valley, and much of his early wealth came from his ability to translate important commercial documents between English and Dutch.

The New Restoration Colonies

Charles II had spurred England's seizure of New Netherland by issuing a charter for control of the contested region to his brother, the Duke of York. To reward supporters, he continued to issue royal charters granting American land. By drawing on England's early claims in North America that dated back to the explorer John Cabot, the king hoped to expand trade and colonization at no cost to the crown. In 1670, for example, he granted a charter to the Hudson's Bay Company. The deal gave the company's proprietors a monopoly on trade, minerals, and land across northern Canada. Farther south, Charles used charters to redistribute control along major portions of the Atlantic coast. His actions prompted an unprecedented scramble for colonial property and profits. Within decades, the English launched important settlement clusters in two regions: the Delaware River valley and the Carolina coast. Each offered lucrative charters to a small network of friends.

Most of these well-placed people belonged to the Councils for Trade and Plantations in London. Created in 1660, these advisory groups linked England's powerful merchants with crown officials. When Charles II issued a charter for Carolina in 1663, five of its eight initial proprietors served on those councils. In 1665, two of these same eight men became the proprietors of New Jersey. In addition, three of the eight played an active role in the Royal African Company, four became founders of the Hudson's Bay Company, and five became initial proprietors of the Bahamas. But Charles reached beyond this small group as well. In 1679 he made New Hampshire a proprietorship (an ill-fated experiment that lasted to 1708). In 1681 he paid off a debt to Quaker aristocrat William Penn by granting him a charter for Pennsylvania. (The generous arrangement included the "Lower Counties" that became Delaware in 1704.)

Penn's "holy experiment" to create a Quaker refuge benefited from earlier colonization south of New York. Dutch and Swedish settlers had inhabited the lower Delaware Valley for more than a generation. In 1665 the Duke of York carved off a portion of his vast proprietorship, granting the area between the Delaware and the Hudson to two friends: Lord John Berkeley and Sir George Carteret. They named the area New Jersey because Carteret had been born on the Isle of Jersey in the English Channel and had harbored Charles II when he took refuge there in 1649. Berkeley and Carteret promptly announced liberal "Concessions"—a representative assembly and freedom of worship—to attract rent-paying newcomers from England and the existing colonies. But their plans for profit made little headway.

In 1674 the proprietors divided these fertile lands into two separate provinces. East Jersey—where Newark was established in 1666—attracted Puritan families from New England,

> *Charles II had spurred England's seizure of New Netherland by issuing a charter for control of the contested region to his brother, the Duke of York.*

Dutch farmers from New York, and failed planters from Barbados. West Jersey was sold to members of the Society of Friends (including William Penn) who inaugurated a Quaker experiment along the Delaware River. Filled with egalitarian beliefs, the Quakers created a unicameral (single body) legislature, used secret ballots, and gave more power to juries than to judges. Their idealistic effort foundered within decades, and by 1702 all New Jersey came under crown control as a royal colony.

But by then, the Quakers had established a foothold in the neighboring colony of Pennsylvania. Its capital, the market town of Philadelphia, laid out by proprietor William Penn in 1682, already had more than 2000 inhabitants. An earnest Quaker, Penn professed pacifism. He made it a point to deal fairly with the Lenni-Lenape (Delaware) Indians. After purchasing their land, he resold it on generous terms to English, Dutch, and Welsh Quakers who agreed to pay him an annual premium, called a quitrent. He also emphasized religious toleration. A growing stream of German Protestants and others facing persecution in Europe began to flow into Pennsylvania after 1700.

Penn drew inspiration from James Harrington, the English political philosopher. Harrington's book *Oceana* (1656) argued that the best way to create an enduring republic was for one person to draft and implement its constitution. After endless tinkering, Penn devised a progressive "Frame of Government" that allowed for trial by jury, limited terms of office, and no use of capital punishment except in cases of treason and murder. But he remained ambivalent about legislative democracy. Settlers resented his scheme for a lower house that could approve acts drafted by the governor but could not initiate laws. In a new Charter of Privileges in 1701, Penn agreed to the creation of a unicameral legislature (that is, having only one chamber, or house) with full lawmaking powers. Disillusioned, Penn then departed for England, writing, "The Lord forgive them their great ingratitude." Penn's expansive proprietorship belonged to his descendants until colonial rule ended in 1776.

Anthony Ashley-Cooper, leader of the Carolina proprietors, also drew inspiration from Harrington, but for a very different undertaking. *Oceana* had stressed that distribution of land determined the nature of any commonwealth, and Ashley-Cooper (later the first earl of Shaftesbury) was eager to establish a stable aristocratic system. With his young secretary, John Locke (later an influential political philosopher), he drew up a set of "Fundamental Constitutions" in 1669. They proposed a stratified society in which hereditary nobles controlled much of the land and wealthy manor lords employed a lowly servant class of "leetmen." Their unrealistic document tried to revive the elaborate feudal hierarchy of medieval times.

The new government framework also endorsed racial slavery, declaring that "Every Freeman of Carolina shall have absolute Power and Authority over his Negro Slaves." This endorsement was not surprising, given the proprietors' involvement with England's new slave-trading monopoly in Africa and their initial recruitment of settlers in 1670 from the sugar island of Barbados. When Carolina colonists founded Charlestown (later Charleston) between the Ashley and Cooper rivers in 1680, the proprietors had already modified aspects of their complicated scheme, setting aside feudalism to encourage greater immigration. Nevertheless, their endorsement of slavery shaped the region's society for hundreds of years.

Bloodshed in the English Colonies: 1670–1690

The appearance of isolated English settlements along the Atlantic coast did little in most places, to alter the traditional rhythms of life. Year after year, the daily challenges of subsistence dominated American life for Indians and colonists alike. The demanding seasonal tasks of clearing fields, planting seeds, and harvesting crops remained interwoven with the incessant chores of providing clothing, securing shelter, and sustaining community.

Over time, however, changing circumstances in America and Europe introduced new pressures up and down the Atlantic seaboard. On occasion after 1670, familiar routines gave way

■ **MAP 3.3** METACOM'S WAR IN NEW ENGLAND, 1675–1676 In 14 months of war, New England Indians destroyed more than two dozen colonial towns and suffered their own heavy losses. The brutal conflict ended after the death of Metacom (the Wampanoag leader, also known as King Philip), near Mt. Hope, on August 12, 1676.

to episodes of bloodshed that threatened to tear whole colonies apart. Elsewhere in North America, Pueblo rebels were resisting the Spanish in New Mexico, and Iroquois warriors were challenging the French in Illinois country. The English, with their larger numbers, posed an even greater cultural and economic problem for Indian inhabitants.

In 1675, the Wampanoags and their allies rose up across southern New England in Metacom's War (or King Philip's War). The next year, frontier tensions in Virginia sparked the upheaval known as Bacon's Rebellion. A decade later, events in England prompted further tremors. In London, mounting opposition forced the unpopular James II to surrender the English throne to William of Orange, and Parliament emerged from the "Glorious Revolution" with enhanced powers. In America, the end of rule by the Stuart dynasty was punctuated by controversy and violence in one colony after another. Colonial isolation had already diminished, and European events intruded more forcefully in the decades ahead.

Metacom's War in New England

By 1675 the Native Americans of southern New England, like the Pueblos in New Mexico, had endured several generations of colonization. Yet they disagreed over how much English culture they should adopt. Many Indians used English words for trading, English pots for cooking, and English weapons for hunting. Some had converted to Christianity, living in protected "praying towns." Several young men had enrolled in Harvard's

Homeland Security and Deep Fears of the Enemy Within

After the terrorist attacks on the World Trade Center and the Pentagon in September 2001, Americans wondered whether extremists operating inside the United States might take additional lives. Because all the original suicide hijackers were young Muslim men with Middle Eastern backgrounds and appearances, would it be "racial profiling" to check the credentials closely for thousands of people in the country who fit that broad description? Could a person be suspected solely on the basis of identification—real or perceived—with a particular nationality, religion, or ethnic

group? And what kinds of patriotic acts, if any, must one perform to overturn such suspicions?

In a nation learning to take pride in its immigrant origins and diverse make-up, the problem seemed deeply troubling. Feelings ran high, but most citizens could see both sides of the question. National safety, perhaps even survival, appeared to hang in the balance, weighed against cherished constitutional rights and fundamental American presumptions of individual innocence. The problem also seemed novel, as symbolized by the creation of a new government bureaucracy: the Office of Homeland Security. The name itself sounded strange to Americans who remembered war only as something that occurred far away: Europe, the South Pacific, Korea, Vietnam, the Persian Gulf.

However, "homeland security" issues were older than the Constitution itself. When Metacom's War erupted in

1675, it was the Christian Indians living among the English who looked like the enemy and aroused sharp suspicion among Massachusetts colonists. Anxious officials relocated whole "praying towns" of Indian converts to windswept Deer Island in Boston Harbor. "When the Indians were hurried off to an iland at half an hours warning," recalled their advocate, John Eliot, the "pore soules," overcome with terror, left behind almost all "their goods, books, bibles."

After Metacom's attackers burned the villages of Medford and Lancaster, Daniel Gookin noted that the grim events "gave opportunity to the vulgar to cry out, 'Oh, come, let us go down to Deer Island, and kill all the praying Indians.'" Bitter townsfolk never followed through, but they threatened Gookin and Eliot for protecting the Indians. The two men visited the relocation camp in the dead of winter, where they reported seeing 500 people

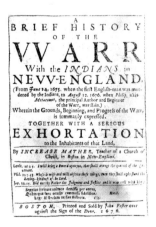

Indian College, where they learned to write English, Latin, and Greek with an eye toward entering the ministry.

Massasoit, the Wampanoag sachem (leader) who had assisted the Pilgrims at Plymouth, made sure that his two sons, Wamsutta and Metacom, learned English ways. The two men raised pigs and fired guns, and the colonists called them Alexander and Philip, after the kings of ancient Macedon. But when Wamsutta died in the 1660s, shortly after succeeding his father, Metacom (now called King Philip) suspected foul play by the English.

Metacom's grievances mounted over the next decade. Colonial traders made the Indians drunk and then cheated them. English livestock trampled Wampanoag corn, and if Indians shot the cattle, colonial courts imposed punishments. Worst of all, colonists now outnumbered the remaining 20,000 Indians in southern New England by more than two to one. When Rhode Island delegates visited Metacom's stronghold near Narragansett Bay, he told them bitterly that "the English should do for us as we did when we were too strong for the English." His own father, Massasoit, had "let them have a hundred times more land" than he now "had for his own people."

The mysterious death of a Christian Indian named John Sassamon sparked open warfare. Sassamon had learned to write English during a brief stint at Harvard. He then crossed back into the Wampanoag world to serve as a secretary for Metacom, who could write his English name only as a labored P, for Philip. Caught between two cultures, Sassamon alerted the English to Metacom's war plans in January 1675. Within days, his corpse was found in a pond near Plymouth. The English accused three Wampanoags of Sassamon's murder, convicted them, and hanged them in early June.

Outraged Indians protested that Sassamon's betrayal of his people and his subsequent death were their own affairs. When a white man shot and wounded a Native American,

Henry Sugimoto was among the artists who documented life in Japanese-American internment camps during World War II.

in need of food and shelter: "The Island was bleak and cold, their wigwams poor and mean, their clothes few and thin." Half the detainees died before spring. With little likelihood that the survivors could "plant or reap any corn" on the barren island, authorities finally freed them. Despite the painful internment, some of the Christian Indians joined the colonial forces in the final months of the war.

For more than two centuries, Native Americans, no matter what their political or religious beliefs, remained subject to recurrent suspicion while Indian Wars raged across the West. In the twentieth century, racial suspicions in wartime shifted to other groups, especially after the Japanese attack on Pearl Harbor during World War II. Fearful of nonwhites in the Pacific War Zone, the U.S. Army removed Aleutian Islanders from their homes in Alaska. And President Franklin Roosevelt signed an executive order that sanctioned the forced relocation of more than 100,000 Americans of Japanese descent living on the West Coast.

Hastily, the U.S. government transported the Japanese Americans to ten barren internment camps in eight western states, trampling the rights of its citizens. Like the Christian Indians in colonial Massachusetts, these victims of wartime hysteria had little time to pack their belongings. Miné Okubo, an art student at Berkeley, remembered being shipped by train to the Central Utah Detainment Center near Topaz Mountain. Finding it "impossible to see anything through the constant dust," Okubo and others sarcastically took to calling the Topaz camp "the jewel of the desert." Reduced to a number by her own government, Okubo made pictures and kept notes of her experience, which she later published as a book: *Citizen 13660*. Some were allowed out to become soldiers, and many lost their lives fighting in Europe. As World War II neared its end, Roosevelt rescinded his order, and the camps emptied. But it took the government a generation to admit that, in this instance, ideas of homeland security had gone badly awry. ∎

the long-expected war was under way in earnest. Irate braves raided the town of Swansea, killing nine residents. In the summer and fall, Metacom's warriors ravaged town after town along the Connecticut River valley and closer to the coast. Metacom used the victories to recruit additional Indian allies. The colonists, unprepared after 40 years of peace and unchallenged dominance, were caught off guard. Distrusting even the Christian Indians, Massachusetts officials relocated whole praying towns of Indian converts to windswept islands in Boston Harbor.

By December, the Connecticut and Rhode Island colonies, terrified of being wiped out, united with Plymouth and Massachusetts Bay to create a force of more than a thousand men. An Indian captive led them to a stronghold of the still-neutral Narragansetts in a remote swamp a dozen miles west of Newport, Rhode Island. The colonists surprised and overwhelmed the fortified village, setting it ablaze during the fierce fighting. Indian survivors fled, leaving behind more than 600 dead. Many of the men, women, and children were "terribly Barbikew'd," minister Cotton Mather later recorded.

This "Great Swamp Fight," reminiscent of an earlier battle in the Pequot War, infuriated the Narragansetts, who joined Metacom's growing alliance. During the late winter of 1676, this loose confederacy continued to wreak havoc on New England villages. But as spring arrived, the coalition weakened and the tide turned. Sickness broke out among the fighters, who lacked food and gunpowder. The powerful Mohawks of the Iroquois Confederacy opposed Metacom from the west. In Boston, Christian Indians joined the colonial forces, despite their painful internment. As Metacom's situation worsened, defections and betrayals increased. In August, a former ally shot the resistance leader and delivered the sachem's head to the English.

■ Green Spring, the largest mansion in Virginia at the time of Bacon's Rebellion, symbolized the autocratic rule of Governor William Berkeley and his "Green Spring Faction." The estate was seized by Bacon's forces in 1676 and later restored by Berkeley's widow.

As the horrific struggle ground to a close, the colonists captured Metacom's wife and child, selling them into slavery in the West Indies along with hundreds of other prisoners of war. New England's remaining Indians became second-class inhabitants, confined to enclaves in the areas they had once dominated. The colonists soon rebuilt and extended their domain. However, the trauma of the war lived on in the minds of the survivors and the sermons of their ministers. For years afterward, Metacom's severed head was displayed on a pole at Plymouth.

Bacon's Rebellion in Virginia

While smoke still billowed over New England, new flames broke out in Virginia. Social unrest had been growing under the stern governorship of Sir William Berkeley. England's wars with the Dutch cut into the tobacco trade and drew enemy ships into Chesapeake Bay. Unfree tobacco workers—more than 6000 indentured Europeans and nearly 2000 enslaved Africans—chafed against their harsh treatment. On the frontier, colonists resented the dependent Indians (Occaneechis, Pamunkeys, and others) who traded furs in exchange for protection from other tribes. Settlers also feared the well-armed Susquehannocks living near the Potomac River. "Consider us," Berkeley wrote to the king in 1667, "as a people press'd at our backes wth Indians, in our Bowills with our Servants . . . and invaded from without by the Dutch."

By 1676 tensions in Virginia reached the breaking point. Officials had increased taxes to pay for fortifications, servant plots and mutinies abounded, and corruption ran rampant among Berkeley's close associates. The aging governor ruled from Green Spring, his huge estate near the capital, Jamestown. Fearing the hostile views of free men who did not own property, Berkeley had revoked their right to vote. He had not dared to call an election in 14 years. He also dreaded outspoken preachers, free schools, and printing presses. "How miserable that man is," he wrote, "that Governes a People where six parts of seaven at least are Poore Endebted Discontented and Armed."

Even wealthy newcomers such as Nathaniel Bacon had trouble gaining access to Berkeley's tight inner circle. When Bacon arrived from England in 1674 at age 27, he received a council seat because of his connections and money. But rivals denied the ambitious gentleman a license to engage in the profitable fur trade. Impatient, Bacon soon condemned Berkeley's ruling Green

Spring faction as sponges who "have sukt up the Publique Treasure." When frontier tensions erupted into racial violence, Bacon threw himself into the conflict, challenging Berkeley's leadership and launching aggressive campaigns. His frontier followers, eager for Indian land, killed friendly Occaneechis as well as hostile Susquehannocks.

The governor, aware of the damage that Metacom's War had inflicted on New England, refused to sanction these raids. He feared "a Generall Combination of all the Indians against us." But Bacon's army continued to grow as backcountry leaders joined landless poor and runaway workers—both black and white—to support his anti-Indian cause. When the desperate governor called for a rare election to assert his strength, Bacon's supporters dominated the new House of Burgesses. Berkeley retreated across Chesapeake Bay and hid on Virginia's eastern shore.

Throughout the summer of 1676, rumors swirled that Bacon might join with malcontents in Maryland and in the newly settled Albemarle region of northeastern North Carolina to carve out an independent enclave and seek aid from the Dutch or the French. The new assembly quickly restored the vote to propertyless men and forbade excessive fees. It limited sheriffs to one year in office and passed other measures to halt corruption and expand participation in government. As an incentive for enlistment in the frontier war, the assembly granted Bacon's recruits the right to sell into slavery any Indians they captured.

For their part, slaves and indentured servants took advantage of the breakdown in public controls to leave their masters and join Bacon. Networks of "news wives" (women who used facts and rumors effectively to fan worker discontent) spread stories of oppressive conditions. In June rebel soldiers talked openly of sharing estates among themselves, and in August they took over Green Spring Plantation, where Berkeley kept 60 horses and 400 head of cattle. A month later, Bacon's army burned Jamestown to the ground.

But by October Bacon was dead, struck down by dysentery, and reinforcements for Berkeley were on the way from England. With armed vessels patrolling the rivers, Berkeley worked up enough nerve to return from the eastern shore. Soon propertied men who had joined with Bacon were changing sides again and receiving amnesty from the governor.

The revolt had been crushed, but the impact of the tumult proved huge. On the frontier, Bacon's violent campaign against the Indians had killed or enslaved hundreds and fostered bitter hatreds. In the Tidewater, the uprising had raised a frightening prospect for wealthy tobacco planters: a unified and defiant underclass of white and black workers. From then on, Virginia's gentry applied themselves to dividing the races and creating a labor force made up of African slaves. In London, the recently formed Royal Africa Company stood ready to further such a design.

The "Glorious Revolution" in England

No sooner had peace returned to New England and Virginia than Stuart policies brought a new round of turmoil on both sides of the Atlantic. In England, debate revived over who would succeed Charles II on the throne. The irreligious Charles, an Anglican in name only, had no legitimate children. Therefore, his brother James, a convert to Catholicism, was first in line to inherit the crown.

In 1678, rumors spread regarding a "Popish Plot" by Catholics to kill the king so that James could take power. The House of Commons, fearful of rule by a Catholic king, urged that James be excluded from the line of succession. Instead of James, House members argued, why not consider James's Protestant daughters by his first marriage: either Mary (recently wedded to her Dutch cousin, William of Orange) or Anne?

Angered by such interference, Charles II dissolved Parliament in 1681 and ruled on his own for the last four years of his life. When he died, the traditional rule of succession prevailed: James II took over the throne in 1685. In France that same year, Louis XIV revoked the Edict of Nantes, which had protected French Protestants. Fear spread among England's Protestant majority that their country's new Catholic ruler, James II, might also sanction persecution of non-Catholics.

These concerns mounted when James disbanded Parliament, raised a standing army, and placed a Catholic in command of the navy. Then in 1688, James's queen gave birth to a male

Jan Wyck, *William III Landing at Torbay*, 1688. National Maritime Museum Picture Library

■ **Protestants in England and America opposed to King James II welcomed news that William of Orange had arrived from Holland with his army in 1688 to take over the English throne.**

heir. Protestant anxieties about a pending Catholic dynasty erupted into open resistance.

United by their fear of Catholicism, rival factions among England's political elite (known for the first time as "Whigs" and "Tories") papered over their differences temporarily. They invited the Protestant William of Orange, James's Dutch son-in-law, to lead an army from Holland and take the English crown. In November 1688, he crossed the English Channel with 15,000 men. Confronting a successful invasion of England (it has never happened since), James abdicated the throne, threw the great seal into the Thames, and escaped into exile. William and Mary were proclaimed joint sovereigns in 1689, accepting a Bill of Rights that limited royal power.

Its position now enhanced, Parliament moved to grant toleration to Protestant dissenters, establish limited freedom of the press, and ensure regular parliamentary sessions. It also imposed limits on any permanent, paid military forces, known as standing armies, because they could accrue their own power and jeopardize civil authority. The English had thus preserved Protestantism and curtailed royal absolutism, all without bloodshed. Parliament hailed King William III as "our great Deliverer from Popery and Slavery." The propertied classes, who benefited most from the peaceful transition, hailed it as "The Glorious Revolution."

The "Glorious Revolution" in America

The succession of James II in 1685 did not bode well for England's American colonies. The new king not only professed the Catholic faith, he also cherished absolute monarchy and distrusted elected assemblies. In colonial affairs, James favored revenue-generating reforms and direct obedience to the crown. He detested the powerful leaders in Massachusetts, for, as Congregationalists, they believed in a decentralized Protestant church. James also resented the fact that they disobeyed the Navigation Acts and asserted their right to self-rule, even after the crown revoked their charter in 1684. Moreover, he rejected the notion that colonists possessed the precious right claimed by the English at home: not to be taxed without giving their consent. The king envisioned an extensive reorganization of the American colonies.

When James assumed the throne, his own colony of New York automatically became a royal province. Convinced of his divine right to set policy, the king nullified the charters of certain colonies in order to bring them under his control. As the cornerstone of his reorganization plan, James linked the New England colonies (plus New York and New Jersey in 1688) into one huge *Dominion of New England*. This consolidation, under an appointed governor general, would make it easier for England to suppress dissent, enforce shipping regulations, and defend the Dominion's frontiers—at least in theory.

In practice, the effort to forge a Dominion of New England proved a disaster. The move met such stiff resistance in America that a similar design for England's southern colonies never materialized. Control of the Dominion went to a military officer, Sir Edmond Andros. The heavy-handed Andros attempted to rule from Boston through a council he appointed, made up of loyal associates, without aid or interference from any elected legislature. He asserted the crown's right to question existing land patents, and he requisitioned a Congregational church for Anglican services. Worse, he offended local leaders by strictly enforcing the Navigation Acts to collect revenue. When participants in democratic town meetings raised objections, he jailed the leaders.

Colonists seethed with resentment toward this revival of Stuart absolutism, which claimed total obedience to the king and his officers as a divine right for the Stuart monarchy. Rumors of French invasions and Catholic plots swirled among staunch Protestants. In April 1689, welcome news that the Protestant William of Orange had invaded England inspired a revolt in Boston. Mobs showed public support for overthrowing the Stuart regime, and local leaders locked Governor Andros in jail.

The success of William and the demise of the Dominion of New England did not end royal efforts to tighten imperial control over New England. The new Massachusetts charter of 1691 consolidated neighboring Plymouth and Maine into the Massachusetts Bay colony. Moreover, it proclaimed that future governors would be appointed by the monarchy, as in other colonies. The men of Massachusetts, who had elected their own governor since the days of John Winthrop, would no longer have that right.

Emboldened by Boston's actions in 1689, New Yorkers ousted their own Dominion officials and set up a temporary government headed by militia captain Jacob Leisler. In Leisler's Rebellion, long-standing ethnic and economic rivalries between English and non-English New Yorkers merged with wider issues of empire. A German Calvinist, Leisler played on Protestant fears of "Popish Doggs & Divells" and on Dutch residents' resentment of English domination to attack the Dominion government.

Leisler's movement also drew on lower-class hostility toward the town's growing elite. His supporters resented their treatment at the hands of the rich. They freed imprisoned debtors and attacked the houses of leading merchants. After a new governor arrived to take charge in 1691, the elite fought back. They lowered artisan wages and executed Leisler as a rebel, although they could find no carpenter willing to provide a ladder for the gallows.

Similar tremors shook the Chesapeake region. In Maryland, where the Catholic proprietor ruled over a large and restive Protestant population, the governing Calvert family waited too long to proclaim its loyalty to King William. Fearing a "Popish" plot, assemblyman John Coode and a force of 250 armed Protestants marched on St. Mary's City and seized the government by force. The "happy Change in England" had replaced divine right rule with a more balanced constitutional monarchy, and Maryland settlers were determined to show their support.

Consequences of War and Growth: 1690–1715

The success of the Glorious Revolution hardly brought peace to England or its empire. On the contrary, warfare marked the reign of William and Mary and also that of Mary's sister, Queen Anne, who ruled from 1702 until her death in 1714. William immediately became involved in bloody campaigns to subdue highland clans in Scotland and overpower Catholic forces in Ireland. Moreover, English involvement against France in two protracted wars on the European continent had implications for colonists and Indians living in eastern North America. The War of the League of Augsburg in Europe became known to English colonists in America as King William's War (1689–1697), and the protracted War of Spanish Succession was experienced in America as Queen Anne's War (1702–1713).

Nowhere was the impact of these imperial wars more evident than in the rapidly growing colonies of the Northeast. Indeed, the earlier bloodshed of Metacom's (King Philip's) War, starting in 1675, had already aroused consternation and soul-searching in Bible-reading New England, and the violent decades that followed were viewed by many as a harsh test or a deserved punishment from the Almighty. They believed that the initial Puritan errand into the wilderness had been closely watched by God. Could it be, ministers now asked from the pulpit, that the Lord had some special controversy with the current generation? As communities grew more prosperous and became caught up in the pursuit of worldly success, were church members forgetting their religious roots and leading less pious lives? Invoking the Old Testament prophet Jeremiah, clerics interpreted personal and collective troubles as God's punishment for the region's spiritual decline.

But such a sweeping explanation of misfortune only raised deeper questions. New Englanders could see clearly that the consequences of rapid change were not spread equally among all towns, congregations, and families. As in most war eras—and moments of economic and demographic growth—some people and localities suffered more than others. Certain individuals and groups seemed to benefit while others fell behind. Some anxious believers saw the hand of Satan in the day-to-day struggles of village life. Others argued that the worldly success and wartime profits of an expanding elite had undermined the community ideals of earlier generations. While flames engulfed isolated Massachusetts communities such as Deerfield and portions of the Maine frontier, fiery passions were also being aroused in older settlements, such as Salem and Boston.

Salem's Wartime Witch Hunt

One of the most memorable disruptions, the Salem witch hunt, occurred in Essex County, Massachusetts, a two-day ride on horseback from the embattled Maine frontier. In 1692 an outburst of witchcraft accusations engulfed Salem Village (now Danvers), a farm community formed as a separate parish in 1672 from the prosperous port of Salem Town, six miles east. The strange episode remains one of the most troubling in American history.

Numerous premodern cultures in Asia, Africa, Europe, and America believed in varieties of witchcraft. Among Christians, the assumption that there are witches who possess supernatural power to inflict harm stretched back for centuries. In the 1600s, witchcraft trials abounded in Europe, and in New England zealous believers had prosecuted scores of supposed witches. They had even executed several dozen people in isolated cases. Three-fourths of those accused (and even more of those executed) were women. Most were beyond childbearing age, often poor or widowed, with limited power to protect themselves in the community. But the hysteria in Salem went far beyond other colonial incidents, with more than 200 people accused and 20 put to death.

Early in 1692, more than half a dozen young women in Salem Village, ranging in age from 9 to 20, began to suffer violent convulsive fits. With reduced appetites and temporary loss of hearing, sight, and memory, they also experienced choking sensations that curtailed their speech. Vivid hallucinations followed. "These calamities first began in my family," wrote Reverend Samuel Parris. A Harvard dropout, Parris had failed as a merchant in Barbados and had later agreed to lead the parish. It was "several weeks before such hellish operations as witchcraft were suspected." The first to appear tormented were Parris's daughter and niece, ages 9 and 11. The children had spent time with Tituba and John, a slave couple of uncertain Indian or African origin whom Parris had brought from Barbados. Tituba often spoke of the supernatural, and soon several of the afflicted girls accused her and two elderly Salem women of witchcraft.

■ A petition from accused women in Salem, addressed to the Governor and General Assembly in Boston.

Library of Congress

By April the girls had accused seven more people. Then some of the seven named others in their elaborate confessions, and the hysteria snowballed. In a world where people considered satanic influence very real, frightened authorities seriously weighed the girls' stories of people appearing to them as devilish specters and apparitions. Overriding tradition, jurists allowed such "spectral evidence" in court. And because all believed that the devil could not inhabit a pious person, protests of innocence from those accused only seemed to confirm the enemy's diabolical ways. The court ordered public hangings of the condemned on Gallows Hill. The hangings continued through September. One poor and elderly farmer, Giles Cory, was pressed to death under heavy stones. Only when accusations reached too high in the social hierarchy and when several accusers recanted their stories did the new governor finally intervene. He emptied the jails, forbade further imprisonments, and pardoned the surviving accused until the tremor could subside.

Why this terrible outburst? Some writers wonder whether the girls' symptoms suggest food poisoning (perhaps from a fungus on rye used in baking bread) or an epidemic of mosquitoborne encephalitis (an inflammation of the brain). Others note political factions within the village. Strained relations between farm families and the more prosperous urban residents of nearby Salem Town may have influenced the craze. Still others emphasize the zeal and gullibility of those first assigned to investigate. Some speculate that the absence of central authority, until Governor Phips arrived in the colony in May, allowed a troubled situation to spin out of control. Finally, commentators stress a perverse psychological dynamic that arises in any witch hunt, ancient or modern. In such cases, accused suspects often can save their own lives by supplying damaging and vivid confessions implicating others rather than by offering heartfelt denials of guilt. One or more of these factors surely came into play.

Yet devastation on the Maine frontier also contributed to what happened in Salem Village. The little Massachusetts town had numerous links to the war zone. George Burroughs, Parris's much-disliked predecessor as minister, had come from Maine. He had returned there when the contentious parish refused to pay him. Traumatized survivors from King William's War—the current conflict with the Abenaki and French—had trickled into the community. Significantly, more than half the young women who had accused others of witchcraft had lost one or both parents in the brutal frontier wars. On February 5, just weeks before the first accusations, attackers had burned the Maine village of York 80 miles north of Salem. The raiders destroyed livestock, killed 48 people, and took 73 captives. Word of the renewed violence no doubt triggered shocking memories among Salem's war refugees, especially the orphans who worked as servants in local households.

Fears deepened in April when one of the accused confessed that the Devil had tempted her while she had been living in Maine. Then the specter of Reverend Burroughs "appeared" to an accuser. Charged with promoting witchcraft and encouraging the hostile Indians (whom the colonists saw as Satan's helpers), Burroughs was arrested in Maine and hanged on Gallows Hill. In Boston, a 17-year-old servant named Mercy Short told of disturbing dreams of the Devil. Short had been captured and orphaned by Indians. She told minister Cotton Mather that in her dreams Satan and his minions had made "hideous assaults" upon her. And, she said, they were "of a tawney, or an Indian colour." Much of what Mather and others recorded as the work of Satan may have spun from posttraumatic stress in a frayed community during wartime.

The Uneven Costs of War

Throughout the 1690s and beyond, England remained entangled in imperial conflict abroad and dynastic struggles at home. The Act of Settlement, passed by Parliament in 1701, ensured that King William, who died the next year, would be succeeded by his wife's sister Anne, who ruled until her death in 1714. King William's War and Queen Anne's War made conflict a constant element in both reigns, and colonists found themselves subject to these winds.

The New York Public Library

■ For protection, the pirate Blackbeard often brought his ship into the shallow waters behind the barrier islands that form North Carolina's Atlantic coast. There, his crew bartered stolen goods at Ocracoke Island and reveled on the beach with local inhabitants.

As in all wars, the burdens fell unevenly. For many colonial families, incessant warfare brought only death and dislocation. But for others, it offered new opportunities. Farmers with access to port towns shifted away from subsistence agriculture and grew crops for commercial sale. In doing so, they exposed themselves to greater financial risks, given transportation costs and market fluctuations. But they hoped to reap large profits.

Overseas trade and wartime smuggling offered investors even higher gains and larger risks. These activities, in turn, boosted demand for sailing vessels. Boston alone supported more than a dozen busy shipyards. They employed hundreds of shipwrights, caulkers, and other skilled workers who crafted hulls, ropes, masts, and sails. Military campaigns, such as the successful ones against the French at Port Royal in Acadia in 1690 and again in 1710, engaged hundreds of colonial soldiers and sailors. When an English fleet of 60 ships carrying 5000 men docked at Boston in 1711, local provisioners (those who sold food and other provisions) reaped the rewards.

The crews of privateers (boats licensed to harass enemy shipping in wartime) made money if they captured a foreign vessel as a prize, and many chose to become buccaneers, pirates who operated for their own gain while avoiding the arm of the law. Englishman Edward Teach (known as Blackbeard) won notoriety as a privateer-turned-pirate, haunting the Carolina coast until his death in 1718. In the brief heyday of buccaneers, numerous colonial sailors also shifted from privateering to pirating.

Everywhere, poorer families were most likely to sink under the burdens of war. Regressive taxes, requiring the same amount from a poor carpenter as from a rich merchant, obviously hurt impoverished people the most. So did high wartime prices for food and other basic necessities. Furthermore, many of the poor men recruited by the military became casualties of combat or disease, increasing the number of widows living in poverty. Such conditions bred discouragement, and struggling communities were struck by the growing distance between rich and poor as towns expanded and interests diverged.

The moral ties and community obligations—known as the social covenant—that Puritan elders had emphasized two generations earlier were loosening. In their place emerged a focus on secular priorities and a new, individualistic spirit. In Boston, troubled ministers decried the hunger and poverty that they saw deepening in their parishes alongside unprecedented displays of wealth. Between 1685 and 1715, the share of all personal wealth in the town controlled by the poorest 60 percent of the population fell from 17 percent to 13 percent. At the same time, the portion belonging to the richest 5 percent climbed from 26 percent to 40 percent. Printers began to publish irate pamphlets protesting these troubling conditions. Angry writers encouraging working people to take political action and charged once-respected elites with studying "how to oppress, cheat, and overreach their neighbours."

No Bostonian wielded more economic power than Andrew Belcher, who first made money supplying provisions to troops during Metacom's War. Each succeeding war brought Belcher larger contracts and greater profits. To the dismay of devout churchgoers and the working poor, he built a mansion on State Street and rode in an imported coach, attended by black slaves dressed in fancy livery. He owned 22 ships and invested in many more. He also repeatedly cornered the wartime grain market, spawning food shortages and raking in inflated profits as prices rose.

In 1710 Belcher asserted his right to ship 6000 bushels of grain on the open market rather than sell flour at home, where people desperately needed bread. Indignant residents rebelled against Belcher's outright defiance of traditional community values. In the dark of night, they disabled his ship by sawing through the rudder. A grand jury declined to indict the protesters. Did ambitious and aggressive merchants such as Belcher cause the city's calamities, or did the townsfolk bring on their own troubles? Using a refrain that recurred in later generations, one godly conservative pointed a finger at the poor and implied they must be sinful if they could not subsist. "There was Corn to be had," he argued; "if they had not impoverished themselves by Rum, they might buy Corn." Only "the Devil's people" lacked food.

Storm Clouds in the South

Peace returned to New England's frontier villages and port towns in 1711, as negotiations began for ending Queen Anne's War in America and the related War of Spanish Succession in Europe. British diplomats managed to gain favorable terms from France and Spain when they signed a treaty at Utrecht two years later. (The formal union of England and Scotland in 1707 under the name *Great Britain* had transformed the *English* empire into the *British* empire.) But London officials could not prevent fresh violence in North America, given the steady expansion of their British colonies. The Wampanoags, Narragansetts, and Abenaki Indians had attempted to roll back the advancement of northeastern settlers into Connecticut, Massachusetts, and Maine. Now Native Americans in the Southeast sought to counter the encroachments of newcomers along the Carolina coast.

By the 1670s, settlers were filtering into what would become the colony of North Carolina. Some were radicals fleeing the Restoration in England. Others, such as John Culpeper, had moved north from the Carolina settlement on the Ashley River, where they disapproved of the hierarchical plans drawn up by Shaftsburg and Locke giving the Carolina proprietors firm control over the new colony. Still others were runaway servants from Virginia and refugees escaping the aftermath of Bacon's uprising. In 1677 these newcomers, led by Culpeper, seized control in the Albemarle region. The proprietors suppressed "Culpeper's Rebellion," but in 1689 they agreed to name a separate governor for the portion of Carolina "That Lies north and east of Cape Feare." Another disturbance, "Cary's Rebellion" in 1710, led to official recognition of "North Carolina, independent of Carolina," the next year. (Surveyors marked off the dividing line with Virginia in 1728.)

In 1680 Native Americans still outnumbered newcomers in eastern North Carolina by two to one, but within 30 years that ratio had been reversed. The Naval Stores Act of 1705, passed by Parliament to promote colonial production of tar and pitch for shipbuilding, drew a stream of settlers to the pine forests of eastern North Carolina. By 1710, English communities existed on Albemarle Sound, at what is now Edenton, and on Pamlico Sound, at Bath (where Blackbeard and other pirates were frequent visitors). Further south, on the site of a

"They Are Really Better to Us Than We Are to Them": Tension on the North Carolina Coast

On one frontier after another from New Mexico to New England, tensions mounted between Indian inhabitants and European intruders. In North Carolina, English settlers William Powell and John Lawson watched as animosities grew from verbal exchanges to open conflict in the Tuscarora War (1711–1713). As colonizers, the two contributed to the escalation and left behind revealing documents about it.

John Lawson provided a published record. In 1700, the young explorer–naturalist made an extensive tour through North and South Carolina, living among the Indians and assessing the land for colonization. His narrative of the journey, A New Voyage to Carolina; Containing the Exact History and Natural History of That Country; Together with the Present State Thereof (London, 1709) became a popular tool for recruiting settlers.

William Powell, Lawson's acquaintance, lacked the skill to be a published writer. But he could look out for his interests. So when angry Indians threatened his household and cursed him for invading their land, he scrawled an account to the governor, with a plea for action. His blunt appeal gives a front-line view of the mounting tensions from one perspective. Some punctuation has been improved, but the

Frontispiece from John Lawson's *New Voyage to Carolina* (London, 1709)

Courtesy, Dartmouth University Library

spelling and language remain as written to the governor.

> October ye 20 1704
> Honorable Sir:
> These Comes to aquaint your honour about the . . . Indians That Came on Thursday Last to my house. There was about sixteen with King Louther all with there guns. I was att worke in the Woods with one Cristopher Gold. I made what hast I could, but they ware to quick for me: for my wife & Children had Left the house. They took away Severall Things that we miss: they have Taken all my Aminition. King Louther strook me with a how. I told him I would Tell yr honour of itt. He said you might kiss his arse. They stod with there guns Cocked So yt I could not gett into my house Tell They had Done what they pleased. I beleve itt is through the Instegation of one John Elderedge for he Told the Indians when I Brought a

Letter to your honour from Mr Lawson that It was to Cutt them of[f] which made them lay [in] wait for me att Seder Island. This they told me & then They Called me sonn of a Bitch & said they would burne my house & when itt was Light Moone the[y] would gather my corne & ye Englishmen's corne. Elderedge Told them further yt the Englishmen would . . . not sell them no Amunition because they would Cutt them of[f]. So we humbly crave that your honour would Take Some Corse or Other with them or Else here will be no Living. . . . Wiliam Powell

Lawson, like Powell, was unsure what the proper "Corse" should be. On one hand, he seems to have been sending messages to the governor urging the English to curtail trade with the Indians. On the other hand, he could write sympathetically about the troubles of Native Americans, whose aggressive new neighbors showed little respect for them:

> They are really better to us than we are to them; they always give us Victuals [food] at their Quarters, and take care we are arm'd against Hunger and Thirst: We do not do so by them (generally speaking) but let them walk by our Doors Hungry, and do not often relieve them.

But eventually, Lawson threw in his lot with Powell and the other settlers. Named surveyor general of North Carolina, he laid out the towns of Bath and New Bern and sketched a precise map of the entire Carolina region to assist further settlement. He soon became a focus of the Indians' resentment. They believed that the naturalist and promoter, "under Colour of being a Surveyor Gen'l, had encroacht too much upon their Territories." When the Tuscarora War erupted in 1711, "they were so enrag'd" that they took Lawson prisoner and put him to death. ∎

■ **MAP 3.4   VIRGINIA AND THE CAROLINAS, c. 1710**   After John Lawson made a 1,000-mile journey through the Carolina interior (1700–1701), he became an advocate for colonial growth. The expanding settlements of North Carolina and South Carolina pressed the Tuscarora and Yamasee Indians, who staged wars of resistance after 1710.

Native American village at the mouth of the Neuse River, Protestant immigrants from Bern, Switzerland, had staked out the town of New Bern.

All this was too much for the Tuscarora Indians. Frustrated by corrupt traders and land encroachment, they launched a war in 1711 to drive out the intruders. But they had waited too long. Within two years, the settlers—aided by a South Carolina force of several dozen whites and nearly 500 Yamasee Indians—had crushed Tuscarora resistance. Most of the Tuscarora survivors migrated north, where they became the sixth nation within the powerful Iroquois Confederacy.

Yamasee warriors from the Savannah River region helped British colonists quell the Tuscarora uprising. But in 1715 they led their own rebellion against advancing settlers and corrupt traders linked to Charleston. They received support from neighboring Creek Indians, Spanish settlers in Florida, and French traders at the new Alabama outpost of Fort Toulouse. The still-powerful Cherokees in southern Appalachia opted not to join in the Yamasee War. Otherwise, the Indians might have overwhelmed the South Carolina colony.

Conclusion

Along the length of eastern North America, from the Kennebec River to the Savannah, hundreds of settlers and Indians perished during the half-century before 1715. Often the frontier struggles became entwined with wider conflicts between the rival European empires. These wilderness skirmishes seem minute compared with the battles raging in Europe at the same time. (One hundred thousand soldiers clashed when England's Duke of Marlborough defeated the French at Blenheim near the Danube River in 1704. Battle lines stretched for 4 miles, and casualties ran to more than 40,000 killed or wounded.) Despite the small scale of the conflicts in North America, Europe's imperial wars had started to influence developments in the English colonies.

Another element of Europe's expansion overseas—the trans-Atlantic slave trade—had also begun to alter the shape of England's North American colonies. What had seemed only a small cloud on the horizon in the early seventeenth century had grown into an ominous force, with a momentum of its own, by the early eighteenth century. The storm hit hardest along the Southeast Coast, where the arrival of thousands of Africans soon shaped a distinctive and depressing world of enslavement and exploitation that endured for generations. No sooner had the English gained control along the Atlantic edge of North America than they orchestrated a "terrible transformation" that placed thousands in bondage and altered the shape of American history.

Sites to Visit

Mission San Xavier del Bac

Lying 7 miles south of Tucson, Arizona, off Interstate 19 is the mission Father Eusebio Kino founded in 1700. The current church was created in 1783. A short drive south on Highway 19, the Tumacacori National Historical Park preserves ruins of three early Spanish missions.

Jesuit Missionary Records

puffin.creighton.edu/jesuit/relations/

In the late nineteenth century, Reuben Gold Thwaites compiled and edited more than 70 volumes titled *The Jesuit Relations and Allied Documents*. Creighton University has made almost the entire English translation of these valuable documents available on this Web site. The documents are also available on CD-ROM from Quintin Publications.

Fort Toulouse

In 1717, the French built Fort Toulouse where the Coosa and Talapoosa rivers converge, just north of Montgomery, Alabama. On the third weekend each month between April and November, volunteers conduct a French Colonial Living History program in and around the reconstructed French fort, with displays of blacksmithing and musket firing.

The Straits of Mackinac

The Straits of Mackinac joining lakes Huron and Michigan was once a strategic spot. Here, Interstate 75 now links Upper and Lower Michigan. North of the Mackinac Bridge, a memorial at St. Ignace honors Father Marquette. At the south end, Colonial Michilimackinac is a reconstructed village reflecting French and English frontier life.

Castillo de San Marcos

This stone fort guarding St. Augustine, Florida, was built in 1672–1695. The National Park Service maintains this fortress as a national monument and also provides a virtual tour online at www.nps.gov/casa/home/home.htm

The Old Deerfield National Historic Landmark

This site lies just east of Interstate 91 and surrounds a beautiful village in the hills of northwestern Massachusetts. Historic Deerfield, incorporated in 1952, maintains 14 restored houses, open for a self-guided walking tour, and the Flynt Center of Early New England Life displays New England life from 1650 to 1850.

Salem Village Witchcraft

www.nhc.rtp.nc.us:8080/tserve/eighteen/ekeyinfo/
salemwc.htm

A good Web introduction to "Witchcraft in Salem Village" appears as part of a project on "Religion and the National Culture" at this Web site of the National Humanities Center. Salem Village (Danvers, Massachusetts) has a memorial to victims of the 1692 witchcraft persecutions.

Eastern North Carolina

www.ah.dcr.state.nc.us/sections/hs/bath/bath.htm

North Carolina's earliest colonial ports at Edenton, Bath, and New Bern (ranging from north to south) still contain rich evidence of eighteenth-century life. This Web site for Historic Bath has links on explorer–naturalist John Lawson, Blackbeard the Pirate, and the Tuscarora War.

For Further Reading

General

Elaine G. Breslaw, *Witches of the Atlantic World: A Historical Reader and Primary Source Book* (2000).

Wesley Frank Craven, *The Colonies in Transition, 1660–1713* (1968).

Elizabeth A. H. John, *Storms Brewed in Other Men's Worlds: The Confrontation of Indians, Spanish, and French in the Southwest, 1540–1795* (1975).

Alvin M. Josephy, Jr., *The Patriot Chiefs: A Chronicle of American Indian Resistance* (1969).

John Lawson, *A New Voyage to Carolina* (1967).

France and the American Interior

Marcel Giraud, *A History of French Louisiana, Volume One: the Reign of Louis XIV, 1698–1715* (1974).

Jay Higginbotham, *Old Mobile, Fort Louis de la Louisiane, 1702–1711* (1977).

Eric Hinderaker, *Elusive Empires: Constructing Colonialism in the Ohio Valley, 1673–1800* (1997).

Robert S. Weddle, *The Wreck of the Belle, the Ruin of La Salle* (2001).

Richard White, *The Middle Ground: Indians, Empires, and Republics in the Great Lakes Region, 1650–1815* (1991).

The Spanish Empire on the Defensive

Ramón A. Gutiérrez, *When Jesus Came, the Corn Mothers Went Away: Marriage, Sexuality, and Power in New Mexico, 1500–1846* (1991).

John H. Hann, *A History of the Timucua Indians and Missions* (1996).

Andrew L. Knaut, *The Pueblo Revolt of 1680: Conquest and Resistance in Seventeenth-Century New Mexico* (1995).

Jerald T. Milanich, *Florida Indians and the Invasion from Europe* (1995).

David J. Weber, editor, *What Caused the Pueblo Revolt?* (1999).

England's American Empire Takes Shape

Joyce D. Goodfriend, *Before the Melting Pot: Society and Culture in Colonial New York City, 1664–1730* (1992).

J. R. Jones, *Country and Court: England, 1658–1714* (1978).

Brendan McConville, *These Daring Disturbers of the Public Peace: The Struggle for Property and Power in Early New Jersey* (1999).

Gary B. Nash, *Quakers and Politics: Pennsylvania, 1681–1726* (1968).

Robert M. Weir, *Colonial South Carolina: A History* (1983).

Bloodshed in the English Colonies: 1670–1690

John Demos, *The Unredeemed Captive: A Family Story from Early America* (1994).

Jill Lepore, *The Name of War: King Philip's War and the Origins of American Identity* (1998).

David S. Lovejoy, *The Glorious Revolution in America* (1972).

Stephen S. Webb, *1676: The End of American Independence* (1984).

Stephen S. Webb, *Lord Churchill's Coup: The Anglo-American Empire and the Glorious Revolution Reconsidered* (1995).

Consequences of War and Growth: 1690–1715

Paul Boyer and Stephen Nissenbaum, *Salem Possessed: The Social Origins of Witchcraft* (1974).

Verner W. Crane, *The Southern Frontier, 1670–1732* (1928).

Carol F. Karlsen, *The Devil in the Name of a Woman: Witchcraft in Colonial New England* (1987).

James H. Merrell, *The Indians' New World: Catawbas and Their Neighbors from European Contact Through the Era of Removal* (1989).

Gary B. Nash, *The Urban Crucible: The Northern Seaports and the Origins of the American Revolution* (1986, abridged edition).

Online Practice Test

Test your understanding of this chapter with interactive review quizzes at

www.ablongman.com/jonescreatedequal/chapter3

PART TWO

A Century of Colonial Expansion to 1775

O N APRIL 19, 1775, NEW ENGLAND FARMERS BATTLED BRITISH SOLDIERS at Concord Bridge. The confrontation marked the start of the American Revolution. (Each spring in Massachusetts, the date is still set aside as Patriots' Day and celebrated with the running of the Boston Marathon.) But how did colonies that remained weak outposts before 1700 become strong enough to challenge the power of the British empire in the second half of the eighteenth century? The answer is not a simple one. Life changed in dramatic ways during the century before 1775, not only in New England but throughout much of North America.

The rapid spread of Spanish horses across the West allowed Native Americans, such as the Comanche and Sioux, to become mounted buffalo hunters on the Great Plains. The arrival of Russian fur traders disrupted traditional cultures on the Aleutian Islands and the coast of Alaska. At the same time, the gradual success of the new Louisiana colony gave France access to much of the Mississippi River valley. But the potential for a dominant French-speaking empire in America evaporated with the stunning defeat of French forces by the British in the Seven Years' War. As that global conflict ended in 1763, the Spanish also lost ground in North America. After claiming Florida for 200 years, they finally ceded the peninsula to the British, even as they began to extend Spanish missions up the coast of California.

Other changes were even more dramatic. In the eighteenth century race slavery became an established aspect of colonial society in North America. The process began early, well before 1660, and evolved over several generations. In the coastal Southeast, it rapidly took hold as a dominant institution. The English had come late to the trans-Atlantic slave trade, but they became aggressive participants in the lucrative traffic in human beings. English colonizers fashioned harsh slave-based societies in the Caribbean, then in the Chesapeake colonies of Virginia and Maryland, next in North and South Carolina, and finally, after 1750, in the recently established colony of Georgia.

This terrible transformation to mainland colonies based on race slavery had far-reaching results. Thousands of Africans arrived in North American ports in the eighteenth century. Strikingly, they were only a small fraction of the much greater transport of Africans to the Caribbean and Central and South America. Nevertheless, by 1750 there were nearly 250,000 African Americans living in North America. Most lived in the South, and most were enslaved, including several hundred in Spanish East Florida and several thousand in French Louisiana. By 1775 the number exceeded half a million. By then, blacks made up more than 20 percent of the population of the British colonies, and the legal and social constraints that bound them remained tighter than ever.

Newcomers from Europe, as well as from Africa, altered the make-up of Atlantic colonies that had once been almost entirely English. Many of these newly arrived Europeans, unable to afford the cost of passage, had to pledge their labor for a period of years. But in contrast to the Africans, most European migrants came to America voluntarily and were free from obligations within a few years. The Atlantic crossing could be harrowing, of course, but for thousands the long-term advantages outweighed the short-term drawbacks. Artisans of all kinds were in high demand, and land was cheap. Colonial governments ruled with a light hand in comparison to the monarchies of Europe, and they competed with one another to attract newcomers. This competition, in turn, bred relative religious and ethnic tolerance.

Pushed by events in Europe and drawn by opportunities in America, non-English families flocked to Britain's North American colonies. Combined with the African slave trade, this new flow from Europe and the British Isles quickly generated a far more diverse colonial society on the foundations laid by earlier English immigrants. Prior generations of colonists had laid out towns, formed governments, and founded the rudimentary institutions of colonial social life. They had established an ambiguous pattern of interaction with Native Americans that involved warfare and displacement as well as trade and intermarriage. Also, they had located harbors, carved out roads, and started to build an economic infrastructure.

As numbers rose and diversity increased, a series of regional economies emerged along the eastern seaboard. Each sustained the local inhabitants while also serving the wider needs of the British empire. For much of the eighteenth century, the British crown promoted economic growth in the colonies through a workable combination of protectionist controls and benign neglect.

But the British victory over the French brought drastic new problems to eastern North America after 1763. Native Americans lost a valued trading partner and military ally when the French withdrew. Britain faced an enormous war debt and looked to its burgeoning colonies as a source of much-needed revenue. Within little more than a decade, Britain's North American colonists went from resentment and resistance to overt rebellion and an anticolonial war of independence.

1755 Braddock is defeated near Fort Duquesne.

1758 Comanches attack Spanish at San Saba Mission.

1759 Quebec falls to the British.

1760 George III becomes king of England.
France surrender Montreal to British.

1763 Treaty of Paris ends the French and Indian War.
Proclamation Line limits expansion of British colonies.
Pontiac's Rebellion.

1764 Sugar Act; Currency Act.

1765 Quartering Act; Stamp Act.
Virginia Resolves; Stamp Act demonstrations.
Tenant riots in Hudson Valley.

1766 Stamp Act repealed.
Declaratory Act.
Bougainville explores the South Pacific.

1767 Townshend Acts.

1768 James Cook makes first of three voyages to explore the Pacific.
Massachusetts Circular Letter.

1770 Boston Massacre.

1771 Battle of Alamance ends the Regulator Movement in North Carolina.

1772 Burning of the *Gaspée*.

1773 Boston Tea Party.

1774 Intolerable Acts.
First Continental Congress meets.
The Suffolk Resolves.

1775 Battles of Lexington and Concord.
Spanish enter San Francisco Bay.

African Enslavement: The Terrible Transformation

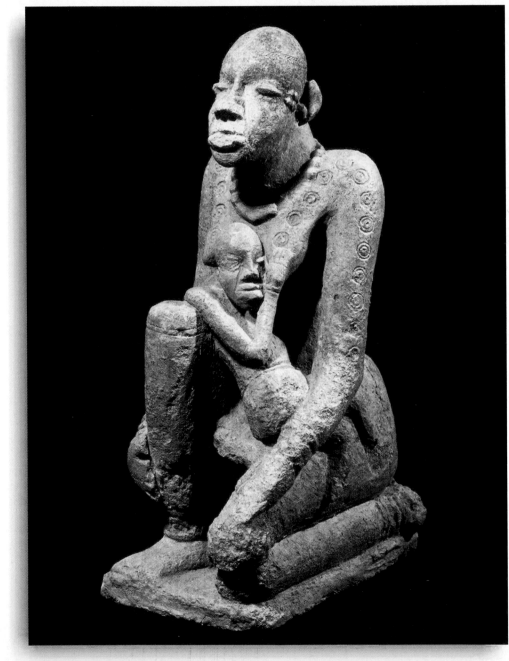

The Menil Collection, Houston

■ Ancient terra-cotta sculpture from Mali depicting an African mother and child.

On a cool day in January 1656, a mulatto servant named Elizabeth Key went before the local court in Northumberland County, Virginia. She was 25 years old. The late Colonel John Mottrom, a justice of the peace, had held Elizabeth as a slave, kept in perpetual bondage. She objected strongly, and she wanted to sue the executors of Mottom's estate for her freedom and back pay. Bess, as she was known, presented a threefold argument. First, as the daughter of a free man, she should inherit her father's legal status according to English law. Second, as a baptized Christian, she should not be enslaved. And third, she could produce a document showing that as a small child she had been "put out" to work until she was 14, following local custom. Such contracts for apprenticing a child for a fixed number of years were common in America, where labor was in short supply. But her term of work had expired long ago.

Key was accompanied in court by her white attorney and lover, William Greensted. They had had two children together and would marry six months later, when they finally won a favorable verdict. The executors of Mottrom's estate, eager to show that Bess's father was neither free nor Christian, implied that a Turkish crewman off a visiting ship was the girl's father. But the young couple produced witnesses who testified that Bess was indeed the daughter of Thomas Key, a white man serving in the Virginia General Assembly, and his "Negro woman." One witness, though only 13 at the time of Elizabeth's birth in 1631, told the jury she remembered Bess's mother well. The witness knew that she lived openly with Mr. Key and had heard her say that the girl was Key's daughter.

Other witnesses recalled that Bess Key's mixed parentage "was a common Report amongst the Neighbours." Mrs. Newman, the 80-year-old midwife who had delivered Bess's own children, contributed additional testimony. She recalled that 25 years earlier, Mr. Key was brought to court and "fined for getting his Negro woman with child." Further testimony established that in 1636, not long before he died, Key had bound little Bess to Humphrey Higginson, a member of the Council of State. Higginson "promised to use her as well as if shee were his own Child"; that is, "more Respectfully than a Comon servant or slave." He even stood as her godfather when Bess was christened.

To be raised in a Christian church was no small matter at a time when Europeans viewed non-Christians captured in wars to be uniquely vulnerable to legal enslavement. For Bess, this circumstance helped her cause greatly, for she proved "able to give a very good account of her fayth." Furthermore, she produced clear evidence that her father had sold her to Higginson for nine years. Mr. Key had demanded that Higginson not dispose of her to any other person, such as to Colonel Mottrom. Rather, he was to give her the usual "freedom portion" of corn and clothes "and lett her shift for her selfe," either in England or Virginia, when her term expired.

Africans arriving in America often had ornamental scarification (known as "country marks") on their bodies, as well as brands inflicted by slave traders and physical scars from the middle passage.

The local jury accepted Elizabeth Key's three-part argument and pronounced her free. But the General Court overturned the verdict on appeal, only to be overruled in turn by a committee of the General Assembly. In the end, the committee determined that "Elizabeth ought to bee free." The assemblymen also argued that her last master owed her a "freedom portion," plus back pay "for the time shee hath served longer than Shee ought to have done." Still, the matter generated debate among settlers. Several decades later, Elizabeth's case would have been decided differently. Moreover, the courts of Virginia might well have enslaved her children for life. And their own offspring would have inherited slavery status as well.

A terrible transformation was under way in English colonial culture that would warp American society for centuries to come. It did not become obvious overnight. Instead, it spread gradually, like a cancer, revealing a different pace and pattern in each mainland colony. During the 1620s and 1630s, a few black servants were working alongside white servants in Virginia and New England. All worked for fixed periods of service, with equal expectations of eventually becoming free residents and property holders. But well before the end of the century, a fateful transition had occurred, and the grandchildren of those workers had been separated into two distinct categories based upon skin color and physical appearance, or race. Free blacks persisted in the English colonies, but in most communities they became anomalies, for the tide was flowing against them. From now on, people of African ancestry were to be legally enslaved for life.

The earliest signs of lifetime enslavement definitely predate 1660, and the dark consequences would play out across American history down to the present day. But in scarcely half a century, during the late 1600s and early 1700s, this malignant condition developed from possibility to reality. Elizabeth Key and her children and grandchildren experienced the painful transition first-hand and glimpsed its horrendous consequences.

The Descent into Race Slavery

Some grim transitions in human affairs evolve slowly, even imperceptibly. In the mid-twentieth century, western societies recovering from World War II looked back at the havoc that fascism had spawned in Europe and wondered how Germany had moved from anti-Jewish prejudice, to hatred, to death camps in just two generations. In the mid–twenty-first century, we may look back and wonder how global warming, population expansion, religious fanaticism, weapon proliferation—or some difficulty we cannot now see—went from a negligible problem to a debatable issue to a rampant disaster during our lifetimes. How North American society sank into the pit of race slavery is just such a difficult topic. But the slippery slope sanctioning perpetual servitude based on race demands attention. Nothing shaped colonial cultures more forcefully than the European colonists' gradual commitment to the legalized enslavement of hundreds of thousands of people and their descendants.

The Caribbean Precedent

The roots of race slavery in the Americas extend back to the era of Columbus, when warfare, sickness, and exploitation quickly decimated the native populations of the Caribbean after 1492. Hungry for human labor, the Spanish intruders began to import people from Africa to grow crops and dig for gold in the Caribbean islands. As the native population declined sharply through epidemics, the traffic in black newcomers expanded.

Spanish pressure for labor in the New World intensified further with the discovery of additional mines in Mexico and Peru. To meet the growing demand, Spain's king even issued a contract (called the *asiento*) that allowed other European powers—such as Portugal, France, or the Netherlands—to import African slaves to the Spanish colonies. High profits drew eager participation. In the half-century between 1590 and 1640, more than 220,000 people arrived in chains from Africa at the empire's ports in Central and South America.

Meanwhile, the Portuguese purchased enslaved Africans to work their own expanding sugar plantations. They imported more than 75,000 slaves, mostly from the Congo Rver region of West Central Africa, to the Atlantic island of São Tomé in the sixteenth century. And when Portuguese sugar production spread to coastal Brazil, so did the exploitation of African labor. By 1625 Brazil imported the majority of slaves crossing the Atlantic each year and exported most of the sugar consumed in Europe.

Long before the 1660s, therefore, Europeans had set a precedent for exploiting African workers in New World colonies. Over more than a century, Spain and Portugal had learned to purchase, transport, market, and exploit enslaved workers from ports along the West African coast. Moreover, they had found ways to justify in their own minds a deep involvement in this brutal but lucrative system. Religious and secular authorities frowned on actively enslaving people, especially if they were fellow Christians, but purchasing so-called infidels (those who followed other religions or opposed Christianity) could be tolerated, particularly if slavery had already been imposed on them by someone else. These West African victims were non-Christians, and most had already been enslaved by others, captured by fellow Africans in war.

> *As late as 1660, it was not at all clear that African slavery would gain a prominent place, or even a lasting foothold, in any North American colonies.*

Confident in this rationale, the Spanish and Portuguese adapted their laws to accept the enslavement of Africans. Moreover, the condition would be hereditary, passed on from mother to child, and the new labor system had backing from the Catholic Church. Catholic priests occasionally worked to alleviate suffering among Africans in the Americas, and they reached out regularly for the conversion of souls, but the papacy did nothing to condemn the growing traffic. Nor did the Protestant Reformation have a dampening effect. On the contrary, the rising Protestant sea powers of northern Europe proved willing to assist in the slave trade and compete in what historians call the "sugar revolution," growing sugar on a massive scale for expanding Atlantic markets.

Ships of the Dutch West India Company, for example, played an increasing role in the Brazilian trade, transporting both slaves and sugar. Indeed, for a generation in the first half of the seventeenth century, the Dutch ruled the South American colony. When the Portuguese regained control of Brazil at mid-century, they pushed out Dutch settlers who had long experience in managing sugar plantations. These outcasts traveled the islands of the Caribbean, bringing their knowledge with them. Some appeared in the new English possessions of Barbados and Jamaica, and soon they were directing African slaves in cutting, pressing, and boiling sugar cane to make molasses. The thick molasses could then be processed further to make the rum and refined sugar that these English colonies exported. By the 1650s slavery and sugar production were engulfing England's West Indian possessions, just as these twin features had already become central to the New World colonies controlled by Spain and Portugal. But as late as 1660, it was not at all clear that African slavery would gain a prominent place, or even a lasting foothold, in any North American colonies.

Ominous Beginnings

As far back as the sixteenth century, African men had participated in Spanish explorers' forays into the Southeast, and some had remained, fathering children with Indian women. African slaves had helped to establish the small Spanish outpost at St. Augustine in 1565, but a century later no additional coastal colonies had yet appeared on the mainland anywhere south of Chesapeake Bay. Granted, Africans were present farther north in the fledgling settlements of the French, Dutch, and English. But their numbers remained small—several thousand at

Anonymous, *Vue du Cap Francais et Du nvr La Marie Seraphique de Nantes, 1772–1773. Le jour de l'Ouverture de sa Vente, Troisieme Voyage d'Angole.* Musée du Château des Ducs de Bretagne (950.4.3)

■ This summary of an African slave-trading voyage shows wealthy planters boarding a French ship upon its arrival in the West Indies in order to buy slaves newly arrived from Angola. The crew has used an iron fence dividing the deck to protect against revolt during the voyage. The captain conducts business under an awning in the stern.

most—in comparison to the expanding black populations of the older sugar colonies near the equator. In addition, few of these newcomers had come directly from Africa. Most had lived for years in the Caribbean or on the mainland, absorbing the languages, customs, and beliefs of the majority population. So they and their children, like Bess Key, were not viewed as complete outsiders by the European colonists.

The legal and social standing of these few early African Americans remained vague before the 1660s. Local statutes regarding labor were crude and contradictory; their interpretation and enforcement varied widely. Everywhere, workers were in demand, and most black newcomers found themselves indentured for a period of years alongside European servants in a similar unfree condition.

In the Massachusetts Bay colony, early Puritan settlers, casting about for sources of labor and for markets, exchanged goods for slaves in the Caribbean. In 1644, seafaring New Englanders even attempted direct trade with Africa. But the following year, Massachusetts authorities ordered a New Hampshire resident to surrender a black worker he had purchased in Boston. They argued that the man had been stolen from Africa, not captured in war, and should be returned to his home. For the earliest handful of black New Englanders, their standing proved uncertain in a region where religious status mattered far more than language, dress, or outward physical appearance. In 1652 Rhode Island passed a law clearly limiting all involuntary service—whether for Europeans or Africans—to no more than 10 years.

Along the Hudson River, the Dutch colonists had close ties with the sugar islands of the West Indies where race slavery was already an accepted system. In New Netherland, therefore, the laws discriminated against black workers and limited their rights. But the statutes also provided loopholes that permitted social and economic advancement to the community's Africans, most of whom spoke Dutch.

Chesapeake Bay lay even closer to the main routes of the Atlantic slave traffic. In 1619 a Dutch warship that had acquired slaves during a season of raiding in the Caribbean brought more than 20 African men and women to Virginia. They were put up for sale as servants, along with people deported from England to build up the Chesapeake's labor force. Terms of service varied, and some black newcomers earned their freedom quickly and kept it. But others saw their terms extended arbitrarily. In 1640 Virginia's General Court considered punishment for "a negro named John Punch" and two other servants who had escaped to Maryland and had been apprehended together. The Dutchman and the Scotsman each received four additional years of service, but the African was sentenced to unending servitude "for the time of his natural life." That same year, Virginia passed a law that prevented blacks from bearing arms. And a 1643 law taxing productive field hands included African American women but not white women.

These early efforts to separate Africans from Europeans by law set an ominous precedent in the use of skin color as a distinguishing marker. Throughout the 1640s and 1650s, aggressive English tobacco farmers in Virginia and Maryland, in imitation of planters in Barbados, attempted to purchase the labor of Indians and Africans for life. They even claimed rights to the future children of nonwhite women in their possession. Still, rules governing the lives of people of color and their offspring remained ambiguous for several decades, and (as the case of Bess Key makes clear) efforts at exploitation could often be undone in court. But new forces would come into play in the mainland American colonies after 1660, consolidating the transition to hereditary African slavery.

Alternative Sources of Labor

For African newcomers to English North America, their legal status became distinctly clearer and less hopeful in the decades after 1660. This shift was linked to the fact that colonial efforts to exploit two other supplies of affordable workers—captured Native Americans and impoverished Europeans—were running into increasing difficulty. The transatlantic slave trade, already more than a century old, provided certain English colonies with a ready source of African workers at a time when more obvious streams of inexpensive labor were dwindling or drying up.

For labor-hungry colonists, Native Americans had much to recommend them, since they were close at hand and knew the country well. Throughout the century, English newcomers often paid an Indian hunter to keep them supplied with fresh meat. But it was a different matter if European strangers tried to force that neighbor to cut down trees and cultivate unfamiliar crops endlessly, with little or no reward. Native Americans took captives when fighting one another, so colonists could buy Indian prisoners or seize them in frontier warfare. Europeans felt they could enslave such people in good conscience, since they were non-Christians who had been taken captive in war. But Native American numbers were declining steadily, owing to epidemics. And those who did become enslaved knew the countryside well enough to escape. Besides, traffic in Indian slaves worked against other goals of the colonists. It disrupted the profitable deerskin trade, undermined wilderness diplomacy, and sparked conflict on the frontier.

Efforts to maintain a steady flow of cheap labor from Europe ran into different problems. The Great Plague of 1665 devastated the English population, and the London Fire the following year created a new need for workers of all kinds to rebuild the capital. England's labor surplus, which had been a boon to the initial colonies half a century earlier, rapidly disappeared. Those who made their living in English ports by procuring labor for America were forced to nab youngsters off the streets. But even this practice (called by the new word, *kidnapping*) was soon outlawed. The use of indentures persisted, whereby the poor could buy their passage by agreeing to sell their labor for a fixed term. But when these workers reached America, they served for only a few years and then had to be replaced. Moreover, when their terms of indenture expired, they expected "freedom dues" (clothes, tools, and food from their former master) and their own land to farm. Once free, therefore, they competed for acreage that large planters hoped to control.

Equally important, when indentured servants were mistreated, they had little difficulty in relaying their complaints home to other potential workers. The flow of ships back and forth between Europe and North America grew steadily in the century after 1660, so word of places where indentured servants were regularly abused or swindled quickly reached the other side of the Atlantic. As Europeans mulled over private letters, coffeehouse gossip, and sailors' reports, they could adjust their own plans for migration. Depending on what they heard or read, they might postpone a voyage or seek a more promising destination.

In contrast, the African slave trade lacked any similar "feedback loop." People swept up in the growing stream of unfree African labor had no access to information regarding New World conditions. On New World plantations—as in Siberian slave labor camps and German extermination centers in the twentieth century—people and information flowed in only one direction. A mere handful, among hundreds of thousands of enslaved Africans, ever managed to communicate with their homeland. One can only speculate how different the procurement and treatment of colonial labor might have been if generations of Europeans had received no knowledge of conditions in North America, or if Africans had received a great deal. As it was, the brutal treatment of black workers across the Atlantic never had a chance, through accurate feedback, to influence the future flow of deportations from Africa.

Reparations for Slavery?

The small plaque reads, "In memory of the courage, pain and suffering of enslaved African people." But you probably will never see it. In 1993, members of the National Association of Black Scuba Divers lowered it to the bottom of the Atlantic Ocean off Key West, Florida. There it marks the resting place of the *Henrietta Marie,* an English slave ship built in 1699 that sank the next year, during its second voyage. Similarly, civic leaders in South Carolina unveiled a marker at Sullivan's Island in Charleston Harbor. It honors thousands of eighteenth-century Africans who faced enslavement, rather than opportunity, when they arrived at "the Ellis Island of Black America."

Other markers will follow as Americans continue to reexamine the country's long involvement with slavery and the slave trade. But many people now say that memorials, even official apologies, are not enough. Instead, they believe, formal reparations are overdue. The passions stirred by their suggestion show that the matter of slavery in America has not yet been laid to rest.

Payment of reparations—repairing a wrong through some compensation for damages—is an old and honored concept. It can sometimes bring legal satisfaction and moral closure to both the abused and the abuser. And it applies whether individuals, groups, or nations are involved. Germany has paid extensive reparations for Nazi

Bell recovered from the *Henrietta Marie,* a slave ship that sank in 1700.

atrocities during World War II, and the German government and private industries are compensating people who were forced to work without pay in slave labor camps.

Inevitably, the issue of reparations sparks controversy whenever it appears. It applies most readily to offenses that are short-lived and recent. For example, after much deliberation, Congress began paying reparations in 1991 to U.S. citizens of Japanese descent who were placed in internment camps during World War II. But reparations have also been argued for human wrongs that lasted much longer and lie buried deeper in the past, such as the enslavement of African Americans over centuries.

Talk of slavery reparations is hardly new. English lawyer James Grahame published a book in 1842 criticizing U.S. hypocrisy and claiming reparations on behalf of African Americans. A generation later it looked as though the country's 4 million slavery survivors might at least get the simple "freedom dues" that had gone to indentured servants in colonial times for beginning free life after servitude. But promises of "40 acres and a mule" fell through when the federal government refused to redistribute the land of planters who had declared war against the United States. Congressional aid offered through the Freedmen's Bureau proved small and uneven. It was also short-lived. Congress cut off funds for the agency in 1872.

In recent years, opposition to renewed talk of slavery reparations has been swift and varied. How do you calculate such a huge price tag, and who foots the bill? Should compensation go to slavery's descendants (numerous and not always easy to define) or to the African lands that suffered such colossal losses? Would a token payment, spread widely, be useless and insulting all at once? And doesn't the entire notion reopen old wounds and revive talk of victim status long after it is time to move on?

Not so, says John Conyers, a black representative from Michigan who has been prodding Congress for more than a decade to form a commission to study the issue. Frustrated on Capitol Hill, he points to a coalition of lawyers who hope to force the issue in court. They see the primary obstacle not as money but as public ignorance and apathy. Most Americans, they argue, are still in denial about the true nature of slavery and its enormous scope. "We just want the history to be told a little more accurately," Conyers observes. "I think if it's told, we'll have our day in court and we'll win." ∎

The Fateful Transition

In general, powerful Chesapeake tobacco planters had opposed challenges to the monarchy from Puritans and Parliament during England's recent civil wars. Many had close ties to the royalists and courtiers (known as "Cavaliers") who had remained faithful to the Stuart cause after King Charles I had been executed and his son had gone into exile. They were encouraged in 1660 by news of the Restoration of Charles II, since he was likely to support their interests and reward their loyalty. These men had noticed the rising profits that sugar growers were making by using slaves in the Caribbean. In Virginia and Maryland, therefore, planters passed a series of laws that sharpened distinctions between servants working for a fixed period and slaves consigned to labor for life. Officials who had objected to the verdict that freed Elizabeth Key in 1656 moved in the following decade to implement their own harsher views as law.

In shaping new legislation, they even challenged long-standing English legal traditions, such as the right of children to inherit their father's status. In 1662 Virginia's General Assembly considered whether any child fathered "by an Englishman upon a negro woman should be slave or Free." In a crucial reversal of precedent, the legislature said that in such cases "all children borne in this country" shall be "held bond or free *only according to the condition of the mother.*" From now on, the infant of any female slave would be enslaved from birth, an obvious boon for masters who wanted additional long-term labor at little cost. Slavery was becoming a hereditary condition.

If enslaved persons accepted Christianity, could they receive their freedom, as sometimes happened in Spanish colonies? A Maryland law of 1664 closed off that prospect. The act made clear that the legal status of non-Christian slaves did not change if they experienced religious conversion. Three years later, Virginia's government agreed that "the conferring of baptisme doth not alter the condition of the person as to his bondage." By taking religion out of the question, legislators shifted the definition of who could be enslaved from someone who was not Christian to someone who did not look European. In 1680, Reverend Morgan Godwyn observed that the "two words, *Negro* and *Slave,*" had already "by custom" grown interchangeable in Virginia. Because nobody could alter their skin color but anyone could change faith, planters moved to categorize colonial workers by their appearance rather than their religion.

In scarcely a generation, black bondage had become a hereditary institution, and the conditions of life had grown markedly worse for African Americans. Europeans receiving wages for work could pay fines for misbehavior; servants indentured for a term could be required to work additional months or years as a punishment. But enslaved Africans, condemned to unpaid labor for life, had no money or time to give up when disciplined for misdeeds, whether real or imagined. Therefore, they found themselves subjected increasingly to corporal punishments: whippings, torture, and even mutilation. In the generation after Elizabeth Key, black slaves—and often free blacks as well—lost their right to accuse, or even testify against, a white person in a court of law. "And further," stated Virginia's formative slave law of 1680, "if any Negro" so much as raises a hand, even in self-defense, "against any Christian, he shall receive thirty lashes, and if he absent himself . . . from his master's service and resist lawful apprehension, he may be killed."

The Growth of Slave Labor Camps

In the second half of the seventeenth century, those who ran the South's emerging staple crop economies undertook a drastic change of course. Step by step, over two generations, tobacco growers in the Chesapeake and rice producers in the new colony of South Carolina embraced the system of hereditary race slavery that had developed in the Caribbean. Within a matter of decades, they made it central to their way of life.

Traditionally, historians had described this change as the rise of plantation agriculture. But for those forced to cut the trees, drain the swamps, and harvest the crops, the shift in production strategy represented—in modern terminology—the emergence of slave labor camps. After all, the plantations of varying sizes that came to dot the southern coastline and the interior river valleys exploited a captive workforce. These people received no wages for their labor, had no legal rights, and could be deported to some other location at any time. This deterioration in

Alice Ravenel Huger Smith, *The Threshing Floor with a Winnowing-House (The Carolina Rice Plantation Series).* Gibbes Museum of Art/CAA, 37.09.22

■ Rice plantations that emerged in coastal South Carolina around 1700 became labor camps where enslaved blacks were confined for generations, without wages or legal rights. In the 1850s, distant descendants of the region's first African workers were still being forced to plant, harvest, and process the huge rice crops that made their masters rich.

conditions occurred first, and most dramatically, in Virginia, where several thousand African Americans lived and labored by the 1670s.

Black Involvement in Bacon's Rebellion

Nothing did more to consolidate Virginia's slide toward race slavery than Bacon's Rebellion, the major uprising that shook the Chesapeake region in 1676 (see chapter 3). The episode pitted aspiring gentry, led by Nathaniel Bacon, against beleaguered Indian groups on the frontier and an entrenched oligarchy in Jamestown. The rebellion underscored the dilemmas inherent in Virginia's reliance on a steady flow of white indentured servants to cultivate tobacco. That labor supply was uneven at best, and employers constantly needed new recruits, since terms of service lasted only several years. Workers who earned their freedom—hundreds every year—were young, armed men who demanded property of their own. Whether they had to take it from rich landholders or neighboring Indians made little difference to them.

These free men, would-be farmers in search of land, made up part of Bacon's following, but a diverse group of unfree workers also proved eager recruits. These ill-treated individuals remained legally bound to large landholders for varying terms, and many of the Africans were undoubtedly bound for life. Together, they raised much of the colony's annual tobacco crop. The backbreaking labor—planting, hoeing, suckering, topping, picking, curing, and packing tobacco—prompted frequent unrest. These ragged workers, however long their term of service might be, had the most to gain and the least to lose from Bacon's revolt. According to the Virginia Assembly, "many evill disposed servants...taking advantage of the loosenes of the tymes...followed the rebells in rebellion." When Bacon fell ill and died in October 1676, many of his wealthier supporters reasserted their loyalty to the colonial government in order to emerge on the winning side. But bound workers who had escaped from their masters continued the fight.

A letter reaching London that fall suggested that at the height of the rebellion Bacon had "proclam'd liberty to all Servants and Negro's." Whether or not Bacon had actually declared freedom to servants and slaves of all sorts, the widespread unrest clearly had given hope to the most downtrodden tobacco pickers, about a quarter of whom were black. As a Royal Commission put it, "sundry servants and other persons of desperate fortunes" had "deserted their masters and run into rebellion on the encouragement of liberty." When military reinforcements arrived in Chesapeake Bay from England in November, their commanding officer, Captain Thomas Grantham, found hundreds of laborers still in active revolt.

Impressed by their strength, Grantham chose to use deceit when he met with eight hundred heavily armed rebels, both white and black, at their headquarters near the York River in Virginia. By distributing brandy and making vague promises regarding pardons and freedom, he persuaded most of the white men to surrender and return home. Only about "Eighty Negroes and Twenty English...would not deliver their Armes." According to Grantham, they threatened to kill him, asserting that they wanted "their hoped for liberty and would not quietly laye downe their armes." But when these last holdouts boarded a sloop to head down river, Grantham managed to lure them within range of his ship's cannons. He disarmed the rebels and chained them below decks for return to their masters.

The Rise of a Slaveholding Tidewater Elite

With Bacon's death and the arrival of British ships, propertied Virginians had narrowly averted a successful multiracial revolution, fueled from below by workers who resented their distressed condition. But it was clear that another revolt might succeed in the future, and the great planters of the Chesapeake region moved to tighten their hold on political and economic power. After Bacon's Rebellion, a strategy of divide and conquer seemed in order. They moved to improve conditions for poor whites in ways that would reduce tension between classes and ensure deference and racial solidarity among Europeans. At the same time, they moved to reduce further the legal status of blacks and solidify their full enslavement. Africans would regularly be forced to serve for life, with increasingly harsh penalties for any show of opposition or dissent.

For precedent, the planters had the model provided by slavery-based colonial societies in the West Indies, including the English sugar island of Barbados. The notion of treating Africans separately, based on their customs, speech, and appearance, became an article of faith among aspiring planters. Their uneasiness continued over importing non-Christian strangers who spoke little, if any, English. But such doubts were more than offset by the prospect of laying claim to the children of slaves and to the lives and labor of all generations to come. In short, enslaved African women gave birth to additional workers, acquired by the master at no extra cost. These same women, moreover, were often more familiar with agricultural tasks than their European counterparts. Besides, planters could exploit black women and men more ruthlessly than they could whites without affecting future labor supplies.

Increasing life expectancy in the Chesapeake region, resulting from sturdier dwellings and more stable living conditions, further motivated planters to move away from a workforce of indentured servants. For a self-interested planter, longer lives meant that a white indentured person, after serving only a few years, would become yet another long-term competitor in the crowded tobacco market. In contrast, Africans enslaved for life would yield profitable service for an increasingly long time. And they would be more likely than ever to produce healthy offspring. Boys and girls who survived childhood could then be forced to clear more land to grow additional crops.

■ **A small minority of enslaved Africans became house servants to wealthy families in England and America. Though set apart from the black community and denied entry into white society, many traveled widely and described the outside world to fellow slaves confined to field labor.**

Among a circle of wealthy investors, the enticement of such an economic bonanza overcame any cultural anxieties or religious scruples. Seizing the moment, these aggressive entrepreneurs established themselves as the leading families of Virginia. William Byrd was an apt example. The son of an English goldsmith, Byrd took over his uncle's trading post near the falls of the James River at age 18 and soon married into a prominent family. As a frontier resident, he joined briefly in Bacon's uprising. But by the 1680s, he occupied a seat on Virginia's council and held several high financial posts. With his salary, he bought up his neighbors' tobacco and shipped it to England. He then used the proceeds to purchase cloth, kettles, muskets, and beads for the Indian trade. After exchanging these goods for deerskins, he exported the skins at a profit. In return, he imported trade goods from London and slaves and rum from the Caribbean, all of which he sold to small planters for more tobacco so the lucrative cycle could begin again.

In the 1690s, Byrd moved his operations closer to the seat of power, which remained at Jamestown until the capital shifted to nearby Williamsburg in 1699. He established a large estate at Westover, on the north bank of the James River, where he used scores of imported slaves to expand his wealth and launch a family dynasty. By the 1730s, Byrd's son, like other wealthy slave owners, came to fear a "servile war" so violent that it would "tinge our rivers, as wide as they are, with blood."

But for early merchant-planters, the enormous profits offered by slavery outweighed the calculated risks. These ambitious men expected that the English-speaking Africans already present could assist in teaching newcomers to receive orders. They also assumed that slave laborers from diverse African societies could not communicate well enough with one another to cause dangerous disturbances. And of course, having now made skin color a determining feature of social order, they knew that black runaways could be spotted and apprehended readily in the free white community.

Closing the Vicious Circle in the Chesapeake

As the profitability of the slavery option increased, so did its appeal. In 1664 Maryland's governor had been unable to find a hundred planters whose "purses would endure" a scheme in which each bought one slave per year. As yet, there were "nott men of estates good enough to undertake such a buisnesse." But 40 years later, some 4500 people were enslaved in Maryland in a total population of 35,000. And the colony's assembly was taking further measures to encourage the importation of slaves. Growing demand meant that merchants and sea captains who had only occasionally dabbled in the transportation of slaves now devoted more time and larger ships to the enterprise. Expansion of the slave-trading infrastructure made African workers readily available and affordable.

As the supply of enslaved black newcomers grew larger, planters eager to strengthen their position manipulated the established headright system. Traditionally, under this system, the colonial government granted to any arriving head of household 50 acres for every family member or hired hand he brought into the colony. The incentive was intended to spur emigration from Europe, expand the free population, and develop the land through the establishment of family farms. But the wealthy planters who saw African slavery as a profitable labor source also controlled Virginia's legal system. For their own benefit, therefore, they extended the headright system so that a land bonus also went to anyone who purchased an African arrival as a lifelong slave. Thus, before the seventeenth century closed, a Virginia investor buying 20 slaves could also lay claim to headrights worth 1000 acres of land.

To consolidate their new regime, planters worked through the church and the legislature to separate whites from blacks legally and socially. They stigmatized interracial ties and undermined the position of free blacks. A 1691 Virginia statute decried the "abominable mixture and spurious issue" that resulted from "Negroes, mulattoes and Indians intermarrying" with English or other white people, as Bess Key and William Greensted had done. All such couples were "banished from this dominion forever." It also prohibited masters from granting freedom to any black or mulatto unless they provided that person's transportation out of the colony within six months.

Virginia's Negro Act of 1705 further underscored the stark new boundaries. It mandated that white servants who were mistreated had the right to sue their masters in county court. Slaves, in contrast, had no such right. Any enslaved person who tried to escape could be tortured and even dismembered in hopes of "terrifying others from the like practices." When masters or overseers killed a slave while inflicting punishment, they were automatically free of any felony charge, "as if such accident had never happened." And if slaves were killed or put to death by law, the owners would be paid public funds for the loss of their "property." In scarcely 40 years, a dire and long-lasting revolution had transformed the labor system of the Chesapeake with the full backing of the law.

England Enters the Atlantic Slave Trade

By the time planters in North America began to consider aggressively importing African labor in the last decades of the seventeenth century, the trans-Atlantic slave trade had been operating for more than a hundred years. The scope and duration of this forced exodus from Africa remain difficult to conceive. In nearly four centuries, more than 10 million people

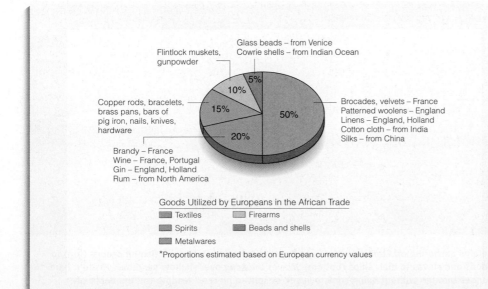

Goods Utilized by Europeans in the African Trade

- Textiles
- Firearms
- Spirits
- Beads and shells
- Metalwares

*Proportions estimated based on European currency values

■ **FIGURE 4.1**
GOODS TRADED IN AFRICA As European ship captains expanded trade along the African coast, they tailored their cargoes to suit the demands of local markets.

were torn from their homelands against their will and transported to the Caribbean and to Central, South, and North America. Several million more perished during their abduction. The Atlantic slave trade remains the largest and longest-lasting deportation in human history. By 1700, more Africans than Europeans had already crossed the Atlantic to the Americas. Their numbers grew over the following century as the traffic reached its height and North America became an added destination in the trade.

England took little part in the trade at first. However, the development of Barbados as a lucrative sugar colony and the expansion of English overseas ambitions changed matters quickly after 1640. In 1652 Prince Rupert, a nephew of the late Charles I, visited Gambia in sub-Saharan Africa and saw profits to be made. With the restoration of the English monarchy in 1660, Rupert's cousin Charles II immediately granted a monopoly on African trade to a small group of adventurers, and in 1672 he chartered the powerful new Royal African Company (RAC). The RAC dispatched a steady flow of merchant ships to West Africa. Reaching English outposts along the coast on the first leg of a triangular trade pattern, the ships exchanged textiles, guns, and iron bars for gold, ivory, and enslaved Africans. After a trans-Atlantic "middle passage" of one to three months, the captains sold slaves and took on sugar in the West Indies before returning to England on the final leg of the triangle.

■ Captains anchoring off Elmina on the Gold Coast relied on Africans with fishing canoes (top) to ferry goods and slaves to their ships (bottom). Waves breaking over shallow sand bars made it hard "to carry canoes through without being sunk, overset, or split to pieces," leading to "the death of many...and considerable losses of goods."

■ **MAP 4.1**
REGIONS OF THE AFRICAN SLAVE TRADE IN 1700

Demand for labor in the English Caribbean often exceeded supply, so the price of African workers rose. The lure of profits prompted interlopers to horn in on the RAC monopoly with increasing success. Of 76,000 Africans delivered in English vessels during the 1690s, scarcely 16,000 boarded RAC ships. All the others were carried by independent traders. When the company's monopoly ended officially in 1698, English slave trading ballooned. In the mainland colonies, boat builders and ship owners from Boston to Charleston sought out a portion of the trade, concentrating first on links to the Caribbean. In 1713 England obtained the lucrative contract to deliver Africans to Spain's colonies in America. By the 1730s, British ships controlled the largest share of the Atlantic slave trade. They continued to dominate the traffic for the next 70 years.

The Slave Trade on the African Coast

By the 1680s, it had been two centuries since Portuguese sailors had visited Africa's western shores on both sides of the equator and established a factory at Elmina, in modern-day Ghana. Dozens of depots controlled by rival European powers and their local allies dotted the sub-Saharan coastline. In the northwest, this string of primary ports and secondary "entrepots" (trading posts) began at the mouth of the Senegal River, just above Cape Verde, the continent's westernmost point. It ended more than 3000 miles to the southeast at outposts below the mouth of the Congo River, in present-day Angola. In between, the coastline curved some 5000 miles from the southwestern edge of the Sahara Desert almost to the Skeleton Coast in present-day Namibia. It embraced diverse geographic environments—from open savannas to thick forests—

■ Slaves were held as prisoners in the interior before being marched to the African Coast in groups known as coffles.

and scores of distinctive cultures. All along this coastline, villagers caught fish and gathered salt for trade with herders and farmers living farther inland.

Generations of contact with oceangoing ships brought new pressures and opportunities to African coastal communities. Local merchants, who traded gold and ivory to sea captains for imported textiles and alcohol, expanded their wealth and power. Some formed alliances with European trading partners. As sugar production expanded across the Atlantic, African traders responded to the growing demand for human labor. They consolidated their positions near suitable harbors and navigable rivers. From there, they bartered local servants and war captives to white agents (factors). In return, they obtained linen, beads, metalwares, and muskets, items that enhanced their prestige and let them extend their inland trading networks.

Inland traders, alert to the rising demand for slaves in the port towns, annually brought thousands of captives from the backcountry to the coast. The traders traveled by land and water, binding their prisoners together in small groups to form a coffle (from the Arabic word for "caravan"). The overseas goods they received as payment included firearms, gunpowder, and knives, which they used to prosecute additional wars and raids in their homelands and to secure more captives.

By the 1660s and 1670s, the pace of deportation across the Atlantic had doubled from the previous generation to an average rate of nearly 15,000 people each year. It rose steadily to a high of more than 65,000 people per year a century later. As the traffic grew, it became increasingly organized, competitive, and routine. Shrewd African traders played one European vessel against another for the best deals and hid illness among captives. When they saw that a ship was eager to depart, they increased their prices. Hardened European agents stockpiled the wares that African traders most wanted. They also learned to curry favor with local officials and to quell unrest among captives, confined in the holding pens known as barracoons. Experienced captains mastered prevailing winds and currents and modified the holds of their ships to pack in larger cargoes. Increasingly, they timed their ventures to avoid the months when sickness was most rampant in the tropics. Through repeated voyages, improved charts, and accumulated lore, they came to differentiate and exploit half a dozen major slaving regions along Africa's Atlantic coast. On occasion, they even ventured to Mozambique in southeast Africa and the nearby island of Madagascar.

The closest market where Europeans bargained for goods and slaves was Senegambia, or the northern parts of Guinea, between the Senegal River and the Gambia River. Gorée Island, off the coast of Senegal, and James Fort, located in the mouth of the Gambia, served as slave trading centers. The long Windward Coast extending to the southeast beyond Sierra Leone became known for its pepper and grain and for ivory in the south beyond Cape Palmas. Due east on both sides of Cape Three Points stretched the Gold Coast. There, the Portuguese had established Elmina to draw trade from the Asante gold fields in the interior. Farther east, the Slave Coast reached along the Bight of Benin to the huge delta of the Niger River. Trading depots at Whydah, Ardra, and Lagos drew captives from secondary ports in between. Beyond the Niger, where the African coast again turns south near Cameroon, lay the Bight of Biafra. English captains quickly learned the preferences for trade goods in each district, carrying textiles to the Gold Coast, cowrie shells to the Slave Coast, and metals to the Bight of Biafra.

The largest and most southerly region, known as Congo-Angola or West Central Africa, was the only one below the equator. Elsewhere, Europeans did not exert direct control beyond an isolated coastal fortress or trading depot. But here, they held sway over a wider reach. Catholic missionaries had established early footholds. And Portuguese traders had exported slave labor for sugar production, first on the Atlantic island of São Tomé and later in Brazil and the Caribbean. Before 1700, more than half of all Atlantic slaves departed from West Central Africa. In the eighteenth century the proportion remained over one-third.

North of the Congo River, French and English interests came to dominate the slave traffic out of Loango and Cabinda. South of the great waterway, the Portuguese continued to hold the upper hand at Luanda and Benguela. During the entire span of the slave trade, the Congo-Angola hinterland furnished roughly 40 percent of all Atlantic deportees: more than 4.5 million men, women, and children.

The Middle Passage Experience

For every person the exodus was different, a harrowing personal story that depended on the particulars of how old the captives were, where they had lived, and how they were captured. Nevertheless, the long nightmare of deportation contained similar elements for all who fell victim to the trans-Atlantic trade. The entire journey, from normal village life to enslavement beyond the ocean, could last a year or two. It unfolded in at least five stages, beginning with capture and deportation to the African coast. The initial loss of freedom—the first experience of bound hands, harsh treatment, and forced marches—was made worse by the encounters with strange landscapes and unfamiliar languages. Attempts to escape usually proved futile, and initial thoughts of returning home gave way to worries about immediate survival. Hunger, fatigue, and anxiety took a steady toll as coffles of young and old were conveyed slowly toward the coast through a network of traders.

The next phase, sale and imprisonment, began when a contingent reached the sea. During this stage, which could last several months, African traders transferred "ownership" of the captives to Europeans. Many buyers subjected their new property to demeaning inspections and burned brands into their skin. In the confusion, prisoners often lost sight of kinfolk or fellow villagers for a final time. When the buyer was an independent trader, he had the Africans transported through the surf to his waiting vessel. (Their hands were bound, so if a canoe capsized in the waves, it meant certain drowning.) Once aboard, they might languish in the sweltering hold for weeks while the captain cruised the coast in search of additional human cargo.

Often, however, the European purchaser was an agent for a large company. His assignment was to gather up prisoners at small ports and carry them by coastal vessel to a major trade fort. There they were put in irons alongside hundreds of other captives and guarded in a secure spot to prevent escape. For example, the underground dungeon at Cape Coast Castle on the Gold Coast had walls 14 feet thick. A visitor in 1682 observed that the RAC's fortress provided

ATLANTIC OCEAN

NORTH AMERICA

4% Chesapeake

16% 15%
11%
38% 16%

Origin of Africans, 1700–1800
- Senegambia
- Windward Coast
- Gold Coast
- Bight of Benin
- Bight of Biafra
- West Central Africa
- Mozambique

23%
40% 18%
7% 9%
3% Carolinas

Over 5,800,000 Africans arrived in the Americas (1700–1800)

The Atlantic Slave Trade during the 18th Century

9%
1% 25% 25%
3% 18% 19%

Africans reaching the New World, 1700-1800

British North America (522,400)	Dutch Americas (208,960)
British Caribbean (1,439,500)	Danish Americas (46,450)
Spanish Americas (1,114,460)	Portuguese Brazil (1,427,900)
French Americas (1,044,800)	

SOUTH AMERICA

PACIFIC OCEAN

■ **MAP 4.2**
ONE CENTURY IN THE TRANSATLANTIC SLAVE TRADE (1700–1800):
AFRICAN ORIGINS, EUROPEAN CARRIERS, AMERICAN DESTINATIONS
The Atlantic slave trade reached its greatest size in the eighteenth century, and Britain replaced Portugal as the largest transporter. Between 1700 and 1800, ship captains purchased more than 6.6 million Africans. Of these, nearly 800,000, or 12 percent, died during the middle passage. Therefore, just over 5.8 million captives survived the Atlantic crossing during the century.

Of these middle passage survivors, only about 9 percent (over half a million Africans) were sent to North America during the eighteenth century. Their ethnic backgrounds varied from colony to colony. In South Carolina, people from Senegambia and West Central Africa made up nearly two-thirds of the new black population; in the Chesapeake region, 38 percent of African arrivals came from the Bight of Biafra.

"a good security . . . against any insurrection" before a ship arrived and the prisoners could be loaded aboard. According to one English trader, "the negroes were so wilful and loth to leave their own country, that they often leap'd out of the canoos, boat and ship, into the sea, and kept under water till they were drowned." Crew members sometimes raised nets surrounding the deck to prevent such attempts at escape or suicide.

The ship's captain decided when to begin crossing the Atlantic, the harrowing third phase that constituted the middle passage. Drawing on his sponsors' instructions, advice from local agents, and his own experience, he weighed the variables. If he lingered too long to obtain more

ATLANTIC OCEAN

EUROPE

AFRICA

INDIAN OCEAN

Nations participating and their share in the slave traffic, 1700-1800

- Britain (3,100,100)
- The Netherlands (349,600)
- Portugal (1,846,900)
- Denmark (52,770)
- France (1,028,950)
- British Colonies/U.S.A. (211,100)

5% 1% 3%
16%
28%
47%

Roughly 800,000 Africans perished at sea

Approximately 6,600,000 departed from Africa (1700–1800)

SENEGAMBIA

WINDWARD COAST

GOLD COAST

BIGHT OF BENIN

BIGHT OF BIAFRA

WEST CENTRAL AFRICA

MOZAMBIQUE

2%
6% 8%
11%
37% 18%
18%

Africans taken to the Americas, 1700-1800

- Senegambia (389,150)
- Bight of Biafra (1,174,050)
- Windward Coast (521,100)
- West Central Africa (2,440,000)
- Gold Coast (758,550)
- Mozambique (131,000)
- Bight of Benin (1,187,300)

slaves at lower prices, he risked depleting his food supplies and raising the death toll among his crew and prisoners. If he departed too soon in an effort to shorten the voyage and preserve lives, including his own, he risked missing a drop in prices or a new contingent of slaves that could absorb his remaining stock of trade goods and bring more profits. He had to balance the danger of late summer hurricanes in the Caribbean against the need to arrive in America when harvests were complete—the time when planters had crops to send to Europe and money or credit to invest in African workers.

The Africans aboard each ship knew nothing of such calculations. Even those who had spent time as slaves among fellow Africans or as fishermen in coastal waters now faced an utterly alien plight, trapped in a strange wooden hull. When the crew finally raised anchor and unfurled the vessel's huge sails, the captives could only anticipate the worst. Already the crowded hold had become foul, and the large wooden buckets used as latrines had taken on a loathsome smell. Now the rolling of the ship on ocean swells brought seasickness and painful chafing from lying on the bare planks. Alexander Falconbridge, who sailed as a surgeon on several slave ships, recorded that "those who are emaciated frequently have their skin and even their flesh entirely

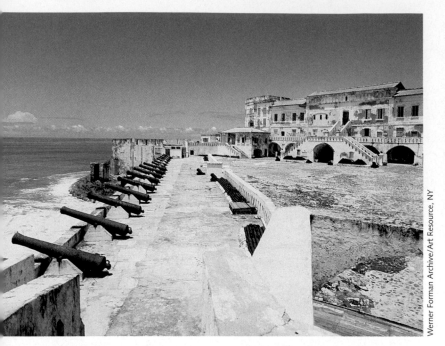

Werner Forman Archive/Art Resource, NY

■ **England's Royal African Company maintained more than a dozen small posts along the Gold Coast. Each outpost funneled slaves to this strong 74-gun fortress known as Cape Coast Castle. Cut into rock beneath the parade ground, the vaulted dungeon inside could "conveniently contain a thousand Blacks...against any insurrection."**

rubbed off, by the motion of the ship, from the...shoulders, elbows and hips so as to render the bones quite bare."

In its details, every crossing from Africa to the Americas was different. Historians have documented more than 27,000 slave voyages, and in each one an array of variables came into play to shape the Atlantic crossing. These included the exact point of departure, the planned destination, the season of the year, the length of the journey, the supplies of food and fresh water, the temperament of the captain and crew, the condition of the vessel, the health and resolve of the prisoners, the vagaries of piracy and ocean warfare, the ravages of disease, and the challenges of weather and navigation.

A change in weather conditions or in the captain's mood could mean the difference between life and death. The *Emperor,* crossing from Angola to South Carolina in 1755 with 390 Africans aboard, encountered a storm that lasted for a week. By the time the heavy seas subsided, 120 people had died in the hold. The surgeon sailing aboard the brig *Ruby* described the repeated flogging of one African man "for two or three days by both the captain and the chief mate until his body was so lacerated that it was a gory mass of raw flesh."

While the grim details varied, the overall pattern remained the same. Ship after ship, year after year, the attrition continued. The constant rolling of the vessel; the sharp changes in temperature; the crowded, dark, and filthy conditions; and the relentless physical pain and mental anguish took a heavy toll on people already weakened by their earlier ordeals. Pregnant mothers gave birth or miscarried; women were subjected to abuse and rape by the crew. Crews threw the bodies of those who died to the sharks or, worse still, used them as bait to catch sharks, which they fed to the remaining captives.

Saltwater Slaves Arrive in America

For the emaciated survivors of the Atlantic ordeal, two further stages remained in their descent into slavery: the selling process and the so-called time of seasoning. The selling process on American soil varied widely and could drag on for weeks or months. The colonial slave merchant or his agent came aboard soon after the ship dropped anchor, eager to inspect the human cargo. Once he assessed their origins, numbers, and condition, he saw to it that the crew washed and nourished the prisoners, oiled their bodies, and disguised their scars. Then the healthiest were paraded on deck for wealthy buyers or preferred customers. Those not sold immediately were transported to dockside holding pens, where they languished while advertisements circulated announcing their arrival and date of sale. Prospective owners examined and prodded the newcomers. Those purchased were wrenched away from their compatriots and the shipmates with whom they had formed strong links during their shared miseries at sea. Slaves often were auctioned off in groups, or parcels, to ensure sale of the weak along with the strong. Then another journey brought them to the particular slave labor camp where they were fated to work and probably to die.

If slaves arrived in the fall or winter, when spring planting was still a good way off, most newcomers did not begin their forced labor immediately. Instead, they entered a final stage, known as seasoning, which lasted several months or longer. The strangers were distinguished as "saltwater slaves"—in contrast to "country-born slaves" who had grown up in America from birth—and seasoning gave them time to mend physically, regain their strength, and begin absorbing the rudiments of a new language. Inevitably, many suffered from what we would now describe as posttraumatic stress syndrome.

As adults and children recovered from the trauma of the middle passage, they faced a series of additional shocks. Around them they found other Africans who had survived earlier voyages and still spoke their traditional languages. In conversation, they gradually learned where they were and what lay in store for them. They confronted strange foods, unfamiliar tasks, and even new names. They faced alien landscapes and unfamiliar diseases. Worst of all, they encountered a master or his overseer who viewed the seasoning phase as a time to test the spirit of the saltwater newcomers. He made every effort to break the wills of these fresh arrivals and to turn them into compliant bondservants. Repeatedly, the powerful stranger used arbitrary force to demand the slaves' obedience, destroy their hope, and crush any thoughts of resistance.

Survival in a Strange New Land

By 1700 race slavery was accepted throughout the mainland colonies, so Africans found themselves scattered from northern New England to the Carolinas. But their distribution was far from even, for northern locations received only a small portion of the slave traffic to the North American continent. Among roughly 247,000 slaves in the colonies in 1750, only 30,000 (or 12 percent) resided in the North, where they made up just 5 percent of the overall population from Pennsylvania to New Hampshire. More than one-third of these northerners (11,000) lived in the colony of New York, where they made up as much as 14 percent of the inhabitants. All the rest of the people of African descent in North America— some 217,000 men, women, and children by the mid-eighteenth century—lived and worked in the Chesapeake region and the lower South. (Fewer than 5000 of these black southerners resided in French Louisiana.)

African Rice Growers in South Carolina

Throughout the eighteenth century, by far the most North American slaves lived in Virginia or Maryland: 150,000 African Americans by 1750. But the highest *proportion* of enslaved workers lived in South Carolina, where Africans began outnumbering Europeans as early as 1708. By 1750 this black majority (40,000 people) constituted more than 60 percent of the colony's population. Almost all had arrived through the deepwater port of Charleston. Sullivan's Island, near the entrance to the harbor, with its so-called pest house to quarantine incoming slaves and reduce the spread of shipborne disease, has been called the Ellis Island of black America.

What explains the emergence of South Carolina's slave concentration? For one thing, the colony was closer than Virginia to Africa and to the Caribbean. Moreover, it had been founded in 1670, just as the English were embracing plantation slavery and the African trade. Indeed, some of the colony's original proprietors had a stake in the Royal African Company. Also, some of Carolina's influential early settlers came directly from Barbados, bringing enslaved Africans and planter ambitions with them.

In the earliest days of colonization in South Carolina, however, workers of any kind were few in number. The colonists lacked sufficient labor to clear coastal forests and plant crops. Instead, they let their cattle and pigs run wild. With easy foraging and warm winters, the animals reproduced rapidly. The settlers slaughtered them and shipped their meat to the

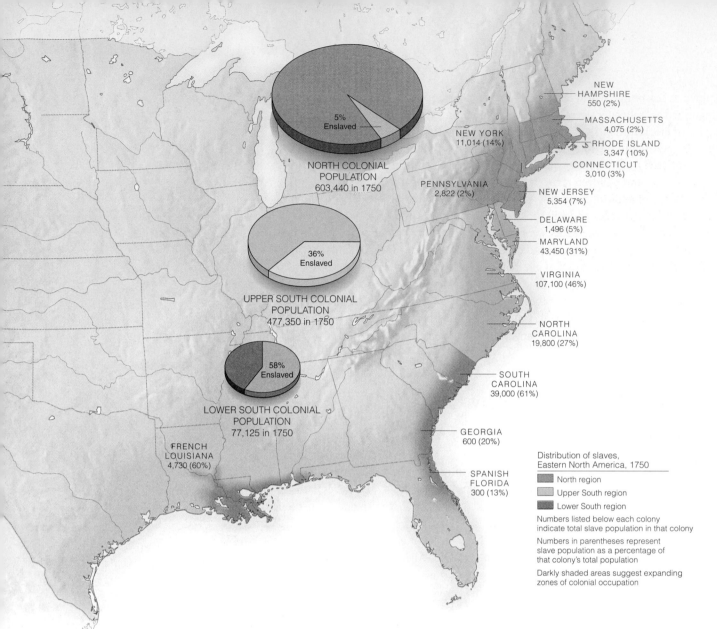

NEW
HAMPSHIRE
550 (2%)

MASSACHUSETTS
4,075 (2%)

RHODE ISLAND
3,347 (10%)

CONNECTICUT
3,010 (3%)

NEW YORK
11,014 (14%)

PENNSYLVANIA
2,822 (2%)

NEW JERSEY
5,354 (7%)

DELAWARE
1,496 (5%)

MARYLAND
43,450 (31%)

VIRGINIA
107,100 (46%)

NORTH
CAROLINA
19,800 (27%)

SOUTH
CAROLINA
39,000 (61%)

GEORGIA
600 (20%)

SPANISH
FLORIDA
300 (13%)

FRENCH
LOUISIANA
4,730 (60%)

NORTH COLONIAL POPULATION
603,440 in 1750
5% Enslaved

UPPER SOUTH COLONIAL POPULATION
477,350 in 1750
36% Enslaved

LOWER SOUTH COLONIAL POPULATION
77,125 in 1750
58% Enslaved

Distribution of slaves,
Eastern North America, 1750

- North region
- Upper South region
- Lower South region

Numbers listed below each colony
indicate total slave population in that colony

Numbers in parentheses represent
slave population as a percentage of
that colony's total population

Darkly shaded areas suggest expanding
zones of colonial occupation

■ **MAP 4.3**

ENSLAVED PEOPLE LIVING IN NORTH AMERICA IN 1750: DISTRIBUTION BY COLONY, PERCENTAGE OF TOTAL POPULATION By 1750 nearly a quarter of a million people lived as slaves in eastern North America—more than 21 percent of the colonial population. Almost all were Africans or the descendants of Africans, along with a few thousand Native American and mixed-race slaves. In the North, slaves made up a small fraction of a large population. By far the greatest number of slaves lived in the Chesapeake area, where they made up more than a third of the total population. Enslaved people were less numerous but much more concentrated in the lower South, making up a clear majority of the overall inhabitants. White settlers had already smuggled several hundred slaves into the fledgling colony of Georgia, even though the exploitation of slave labor did not become legal there until 1751.

Caribbean, along with firewood for boiling sugar cane and barrels for transporting sugar. Ship captains also carried enslaved Native Americans to the West Indies and brought back African slaves.

The new arrivals understood South Carolina's subtropical climate, with its alligators and palmetto trees, better than their European owners did. Many of these enslaved newcomers were already familiar with keeping cattle. Others, obliged to feed themselves, began growing rice in the fertile swamplands just as they had in West Africa. Slave owners quickly realized that this plant, unfamiliar to much of northern Europe, held the answer to their search for a profitable staple crop. Soon, people who had tended their own irrigated rice crops near the Gambia River were obliged to clear cypress swamps along the Ashley and Cooper rivers to grow rice for someone else. Women who had prepared small portions of rice daily for their families in West Africa—pounding the grains with a wooden pestle to remove the husks, then tossing them in a broad, flat basket to winnow away the chaff—now had to process vast quantities of rice for export.

Before long, people in England had developed a taste for rice pudding, and London merchants were shipping tons of Carolina rice to other European countries, where it proved a cheap grain for feeding soldiers, orphans, and peasants. By the middle of the eighteenth centruy, South Carolina's white minority had the most favorable trade balance of any mainland colonists. Their fortunes improved even more when indigo, another African crop, joined rice as a profitable export commodity. Outnumbered by their enslaved workers, South Carolina's landowners passed strict Negro Acts patterned on those of the Caribbean. Legislation prohibited slaves from carrying guns, meeting in groups, raising livestock, or traveling without a pass. Statutes controlled everything from how they dressed to when they shoveled the dung off of Charleston streets. Everywhere, mounted patrols enforced the regulations with brutal severity.

Patterns of Resistance

In South Carolina and elsewhere, enslaved African Americans pushed against the narrow boundaries of their lives. Like any other imprisoned population, they pressed steadily for small indulgences. Then they worked, individually and collectively, to turn occasional concessions into customary rights. And like others held prisoner, they used every possible means to negotiate slivers of freedom, including spreading rumors, refusing to work, breaking tools, feigning illness, and threatening violence. In response, their owners tried to divide them in order to control them. Masters rewarded workers who acted obedient and diligent or who informed on fellow slaves. They imposed harsh punishments—whipping, mutilation, sale, or death—on those suspected of taking food, sowing dissent, or plotting revolt. And they encouraged the formation of black families, not only to gain another generation of laborers at no cost but also to create the emotional ties that they knew would hold individuals in check for fear of reprisals against loved ones.

Owners confined residents in the slave labor camps with curfews and pass systems and kept them from learning to read and from communicating freely with neighbors and relatives. They also refused to allow any impartial system for expressing grievances or appealing arbitrary punishments. Faced with such steep odds, many slaves submitted to the deadening routine of the prison camp to survive. But others resorted to diverse strategies to improve their situation or undermine their masters' dominance. Running away, even for a brief period, provided relief from forced work and deprived owners of the labor they depended on. Frequent newspaper advertisements regarding runaways reveal that thousands risked their lives, alone or in groups, in attempts to escape. Because arson created serious damage and was difficult to detect, some slaves burned down barns at harvest time. Others succeeded in killing their masters or overseers. Such acts of pent-up rage usually proved suicidal, but they also confirmed slave owners' worst fears. Aware that Africans knew how to communicate with one another with drums and could concoct poisons from herbs, white planters became even more fearful of blacks.

Above all, the prospect of open rebellion kept burning in the minds of prisoners and jailers alike. In light of this constant tension, it is hard to untangle episodes of white paranoia from incidents of actual revolt. Many innocent slaves were falsely accused. But countless others did discuss plans for resistance, and a few freedom fighters avoided detection or betrayal long enough to launch serious uprisings. Word of one upheaval, real or imagined, could spark others.

An early wave of slave unrest erupted in the dozen years after 1710, highlighted by violence in New York City in the spring of 1712. The leaders of the conspiracy were "Coromantee," or

■ **FIGURE 4.2**
REWARD NOTICES FOR ESCAPED SLAVES, PRINTED IN THE *PENNSYLVANIA GAZETTE*
The Philadelphia newspaper published more than 1000 such advertisements between 1728 and 1790. They provide historians with detailed information about the lives of slaves.

June 27, 1734

RUN away on Thursday last from the House of John Richardson, Shoemaker, a new Negroe Girl about 16 or 18 Years of Age, short Stature, branded upon the Breast N R mark'd round the Neck with three Rows like Beads, suppos'd to be a Whedaw Negroe; had on a check'd Cotten Petticoat and a Seersucker Jacket. Her Name is Rose.
    Whosoever takes up said Negroe, and brings her to John Richardson aforesaid, or B. Franklin Printer, shall have Twenty Shillings Reward and reasonable Charges paid by   John Richardson.

November 2, 1749

Philadelphia, November 2, 1749.
RUN away three weeks ago, from Marcus Kuhl, of Philadelphia, baker, a Negroe man, named Scipio, wears a blue broad cloth coat, or a black ditto, old shoes, and stockings, of a short stature, plays on the banjou, and sings with it, speaks but indifferent English. Whoever takes up and secures said slave, so that his master may have him again, shall have Fifteen Shillings reward, and reasonable charges, paid by
                                MARCUS KUHL.

October 26, 1758

Philadelphia, October 24, 1758
RUN away, on the 21st Instant, from Robert Wakely, of this City, a Negro Woman, named Anne, about 18 or 20 Years of Age, is short and well set, and had on a blue Jacket and Petticoat, Ozenbrigs Apron, and an old Cap, but no Shoes or Stockings. Also run away, at the same Time, a Negroe Man, named Frank, belonging to Alexander Collay, of Whitemarsh, about 30 or 35 Years of Age, is a slender middle sized Fellow, and had on a new Wool Hat, Bearskin light coloured Coat, a Snuff coloured Jacket, without Sleeves, a striped Shirt, Leather Breeches, blue Stockings and good Shoes. They are Man and Wife, and supposed to be gone together. Whoever takes up said Negroes, and brings them to either of the Subscribers, shall have fifty Shillings Reward for both, or if put into the next Goal where taken up Forty Shillings, paid by
                ROBERT WAKELY, or ALEXANDER COLLAY.

Akan people from Africa's Gold Coast region. Several dozen enslaved Africans and Indians, determined to obtain their freedom and kill all the whites in the town, set fire to a building. As citizens rushed to put out the blaze, the rebels attacked them with guns, clubs, pistols, staves, and axes, killing eight and wounding more. When the militia finally captured the insurgents, six of them committed suicide. Authorities condemned 21 others and executed 18. They burned several at the stake, hanged others, and left their bodies on display. Eager to curtail slavery following such unrest, the governor called for "the Importation of White Servants." New York's elected colonial assembly, expressing growing racial hatred, chastised free blacks and prohibited freed slaves from owning property.

A Wave of Rebellion

A second wave of black resistance swept the mainland colonies after 1730, fueled by the largest influx of Africans to date. In Louisiana, the French had moved their capital to the new town of New Orleans on the Mississippi River (1722) and had joined their Choctaw allies in a devastating war to crush the Natchez Indians and seize their lands (1729–1731). As French landowners staked out riverfront plantations, they also imported African slaves. The several thousand black workers soon outnumbered European settlers. Fearful of attack, the whites broke up two presumed slave plots in 1731. One involved a scheme to rebel while Catholic colonists attended a midnight mass on Christmas.

Another apparent plot was revealed by the careless boast of a black servant woman in New Orleans. It included several hundred Bambara newcomers from Senegal who were determined to massacre whites, enslave other Africans, and take control of the region. The leader among eight captured plotters was a man known as Samba Bambara. A former interpreter at Galam on the Senegal River, Bambara had recently lost that post and been deported to Louisiana. There, he became a trusted slave, supervising workers owned by the French Company of the Indies. When torture by fire failed to force confessions from the captives, officials hanged the servant woman and broke Bambara and half a dozen other men on the wheel.

The largest slave uprising in colonial North America broke out in 1739 near the Stono River, 20 miles southwest of Charleston. Several factors fueled the Stono Rebellion. By 1739, blacks exceeded whites nearly two to one among South Carolina's 56,000 people. The proportion of recently imported slaves had reached an all-time high. In addition, working conditions had worsened steadily as rice production expanded. Moreover, for several decades the Spanish in Florida had been luring slaves from South Carolina, knowing that the promise of freedom might destabilize Carolina's profitable slave regime. More than a hundred fugitives had escaped to Florida by 1738, when Florida's governor formed them into a free black militia company at St. Augustine. Hoping to win more defections, he allowed 38 African American households to settle north of the city and build a small fortress—Fort Mose.

Courtesy, Florida Museum of Natural History Photo by James Quine

■ **Archaeologists have recently excavated the site of Fort Mose, near St. Augustine, Florida. Dozens of slaves who escaped from South Carolina received their freedom from the Spanish and established an outpost there in the 1730s.**

Meanwhile, the wider commercial rivalries of the British and Spanish continued elsewhere, leading to open warfare between the two Atlantic empires in 1739. The slave uprising at Stono erupted just after word reached Charleston that war had broken out between Spain and Britain. Perhaps this was mere coincidence. Or perhaps the news sparked hopes among slaves that Carolina authorities would be preoccupied and vulnerable, or that Spanish neighbors would assist a revolt in the colony. Other factors may also have influenced the rebels' timing. An epidemic in Charleston had disrupted public activities, and a new Security Act requiring all white men to carry arms to church was to take effect before the end of September.

Early on Sunday, September 9, 1739, 20 slaves from a work crew near the Stono River broke into a local store. There they seized weapons and executed the owners. Led by a man named Jemmy, they raised a banner and marched south, beating drums and shouting "Liberty!" The insurgents burned selected plantations, killed a score of whites, and gathered more than 50 new recruits. But armed colonists overtook them near the Edisto River and blocked their escape to St. Augustine. Dozens of rebels died in the ensuing battle. In the next two days militia and hired Indians killed 20 more and captured an additional 40 people, whom they immediately shot or hanged.

Yet even these reprisals could not quell black hopes. In June 1740 several hundred slaves plotted to storm Charleston and take arms from a warehouse. However, a comrade revealed the plan. According to a report, "The next day fifty of them were seized, and these were hanged, ten a day, to intimidate the other negroes." In November, a great fire of suspicious origin consumed much of Charleston.

Fire also played a role in hysteria that broke out in New York City in 1741. Britain's ongoing conflict with Spain (1739–1743) fanned wild Protestant fears that Jesuit spies and Catholic slaves planned to burn the major towns in English North America. In March, a blaze consumed the residence of New York's governor and a local fort. Other fires soon focused suspicions on a white couple, John and Sarah Hughson, who had often entertained blacks at their alehouse. The Hughsons—thought to fence stolen goods for a black crime ring, the Geneva Boys— were accused of inciting working-class unrest. In exchange for her freedom, Mary Barton, a 16-year-old Irish indentured servant at the Hughsons' tavern, testified that she had overheard the planning of an elaborate "popish plot."

In a gruesome spiral of arrests and executions, New York authorities put to death 34 people, including 4 whites, and banished 72 blacks. On one hand, the debacle recalled the Salem witch trials, as a fearful community engaged in judicial proceedings and killings on the basis of rumors and accusations. On the other hand, the New York Slave Plot recalled Bacon's Rebellion, for evidence emerged of cooperation between impoverished blacks and whites eager to see a redistribution of property. According to his accusers, a slave named Cuffee had often observed that "a great many people had too much, and others too little." He predicted that soon his master "should have less, and that he (Cuffee) should have more." Instead, he was burned at the stake.

The Transformation Completed

Word of the Stono Rebellion and the New York Slave Plot, plus rumors of uprisings in the West Indies, brought renewed hope to enslaved Americans and renewed fear to their captors. The mechanisms for extorting labor from tens of thousands of people were firmly in place. But to maintain this repressive system, local governments and the white population had to keep up constant vigilance and continually threaten blacks. In South Carolina, officials displayed the heads of slain rebels on poles, stepped up night patrols, and passed an even harsher Negro Law.

Some colonists saw slavery as too morally degrading and physically dangerous to maintain, but others found it too rewarding to give up. As in later generations, powerful supporters of the institution suggested modifications in response to calls for outright abolition. For example, white officials in Charleston imposed a heavy duty on new African arrivals for several years, hoping to increase the ratio of white to black slaves in the lowcountry of coastal South Carolina. They also opened a school to provide rudimentary education to a handful of obedient black Christians. At a time of growing humanitarian concerns in Enlightenment Europe, it took great effort to maintain the rationale for enslavement in America. But free people who

"Releese Us out of This Cruell Bondegg"

As researchers pay increasing attention to African bondage in the colonial era, new pieces of evidence continue to appear. This appeal, written in Virginia in 1723 by a mulatto Christian slave, was rediscovered in a London archive in the 1990s and transcribed by historian Thomas Ingersoll. It is addressed to Edward Gibson, the newly appointed bishop of London, whose position gave him religious oversight over all the Anglican parishes in England's American colonies, including Virginia. Gibson, through his pamphlets, had shown an interest in the Christianization of enslaved Africans, but like many contemporary church leaders, he had less interest in the liberation of slaves. This heartfelt document, prepared with great labor and at enormous risk, was simply filed away with the bishop's vast correspondence. It never received a response or prompted any further inquiry into conditions in Virginia.

George Morland, *Traite Des Negres*, 1790–91. Colonial Williamsburg Foundation

When abolition of the slave trade finally became a public issue in England in the 1780s, British artists painted scenes criticizing the traffic. But two generations earlier, pleas from New World slaves aroused no response, even from the Bishop of London, who supervised the Church of England in the American colonies.

August the forth 1723
    to the Right Raverrand father in god my Lord arch Bishop of Lonnd. . . .
    this coms to sattesfie your honour that there is in this Land of verJennia a Sort of people that is Calld molatters which are Baptised and brouaht up in the way of the Christian faith and followes the ways and Rulles of the Chrch of England and sum of them has white fathars and sum white mothers and there is in this Land a Law or act which keeps and makes them and there seed Slaves forever. . . .
    wee your humbell and poore partishinners doo begg Sir your aid and assisttancce in this one thing . . . which is that your hon-our will by the help of our Sufvering [i.e., sovereign] Lord King George and the Rest of the Rullers will Releese us out of this Cruell Bondegg. . . . /and here it is to bee notd that one brother is a Slave to another and one Sister to an othe which is quite out of the way and as for mee my selfe I am my brothers Slave but my name is Secrett/
    wee are commandded to keep holey the Sabbath day and wee doo hardly know when it comes for our task mastrs are has hard with us as the Egypttions was with the Chilldann of Issarall. . . . wee are kept out of the Church and matrimony is deenied us and to be plain they doo Look no more upon us then if wee ware dogs which I hope when these Strange lines comes to your Lord Ships hands will be Looket in to. . . .
    And Sir wee your humble per-ticners do humblly beg . . . that our childarn may be broatt up in the way of the Christtian faith and our desire is that they may be Larnd the Lords prayer the creed and the ten commandements and that they may appeare Every Lord's day att Church before the Curatt to bee Exammond for our desire is that godllines Shoulld abbound amongs us and wee desire that our Childarn be putt to Scool and Larnd to Reed through the Bybell
    My Riting is vary bad. . . . I am but a poore Slave that writt itt and has no other time butt Sunday and hardly that att Sumtimes. . . . wee dare nott Subscribe any mans name to this for feare of our mas-ters for if they knew that wee have Sent home to your honour wee Should goo neare to Swing upon the gallass tree. ∎

Source: Thomas N. Ingersoll, "'Releese Us out of This Cruell Bondegg': An Appeal from Virginia in 1723," *William and Mary Quarterly,* Third Series, 51 (October 1994):776–782.

questioned the institution met stiff resistance from those with vested interests, as the experience of the new colony of Georgia demonstrates.

Voices of Dissent

As race-based slavery expanded numerically and geographically, white colonists treated the continuing presence of free blacks as a contradiction and a threat. As early as 1691, the Virginia assembly passed an act restricting manumissions (grants of individual freedom by masters) because "great inconvenience may happen to this country by setting of negroes and mulattoes free." According to the act, such people fanned hopes of freedom among enslaved blacks by their mere presence. Since most free blacks were quite poor, they were often accused of having links to the slave community and trafficking in stolen goods. Besides, when they grew old and infirm, their care at public expense could constitute "a charge upon the country." By 1723, additional Virginia statutes prevented free people of color from voting, taxed them unfairly, and prevented them from owning or carrying firearms. Lawmakers went on to prohibit manumissions altogether, except when the governor rewarded "meritorious service," such as informing against other enslaved workers.

While the southern slave colonies labored to intimidate, divide, and reduce their free black communities, free blacks in the North faced growing discrimination in their efforts to hold jobs, buy land, obtain credit, move freely, and take part in civic life. Northern slave populations, though small in comparison to those in the South, were growing steadily. As the North's involvement in the Atlantic slave trade expanded, its economic and legal commitment to race slavery increased. Rhode Island's slave ranks jumped from 500 in 1720 to more than 3000 in 1750. Everywhere, new laws made manumission more difficult and African American survival more precarious. In Philadelphia, only 90 slaves gained their freedom between 1698 and 1765. Of the few hundred free blacks living in Boston in 1742, 110 resided in the church-supported almshouse and another 36 in the public workhouse. Only in the century after 1760 did northern free black communities gain the numerical and social strength to offer effective opposition to enslavement.

Whereas free blacks lacked the means to oppose slavery, prominent white Christians lacked the will. Even in Massachusetts, where religion remained a dominant force at the turn of the century and the number of slaves had scarcely reached 1000 people, many leaders already owned black servants. They used them more to flaunt their prosperity than to expand their wealth. When Boston merchants purchased black attendants to serve as coachmen, few citizens objected.

The protests that did appear were ambivalent at best. In 1700 Judge Samuel Sewell questioned African enslavement in a tract titled *The Selling of Joseph*. But he also revealed his sense of superiority and his skepticism that blacks could play a part in "the Peopling of the Land." African Americans, Sewell commented, "can seldom use their freedom well; yet their continual aspiring after their forbidden Liberty, renders them unwilling servants." Reverend Cotton Mather, a slave owner who once berated Sewell as one who "pleaded much for Negroes," was even more ambivalent. In *The Negro Christianized* (1706), the influential Puritan stressed that conversion and Christian instruction, far from earning African slaves their freedom, would make them into "better servants."

The conversion and instruction of slaves, rather than the abolition of slavery, also became a mission for pious English philanthropist Thomas Bray, a well-to-do Anglican committed to religious education and prison reform. In 1699, Bray founded the Society for Promoting Christian Knowledge to organize libraries in the fledgling colonies. The following year, the bishop of London sent Bray to Maryland. He soon returned to England with a desire to train better ministers and to spread the Anglican faith in America among Europeans, Indians, and Africans. In 1701 Bray established the Society for the Propagation of the Gospel in Foreign Parts (SPG).

The SPG strengthened the Church of England abroad in the eighteenth century by providing dozens of ministers to serve in the colonies. But this improved foothold came at a steep price. Southern planters made SPG ministers agree that any promise they offered to slaves regarding heavenly salvation would not include hints of earthly freedom. With few exceptions, the Anglican clergy gave in, strengthening religious support of race slavery. In 1723 a heartfelt petition from a mulatto slave to the bishop of London, in which the author protested "Cruell Bondegg" in Virginia, went unanswered. That same year, Bray set up a trust of "Associates" to carry on his work. With limited success, they focused on converting blacks in the British plantation colonies. By the 1730s, only a few whites in Europe or America dared to press publicly for an end to slavery.

Christian Priber, who arrived in the South in 1735, was one such activist. The idealistic German hoped to start a utopian community in southern Appalachia. But his radical proposal for a multiracial "Paradise" uniting Indians, Africans, and Europeans posed a huge threat to South Carolina authorities. "He enumerates many whimsical Privileges and natural Rights, as he calls them, which his citizens are to be entitled to," wrote a scornful detractor, "particularly dissolving Marriages and allowing Community of Women and all kinds of Licentiousness." Worst of all, according to the coastal elite, this egalitarian haven at the "Foot of the Mountains among the Cherokees" was to be "a City of Refuge for all Criminals, Debtors, and Slaves who would fly thither from [the] Justice of their Masters." Priber's brief career as a social agitator challenging the status quo ended in 1743, when he was arrested and brought to jail in Charleston. He died—or was killed—before his case could be heard in court.

At the same time, a New Jersey tailor and bookkeeper named John Woolman posed a less defiant but more enduring threat to race slavery. In 1743, at age 23, this shy Quaker began to question his role in writing out bills of sale when his fellow Quakers purchased slaves. It struck him forcefully that "to live in ease and plenty by the toil of those whom violence and cruelty have put in our power" was clearly not "consistent with Christianity or common justice." Woolman traveled widely to Quaker meetings, north and south, pressing an issue that most Quakers preferred to ignore. "The Colour of a Man avails nothing," Woolman insisted, "in Matters of Right and Equity." When he drafted *Some Considerations on the Keeping of Negroes* (1754), members of the Quaker Yearly Meeting in Philadelphia published his booklet and circulated it widely in several editions. Four years later, led by Anthony Benezet, this group outlawed slaveholding among its local members. They set a precedent that many Quakers followed in the next generation, and they challenged other denominations to do the same.

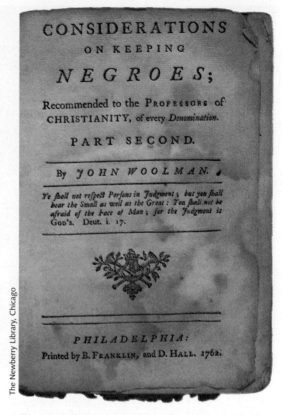

The Newberry Library, Chicago

■ **Pennsylvania Quaker John Woolman published a pioneering tract against slavery in 1754. He traveled widely to oppose the institution, and he encouraged people not to use products created by enslaved labor. Benjamin Franklin published the 1762 edition.**

Oglethorpe's Antislavery Experiment

The most sustained early challenge to the slavery system in the American South came in the Georgia colony. In 1732 a group of well-connected London proprietors (known as trustees) obtained a 20-year charter for the region between English South Carolina and Spanish Florida. Ten of the 21 initial trustees were members of Parliament. They included James Oglethorpe, who had recently organized and chaired a "committee on jails" to investigate the condition of debtors in English prisons. The trustees foresaw three related purposes—charitable, commercial, and military—for their experimental colony, which they named after King George II. Georgia would provide a haven for England's worthy poor, selected members of the neediest classes who could be transported across the Atlantic and settled on small farms. These grateful newcomers would

William Hogarth, To Inquire Into the State of the Gaols of This Kingdom. The National Portrait Gallery, London

■ In 1729, James Oglethorpe (seated, right front) chaired a Parliamentary committee exposing the harsh conditions in English jails. When William Hogarth portrayed the committee's visit to Fleet Street Prison, the artist showed Oglethorpe's concern for a dark-skinned prisoner, a hint of Oglethorpe's future opposition to slavery in Georgia.

then produce warm weather commodities—olives, grapes, silk—to support the empire. And their prosperity would create a growing market for English goods. Finally, their presence would provide a military buffer to protect South Carolina from further warfare with the Yamasee and Creek Indians and from possible invasion by the Spanish in St. Augustine.

With Oglethorpe as their governor, an initial boatload of 114 settlers arrived in 1733 and began building a capital at Savannah. By 1741 the town, located on a bluff 15 miles up the Savannah River, boasted more than 140 houses. It also had a wharf, a jail, a courthouse (which doubled as a church), and a building for receiving delegations of neighboring Indians. By then, more than a thousand needy English, plus 800 German, Swiss, and Austrian Protestants, had journeyed to Georgia at the trustees' expense. Another thousand immigrants had paid their own way. Like earlier colonizers, Georgia's first arrivals had trouble adjusting to a strange environment. Alligators, rattlesnakes, and hurricanes tested their resolve. Tension over governance only deepened their discouragement.

The idealistic trustees in London declined to accumulate property and profits for themselves in the colony, but they felt justified in controlling every aspect of Georgia's development. For example, they knew that gin was becoming a source of debt and disruption in Europe and that rum and brandy sold by traders was poisoning colonial relations with southeastern Indians. So in 1735 they outlawed the use of every "kind of Spirits or Strong Waters" while still allowing consumption of wine and beer. Georgia's early experiment with prohibition of hard liquor proved difficult to implement, and officials quietly stopped enforcing the law in 1742.

Other efforts at control from above went further. The trustees refused to set up a legislature or to let settlers buy and sell land. Instead, they gave 50 acres to each family they sent over, including a house lot in town to ensure defense for each new village. But they parceled out land with little regard for variations in soil fertility. They also stipulated that owners could pass land on to sons only. Denying daughters the right to inherit, the trustees reasoned, would prevent men from creating large estates simply by marrying women who were likely to inherit big tracts of land. In a further effort to prevent the concentrations of wealth that they saw developing in other colonies, the trustees said that no one could own more than 500 acres. Prohibiting massive estates would allow for thicker settlement and therefore greater manpower to defend the colony militarily.

But the most important prohibition, by far, involved slavery. Oglethorpe began his career as a deputy governor of the Royal African Company, but he died in 1785 opposing the slave trade. His sojourn in Georgia turned him against slavery. In neighboring South Carolina, he saw first-hand how the practice degraded African lives, undermined the morals of Europeans, and laid that colony open to threats of revolt and invasion. More friendly to Indians than to African Americans, Oglethorpe persuaded the trustees to create a free white colony. Specifically, he convinced them to enact a law in 1735 that prohibited slavery and also excluded free blacks. He believed that this mandate would protect Georgia from the corruptions of enslavement while also making it easier to apprehend black runaways heading to Florida from South Carolina.

The Stono Rebellion, and the outbreak of war between England and Spain in 1739, strengthened Oglethorpe's belief that slavery undermined the security of the English colonies by creating internal enemies who would support any foreign attackers. He saw further evidence in 1740, when he failed in a wartime attempt to capture St. Augustine from Spain. Unable to take the Florida stronghold, the governor managed to seize neighboring Fort Mose, which had been erected by anti-English slaves who had escaped from Carolina. But a Spanish force regained the fort, relying heavily on Indian and African American fighters to win a fierce dawn battle. Oglethorpe's army withdrew in disarray, but he had seen the intensity with which ex-slaves would fight the English, their former masters.

The next year, fearing a counterattack, Oglethorpe issued a warning to imperial officials. He predicted that if Spanish soldiers captured Georgia, a colony inhabited by "white

■ Savannah, the capital of Oglethorpe's Georgia, was one year old when this view was sketched in 1734. The following year, Georgia's trustees officially outlawed slavery, creating a sharp contrast with the other British colonies in North America, especially neighboring South Carolina on the opposite bank of the Savannah River.

■ **MAP 4.4**
ENGLISH–SPANISH COMPETITION AND THE EXPANSION OF SLAVERY INTO GEORGIA The Spanish and the British had competing land claims along the southeast coast after 1670. Creation of the Georgia colony in 1732 intensified the rivalry. The Spanish in Florida offered freedom to any slaves who escaped from South Carolina to St. Augustine, sparking the Stono Revolt in 1739. During the war between Britain and Spain (1739–1743) Georgians defeated the Spanish at Bloody Marsh and secured the disputed "Sea Island" region for the British. Within a decade, slavery became legal in Georgia, and scores of new labor camps appeared between the Savannah and the St. Mary's River, producing rice for export.

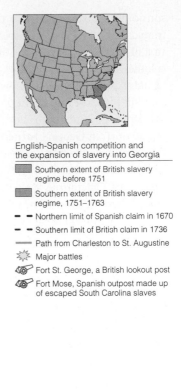

Protestants and no Negroes," they would then send agents to infiltrate the vulnerable colonies farther north and stir black rebellion. The Spanish, he argued, understood that the thousands of embittered slaves "would be either Recruits to an Enemy or Plunder for them." No sooner had he written his wartime prediction in 1741 than suspicious fires broke out in New York and Charleston.

The End of Equality in Georgia

As Britain's war with Spain continued, few whites could deny the Georgia governor's assertion that slavery elsewhere in British America was a source of internal weakness and strategic danger. In 1742, as the governor had predicted, Spain pushed from Florida into Georgia with an eye toward destabilizing the colonies farther north. Oglethorpe's troops repulsed the invading Spanish force in the crucial Battle at Bloody Marsh on St. Simon's Island. The victory reduced the immediate threat to Britain's North American colonies, especially neighboring South Carolina, where Oglethorpe and his idealistic policies had numerous powerful opponents. These opponents now joined a group of so-called Malcontents in Savannah to question Georgia's continued prohibition against slavery. When this coalition challenged the trustees' antislavery stance, it prompted the first protracted North American debate about enslavement. It dragged on for more than a decade.

In the face of numerous ills—including a sickly climate, poor soil, restrictive land policies, and lack of representative government—a well-organized Georgia faction argued that slavery was the one thing needed for the colony to prosper, since it would provide profits to slaveowners regardless of Georgia's many drawbacks. Not everyone agreed. In 1739 Scottish Highlanders living at Darien on the Altamaha River had contacted Oglethorpe to lay out their practical arguments against importing Africans. Their petition expressed shock "that any Race of Mankind, and their Posterity, Should be sentenced to perpetual slavery." Immigrants from Salzburg, Germany, residing at Ebenezer on the Savannah River drafted a similar statement. But Georgia's Malcontents pushed back. These several dozen English and Lowland Scot adventurers, led by the disgruntled son of a colonial official, wrote letters and circulated petitions demanding the right to import slaves. They drew encouragement and support from powerful merchant-planters in South Carolina. Eager to expand their trade in slaves from Africa and to open up new lands for profitable plantations, these well-to-do Carolinians dreamed of extending their successful rice operations into coastal Georgia.

Oglethorpe warned that the proslavery lobby, hungry to create large estates, seemed bent on "destroying the Agrarian Equality" envisioned in Georgia's initial plan. But the colony's trustees in London grew less unified, committed, and informed over time. Eventually, the persistent efforts of the proslavery pamphleteers bore fruit. In 1750 the trustees gave in on the matter of land titles. They allowed acreage to be bought and sold freely in any amount, which opened the door for the creation of large plantations. From there, it was just one more step to allowing slavery. The trustees finally gave in on the question of bondage, letting Georgians exploit slaves after January 1, 1751. The 1750 law permitting slavery made futile gestures to ensure kind treatment and Christian education for slaves, but the dam had broken. Hundreds of slave-owning South Carolinians streamed across the Savannah River to invest in land. In 1752 the trustees disbanded, their patent expiring, their vision undone. By 1754 Georgia had become a royal colony.

Some argued that Georgia should simply be incorporated into South Carolina. In a sense it was: slave labor camps producing rice and indigo for export soon dotted the lowcountry on both sides of the Savannah River. Georgia's assembly passed a harsh slave code in 1755, based on South Carolina's. Two years later, it legislated a system of patrols to keep the brutal new regime in place. Georgia's effort to counter race slavery in North America had failed, a case of too little too late. After holding out for nearly two decades, the colony fell victim to the same divisive institution that had already taken root more slowly elsewhere along the Atlantic seaboard.

Conclusion

Two final observations provide a wider Atlantic context regarding the people swept up in the North American portion of the gigantic African traffic. First, their odyssey began comparatively late, for this dimension of the trade did not expand rapidly until after the 1670s. In the broader history of North American immigration, of course, their forced migration from Africa came relatively early. Indeed, the proportion of blacks in the colonial population on the eve of the American Revolution (over 20 percent) was higher than it has ever been in the United States since then. But in terms of the entire African slave diaspora, or dispersion, the influx to English North America occurred long after the traffic to Mexico, Brazil, and the Caribbean was well established.

Second, even at its height, the North American trade remained marginal in relation to the wider Atlantic commerce in African labor. For example, whereas roughly 50,000 enslaved men and women reached all the docks of North America between 1721 and 1740, the small West Indian islands of English Barbados and French Guadeloupe *each* received more than 53,000 Africans during the same period. In the next two decades, while Britain's mainland colonies purchased just over 100,000 Africans, Caribbean Islands such as English Jamaica (120,000) and French Saint Domingue (159,000) absorbed many more slaves.

During this single 40-year span (1721–1760), Brazil bought 667,000 African workers—more than would reach North America during the entire slave trade. All told, scholars currently estimate that some 650,000 Africans were brought to North America over several centuries. They represented roughly 6 percent of the total Atlantic commerce in enslaved people. Still, the number of mainland slaves expanded from scarcely 7000 in 1680 to nearly 29,000 in 1700 and to more than 70,000 in 1720. Half a century later in 1770, because of importation and natural increase, 470,000 individuals were confined to enslavement from New Hampshire to Louisiana.

A century had passed since Elizabeth Key's generation saw the terrible transformation begin. Relative openness had given way to systematic oppression, and slavery's corrosive effects were felt at every level of society. An English visitor to the South in 1759 found provincial planters "vain and imperious," subject "to many errors and prejudices, especially in regard to Indians and Negroes, whom they scarcely consider as of the human species." It took another century before pressures developed that could unseat race slavery, sanctioned by law, as a dominant institution in the land.

Sites to Visit

Colonial Williamsburg

More than half the residents of colonial Williamsburg were black. Increasingly, their lives are being explored and discussed at this reconstructed historic town in tidewater Virginia. The Slave Quarters at nearby Carter's Grove Plantation contain four cabins and provide an interpretation of African American life before the Revolution.

Fort Mose
www.fortmose.org/

Under Spanish protection, slaves who had escaped from colonial South Carolina built Gracia Real de Santa Teresa de Mose, or Fort Mose, on the eastern edge of a marsh, 2 miles north of St. Augustine, Florida. Archaeologists rediscovered the site of this early free black community, and it is being made into an exhibition area.

Africans in America
www.pbs.org/wgbh/aia/home.html

This four-part television series prepared for PBS provides an overview of slavery from its beginnings to the end of the Civil War. Part One deals with "The Terrible Transformation," offering resources and insights on the era from 1450 to 1750.

SeacoastNH.com

Billed as "the biggest website for America's smallest seacoast," this site contains an excellent section on New Hampshire's black history, which stretches back more than 350 years. Links connect to the Portsmouth Black Heritage Trail, which leads to two dozen sites in Portsmouth, describing where black New Englanders lived and worked.

Drayton Hall

This National Trust historic site on the Ashley River outside Charleston, South Carolina, features the oldest plantation house in America open to the public, built by Europeans and African Americans at the time of the 1739 Stono Rebellion. The staff has developed a "Gullah Connection" to explore black culture with local schools.

The Cultural Landscape of the Plantation
www.gwu.edu/~folklife/bighouse/intro.html

American studies professor John Michael Vlach has created this online exhibition using images of plantation buildings from the Library of Congress and linking them with the testimonies of former slaves recorded during the 1930s.

Somerset Place

This is just one of many historic plantations across the South steadily improving the ways in which they present the slave experience. Somerset Place is a huge estate created after the American Revolution beside Lake Phelps, in Creswell, North Carolina. The site has reconstructed slave buildings, and it hosts a biannual black homecoming.

Mel Fisher Maritime Museum

This museum in Key West, Florida, has a Traveling Trunk of artifacts relating to the slave ship *Henrietta Marie*, which sank near Key West in 1700. For rental of these materials, go to www.melfisher.org.

Pictorial Images of the Transatlantic Slave Trade
gropius.lib.virginia.edu/SlaveTrade/index.html

This database from the Virginia Foundation for the Humanities and Public Policy contains numerous images relating to the trans-Atlantic slave trade.

For Further Reading

General

Ira Berlin, *Many Thousands Gone: The First Two Centuries of Slavery in North America* (1998).

David Eltis, *The Rise of African Slavery in the Americas* (2000).

A. Leon Higginbotham, Jr., *In the Matter of Color: Race and the American Legal Process, the Colonial Period* (1978).

Evelyn Brooks Higginbotham, *The Harvard Guide to African-American History* (2001).

John Thornton, *Africa and Africans in the Making of the Atlantic World, 1400–1800* (1992).

Peter H. Wood, *Strange New Land: Africans in Colonial America* (2002).

The Descent into Race Slavery

T. H. Breen and Stephen Innes, *"Myne Owne Ground": Race and Freedom on Virginia's Eastern Shore, 1640–1676* (1980).

Kathleen M. Brown, *Good Wives, Nasty Wenches, and Anxious Patriarchs: Gender, Race, and Power in Colonial Virginia* (1996).

Edward Countryman, ed., *How Did American Slavery Begin?* (1999).

Winthrop D. Jordan, *White over Black: American Attitudes Toward the Negro, 1550–1812* (1968).

Edmund S. Morgan, *American Slavery, American Freedom: The Ordeal of Colonial Virginia* (1975).

The Growth of Slave Labor Camps

Madeleine Burnside, *Spirits of the Passage: The Transatlantic Slave Trade in the Seventeenth Century* (1997).

Clifford Dowdey, *The Virginia Dynasties: The Emergence of "King" Carter and the Golden Age* (1969).

Sylvia R. Frey and Betty Wood, *Come Shouting to Zion: African American Protestantism in the American South and British Caribbean to 1830* (1998).

Allan Kulikoff, *Tobacco and Slaves: The Development of Southern Cultures in the Chesapeake, 1680–1800* (1986).

England Enters the Atlantic Slave Trade

Jay Coughtry, *The Notorious Triangle: Rhode Island and the American Slave Trade, 1700–1807* (1981).

Philip D. Curtin, *The Atlantic Slave Trade: A Census* (1969).

Douglas Grant, *The Fortunate Slave: An Illustration of African Slavery in the Early Eighteenth Century* (1968).

Herbert S. Klein, *The Atlantic Slave Trade (New Approaches to the Americas)* (1999).

James A. Rawley, *The Transatlantic Slave Trade: A History* (1981).

James Walvin, *Black Ivory: A History of British Slavery* (1994).

Survival in a Strange New Land

Kathleen Deagan and Darcie MacMahon, *Fort Mose: Colonial America's Black Fortress of Freedom* (1995).

Michael A. Gomez, *Exchanging Our Country Marks: The Transformation of African Identities in the Colonial and Antebellum South* (1998).

Jane Landers, *Black Society in the Spanish Florida* (1999).

Daniel Littlefield, *Rice and Slaves: Ethnicity and the Slave Trade in Colonial South Carolina* (1981).

Philip Morgan, *Slave Counterpoint: Black Culture in the Eighteenth-Century Chesapeake and Lowcountry* (1998).

Peter H. Wood, *Black Majority: Negroes in Colonial South Carolina from 1670 Through the Stono Rebellion* (1974).

The Transformation Completed

Harold E. Davis, *The Fledgling Province: Social and Cultural Life in Colonial Georgia, 1733–1776* (1976).

Gwendolyn Midlo Hall, *Africans in Colonial Louisiana: The Development of Afro-Creole Culture in the Eighteenth Century* (1992).

Kenneth A. Lockridge, *On the Sources of Patriarchal Rage: The Commonplace Books of William Byrd and Thomas Jefferson and the Gendering of Power in the Eighteenth Century* (1992).

Phillips P. Moulton, ed., *The Journal and Major Essays of John Woolman* (1997).

Betty Wood, *Slavery in Colonial Georgia, 1730–1775* (1984).

Online Practice Test

Test your understanding of this chapter with interactive review quizzes at

www.ablongman.com/jonescreatedequal/chapter4

Additional Photo Credits

Page 115: *Voyage Pittoresque dans le Bresil*, Rugendas plate 10, 2nd part. The Newberry Library, Chicago
Page 116: The British Museum, Museum of Mankind-The Ethnology Collection
Page 129: Courtesy, Antiquarian & Landmarks Society
Page 133: Library of Congress
Page 135: Chicago Historical Society, ICHi-x.1354

CHAPTER 5

An American Babel, 1713–1763

John Greenwood, *Portrait of John Clarke*, 1745–50. Peabody Essex Museum (Acc. #125717). Photo by Mark Sexton

■ Captain John Clarke (1701–1764), a Massachusetts merchant, posed for his portrait with Salem's harbor and fort in the background.

IN 1749, PEACE SEEMED A WELCOME PROSPECT IN THE SPANISH SETTLEMENT OF SAN Antonio in south-central Texas. On an August morning, hundreds of people gathered in the plaza in front of the town's presidio, or military post. Captain Turibio de Urrutia, the presidio's commander, was there with a contingent of soldiers. Father Santa Ana, who had presided over the local missions for 16 years, was also present, along with other missionaries and lay residents. Across from them stood four Apache Indian chiefs with several hundred of their people. Between the two groups, in the center of the plaza, Spanish and Indian workers began to dig a deep pit with steep sides. Those attending were about to witness one of the most important events in the town's brief history.

Three decades earlier, in the spring of 1718, a small expedition of Spanish soldiers, missionaries, women, and children had built the presidio and a mission next to the San Antonio River. They constructed rough houses and excavated irrigation ditches to divert river water onto their fields. But they had occupied contested ground, on which the French and Indians also had designs. Undaunted by the failure of LaSalle's Texas colony, the French had established Natchitoches on the Red River in 1716 and New Orleans on the lower Mississippi in 1718. French explorers began probing west along Louisiana's western frontier and trading with Indians in eastern Texas. Then in 1720, Apache bands, moving down from the north under pressure from the Comanches, suddenly made their presence known. When they attacked two San Antonians out looking for missing horses, it marked the start of warfare.

Detail from an eighteenth-century Spanish map showing San Antonio and nearby missions.

Fresh support for the beleaguered settlers arrived at San Antonio in 1731, and additional friars laid out four new missions. But other conflicts arose. Sixteen families who had migrated all the way from the Canary Islands in the Atlantic Ocean received little support from local authorities. Religious leaders jostled with military personnel over how to use scarce resources and deal with raiding parties of neighboring Native Americans. An outbreak of smallpox in 1739 killed scores of mission Indians and forced others to depart in fear, but the cycle of war intensified. When Apache bands stole horses and killed settlers, Spanish officers responded with raids of their own. They captured Apache women and children and sold them into slavery in Mexico.

Captain Urrutia conducted one such campaign northwest from San Antonio in 1745, taking enough captives to earn a profit. Father Santa Ana protested such harsh tactics. When the Apaches retaliated against the presidio, Santa Ana's mission Indians from small local tribes helped fend off the attack. But in the end, the cleric hoped not only to make peace with the Apaches but to draw them into the expanding mission system, where they would accept Christianity, learn Spanish, and take up agriculture under the direction of missionaries. He called on Urrutia to stop selling slaves and provoking reprisals.

At Santa Ana's urging, the captain modified his approach in 1749. During the spring raids and counter-raids, Urrutia used mission Indians as fighters and translators, and he issued orders for humane treatment of the 175 prisoners brought back to San Antonio.

Theodore Gentilz, San Francisco del Espada en 1844. Yanaguana Society Collection. Daughters of the Republic of Texas Library at the Alamo

■   Mission San Francisco de la Espada, at San Antonio, had 1100 cattle, 80 horses, and 16 pairs of oxen when this chapel was being constructed in the 1740s. By the time the United States annexed Texas a century later (1845), the church had fallen into disrepair.

Rather than sell them as slaves, the Spanish locked up the men and dispersed the women and children among the missions and local households for "safe-keeping." Then Urrutia and Santa Ana chose two women and a man from among the captives and sent them back to Apache country with a proposal for peace. When the messengers returned with word that four important Apache chiefs were prepared to negotiate, preparations began for a major parley.

On August 16, 1749, Captain Urrutia and Father Santa Ana rode north from San Antonio, accompanied by most of the townsfolk, to welcome the Apache delegation. Both sides were eager for peace, and the negotiations went smoothly. There was ceremonial feasting, important for such occasions, and the four chiefs attended a mass conducted by Father Santa Ana. After two days of discussion through translators, the Spanish released some of their Apache prisoners as a goodwill gesture, and both sides agreed to hold a formal peace ceremony in the presidio plaza the next morning.

The next day all gathered to watch the workers digging the deep pit. Then the longtime adversaries buried their differences in an elaborate symbolic ritual. They lowered a live horse into the hole, along with other emblems of warfare: a lance, a hatchet, and a bundle of arrows. Next, the four chiefs linked hands and walked solemnly around the pit, accompanied first by Captain Urrutia, then by the missionaries, and finally by a resident of the town. Suddenly, at a set moment, all the onlookers grabbed up loose earth and tossed it into the hole. The horse was soon completely buried—a sacrifice for peace in the region—and the ceremony broke up with shouts and celebration.

Though striking, the encounter between the Spanish and Apaches at San Antonio was not unique. During the same era, Europeans and Native Americans met to parley and trade in other colonial towns such as Albany, Philadelphia, Charleston, St. Augustine, Mobile, and New Orleans. Such formal occasions highlight a far wider process of contact and interaction that was going on throughout the North American colonies in the half-century between 1713 and 1763. Everywhere, on a daily basis, the process of colonial expansion brought together Europeans, Africans, and Native Americans in surprising new contacts. Equally important, it forced different peoples *within* each of these three categories, despite contrasting backgrounds and customs, to rub shoulders with one another in unprecedented and unfamiliar ways.

These constant encounters had all been set in motion by the colonization process itself. Spanish missionaries lived among Tejas Indians in eastern Texas; French explorers dominated, and then lost, the Mississippi Valley; escaped African slaves fought militiamen from Georgia on the outskirts of St. Augustine. Some day-to-day meetings proved rewarding—a sound bargain, a helpful remedy, or a happy marriage. But other mixing was strained and uneasy at best—full of verbal misunderstandings, competing claims, and harsh commands.

Everywhere, motives differed, accents jarred, and cultures clashed. In Philadelphia, printer Benjamin Franklin, himself a newcomer from Boston, protested the way in which German-speaking Europeans "swarm into our settlements, and by herding together establish their language and manner to the exclusion of ours."

For many Christians, the new confusions recalled the story of Babel. Despite ambitious plans, the people in that biblical city could not understand one another well enough to work together. Eventually, they scattered abroad across the face of the earth. Bible-reading European-Americans no doubt recalled that tale, especially during the great religious awakening that shook the English colonies in the 1740s, when the prospect of building something new and transcendent seemed close at hand. The German-born utopian Christian Priber even attempted to establish an egalitarian realm in Appalachia where Europeans, Africans, and Native Americans could live peaceably together. Such dreams were not to be, however. Instead, the existing colonies continued to build up regional economies of their own, under British protection, and elements of a dominant Anglo-American culture began to emerge amid the Atlantic Babel's many voices.

New Cultures on the Western Plains

I t makes sense that the Apaches chose to bury a horse during their elaborate ceremony at the Spanish presidio in 1749. By this time, the horse, recently introduced to the Indians was transforming life on the Great Plains. It also makes sense that they buried arrows and hatchets rather than guns. Traditionally, the Spanish aspired to make the Indians into loyal subjects and Christian converts. From the time of Spain's arrival in the New World, therefore, official policy had forbidden the sale of firearms to Native Americans.

In contrast, the French, Dutch, and English desired trade at almost any cost. From the beginning, they showed less hesitation about supplying Indians with guns in exchange for furs. Firearms had become familiar to many eastern Indians in the seventeenth century. In the eighteenth century, guns began to spread across the Mississippi River as well. Combined with the

Harrison Begay, "Night Chant Ceremonial Hunt," 1947. Museum purchase, The Philbrook Museum of Art, Tulsa Oklahoma (1947.40)

■ The horse offered new mobility for hunting, as in this modern painting of Navajo riders. Tribes that had once tracked buffalo on foot at the edge of the Great Plains could now pursue herds across miles of open grassland. This was true for the Cheyenne, who were living in fixed villages in what is now South Dakota in the early eighteenth century. "After they got the first horses," recalled John Stands-in-Timber, "they learned there were more of them in the South and they went there after them." Cheyenne life would never be the same again.

movement of horses from the south, this development had enormous consequences. New patterns of warfare altered Indian cultures, and more powerful hunting techniques affected the regional economies and ecologies of the Native American West.

The Spread of the Horse

Although small horses once roamed the ancient West, they migrated into Asia thousands of years ago and became extinct in America. They returned with the early Spanish explorers, but Coronado's soldiers preferred to ride male horses. Only around 1600, when New Mexico's early colonists brought mares north for breeding, did horse herds develop in the Rio Grande valley. After the Pueblo Revolt in 1680, horses taken from the Spanish entered Indian trading networks and rapidly moved north from one culture to another.

By 1690 the Utes had obtained horses and traded them to the Shoshones. Before the mid-eighteenth century, horses had moved west of the Rocky Mountains to the Nez Perce and north to the Blackfeet. The Apaches brought horses east along other routes to the Caddoan cultures near the Red River and then north to the Pawnees, Arikaras, and Hidatsas. Even tribes in the Southeast acquired Spanish horses from the West before they obtained English horses from the Atlantic coast. When La Salle descended the Mississippi in 1682, he met Indians who had heard rumors from the West about a mysterious animal. And when a Chickasaw leader drew a regional map on deerskin in 1723, he showed a Native American leading a horse east of the Mississippi River.

For all Indians, the first horses seemed utterly strange. One elder recalled that "the people did not know what they fed on. They would offer the animals pieces of dried meat." "He put us on mind of a Stag that had lost his horns," another remembered, "and we did not know what name to give him. But as he was a slave to Man, like the dog, which carried our things, he was named the Big Dog." For generations, Native Americans had used dogs to pull provisions and bedding on a travois, an A-frame device made with tent poles. A larger animal could haul bigger loads, including longer tent poles. The long poles, in turn, allowed each family to live in a more spacious tipi.

Whether or not a tribe used tipis as dwellings, it could readily use the horse as a new source of tasty food and as an aid in hunting. The first few horses were far too valuable to risk in warfare. As herds expanded, however, warriors rode into battle, adapting their tactics to take advantage of their new swiftness. On horses, they could conduct lightning raids over long distances to attack rivals. They could also earn respect by stealing horses or by riding close enough to touch an enemy warrior, an act of bravery known as counting coup. Soon, raising and trading horses became important activities, and a family's wealth and status depended partly on the number of horses at its command.

The Rise of the Comanches

By the time of the American Revolution in the 1770s, mounted Comanche warriors commanded respect and fear across a vast domain. Their territory stretched south nearly 600 miles from western Kansas to central Texas, and it spanned 400 miles from eastern New Mexico to what is now eastern Oklahoma. This area, known as the Comanchería, roughly equaled all the English settlements on the Atlantic coast in size, but its origins were recent and humble. The Comanches' ancestors had been hunter–gatherers on the high plains of Wyoming, living on small game, roots, and berries.

The arrival of the horse around 1690 changed everything. It allowed family bands to migrate southeast from the Rockies. They joined with other Shoshone-speakers to hunt the buffalo herds that grazed along the western edges of the Great Plains. From there, it was not a long ride through the Sangre de Cristo Mountains to northern New Mexico, where they could trade buffalo hides for additional horses at Taos and Santa Fe. The Spanish noted the Shoshone-speaking arrivals in 1706, referring to them as Comanches in their records.

European horses reach the Western Plains, 1675–1750

― Present-day political boundaries

━ Routes for introduction of horses to Native American people, with approximate dates

⇨ Comanche migration to the Southern Plains

Dates show the year that horses reached certain Indian groups

■ **MAP 5.1**
THE RAPID SPREAD OF SPANISH HORSES ACROSS THE WESTERN PLAINS, 1675–1750

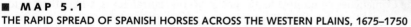

The Comanches were not the first to make their homes in what is now eastern Colorado. For generations, groups of Apaches had settled in the region near the upper reaches of the Platte and Arkansas rivers. Their ancestors had been Athapascan-speakers who had migrated south from Alaska centuries earlier and adjusted well to the warmer climate. Eventually, they had adopted some of the agricultural ways of the Pueblos and learned to ride horses from the Spanish. For Comanche newcomers, the Apache settlements—with their irrigated gardens and herds of horses—provided easy targets. Soon, Comanche raids caused such destruction that the Apaches sought assistance from the Spanish in the New Mexico colony to protect their homeland.

Officials in Santa Fe, fearful about their own defenses, looked for ways to halt Comanche aggression. They also hoped to convert the Apaches to Christianity and stop French traders from moving up the Missouri River onto the Plains. In 1720 the Spanish sent soldiers northeast from Santa Fe to check the latest rumors of French incursions. But they pushed too far. An Indian war party, with French support, routed the force somewhere near present-day North Platte, Nebraska. The Spanish defeat only encouraged the Comanches to launch further attacks on Apache settlements.

Within two decades, the Comanches had hammered their enemies south through one river valley after another: the Arkansas, the Red, the Brazos, the Colorado. Desperate Apache bands

Jean-Pierre Lassus, *Vue et Perspective de la Nouvelle-Orléans*, 1726. C.A.O.M. Aix-en-Provence (France) DFC Louisiane 71 (pf6B)

soon reached the vicinity of San Antonio, where they stole livestock from the new Spanish settlement to survive. Comanche power also pressed the Apaches west, where they raided Spanish outposts in New Mexico. As in Texas, Spanish campaigns against Apache intruders netted captives for the colonial slave trade. When Comanches visited a trade fair at Taos in 1731, they saw first-hand the commerce in Native American captives at the annual *rescate*, or ransoming. Comanche bands then stepped up raids on Apaches and carried the captives to market.

At first, New Mexico resisted the additional trade in slaves. The colony had not been able to protect Apache families or convert them; now it was being asked to buy them. But in the 1740s, officials in Santa Fe discovered that if they turned away Comanche traders, they faced the increasing power of Comanche war parties. So they granted the Comanches access to the *rescate* at Taos in exchange for assurances of peace. With a secure market for their hides, meat, and captives, the Comanches could now focus their raids on central Texas, where their hard-pressed Apache enemies had sealed a pact with the Spanish in 1749.

Not long after they buried the horse in the plaza, the Spanish began plans for a mission and presidio among their new Apache allies. The outpost would lie 150 miles northwest of San Antonio on the San Saba River, near present-day Menard, Texas. But the post had been established for less than a year when the Comanches attacked it in 1758. They returned the next year, capturing 700 horses. "The heathen of the north are innumerable and rich," exclaimed a Spanish officer at San Saba. "They dress well, breed horses, [and] handle firearms with the greatest skill."

Over the next eight years, the Comanche onslaught continued. Their raiders even stole a horse herd from San Antonio itself. Repeated attacks finally forced the Spanish to withdraw from San Saba in 1767. In less than two decades, the Comanches had overrun most of Texas. They continued to absorb smaller Native American groups and swell in numbers. By 1780 they had grown into a proud Indian nation of more than 20,000 people. Their domain, the so-called Comanchería, remained a powerful entity in the Southwest for decades.

The Expansion of the Sioux

Comanche strength depended not only on mounted warfare but also on using the horse as a trade commodity to obtain guns. Because Spanish policy prohibited the sale of firearms to Native Americans, the Comanches looked east for weapons. They quickly discovered that by

FLEVVE   DE   St LOVIS   OV MISSISSIPI

■ By 1726 New Orleans, with 100 cabins and nearly 1000 inhabitants, was receiving shipments of trade goods from France and distributing them up the Mississippi River and its tributaries. Following a Louisiana hurricane in 1722, the levies along the waterfront were expanded, but flooding remains a threat to the low-lying city even today.

selling horses to their eastern allies, such as the Wichita Indians along the Arkansas River, they could receive French muskets from Louisiana in return. But the Comanches were not the only Indian nation to take advantage of the gun frontier as it inched steadily west.

By 1720 the French had established settlements at Peoria, Cahokia, and Kaskaskia in Illinois and at New Orleans, Natchez, and Natchitoches in Louisiana. French traders at these sites provided guns and other metal goods to Indians in exchange for salt, deerskins, beaver pelts, horses, or even war captives to serve as laborers and concubines. Native American groups that took advantage of this trade included the Tunicas beside the lower Mississippi, the Caddos and Wichitas along the Red and Arkansas rivers, and the Osage, Pawnee, and Omaha tribes near the Missouri.

Further north, muskets carried west from French posts on the Great Lakes and south from English bases in subarctic Canada proved more significant than any traffic from Louisiana or Illinois. This northern trade was especially important among the Sioux peoples, who trapped game and gathered wild rice by the lakes of their northern Minnesota homeland. The Comanches had mastered horses and then acquired guns; the Sioux, given their different location, first absorbed firearms and then adopted the horse. But the results proved equally dramatic.

When the Sioux first encountered a gun from French voyageurs in the mid-seventeenth century, they called it *mazawakan,* meaning "mysterious or sacred iron." Initially, they used the few muskets they could obtain to fight their less well-armed Indian neighbors to the north. But in 1682, English agents established an outpost at the mouth of the Nelson River on Hudson Bay, trading muskets to Native Americans for furs. Supplied with shiploads of guns by the Hudson's Bay Company, Cree and Assiniboine Indians pushed southwest, expanding their hunting territory as they depleted the fur supply.

Pressured by these northern rivals, several Sioux bands (the Teton and Yanktonai) migrated to the prairie country of southwest Minnesota, learning to hunt for buffalo on foot. They also sought beaver for an expanding European market. Ready access to firearms facilitated the Sioux migration, giving them a military advantage over tribes to their west. By 1700 French traders, moving from the east, had established direct trade with the Sioux, offering a steady supply of guns and powder in exchange for furs.

For several generations, the Sioux walked between two worlds. In the summers, they followed the buffalo onto the prairies, with dogs pulling travois and women carrying heavy burdens. As cold weather approached, they retreated to the edge of the woodlands to gather

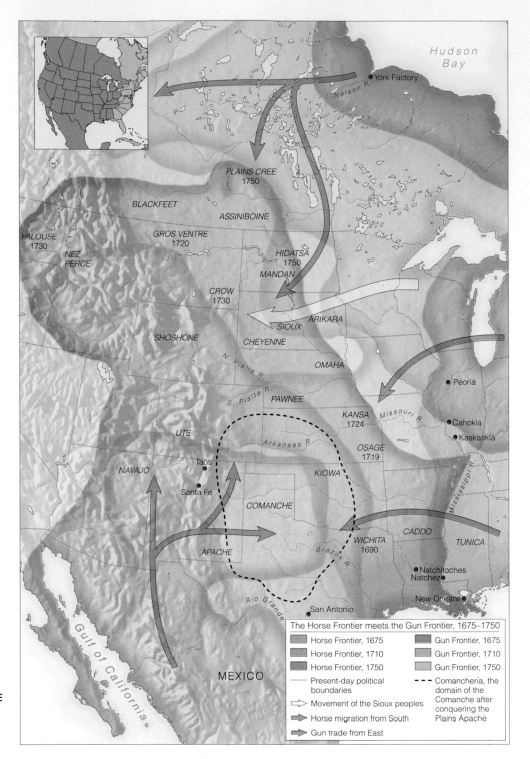

■ MAP 5.2
THE HORSE FRONTIER MEETS THE
GUN FRONTIER, 1675–1750

firewood and seek beaver. In the spring, after trading meat and pelts to the French for guns and ammunition, they returned to the edge of the plains. They glimpsed their first horses not long after 1700. But it was several generations before the western Sioux had acquired enough mounts and developed sufficient confidence to drop their old customs and adopt a horse-centered way of life.

By midcentury, the horse frontier on the northern Great Plains had met the gun frontier, just as it had in what is now Texas, Arkansas, and Missouri. Saukamappee, a Cree Indian living with the Blackfeet, remembered vividly the surprise of the initial encounter. When he was a young man, his war party—well armed and on foot—had gone into battle against the Shoshones. "We had more guns and iron headed arrows than [ever] before," he recalled years later. "But our enemies . . . and their allies had Misstutim [Big Dogs, that is Horses] on which they rode, swift as the Deer."

Indian women remembered the arrival of the horse and the gun with ambivalence. These new assets improved food supplies and made travel less burdensome, but the transition brought disadvantages as well. Violent raids became more common, and young men who fought as warriors gained status in the community compared to older men and women. Also, the hard task of processing slain buffalo increased, creating new work for women even as it provided fresh resources for the whole community.

As the overlap of horse and gun proceeded after 1750, Sioux men bearing muskets continued to acquire mounts and fight for control of the buffalo grounds. Their competitors, all of whom had recently acquired horses, now had guns as well. But within several decades, the Sioux had pushed their domain west to the Missouri River. Like the Comanches farther south, they had emerged as the dominant power across a wide portion of the Great Plains—a force to be reckoned with in the century ahead.

Britain's Mainland Colonies: A New Abundance of People

East of the Rockies, horses and guns brought dramatic shifts as the eighteenth century progressed. But east of the Appalachian Mountains, a different force prompted striking change: population growth. Several factors came together to push the demographic curve upward at an unprecedented rate after 1700. From our vantage point in the twenty-first century, the colonial seaports and villages appear tiny, and rural settlement seems sparse. But by the mid-eighteenth century, the coastal colonies represented the largest concentration of people that had ever occupied any portion of the continent.

On both sides of the North Atlantic, steady population growth characterized eighteenth-century life. In Europe, improvements in agriculture led to larger harvests and more fodder for keeping livestock alive through long winters. These changes prompted better diets, and they were accompanied by improvements in food distribution and sanitation that also assisted population growth. But as European numbers rose at a more or less steady pace, the population of Atlantic North America surged. A comparison with England demonstrates how astounding American demographic growth was along the eastern seaboard. England in 1700 had 5.1 million people, and that figure increased a mere 14 percent to 5.8 million by 1750. In the same half century, the colonial population in British North America more than quadrupled, from 260,000 to nearly 1.2 million.

This enormous expansion in numbers contained an additional change. During the first two thirds of the eighteenth century, the Atlantic seaboard colonies made a permanent and dramatic shift away from a population that was almost entirely of English origin. Never before had North America seen such extensive ethnic and racial diversity. As the numerous cultures and languages indigenous to western Europe, western Africa, and eastern North America mixed and mingled, they gave rise to an American Babel.

Population Growth on the Home Front

Natural increase—more births than deaths—played an important role in colonial population growth. Marriages occurred early, and the need for labor created an incentive for couples to have large families. Benjamin Franklin, who rose to become the best-known colonist of his generation, was born in Boston in 1706. He grew up in a household of 17 children. Large

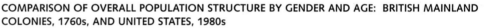

■ **FIGURE 5.1**
COMPARISON OF OVERALL POPULATION STRUCTURE BY GENDER AND AGE: BRITISH MAINLAND
COLONIES, 1760s, AND UNITED STATES, 1980s

families had long been commonplace, to compensate for frequent deaths among children. What made the Franklin family unusual was that all the children survived childhood and started families of their own. (Such success would have been highly unlikely in the previous century, when 28 percent of young people in New England died before age 20, and the mortality rate was far higher in Virginia.)

Although a high birth rate typified most preindustrial cultures, it was the low death rate and long average life span that pushed up American population numbers. With no huge urban centers, the colonial populace remained dispersed, so epidemics proved less devastating and of shorter duration than in Europe. Food was plentiful, and housing improved steadily. Newborns who survived infancy could live a long life. Franklin himself lived 84 years, and his publications, the *Pennsylvania Gazette* and *Poor Richard's Almanack,* offered frequent advice and encouragement for readers to become healthy as well as "wealthy and wise."

The 1720s and 1730s proved generally peaceful, in contrast to most earlier decades, so soldiering did not disrupt work and endanger lives among men of military age. For women, death related to pregnancy and childbirth still loomed as a constant threat. (Franklin's own mother was his father's second wife; the first wife died after bearing seven children.) Yet women still outnumbered men among people living into their sixties, seventies, and eighties. Although grandparents often endured far into old age, the average age for the total population stayed remarkably young. In the mid-eighteenth century, fully a third of all people in the British mainland colonies were under age 10, and more than half were under age 20. In the late twentieth century, in contrast, barely one-seventh of all living Americans were below 10 ten years of age, and fewer than one-third were below 20.

The reasons for such a young overall population seem clear. The ratio between men and women was becoming more even over time, the marriage rates for women remained extremely high, and there was no effective means of contraception. Women could resort to sexual abstinence to avoid pregnancy, and mothers could extend the time between births by nursing their infants for a long period (since lactation reduces the chances of conception). Not surprisingly, children abounded.

"Packed Like Herrings": Arrivals from Abroad

Frequent births and improving survival rates were only part of the population story. Immigration—both forced and free—also contributed mightily to the colonies' growth. The unfree arrivals came in two different streams from two separate continents and faced very different prospects. The largest flow of unfree arrivals came from Africa, and these forced migrants faced a bleak new life with few options for improvement. Well before the 1720s, the system of race-based slavery was sanctioned by law. By the 1730s, the expanding trans-Atlantic slave trade brought at least 4000 Africans to the colonies every year, and the rate increased steadily. In 1756, Charleston, South Carolina, received more than 2200 slaves aboard 14 ships (including vessels that bore grimly ironic names such as *Relief, Hope,* and *Success*).

A separate stream of unfree laborers came to the colonies from Europe. It included prisoners forced from crowded jails and also indentured servants unable to pay their own way to America. By comparison to enslaved Africans, the long-term prospects of these European migrants were far more promising. Every year, hundreds of detainees in British jails were offered transportation to the colonies and a term of service laboring in America as an alternative to prison time or execution. In Daniel Defoe's romance *Moll Flanders* (1722), English authorities deport the fictional heroine to Virginia for her crimes as a pickpocket, and she ends up inheriting considerable wealth. Most real-life convicts had no such luck, but most earned their freedom and found ways to blend in to colonial society.

Deported felons joined the larger flow of unfree migrants from Europe: poor people, unable to pay for their own passage, who accepted transportation to America as indentured servants. All were sold to employers to serve as workers, with scant legal rights, until their indenture expired, usually after three to six years. In the 1720s, Philadelphia shippers devised a variation on indentures known as the redemption contract. Under this redemption system, agents in Europe recruited migrants by contracting to loan them money for passage and provisions. On arrival in America, the recruits could then sign a pact with an employer of their own choosing. That person agreed to pay back the shipper, "redeeming" the original loan that had been made to the immigrant. In exchange, the newcomer (called a redemptioner) promised to work for the employer for several years, receiving no more than room and board. After that, the redemptioners were on their own, and their prospects usually improved.

> *Detainees in British jails were offered transportation to the colonies and a term of service as an alternative to prison time or execution.*

Besides Africans who remained unfree for life and Europeans who gained freedom after a period of service, a smaller stream of newcomers involved free families arriving from Europe who could pay their own way. Poor conditions at home pushed these risk-takers to try their luck in the New World, and glowing descriptions of abundant land at bargain rates caught their attention. American land speculators hoped to rent or sell forest tracts to immigrant farmers who would improve the value of the land by clearing acreage, constructing fences, and building homes. For example, Boston merchant Samuel Waldo, infected by this "speculative fever," induced several hundred Germans and Scots to come to America in the 1740s. He transported them to his extensive wilderness lands east of the Damariscotta River, where they became the early inhabitants of what is now Waldoboro, Maine.

Britain's imperial administrators also sought to recruit Europeans to the American colonies. The settlements these immigrants established could bolster colonial defenses against foreign rivals and provide a buffer on the frontier to ward off Indian attacks. In one of many pamphlets for German immigrants, Joshua von Kocherthal explained how South Carolina's proprietors would give a 65-acre plot to each head of household, with the promise of more land if they needed it or if they came with a large group.

Even with such enticements, South Carolina's enslaved African community expanded faster than its free population. By 1760 blacks outnumbered whites 58,000 to 39,000. The next year, fearing the prospect of a slave revolt, the South Carolina government offered a bounty of £4 sterling ($360) to anyone importing a Protestant European, and it provided a smaller amount

"Pastures Can Be Found Almost Everywhere": Joshua von Kocherthal Recruits Germans to Carolina

Joshua von Kocherthal grew up near Heidelberg, capital of the Electoral Palatinate in southern Germany, and trained to be a Lutheran minister. On a visit to London at the start of the eighteenth century, he learned of England's desire to recruit settlers to its American colonies. Because fellow Germans faced hard times at home, he led several groups to New York, where they established Neuberg (Newburgh) on the Hudson River. In 1706, Kocherthal also published a German-language tract promoting migration to South Carolina. The popular booklet went through several editions in his Palatinate homeland east of the Rhine River.

The winter of 1708–1709 was especially harsh in the Palatinate. In the spring of 1709, a stream of desperate refugee families migrated north along the Rhine and then west to England. From there, they hoped to obtain passage across the Atlantic to South Carolina. Many carried Kocherthal's simple pamphlet, and they focused on the numerous advantages outlined in his brochure, especially the abundance of land. According to Kocherthal, the colonial government registered all land grants "to prevent errors or future arguments," and it exempted newcomers from taxes for several years. Best of all, food was plentiful, no feudal obligations or serfdom existed, and members of Protestant denominations had "freedom of religion and conscience."

South Carolina is one of the most fertile landscapes to be found . . . preferable in many respects to the terrain in Germany, as well as in England. . . . Game, fish, and birds, as well as waterfowl such as swans, geese, and ducks, occur there in such plentiful numbers that . . . newcomers can sustain themselves if necessary . . . until they have cleared a piece of land, sown seeds, and gathered in a harvest. . . . Among other things, there can be found in the wild so-called "Indian chickens" [turkeys], some of which weigh about 40 pounds or even more. These exist in incredible numbers. . . .

Hunting game, fishing, and bird-catching are free to anyone, but one shouldn't cross the borders of neighbors or of the Indians [who] live in complete peace and friendship with our families. In addition, their number decreases while the number of our people (namely the Europeans) increases. . . . Lumber can be found there in abundance, especially the most beautiful oaks, but also many of the nicest chestnuts and nut trees which are used by many for building and are considered better than oaks. One can also find beeches, spruces, cypresses, cedars, laurels, myrtle, and many other varieties.

Hogs can be raised very easily in great numbers at little cost, because there are huge forests everywhere and the ground is covered with acorns. . . . Above all, the breeding of horses, cows, sheep, hogs and many other kinds of domestic livestock proceeds excellently, because pastures can

($90) to help the new immigrant get started. These incentives prompted importers to seek out migrants, using kidnapping if necessary, and move them at the least possible expense. Importers' only aim, according to one local observer, was "to deliver as many as possible alive on Shoar upon the cheapest terms, and no matter how they fared upon their Voyage nor in what condition they were landed." More than 3000 newcomers reached South Carolina under this system, but the abuses proved so shocking that it was discontinued after seven years.

Even for those who could pay their own way, the Atlantic passage was a life-threatening ordeal. "The people are packed densely, like herrings," Lutheran minister Gottlieb Mittelberger recorded after a voyage to Pennsylvania. "During the journey the ship is full of pitiful signs of distress—smells, fumes, horrors, vomiting, various kinds of sea sickness, fever, dysentery, headaches, heat, constipation, boils, scurvy, cancer, mouth-rot, and similar afflictions." Despite such hardships, newcomers found economic opportunities awaiting them in America. They often wrote home glowing accounts of colonial life, and their letters helped boost the rising population further. In 1773 English customs officials quizzed 29-year-old Elizabeth McDonald about why she was departing for Wilmington, North Carolina. The unmarried Scottish servant replied that she was setting out "because several of her friends, having gone to Carolina before her, had assured her that she would get much better service and greater encouragement in Carolina than in her own country."

In 1709, roughly 13,000 German immigrants seeking passage to America encamped for months at Blackheath, near London. The British government supplied the Palatines with tents, blankets, bread, and cheese, and churchgoers prayed for their welfare. But other Britons protested that the German strangers took "bread out of the mouths of our native handicraft men and laboring people, and increase the number of our poor which are too many and too great a burden to our nation already." Most of the refugees reached North America, serving as the vanguard for later German migration.

be found almost everywhere, and the livestock can remain in the fields the whole year, as it gets no colder in Carolina in the middle of winter than it does in Germany in April or October. . . . Because of the multiplication of livestock, almost no household in Carolina (after residing there a few years) can justifiably be called poor.

As far as vegetables and fruits are concerned, Indian corn predominates, thriving in such a way that one can harvest it twice a year and grow it wherever one wants to. Our local cereals such as wheat, rye, barley, and oats do well, but above all, rice thrives there as excellently as in any other part of the world, and it grows in such

amounts that it can be loaded on ships and transported to other places. And as the inhabitants use rice so much and make much more profit from it than any other cereal, they are most keen on growing rice and there has been very little cultivation of other cereals.

All kinds of our fruits can be planted there, but . . . future arrivals would do well to bring along seedlings of any kind, or at least the seeds. . . . There can already be found different kinds of our local apples. . . . As far as cabbage, beets, beans, peas, and other garden plants are concerned, not only do our local plants grow very well, but there are also many other varieties with excellent taste that are completely unknown to us. . . . Newcomers will do well to acquire all sorts of iron tools and bring these along. . . . If someone has lived in Carolina for a time and he wants to go to another country, he may do so freely at any time. ∎

Source: Translations by Dorothee Lehlbach from Joshua von Kocherthal, *Ausfeuhrlicher und umstaendlicher Bericht von der beruehmten Landschaft Carolina, in dem engellaendischen American gelegen* (Frankfurt: Georg Heinrich Oehrling, 2nd ed., 1709), in the Special Collections Library of Duke University.

Non-English Newcomers in the British Colonies

Colonies that were thoroughly English at their origin became decidedly more varied after 1700. By far the largest and most striking change came from North America's increasing involvement in the Atlantic slave trade. By 1750, some 240,000 African Americans made up 20 percent of the population of the British colonies. Native Americans had been drawn into the mix in small numbers as slaves, servants, spouses, and Christian converts. But roughly four out of five colonists were of European descent. Among them, as among the Africans and Indians, many spoke English with a different accent, or as a second language, or not at all.

No area went untouched by this change. The New England colonies remained the most homogenous, but even there, 30 percent of the residents had non-English roots by 1760. The new diversity, which increasingly characterized American society in future centuries, was most visible in New York because of the colony's non-English origins. A 1703 census of New York City shows that the town had no single ethnic majority. It remained 42 percent Dutch, with English (30 percent) and Africans (18 percent) making up nearly half the population. The rest of the population included a small Jewish community (1 percent) and a growing number of French Protestants (9 percent).

The French New Yorkers had fled to America after Louis XIV ended protection for the Protestant minority of France. When the king revoked the long-standing Edict of Nantes in

The DePeyster Painter, *Maria Maytilda Winkler*, c.1730. Fine Arts Museum of San Francisco, Gift of Mr. and Mrs. John D. Rockefeller 3rd, 1979.7.34

■ Colonial artists often copied engravings of well-known European pictures and then inserted a likeness of their client's head. That was the case in this New York portrait of Maria Maytilda Winkler, made around 1730 by a Dutch-American "limner," or painter.

John Wollaston, *Mary Spraat Provoost Alexander*, undated. Museum of the City of New York, Gift of William Hamilton Russell (50.215.4)

■ Like many New Yorkers of her generation, shopkeeper Mary Spratt Provoost Alexander (1693–1760) spoke both Dutch and English. Her Dutch mother had married a Scottish immigrant, and Mary was the wife of a local attorney who also came from Scotland.

1685, he also prohibited Huguenot emigration, but several thousand French Protestants escaped illegally and sought refuge in America. They established small communities such as those at New Rochelle in New York and along South Carolina's Santee River. South Carolina's governor protested against the Huguenots' early political activity: "Shall the Frenchmen, who cannot speak our language, make our laws?" But everywhere, they intermarried with the English and prospered in commerce. By the 1760s, several families with humble Huguenot origins—among them the Faneuils in Boston and the Laurenses, Manigaults, and Ravenels in Charleston—had amassed enormous fortunes.

At a time when France and Great Britain were at war, another infusion of French-speaking refugees, the Acadians, fared less well. In 1755, authorities evicted French colonials from Acadia in British Nova Scotia, fearing they might take up arms for France. Officials burned their homes and deported more than 6000 of them further south, allotting shiploads to the various coastal colonies so that widely dispersed groups could pose no threat. Mistreated for their Catholicism and feared as enemies during wartime, the Acadians struggled to make ends meet. Most had lost all their property. Some, who could not support themselves, were sold into indentured servitude, adults and children alike. Feeling unwelcome in their new homes, many eventually moved on to French Louisiana, where the Acadians, or Cajuns, became a lasting cultural force.

Scotland provided a much larger flow of migrants than France, stemming from two different sources. A growing stream of families, at least 30,000 people by 1770, came from Scotland itself. They were pushed by poverty, land scarcity, famines, and a failed political rebellion in 1745. In addition, a larger group known as the Scots-Irish came from Ulster in Ireland. The British had encouraged these Scottish Presbyterians to settle in Northern Ireland in the seventeenth century, displacing rebellious Irish Catholics. But the Scottish newcomers in Ulster soon faced commercial and political restrictions from Parliament and the Anglican church. By 1770 nearly 60,000 Scots-Irish had opted to leave Ireland for America. Scottish immigrants became farmers and traders throughout the colonies. In Georgia, for example, they established New Inverness (now Darien) on the southern coastal frontier in 1736.

Another stream, German-speaking immigrants from the heart of Europe, nearly equaled the combined flow of Scots and Scots-Irish settlers. They began to arrive shortly after 1700 as religious persecution, chronic land shortages, and generations of warfare pushed whole communities out of the so-called Palatinate in southern Germany and also neighboring Switzerland. Roughly 30,000 migrated in the 1750s alone, and by 1770 the total had reached 85,000. Even more than other European newcomers, these refugees generally came as whole families, and they usually took up farmland on the fringes of the colonies. Germans occupied the Mohawk Valley in New York and the Shenandoah Valley in Virginia, and they fanned out from Germantown across the rich farmland of Pennsylvania. Swiss founded New Bern, North Carolina, in 1710, and migrants from Salzburg established New Ebenezer near Savannah, Georgia, in 1734.

Almost all of the white, non-English newcomers, including several thousand migrants from Wales, were Protestant Christians. Many clung to their language and traditions. (Because the new Pennsylvanians spoke

German, or *Deutsch,* they became known as Pennsylvania Dutch.) But most arrivals learned English, and many of their children intermarried with the English settlers. An eighteenth-century Frenchman wrote of meeting a typical American "whose grandfather was an Englishman, whose wife is Dutch, whose son married a French woman, and whose present four sons have now four wives of different nations."

The Varied Economic Landscape

Population growth had consequences, and the changes began at the water's edge. Ships carrying newcomers docked most often at Boston, New York, Philadelphia, or Charleston. Each of these deepwater ports grew from a village to a bustling commercial hub, absorbing manufactured goods from Britain and shipping colonial produce abroad. All four towns spawned secondary ports located on neighboring rivers, where small boats carried on an active coastal trade. Chesapeake Bay, with no single dominant port, was the exception. There, Baltimore, Annapolis, Alexandria, and Newport all expanded. But given the bay's many rivers, Atlantic ships often visited separate riverside plantations and villages to do business.

In Chesapeake Bay and elsewhere, inland commerce was conducted by boat wherever possible. Hartford and Springfield on the Connecticut River, Kingston and Albany on the Hudson, Wilmington and Trenton on the Delaware, and Savannah and Augusta on the Savannah all become active riverside trading centers. Richmond, Virginia, which began as a trading post at the falls of the James River, already had 250 inhabitants when it incorporated as a town in 1742. Trails

Thomas Davies, Prospect of the City of Albany in the Province of New York in America, 1763. Albany Institute of History and Art, Gift of Mrs. Richard C. Rockwell (#1980.17)

PROSPECT of the *CITY of ALBANY* in the *PROVINCE of NEW YORK* in AMERICA.

■ Albany, a fur-trading center for generations, prospered in the mid-eighteenth century. The Hudson River town would become the capital of New York in 1797 and the starting point for the Erie Canal, completed in 1825.

■ A 1752 sketch of Baltimore by John Moale. In 1729 Maryland planters founded Baltimore to provide a port on Chesapeake Bay for shipping tobacco. The town had only 50 homes and 200 inhabitants when this early sketch was made, but it grew rapidly after that.

and former Indian paths connected these river-based communities, easing the way for travelers in the hinterland. By the 1740s, a pathway known as the Great Wagon Road headed southwest from Philadelphia to Winchester in Virginia's Shenandoah Valley and then south through gaps in the Blue Ridge Mountains to the Piedmont region of central Carolina.

Widening networks of contact, using boats and wagons, extended inland from the primary ports. And expanding fleets of ships tied each major hub to distant Atlantic ports. As a result, farmsteads and villages that had been largely self-sufficient before 1710 gradually became linked to wider markets. Local production still met most needs. But increasingly, the opportunity existed to obtain a new tool, a piece of cloth, or a printed almanac from far away. These and scores of other items might come from a larger town in the colony or from abroad. The new possibility of obtaining such goods lured farmers to grow crops for market rather than plant only for home consumption.

As local commercial systems gained coherence and strength, a string of regional economies developed along the Atlantic seaboard. Coastal vessels and a few muddy roads linked them tenuously to one another. But geographical and human differences caused each to take on a character of its own, and this distinctiveness increased over the years. Migration patterns reinforced this diversity, since arrivals from Europe often sought out areas where others already spoke their language or shared their form of worship. The growing influx of German farmers through Philadelphia, for example, gave unique traits to life in colonial Pennsylvania. Likewise, the rising importation of Africans helped shape the economy and culture of Chesapeake Bay, and the same held true for coastal South Carolina. Besides the diversity among arriv-

New England
Limited by rocky soil and long winters, New Englanders supplemented their farm production with ship building, fishing, and distilling West Indian sugar into rum.

Middle colonies
With rich land and abundant water power for milling, the middle colonies exported excess wheat, corn, and flour, along with flax, tobacco, oats, meat, and wood products.

Chesapeake Bay
Tobacco, grown and picked by enslaved African Americans, dominated the Chesapeake Bay economy. Beyond the Tidewater region, farmers raised hogs, wheat, and corn.

North Carolina
Colonists in coastal North Carolina used ample pine forests to manufacture naval stores: tar, pitch, turpentine, and resin. Farms farther west, lacking access to major ports, sent produce to Virginia and South Carolina from the fertile Piedmont region.

South Carolina and Georgia
Rice and indigo, two African crops, became the staples of the South Carolina and Georgia economy, along with deerskins from the interior. Georgia permitted slavery after 1750.

Economic regions of the British Colonies

- New England
- Middle colonies
- Chesapeake Bay
- North Carolina
- South Carolina and Georgia
- The Great Wagon Road
- Major ports
- Flow of goods from NC Piedmont region

ATLANTIC OCEAN

■ **MAP 5.3**
ECONOMIC REGIONS OF THE BRITISH COLONIES

ing peoples, American ecological differences played a role as well. Variations in land and climate contributed to the emergence of five distinctive economic regions along the Atlantic coast.

Sources of Gain in the Southeast

Two related but distinctive regions took shape along the southeastern coast, linked respectively to the two Carolina colonies. The larger of the two centered on the lowcountry of coastal South Carolina. There, the warm current of the Gulf Stream moving north from Florida along the

Sea Islands provided a long growing season. It also assured very mild winters, in contrast to Europe, and this meant that cattle and hogs could forage in the woods unattended for most of the year. As livestock multiplied, settlers sold meat, barrel staves, and firewood to the sugar islands of the West Indies, purchasing African slave labor in return.

Some of the newcomers had grown rice in Africa before their enslavement, and in planting it for their own use they soon demonstrated that the crop, unfamiliar to the English, could thrive in Carolina. Once African know-how made clear the potential for rice cultivation, a system of plantation agriculture, imported from Barbados, took hold quickly after 1700. Rice production spread to Georgia after that colony legalized slavery in 1751. Another African plant, indigo, also took root as a money-making staple crop. For several generations after 1740, cakes of indigo from South Carolina provided the blue dye for England's rising textile industry.

On Charleston's busy docks, casks of deerskins piled up beside the barrels of rice and indigo. The extensive deerskin trade in South Carolina and Georgia depended on the Creek and Cherokee men who hunted the animals and the women who processed the hides. Keeping some skins for domestic use, the Indians sold the rest to traders in exchange for guns, blankets, cloth, knives, kettles, and rum. Native American bearers, often women, carried the heavy packs of skins to the trading posts until packhorses became available in the region. At the height of the trade in the 1730s, Indian and white hunters killed more than a million deer per year, often leaving the meat and selling the skin. When colonial laws against overhunting failed to stem the onslaught, the deer population and the southern deerskin trade declined.

In North Carolina, a second regional economy evolved. North of Cape Fear, the sandy barrier islands known as the Outer Banks prevented easy access for oceangoing vessels and gave protection to pirates who harassed Atlantic shipping. Because the coastal geography hindered efforts to promote staple crop agriculture, colonists turned to the pine forest to make a living. An extensive band of longleaf pine rimmed the southern coastal plain from Virginia to Texas, and in North Carolina it stretched inland for a hundred miles. With labor, this longleaf forest yielded an abundance of naval stores: the tar and pitch used by sailors to protect their ships and rigging. Workers hauled the finished products to Wilmington on the Cape Fear River, the colony's best outlet to the sea. By the 1770s, the port was well known for exporting naval stores, and a dozen sawmills dotted the river.

Further inland, Scots-Irish and German families moved down the Great Wagon Road after 1740 to carve out farms across the Carolina Piedmont on lands controlled largely by several absentee owners in Britain. By 1763 Ben Franklin estimated that Pennsylvania had lost 10,000 families to North Carolina. Typical of this migration were the Moravians, a German-speaking religious group who established towns at Nazareth and Bethlehem, Pennsylvania, in the 1740s. In 1753 members of the expanding Moravian community bought a tract of 100,000 acres near modern-day Winston-Salem, North Carolina. They named it Wachovia, meaning "Peaceful Valley," and within several years they had developed prosperous farms, a pottery shop, and a tannery around their initial settlement, called Bethabara. The newcomers bartered seeds and tools with one another and shipped extra produce overland to South Carolina and Virginia.

Chesapeake Bay's Tobacco Economy

North of the Carolinas, farmers in the colonies bordering Chesapeake Bay committed to tobacco production in the seventeenth century. They clung to that staple crop despite a long decline in its market price. After 1710, demand for tobacco revived and prices rose again, in part because snuff (pulverized tobacco inhaled through the nostrils) became increasingly popular among Europeans. An additional boost came from the French government. It granted a monopoly to a company that bought large amounts of Chesapeake tobacco and distributed it efficiently across Europe. Tobacco prices remained strong, and the leaf continued to dominate the Chesapeake economy. But local conditions in parts of Virginia and Maryland prompted crop diversification as the century progressed.

For one thing, constant tobacco planting depleted the soil and reduced yields. For another, certain soils proved poorly suited for the crop. In addition, most new farmland lay far from any navigable river, and rolling huge casks of tobacco many miles to market became an expensive chore. Wheat and corn thus emerged as important secondary staples. These new crops, along with flax, hemp, and apples for making cider, provided a buffer against poor tobacco harvests. They also spurred related economic activities such as building wagons, making barrels, and constructing mills. These trades, in turn, produced widening networks of local exchange and prosperity for white yeoman families, with or without slaves.

Before 1700, all the mainland colonies could be described as *societies with slaves.* After that, the northern colonies continued to allow enslavement, but they never relied on it. In contrast, the southern colonies, except for certain inland farmlands settled from the north, shifted early in the eighteenth century to become something different: full-fledged *slave societies,* tied economically and culturally to slavery. The system of forced labor created constant tension and violence. But it also created widespread wealth in the white community. In a circular fashion, planters exporting staple crops to Britain reaped sufficient profits to invest in additional African labor to grow more tobacco and rice.

Schomburg Center for Research in Black Culture, New York Public Library

■ **In North Carolina, black workers cut pine trees and then burned the wood in closed ovens to turn pine resin into tar and pitch. These so-called naval stores were sealed into barrels and later used by seamen to protect the ropes on ships.**

By midcentury, plantation owners remained less wealthy than their counterparts in the West Indies who lived off the profits of slave-grown sugar. But on average, members of the southern elite controlled far more wealth than their counterparts in the North. The profits of the plantation system spread widely through the rest of the European American community. By the 1770s, whites in the South averaged more than twice as much wealth per person as whites in the North. An estimate for 1774 puts the white southerner's average net worth at £93, a sharp contrast to their counterparts in the middle colonies (£46) and New England (£38).

New England Takes to the Sea

North of Chesapeake Bay, two overlapping economic regions emerged: the long-established New England colonies and the somewhat newer and more prosperous middle colonies. New England faced peculiar disadvantages, beginning with the rocky soil. Ancient glaciers had strewn stones across the landscape, and it was tedious work to haul them off the fields to build endless stone walls. As imports from London increased, New Englanders found no staple crop that could be sold back directly to Britain to create a balance of trade. All the beaver had been hunted, and much of the best land had been occupied. The region's farm families had adapted well to the challenging environment and short growing seasons. Both men and women worked on handicrafts during the long, hard winters, and networks of community exchange yielded commercial prosperity in many towns. But with a rapidly growing population, each successive generation of parents had less land to pass on to their children. Increasingly, New England's young men with little prospect of inheriting prime farmland turned to the sea for a living.

In timber-rich New England, shipbuilding prospered. Colonists established shipyards at the mouth of nearly every river, drawing skilled carpenters and willing deckhands to the coast. By 1763, Marblehead, Massachusetts, with a fleet of a hundred ships, had grown to 5000 people. That made it the sixth largest town in the 13 colonies, behind only Philadelphia, New York, Boston, Charleston, and Newport, Rhode Island. By 1770, three out of every four ships sailing from New England to a British port was owned by colonial residents. In contrast, in the southern colonies from Maryland to Georgia, the proportion was only one in eight.

On Nantucket Island off Cape Cod, whaling became a new source of income. For generations, the islanders had cooked the blubber of beached whales to extract oil for lamps. In 1715, they outfitted several vessels to harpoon sperm whales at sea and then return with the whale blubber in casks to be rendered into oil. In the 1750s, they installed brick ovens on deck and began cooking the smelly blubber at sea in huge iron vats. This change turned the whaling vessel into a floating factory, and it allowed longer voyages in larger ships. By the 1760s, Nantucket whalers were cruising the Atlantic for four or five months at a time and returning loaded with barrels of oil.

The fishing industry prospered as well. All along the coast, villagers dispatched boats to the Grand Banks, the fishing grounds off Newfoundland. When the vessels returned, laden with fish, the townspeople graded, dried, and salted the catch. They sent the best cod to Europe in exchange for wine and dry goods. Yankee captains carried the lowest grade to the Caribbean sugar islands, where planters bought "refuse fish" as food for their slaves. In return, skippers brought back kegs of molasses to be distilled into rum. By 1770, 140 American distilleries, most of them in New England, produced 5 million gallons of rum annually. Much of it went to colonial taverns and Indian trading posts. But some also went to Africa, aboard ships from Britain and New England. American rum, along with various wines and spirits from Europe, made up one-fifth of the total value of goods utilized to purchase African slaves.

As the New England economy stabilized, it became a mixed blessing for women. On the farm, their domestic labors aided the household economy and helped to offset bad harvests. Mothers taught their daughters to spin yarn, weave cloth, sew clothes, plant gardens, raise chickens, tend livestock, and churn butter. The products from these chores could be used at home or sold in a nearby village to buy consumer goods. While the husband held legal authority over the home, a good wife served as a "deputy husband," managing numerous household affairs, or perhaps earning money as a midwife to help make ends meet. She took charge entirely if her husband passed away or went to sea.

But for all their labors, women seemed to lose economic and legal standing to men as New England towns became larger and more orderly. The creation of public buildings meant that community business was no longer conducted in the home, and so women did not get to participate as frequently as they once had. Networks of local officials, consisting entirely of men, drafted statutes and legal codes that reinforced male privileges. Women found it difficult to obtain credit or receive a business license. In addition, the law barred married women from making contracts, limiting the chance for independent activities outside the home. Increasingly, male apothecaries and physicians with a smattering of formal training shouldered traditional midwives away from the bedside. Even in the port towns, where women outnumbered men, their rights were limited, and poor women faced particular scrutiny. Selectmen and Overseers of the Poor had the power to remove children from a widowed mother and place them in the almshouse.

Economic Expansion in the Middle Colonies

The fifth regional economy, the one that flourished in the middle colonies between New England and Chesapeake Bay, represented the best of two worlds. The Europeans who resettled Indian lands in Delaware, Pennsylvania, New Jersey, and New York found a favorable climate, rich soil, and an abundance of millstreams. Unlike New Englanders, they developed a reliable staple by growing an abundance of grain. They exported excess wheat, flour, and bread as effectively as southerners shipped tobacco and rice. But unlike the planters in Virginia and South Carolina, middle-colony farmers did not become locked in the vicious cycle of making large investments in enslaved workers and exporting a single agricultural staple. Instead, they developed a more balanced economy, using mostly free labor. Besides grain products, they also exported quantities of flaxseed, barrel staves, livestock, and pig iron. Large infusions of money from Britain during its long war against France in the 1750s gave a further lift to this prosperous economy.

Whereas the Chesapeake had no dominant seaport, the middle colonies boasted two major ports of entry. Europeans eager to ply their crafts in America saw little likelihood of competing with unpaid slave artisans in the south. So they flocked to the middle colony seaports instead. Both Philadelphia and New York grew faster than rival ports in the mid-eighteenth century, passing Boston in size in the 1750s. Each city doubled its number of dwellings in the two decades after 1743 as brick structures with slate roofs replaced older wooden homes covered with inflammable cedar shingles. But new houses could not meet the ever-increasing demand. By 1763, Philadelphia had more than 20,000 people, New York had nearly as many, and both cities faced a set of urban problems that had already hit Boston.

As the port towns grew, they became more impersonal, with a greater economic and social distance between rich and poor. Large homes and expensive imports characterized life among the urban elite. In contrast, the poorest city dwellers increasingly lacked property and the means to subsist. By the 1760s, Philadelphia's almshouse and the new Pennsylvania Hospital for the Sick Poor were overflowing. In response to the crisis, Philadelphia's Quaker leaders established a voluntary Committee to Alleviate the Miseries of the Poor, handing out firewood and blankets to the needy. They also built a "Bettering House," patterned on Boston's workhouse, that provided poor Philadelphians with food and shelter in exchange for work.

Soon after the Delaware chief, Tishcohan, posed for this 1735 portrait, his people lost valuable land due to Pennsylvania's notorious Walking Purchase.

In an effort to limit urban poverty, authorities in New York and Philadelphia continued to move newcomers to the countryside. Dutch and German settlers had already established an efficient farming tradition in the area over several generations. With rising immigration after 1730, the burgeoning region slowly expanded its economic reach far up the Hudson Valley, east into much of Connecticut and Long Island, and south to Baltimore and parts of Maryland.

The farm frontier pushed west as well. The acquisitive Thomas Penn had inherited control of Pennsylvania from his more idealistic father, founder William Penn. In 1737 the young proprietor defrauded the Delaware Indians out of land they occupied west of the Delaware River. In the infamous Walking Purchase, Penn claimed a boundary that could be walked in a day and half. Then Penn's men cleared a path through the woods and sent horsemen along to assist his runners, who covered more than 55 miles in 36 hours. In all, the fast-moving agents took title to 1200 square miles of potential farmland near modern Easton and Allentown, Pennsylvania. Land-hungry settlers pressed the reluctant Delawares west toward the Allegheny Mountains and occupied the rich river valleys of eastern Pennsylvania. Land agents and immigrant farmers called the fertile region "the best poor man's country."

Matters of Faith: The Great Awakening

Philadelphia epitomized the commercial dynamism of the eighteenth-century British colonies. The city was a hub in the fastest-growing economic region on the Atlantic seaboard. Ben Franklin, arriving there in 1723 at age 17, achieved particular success. Within seven years he owned a printing business. Within 25 years he was wealthy enough to retire, devoting himself to science, politics, and social improvement. He created a lending library, developed an efficient stove, promoted schools and hospitals, supported scientific and philosophical organizations, and won fame in Europe for his experiments with electricity. The outburst of scientific inquiry and religious skepticism spreading through European

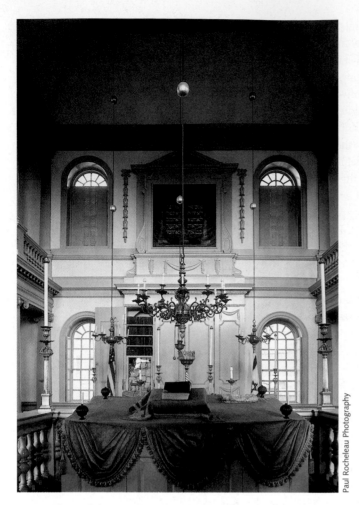

■ Members of the Jewish community in Newport started Touro Synagogue in 1759, a century after the arrival of their first ancestors in the Rhode Island seaport. Completed in 1763, this gem of colonial architecture is the oldest existing synagogue in the United States.

intellectual circles at the time became known as the Enlightenment. Its spirit of rational questioning and reason was greatly aided by the printing press. In America, Franklin and his fellow printers personified the new Age of Enlightenment.

By 1760 the British mainland colonies had 29 printing establishments, more presses per capita than in any country in Europe. These presses squeezed out 18 weekly newspapers and a variety of public notices, commercial broadsides, fictional pieces, farmers' almanacs, and scientific treatises. They fostered political and business communication throughout the colonies. But they also performed a very different public function, publishing an array of religious material. In Britain's eighteenth-century North American colonies, the spirit of enterprise and worldly achievement existed side by side with a longing for spiritual community and social perfection. The story of another Pennsylvania printer is an apt example.

In 1720, three years before Franklin arrived in Pennsylvania, Conrad Beissel migrated to Philadelphia from the Palatinate in Germany. He lived and preached in nearby Germantown; in 1738 he withdrew farther west to lead a life of unadorned simplicity. Soon other men and women joined him at his retreat near modern-day Lancaster, Pennsylvania. There they created Ephrata Community, the earliest of many wilderness utopias in North America. The communal experiment lasted for more than a generation, supporting itself by operating a printing press. Although Beissel pursued the same trade as Franklin, his experience as a dedicated seeker of spiritual truth represents a very different and important side of colonial life. In the first half of the eighteenth century, colonists witnessed surprising breakthroughs in religious toleration and bitter controversies within the ministry. They also experienced a revivalist outpouring, with roots in Europe and America, that later became known as the Great Awakening. This stirring began in the 1730s, and it gained momentum through the visits from England of a charismatic preacher named George Whitefield (pronounced Whitfield). In most colonies, the aftershocks of the Awakening persisted for a full generation.

Seeds of Religious Toleration

The same population shifts that made Britain's mainland colonies more diverse in the eighteenth century also created a new Babel of religious voices that included many non-Christians. Africans, the largest of all the new contingents, brought their own varied beliefs across the Atlantic. Some slaves from Portuguese Angola had had exposure to Catholicism in their homeland. But most Africans retained as much of their traditional cultures as possible under the circumstances, and they showed skepticism toward initial efforts to plant Christianity among them. An Anglican missionary recalled one black South Carolinian saying that he "preferred to live by what he could remember" from Africa. Christian efforts to convert Native Americans also had mixed results. A minister living near the Iroquois reported that Indians would beat a drum to disrupt his services and then "go away Laughing."

Another non-Christian contingent, Jewish immigrants, remained few in number, with only several hundred families by 1770. Merchants rather than farmers, they established communities in several Atlantic ports, beginning in Dutch New Amsterdam (1654) and Newport

(1658). Most were Sephardic Jews; that is, their ancestral roots were in Spain and Portugal. They came by way of the Caribbean, reaching Charleston in 1697, Philadelphia after 1706, and Savannah in 1733. A few of their children merged into the Protestant culture. In 1743, for example, Phila Franks, daughter of a leading Jewish merchant in New York, wed the son of Stephen DeLancey, a wealthy Huguenot who had married into the city's Dutch aristocracy and then joined the Anglican church. But more than 80 percent of Jewish young people (including a handful of Ashkenazi Jews with ties to central Europe) found partners within their congregations, creating small but lasting communities.

The majority of the colonies' newcomers in the eighteenth century were Christians. A few, such as the Acadians, were Catholics, but the rest had some Protestant affiliation. In the two centuries since the Reformation, numerous competing Protestant denominations had sprung up across Europe. Now this wide array made itself felt in America, as Presbyterians, Quakers, Lutherans, Baptists, Methodists, and smaller sects all increased in numbers. To attract immigrant families, most colonies did away with laws that favored a single established church. Nevertheless, New England remained firmly Congregational, while the merchant elite everywhere, and southern gentry in particular, concentrated increasingly within the Anglican church.

Rhode Island had emphasized the separation of church and state from the start, and Pennsylvania had likewise favored toleration, both as a matter of principle and as a practical recruitment device to attract new settlers. In Europe, Enlightenment thinking gave ideas of religious tolerance greater force as the eighteenth century progressed. So new colonists looked for assurances that they could indeed practice their religion freely and avoid burdensome taxes to support other faiths. In fact, migration from Europe was a demanding ordeal that discouraged the fainthearted. Those willing to take the risk were often people with strong religious hopes and convictions, and various colonies competed to accommodate them. In many places, religious tests still limited who could hold public office, according to the acceptability of their beliefs, but tolerance for competing religious views was definitely expanding.

Ironically, if any institution threatened the growing religious toleration in the colonies, it was the British king's own denomination. The monarch headed the Anglican church, and it had influential American members, including almost every colonial governor. Therefore, repeated talk by the Church of England about installing a resident bishop in America aroused suspicions among loyal colonists who worshipped in other denominations. This was especially true in New England, where Congregationalists had long opposed hierarchies within the Christian faith. Boston, which had 18 churches, rose up against a plan for an Anglican bishop in 1750. In a passionate sermon, Reverend Jonathan Mayhew preached that the town must keep "all imperious bishops, and other clergymen who love to lord it over God's heritage, from getting their feet into the stirrup."

The Onset of the Great Awakening: Pietism and George Whitefield

As relative toleration became a hallmark of the British colonies, no one benefited more than German-speaking Protestant groups. Numerous religious sects, such as the Moravians, Mennonites, Schwenkfelders, and Dunkers, were escaping from persecution as well as poverty at home. Their numbers multiplied after 1730, and hymns in German became a common sound on Sabbath day. In 1743, before any American printer produced an English-language Bible, a press in Pennsylvania put out a complete German edition of Luther's Bible, using type brought from Frankfurt.

Courtesy, Winterthur Museum (63.639)

■ **When George Whitefield visited America in 1739, his preaching spurred the Great Awakening.**

Sounds Around Us: The Lost World of High Fidelity

George Whitefield was as much a performer as a minister. He preached extemporaneously, mesmerized his listeners, and rarely declined an opportunity to address a crowd. Besides his 7 trips to America, he made 3 tours in Ireland and 15 in Scotland. He preached roughly 18,000 times before his death in New England in 1770, so hundreds of thousands of people heard him on both sides of the Atlantic. Because dozens of his sermons were transcribed and published, we are able to read what he said. But what did he sound like? And for that matter, what did anything sound like in the eighteenth century?

Whitefield had "a clear and musical voice," one listener recalled, "and a wonderful command of it." He squeezed every word for full effect. Some said he could move his listeners to tears with his dramatic enunciation of a single word, such as *Mesopotamia*. England's most famous actor observed, "I would give a hundred guineas if I could only say 'O!' like Mr. Whitefield." Benjamin Franklin, a skeptic and deist in matters of religion, told how he had gone to hear Whitefield preach at Philadelphia's Market Street, determined to hold onto the gold and silver coins he was carrying. "As he proceeded I began to soften," Franklin wrote, "and he finished so admirably that I emptied my pocket wholly into the collector's dish, gold and all."

"The multitudes of all sects and denominations that attended his sermons were enormous," Franklin reported, and their numbers challenged Whitefield's exceptional voice. Ever the rational experimenter, Dr. Franklin set out to measure the preacher's range. He backed down Market Street until he could not hear the sermon distinctly, then calculated the radius of the circle Whitefield could reach, allowed 2 feet for every potential listener, and concluded "that he might well be heard by more than thirty thousand." The estimate may be generous, but it speaks to the strength of Whitefield's operatic voice and the hushed attentiveness of his audience. It also reflects a wider point: the very different quality of hearing three centuries ago.

Of all the five senses, hearing may be the one that historians think and write about least of all. For years they have studied the rich world of musical history, of course, and recently they have awakened to disability history, exploring the complicated saga of social responses across time to hearing loss and other physical impairments. But the broader history of hearing remains so unexamined that few even recognize it as a fit topic of inquiry. Still, if each environment has a distinctive landscape that changes over time, it must have a discernible soundscape as well.

If we could join the residents of Franklin's Philadelphia, or if they could join us, the contrasts in sight, smell, taste, and touch between our two worlds would be fascinating to discuss. When you explore the history of these senses by listing differences, they mount up quickly. The same is true with sound. Rasping handsaws, creaking pump handles, and airy harpsichords would sur-

Collectively, these newcomers were part of a European reform movement to renew piety and spiritual vitality among Protestant churchgoers in an age of increasing rationalism and worldliness. Pietism, as this "Second Reformation" was called, had roots in eastern Germany and stressed the need to restore emotion and intensity to worship that had become too rational, detached, and impersonal. The German pietists reached out after 1700 to inspire Huguenots in France and Presbyterians in Scotland. They influenced reformers in the Church of England such as John Wesley, the founder of Methodism and a teacher at Oxford University. Through Wesley, pietist ideas touched George Whitefield, a lively college student in the class of 1736. Over the next decade, "the boy parson" became the first trans-Atlantic celebrity. Hailed as a preaching prodigy, he sparked a widespread religious awakening in the American colonies.

As a boy growing up in England, George Whitefield left school at 12 to work in the family tavern. But he still managed to attend college, and at Oxford he discovered Wesley and the pietists. He also discovered two other things: the lure of America and his calling to be minister. His mentor, Wesley, had preached briefly in Georgia. So in 1738, at age 23, Whitefield spent several months in the new colony, where he laid plans for an orphanage near Savannah.

Arriving back in England, Whitefield quickly achieved celebrity status. He drew large crowds with fiery sermons that criticized the Anglican church. The evangelist's published *Jour-*

While colonial life featured clear, isolated sounds, modern existence creates constant background noise. This mid-nineteenth-century painting about early industrialization in Pennsylvania suggests the shift. Soon steady noise from the distant factory and the advancing steam engine will blur smaller, sharper sounds.

prise us; droning lawnmowers, honking taxicabs, and pulsating electric guitars would startle them. But with sound, the differences go deeper than simply comparing one set of activities and instruments with another. There is a more fundamental contrast.

Just as the cars, trucks, machines, and factories of our ever-widening industrial world have spawned physical pollution around the globe, they also generate noise as a universal byproduct. These sounds are so numerous and constant that we hardly recognize them as noise pollution because we know no other soundscape. But Murray Schaffer explained the shift in a pioneering work of sound history, *The Tuning of the World* (1977). In the preindustrial world (most of history) humans lived in a high-fidelity soundscape with very little background noise. Distinct sounds traveled clearly and far, whether a tolling bell, a ringing axe, a singing bird, a shouting preacher, or a clap of thunder.

In contrast, we grow up in a low-fidelity world. From birth, our soundscape is filled with a steady array of background noises, large and small, day and night. Even in a rural field or a wilderness campsite, the roar of a snowmobile, the whine of a chainsaw, or the hum of distant tires or a passing jet plane can alter the near silence. The whir and buzz of countless devices is so much a part of our sound envelope that we amplify and blast voices to make them heard. Or we slip on headphones so we can lock out background noise and listen only to what we want to hear. Colonial visitors would marvel at how noisy our world seems but also at how scrambled and indistinct specific sounds become in this modern cacophony. "How do you hear yourselves think?" they might well ask. ■

nals, priced at only sixpence, went through six editions in nine months. Moreover, he recruited an experienced publicist, so word of his popularity preceded him in 1739 when he returned to America for an extended tour, the second of seven trans-Atlantic journeys during his career. Building upon religous stirrings already present in the colonies, Whitefield preached to huge and emotional crowds nearly 350 times in 15 months. He made appearances from Savannah to Boston, something no public figure had ever done. "God shews me," he wrote in his journal, "that America must be my place for action."

The timing was perfect. Whitefield, whose brother was a wine merchant, understood the expanding networks of communication and consumption in the British Atlantic world. He saw that in America, as newspapers multiplied and roads increased, he could advertise widely and travel extensively. Other ministers from England had remarked in frustration that most colonists knew "little of the nature of religion, or of the constitution of the church." At times, each person seemed to hold to "some religious whim or scruple peculiar to himself." Whitefield thrived on this vitality and confusion. He had little taste for Protestant debates over church structures and sectarian differences. Instead, he believed that an evangelical minister should simply preach the Bible fervently to a wide array of avid listeners. Everywhere he went, Whitefield served as a catalyst for religious activity.

"The Danger of an Unconverted Ministry"

The heightened commotion in American churches had local origins as well. The same tension felt in European parishes—between worldly, rational pursuits and an emotional quest for grace and salvation—also troubled colonial congregations. Occasional local revivals had taken place in America for decades. The most dramatic "harvest" of committed converts to the church took place in Northampton, Massachusetts, in 1734–1735 under the able guidance of

a local minister named Jonathan Edwards. As the colonies' most gifted theologian, Edwards anticipated Whitefield's argument that dry, rote "head-knowledge" made a poor substitute for "a true living faith in Jesus Christ." "Our people do not so much need to have their heads stored," Edwards observed, "as to have their hearts touched."

In a fast-growing society, who would prepare suitable church leaders for the next generation? Candidates for the ministry could train at Harvard College (founded 1636), William and Mary (1693), Yale (1707), or one of several small academies. But these institutions could not instruct a sufficient number and variety of church leaders. The shortage of educated ministers, combined with steady geographic expansion, meant that pulpit vacancies were common. A minister might oversee several parishes, and even if he tended only one parish, it often had broad boundaries. Rural families found it difficult to attend church regularly, and the great distances separating parishioners made it hard for any pastor to travel widely enough to address their needs. Feeling neglected, people voiced their dissatisfaction over the shortage of ministers.

The problem in the pulpit went beyond the matter of quantity. It included the issue of quality as well. Many college graduates had too much "head-knowledge." Their fluency in Latin and Greek often earned them more disdain than respect from down-to-earth congregations. Most foreign-born ministers, such as Anglicans sent from England and Presbyterians from Scotland, had failed to land good positions at home. Some resented their assignments to the colonies, and others felt overwhelmed by the task they confronted. Too often, they showed limited appreciation for the local church members who paid their salaries, and they resented those who criticized their ministries. One such critic was the Scots-Irish immigrant William Tennent, who arrived in Pennsylvania with his family in 1716. Dismayed by the small numbers and cold, unemotional outlook of Presbyterian ministers, Tennent opened a one-room academy in a log house to train his four sons and other young men for the ministry. But local Presbyterian authorities challenged his credentials and disparaged the teachings of his "Log College." Eventually, the school moved and grew, becoming linked to the new College of New Jersey in 1746, which later evolved into Princeton University. But before this happened, Tennent's preacher sons allied themselves with Whitefield and managed to shake the colonial religious establishment to its roots.

One of Tennent's sons, Gilbert, eventually led a Presbyterian church in Philadelphia created by Whitefield's supporters. In 1740, at the time of Whitefield's triumphal tour, young Gilbert Tennent delivered a blistering sermon entitled "The Danger of an Unconverted Ministry" that became a manifesto for the revival. Cutting to the heart of the matter, he condemned the "sad security" offered by incompetent, uncaring, and greedy ministers. "They are as blind as Moles, and as dead as Stones," he charged, "without any spiritual Taste and Relish." He argued that congregations had the right to turn away from these "Orthodox, Letter-learned . . . Old Pharisee-Teachers." It was "an unscriptural Infringment on Christian Liberty," Tennent proclaimed, "to bind men to a particular Minister, against their Judgement and Inclinations."

The Consequences of the Great Awakening

Whitefield hailed Gilbert Tennant and his brothers as "burning and shining lights" of a new kind. All the ministers and worshipers who joined in the movement began to call themselves "New Lights." Opponents, whom they dismissed as "Old Lights," continued to defend a learned clergy, emphasized head-knowledge on the difficult road to salvation, and opposed the disruptions caused by itinerant ministers who moved freely from parish to parish without invitation. The New Lights, in contrast, appealed to people's emotions and stressed the prospect of a more democratic salvation open to all. They defended their itinerant wanderings, which made them more accessible to a broader public and less likely to become set in their ways. "Our Blessed Saviour was an Itinerant Preacher," they reminded their critics; "he Preach'd in no other Way."

Just as New Light preachers moved readily across traditional parish boundaries, they also transcended the lines between different Protestant sects. Their simple evangelical message reached across a wide social spectrum to diverse audiences of every denomination. Moreover, their stress on communal singing, expressive emotion, and the prospects for personal salvation inevitably drew special attention from those on the fringes of the culture, such as young people, women, and the poor. It is important, but not surprising, that New Light ministers and their supporters made headway in spreading Christianity within various African American and Native American communities.

> *Some of the most zealous New Light men and women tried to transcend the competing denominations altogether and create a broad community of Protestant believers.*

Faced with such a broad awakening, members of the religious establishment, once secure as unchallenged leaders within their own church communities, now faced a stark choice. Some reached out to the itinerants who attacked them so vehemently. These powerful churchmen acknowledged their New Light critics and reluctantly welcomed the popular renegades into the local pulpits. Such a strategy might blunt the thrust of the revival, and it would surely raise church attendance. Other Old Lights, however, took the opposite approach; they clung to tradition and stability, challenging their new rivals openly. They condemned itinerancy and disputed the interlopers' right to preach. They mocked the faddish popularity of these overemotional zealots and even banned the New Light itinerants from local districts for the good of the parishioners.

In the end, neither tactic stemmed the upheaval. The arguments of the Great Awakening reverberated through the colonies for a full generation, peaking in the North in the 1740s and in the South during the 1750s and 1760s. But its long-term consequences were mixed. Some of the most zealous New Light men and women tried to transcend the competing denominations altogether and create a broad community of Protestant believers. But for all their open-air preaching, the itinerant reformers could never create such unity, and they left behind no new set of doctrines or institutional structures. Nevertheless, they created an important legacy. First, they infused a new spirit of piety and optimism into American Christianity that countered older and darker Calvinist traditions. Second, they established a manner of fiery and popular evangelical preaching that found a permanent place in American life. Finally, and most importantly, they underscored democratic tendencies in the New Testament gospels that many invoked in later years when faced with other apparent infringements of their liberties.

The French Lose a North American Empire

In 1739 Pierre and Paul Mallet set out up the Mississippi River from New Orleans. The two French Canadians hoped to test rumors that the Missouri River, the Mississippi's mightiest tributary, stretched into New Mexico and to claim the new trading route for France. Far to the east that same year, George Whitefield launched his tour of the English colonies, and the Stono slave rebellion erupted in South Carolina. But in the heart of the French empire thoughts were on expansion. Pausing in the Illinois country to gather seven French Canadian recruits, the Mallet brothers pushed up the Missouri. They finally abandoned the river in northeastern Nebraska, purchased horses at an Omaha Indian village, and set off across the plains. Clanging church bells greeted the French when they reached Santa Fe in July. After a nine-month stay, most of them returned east across the southern plains the next year.

At a stream in central Oklahoma, the explorers exchanged their horses with local Indians for elm bark canoes. (They named the water the Canadian River, a reference to their roots.) Farther east, they stopped at the old Arkansas Post near the mouth of the Arkansas River and then at Fort Rosalie on the lower Mississippi, where Louisiana colonists and their Choctaw allies had put down a revolt by the Natchez Indians a decade earlier. When the Mallet brothers completed their enormous circuit and returned to New Orleans, they brought word from the West of Indian and Spanish eagerness to engage in greater trade. From their perspective, the future of France in America looked bright indeed. But the promise disappeared entirely within their lifetimes.

Prospects and Problems Facing French Colonists

In 1740 French colonists had grounds for cautious optimism. France already claimed a much bigger expanse of North America than Britain or Spain had, and the French wilderness empire ran strategically through the center of the continent. The available resources and potential for agriculture seemed boundless, as a small community of settlers in the Illinois region had already discovered. Moreover, no Europeans had shown greater skill in forging stable and respectful relations with Native American peoples. North of Fort Rosalie and the Arkansas Post, a chain of isolated French forts stretched up the Mississippi River and then east to the lower Great Lakes and the St. Lawrence Valley. These posts facilitated trade with Native Americans and secured ties between Canada and Louisiana. With Indian support, more outposts could be built farther east near the Appalachian mountain chain to contain the English settlers and perhaps one day to conquer them.

At least three problems marred this scenario. First, the French population in America remained small, and the flow of new immigrants paled by comparison to the large number of English settlers. Canada still had fewer than 50,000 colonial inhabitants in 1740, whereas Britain's mainland colonies were rapidly approaching a million. Likewise, the Louisiana colony contained only 3000 French people, living among nearly 4000 enslaved Africans and 6000 Native Americans. Second, colonists lacked sufficient support from France to develop thriving communities and expand the valuable Indian trade. The importation of European goods was still meager and unpredictable, to the dismay of colonists and Native Americans alike. Finally, an ominous trickle of British hunters and settlers was beginning to cross the Appalachian chain. Carolina traders already had strong ties with the Chickasaw Indians living near the Mississippi River, and Virginia land speculators were eyeing lands in the Ohio Valley.

What seemed a promising situation for the French in 1740 was soon put to the test. Britain and France had long been on a collision course in North America. Colonial subjects of the two European superpowers had already clashed in a series of wars, with Indian allies playing crucial roles. After several decades of peace, the conflicts known in English-speaking America as King William's War (1689–1697) and Queen Anne's War (1702–1713) seemed distant memories, but warfare was about to resume. Two more contests, King George's War (1744–1748) and the French and Indian War (1754–1763) preoccupied colonists and Native Americans alike over the next two decades. In 1763 the Treaty of Paris ended the French and Indian War, part of a far wider conflict known in Europe as the Seven Years' War. At that point, less than a quarter century after the Mallet brothers' optimistic journey through the heartlands, the expansive French empire in North America suddenly vanished.

British Settlers Confront the Threat from France

These colonial conflicts of the mid-eighteenth century, generally linked to wider warfare in Europe, had a significant impact on everyone living in the British mainland colonies. A few people took advantage of the disturbances to become rich. They provisioned troops, sold scarce wartime goods, sponsored profitable privateering ventures, or conducted forbidden trade with the enemy in the Caribbean and elsewhere. But many more people paid a heavy price because of war: a farm burned, a job lost, a limb amputated, a husband or father shot in battle or cut down by disease. From London's perspective, the Americans made ill-disciplined and reluctant soldiers. But from the colonists' viewpoint, they received too little respect and inadequate assistance from Britain.

Adding insult to injury, a hard-won victory on North American soil could be canceled out at the peace table in Europe. In 1745, during King William's War, Massachusetts called for an attack on Louisburg, the recently completed French fortress on Cape Breton Island that controlled access to the St. Lawrence River and nearby fishing grounds. Because they had less at stake, other colonies refused to assist the Massachusetts fleet in this endeavor. (George Whitefield, sensing a Protestant crusade against French Catholicism, preached a fiery sermon to the troops before their departure from Boston.) After a lengthy siege, the New England forces prevailed. But the cost was high—dysentery slaughtered the soldiers—and British diplomats soon rescinded the colonial victory. In 1748, at treaty negotiations ending the war, they handed Louisburg back to France in exchange for Madras in India.

Whatever their differences, the American colonists and the government in Britain saw potential in the land west of the Appalachian mountains, and both were eager to challenge French expansion in the region. In 1747, a group of colonial land speculators formed the Ohio Company of Virginia, seeking permission to develop western lands. Two years later the crown granted them rights to 200,000 acres south of the Ohio River if they would construct a fort in the area. Moving west and north, the Virginians hoped to occupy a valuable spot (modern-day Pittsburgh, Pennsylvania) where the Monongahela and Allegheny rivers come together to form the Ohio River. But the French had designs on the same strategic location as they extended their holdings toward the upper Ohio from the Great Lakes region.

In 1753 the Virginia governor sent a promising young major in the colonial militia named George Washington—at age 21 already regarded as a distinguished soldier— to warn the French to leave the area. The next spring Virginia workers began erecting a fort at the forks of the Ohio, but a larger French force drove them from the site and constructed Fort Duquesne instead. When Major Washington returned to the vicinity with troops in April, he probed for enemy forces. In a skirmish on May 28, 1754, 5 miles east of modern Uniontown, Pennsylvania, his men killed ten French soldiers, the first casualties in what eventually became history's first truly global war. Fearing a counterattack, he fortified his camp, calling it Fort Necessity. With 450 men and meager supplies, he dug in to prepare.

> *"Everyone cries, a union is necessary, but when they come to the manner and form of the union, their weak noodles are perfectly distracted."*

Throughout the British colonies in the early summer of 1754, fears spread about the dangers of French attack and the loyalties of Native American allies. Officials in London requested that all the colonies involved in relations with the Iroquois send delegates to a special congress in Albany, New York, to improve that Indian alliance. Virginia and New Jersey abstained, but seven other colonies sent 23 representatives, who hoped to strengthen friendship with the Iroquois nations and also discuss a design for a union of the colonies.

With these goals in mind, the delegates to the Albany Congress explored and adopted a proposal by Benjamin Franklin. It called for a colonial confederation empowered to build forts and repel a French invasion. The colonies would be unified by an elected Grand Council and a president general appointed by the crown. The delegates hoped the design would be debated by colonial assemblies and implemented by an act of Parliament. But Franklin's far-sighted Albany Plan never received the attention it deserved, and no colonial legislature ever ratified the idea. "Everyone cries, a union is necessary," Franklin wrote, "but when they come to the manner and form of the union, their weak noodles are perfectly distracted."

The main distraction came from Pennsylvania, with word that on July 3 the French had attacked Major Washington at Fort Necessity. After a brief fight, he had no alternative but to surrender to a larger force and then withdraw. But the British colonists were not willing to give up their claims to the Ohio Valley without a fight. Taking the lead, the Virginia government asked for help from Britain in conducting a war against the French and their Native American allies. The crown responded by dispatching General Edward Braddock and two regiments of Irish troops. Early in 1755, his force arrived in Virginia, where preparations were already under way for a campaign to conquer Fort Duquesne. Washington accepted an unpaid position as an aide to Braddock, and in June the combined British and colonial army of 2500 began a laborious march west to face the French.

An American Fight Becomes a Global Conflict

The early stages of the war in America could hardly have been more disastrous for Britain or more encouraging for France. According to his own secretary, the aging Braddock was poorly qualified for command "in almost every respect." A French and Indian force ambushed his column in the forest near Fort Duquesne, cutting it to pieces in the most thorough defeat of the century for a British army. When Braddock died of his wounds during the hasty retreat, Washington oversaw the burial and then wrote in his diary, "We have been most scandalously beaten by a trifling body of men."

Elsewhere, the British fared little better. Indian raids battered the frontiers, spreading panic in the northern colonies. With the local militia away at war, fears of possible slave uprisings swept through the south. The French commander, the Marquis de Montcalm, struck into New York's Mohawk Valley from Lake Ontario in 1756 and then pushed south down Lake Champlain and Lake George in 1757. After a seven-day siege, he took 2000 prisoners at Fort William Henry. In an episode made famous in *The Last of the Mohicans*, his Huron Indian allies killed more than 150 men and women after their release.

The change in British fortunes came with the new ministry of William Pitt, a vain but talented member of the House of Commons. Pitt was an expansionist committed to the growth of the British empire at the expense of France. He brought a daring new strategy to the war effort, and he had the determination and bureaucratic skill to carry it out. In recent contests with France, the military might of the French army in Europe had stymied the British. Now, British forces would instead concentrate on France's vulnerable and sparsely populated overseas colonies. Under Pitt, the British broadened the war into a global conflict, the first in history, taking advantage of their superior naval power to fight on the coasts of Asia and Africa and in North America as well. By 1758, Britain had undertaken a huge military buildup in America (nearly 50,000 troops) and funded it with vast amounts of money.

To win colonial support for his plan, Pitt promised to reimburse the colonies generously for their expenses. In the South, guns, ammunition, and trade goods flowed freely to Britain's Native American allies through Charleston and Savannah, while desperate French officials in Louisiana waited anxiously for supplies that would help them retain the wavering support of their Choctaw and Creek allies. In the North, France lost Louisburg again in July 1758. Fort Frontenac on Lake Ontario fell in August. In November, faced with a powerful force, the French abandoned their valuable position at the Fork of the Ohio, blowing up Fort Duquesne to keep it out of enemy hands. Even without fortifications, the British were glad to possess the strategic site at last. They erected a new post, aptly named Fort Pitt, and laid out the village of Pittsburgh beside it.

In Canada, autumn brought a poor harvest, followed by the worst winter anyone could remember. The Marquis de Montcalm huddled in the provincial capital at Quebec with his ill-equipped army. Ice in the St. Lawrence combined with a British blockade to cut off overseas support from France during the long, cold winter.

In the spring of 1759, the British pressed their advantage, moving against Canada from the West and the South. As Britain's superintendent of Indian affairs in the region, Sir William Johnson had lived among the Iroquois nations for 20 years. His Mohawk Indian wife, Molly Brant,

■ MAP 5.4
THE BRITISH CONQUEST OF NEW FRANCE, 1754–1760

British conquest of New France

- French settlements
- British settlements
- Iroquois settlements
- - - Land claimed by the Ohio Company of Virginia
- French victories
- British victories
- French forts
- British forts

1. Washington gives up Ft. Necessity to French, July 3–4, 1754
2. Braddock's army destroyed near Ft. Duquesne, July 9, 1755
3. British yield Ft. William Henry to Montcalm, Aug. 9, 1757
4. British capture French fort at Louisburg, July 26, 1758
5. British take Ft. Frontenac from the French, Aug. 27, 1758
6. Johnson captures Ft. Niagara from the French, July 25, 1759
7. Wolfe defeats Montcalm, Plains of Abraham, Sept. 13, 1759
8. Amherst accepts French surrender of Montreal, Sept. 8, 1760

was the sister of Chief Joseph Brant. As British successes mounted, the Mohawks and other Iroquois became increasingly eager to support the winning side in the war. Sensing this, Johnson recruited 1000 formerly neutral Iroquois to join 2000 British regulars on the shores of Lake Ontario. With Johnson in command, they laid siege to Fort Niagara. The fort fell in July, a British victory that effectively isolated enemy posts farther west and obliged the French to abandon them. In August, a British force under Jeffery Amherst captured Ticonderoga and Crown Point on Lake Champlain. The stage was set for an assault on Quebec itself.

Quebec Taken and North America Refashioned

In London, William Pitt knew that capturing Quebec would conquer Canada. Months earlier, he had ordered James Wolfe "to make an attack upon Quebeck, by the River St. Lawrence." Wolfe's flotilla, with 8500 troops, anchored near the walled city in late June. But the French held their citadel despite weeks of heavy shelling. Desperate and sick, Wolfe resorted to a ruthless

Thomas Johnson, engraving, 1759. The I.N. Phelps Stokes Collection of American Historical Prints, Prints Division, The New York Public Library

■ *Quebec, the Capital of New France,* by Thomas Johnson. Eager to celebrate the fall of Quebec in 1759, a Boston printer took an old image of the city from a French map. He highlighted the Catholic churches and seminaries that Protestant New England found so threatening.

campaign against the countryside that left 1400 farms in ruins. Even this strategy failed to draw Montcalm's forces out to fight. Cold weather was approaching, and the British realized that they would soon need to reboard their ships and retreat to the Atlantic to avoid being trapped by winter ice on the river.

As a last resort, Wolfe adopted a risky plan to climb a steep bluff and attack the vulnerable west side of the city. On the night of September 12, 1759, he dispatched troops to float quietly past French sentries and scale the formidable cliffs. At daybreak, 12 British battalions emerged on a level expanse known as the Plains of Abraham. The future of the continent and its inhabitants hinged on a pitched battle between opposing European armies. Montcalm and Wolfe staked everything in the clash, and both lost their lives in the encounter. By nightfall, the British had won a decisive victory, and four days later the surviving French garrison surrendered the city of Quebec.

Montreal fell to Britain the following year, and fighting subsided in America. But Pitt continued to pour public money into the global war, and one military triumph followed another. The British conquered French posts in India, took French Senegal on the West African coast, and seized the valuable sugar islands of Martinique and Guadeloupe in the French West Indies. When Spain came to France's aid in 1762, British forces captured the Philippines and the Cuban city of Havana. As Londoner Horace Walpole put it, "Our bells are worn threadbare with ringing of victories." But with 160,000 men under arms, British taxpayers resented the huge costs of the war. Many also worried that the effort to humiliate France and Spain and undo their empires could spark retaliation in the years ahead. Rising criticism pushed Pitt from office, and peace negotiations began.

In a matter of months, the European powers redrew the imperial map of North America. Their complex swaps constituted the largest single rearrangement of real estate in the history of the continent. First, France ceded to Spain the port of New Orleans and all of the Louisiana territory west of the Mississippi River. Then, in the 1763 Treaty of Paris, more transactions followed. Spain turned over East Florida to Britain, receiving back Havana and the Philippines in return. France gave Britain its holdings between the Appalachians and the Mississippi River as well as the parts of Canada not already claimed by the Hudson's Bay Company. In exchange for this vast acquisition, the British returned the sugar islands of Martinique and Guadeloupe to the French. They also allowed France to retain fishing rights off the coast of Newfoundland and two small islands in the vicinity.

Those negotiating the peace agreed that French Canadians could choose between leaving Canada or becoming British subjects. But the Paris treaty made no mention of the thousands of Native Americans whose bountiful homelands were being reassigned. The final results were striking. Britain emerged as the world's leading colonial power, and, after two centuries, the empire of France in North America abruptly disappeared.

Conclusion

For half a century, the complex currents of colonial life had recalled the ancient tale of Babel, as told in the Book of Genesis in the Bible. A confusion of voices, interests, and cultures competed and interacted over a wide expanse in North America. In the process, a string of related economic regions emerged along the eastern seaboard. The colonies that composed these regions varied in ethnic make-up, but they all owed political allegiance to Britain, and they were all expanding rapidly in population. This demographic growth was crucial. Beneath the commercial striving and religious debate, a deeper and less visible change in numbers was underway that would alter the power and place of the Atlantic colonies.

Unprecedented population growth along the Atlantic coast stands out dramatically in hindsight. In 1763 Britain's mainland colonies contained more than 1.6 million people. The figure had quickly come to dwarf all the other population totals on the continent. The Spanish in New Mexico and Texas and the Comanche and Sioux on the Great Plains all controlled wide stretches of territory. But their numbers remained only a minute fraction of the people in the East Coast colonies who had recently managed, despite all their regional differences, to support the British armed forces in ousting the French from North America.

Amazingly, in the 13 years between 1750 and 1763 more than 400,000 people were added to the British mainland colonies. This number of new people—reflecting natural increase and migration combined—exceeded the entire population that had been living in those same British colonies five decades earlier, in 1713. The growth in numbers during the decades to come was equally rapid, and the changes for the continent were even more dramatic and long-lasting.

Sites to Visit

San Saba Mission

The ruins of the mission, abandoned by the Spanish after Comanche attacks in the 1750s, lie 2 miles east of Menard, Texas, off US-190, near the San Saba River. Two miles west of Menard, on Highway 29, the fully restored San Saba Presidio contains a small museum in the rebuilt chapel. Menard is 150 miles northwest of San Antonio.

The Ephrata Cloister

One of America's earliest communal societies was the Ephrata Cloister, founded by Conrad Beissel in 1732. It is located on West Main Street in Ephrata, Pennsylvania, 2 miles west of Highway 222 between Lancaster and Reading. Guided tours include the Meetinghouse, Bake House, and Print Shop.

Winchester, Virginia

Founded in 1744 as a stop on the Great Wagon Road, Winchester is located 70 miles west of Washington, D.C., at Interstate 81, "where the Shenandoah Valley begins and history never ends." Young George Washington worked as a land surveyor in this frontier town, and his office is now a museum.

Old Salem
www.oldsalem.org

This reconstruction of a village founded in 1766 is in Winston-Salem, North Carolina. The site includes the Winkler Bakery, a cemetery, and the Museum of Early Southern Decorative Arts (MESDA). Take a virtual tour of the site at www.oldsalem.org. Nearby is Bethabara, a Moravian community founded in 1753, also open to the public; see www.bethabara.org.

Sermons of the Reverend George Whitefield
www.crta.org/documents/Whitefield.html

The texts of 59 sermons of the Reverend George Whitefield are available online at this Web site. The Bethesda Orphanage, founded by Whitefield in 1740, is located on 650 acres beside the Moon River outside Savannah, Georgia. It is now the Bethesda Home for Boys, America's oldest existing children's home.

The Rice Museum

Located in the Old Market Building in Georgetown, South Carolina, the museum contains dioramas and exhibits describing rice cultivation. The Caw Caw Interpretive Center, west of Charleston on the Savannah Highway (Route 17S) in Ravenel, South Carolina, provides a fascinating view of eighteenth-century rice fields.

Fort William Henry

This fort, at the south end of Lake George, was the location for events in 1757 depicted in *The Last of the Mohicans*. Guided tours relating to the British–French struggle during the Seven Years' War are available at Fort William Henry and at larger Fort Ticonderoga, on Lake Champlain. Both sites are east of Interstate 87, north of Albany, New York. Visit Fort Ticonderoga online at www.fort-ticonderoga.org/.

Seven Years' War Association Journal
www.sywajournal.com/

The online journal of the Seven Years' War Association has links to numerous sites and documents connected to the American portion of the conflict, often known as the French and Indian War. For a Web Index of the French and Indian War, go to www.geocities.com/Athens/Parthenon/1500/fiw.html.

For Further Reading

General

John J. McCusker and Russell R. Menard, *The Economy of British America, 1607–1789* (1991).

Gary B. Nash, *The Urban Crucible: The Northern Seaports and the Origins of the American Revolution* (abridged edition, 1986).

Carla Gardina Pestana, *Liberty of Conscience and the Growth of Religious Diversity in Early America, 1636–1786* (1987).

Marcus Rediker, *Between the Devil and the Deep Blue Sea: Merchant Seamen, Pirates, and the Anglo-American Maritime World, 1700–1750* (1987).

New Cultures on the Western Plains

Gary Clayton Anderson, *Kinsmen of Another Kind: Dakota–White Relations in the Upper Mississippi Valley, 1650–1862* (1984).

Elizabeth A. H. John, *Storms Brewed in Other Men's Worlds: The Confrontation of Indians, Spanish, and French in the Southwest, 1540–1795* (1975).

Frank Raymond Secoy, *Changing Military Patterns of the Great Plains Indians* (1953).

Britain's Mainland Colonies: A New Abundance of People

Kirsten Fischer, *Suspect Relations: Sex, Race, and Resistance in Colonial North Carolina* (2002).

James T. Lemon, *The Best Poor Man's Country: A Geographical Study of Early Southeastern Pennsylvania* (1972).

Harry Roy Merrens, *Colonial North Carolina in the Eighteenth Century: A Study in Historical Geography* (1964).

A. G. Roeber, *Palatines, Liberty, and Property: German Lutherans in Colonial British America* (1993).

Laurel Thatcher Ulrich, *Good Wives: Image and Reality in the Lives of Women in Northern New England, 1650–1750* (1982).

Marianne S. Wokeck, *Trade in Strangers: The Beginnings of Mass Migration to North America* (1999).

The Varied Economic Landscape

Kathryn E. Holland Braund, *Deerskins and Duffels: Creek Indian Trade with Anglo-America, 1685–1815* (1993).

Elaine Forman Crane, *Ebb Tide in New England: Women, Seaports, and Social Change, 1630–1800* (1998).

Margaret Ellen Newell, *From Dependency to Independence: Economic Revolution in Colonial New England* (1998).

Frederick B. Tolles, *Meeting House and Counting House: The Quaker Merchants of Colonial Philadelphia, 1682–1763* (1948).

Daniel Vickers, *Farmers and Fishermen: Two Centuries of Work in Essex County, Massachusetts, 1630–1850* (1994).

Michael Zuckerman, *Peaceable Kingdoms: New England Towns in the Eighteenth Century* (1970).

Matters of Faith: The Great Awakening

Patricia U. Bonomi, *Under the Cope of Heaven: Religion, Society, and Politics in Colonial America* (1986).

Carl Bridenbaugh, *Mitre and Sceptre: Transatlantic Faiths, Ideas, Personalities, and Politics, 1689–1775* (1962).

Philip Greven, *The Protestant Temperament: Patterns of Child-Rearing, Religious Experience, and the Self in Early America* (1977).

Timothy D. Hall, *Contested Boundaries: Itinerancy and the Reshaping of the Colonial American Religious World* (1994).

Jacob R. Marcus, *The Colonial American Jew* (1970).

Mechal Sobel, *The World They Made Together: Black and White Values in Eighteenth-Century Virginia* (1987).

The French Lose a North American Empire

Fred Anderson, *Crucible of War: The Seven Years' War and the Fate of Empire in British North America, 1754–1766* (2000).

Fred Anderson, *A People's Army: Massachusetts Soldiers and Society in the Seven Years' War* (1984).

Francis Jennings, *Empire of Fortune: Crowns, Colonies, and Tribes in the Seven Years' War in America* (1988).

Ian K. Steele, *Betrayals: Fort William Henry and the "Massacre"* (1990).

Daniel H. Usner, Jr., *Indians, Settlers, and Slaves in a Frontier Exchange Economy: The Lower Mississippi Valley Before 1783* (1992).

Online Practice Test

Test your understanding of this chapter with interactive review quizzes at

www.ablongman.com/jonescreatedequal/chapter5

CHAPTER 6

The Limits of Imperial Control, 1763–1775

Benjamin Blyth, *Abigail Adams*, c.1766. Courtesy of the Massachusetts Historical Society, MHS #73

■ The astute Abigail Adams (like Barbara Bush in our own time) was the wife of one American president and the mother of another.

B Y THE 1760s, BOSTON HAD GROWN INTO A BUSY SEAPORT OF 16,000 PEOPLE. ALTHOUGH tiny by modern urban standards, the city was much larger and less intimate than it had been a century earlier. The gap between the rich and the poor had expanded steadily, until a mere 5 percent of the city's taxpayers controlled as much wealth as the other 95 percent combined. The Seven Years' War had only worsened the growing inequality. During the war, wealthy Boston families such as the Apthorps and Hancocks multiplied their fortunes, building stately homes and importing elegant fashions. In 1764 young John Hancock, heir to his uncle's vast shipping business, inherited an immense fortune of £80,000.

However, most Bostonians lived in a very different world, made worse by a terrible fire that swept the port in 1760 and the depression that gripped the region after the war ended in 1763. Half the townspeople had lifetime property and savings worth less than £40, and half of those possessed £20 or less. George Hewes, five years younger than Hancock, was born into this other Boston in 1742. Hewes lost his father, a struggling butcher who also sold soap and candles, at age seven. But unlike Hancock, he had no rich uncle. Hewes's mother died in 1755, and when her own father died the next year after a life toiling as a shoemaker, he left behind only £15. George inherited less than £3 from his grandfather, and perhaps his tools and his familiarity with leatherworking as well. The boy became an apprentice shoemaker at age 14.

At 93, cobbler George Hewes still recalled his part in the "Boston Tea Party" of 1770.

Despite the town's growth, rich and poor still encountered one another on occasion. If anything those contacts increased during the tumultuous decade that gave rise to the American Revolution. Politics—both imperial and local—heated up in the 1760s, opening up rifts within the ruling elite. Throughout the colonies, British officials and other people who supported the crown's policies became known as Loyalists, or Tories. The wealthy among them saw social and economic dominance as their birthright and scorned their rivals for courting favor with the poor. In contrast, leaders of the emerging opposition (known as Whigs or Patriots) consisted of less conservative—often young and ambitious—members of the educated and professional classes. These people downplayed their rank and privilege to win popular support from those beneath them on the social scale.

In Boston, Hancock was one such person. In 1763, after Hewes repaired an expensive shoe for John Hancock, the merchant invited the young cobbler to a New Year's open house at his impressive mansion. In his old age, Hewes still recalled the occasion vividly. Intimidated by the wealth around him, he remembered being scared "almost to death" when the magnate toasted him and gave him a silver coin.

According to Hewes, the two men met again on very different terms after a decade had passed. In December 1773, the shoemaker painted stripes on his face and then joined other activists, also disguised as Native American warriors, in a risky nighttime action. To protest imperial policies, these patriots in war paint emptied chests of British tea into Boston Harbor. Recalling that night as an elderly man, Hewes was one of the first to refer to the event as a "tea party." And he swore that in the darkness he had rubbed elbows with Hancock himself and had joined him in smashing a crate of tea.

Edward Savage, *John Hancock and his Wife*, n.d., (48.8). In the Collection of The Corcoran Gallery of Art, Bequest of Woodbury Blair

■ Some wealthy colonists, like the Hancocks of Boston, joined the Patriot opposition during the 1760s and 1770s. Gradually, out of necessity, these merchants and planters forged a loose and convenient alliance with colonial artisans and workers who came from a very different world.

Whether the man beside Hewes—also disguised as an Indian yet wearing a ruffled shirt—was actually Hancock remains doubtful. But symbolically, the two men were now working shoulder to shoulder. They came together across class lines in a coalition that would soon challenge Europe's strongest empire, Britian, and spark the Atlantic world's first successful anticolonial revolution.

Few could have predicted the growth of solidarity between a portion of the colonial elite and a wide spectrum of working people; this implausible alliance developed gradually and imperfectly. During the decade before 1776, there were numerous occasions when class and regional interests still sharply divided the British colonists. Urban artisans, rural farmers, enslaved African Americans, and numerous wives and widows, for example, did not necessarily share common views and concerns. Indeed, they were frequently at odds. Nevertheless, within half a generation enough of these diverse people— many as distant from one another socially as Hancock and Hewes—came together to stage a successful struggle to separate politically from Britain.

What shared experiences and beliefs caused this unstable partnership to emerge against the odds? What events shaped it and prompted it to gather momentum by July 1776, when John Hancock, as president of the Second Continental Congress, applied the first and largest signature to the American colonies' Declaration of Independence? In retrospect, we know that between 1763 and 1775 a significant change in identity took place. Little by little, for the first time, colonists from separate regions and different countries of origin began to speak of themselves as Americans. Gradually, they adopted a term that had previously applied only to Indians. (Indeed, it may be a sign of the increasing identification with North America that they occasionally adopted symbolic Indian garb, as when Hewes and Hancock joined others in dumping tea in Boston Harbor.)

At times, of course, this self-conscious new identification with North America went too far, as in the creation of a *Continental* Congress. In fact, it was not a body of the entire North American continent at all. The tumult and debate that led up to the revolt against Britain touched communities all up and down the Atlantic seaboard, linking them through shared debates and energetic Committees of Correspondence. So it is not surprising that the delegates to Philadelphia boldly called themselves a Continental Congress. Still, the familiar terminology is clearly misleading in any wider, literal sense. Eventually, a new American nation would come to control much of the continent. But that unlikely prospect lay far in the future, and few obvious signs pointed in that direction.

In 1763 thousands of Native Americans in the Midwest, under the leadership of Pontiac, were fighting to assert their own independence from European encroachment. While Indians on the Great Plains, including the Comanche and the Sioux, continued to contend for new territories, other peoples still farther west experienced the initial shocks of colonial contact. Suddenly, inhabitants of the Hawaiian Islands and the Alaskan coast were encountering European intruders for the first time. The rival European empires, meanwhile, competed globally on the high seas, seeking mastery in the Atlantic, the Pacific, and the Indian Oceans. For them, North America, the resources of its rich interior still largely unexplored and unexploited, remained only one piece in a larger puzzle, one prize in a wider imperial game.

Following the departure of the French, the push of rival powers to establish permanent control over the North American continent continued. But the limitations that constrained imperial control were more evident than ever. Geographic ignorance, limited resources, weak bureaucracies, huge distances, strong-willed colonists, and resilient native inhabitants all posed limits for maintaining and expanding far-flung empires. Russia's foothold in Alaska and Spain's presence in California were new and tenuous at best. Spanish dominance at older outposts in Arizona, New Mexico, and Texas remained partial, and Spain's grip on its newly acquired Louisiana territory was even more nominal. East of the Mississippi River, long-term British control finally seemed to be assured. But appearances can be deceiving. Even Britain, secure after its decisive victory over France, would soon be fighting a losing battle to retain much of the American continent that it confidently claimed to control.

New Challenges to Spain's Expanded Empire

With Spain's acquisition of Louisiana from France in 1763, the Spanish held nominal title to the entire West, from the Mississippi to the Pacific. Populated by more than 1 million Native Americans, this expanded empire reached north into the uncharted realms where Russian Siberia faced Alaska. But whether Spain could settle and exploit, or even explore and defend, this vast domain remained an open question. After all, envious rivals were already probing North America's Pacific coast. Exploration voyages by the French and the British challenged Spain's dominance in the Pacific, and Russian colonization in Alaska spurred the Spanish to establish posts along the coast of California. These rivalries, in turn, brought new pressures to bear on the West's diverse Indian peoples, even before the United States emerged as a separate entity with expansionist ambitions of its own.

Pacific Exploration, Hawaiian Contact

Defeat in the Seven Years' War removed the French from North America in 1763. Lamenting the loss and burdened with heavy war debts, France sought fresh prospects in the unexplored

John Webber, A View of Kealakekua Bay, c. 1781–1783. Dixson Library, State Library of New South Wales, Sydney

■ When Captain Cook anchored at Hawaii's Kealakekua Bay in 1779, he wrote in his journal that the islanders crowded aboard his two vessels and paddled around them in "a multitude of Canoes." Hundreds of others swam around the ships, along with "a number of men upon pieces of Plank." One such surfboarder is visible in the foreground.

South Pacific. As one Frenchman observed, the discovery of a new continent might furnish "opportunities for profit to equal all that has been produced in America." The task of finding such a bonanza fell to Louis Antoine de Bougainville, a gifted French officer who had served with General Montcalm in Canada during the war. In 1766 Bougainville set out to search for "Terra Australis Incognita," the Pacific's fabled unknown southern land. His voyage marked the first French circumnavigation of the world. Nevertheless, it revealed no continent—only small, lush islands such as Tahiti and Samoa. French hopes for immediate wealth from a new Pacific landmass went unfulfilled.

Not to be outdone, British captains pressed their own Pacific explorations. The most skilled and successful was James Cook, who ranged from the Arctic Circle to Antarctica during three momentous voyages beginning in 1768. In January 1778, during Cook's final voyage, his two vessels happened upon the Hawaiian Islands, eight volcanic isles stretching over 300 miles. More than 13 centuries earlier (A.D. 300–500), seafaring Polynesians had migrated here in remarkable ocean-sailing canoes. They had arrived from the Marquesas Islands far to the south, and their descendants, perhaps as many as 300,000 people, lived in agricultural and fishing communities dominated by powerful chiefs.

The Hawaiians mistook Captain Cook for Lono, a deity they had expected to reappear, and treated him with hospitality and respect. "No people could trade with more honisty," the navigator scrawled in his journal when he departed. During the next 12 months, Cook cruised up the west coast of North America, starting in what is now Oregon. Two centuries had passed since Francis Drake's earlier visit to the California coast. But English mariners still hoped to find a sea passage through North America that might drastically shorten voyages from the Atlantic to Asia. Cook brought an end to the speculation. He encountered a solid coastline that stretched all the way to Alaska. Along the way, he traded with Northwest Coast Indians for sea otter pelts and other furs. In Alaska, he gave his own name to Cook Inlet, near present-day Anchorage. Then he sailed north into arctic waters, pausing at Asia's easternmost tip.

Cook's vessels returned south in 1779, and they were again greeted with fanfare on the big island of Hawaii. But admiration turned to resentment as the English outstayed their welcome at Kealakekua Bay. When an incident of petty pilfering erupted into violence, an angry crowd of Hawaiians killed Cook and four of his mariners. After the captain's death, his two sloops returned to the North Pacific and then stopped at the Chinese port of Macao. There, the crew sold their furs at an enormous profit. They then sailed back to England in 1780 with word of the money to be made selling North American sea otter pelts in China. The voyagers also confirmed a disturbing rumor: Russia already had a foothold in this lucrative Pacific traffic.

The Russians Lay Claim to Alaska

In 1728 Vitus Bering, a Danish captain hired to serve in the Russian naval service, completed a three-year trek east across Siberia. Reaching the Kamchatka peninsula on the Pacific Ocean, he built a boat and sailed north between Asia and America through the strait that bears his name today. The journey ended European speculation that Asia was linked to North America. On a second expedition in 1741, Bering visited the Alaskan mainland and claimed it for Russia. He lost his life on the return voyage after a winter shipwreck on a frozen island.

Bering's crew managed to return to Kamchatka with valuable pelts. Their feat proved that round trips between Russia and America were both possible and profitable. Over the next generation, merchants in Asian Rus-

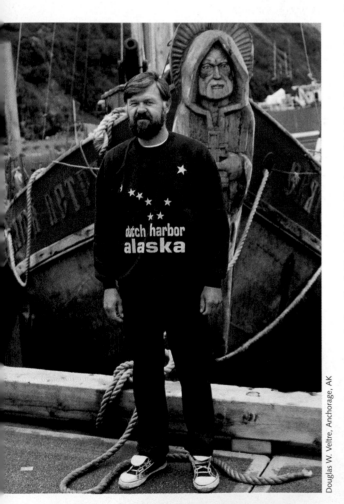

■ In 1991, 250 years after Vitus Bering's voyage to Alaska, Russians from Kamchatka sailed replicas of Bering's three small vessels across the North Pacific to Alaska. Aleksandr Maslov-Bering, a descendant of the explorer, poses beside the carved bow of one boat.

Douglas W. Veltre, Anchorage, AK

sia sent several expeditions to Alaska each year, bringing back furs that they traded with the powerful Chinese empire. One typical journey east along Alaska's Aleutian Island chain in 1752 brought back the pelts of 1772 sea otters, 750 blue foxes, and 840 fur seals.

Before reaching Alaska, these rough Russian trappers (known as *promyshlenniki*) had gathered furs in Siberia for generations using a cruel and effective system. They captured native women and children as hostages, then ransomed them back to their men in exchange for a fixed number of furs. In Alaskan waters, the trappers lacked the numbers, the boats, and the skill to collect large supplies of furs on their own. So they put their brutal hostage system into practice there as well. "They beach their vessels and try to take hostages, children and women from the island or nearby islands. If they cannot do this peacefully, they will use force," one Russian captain explained. "No matter where the Natives hunt, on shore or at sea, they must give everything" to the trappers. Native Alaskans resisted these intruders where possible, but many eventually submitted in a desperate effort to survive.

In the quarter century before 1780, 30 different companies sponsored expeditions to Alaskan waters. Harsh conditions and stiff competition between ships made the traffic risky for the Russians and far worse for the Aleutian Islanders. The newcomers, bringing diseases, firearms, and their brutal hostage-taking system, reduced the population of the islands. The remaining Aleuts were forced to overhunt their valuable wildlife, making their own survival even more precarious. As the human and animal population of the Aleutian Islands declined, the Russians pushed farther east in search of new hunters and hunting grounds.

As the voyages from Kamchatka grew longer and more expensive, a Russian organizer named Grigorii Shelikov gave serious thought to establishing an Alaskan base to facilitate operations. Shelikov and a partner formed a new company in 1781, and in 1784, founded a permanent colonial settlement on Kodiak Island east of the Aleutians, despite fierce opposition from the island's native residents. By 1799 the firm would absorb smaller competitors to become the Russian-American Company, with a monopoly from the czar.

In 1790, with the Kodiak base secure, Russians forced more than 7000 island inhabitants to embark on six enormous fur hunts in their versatile two-seat kayaks. That same year, Shelikov hired Alexander Baranov to oversee the Kodiak post and expand operations down the Alaskan coast. In 1799 Baranov established an additional outpost at Sitka in southeast Alaska. When a raid by Tlingit Indians destroyed the fort in 1802, he rebuilt the post. Sitka, called New Archangel at the time, became the capital of Russian America in 1808. From here, Baranov eventually extended the company's reach south toward Spanish California, seeking new hunting grounds and a climate warm enough to grow food crops.

Spain Colonizes the California Coast

The Seven Years' War had left Spain's king, Carlos III, with vast new land claims in western North America and only limited resources to explore or defend them. The Spanish ceded Florida to the British in 1763, evacuating St. Augustine and Pensacola. But Spain acquired from France the port of New Orleans and all of upper and lower Louisiana west of the Mississippi.

The bureaucrats charged with administering Spanish America struggled to oversee the vast and unfamiliar portions of the extended realm. But they faced numerous obstacles in controlling the huge domain. To their dismay, many of the Native Americans were not intimidated by force. Apaches and Comanches resisted several decades of military suppression and slave raids across the Southwest. In addition, clerics offered their own resistance to government designs. Carlos III expelled the powerful Jesuit order from the Spanish realm in 1767 for opposing administrative reform in the colonies. Unruly colonists posed a threat of their own. French inhabitants of New Orleans led a brief rebellion against Spanish rule in 1768. Finally, officials feared challenges in the Pacific from the British and the Russians. It was not until 1812 that Baranov finally established a Russian outpost at Fort Ross on the California coast, just north of San Francisco Bay. But as early as 1759, a Spanish Franciscan had published *Muscovites in California,* warning of Russian settlements.

With the threat of Russians in mind, Spanish leaders in America concentrated on establishing a token presence along the Pacific coast. Responsibility for this difficult task fell to

■ Jesuit missionary Ignacio Tirsch drew this view of his mission at the southern tip of Baja California in the 1760s. A Spanish ship that has crossed the Pacific from the Philippines is anchored offshore. When all Jesuits were ejected from Spain's American empire in 1767, Tirsch returned to his home near Prague in eastern Europe.

The Spanish entry into Alta (upper) California

- Fort
- † Mission
- ▪ Presidio
- ● Town
- ⊞ Mission and Presidio
- ⊡ Town and Presidio
- —— Portolá, 1769
- —— Anza and Garcés, 1774
- —— Anza, 1775–1776
- —— Garcés, 1776
- —— Domínguez and Escalante, 1776
- ------ Modern state boundaries
  shown for orientation
- (1769) Years indicate the date of founding

■ **MAP 6.2**

**SPANISH EXPLORATION AFTER 1760 AND THE START
OF THE CALIFORNIA MISSIONS**

José de Gálvez, a dedicated administrator who literally drove himself mad with concern for securing this bountiful region. In 1769
Gálvez sent a small vanguard north from lower (Baja) California, led
by Gaspar de Portolá and Franciscan friar Junípero Serra. They established an initial outpost at San Diego Bay. Portolá then pressed farther
up the coast, building a presidio (or military garrison) at Monterey in 1770 to
"defend us from attacks by the Russians, who," he believed, "were about to invade us."

After the removal of all Jesuits from Spanish America in 1767, numerous Franciscan missionaries, members of a competing Catholic order, expanded their work and took on new
responsibilities. Following the lead of Father Serra, other Franciscans soon planted several missions between San Diego and Monterey. These included the San Gabriel mission in 1771, where
colonists established the town of Los Angeles ten years later. In 1775 a Spanish captain sailed
through the Golden Gate into spacious San Francisco Bay, and the next year a land expedition laid out the presidio and mission of San Francisco. A town sprang up at nearby San José
the following year. Isolated Franciscan fathers labored to convert the coast's diverse Indian
inhabitants. Meanwhile, Spanish vessels pushed far up the Pacific shoreline. They established
contact with the Northwest Coast Indians in 1774, and Captain Ignacio de Arteaga reached
the Gulf of Alaska in 1779, 14 months after Captain Cook had been there.

But Spanish ships traveling north from Mexico had difficulty supplying the few dozen settlers in California. Authorities therefore looked to open an overland supply route to the coast
from Santa Fe or Sonora. In 1774, Juan Bautista de Anza set out in search of a land route to
California from the Sonoran presidio he commanded at Tubac, south of Tucson. Accompanied

by a Franciscan named Father Garcés, he forded the Colorado River with the help of Yuma Indians. He then crossed desert and mountains to reach the coast at San Gabriel. The next year, Anza led 240 reinforcements—mostly Spanish women and children—along a similar route, pausing at San Gabriel and heading north to San Francisco Bay.

Further explorations in 1776 proved less successful. Trying to find a usable route between California and New Mexico, Father Garcés meandered through the southwestern deserts. He traveled north along the Colorado River from Yuma country and then probed west across the Mohave Desert and east near the Grand Canyon without success. Two other Franciscans, Fathers Domínguez and Escalante, left Santa Fe on horseback in July 1776. They headed northwest across Colorado and Utah in search of a more northern route to avoid hostile Indians and lead to Monterey on the Pacific coast. But no such trail existed, and eventually they turned back. Instead of a west-flowing river, their five-month, 1800-mile trek revealed the huge expanse of the Great Basin. A passable route linking Santa Fe to the West Coast would have to wait for another half century.

Moreover, the Sonoran path to California that Anza had established proved short-lived. The same Yuma Indians who had helped his party cross the Colorado River in 1774 quickly grew to resent the Spanish trespassers. The last straw came in the summer of 1781, when a party of Spanish soldiers and settlers arrived at the river, heading for California with nearly a thousand head of livestock. When a sergeant demanded food from the Yumas, he reported that "the Indians screamed out to me that the cows and horses destroyed their mesquite [trees] and corn fields." The irate inhabitants asked him why the animals "were not fenced in," and within weeks they retaliated. Father Garcés and more than 100 Spanish men, women, and children died in the bloody Yuma Revolt, and hopes for a rapid expansion of the Spanish colony in California died with them.

Despite all these problems, the tiny California settlements endured. With difficulty, Spain managed to retain some control over its recently expanded North American empire. The same could not be said for the British in their own newly enlarged empire farther east. They had taken Canada from the French, and their military might dominated the Atlantic world. But their fortunes in North America were about to change.

New Challenges to Britain's Expanded Empire

In September 1760, French forces at Montreal submitted to British commander Jeffery Amherst in the final surrender of the Seven Years' War. For Native Americans living east of the Mississippi, the French defeat had an immediate impact. General Amherst, who despised Indians as "treacherous" and "contemptible," intended to alter Native American relations in the interior to reflect the new balance of power.

Immediately, Amherst dispatched James Grant to South Carolina with instructions "to chastise the Cherokees," who had taken up arms against the growing number of English traders and settlers in western Carolina. With 2800 soldiers—and more than 80 blacks to tend 700 packhorses and 400 beef cattle—Grant invaded Cherokee country in 1761. His men burned 15 villages and destroyed 1500 acres of beans and corn. The attackers had orders "to put every Soul to Death" without sparing women or children. The Indians who escaped Grant's force retreated in defeat.

With the Cherokees chastened in the South, Amherst turned his attention to the Indians living north of the Ohio River. Here his harsh policies brought a sudden retaliation from the Native Americans that took many lives and cost Amherst his command. And if Indians in the Midwest posed fresh challenges to Britain's expanded American empire, so did the colonists themselves.

Midwestern Lands and Pontiac's War for Indian Independence

As soon as the British unseated their French competitors in the Ohio River Valley, they prohibited traffic with Indians in such goods as knives, tomahawks, muskets, lead, and powder.

They also cut back on the use of ceremonial gifts. When the French were still powerful, the British had been generous, but now, one Native American complained, "you Look on us as Nobody." As French traders withdrew, the British took over their strategic posts at Detroit and at Michilimackinac. English settlers built new forts in the Ohio Valley and erected massive Fort Pitt over the ruins of Fort Duquesne. Indians at Niagara Falls commented in dismay at "so many Men and so much artillery passing by."

In 1761 wary Senecas proposed a preemptive strike against the British intruders. They failed to recruit their former enemies—the Ottawas, Potawatomies, and Hurons—so the plan died. But the next year brought poor harvests, a harsh winter, and a deadly epidemic. Hard conditions, plus the lack of French trade, weakened these "three fires" of the Great Lakes region and made them more willing to take up arms. Then, early in 1763, rumors spread through the Indian communities regarding peace negotiations in Europe. Reportedly, France would cede Louisiana to Spain and give up Canada and the entire Midwest to Great Britain. Among Native Americans, this shocking news undercut moderate leaders who were willing to accommodate the English and strengthened the hand of war factions.

Word that a remote treaty in Paris might disrupt the entire region also drew attention to Neolin, a Delaware Indian prophet who urged a return to ancient ways and a separation from the corrupting Europeans. Neolin's vision of gaining independence from white control by driving out the British held wide appeal for Native Americans in the Midwest. Among those influenced by it was Pontiac, a militant Ottawa warrior. In April, Pontiac addressed a great council of more than 400 Ottawas, Potawatomies, and Hurons, meeting secretly within 10 miles of Fort Detroit. Invoking the Delaware Prophet's vision, he told the gathering that the Master of Life resented the British and wanted them removed: "Send them back to the lands which I have created for them and let them stay there." By May, he had mobilized a coalition and laid siege to Detroit.

Pontiac's uprising ignited other attacks, as Indians from 18 nations joined in a widespread war of liberation. By mid-June 1763, both Detroit and Fort Pitt were under siege. Moreover, the British had lost every other Ohio Valley and Great Lakes outpost. As Indian raiding parties ravaged white communities in western Virginia and Pennsylvania, embittered settlers responded with indiscriminate racial killing. In December, white men from Paxton Creek descended on families of peaceful Conestoga Indians near Lancaster, Pennsylvania, executing more than 30 Christian converts in cold blood. When eastern Pennsylvanians protested this outrage, the "Paxton Boys" marched on Philadelphia to demand increased protection on the

■ Violence on Pennsylvania's frontier prompted turmoil in Philadelphia, where Quakers had pressed for peaceful relations with Native Americans. In 1764 the Paxton Boys marched to the city to demand support for frontier settlers from the government. Ironically, as this cartoon shows, local pacifists prepared to resist them with force.

frontier. General Amherst ordered his officers to take no Indian prisoners, spread smallpox if possible, and treat the Native Americans as "the vilest race of beings that ever infested the earth." They deserved extermination, he ranted, "for the good of mankind."

The violence ended in a stalemate. Without French support, Native American munitions ran short, and Detroit and Fort Pitt endured. Indian militancy waned, and fighters deserted the coalition. Then in 1765, Pontiac was assassinated by a Peoria Indian in Illinois. Although the Native Americans had not won, they also had not lost, for the costly uprising prompted a shift in British policy. To avoid further expensive warfare, officials moved to restore the Indian trade, keep squatters and debt evaders out of Indian country, and prevent colonial speculation in western lands. In October 1763, Major General Thomas Gage replaced Amherst in command of British forces.

In England, the crown went further. Late in 1763, it issued a proclamation forbidding colonial settlers from moving west across the Appalachian Divide. They were not to go past the headwaters of the familiar rivers that ran east into the Atlantic Ocean. Beyond that line, where the streams flowed west into the Mississippi River or south into the Gulf of Mexico, all the land east of Spanish Louisiana would be reserved for Native Americans and a few authorized British soldiers, Indian agents, and traders.

In practice, the Proclamation Line of 1763, drawn in London, had only limited success. But it managed to frustrate aspiring members of Virginia's gentry, such as George Washington and Thomas Jefferson. These prominent men were investors in land companies that speculated in large western tracts, hoping to obtain property cheaply from Native Americans and sell small parcels to eager settlers at a steady profit. One place they did this was Kentucky, a region that had been disputed among Indians for generations.

Conflicting treaties in 1768 only sharpened the disagreement. At the Treaty of Hard Labor in South Carolina, the Cherokees retained control of the Kentucky region for hunting. Yet at the Treaty of Fort Stanwix in New York, the Iroquois ceded the same area to the British in exchange for a large payment. They did so even though the Kentucky lands were not theirs to sell. Virginia investors, hoping that this latter deal would open the region for purchase, pressed their case. But the British government, fearful of sparking unified Indian opposition and additional warfare, denied the Virginians' wishes and aroused their resentment.

Grenville's Effort at Reform

In 1763, the same year as the Proclamation Line, King George III also appointed Robert Grenville to head a new government in London. Grenville's ministry immediately faced a series of intertwined problems. Britain's victory over the French in the Seven Years' War had proved costly, nearly doubling the national debt to a staggering £146 million. As England's postwar depression deepened, returning soldiers swelled the ranks of the unemployed. Aggressive imperialists objected to what they saw as a timid peace settlement with France. In addition, rural mobs protested a new tax on domestic cider, imposed to help whittle away at the war debt.

No one promoted opposition to the government more than John Wilkes, a flamboyant member of Parliament (MP) who published an outspoken periodical. In issue number 45 of the *North Briton*, Wilkes attacked the king's peace settlement and the king himself. Grenville reacted quickly, issuing a general warrant to search the homes of all those connected to the paper. He also arrested the publisher, despite his status as an MP. Angered by the government's sweeping suppression of dissent, protesters made "Wilkes and Liberty!" and "45" into popular rallying cries.

Pressured at home, Grenville set out to impose order on Britain's growing American colonies through a series of reforms. The first step was to maintain a considerable military presence. Even with the Proclamation Line in place, Grenville's ministry kept nearly 7000 troops in North America. Leaving them there could help enforce peace with the Indians, protect the newly acquired territories of Canada and Florida, and keep young British men employed overseas rather than jobless at home. Grenville also saw another positive aspect to this move that helped to justify it. Strapped for funds, he considered paying for the trans-Atlantic forces with money drawn from the very colonies these troops were defending.

Raising money in this way would also remind the British colonies of their subordination to the sovereign power of Parliament. Colonists had grown wealthy by sidestepping the elaborate Navigation Acts and trading illegally with foreign powers, even during wartime. Sympathetic colonial juries had looked the other way. Worse, American legislatures had used their power of the purse to withhold money from any British governor who ignored local interests. Finally, lax customs officers assigned to colonial ports often collected their salaries while remaining in England, without even occupying their posts.

As a preliminary step, Grenville ordered absentee customs officials to their colonial stations and dispatched 44 navy ships to assist them. Next, he moved his first reform through Parliament: the American Duties Act of 1764, also known as the Revenue Act or the Sugar Act. The new law increased the duty on sugar and other products, such as wine, spirits, cloth, coffee, and indigo, entering the empire from non-British ports. But most important, it cut in half the long-standing import duty of sixpence per gallon on foreign molasses. Officials hoped that New England rum distillers, who had been secretly importing cheap molasses from the French West Indies without paying customs, would be willing to pay threepence per gallon to import the ingredient legally. If fully enforced, the act would reduce smuggling and boost revenues while saving merchants from the heavy costs of bribing port officials and courtroom participants.

> *"What has America done,"* protested critics, *"to be stripped of so invaluable a privilege as the trial by jury?"*

To ensure compliance, the Sugar Act strengthened the customs officers' authority to seize goods off arriving ships, and it established the first of several vice-admiralty courts. The court sat at Halifax, Nova Scotia, so defendants had large travel expenses and no hope of a favorable local jury. Instead, they faced a single appointed judge and no jury. Shockingly, a captain or shipowner accused of smuggling was presumed guilty until he could prove his innocence. If he failed to do so, he lost his seized property. "What has America done," protested critics, "to be stripped of so invaluable a privilege as the trial by jury?"

Additional statutes followed quickly. The Currency Act of 1764 prohibited colonial assemblies from issuing paper money or bills of credit to be used as legal tender to pay off debts. The move only worsened the money shortage in British America, where trade languished in a postwar depression. A lopsided trade balance was already draining gold and silver from the colonies to England annually, and colonial merchants had to pay Grenville's new duties using the same scarce hard money.

The next year, after resentful New Yorkers refused to provide firewood for General Gage's troops, Parliament passed a Quartering Act that obliged colonists to assist the army. Soldiers could not be quartered in private homes, as Gage had requested, but officers could requisition vacant barns and other buildings as temporary quarters when regular barracks and alehouses could not accommodate all their men. The local governor was to supply the soldiers, at colonial expense, with certain basic necessities they would expect at any inn: firewood, candles, bedding, salt, vinegar, utensils, and rations of beer and cider. Colonial assemblies had willingly voted such support during the Seven Years' War. However, these peacetime requisitions, ordered by a distant Parliament, seemed to challenge their authority and smacked of indirect taxation.

The Stamp Act Imposed

There was nothing indirect about Grenville's most important reform: the Stamp Act. Early in 1765, Parliament approved the new statute "for raising a further revenue" to pay for "defending, protecting, and securing" the British colonies in America. Grenville patterned his legislation on a similar law already in place in England. The new act was a complex measure that required stamps (rather like those on modern packs of cigarettes) to appear on a wide variety of articles in America after November 1, 1765. The list included all legal contracts and commissions, plus countless other paper documents from land deeds and liquor licenses to servant indentures and academic degrees. Newspapers, pamphlets, almanacs, playing cards, and dice also had to bear a stamp.

Colonial lawyers and printers were supposed to purchase these stamps from designated agents and pass the additional cost on to their clients and customers. The official stamp distributor in each colony would receive a handsome fee equaling 7.5 percent of all stamp sales. The British Exchequer (Treasury) anticipated taking in at least £100,000 per year, to be held in a separate account and spent only for government operations in America.

The proposed stamp bill generated little debate in Parliament. William Pitt, the leader of the opposition party and a friend of the colonists, did not even attend the session. Only Isaac Barré, a veteran of the Quebec campaign, protested. Claiming to "know more of America than most of you," Barré challenged the assertion of Stamp Act supporters that England had nurtured and protected the colonies from earliest times. He defended the Americans as true "Sons of Liberty": loyal British subjects protective of their rights and quick to "vindicate them, if ever they should be violated."

But Grenville countered Barré's claims. Americans, the minister argued, had nothing to fear from England. Granted, colonists had no actual representation in the Parliament that had enacted this tax. But in this they were like the majority of subjects in England. Most of them did not have the right to cast a ballot, yet all of them were said to be "virtually" represented by MPs, who supposedly had the interests of the entire country at heart. If members of Parliament could look out for nonvoting subjects at home, surely they could provide the same sort of "virtual representation" for all British subjects throughout the realm.

Whether or not they spoke for colonists in America, most MPs viewed Grenville's stamp measure as appropriate, moderate, and well conceived. They saw no legal distinction between external duties used to regulate trade and enforce the nation's navigation acts and internal taxes imposed by Parliament within the colonies themselves to raise revenue. Besides, because the stamp tax applied to numerous daily articles used throughout the colonies, it would be widely and evenly distributed. Even better, revenues would grow steadily and automatically as colonial economic activity continued to expand.

So as not to cause alarm in the colonies, Parliament set initial stamp prices in America lower than those charged in England, although it could always raise the rates as colonists grew accustomed to the tax. Moreover, the tax was to be gathered quietly by Americans themselves in the course of doing business rather than extracted from individual citizens by tax collectors. In drafting the act, the ministry had consulted agents serving as lobbyists for the American colonies in London, including Benjamin Franklin. According to these public figures, prominent colonists were eager to accept the lucrative stamp distributorships. No one predicted the upheaval that the Stamp Act would instigate. But it soon unleashed a storm of organized, militant resistance in the colonial ports where the stamps were to be sold.

The Stamp Act Resisted

At first, most colonial assemblies had mixed responses to the burdensome new tax. But in late May, the youngest member of the Virginia House of Burgesses—a rising country attorney named Patrick Henry—galvanized American resistance to the Stamp Act. Henry introduced a series of fiery resolves regarding the mandate. The House session was winding down, and many conservative members who endorsed Parliament's right to impose taxes had already departed from Williamsburg. With impressive oratory, the 28-year-old Henry managed to gain narrow passage of five separate resolutions. Young Thomas Jefferson recalled listening to the heated debate from a hallway, with other students from the College of William and Mary.

Henry's fifth and most provocative resolve asserted that Virginia's assembly had the "sole exclusive right and power to lay taxes" on the colony's inhabitants. The resolution passed by just one vote. In fact, opponents reintroduced it the next day, after Henry himself left town, and voted it down. But the spark had been struck. Within a month, distant newspapers were reprinting Henry's "Virginia Resolves." The papers included not only the resolution that had been voted down but also two ominous-sounding ones that had been drawn up but never introduced for a vote, since approval seemed unlikely. According to these two added resolutions, Virginians were "not bound to yield obedience" to any such tax, and anyone arguing otherwise must "be deemed an enemy" to the colony.

In Massachusetts, the assembly took a different approach. It issued a call for each colony to send delegates to a Stamp Act Congress in New York in October 1765 to "implore relief" from Parliament. Local citizens, inflamed by Virginia's resolutions and squeezed by an economic depression, prepared to take more direct action. In Boston, a small group of artisans and merchants known as the Loyal Nine mobilized to halt the new tax before it could even be implemented. They hatched a plan to force the designated stamp distributor, Andrew Oliver, to resign before the stamps arrived from England.

The Loyal Nine persuaded Ebenezer McIntosh, leader of the well-organized Pope's Day demonstrations in that city's South End, to join forces with North End rivals in a demonstration against Oliver. On August 16, a crowd of several thousand hanged an effigy of Oliver and tore down his newly erected Stamp Office. That night, the protesters ransacked Oliver's elegant house, drinking his wine and smashing his furniture. The next day, Oliver resigned his appointment.

As word of the protest spread, crowds took to the streets in scores of towns. Often the mobs were encouraged by local leaders who opposed the Stamp Act. These prominent citizens had started to organize themselves in secret groups, which they called the Sons of Liberty, borrowing the phrase first used by Isaac Barré in Parliament. With speeches and additional prompting, they aroused angry demonstrators. The crowds, in turn, forced the resignation of potential stamp distributors in ports from New Hampshire all the way down to the Carolinas. When a shipment of stamps finally arrived in New York City, a crowd of nearly five thousand risked open warfare to confiscate the hated cargo on Guy Fawkes Day, November 5.

Library of Congress

■ Lawyers and artisans in the Sons of Liberty encouraged demonstrations against the Stamp Act. But they ran the risk, suggested here, that poor workers, black slaves, and women in the crowds might give their own meanings to the shouts of "Liberty!"

Throughout the second half of 1765, the Sons of Liberty promoted street violence against specific targets. But they quickly learned that they could not always contain and control the demonstrations, since the debtors, sailors, blacks, and women drawn to such crowds all had separate grievances of their own. For example, on August 26 in Boston, just 10 days after the raid on Oliver's house, a second mob launched a broader assault. Without sanction from the Loyal Nine or the Sons of Liberty, the crowd went after the homes of several wealthy office holders, including the house of Lieutenant Governor Thomas Hutchinson. Because he also served as chief justice of the Superior Court, Hutchinson had offended townspeople by issuing numerous warrants for debtors and collecting large fees for administering bankruptcies. He recounted how he fled when "the hellish crew fell upon my house with the Rage of devils and…with axes split down the doors." By the time the assault ended, the attackers had pillaged Hutchinson's entire estate.

In South Carolina several months later, the spirit of insurrection also went well beyond the careful boundaries intended by the Sons of Liberty. They were pleased when Charleston artisans hanged a stamp distributor in effigy, with a sign reading, "Liberty and no Stamp Act." And they gave tacit approval when white workers harassed the wealthy slave trader and potential stamp distributor Henry Laurens with chants of "Liberty, Liberty!" Soon, however, enslaved African Americans also took to the streets, raising their own defiant cry of "Liberty, Liberty!" Fearing an insurrection by South Carolina's black majority, the same people who had sanctioned earlier street demonstrations quickly shifted their focus, believing that ideas of freedom had spread

Hudson Bay
Company

Quebec

Three Rivers

Nova Scotia

Halifax

Lake
Nipissing

Quebec

Montreal

ME
(part of Mass.)

Annapolis
Royal

NH

Ft. Edward Augustus,
abandoned June 15, 1763

Portsmouth
Windham
Salem
Marblehead

Ft. Michilimackinac,
June 2, 1763

Albany

Lebanon
Hartford
Wethersfield

MA

Boston
Pomfret
Plymouth

NY

RI

Ft. Niagara

Wallingford
New Haven
West Haven

CT

Norwich

Newport

New London

Ft. Presque Isle,
June 14–17, 1763

PA

Milford

Lyme
Stratford
Fairfield
New York

Ft. Detroit

Ft. Venango,
June 13, 1763

Woodbridge

Paxton
Amwell Twp.

Piscataway

Ft. St. Joseph,
May 25, 1763

Ft. Le Boeuf,
June 18, 1763

Elizabeth Town
Perth Amboy
Brunswick

Ft. Sandusky,
May 16, 1763

Ft. Pitt

Lancaster
Conestoga

NJ

Salem

Philadelphia

Ft. Miami,
May 27, 1763

Frederick Town

Baltimore

Elk Ridge Landing

Ft. Ouiatenon,
May 31, 1763

Annapolis

Talbot

DE

Lewes

Dumfries

MD

Ft. Chartres

Indian
reserve
(by proclamation 1763)

Leeds
Tappahannock

VA

ATLANTIC
OCEAN

Williamsburg

Norfolk

Spanish
Louisiana

NC

New Bern

Cross Creek

Duplin

Mississippi R.

Wilmington
Brunswick
Fort Johnson

SC

Charleston

Proclamation Line 1763

GA

Savannah

British dominance in eastern North America

Acquired by Britain from France

Acquired by Britain from Spain

Prior British colonies, as of 1763

Reserved to Indians under British rule

Spanish Louisiana

Points of violence, 1763–1766

British forts seized during Pontiac's Rebellion in 1763

Towns demonstrating against the Stamp Act in 1765

Distribution of British troops

British posts 100–250 soldiers

British posts 250–600 soldiers

British posts over 600 soldiers

Boundary after 1764

West Florida

St. Mary's R.

Boundary in 1763

Mobile

New Orleans

Pensacola

Ft. Apalachee

St. Augustine

East
Florida

Gulf of
Mexico

■ **MAP 6.3**
BRITISH NORTH AMERICA, 1763–1766 In 1763, the British
worked to govern their new provinces in Canada and Florida,
while suppressing an Indian uprising in the Midwest. With widely
dispersed troops, they also tried to keep colonists out of the
Mississippi Valley and halt opposition to the 1765 Stamp Act.

too far. The colonial assembly banned further importation of Africans temporarily, while local leaders expanded slave patrols and placed Charleston briefly under martial law.

Elsewhere, too, the colonial elites took steps to contain the turbulence. Many moved—often reluctantly—toward more radical positions, joining the Sons of Liberty and ridiculing the British concept of virtual representation. Colonial assemblies condemned Grenville's intrusive reforms, and the Stamp Act Congress passed resolutions vehemently protesting both the Sugar and Stamp acts. But even as they challenged Parliament, these same local leaders counseled caution and restraint. They stressed their continuing loyalty to the crown and moved to control the violence, some of which was directed at them. Such moderation appealed to cautious merchants in Boston, New York, and Philadelphia. Reluctantly, they agreed to stop ordering goods from Britain. As they saw it, British exporters, feeling the boycott's economic pinch, might use their political strength to force a repeal of the Stamp Act and defuse the tense situation.

When politics in London prompted Grenville's sudden removal from office, hopes rose in America for a possible compromise resolving the Stamp Act crisis. In March 1766, these hopes were nearly fulfilled. The new ministry of Lord Rockingham, responding to merchant pressure as predicted, and also to the compelling rhetoric of William Pitt, persuaded Parliament to repeal the Stamp Act. But colonial victory had a hollow ring to it, for the repeal bill was accompanied by a blunt Declaratory Act. In it, the members of Parliament declared clearly that they reaffirmed their power "to make Laws…to bind the Colonists and People of America…in all Cases whatsoever."

"The Unconquerable Rage of the People"

As news of Stamp Act repeal spread, the Sons of Liberty organized elaborate celebrations in British America. In Charleston and Philadelphia, citizens staged public "illuminations," placing lighted candles in the windows of their homes. In Boston, they lit so many fireworks that the town shone like day, and John Hancock treated the public to casks of Madeira wine. But word of the Declaratory Act had a sobering effect. Clearly, the problems surrounding colonial taxation and representation remained unresolved. The atmosphere of mutual suspicion and righteous indignation that had erupted during the Stamp Act crisis divided colonists further in the years ahead.

A flurry of pamphlets from colonial presses broadened awareness of the issues, sharpened arguments, and inspired new coalitions. For the first time, colonists from separate regions and different countries of origin began to identify themselves as Americans, gradually adopting a term that had previously applied only to Indians. Most importantly, as colonial leaders collaborated with one another, they discovered a shared viewpoint that gave heightened meaning and importance to each new event. This emerging ideology had a logic of its own, with common assumptions and unifying principles. It also had deep roots stretching back into earlier periods in English history.

Expanding the Framework for Revolution

The radical ideas that had emerged during England's Civil War in the 1640s, when English subjects briefly overthrew their monarchy and proclaimed a Puritan Commonwealth, lived on long after the Restoration in 1660. Decades later, the English Whigs who led the Glorious Revolution invoked some of these same principles when they limited the monarchy's power and strengthened Parliament's authority in 1688. Succeeding generations of mainstream publicists hailed the rights of all freeborn English subjects and congratulated themselves that Great Britain (as England and Scotland became known in 1707) had achieved a truly balanced government. They drew on the ancient Greek philosopher Aristotle to explain their accomplishment.

Aristotle, his modern readers noted, had observed a cycle in politics. He believed that too much power vested in a king could eventually corrupt the monarchical form of government.

Movement Building Against the Odds

Few popular protests, no matter how novel, start from scratch. Social movements regularly build on their predecessors. Even when protesters address new issues, they borrow many of their strategies from the past. Consciously or unconsciously, they adopt tactics that have proven effective at other times in undermining powerful opponents and rallying public support. Old songs are rewritten for fresh causes or adopted by new generations. The Civil Rights anthem "We Shall Overcome" began as a slave protest song and spread into the modern labor movement before returning to the black freedom struggle in the 1950s. In the late twentieth century, it circled the globe from Poland to South Africa to the Philippines as a universal hymn of liberation.

But each era of conflict contributes its own fresh additions to the arsenal of protest. Nineteenth-century slavery opponents and advocates for women's rights raised the ancient art of petition writing to a form of public demonstration. Withholding local tax payments also became a viable protest action. Author Henry David Thoreau went to jail for this act in 1846, as a gesture to oppose the Mexican–American War. In a famous essay, Thoreau popularized the general idea of civil disobedience and influenced the nonviolent protest tactics of Mahatma Gandhi in India a century later. In the twentieth century, American autoworkers and civil rights activists perfected the sit-in, drawing inspiration from Gandhi.

The Atlantic world of the late eighteenth century made key contributions to the list of effective protest tactics. Strikes, the organized work stoppages that became a central weapon for organized labor in the industrial era, draw their name from earlier acts by British deck hands. As far back as the 1760s, militant sailors in London would "strike" (take down) the sails and the horizontal yardarms of their square-rigged ships. By keeping vessels in the world's busiest port, they could halt English trade until their demands were met.

In North America, meanwhile, colonists experimented with the same boycott tactics used more recently by farm workers, environmentalists, and opponents of movie violence and record industry obscenity. Groups of irate colonists combined in formal associations, using their collective buying power to withhold purchases of certain imported goods. These nonimportation agreements were intended to cripple commerce with Britain until the government altered its policies. Such associations, though supposedly voluntary, put heavy social pressure on nonmembers who refused to join, ignoring them at church and in the streets. (Such boycotts, both commercial and social, did not earn their current name until a century later, when Irish protesters used them effectively against a landlord named Captain Boycott in 1880.)

Unbounded royal power sooner or later led to a tyranny, misrule by a despot wielding absolute control. When nobles then asserted themselves against the tyrant (as English barons had done when they forced King John to sign the Magna Carta in 1215), the resulting aristocracy could easily turn corrupt as well. Abuse of power by such an oligarchy of self-serving nobles could then prompt the common people, known as the commons, to rise up. If the commons gained sway, they might build a democracy, but it too could degenerate, leaving only anarchy. Such a "mobocracy" only paved the way for an opportunistic leader to once more seize the scepter of royal power and start the cycle over again.

Confident Whigs claimed that England had halted this vicious cycle by balancing the power of the nation's three estates: the king epitomized the legitimate interests of monarchy, the House of Lords represented the aristocracy, and the House of Commons represented the rest of the population. A few of the more radical Whig theorists continued to oppose this consensus view long after 1700, however. Calling themselves the Real Whigs, these skeptics argued that the existing mixed government—which claimed an ideal and lasting balance between monarchy, aristocracy, and commons—was actually much less perfect and more vulnerable than most people suspected.

A truly balanced government, they argued, is hard to achieve and difficult to maintain, for if power inevitably corrupts, then schemers who obtain undue control can readily disrupt such a fragile system. So its protection, these critics argued, demanded constant vigilance. They urged

©1965 Hiroji Kubota/Magnum Photos, Inc.

Ever since the era of the Boston Tea Party, Americans have organized symbolic demonstrations to challenge official policies and attract public attention. In November 1965, protestors in Washington, DC, donned death masks to draw media coverage to a rally opposing the Vietnam War.

Colonists also went beyond nonimportation agreements to engage in concerted attacks on property. But these volatile actions rarely spun far out of control. If there was one thing that the protesters knew from experience and passed on to their successors, it was the need for patience in building a movement. Premature or excessive action by a few enthusiasts could draw down reprisals, turn away potential supporters, and discredit the cause. So organizers who worked to stir up cautious or complacent citizens also worked to rein in overzealous dissidents.

In any era, deadly acts of violence such as seizing a federal arsenal, bombing a public building, or attacking an abortion clinic can be viewed as a wake-up call by those committing the act. But they can also provoke a strong backlash in public opinion. For movements building a broad base of support, therefore, it often seems best if violence and deadly force come first from the powers that be. That was true when British soldiers fired into a Boston crowd on March 5, 1770, and equally true two centuries later when troopers on horseback attacked peaceful civil rights marchers at Selma, Alabama, on March 9, 1965.

So colonial protesters, like modern antiglobalization activists, preferred mock hangings to real ones. And like their descendants with cell phones, they stressed coordination, knowing that communication was essential to the movement's success. It is no surprise that printer Ben Franklin and messenger Paul Revere played central roles. The Committees of Correspondence that linked Whig leaders in separate colonies have present-day counterparts in the campus networks that spur antisweatshop activism. ■

citizens to watch for the two surest signs of decay: the concentration of wealth in few hands and the political and social corruption that inevitably follows. Where others saw grandeur and stability in England's exuberant growth, these Real Whigs perceived sure signs of danger in the powerful new Bank of England, the expanding stock market, and the rise in public debt.

No Real Whigs proved more vigilant than John Trenchard and Thomas Gordon. The two men sensed around them the same luxury and greed that had undermined the Roman Republic. They pored over the works of ancient historians and social critics, including the Roman statesman Cato, whose correspondence described and challenged corrupt behavior. In 1721 they published *Cato's Letters: Essays on Liberty*, in which they cautioned against "the Natural Encroachments of Power" and warned that "public corruptions and abuses have grown upon us."

One abuse that offended Trenchard and Gordon was Britain's expanding patronage system. New public positions seemed designed to reward loyal support, and too many people appeared to gain office through political ties rather than through skill or training. The two writers warned that this system of patronage, when carried to an extreme, put private advancement ahead of the public good. Far from being independent civil servants, the patronage appointees supported and protected some important figure high up in the government. They dutifully filled a post (often in the colonies) and took direction from their patron in exchange for the chance to line their pockets with public money.

The authors of *Cato's Letters* saw each individual act of corruption as representing a dangerous precedent, if unopposed. They reminded their readers that tyranny is often imposed through small, subtle steps, for "if it is suffered once, it is apt to be repeated often; a few repetitions create a habit." Soon, before the citizens realize that they are losing their liberties, the permanent "Yoke of Servitude" is in place, supported by military force, and all hope of successful protest has disappeared. Equally insidious, would-be tyrants may actually "provoke the People to Disaffection; and then make that Disaffection an Argument for new Oppression…and for keeping up Troops." The encroachment of power over liberty, Trenchard and Gordon concluded, is "much easier to prevent than to cure."

During the 1760s, colonists saw disturbing parallels between the warnings of Real Whig authors and current events in America.

Though these writers attracted only limited attention in England, they earned a wide American following. The popularity of *Cato's Letters* and related tracts continued to spread in the colonies during the 1760s, for colonists saw disturbing parallels between the warnings of Real Whig authors and current events in America. Throughout history, the essayists warned, corrupt ministers have encouraged expensive wars, negotiated damaging treaties, and promoted "worthless and wicked" officials whose only qualification is to "show stupid alacrity to do what they are bid." When tainted by corruption, a government might deny adequate representation, initiate unjust taxes, or replace jury trials with arbitrary proceedings such as the vice-admiralty courts. If public officials curtailed freedoms of press or religion, that only confirmed their schemes to consolidate power. Moreover, weak and unprincipled ministers might advise the monarch poorly or keep citizens' pleas from reaching their king's ears. If the populace relaxed its guard, these ministers might even sanction a standing army in peacetime to impose arbitrary rule over their own population.

According to Real Whig doctrine, ordinary people must be alert but circumspect; a measured response to these threats was all-important. After all, one stubborn or mistaken act by officials did not necessarily indicate a pattern of conspiracy. Also, it could be counterproductive to raise alarms too often. So prudent citizens should turn first to accepted, legal methods of appeal and redress. If the system was functioning properly, claims of real abuses would bring forth proper corrections. Even if forced to take to the streets as a last resort, crowds should be organized and purposeful, not riotous and uncontrolled. They should threaten property before people and hang effigies, not actual office holders.

For the most part, the Stamp Act demonstrations had followed this logic of restraint and had gained the desired effect. "In every Colony," wrote John Adams, "the Stamp Distributors and Inspectors have been compelled, by the unconquerable Rage of the People, to renounce their offices." But did individual demands for liberty have limits? If so, what were they? Could slaves seek liberty from their masters? What about wives from their husbands? Could tenants press for redress from rich landlords, or debtors from powerful creditors? Such questions generated widespread, heated debate in the turbulent quarter-century ahead.

Rural Unrest: Tenant Farmers and Regulators

For a growing number of colonists, international events in the years after 1765 seemed to confirm the views that the Real Whigs had passed down. When John Wilkes was repeatedly elected to Parliament but expelled from the Commons for his radical views, his English supporters cried foul and demanded political reform. Americans saw Wilkes as their champion. In 1768, when troops in London fired on a huge mob protesting Wilkes's imprisonment—killing half a dozen people and wounding innocent bystanders—colonists joined in condemning "the massacre of St. George's Field." South Carolina's Assembly even tried to contribute public money to support Wilkes. Similarly, Americans embraced the short-lived cause of Pasquale Paoli, who fought to free the Mediterranean island of Corsica from domination by Genoa.

Many colonists christened their sons after Wilkes or Paoli, and Pennsylvanians named new towns after these overseas heroes. The two men seemed to embody a broader struggle of liberty against tyranny. But often that contest flared up closer to home as well. Local occurrences, large and small, seemed to fit a pattern described by the Real Whigs. On the religious front, for example, New England colonists bemoaned rumors that the Church of England—which had persecuted their Puritan ancestors—hoped to install an American bishop in Boston. Similar talk of a resident bishop in Virginia, where the Church of England had long dominated, also provoked debate. Controversy intensified with the work of Virginia's Separate Baptist ministers, who won over thousands of recruits with their staunch opposition to the colony's established church.

After 1765, as local controversies simmered, the "Rage of the People" often seemed to boil up from below, especially in rural areas, where most colonists lived. "The People, even to the lowest Ranks, have become more attentive to their Liberties," John Adams observed with some worry, "and more determined to defend them" than ever before. For example, while stamp protesters demonstrated in New York City, aggrieved tenant farmers staged a violent revolt against powerful landholders in the Hudson River Valley. They chose an Irish immigrant named William Prendergast as their leader, established a council, and organized militia companies with elected captains. Calling themselves Levellers, they broke open local jails to free debtors, and they set up their own people's courts to try captured gentry.

British troops finally suppressed the Hudson Valley revolt, but not before the land rioters proclaimed themselves Sons of Liberty and sought aid from Stamp Act rebels in New York City. A participant named Moss Kent recalled that "when they went to New York they expected to be assisted by the poor people there." However, leaders in New York City's antistamp protests rebuffed the request for assistance from upriver. These prominent figures were also Hudson River land moguls who had evicted scores of tenants from their manors. Such men proved "great opposers of the Rioters," according to one observer, "as they are of opinion no one is entitled to Riot but themselves." (For example, one New York judge condemned land rioters who were brought before him, even while he was taking an active role in the Stamp Act Congress.) A special court convicted Prendergast of high treason and sentenced him to be disemboweled and then beheaded. Luckily for him, the king spared his life.

While tenant farmers protested in the Hudson Valley, unrest also shook the Carolinas in the interior region known to colonists as the backcountry, or the Piedmont. In South Carolina, the absence of civil government beyond the coastal parishes fostered lawlessness and disunity among white settlers until the governor extended circuit courts into the interior in 1769. In North Carolina, migrants seeking land were moving south from Virginia and Pennsylvania into the fertile backcountry in a steady stream. When they arrived in the Piedmont, they found a local elite already in place. Appointed to county offices by the governor, these officials possessed strong family and financial ties to powerful planters and merchants farther east. (Their high-handed and self-serving ways epitomized, at the local level, the sorts of corruption that had long troubled Real Whig pamphleteers.)

The newcomers disliked the grasping officeholders and corrupt courts. As their numbers rose, they protested against inadequate representation for backcountry counties in the colonial assembly. They began organizing into local groups to better "regulate" their own affairs, and they soon became known as Regulators. These small farmers, many of them in debt after moving to a new region, protested loudly against regressive taxes that imposed the same burden on all colonists, regardless of their wealth or poverty. The Regulators' discontent turned into outrage when they heard that coastal planters who dominated the assembly had voted public funds to build a stately mansion in New Bern for William Tryon, the colonial governor. By this act, the slaveholding elite in eastern North Carolina would establish the colony's permanent capitol building on the coast, rather than in the expanding interior town of Hillsborough. What's more, farmers who would never see the stately mansion would bear most of the cost of constructing it.

The decision to erect "Tryon's Palace" at public expense confirmed the worst suspicions of backcountry settlers. The governor and his associates, they decided, were concerned primarily with their own wealth, at the expense of the public interest. Hundreds, then thousands, of aroused Piedmont farm families joined local alliances that swelled into the well-organized Regulator Movement. They filed petitions, withheld their tax money, closed courts, and

The·TIMES are Dreadful, Dismal Doleful Dolorous, and DOLLAR-LESS.

"Exert Your Selves This Once in Our Favour": Petition Signed by 30 North Carolina Regulators, October 4, 1768

Tryon Palace, the governor's mansion in New Bern, North Carolina, erected in 1768.

In the 1760s, corruption prevailed among appointed officials in central North Carolina. Often holding numerous offices at once, these men managed elections, controlled courts, and gathered taxes. Apparently not all the tax money they collected made it to the public treasury. Nevertheless, any farmer who resisted payment might lose the plow horse or the milk cow that sustained the family. It could be "seized and sold" to cover a small tax payment or minor debt, with "no Part being ever Return'd" from the proceeds.

Banding together to better regulate their own affairs, these farmers sought relief through every possible legal means. But by 1768, when this document was created, these organized Regulators had exhausted most avenues of peaceful protest. The western counties where they resided were badly underrepresented in the colonial assembly. As a new session prepared to convene in November, they fired off a final round of petitions. They assured the legislators that they were law-abiding citizens willing to pay their legal share of taxes. And they begged for the appointment of honest public officials who would protect their interests. (For greater readability, editorial corrections have been made in this emotional petition.)

To the Worshipful House of Representatives of North Carolina

Your Poor Petitioners [have] been Continually Squez'd and oppressed by our Publick Officers both with Regard to their fees as also in the Laying on of Taxes as well as in Collecting. . . . Being Grieved thus to have our substance torn from us [by] . . . such Illegal practices, we applied to our public officers to give us some satisfaction . . . which they Repeatedly denied us.

With Regard to the Taxes,. . . we labour under Extreem hardships. . . . Money is very scarce . . . & we exceeding Poor & lie at a great distance from Trade which renders it almost Impossible to gain sustenance by our utmost Endeavours. . . .

To Gentlemen Rowling in affluence, a few shillings per man may seem triffling. Yet to Poor People who must have their Bed and Bedclothes, yea their Wives Petticoats, taken and sold to Defray, how Tremenious [tremendous] . . . must be the Consequences. . . . Therefore, dear Gentlemen, to your selves, to your Country, and in Pity to your Poor Petitioners, do not let it stand any longer to Drink up the Blood and vitals of the Poor Distressed.

After seeking relief from existing taxes, the petitioners went on to question new burdens, such as the law imposing an additional tax "to Erect a Publick Edifice" for Governor Tryon in New Bern.

Good God, Gentlemen, what will become of us when these Demands come against us? Paper Money we have none & gold or silver we can Purchase none of. The Contingencies of Government Must be Paid, and . . . we are Willing to Pay, [even] if we [must] sell our Beds from under us. And [yet] in this Time of Distress, it is as much as we can support. . . . If, therefore, the Law for that Purpose can be happily Repealed, . . . May the God of Heaven Inspire you with sentiments to that Purpose.

We humble Begg you would . . . Use your Influence with our Worthy, Virtuous Governor to discontinue . . . such Officers as would be found to be ye Bane of Society, and [instead to] Put in the Common Wealth [officials willing] to Encourage the Poor and . . . to stand [up] for them. This would Cause Joy and Gladness to Spring from every Heart. This would cause Labour and Industry to prevail over Murmuring Discontent. This would Raise your poor Petitioners . . . to a flourishing Opulent and Hoping People. Otherwise . . . disatisfaction and Melancholy must Prevail over such as Remain, and Numbers must Defect the Province and seek elsewhere an Asylum from Tyranny and Oppression. . . .

We leave it to you . . . in your great Wisdom . . . to pass such Act or Acts, as shall be Conducive to the welbeing of a whole People over Whose welfare ye are plac'd as Guardians. . . . For the Lords Sake, Gentlemen, Exert your selves this once in our favour. ∎

Source: William S. Powell, James K. Huhta, and Thomas J. Farnham, eds., *The Regulators of North Carolina: A Documentary History, 1759–1776* (Raleigh: State Dept. of Archives and History, 1971), 187–189.

harassed corrupt office holders, protesting the "unequal chances the poor and weak have in contentions with the rich and powerful."

Both sides dug in their heels. In 1771 Governor Tryon finally called out the militia, marching a thousand men into the Piedmont. After defeating several thousand irate farmers at the battle of Alamance in May 1771, Tryon imposed his will on the dissenters. Half a dozen captured leaders were hanged publicly in Hillsborough, and Tryon forced residents to swear an oath of loyalty. Many refused, migrating farther south to backcountry Georgia or west to the Appalachian Mountains. Their leader, a Quaker named Herman Husband, barely escaped with his life, as Prendergast had done in New York. In North Carolina, just as in the Hudson Valley, well-to-do members of the Sons of Liberty dismissed the organized and militant farmers as misguided rabble.

A Conspiracy of Corrupt Ministers?

Numerous sharp divisions—some leading to armed conflict—continued to separate colonists of different classes and regions. But ill-timed steps by successive administrations in London attracted widening attention throughout British America, prompting uneasy new alliances. Colonists familiar with the dire warnings of Real Whig pamphleteers asked themselves a question: in the weak and short-lived ministries that succeeded Grenville's, were the leaders simply ill-informed, or were they actively corrupt? A widening array of colonists wondered whether some official conspiracy existed to chip away at American liberties. Even loyal defenders of the crown expressed frustration with new policies, fearing that they were too harsh to calm irate colonists, yet too weak to force them into line. "It's astonishing to me," wrote a beleaguered supporter from Boston, "after the Warning and Experience of the Stamp Act Times; that any new Impositions should be laid on the Colonies," especially "without even so much as a single Ship of Warr" to back up new measures.

Parliament's first new imposition after repeal of the Stamp Act was the Revenue Act of 1766. The act offered an additional reduction in the duty on molasses, from threepence per gallon to a single penny, in hopes of further discouraging smuggling and raising revenue. Colonial merchants reconciled themselves to this measure as an external tax designed to regulate imperial trade. They paid the new duty, and customs revenues rose. But Real Whigs reminded them that compliance with even the most innocuous measure could set a dangerous precedent.

The skeptics had a point, for Parliament soon imposed new hard-line measures. These distasteful statutes, put in motion by Chancellor of the Exchequer Charles Townshend before his sudden death in 1767, sparked angry responses from colonists. The most telling came from John Dickinson, a moderate Philadelphia lawyer who drafted a series of widely circulated "Letters from a Farmer in Pennsylvania." Urging colonists to respond "peaceably—prudently—firmly—jointly," he dismissed any distinction between external and internal taxation. He also rejected the idea that Americans had virtual representation in Parliament. "We are taxed without our own consent," Dickinson proclaimed to his readers. "We are therefore—SLAVES."

The Townshend Duties

In search of additional funds for the Exchequer, Townshend persuaded Parliament to pass the Revenue Act of 1767, which created new duties on colonial imports of glass, paint, lead, paper, and tea. Proceeds were to be spent in the colonies for "the administration of justice, and the support of civil government," a seemingly benevolent gesture. But Dickinson and other colonists pointed out what these two phrases actually meant. "The administration of justice" cloaked expanded searches of American homes and shops in which customs officers used hated "writs of assistance" to ferret out smuggled goods. "The support of civil government" ensured that governors and appointed office holders could draw their pay directly from the new duties instead of depending on an annual salary grant from the local assembly. In short, the new act removed

■ **Portrait of Samuel Adams by John Singleton Copley.**

from colonial legislatures one of their strongest bargaining tools in dealing with the crown: the power to pay or withhold yearly salaries for key officials sent from Britain.

Similar acts and instructions followed. Asserting its sovereignty, Parliament disciplined the New York Assembly for its "direct disobedience" in refusing to comply with the Quartering Act of 1765. The crown instructed governors in America, now less dependent for their salaries on colonial lower houses, to disapprove any further measures from legislatures asserting their traditional control over how members were chosen, what their numbers should be, and when they would meet. Equally galling, the Customs Act of 1767 established a separate Board of Customs for British North America. Ominously, the commissioners would live in Boston rather than London. To strengthen the board's hand in customs enforcement, Britain moved in 1768 to expand the number of vice-admiralty courts in North America from one to four. It supplemented the court in Halifax (established by the Sugar Act of 1764) with new courts in Boston, Philadelphia, and Charleston. Furthermore, to look after its troublesome mainland colonies, the British government created a new American Department, overseen by Lord Hillsborough. It also began to move British troops in America from remote frontier outposts to major Atlantic ports, both as a cost-cutting measure and as a show of force.

Whereas most people in England viewed these measures as legal, timely, and efficient, many Americans found them threatening, especially when considered as a whole. In February 1768, the Massachusetts legislature, led by 46-year-old Samuel Adams, petitioned the king for redress. The legislators also circulated a call to other lower houses to voice similar protests. Condemning the Townshend Revenue Act as unconstitutional, they argued that it imposed taxation without representation. By removing control of the governors' salaries from colonial legislatures, they said, Parliament set the dangerous precedent of making royal officials "independent of the people." Lord Hillsborough demanded an immediate retraction of this provocative "Circular Letter" and ordered the dissolution of any other assembly that took up the matter.

In June, just as word arrived of the Wilkes Riot in London, events in Boston took a more radical turn. Defying Hillsborough, the Massachusetts assembly voted 92 to 17 against rescinding its circular letter. "The 92" became instant celebrities, and their opponents were vilified by the Sons of Liberty. On June 5, a dockside crowd faced down a "press-gang" from a British warship and protected local sailors from being forced (or "pressed") into naval service. Five days later, customs officials seized John Hancock's sloop, *Liberty,* and demanded that he pay import duties for a cargo of Madeira wine. This move sparked a huge demonstration as citizens dragged a small customs boat through the streets and then burned it on Boston Common. "Hancock and Liberty" became a rallying cry—"as 'Wilkes and Liberty' is in London!" "Let us take up arms immediately and be free," Sam Adams was heard to say; "We shall have thirty thousand men to join us from the Country."

Emotions ran high. But most leaders sensed that any escalation of the violence would be premature and perhaps suicidal. They managed to rein in demonstrations and initiate efforts to expand their base of support. Organizers turned their attention to implementing a boycott of British goods proposed the previous fall. Spurred by an energetic press, nonimportation plans took hold rapidly. These plans called upon colonists to refrain from imported luxuries and opt instead for virtuous self-sufficiency. The idea held broad appeal, as did the prospect that nonviolent resistance might reverse British policies.

As the nonimportation movement expanded, it drew in men from small towns previously untouched by the imperial controversy. It also engaged women of all ranks in sacrificing for the cause. Self-proclaimed Daughters of Liberty took to making, wearing, and selling homespun garments. Local associations sprang up, pledging to forgo imported tea and London fashions. A dozen colonial assemblies voted to halt importation of selected goods. In New York, the value of imports from Britain shrank from £491,000 to just £76,000 in a single year.

Elsewhere, the novel boycott exerted less impact, but the damage to English shipping proved substantial. Britain was losing far more revenue in colonial trade than it was gaining through the expanded customs duties. Soon influential exporters in England were pressing the government for relief. When Lord North established a new ministry in January 1770, he received the king's consent to work toward a better arrangement with the colonies. On March 5, 1770, North persuaded Parliament to repeal all the Townshend Duties except the one on tea. The move defused the colonial boycott, but it offered too little too late. Like the earlier Declaratory Act, this measure reaffirmed Parliament's disputed right to tax the colonists at will. Moreover, it came at the exact moment when violence and bloodshed were escalating in America.

The Boston Massacre

After the *Liberty* riot in June 1768, tensions had mounted in Boston, especially with the arrival in October of two regiments of British soldiers, well armed and dressed in their traditional red coats. Paul Revere, a local silversmith and member of the Sons of Liberty, crafted an ominous engraving entitled "British Ships of War Landing Their Troops." According to Real Whig beliefs, any appearance by a standing army in peacetime constituted danger, and the issue of how to house and feed unwanted troops quickly became a political hot button. The soldiers pitched their tents on Boston Common, a central gathering place for boisterous crowds. Artisans in a sluggish economy welcomed the increased business that the men in uniform generated, but numerous unemployed workers resented the soldiers' "moonlighting," trying to earn extra pay by applying for local jobs.

Library of Congress

■ In Paul Revere's image of the 1770 Boston Massacre, soldiers defend the hated customs house by moonlight, while a sniper fires from a window clearly labeled "Butcher's Hall." The partisan engraving spread an anti-British view of the bloody event.

With 4000 armed men encamped in a seaport of scarcely 16,000, confrontation seemed inevitable. When rowdy American youths harassed the intruders as "redcoats" and "lobsterbacks," British officers ordered their men not to retaliate. Their refusal to fight only prompted more taunts. Affairs "cannot long remain in the state they are now in," wrote one observer late in 1769; "they are hastening to a crisis. What will be the event, God knows."

In February 1770, the answer came. When a hostile crowd threatened a customs informer, he fired back, killing 11-year-old Christopher Seider. The boy's elaborate funeral brought crowds of demonstrators into the streets. On Friday, March 2, protesters reappeared after a run-in between local workers and job-seeking soldiers. Rumors spread during the weekend that a larger confrontation between the two sides was looming. On Monday morning, a scrawled notice of unknown origin appeared on a wall. It read, "to Inform ye Rebellious people in Boston that ye Soldjers . . . are Determend to Joine to Gether and Defend them Selves against all who Shall Oppose them."

Regardless of who actually posted the notice, both sides were ready for a fight. Around 9 P.M. on March 5, a crowd gathered outside the customs house, where a harassed sentry struck a boy with his rifle butt. As witnesses pelted the guard with snowballs, he called for help. As seven fellow soldiers pushed through the mob to assist him, firebells summoned more townspeople to the scene. The British loaded their rifles and aimed at the crowd, their bayonets fixed.

Into this tense standoff marched a brash contingent of several dozen sailors from Dock Square. Led by Crispus Attucks, an ex-slave, they arrived waving banners and brandishing clubs. Attucks was an imposing figure, standing 6 feet 2 inches. The son of a black man and an Indian woman, he had run away from his master two decades earlier and then taken up a life at sea. John Adams assumed the unpopular task of defending the British soldiers at the trial resulting from this incident. He told the court that "Attucks appears to have undertaken to be the hero of this night." Damning the soldiers and daring them to fire, Attucks pressed his band of sailors to the front, waving a long stick in the moonlight.

A slave witness named Andrew, who had climbed a post to get a better view, testified that Attucks "threw himself in, and made a blow at the officer," shouting, "kill the dogs, knock them over." Adams later showed the court how with one hand the sailor "took hold of a bayonet, and with the other knocked the man down." In the mayhem, a British gun went off, prompting a volley of fire from the other soldiers. The crowd recoiled in disbelief at the sight of their dead and wounded neighbors lying in the street, but they stayed past midnight to demand that the soldiers be jailed for murder. According to a printed report, Attucks and four others had been "killed on the Spot." The anti-British cause had its first martyrs, joining young Christopher Seider.

By grim coincidence, the bloody episode on King Street occurred only hours after Lord North addressed the House of Commons to urge removal of most Townshend Duties. His effort at reconciliation immediately became lost in a wave of hostile publicity. In Boston, Paul Revere captured the incident in an inflammatory engraving that circulated widely. The Sons of Liberty quickly named the event of March 5 the Boston Massacre and compared its martyred victims to the Wilkes demonstrators who had perished in London during the Massacre at St. George's Field. "On that night," John Adams remarked, "the foundation of American independence was laid."

The *Gaspee* Affair

As the 1770s unfolded, citizens in Boston commemorated "Massacre Day" each year with orations. According to speakers, the bloodshed on March 5 had revealed a dark scheme among British cabinet ministers. They seemed intent, the orators proclaimed, to drive America into a state of rebellion, "whereby they might hope to gratify both their malice and avarice."

Besides the aggression of a standing army, the overzealous conduct of customs officers gave colonists further cause for distrust. As traffic with Britain revived, after the repeal of most Townshend Duties and the end of the colonial boycott of English goods, so did the likelihood of conflict between merchants and customs inspectors. In the Delaware River region, local residents thrashed and jailed a customs collector in 1770. The next year, protesters stormed a customs schooner at night, beat up the crew, and stole their sails. Tensions ran especially high in Rhode Island. In 1769 Newport citizens seized the sloop *Liberty*—which crown agents had confiscated from John Hancock the year before and converted into a customs vessel—and scuttled it. In June 1772, the *Gaspee*, another customs boat said to harass local shipping, ran aground near Pawtuxet. In a midnight attack, more than a hundred raiders descended on the stranded schooner in half a dozen boats, driving off its crew and setting fire to the vessel.

The destruction of the *Gaspee* renewed sharp antagonisms between the two sides. Alarmed, the Earl of Hillsborough, secretary of state for the American colonies, sent a royal commission from London to investigate and to transport suspects to England for trial. But many of the attackers, such as John Brown of Providence, came from important Rhode Island families. Even a £500 reward could not induce local inhabitants to name participants. Besides, colonists viewed the order to deport accused citizens to England as a denial of their fundamental right to trial by a jury of their peers. They took action.

Again, Virginia's House of Burgesses led the way, as it had in the Stamp Act crisis. In March 1773, Patrick Henry, Thomas Jefferson, and Richard Henry Lee pushed a resolution through that body establishing a standing committee to look into the *Gaspee* affair and to keep up "Correspondence and Communication with our sister colonies" regarding the protection of rights. Following Virginia's example, ten other colonial legislatures promptly established their own Committees of Correspondence. In Massachusetts, similar committees sprang up linking individual towns. Within months a new act of Parliament, designed to rescue the powerful East India Company from bankruptcy, gave these emerging communication networks their first test.

Launching a Revolution

In 1767, before Parliament imposed the Townshend Duties, Americans had imported nearly 870,000 pounds of tea from England. But the boycott movement cut that amount to less than 110,000 pounds by 1770 as colonists turned to smuggling Dutch blends and brewing homemade root teas. When nonimportation schemes lapsed in the early 1770s, purchase of English tea resumed, even though a duty remained in effect.

Encouraged by this apparent acceptance of parliamentary taxation, Lord North addressed the problem facing the East India Company. The ancient trading monopoly owed a huge debt to the Bank of England and had 18 million pounds of unsold tea rotting in London warehouses. Moreover, many MPs held stock in the company. In May, Parliament passed a new law designed to right the situation and bail out the ailing company.

The Tempest over Tea

The Tea Act of 1773 let the struggling East India Company bypass the expensive requirement that merchants ship Asian tea through England on its way to colonial ports. Now they could send the product directly to the colonies or to foreign ports, without paying to unload, store, auction, and reload the heavy chests. Any warehouse tea destined for the colonies would have its English duty refunded. These steps would reduce retail prices and expand the tea market. They would also quietly confirm the right of Parliament to collect a tea tax of threepence per pound.

The company promptly chose prominent colonial merchants as consignees to receive and distribute more than 600,000 pounds of tea, for which they would earn a hefty 6 percent commission. But wary colonists in port towns, sensing a repetition of 1765, renewed the tactics that had succeeded against the Stamp Act. Sons of Liberty vowed to prevent tea-laden ships from docking, and crowds pressured local distributors to renounce participation in the scheme. "If they succeed in the sale of that tea," proclaimed New York's Sons of Liberty, "then we may bid adieu to American liberty."

In Boston, where tea worth nearly £10,000 arrived aboard three ships in late November, tension ran especially high. The credibility of Governor Thomas Hutchinson, who had taken a hard line toward imperial dissent, had suffered in June when Benjamin Franklin published private correspondence suggesting the governor's willingness to trim colonial rights. When two of Hutchinson's sons were named tea consignees, the appointments reinforced townspeople's suspicions of an elaborate plot. The governor could have signed papers letting the three vessels depart, but that would give victory to the local opposition. Instead, he determined to unload and distribute the tea, by force if necessary. One could scarcely buy a pair of pistols in Boston, a resident observed on December 1, "as they are all bought up, with a full determination to repel force by force."

On December 16, the largest mass meeting of the decade took place at Boston's Old South Church. A crowd of 5000, including many from other towns, waited in a cold rain to hear whether Hutchinson would relent. When word came in late afternoon that the governor had refused, the cry went up, "Boston Harbor a teapot tonight!" Following a prearranged plan, 150 men, disguised as Mohawk Indians and carrying hatchets, marched to the docks and boarded the ships.

As several thousand supporters looked on, this disciplined crew spent three hours methodically breaking open hundreds of chests of tea and dumping their contents overboard. The

The Bostonians Paying the Excise-Man, or Tarring and Feathering (1774). Library of Congress.

■ A 1774 London cartoon expressed anger that Boston's Sons of Liberty, defying British authority, could overturn the Stamp Act, abuse revenue agents, dump East India Company tea, and use their "Liberty Tree" to hang officials in effigy.

quasimilitary operation proved swift, efficient, and well organized. It united participants reflecting all levels of society—from merchants such as Hancock to artisans such as Hewes—and news of it spurred similar acts of defiance in other ports. "This destruction of the Tea is so bold, so daring, so firm," John Adams wrote in his diary the next day, "it must have so important Consequences, and so lasting, that I can't but consider it as an Epocha in History." Sixty years later, as one of the oldest veterans of the Revolution, George Hewes still recalled with special pride his role in "the destruction of the tea."

The Intolerable Acts

"The crisis is come," wrote British general Thomas Gage, responding to the costly Tea Party in Boston Harbor; "the provinces must be either British colonies, or independent and separate states." Underestimating the strength of American resolve, Parliament agreed with King George III that only stern measures would reestablish "the obedience which a colony owes to its mother country." Between March and June 1774, it passed four so-called Coercive Acts to isolate and punish Massachusetts.

The first of the Coercive Acts, the Boston Port Act, used British naval strength to cut off the offending town's sea commerce—except for shipments of food and firewood—until the colonists paid for the ruined tea. By the Administration of Justice Act, revenue officials or soldiers charged with murder in Massachusetts (as in the Boston Massacre) could have their trials moved to another colony or to Great Britain. The Quartering Act gave officers more power to requisition living quarters and supplies for their troops throughout the colonies. Most important, the Massachusetts Government Act removed democratic elements from the long-standing Massachusetts Charter of 1691. From now on, the assembly could no longer elect the colony's Upper House, or Council; the governor would appoint that important body instead. In addition, colonists would have to get written permission from him to hold town meetings.

Lord North's government went even further. It replaced Hutchinson with Gage, installing the commander of British forces in America as the governor of Massachusetts and granting him special powers and three additional regiments. It also secured passage of the Quebec Act. The new legislation addressed nagging problems of governance in Canada after a decade of English rule. It accommodated the Catholic faith and French legal traditions of Quebec's inhabitants. Moreover, it multiplied the size of the colony several times over to draw scattered French settlers and traders under colonial government. Suddenly, Quebec took in the entire Great Lakes region and all the lands north of the Ohio River to the east bank of the upper Mississippi River.

Expanding the province of Quebec to the Ohio River might extend British government to French wilderness outposts and help to regulate the Indian trade there. But as American land speculators in Virginia and elsewhere quickly realized, the move also challenged the western claims of other colonies. The Quebec Act appeared to favor French Catholics and Ohio Valley Indians—both recent enemies of the crown—over loyal English colonists. Resentment ran especially high in New England, where Protestants had long associated Catholicism with despotism. The Quebec Act, which denied that province a representative assembly and jury trials in civil cases, set an ominous precedent for neighboring colonies.

The Coercive Acts and the Quebec Act—lumped together by colonial propagandists as the Intolerable Acts—brought on open rebellion against crown rule. Competing pamphlets debated the proper limits of dissent. In *A Summary View of the Rights of British America,* Jefferson went beyond criticisms of Parliament to question the king's right to dispense land, control trade, and impose troops in America. Sympathy for the economic and political distress of Massachusetts mounted in other colonies. Sam Adams and his Boston colleagues had proven their ability to mobilize large and determined crowds; now they needed to foster wider cooperation among distant colonies that were less directly threatened. At the same time, they had to build resolve among wealthy merchants and cautious gentry. Within months, Massachusetts had called for a congress of all the colonies. It also established its own Provincial Congress at Concord, a small vil-

■ The shots fired at dawn by British troops, dispersing local militiamen from Lexington's town green, were the opening volley of the American Revolution. Amos Doolittle, a Connecticut soldier who responded to the alarm, later depicted the events of April 19, 1775. The date is still honored in New England as Patriots' Day.

lage that lay 17 miles west of Boston and British naval power. Operating as a de facto government, the Massachusetts Provincial Congress reorganized the colonial militia into units loyal to its own Committee of Public Safety. These farmer-soldiers became known as Minutemen for their quick response to Gage's repeated efforts to capture patriot gunpowder supplies.

From Words to Action

While Massachusetts chafed under these new restrictions, shifting coalitions in each colony, ranging from conservative to radical, vied for local political control. Extralegal committees, existing outside the authorized structure of colonial government, took power in hundreds of hamlets. In Edenton, North Carolina, 51 women signed a pact to abstain from using imported products for the "publick good." London cartoonists mocked the action as the "Edenton Ladies' Tea Party," but women in other colonies made similar agreements to boycott British textiles and tea. Towns instructed their representatives to provincial assemblies to support Massachusetts' call for an intercolonial congress. During the summer, all colonies except Georgia selected representatives to the First Continental Congress. In September 1774, 56 delegates convened at Carpenters Hall in Philadelphia. Most had never met before, and they differed as much in their politics as in their regional manners.

At first the delegates disagreed sharply over how best to respond to the Intolerable Acts. Joseph Galloway, a wealthy lawyer and commercial land speculator from Pennsylvania, urged a compromise with Britain modeled on the Albany Congress of 1754. His plan called for the creation of a separate American parliament, a grand council with delegates elected by the colonial legislatures. The less conservative delegates voiced opposition to this idea for a federation of the colonies, under a president-general appointed by the king. Led by Patrick Henry of Virginia, they managed to table the Galloway Plan by a narrow vote.

When Paul Revere arrived from Boston on October 6, bearing a set of militant resolves passed in his own Suffolk County, further rifts appeared. Southern moderates, while expressing sympathy for Massachusetts, still resisted calls for a nonexportation scheme that would withhold

■ MAP 6.4

BRITISH NORTH AMERICA, APRIL 1775 Rising colonial unrest brought strong countermeasures. The British government organized regional vice-admiralty courts to punish smugglers; it greatly expanded Quebec in 1774; and it reallocated troops to the Boston area. When warfare erupted there in April 1775, the news spread throughout the colonies within weeks.

Map labels:

HALIFAX, Regional Vice-Admiralty Court for everything above 43 degrees, 15 minutes

BOSTON, Regional Vice-Admiralty Court for everything between 44 degrees, and 40 degrees 30 minutes

PHILADELPHIA, Regional Vice-Admiralty Court for everything between 41 degrees, and 36 degrees 15 minutes

CHARLESTON, Regional Vice-Admiralty Court for everything below 36 degrees, 15 minutes

British dominance in eastern North America
- British-ruled providence of Quebec, 1774
- Boundary set by Quebec Act of 1774
- British-ruled providence of East Florida
- British-ruled providence of West Florida
- Reserved to Indians under British Rule
- Spanish Louisiana
- Major battles

Distribution of British troops
- British posts 100–300 soldiers
- British posts 300–500 soldiers
- British post 4,800 soldiers

The spread of news concerning the battles of Lexington and Concord, April 19, 1775
- Within 1–7 days
- Within 8–14 days
- More than 14 days

American tobacco, rice, and indigo from Great Britain. But by the time the Congress adjourned in late October, it had issued a Declaration of Rights and passed a range of measures that seemed to balance competing views. On one hand, the Congress endorsed the fiery Suffolk Resolves, which condemned the Coercive Acts as unconstitutional and spoke of preparation for war. On the other, it humbly petitioned the king for relief from the crisis and professed continued loyalty. But in practical terms, Galloway and the more conservative members had suffered defeat. Most importantly, the delegates signed an agreement to prohibit British imports and halt all exports to Britain except rice. They called for local committees to enforce this so-called Association, and they set a date—May 10, 1775—for a Second Congress.

Before delegates could meet again in Philadelphia, the controversy that had smoldered for more than a decade on both sides of the Atlantic erupted into open combat. Predictably, the explosion took place in Massachusetts. The spark came in the form of secret orders to General Gage, which he received April 14, 1775. The confidential letter from his superiors in London urged him to arrest the leaders of the Massachusetts Provincial Congress and regain the upper hand before the strained situation grew worse. He was to use force, even if it meant the outbreak of warfare.

On April 18, Gage ordered 700 elite troops from Boston to row across the Charles River at night, march 10 miles to Lexington, and seize John Hancock and Sam Adams, who had taken refuge with Hancock's relatives. Next, the soldiers were to proceed 7 more miles to Concord to capture a stockpile of military supplies. Alerted by signal lanterns, express riders Paul Revere and William Dawes eluded British patrols and spurred their horses toward Lexington along separate routes to warn Hancock and Adams. Bells and alarm guns spread the word that the British were coming. By the time the British soldiers reached Lexington, shortly before sunrise, some 70 militiamen had assembled on the town green. When the villagers refused to lay down their arms, the redcoats dispersed them in a brief skirmish that left eight militiamen dead.

The British column trudged west to Concord and searched the town for munitions. Four hundred Minutemen who had streamed in from neighboring communities watched from the outskirts of town. By 11 A.M., a fire had broken out in the village. The Minutemen advanced in double file, with orders not to fire until the British fired first. At the small bridge over the Concord River, British regulars opened fire. "The shot heard 'round the world" killed two men. The Americans loosed a volley in return, killing three. By noon, British forces were retreating in disarray. Exhausted, hungry, and short of ammunition, the redcoats made easy targets for the more than 1000 Americans who shot at them from behind stone walls. A relief party prevented annihilation, but the British suffered severe losses: 73 killed and 200 wounded or missing. They encamped briefly at Bunker Hill, but lacking the foresight and strength to retain that strategic height, they soon returned to Boston. The Americans, with only 49 dead, had turned the tables on General Gage, transforming a punitive raid into a punishing defeat.

Conclusion

For the British, festering administrative problems in America had suddenly become a military emergency. A decade of assertive but inconsistent British policies had transformed the colonists' sense of good will toward London into angry feelings of persecution and betrayal. The years of incessant argument and misunderstanding reminded many, on both sides of the Atlantic, of watching a stable, prosperous household unravel into mutual recrimination. A once-healthy family was becoming increasingly dysfunctional and troubled. The assertive children grew steadily in strength and competence; the aging parents chafed at their diminished authority and respect.

Predictably, authorities in London found the once-dependent colonists to be ungrateful, intemperate, and occasionally even paranoid. With equal assurance, the American subjects saw Parliament, government ministers, and eventually the king himself as uninformed, selfish, and even deceitful. For the aggrieved colonists, the moment had come to declare loyalties and muster sustained resistance. They would receive suitable recognition within the family, or they would leave home for good. Britain's overseas empire, which had expanded steadily for two centuries, now seemed on the verge of splitting apart.

From the perspective of Britain's mainland colonies, rapid economic and demographic growth had been a fact of eighteenth-century life. It had created serious growing pains, generating strong tensions across boundaries of region, race, and class. In 1676, near the beginning of this growth process, the colonial tensions that generated Bacon's Rebellion in Virginia had been focused into war against the Indians and conflict against the ruling colonial elite, with independence little more than a remote ideal for a few. A century later, the equation had changed, and the limits of imperial control in North America had become increasingly evident. Colonists could overcome their regional and ethnic differences, and political independence no longer seemed implausible. With effort, class hostilities and urban-rural divisions could also be overcome. Redirecting these long-standing local resentments against the distant and powerful British crown could increase the sense of unity among people with very different personal backgrounds and resources.

Nor would British colonists be alone if they mounted a rebellion. On one hand, they could make the unlikely choice of liberating half a million slaves, empowering colonial women, and embracing the anti-British cause of Pontiac and numerous Native Americans. Such revolutionary moves would increase their strength dramatically in one direction. On the other hand, they could also take a more cautious and less democratic route. If men of substance could gain control of the forces that were being unleashed, they might curb potential idealism among slaves, women, tenant farmers, and the urban poor, giving precedence instead to policies and practices that would win powerful European allies.

Bacon's rebels, after all, had never managed to muster French or Dutch support as hoped. But the new Sons of Liberty might well succeed in enlisting vital support from the continent of Europe in an American fight for independence from Britain. France, recently evicted from North America, and Spain, anxious about British designs in the Pacific, might both be willing allies, despite their commitment to monarchy. Such an alliance, if it ever came about, could push the limits of British imperial control to the breaking point.

Sites to Visit

Anza-Borrego Desert State Park

anza.uoregon.edu

This isolated and beautiful state park covers 600,000 acres 80 miles east of San Diego, California. The Web site, which focuses on the exploration of Alta, California, 1774–1776, contains maps, resources, and documents in both English and Spanish concerning Juan Bautista de Anza's two overland expeditions.

Baranov Museum

Located near the ferry landing in Kodiak, Alaska, the Baranov Museum is housed in one of the few remaining structures from the Russian colonial era. In Fairbanks, the modern University of Alaska Museum, located on Yukon Street overlooking the campus, provides a rich introduction to the region's history and cultures.

Fort Ross State Historic Park

This reconstruction of the outpost built by the Russians on the northern California coast in the early nineteenth century is located on a scenic bluff 11 miles northwest of the town of Jenner on Highway 1, about a two-hour drive from San Francisco.

Pontiac Marker

In 1977, Michigan placed a marker concerning Pontiac on a building at 3321 East Jefferson Avenue, near the Renaissance Center in downtown Detroit. It commemorates the Battle of Bloody Run, in July 1763, which marked the height of Pontiac's siege of Detroit. The city of Pontiac, named for the Ottawa leader, lies 25 miles northwest.

Boston's Freedom Trail

This 2.5-mile self-guided walking tour begins at Boston Common. Stops include the Boston Massacre site, the Old South Meeting House where the Boston Tea Party began, Paul Revere's house, and the Granary Burial Ground, where Revere, John Hancock, Samuel Adams, and Crispus Attucks are all buried.

Colonial Williamsburg

www.history.org

This tourist site in Virginia, suitable for all ages, features shops, homes, and public buildings as they existed in the 1770s. In the Capitol Building on Duke of Gloucester Street, Patrick Henry stirred the House of Burgesses to oppose the Stamp Act in 1765. There are regular tours and candlelight evening programs.

Tryon's Palace

Governor William Tryon erected this building in New Bern, North Carolina, in 1768 over the protests of Regulators. The Georgian mansion, with a handsome garden overlooking the Trent River, served as the colony's first capitol. Now restored, Tryon Palace Historic Sites and Gardens is 112 miles east of Raleigh, the current capital.

Alamance Battleground

At this site, located on Route 62 near Burlington, North Carolina, Governor Tryon's forces defeated the Regulators in 1771. In historic Hillsborough, 30 miles east, a plaque on a hillside at the end of King Street on the east side of the town marks the site where Regulator leaders were hanged.

For Further Reading

General

Jack P. Greene, ed., *Colonies to Nation: A Documentary History of the American Revolution* (1975).

Merrill Jensen, *The Founding of a Nation: A History of the American Revolution, 1763–1776* (1968).

Pauline Maier, *From Resistance to Revolution: Colonial Radicals and the Development of American Opposition to Britain, 1765–1776* (1972).

Robert Middlekauff, *The Glorious Cause: The American Revolution, 1763–1789* (1982).

Alfred F. Young, ed., *The American Revolution: Explorations in the History of American Radicalism* (1976).

New Challenges to Spain's Expanded Empire

John Francis Bannon, *The Spanish Borderlands Frontier, 1513–1821* (1970).

Richard Hough, *Captain James Cook* (1994).

John L. Kessell, *Spain in the Southwest: A Narrative History of Colonial New Mexico, Arizona, Texas, and California* (2002).

Mark Santiago, *Massacre at the Yuma Crossing: Spanish Relations with the Quechans, 1779–1782* (1998).

Barbara Sweetland Smith and Redmond J. Barnett, eds., *Russian America: The Forgotten Frontier* (1990).

New Challenges to Britain's Expanded Empire

John K. Alexander, *Samuel Adams: America's Revolutionary Politician* (2002).

John L. Bullion, *A Great and Necessary Measure: George Grenville and the Genesis of the Stamp Act, 1763–1765* (1982).

Gregory E. Dowd, *A Spirited Resistance: The North American Indian Struggle for Unity, 1745–1815* (1992).

Edmund S. Morgan and Helen M. Morgan, *The Stamp Act Crisis: Prologue to Revolution*, 3rd ed. (1995).

Peter D. G. Thomas, *British Politics and the Stamp Act Crisis: The First Phase of the American Revolution, 1763–1767* (1975).

Peter D. G. Thomas, *John Wilkes: A Friend to Liberty* (1996).

"The Unconquerable Rage of the People"

Bernard Bailyn, *The Ideological Origins of the American Revolution* (1967).

Edward Countryman, *A People in Revolution: The American Revolution and Political Society in New York, 1760–1790* (1981).

Ronald Hoffman, *A Spirit of Dissention: Economics, Politics, and the Revolution in Maryland* (1973).

Marjoleine Kars, *Breaking Loose Together: The Regulator Rebellion in Pre-Revolutionary North Carolina* (2002).

Rachel N. Klein, *Unification of a Slave State: The Rise of the Planter Class in the South Carolina Backcountry, 1760–1808* (1990).

A Conspiracy of Corrupt Ministers?

Bernard Bailyn, *The Ordeal of Thomas Hutchinson* (1974).

Woody Holton, *Forced Founders: Indians, Debtors, Slaves, and the Making of the American Revolution in Virginia* (1999).

John Shy, *Toward Lexington: The Role of the British Army in the Coming of the Revolution* (1965).

Peter D. G. Thomas, *The Townshend Duties Crisis: The Second Phase of the American Revolution, 1767–1773* (1987).

John W. Tyler, *Smugglers and Patriots: Boston Merchants and the Advent of the American Revolution* (1986).

Launching a Revolution

David Hackett Fischer, *Paul Revere's Ride* (1994).

Benjamin Woods Labaree, *The Boston Tea Party* (1964).

Philip Lawson, *The Imperial Challenge: Quebec and Britain in the Age of the American Revolution* (1989).

Peter D. G. Thomas, *Tea Party to Independence: The Third Phase of the American Revolution, 1773–1776* (1991).

Alfred F. Young, *The Shoemaker and the Tea Party: Memory and the American Revolution* (1999).

Online Practice Test

Test your understanding of this chapter with interactive review quizzes at

www.ablongman.com/jonescreatedequal/chapter6

1776 Thomas Paine, *Common Sense.*
Declaration of Independence.
Washington crosses the Delaware.
New Jersey gives women the right to vote.

1777 Burgoyne surrenders
at Saratoga.

1778 U.S. forges an alliance with France.

1779 Sullivan's campaign against the Iroquois.

1780 Charleston falls to the British.

1781 Articles of
Confederaition
are ratified.
Cornwallis surrenders
at Yorktown.

ARTICLES
OF
Confederation
AND
Perpetual Union
BETWEEN THE
S T A T E S
OF
New-Hampshire, Massachusetts-Bay, Rhode-Island and Providence Plantations, Connecticut, New-York, New-Jersey, Pennsylvania, Delaware, Maryland, Virginia, North-Carolina, South-Carolina and Georgia.

LANCASTER:
PRINTED BY FRANCIS BAILEY.
MDCCLXXVII.

1783 Treaty of Paris.
Newburgh Conspiracy
is thwarted.

1785 Land Ordinance of 1785.

1786 Shays's Rebellion.

1787 Constitutional Convention meets in
Philadelphia.
Constitution of the United States is signed.
Northwest Ordinance creates Northwest
Territory.

1788 U.S. Constitution goes into effect after
ratification by nine states.

1789 George Washington
is inaugurated first
president of the U.S.
Judiciary Act of 1789.

1790 First U.S. Census enumerates population of
4 million.
Congress restricts citizenship to "free
white persons."
Northern states take steps
to abolish slavery.
Miami Chief Little Turtle scores victory
over U.S. troops.

P A R T   T H R E E

The Unfinished Revolution, 1775–1803

I
N 1775, GREAT BRITAIN STILL POSSESSED ALL OF NORTH AMERICA EAST
of the Mississippi River, from Hudson Bay to the Gulf of Mexico. If
the British could suppress the troublesome rebellion along the
Atlantic seaboard, their prospects for expansion in America looked promising. Farther west, Spain had recently acquired the vast Louisiana Territory from France. The Spanish retained their dominance in the
Southwest, and they were finally beginning to expand their claim to California by building a series of new missions and presidios.

By 1803, however, the broad picture had changed markedly. In the
Pacific Ocean, Europeans had encountered the Hawaiian Islands for the
first time, Russian fur traders had consolidated their hold in Alaska, and
Spanish vessels along the Pacific coast faced increasing competition from
the ships of rival nations. The British still held Canada and Florida, but
the 13 rebellious colonies had become an independent republic and had
started to acquire new territories. The most spectacular acquisition was
the Louisiana Territory, which the United States purchased in 1803, after
Spain returned the region to the control of France.

Few could have foreseen such an unlikely series of events in such a
brief span of time. Thomas Jefferson drafted the Declaration of Independence in 1776 at age 33. His generation had reluctantly become the effective leaders of a revolutionary movement by the mid-1770s. They
contended ably with those who pushed for greater democratization, those
who desired the stability of military rule, and even those who longed for
the protection of the British monarchy.

These unlikely revolutionary leaders were by no means united in all
their views and actions. They argued fervently over constitutional issues,
domestic policies, and foreign alignments. Most managed to reap personal rewards from the new society's collective success. And they saw to it
that these rewards reached far beyond their own households. Urban artisans, frontier farmers, and immigrant newcomers benefited from the
removal of monarchy.

Such positive developments inspired optimism for many, both at
home and abroad. Yet although the revolutionary era fulfilled the expectations of numerous citizens, it failed to meet the hopes and aspirations of

many Americans. Many American merchants and planters, indebted to British interests before 1776, gained by the separation from Great Britain as creditors and investors in the new society. Many frontier farmers and army veterans, on the other hand, faced burdensome debts after the Revolutionary War.

Women worried that the numerous written constitutions of the period were unresponsive to their interests. In 1776 only New Jersey gave the vote among property holders to "all free inhabitants," including women. But this provision was undone a generation later, in 1807, when New Jersey men objected to the idea of women having the right to vote. From New Hampshire to Georgia, committed "Daughters of Liberty" had made possible colonial boycotts through their industry and had managed families, farms, and businesses during the dislocations of war. Female access to education and the courts improved somewhat in the last quarter of the eighteenth century, but for most American women the advances were more symbolic than real.

For African Americans the disappointments were greater still. British offers of freedom prompted thousands of southern slaves to take up the Loyalist cause at great personal risk. Other free blacks and slaves, primarily in the North, shouldered arms for the Patriots, drawn by the rhetoric of liberty and the prospect of advancement. Even though they had chosen the winning side, they reaped few benefits. Although the number of free blacks expanded after the Revolutionary War, the African slave trade to the United States resumed and gained official protection. Slavery itself gained renewed significance with the transition to cotton production in the South and a federal constitution that sanctioned the power of slaveholders. Even in the North, where gradual emancipation became the norm by the end of the century, free blacks found their welcome into white churches and schools to be so half-hearted that many set about organizing their own separate institutions.

Eastern Indians, like African Americans, had good reason to distrust the Revolution and its leaders. The majority, including most Iroquois and Cherokee warriors, sided with the British and paid a steep price in defeat. Throughout the Mississippi Valley, Native Americans who still remembered the benefits of French trade and British military support faced relentless pressure as American speculators, soldiers, and settlers dissected their homelands. Some government officials promised that the newly acquired lands beyond the Mississippi would become an Indian Territory, providing lasting refuge for displaced eastern tribes. If so, what was to become of the Native American nations that already inhabited the western plains?

Like most political upheavals, the American Revolution left many questions unanswered and much business unfinished. Even the new federal government itself, in operation for little more than a decade by 1803, remained a work in progress. The specific roles and relative power of the government's three separate branches spurred endless debate, as did the proper place of the military and the most suitable direction for foreign policy. The Constitution ratified in 1789 seemed promising, but it remained an uncertain and largely untested framework.

1791 Bill of Rights is ratified.
Saint Domingue slave revolt.
Alexander Hamilton, "Report on the Subject of Manufactures."
Samuel Slater constructs first spinning machine on U.S. soil.
Bank of the United States is chartered.

1792 Washington is reelected president.
Mary Wollstonecraft, *Vindication of the Rights of Woman.*

1793 Washington issues Neutrality Proclamation.
Eli Whitney invents the cotton gin.

1794 U.S. troops defeat forces of Ohio Confederacy.
Whiskey Rebellion.

1795 Jay's Treaty.
Treaty of San Lorenzo.

1796 Washington's farewell address.
John Adams is elected president.

1797 XYZ Affair.

1798 Quasi War with France (to 1800).
Alien and Sedition Acts.
Kentucky and Virginia Resolutions (1798–1799).

1799 Seneca Leader Handsome Lake proclaims gai'wiio, or "Good Message."

1800 Thomas Jefferson is elected president.
Gabriel plot is exposed in Richmond, Virginia.

1801 Judiciary Act of 1801.
War against Barbary pirates.
Spain secretly cedes Louisiana Territory to France.

1803 Louisiana Purchase.
Marbury v. Madison.

CHAPTER 7

Revolutionaries at War, 1775–1783

■ American sharpshooter and Pennsylvania regular infantryman, 1784

IN 1775, AFRICAN-BORN THOMAS PETERS WAS A 37-YEAR-OLD SLAVE IN WILMINGTON, North Carolina. As a young man, this Yoruba speaker had been taken from what is now Nigeria and shipped to Louisiana aboard the slave ship *Henri Quatre*. Forced to cut sugar cane in the French colony, Peters rebelled repeatedly. For this, he endured whipping, shackles, branding, and exile. His owner sold him to a merchant on North Carolina's Cape Fear River, where he received his English name, learned to operate a grist mill, and started a family. Still enslaved, Peters was working as a millwright and living with his wife, Sally, age 22, and their 4-year-old daughter, Clairy, by the eve of the Revolutionary War.

During the 15 years between Peters's abduction from Africa in 1760 and the outbreak of hostilities between America and Britain in 1775, nearly 225,000 people had streamed into the British mainland colonies. More than half came from the British Isles (125,000), and another 15,000 arrived from Europe, mostly German-speaking settlers landing in Philadelphia. But the remaining 85,000 newcomers—or 4 in every 10—had all been purchased in Africa and enslaved in the coastal South. Thomas Peters, entering from Louisiana, was among the recent arrivals in British America.

In the summer of 1775, Peters must have heard talk about possible slave revolts in Virginia and the Carolinas. Before the end of the year, he certainly knew that Virginia's governor, Lord Dunmore, had offered freedom to slaves who would take up arms for the British. The following March, ships of the Royal Navy arrived at the Cape Fear River. The fleet carried a strike force under the command of Sir Henry Clinton, and it offered to provide safe haven for any slaves escaping from Patriot masters. For two months, the ships cruised the Lower Cape Fear, and Thomas and Sally Peters realized that the opportunity would not last. Joining numerous other black families, they risked arrest to gain their personal liberty by bolting to the British vessels.

Escaped slave Thomas Peters took part in the British fleet's unsuccessful attempt to seize control of Charleston Harbor in June 1776.

Peters was with General Clinton when the British fleet tried to take Charleston, South Carolina, in June 1776. Throughout the war, he served in a unit called the Black Pioneers. He was wounded twice and rose to the rank of sergeant. In October 1783, as defeated Loyalists left New York at the end of the Revolutionary War, the British officer in command of Peters's company swore out a certificate attesting to his service and affirming that he had "gained the good wishes of his officers and comrades." By serving, Peters had earned the promise of a farm in British Canada. He joined other members of the Black Pioneers aboard the *Joseph James* in New York harbor, bound for Nova Scotia. With him were Sally, Clairy, and 18-month-old John. Departing in November 1783, the ship was blown off course by foul weather. The ex-slaves spent the winter sheltered at Bermuda before finally joining 3500 other black Loyalists in Nova Scotia the following May.

But reaching Nova Scotia did not mark the end of Thomas Peters's odyssey. In 1790, after he and others had been denied the promised farmland, he ventured to London as an advocate for these former slaves. He protested their treatment, petitioned for relief, and met with British abolitionists who were planning a colony of former slaves in West Africa. Eager to take part in the effort, he returned to Canada and led 1200 African Americans to Sierra Leone, where he died at Freetown in 1792. In 32 years, Peters had seen New Orleans, Wilmington, Charleston, New York, Halifax, and London. He had escaped after 16 years of enslavement and then gone to war, fighting for his belief in freedom and for the safety of family and friends.

Though Thomas Peters's saga is unusual, it helps to illustrate an overriding point about the Revolutionary War. Although it has often been represented as such a simple "family affair," the American War of Independence was not, in fact, a clear, two-sided struggle in which unified English colonists joined together to oppose the English monarchy and Parliament. Instead, like most revolutions, it was a conflict fought by loose and shifting coalitions.

After decades of intensive migration, the mainland colonies had become increasingly complex (and in many ways non-English) societies. At a personal level, innumerable options existed to create fresh personal alliances, marrying someone who differed in language, ethnicity, religion, or class. Similarly, in a time of strife, there were countless possibilities for forging political "marriages of convenience" between different regions, groups, and interests. Where would merchants and sailors, wives and widows, servants and slaves, farmers and shopkeepers wind up in the emerging alignment between the Patriots (or rebels) on one hand and the Loyalists (or Tories) on the other? And what about dozens of other possible groupings, such as debtors, Catholics, young people, or frontier dwellers? Given the diversity of people with a stake in the outcome of the war, almost any combination seemed plausible.

Within each small community, and within the Atlantic theater as a whole, alliances often proved the old adage that "My enemy's enemy is my friend." No doubt Thomas Peters escaped servitude to join the British in part because the man who had been holding him in slavery was a leading member of the local Sons of Liberty. Likewise, powerful colonial merchants like John Hancock and Henry Laurens threw in their lot with the crowds in the streets in part because they had grown disillusioned with the political and commercial controls exerted by Parliament. On the international scale, the monarchies of France and Spain eventually swallowed their dislike for American rhetoric to join in a war that allowed them an opportunity to attack their longstanding rival, Britain. On the other hand, many Cherokee and Iroquois Indians, disillusioned by contact with land-hungry settlers, cast their lot with the British forces from overseas.

Precisely because the alliances were so numerous and complex, they often remained problematic and incomplete. Not all Iroquois warriors or African slaves sided with the British, and by no means all New England merchants or Virginia planters embraced the Patriot cause. In a landscape marked by uncertainty, large numbers of people at all levels of society opted for cautious neutrality as long as they could, while others shifted their allegiance as the winds changed. It was even possible, as the dramatic case of Benedict Arnold made clear, to betray a post of trusted leadership on one side and assume a position of authority on the other.

Not surprisingly, given so many complexities and uncertainties, the final outcome of the conflict remained a source of constant doubt. Looking back, Americans often view the results of the Revolutionary War as inevitable, perhaps even foreordained. In fact, the end result—and thus independence itself—hung in the balance for years.

■ **MAP 7.1**

BRITAIN AT WAR: THE GLOBAL CONTEXT, 1778–1783 For Britain, the war that began in 1775 expanded into a worldwide conflict against rival European powers within three years. By 1783, the British lost American colonies while expanding their hold in India. The lifetime journey of African-born Thomas Peters, shown here, is clearly exceptional, but extensive movements figured in many lives during these years of warfare. General Cornwallis, for example, went on to serve the British in India after his defeat at Yorktown in 1781.

Declaring Independence

New England's Minutemen had rallied swiftly at Lexington and Concord to harry the British. They moved equally quickly to spread news of their success in all directions. A ship carrying the Patriot version of events arrived in England two weeks before the dispatches of General Gage. Word reached Charleston, South Carolina, by early May and soon spread west beyond the Appalachian Mountains. When hunters exploring the blue-grass region heard the news, they named their campsite Lexington, now a city in modern-day Kentucky.

In the ensuing months, Congress took the initial steps to form a Continental Army. It also launched efforts to force the British out of Boston and to pull Canada into the rebellion. If these predominantly Protestant rebels hoped to draw the French Catholics of Quebec into their revolt, would free whites also be eager to include the blacks of Boston, Williamsburg, and Charleston in the struggle for liberty? Or would it be British officials who recruited more African Americans and furnished them with arms? After all, determined ex-slaves like Thomas Peters represented a serious threat to their former masters and a stark reminder to other slave owners who contemplated joining the colonists' rebellion. The answers to such questions became clear in the 15 months between the skirmish at Lexington and the decision of Congress to declare political independence from Britain in July 1776.

Charles Willson Peale, *George Washington in the Uniform of a British Colonial Colonel, c. 1772.* Washington-Custis-Lee Collection, Washington and Lee University, Lexington, VA

■ In June 1775, Congress selected a wealthy Virginia planter to command its army. The choice of George Washington reassured southern slave owners and disappointed blacks and whites in the North who saw slavery as a contradiction in the struggle for freedom.

The Continental Congress Takes Control

Enthusiasm ran high in Philadelphia in May 1775 as the second Continental Congress assembled amid cheers and parades. Delegates moved quickly in the weeks that followed to put the beleaguered colonies on a wartime footing. They instructed New York to build fortifications. They also paid for a dozen new companies of riflemen—recruited in Pennsylvania, Maryland, and Virginia—to be sent north to aid the Minutemen surrounding Boston. They created an Army Department under the command of a New York aristocrat, General Philip Schuyler, and approved an issue of $2 million in currency to fund the military buildup. The Congress also took important steps to ensure a coalition between the southern and the northern colonies.

In late May, word arrived from Lake Champlain in New York of a victory for the Green Mountain Boys (farmers led by Ethan Allen, from the area that became Vermont) and soldiers under Benedict Arnold of Connecticut. They had captured Fort Ticonderoga, along with all its cannon (heavy arms the new Army Department needed badly). This initiative not only secured the Hudson Valley against a British attack from the north; it also allowed Schuyler to propose a strike against Montreal and Quebec via Lake Champlain and the Richelieu River. Congress approved the assault, to be led by General Richard Montgomery. It also approved a daring scheme submitted by Arnold. He planned to lead separate forces up the Kennebec River. They would assist Montgomery in seizing Quebec and winning Canada before the region could become a staging ground for British armies.

But no single action by Congress had greater implications for coalition building among the colonies than the one taken on June 15, 1775. That day, members voted unanimously to appoint George Washington, a 43-year-old delegate from Virginia, "to command all the continental forces." Colonel Washington already headed a committee that was drawing up regulations to run the new army, and he had notable military experience. But his strongest asset may have been his southern roots. Northern delegates—especially John Adams, who had nominated Washington—sensed the need to foster colonial unity by placing a non–New Englander in charge of the army outside Boston. For their part, Southerners sensed keen regional differences, particularly over slavery. They appeared jealous, as one delegate noted, "lest an enterprising New England general, proving successful, might with his victorious army" enforce control over "the southern gentry."

In military and political terms, the selection of Washington proved auspicious. The tall, imposing planter from Mount Vernon emerged as a durable and respected leader in both war and peace. At another level, however, putting a slaveholder in command signaled the beginning of an important alliance between the well-to-do regional leaders of the North and South. Although no one could foresee it at the time, this alliance would contribute to the particular shape of the Federal Constitution a dozen years later, and the bond endured sufficiently to shape the governing of the country until the middle of the next century.

"Liberty to Slaves"

The selection of Washington strengthened the hand of plantation owners in the emerging coalition across regions. But in so doing, it signaled a limit to the prospects for any major or lasting American coalition across racial lines. The move sent a stronger message than Congress realized to some half a million African Americans, increasing their skepticism about the Patriot cause and spurring many of them—including Tom Peters, no doubt—to risk siding with the British.

Quebec, 1775
Montreal, 1775
Ft. Ticonderoga, 1775
Saratoga, 1777   Bennington, 1777
Ft. Stanwix, 1777   Boston, 1775
Newtown, 1777
New York, 1776
Princeton, 1777   Monmouth, 1777
Trenton, 1777
Brandywine, 1777   Germantown, 1777
Vincennes, 1779
Charlottesville, 1781   Naval Battle, 1781
Yorktown, 1781
St. Louis, 1780
Kaskaskia, 1778
Guilford Courthouse, 1781
Moore's Creek
Bridge, 1776
King's Mountain, 1780
Fishing
Creek, 1780
Cowpens, 1781   Camden, 1780
Charleston, 1780
Savannah, 1779
Natchez, 1778   Mobile, 1780
Pensacola, 1781

Mississippi R.

ATLANTIC OCEAN

Overview of the Revolutionary War
✹ British victories
✹ Patriot victories

■ **MAP 7.2**
OVERVIEW OF THE REVOLUTIONARY WAR

For their part, the British gave increasing thought to the idea of befriending enslaved Africans in order to undermine rebellious planters. In June 1775, the British commander in America, Thomas Gage, wrote to London: "Things are now come to that crisis, that we must avail ourselves of every resource, even to raise the Negros, in our cause." One Lutheran minister who spoke to black house servants near Philadelphia the next year noted that they "secretly wished that the British Army might win, for then all Negro slaves will gain their freedom. It is said that this sentiment is almost universal among the Negroes in America."

In the South, rumors of liberation swept through the large African American community during 1775. Slaveholding rebel authorities countered with harsh measures to quell black

"Revoking Those Sacred Trusts Which Are Violated": A Declaration Signed by 15 Grand Jury Members in South Carolina, May 1776

Young Martha Ryan used her cipher-book to do more than practice writing. She also drew American ships and flags and embellished the popular rallying cry, "Liberty or Death."

*T*hroughout the late spring of 1776, provincial assemblies, town meetings, and grand juries in the 13 colonies began issuing their own pronouncements regarding a break with Great Britain. The authors drew on historical precedent, legal tradition, and emotional sentiment. They mixed lofty theory and Real Whig ideology with local concerns. They also incorporated rhetoric and ideas from current pamphlets, speeches, and newspaper essays.

At least 90 of these proclamations survive. Most are more impressive for their strong feelings than for their literary merit. But taken together, they suggest the sentiments, arguments, and words that were in the air when Jefferson drafted the Declaration of Independence. This document was drawn up and signed by 15 members of the Cheraw District grand jury who came together for their regular court session in Long Bluff, South Carolina, on Monday, May 20, 1776.

unrest. In Charleston that spring, they deported an African-born minister, David Margate, for preaching a sermon that hinted at equality. Also, they focused their attention on a prominent free black man named Thomas Jeremiah, who had prospered as a skilled pilot guiding vessels between treacherous sand bars into the busy South Carolina port. In April, Jeremiah supposedly told an enslaved dockworker of a great war coming and urged slaves to prepare to seize the opportunity. Weeks later, nervous Patriot planters made the well-known free black into a scapegoat, accusing him of involvement in a plot to smuggle guns ashore from British ships to support a slave uprising. In August 1775, despite a lack of hard evidence against him, Jeremiah was publicly hanged and then burned.

That September, a Georgia delegate to Congress made a startling comment. If British troops were to land on the southern coast with a supply of food and guns, he said, and offer freedom to slaves who would join them, 20,000 blacks from Georgia and South Carolina would materialize in no time. In November, the beleaguered royal governor of Virginia, Lord Dunmore, attempted just such a scheme. Dunmore issued a proclamation granting freedom to the slaves of rebel masters who agreed to take up arms on behalf of the king. Hundreds responded to Dunmore's proclamation. They formed the Ethiopian Regiment and wore sashes proclaiming "Liberty to Slaves."

I. When a people, born and bred in a land of freedom and virtue . . . are convinced of the wicked schemes of their treacherous rulers to fetter them with the chains of servitude, and rob them of every noble and desirable privilege which distinguishes them as freemen,—justice, humanity, and the immutable laws of *God,* justify and support them in revoking those sacred trusts which are so impiously violated, and placing them in such hands as are most likely to execute them in the manner and for the important ends for which they were first given.

II. The good people of this Colony, with the rest of her sister Colonies, confiding in the justice and merited protection of the King and Parliament of *Great Britain,* ever . . . esteemed such a bond of union and harmony as the greatest happiness. But when that protection was wantonly withdrawn, and every mark of cruelty and oppression substituted; . . . self-preservation, and a regard to our own welfare and security, became a consideration both important and necessary. The Parliament and Ministry of *Great Britain,* by their wanton and undeserved persecutions, have reduced this Colony to a state of separation from her . . . as the only lasting means of future happiness and safety. . . . Cast off, persecuted, defamed, given up as a prey to every violence and injury, a righteous and much injured people have at length appealed to *God!* and, trusting to his divine justice and their own virtuous perseverance, taken the only and last means of securing their own honour, safety, and happiness.

III. We now feel every joyful and comfortable hope that a people could desire in the present Constitution and form of Government established in this Colony; a Constitution founded on the strictest principles of justice and humanity, where the rights and happiness of the whole, the poor and the rich, are equally secured; and to secure and defend which, it is the particular interest of every individual who regards his own safety and advantage.

IV. When we consider the publick officers of our present form of Government now appointed, as well as the method and duration of their appointment, we cannot but declare our entire satisfaction and comfort; as well in the characters of such men, who are justly esteemed for every virtue, as their well-known abilities to execute the important trusts which they now hold.

V. Under these convictions, . . . we . . . recommend it to every man . . . to secure and defend with his life and fortune a form of Government so just, so equitable, and promising; . . . that the latest posterity may enjoy the virtuous fruits of that work, which the integrity and fortitude of the present age had, at the expense of their blood and treasure, at length happily effected.

VI. We cannot but declare how great the pleasure, the harmony, and political union which now exists in this District affords; and having no grievances to complain of, only beg leave to recommend that a new Jury list be made for this District, the present being insufficient.

And lastly, we beg leave . . . that these our presentments be printed in the publick papers.— PHILIP PLEDGER, Foreman [and 14 other signatures] ◼

Source: Pauline Maier, *American Scripture: Making the Declaration of Independence* (New York: Knopf, 1997), 229–231.

The Struggle to Control Boston and Quebec

In the North, British forces had been confined in Boston ever since the Battle of Lexington. They would remain isolated on the town's main peninsula, supported by the Royal Navy, for nearly a year. In early July 1775, Washington arrived at nearby Cambridge to take up his command and oversee the siege of Boston. He quickly set out to improve order among his men. He tightened discipline, enforced punishments, and calmed regional jealousies. He removed nearly a dozen incompetent officers. In addition, he wrote scores of letters to civilian political leaders and the president of Congress to muster support for his meager army.

The Massachusetts legislature alone received 34 messages from the new commander. Washington made clear that nearly everything was in short supply, from tents and uniforms to muskets and cannon. He dispatched 25-year-old Henry Knox, a former bookseller and future general, to retrieve the ordnance captured at Ticonderoga. The Patriots' siege of Boston, he informed Congress, could not succeed without heavy fieldpieces to bombard the city from the heights at Dorchester and Charlestown that lay across the water.

Even before Washington's arrival, the British and the Americans had vied for control of these strategic heights. Indeed, the British General Gage drew up plans to secure Charlestown peninsula by seizing its highest point, Bunker Hill. But the Patriots learned of the scheme. On the night of June 16, 1775, they moved to fortify Breed's Hill, a smaller knoll 600 yards in front of Bunker Hill. The next afternoon, 1500 well-entrenched but inexperienced Patriot volunteers confronted the full force of the British army as thousands watched from the rooftops of Boston.

Although Gage might easily have sealed off Charlestown peninsula with his naval power, he instead used 2500 British infantry, weighed down by heavy packs, to launch three frontal attacks up Breed's Hill from the shoreline. The first two charges fell back before withering volleys at close range. Finally, with adjoining Charlestown ablaze and rebel powder supplies exhausted, a third assault overran the hill and dislodged the Americans. Mistakenly, the engagement became known as the Battle of Bunker Hill. Although it was technically a British victory, success came at a terrible price. Forty-two percent of British troops (1054 men) were wounded or dead—the worst casualty figures of the entire war. Gage lost his command, replaced in October by General William Howe. The Royal Army itself lost its aura of invincibility.

As Washington used the last half of 1775 to organize his rudimentary army in Cambridge, Henry Knox pursued his mission to retrieve the captured British ordnance from Ticonderoga. Using oxen, sledges, and local volunteers, he managed to haul 43 heavy cannon east, across trails covered with snow and ice, from the Hudson Valley to the coast. His men delivered the guns in late winter, and in March 1776 the Americans moved to secure Dorchester Heights. As at Breed's Hill, they made their surprise move at night. But this time, they had cannon that could reach far enough to bombard their enemies huddled in Boston. The British General Howe, who had commanded the charges at Breed's Hill and seen the devastation, drew back from a similar assault on Dorchester Heights. Instead, he evacuated his army, retreating by ship to Halifax, Nova Scotia. There, he made plans to attack the rebels again at New York, where Loyalist support was stronger.

As Washington's forces laid siege to Boston, other Americans converged on British troops in Canada. General Montgomery's troops seized Montreal in November 1775. They then descended the St. Lawrence River to join Benedict Arnold's men, who had struggled north toward Quebec under brutal winter conditions. As one combined force, under Montgomery, they attacked the walled city during a fierce snowstorm on the night of December 30. But their assault failed, and Montgomery perished in the fighting. Smallpox had already broken out in the American ranks, and it spread to new arrivals during the next five months. When British reinforcements showed up at Quebec in May, the Americans beat a hasty retreat toward Lake Champlain. They left behind most of their baggage and hundreds of sick companions.

Hundreds more died of smallpox during the withdrawal of the shattered army, and others spread the deadly pox further as they returned to their New England homes. "I got an account of my johns Death of the Small Pox at Canada," one New Hampshire father scrawled in his diary after learning that his 24-year-old son had died while fighting against the King's forces. "He was shot through his left arm at Bunker Hill." Now, "in defending the just Rights of America," John had been taken "in the prime of life by means of that wicked Tyranical Brute (Nea worse than Brute) of Great Britan." In thousands of American households, strained loyalty was turning to explosive anger.

"Time to Part"

In January 1776, a brilliant pamphlet, *Common Sense,* captured the shifting mood and helped propel Americans toward independence. British corsetmaker Thomas Paine, age 39, had endured a long series of personal and economic failures in England before sailing to Philadelphia. To this passionate man, with his gift for powerful and accessible prose, America represented a fresh start. Arriving late in 1774, Paine poured his energy into bold newspaper essays. In one, he argued that African American slaves deserved freedom and ample land to become productive citizen–farmers.

COMMON SENSE;

ADDRESSED TO THE

INHABITANTS

OF

AMERICA,

On the following interesting

SUBJECTS.

I. Of the Origin and Design of Government in general, with concise Remarks on the English Constitution.
II. Of Monarchy and Hereditary Succession.
III. Thoughts on the present State of American Affairs.
IV. Of the present Ability of America, with some miscellaneous Reflections.

Man knows no Master save creating Heaven,
Or those whom choice and common good ordain.
Thomson.

PHILADELPHIA;

Printed, and Sold, by R. BELL, in Third-Street.
MDCCLXXVI.

■ John Trumbull spent years gathering portraits for his famous painting, *The Declaration of Independence*. This engraving identifies individuals in the painting with their signatures. The artist placed the Drafting Committee in the center (31–35). He omitted signers for whom he had no likeness, and he included several non-signers, such as John Dickinson.

Paine's *Common Sense* was a wildly popular tract, selling 120,000 copies in three months and reaching all sorts of readers. In it, the author promised to lay out "simple facts, plain arguments, and common sense" on the precarious American situation. He then proceeded to lambaste "the so much boasted constitution of England." Not stopping there, he went on to attack hereditary monarchy and the divine right of kings. "One honest man," Paine proclaimed, is worth more to society "than all the crowned ruffians that ever lived." He urged the creation of an independent constitutional republic that could become "an asylum for all mankind." "Reconciliation is now a fallacious dream," he argued: "'TIS TIME TO PART."

Thousands of Paine's avid readers agreed. In the spring of 1776, one colony after another instructed its representatives to vote for independence. But many among the well-to-do still held strong social and economic ties to London; they feared the loss of British imperial protection and the startling upsurge of democratic political activity among the lower orders. At first, Congress vacillated. But with no sign of accommodation from England, most members agreed with Robert Livingston of New York that "they should yield to the torrent if they hoped to direct its course." In early June, young Livingston, age 30, joined the committee assigned to prepare a formal statement declaring independence from Great Britain. The Committee of Five also included Benjamin Franklin, John Adams, Roger Sherman, and the second youngest member of the Continental Congress, Thomas Jefferson.

The 33-year-old Jefferson had recently returned to Philadelphia from Virginia, where his mother had died suddenly in March. Personally independent for the first time, he willingly took responsibility for crafting the document. He framed a stirring preamble, drawing on British philosopher John Locke's contract theory of government. Locke (1632–1702) believed that the sovereign power ultimately resided not in government but in the people themselves, who chose to submit voluntarily to civil law to protect property and preserve basic rights.

According to Locke, rulers held conditional, not absolute, authority over the people. Citizens therefore held the right to end their support and overthrow any government that did not fulfill its side of the contract. For any people facing "a long train of abuses," Jefferson wrote, "it is their right, it is their duty, to throw off such government and to provide new guards for their future security." He went on to catalogue the "repeated injuries and usurpations" committed by King George III. Meanwhile, on July 2, Congress voted on the statement affirming that "these United Colonies are, and of right, ought to be, Free and Independent States." Twelve colonies voted to approve a resolution, with the New York delegation abstaining until it could receive further instructions from home. Having made the fundamental decision, the delegates then considered how to "declare the causes" behind their momentous choice to separate from Great Britain.

Over the next two days, all the Congress members edited the draft declaration submitted by the Committee of Five. They kept Jefferson's idealistic assertion that "all men are created equal." But they removed any reference to slavery, except for the charge that the king had "excited domestic insurrections amongst us," a veiled reference to the Thomas Jeremiah debacle in Charleston and to Lord Dunmore's proclamation. With other changes in place, they finally voted to approve the revised Declaration of Independence on July 4, 1776.

John Hancock, the president of the Congress, signed the document with a flourish, and printers hastily turned it into a published broadside. The other signatures (contrary to folklore) came two weeks later, after New York had offered its approval. Then 56 delegates gathered to sign their names to "The unanimous declaration of the thirteen United States of America." They did so at great risk. As they endorsed the document with their signatures, they knew that they were opening themselves to face charges of treason, punishable by death.

The British Attack New York

While the Continental Congress debated whether to declare independence, the British sharpened their strategies for suppressing the rebellion. Strangling the revolt with a naval blockade appeared impossible, given the length of the American coastline. But two other alternatives emerged in the first year of open warfare. These options shaped British intentions throughout the rest of the conflict. One design involved a southern strategy. It rested on the assumption that loyalty to the crown remained strongest in the South. If the British could land forces below Chesapeake Bay, Loyalist support might enable them to gain the upper hand and push north to reimpose colonial rule elsewhere.

In June 1776 troops under General Henry Clinton arrived off the Carolina coast with such a mission in mind. But Loyalists had already lost a battle to the Patriots at Moore's Creek Bridge near Wilmington, North Carolina, in February, and the British ships sailed to South Carolina instead. On June 28, they bombarded Sullivan's Island, at the mouth of Charleston harbor. But the Americans' cypress log fortress withstood the cannon fire, and the attackers withdrew. The British did not renew their southern design for several years, concentrating instead on a separate northern strategy.

According to Britain's alternative northern plan, troops would seize New York City and then divide the rebellious colonies in two at the Hudson River. By advancing upriver while other forces pushed south from Canada, they would take control of the entire Hudson Valley. Then, having sealed off New England, they could finally crush the radicals in Massachusetts who had spearheaded the revolt while restoring the loyalties of inhabitants farther south. Lord George Germain, the aggressive new British cabinet minister in charge of American affairs, favored this plan. An overwhelming strike, he asserted, could "finish the rebellion in one campaign."

Early in 1776, Germain set out to generate a land and sea offensive of unprecedented scale. He prodded the sluggish Admiralty for ships, and when he could not raise troops swiftly at home, he rented them from abroad. Empress Catherine of Russia declined a request for 20,000 soldiers, but the German states produced 18,000 mercenaries. Eventually, 30,000 German troops traveled to America, so many of them from the state of Hesse-Cassel that onlookers called all of them Hessians. Canada, having already repulsed Montgomery's American invasion, could provide a loyal staging ground in the north. "I have always thought Hudson's River the most proper part of the

■ In July 1776 the largest expeditionary force that the British had ever assembled arrived by sea at New York Harbor. British officer Archibald Robinson sketched part of the fleet and the initial camp at Staten Island. By September, the troops had seized Long Island and occupied New York City.

whole continent for opening vigorous operations," observed "Gentleman Johnny" Burgoyne, the dapper and worldly British general who arrived at Quebec with reinforcements in May 1776.

But plans for a strike south from Canada had to wait. Britain made its first thrust toward the mouth of the Hudson River by sea, using nearly 400 ships. In June, a convoy under General William Howe sailed from Halifax to Staten Island, New York, with 9000 soldiers. By mid-August, the general had received 20,000 reinforcements from across the Atlantic. His brother, Admiral Richard Howe, hovered nearby with 13,000 sailors aboard 70 naval vessels.

On orders from Congress, General Washington moved south to defend New York City, a difficult task made harder by ardent Loyalist sentiment. Rumors swirled of a Loyalist plot to kidnap the general or even take his life. A bodyguard named Thomas Hickey, implicated in the Tory scheme, was hanged before a huge crowd of anxious onlookers in late June. Intrigue aside, Washington's army lacked the numbers, equipment, and naval support to defend New York properly. The general weakened it further by dividing his troops between Manhattan and Brooklyn Heights on nearby Long Island.

A month after Congress members signed the Declaration of Independence, the commander nearly lost his entire force—and the cause itself. General Howe moved his troops by water from Staten Island to the Brooklyn area and then outflanked and scattered the poorly trained Americans in the Battle of Long Island on August 27. Remarkably, the British leader called off a direct attack that almost certainly would have overrun the American batteries on Brooklyn Heights. Perhaps Howe remembered yet again the heavy toll that a similar assault had taken on his forces at Bunker Hill. When his equally cautious brother failed to seal off the East River with ships, rebel troops escaped disaster by slipping back to New York City in small boats under cover of night and fog.

"Victory or Death": Fighting for Survival

Washington's narrow escape to Lower Manhattan from Long Island in August 1776 was only the first of numerous retreats. His army left New York City on September 15. (Congress counseled the American forces against destroying the town as they departed, but a suspicious fire devastated much of the city a week later.) The rebels withdrew from upper Manhattan and Westchester in October and from Fort Washington and Fort Lee on the Hudson—with heavy losses—in November. The Americans "fled like scared rabbits," one Englishman wrote. "They have left some poor pork, a few greasy proclamations, and some of that scoundrel Common Sense man's letters, which we can read at our leisure."

With winter at hand, the ragged Continental forces retreated southeast toward Philadelphia, plagued by deserting troops and low morale. But thanks to the unlikely success of one desperate maneuver—recrossing the Delaware River by night—they survived to renew their efforts in 1777. By the end of the next campaign season, two and a half years after the skirmish at Lexington, their powerful adversaries stumbled badly. Still, it was a long 14 months between the painful withdrawal from New York City and a stunning victory that finally came at Saratoga, 185 miles up the Hudson.

A Desperate Gamble Pays Off

As the American army retreated from New York late in 1776, General Howe repeatedly failed to press his advantage. The British commander and his brother had received a commission from Lord North, who headed the government in London, permitting them to negotiate a peace settlement with the Americans whenever possible. They hoped that a strong show of force, without a vicious offensive that might alienate civilians, could bring the enemy to terms. Howe's troops captured General Charles Lee, second in the American command, as they chased Washington across New Jersey. They also offered pardons to repentant rebels and encouraged desertions form Washington's army. In early December, the dwindling American force hurried through Princeton and slipped across the Delaware River into Pennsylvania. Confident of victory, the British again failed to pursue them, instead making camp at Trenton. Washington realized that unless circumstances changed quickly, "the game will be pretty well up."

Distressed by civilian talk of surrender, Tom Paine again took up his pen. In the *Pennsylvania Journal* for December 19, he launched a new series of essays called "The American Crisis." The series began with the ringing words, "These are the times that try men's souls." Paine mocked "the summer soldier and the sunshine patriot" who shrank from extreme trials, and he chided Lord North's administration for so underestimating "our abilities and disposition." Just when Britain "supposed us conquered," Paine predicted hopefully, "we rose the conquerer."

Action soon followed words. On Christmas Day 1776, Washington issued a new code phrase for sentinels: "Victory or Death." He ordered Paine's words read aloud to the troops. Then, after dark, his men recrossed the windswept Delaware River in a driving snowstorm and advanced on Trenton. Overconfidence, holiday festivities, and the foul weather had left the enemy unprepared. The Americans inflicted a startling defeat, killing several dozen and capturing more than 900 Hessian soldiers.

Few Patriot soldiers could converse with their German-speaking captives, but they could see first-hand that their opponents had superior resources. Both the British and their Hessian mercenaries possessed standardized equipment and ample supplies. The Americans, in contrast, were expected to provide their own firearms, and soldiers who brought a blanket from home earned a bonus. On enlisting, they were generally offered 40 shillings a month and a new issue of clothes, but the cost of their outfit came out of their pay at 10 shillings per month. Food was poor, rifle balls were makeshift, and gunpowder was so scarce that earlier in the year Benjamin Franklin had seriously proposed the use of bows and arrows. Most soldiers had signed up to serve for a brief term and return home, and many had joined the previous January for a one-year stint.

Washington knew that numerous enlistments expired on December 31 and that men would leave if the brief offensive halted. So he advanced again on December 30. Howe sent fresh troops forward under Charles Cornwallis to confront the rebels, pinning them down at Trenton. But when the British paused before attacking, the Americans left their campfires burn-

William Mercer, Battle of Princeton, date unknown. Courtesy of The Historical Society of Pennsylvania Collection, Atwater Kent Museum of Philadelphia

■ **This picture showing the noise and movement of the American victory at the Battle of Princeton was created by deaf painter William Mercer, whose father, Brigadier General Hugh Mercer, died in the battle.**

ing and slipped out of reach. They then circled behind Cornwallis to surprise and defeat his reinforcements at Princeton on January 3. It was not the last time that Washington bested Cornwallis. But for now, the victories at Trenton and Princeton restored a glimmer of hope for the tattered Continental Army as it took up winter quarters at Morristown, New Jersey.

When Howe withdrew his forces from much of New Jersey, anxious civilians who had sworn their loyalty to the crown felt deserted. Public sentiment again swung toward the rebels. More importantly, news of the victories spurred support for the American cause overseas in France. Eager to see their powerful rival bogged down in a colonial war, the French dispatched secret shipments of munitions to aid the revolutionaries. One young aristocrat, the idealistic Marquis de Lafayette, was already on his way from France to volunteer his services to General Washington. But it took a larger show of success to draw forth an official French commitment to the American cause.

Breakdown in British Planning

Among the Americans, two years of grim conflict had dampened the initial zeal for rebellion that had prompted citizen soldiers to enlist. Washington believed that the armed resistance could scarcely continue unless many more men made longer commitments to fight. They needed better pay, he insisted, and tighter discipline. Congress members reluctantly agreed. Though opposed in principle to a professional standing army, Congress expanded the commander's disciplinary powers and approved a bonus for men who enlisted for three-year terms.

Faced with a slumping economy, numerous recruits answered the call, including recent immigrants and unemployed artisans. All lacked training, supplies, and experience; many also lacked immunity to smallpox. Most of the enemy soldiers had acquired immunity from the devastating disease in Europe by surviving frequent epidemics. In contrast, Washington's rural recruits came from isolated townships and had never been exposed to the disease. When smallpox broke out among the American soldiers at Morristown, the commander promptly ordered inoculation. Because the process brings on a mild case of the disease, he anxiously counted the days until his rebuilding army could be ready to fight. "If Howe does not take advantage of our weak state," Washington commented in April 1777, "he is very unfit for his trust."

Despite the Americans' vulnerability, the British were slow to move. By seeking both a decisive blow and a negotiated settlement in 1776, they had achieved neither objective. George Germain and his colleagues in Lord North's ministry had fallen victim to contradictions in their own cumbersome planning process. They had also underestimated the persistence of Washington's army. During the campaigns of 1777, the British learned further hard lessons about the difficulty of the task facing them and the need for tight coordination of plans.

General Burgoyne, returning to London for the winter, won government support for a major new offensive. He planned to lead a large force south from Canada via Lake Champlain, using the Hudson Valley to drive a wedge through the rebellious colonies. In support, a combined British and Indian force would strike east from Lake Ontario, capturing Fort Stanwix (east of modern-day Syracuse, New York) and descending the Mohawk River to meet Burgoyne at Albany. Howe would push north from New York City to complete the design.

But General Howe had formed a different plan. Assuming Burgoyne would not need his help in the Hudson Valley, he intended to move south against Philadelphia. The two generals never integrated their separate operations, and the results were disastrous. In one six-month span, the British bungled their best chance for victory and handed their enemies an opening that permanently shifted the course of the war.

Saratoga Tips the Balance

The isolated operations of Burgoyne and Howe got off to slow starts in late June 1777. Howe used up two months in moving his troops by sea from New York harbor to the headwaters of Chesapeake Bay. This delay gave the Americans time to march south to check the British advance on Philadelphia. But at the Battle of Brandywine Creek (September 11, 1777), Howe bested Washington once again, using the same flanking maneuver that had worked so well on Long Island the year before. The British general finally marched into Philadelphia in late September, only to find that the rebel Congress had retreated to York, Pennsylvania.

With pacifist Quakers and active Tories in the area, Washington could count on little support from local militia. Nevertheless, he launched a surprise attack against the large Hessian garrison at Germantown just north of Philadelphia on the morning of October 4. He hoped to repeat his previous success at Trenton. However, dawn fog created so much confusion that the inexperienced Patriot troops "ran from victory," according to American general Anthony Wayne. Yet as Washington led his battered army to winter quarters at nearby Valley Forge, the defeats at Brandywine and Germantown seemed worth the price. The Americans had gained needed combat experience and had made Howe pay heavily in men and in time for his hollow capture of Philadelphia. "Now," Washington wrote expectantly, "let all New England turn out and crush Burgoyne."

Moving south from Canada in late June, "Gentleman Johnny" saw little likelihood of being crushed. His huge army consisted of 7200 soldiers, with 1500 horses to haul baggage and heavy equipment. The British officers believed their force to be irresistible and foresaw little danger. General Burgoyne even brought his mistress along on the campaign. Weakened by tensions in their own command and knowing the British were on the march, the Americans fell back from Crown Point and Ticonderoga on Lake Champlain.

But as British supply lines lengthened, the crown's army grew less invincible. Burgoyne's soldiers were forced to expend valuable time cutting a roadway through the wilderness. Also,

The Newberry Library, Chicago

■ The surrender of Burgoyne's army at Saratoga, New York, in October 1777 put more than 5000 British soldiers in American hands. Fearing that they would fight again if allowed to return to England, Congress ordered them held at this camp in Virginia until the end of the war. Many escaped and chose to settle in America.

the reinforcements anticipated from the west never arrived; Benedict Arnold turned them back at Fort Stanwix. Even worse, a British unit of 600 sent east to forage for corn and cattle was badly mauled by militia near Bennington. With cold weather approaching and his supplies dwindling, Burgoyne pushed toward Albany, unaware that Howe would not be sending help up the Hudson to meet him.

As Burgoyne's situation worsened, the American position improved. An arrogant British proclamation demanding submission from local residents only stiffened their resolve and drew out more rebel recruits. The Americans' strength grew to nearly 7000 in September after Congress gave command in the Hudson Valley region to Horatio Gates. The new general was an ambitious English-born officer who harbored resentments toward his American superior, Washington, and toward the much-admired Benedict Arnold. While Burgoyne's army crossed to the Hudson River's west bank at Saratoga, Gates's American forces dug in on Bemis Heights, 10 miles downstream.

On September 19, 1777, Patriot units under two aggressive officers, Benedict Arnold and Daniel Morgan, confronted the enemy at Freeman's Farm, not far from Saratoga. In the grueling battle, British forces suffered 556 dead or wounded, nearly twice the American losses. Gates's refusal to commit reinforcements prevented the Patriots from achieving total victory. Nevertheless, he claimed success and saw to it that his nemesis, Arnold, later lost his command.

In the weeks that followed, the American ranks swelled with new recruits who sensed a chance to inflict losses on Burgoyne's forces. On October 7, the beleaguered British tried once more to smash southward, only to suffer defeat in a second battle at Freeman's Farm. Morgan and Arnold once again played key roles, though Arnold suffered a crippling leg wound. When Burgoyne's entire army of 5800 surrendered at nearby Saratoga ten days later, Gates took full credit for the stunning triumph.

Uncanny Similarities: Britain's Vietnam?

Does history repeat itself? Never exactly, of course, yet sometimes the general similarities can be striking. This applies not only to small incidents but also to larger historical events such as the American Revolution. Consider the following six paragraphs:

The **British** had emerged victorious from a major world war just decades earlier. They took pride in their commercial dynamism, military strength, and cultural power. Also, they felt justifiably confident that their political institutions tended more toward liberty than those of their competitors. Still, step by step, they let themselves be drawn into a difficult conflict on a distant continent. At the time, the political and economic reasoning for entering combat made sense to most **British** leaders, especially because they were engaged in an ongoing struggle for global power with their major rival, **France.**

But **British** forces soon discovered that they were unable to exert their full military superiority. Instead, they needed to work incessantly to win the "hearts and minds" of the people (a phrase coined by John Adams). They found the population in the theater of war to be deeply divided politically, although it was often difficult to determine just who supported the **British** presence and who opposed it.

Commandeering local resources might alienate the very people they hoped to support. But supplying a large modern army with food and equipment across a wide ocean posed unprecedented logistical problems. Moreover, **British** recruits who had little personal stake in the conflict had to fight on unfamiliar terrain alongside soldiers of several nationalities. Career army officers found it difficult to maintain high morale among the **British** troops when facing a highly motivated citizen army opposed to colonialism of any kind.

France, the rival superpower, provided extensive support to the enemy's war effort to increase the capacity and willpower of a determined people's army. Officers, diplomats, and politicians in **France** hoped to keep large portions of the **British** army and navy tied up in a long and expensive war. That way, troops and resources were unavailable for engagements in other parts of the world.

At home, despite well-intentioned efforts, charges of corruption and inefficiency within the **British** bureaucracy and military establishment weakened the war effort. Opposition to the war slowly expanded within vocal portions of the **British** public. As casualties rose and the nation's deficit spending increased, the war became a divisive domestic issue. After years of fighting, successful enemy offensives underscored the army's weak position. The **British** concentrated their final efforts in the southern part of the country, where support remained strongest.

Finally, successive defeats (and a desire to protect **British** interests elsewhere in the world) prompted

Forging an Alliance with France

Ever since declaring independence, Congress had maneuvered to win international recognition for the new nation and aid for its military cause. While claiming neutrality, the Dutch supplied gunpowder for the rebellion through their West Indian island of St. Eustatius. In November 1776 they fired cannon there to salute an American ship—the first foreign acknowledgment of American sovereignty. Weeks later, Benjamin Franklin arrived in France as part of a commission sent to seek wider European support.

It was one thing for the Dutch Republic to recognize fellow republicans; it was quite another for the French king, Louis XVI, to endorse a revolution that opposed monarchy. Some in France, like the young marquis de Lafayette, felt enthusiasm for the American cause as an expression of rational enlightenment beliefs. But others, such as France's foreign minister, Comte de Vergennes, saw the colonists' revolt as an opportunity to avenge old grievances against Britain and undermine British power. Uncertain about the rebellion's chances for success, especially after the fall of Philadelphia, the government in Paris moved cautiously. It confined itself to substantial but covert assistance in the form of money and arms.

Word of the American victory at Saratoga suddenly gave Franklin more room to maneuver. When he hinted to the French that he might bargain directly with London for peace, Vergennes moved immediately to recognize American independence. France agreed to renounce

American soldiers in Vietnam, like the British in America two centuries earlier, had superior arms but faced huge logistical problems moving heavy supplies to a distant war zone.

time, for each use of the word *British* read *American,* and for *France* read *the Soviet Union.* Surprisingly, two centuries after the War of Independence, the United States found itself in a situation that bore remarkable similarities to the British position during the American Revolution. Again, a powerful English-speaking empire (this time an informal one) seemed to have overextended its reach across a western ocean.

Americans now have three decades of perspective on the Vietnam War. In a new generation that did not experience the conflict first-hand, many feel a keen interest in understanding its lessons. For historians, comparison is a traditional tool for such inquiry. They often seek out similarities between two historical people or episodes and then test the comparison, seeing where it works best, where it breaks down, and where it leads to new comparisons or deeper insights. Could learning more about Vietnam possibly help to put the American Revolution in a new light—and vice versa? ■

the full-scale evacuation of the army. As the troops departed, they were accompanied by thousands of civilians who had remained loyal supporters. After nearly a decade, the **British** and their enemies negotiated a peace treaty in Paris, and the long war came to a conclusion. But ill will lingered between the

two countries for another generation before they finally resumed peaceful commerce.

This seems a brief and plausible overview of events, at least from a British perspective. But now try going over these six paragraphs again. This

forever any claim to English land in North America, and Franklin promised that the Americans would help defend French holdings in the Caribbean. Both parties pledged to defend the liberty of the new republic, and each agreed not to conclude a separate peace with Great Britain or to cease fighting until U.S. independence had been ensured by formal treaty. In May 1778 the Continental Congress approved this alliance. The next month, France entered the war, adding its enormous wealth and power to the American cause. A year later, Spain—unwilling to ally itself directly with the upstart republic but eager to protect its vast American assets from Great Britain—entered the war on the side of France.

For the British, what had been a colonial brushfire swiftly flared into a global conflict reminiscent of the Seven Years' War. These new hostilities with France meant possible invasions at home. Equally worrisome, they meant inevitable attacks on outposts of Britain's empire around the world, from the Mediterranean Straits of Gibraltar to India's Bay of Bengal. Over several years, French ships seized Senegal in West Africa, took Grenada in the West Indies, and burned trading factories at Churchill and York on Hudson Bay. London's annual war expenditures climbed from £4 million in 1775 to £20 million in 1782.

As these costs mounted, British domestic opposition to the war in America intensified. Some members of Parliament pushed for a swift settlement. In 1778 a peace commission led by Lord Carlisle offered concessions to the Continental Congress, hoping to tear the French alliance apart. But the Carlisle Commission failed to win a reconciliation. Other Britons went

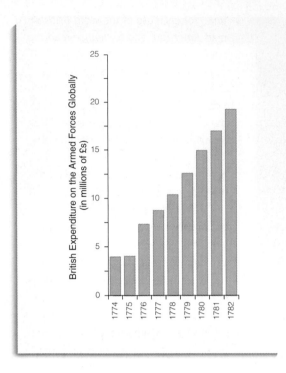

■ **FIGURE 7.1**
BRITISH GOVERNMENT EXPENSES ON ARMED FORCES THROUGHOUT THE WORLD (IN MILLIONS OF POUNDS), 1775–1782 Britain's war budget soared after France entered the conflict in 1778, but major resources flowed toward India and the Caribbean, limiting the share available for North America.

further in opposing the American war. Their diverse reasons included fear of French power, desire for American trade, disgust over war profiteering, hatred of government corruption, ties to friends in America, and idealistic belief in the revolution's ideals. They drank toasts to General Washington and openly supported the American cause.

Faced with growing economic and political pressure, the king and his ministers briefly considered withdrawing all troops from the rebellious colonies and focusing on the French threat. But instead, when General Howe resigned as commander-in-chief in America, they instructed his successor, Sir Henry Clinton, to retreat from Philadelphia to New York and devote his main resources to attacking the French in the Caribbean. Over the next four years, discontent within Britain continued to escalate, and no strategy proved sufficient to pacify the Americans or to crush their rebellion.

Legitimate States, a Respectable Military

Even with a new French alliance in hand, the rebellious American states faced serious challenges on both the civilian and military fronts in the struggle to secure lasting independence. They had thrown out their colonial governors and embarked on a dangerous war, but two fundamental questions still confronted them: How would the once-dependent colonies govern themselves? And even if they devised new forms of self-governance, how could they shape a military force strong enough to defend themselves but not so unchecked as to overthrow their new civil governments? Their colonial experience had taught them to trust representative legislatures over strong executive authority. They had also learned another lesson: Any standing army, even one's own, could pose a danger if not under civilian control. For people who often cited ancient history, one well-known story drove this point home. Colonists knew how Rome's military commander, Julius Caesar, and his legion crossed the Rubicon in 49 B.C. and helped destroy the Roman Republic they had sworn to defend.

The Articles of Confederation

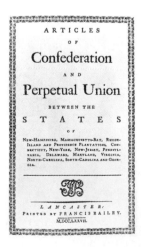

The Continental Congress that the rebelling states created had taken prompt initiative. Without clear authority, it had declared independence, raised an army, issued currency, borrowed money from abroad, and negotiated an alliance with France. Then it moved to bring greater stability and legitimacy to its work. In November 1777, one month after the victory at Saratoga, it approved Articles of Confederation and presented this formal plan for a lasting and unifying government to the states for ratification. In every region, citizens were already debating how much authority each new state government would have in relation to the larger federation. Who would have the power to levy taxes, for example, and who would control the distribution of land?

The Articles declared "The United States of America" to be a "firm league of friendship" between the 13 former colonies that had each become a new state. The final document proposed a weaker confederation than the one outlined in an earlier draft by John Dickinson. According to the finished charter, each state would retain its sovereignty and independence, plus all rights and powers not "expressly delegated" to the Confederation Congress. Indeed, it implied such a loose arrangement of states that the French considered sending 13 separate ambassadors to America. And several European proposals to end the war suggested negotiating separately with each state.

According to the Articles, Congress could not collect taxes or regulate trade; it could only requisition funds from the states. Their proportions would vary depending on relative population. Moreover, the Confederation had no separate executive branch; executive functions fell to various committees of the Confederation Congress. In addition, to the dismay of land speculators, the Congress would not control the western domains that several large states had claimed. Maryland, a small state without western claims, protested this arrangement and refused to ratify. To win approval, drafters changed the plan and granted the Confederation control of western lands. After four years, the Articles finally won ratification in 1781.

Given the importance of the states, the task of designing new state governments seemed a higher priority to many than inventing a confederation structure. Some leaders in the Continental Congress returned home to help implement this reconstruction process. In May 1776, for example, two of Jefferson's friends in the Virginia delegation in Philadelphia departed for Williamsburg. They left their younger colleague behind, but they carried his written draft for a possible state constitution. Those already at work in Virginia accepted Jefferson's proposed preamble, and on June 29, 1776, Virginia led the way, adopting the first republican state constitution.

Virginia had already pioneered in another respect. Two weeks earlier, Virginia representatives approved a Declaration of Rights drawn up by George Mason. In language anticipating Jefferson, Mason affirmed that "all men are by nature equally free and independent," possessing inherent rights "to the enjoyment of life and liberty, with the means of acquiring and possessing property, and pursuing and obtaining happiness and safety." He affirmed the revolutionary concepts that all power derives from the people and that magistrates are their servants. He went on to endorse trial by jury, praise religious freedom, and condemn hereditary privilege. Over the next eight years, each state adopted a similar bill of rights to enumerate the fundamental limits of government power.

Creating State Constitutions

Though diverse, the 13 states shared practical needs. Each had removed a functioning colonial government and needed to reestablish the rule of law under a new system. To do so, they drew on principles they had learned in the previous decade and on English common-law traditions. Britain possessed no written constitution, but the colonists had been ruled under published charters, and they shared a belief in the value of such clear and open arrangements. Thus they readily envisioned an explicit controlling document, or constitution, for each new state. Besides, the novel idea that government flowed from the people—as an agreement based on the consent of the governed—called for some all-encompassing, written legal contract.

A new written constitution, whether for a state or a union of states, represented something more fundamental and enduring than a regular law. It needed to be above day-to-day legal statutes and political whims. Somehow, the people, through chosen representatives, had to prepare a special document that citizens would affirm, or ratify, only one time. After the new government structure was in place, the constitution itself would be difficult, though not impossible, to change.

In 1779, Massachusetts legislators, under pressure from the public, fixed upon a method for providing the elevated status and popular endorsement for such a new document. Local voters in town meetings chose representatives for a specific constitution-drafting convention. These delegates, building on a model suggested by John Adams, crafted a suitable document, and their proposed constitution was then submitted to all the state's free men (regardless of race or property) for ratification. This widened constituency was intended to give special weight to the endorsement process.

John Singleton Copley, *John Adams*, 1783. Courtesy of the Harvard University Portrait Collection, Bequest of Ward Nicholas Boylston to Harvard College, 1828. Photograph by Photographic Services. ©President and Fellows of Harvard College

■ After independence, Americans had to create their own governments, and states experimented with new forms. John Adams of Massachusetts was part of a unique generation of lawyers who became skilled in the art of constitution-making.

Approval of the Massachusetts document was hotly debated. Many objected to the limits on popular power that were part of Adams's novel design. A reluctant revolutionary, Adams had dismissed Tom Paine as "ignorant, malicious, short-sighted." He had even composed a tract titled *Thoughts on Government* to counter the democratic enthusiasm of Paine's *Common Sense*. In his pamphlet, Adams argued that "interests" (like-minded groups), rather than people, should receive equal representation. In addition, he proposed sharing legislative responsibilities between a house, a senate, and a chief executive. Property requirements for these offices were steep, so wealthy interests would have power far beyond their numbers. The Massachusetts state constitution, ratified by a narrow margin, implemented these ideas. They signaled a turn away from the strongest popular radicalism of 1776 and foreshadowed the more conservative balance of interests that Madison championed in the federal Constitution drafted in 1787.

This extended experiment in constitution writing was exhilarating and unprecedented. Never before in history, John Adams observed, had several million people had numerous opportunities "to form and establish the wisest and happiest government that human wisdom could contrive." Initial state efforts yielded varied results as citizens debated novel approaches to self-government. By 1780, the desire of prominent and well-established elites to rein in democratic power was evident. Yet in comparison to the overseas monarchy they had rejected, even the most conservative new state constitutions seemed risky and bold.

At least three common threads ran through all the documents. First, fearing executive might, drafters sharply curtailed the strength of state governors. These men no longer had the power to dismiss assemblies, raise armies, declare war, fill offices, or grant privileges. Colonial governors had been appointed from above, by proprietors or the crown, and they could serve terms of any length. In contrast, state governors would now be elected annually, usually by the assembly. Moreover, their service was subject to impeachment and controlled by term limits. In Pennsylvania, the most radical of the new constitutions did away with a single governor altogether, placing executive power in the hands of a 12-member council elected by the people.

Second, whether out of political belief or an effort to mobilize broad support for the revolutionary cause, drafters expanded the strength of the legislature and increased its responsiveness to the popular will. They enlarged the size of assemblies and increased the frequency of elections to allow greater local involvement. They also reduced property requirements for holding office and changed limits on the right to vote to allow wider participation.

Third, the constitution-makers feared the possible corruptions that came when people held more than one office at the same time. Having experienced these glaring conflicts of interest first-hand, they stressed the separation of executive, legislative, and judicial posts. The decision to prevent members of the executive branch from also holding a legislative seat removed any prospect for a cabinet-style government along the lines of the British model.

Tensions in the Military Ranks

A new republican order, whatever its nature, could not defend itself without a suitable fighting force. Just as defunct colonial administrations gave way to new state governments after serious debate, colonial militia companies transformed into state militia amid intensive arguments. In the state militias, and in Washington's army, controlled and paid by the Continental Congress, inevitable tensions emerged from the start. Heated discussions erupted as to what constituted equitable pay, appropriate discipline, suitable tactics, and a proper distribution of limited supplies. Others argued over whether wealth, popularity, vision, military experience, political savvy, European training, or influential ties should play a role in determining who received, or retained, the cherished right to command.

Two basic tensions underlay all of these debates. One involved the stresses arising between educated gentry and citizen soldiers when different, even opposing, social ranks joined in a coalition across class lines to confront a common enemy. The other concerned strains within the upper levels of society, as status-conscious members of the upper classes wrestled with what constituted appropriate service and recognition for men of their standing. Should they serve in the military at all, and if so, how much should they defer to older soldiers, seasoned frontiersmen, foreign-born officers, or civilian authorities without taking offense.

One heated topic involved the election of officers. Wealthy gentry assumed that they would command their state militia, while citizen soldiers demanded the right to choose their own leaders. Another source of tension concerned an old European tradition—the right of any prosperous individual to buy exemption from military service or to send a paid substitute. Back in December 1776, as Washington's army had retreated into Pennsylvania, militia in Philadelphia had chastised "Gentlemen who formerly Paraded in our Company and now in the time of greatest danger have turn'd their backs." They asked whether state authorities meant "to force the poorer kind into the field and suffer the Rich & the Great to remain at home?"

Three years later, some of these same Philadelphia militia, bitter that the burdens of the war always fell disproportionately on the poor, took part in what became known as the Fort Wilson Riot. Staging a demonstration in October 1779 spurred by soaring food prices, they intentionally marched passed the stately home of James Wilson, where wealthy Patriots had gathered. "The time is now arrived," the demonstrators' handbill proclaimed, "to prove whether the suffering friends of this country, are to be enslaved, ruined and starved, by a few overbearing Merchants,. . . Monopolizers and Speculators." Shots were exchanged, and six died in the melee at "Fort Wilson." (Wilson himself went on to become a leader of the 1787 Constitutional Convention.)

Subtle class divisions had also beset the Continental Army, where jealousies over rank plagued the status-conscious officer corps. Congressional power to grant military commissions, often on regional and political grounds, only intensified disputes. Also, Americans representing Congress abroad were empowered to promise high military posts to attract European officers. Some of these recruits served the American cause well, such as Johann de Kalb and Friedrich von Steuben (both born in Germany) and Thaddeus Kosciusko and Casimir Pulaski from Poland. In France, at age 19, the Marquis de Lafayette secured a commission to be a major general in America, and he assisted Washington impressively throughout the war.

However, other foreign officers displayed arrogance and spread dissension. Irish-born Thomas Conway, for example, courted congressional opponents of Washington and encouraged the desires of General Horatio Gates to assume top command. Whether or not a concerted "Conway Cabal" ever existed, Washington managed to defuse tensions from Valley Forge during the hard winter of 1777–1778. His numerous letters helped to patch frayed relations with Gates and consolidate his position with Congress.

Another rival for command of the army, English-born Charles Lee, met disfavor several months later, when Washington ordered him to attack the rear guard of Clinton's army as it withdrew from Philadelphia to New York. Lee mismanaged the encounter at Monmouth, New Jersey, on June 28, 1778, and only Washington's swift action stopped a premature retreat. The Battle of Monmouth ended in a draw, but American troops claimed victory and took pride in their swift recovery and hard fighting.

Shaping a Diverse Army

The army's improved effectiveness came in large part from the efforts of Friedrich von Steuben, a European officer recruited by Benjamin Franklin after charges of homosexuality disrupted his German military career. He had arrived at Valley Forge in February 1778, offering to serve without pay. There he found soldiers with poor food, scant clothing, and limited training. Many Americans still wanted to see a more democratic citizen army, with elected officers and limited hierarchy. But Washington hoped to mold long-term soldiers into a more "Europeanized" force, using stern discipline to train the Continental Line. Steuben provided the chance to do so. Shouting in several languages—he spoke no English—the newcomer worked energetically to drill soldiers who, in turn, trained others. A written drill manual was drawn up, and the strict training paid off. Alexander Hamilton, who observed the routine and later fought beside Steuben at Yorktown, wrote that "unquestionably to his efforts we are indebted for the introduction of discipline in the Army."

New discipline helped boost morale. Still, terms of service and wage levels remained sources of contention for American soldiers. So did the disparities in treatment and pay between officers and enlisted men. There were other grievances as well. Congressional committees overseeing the war effort appeared inept. Officers with political appointments frequently proved incompetent, and civilians often expressed indifference or hostility toward militia. A steady shortage of new recruits added to the frustrations of enlisted men.

Arguments also persisted over who could serve in the army. Women organized in diverse ways to assist the war effort, making uniforms and running farms and businesses for absent husbands. A few American women, such as Deborah Sampson of Massachusetts, disguised themselves as men and fought. Far more accompanied the troops to cook and wash in the camps. Earning scant pay, they carried water to the weary and wounded on the battlefield. Serving in these capacities, they formed a significant presence in both armies. For example, when Burgoyne launched his campaign from Canada, 2000 women accompanied his 7200 troops.

As many as 20,000 women, many of them wives, may have accompanied the American army during the war. Washington reluctantly accepted the presence of women in camp, reasoning that they freed men for "the proper line of their duty." Mary Hays, wife of a Pennsyl-

Pennsylvania Capitol Preservation Committee

■ **More than a century after the grim winter at Valley forge, artist Edwin Abbey composed this mural of Steuben drilling Washington's soldiers in February 1778.**

■ When British ships trapped an expedition from Massachusetts along the Maine coast in August 1779, the 40 American vessels retreated up the Penobscot River. Before fleeing into the woods, the crews set fire to their boats, creating a spectacular blaze. "When they Blew up," one sailor wrote, "Shott and Timber flew verey thick up and Down the River."

vania soldier, embodied the women's effort and commitment. She endured the winter at Valley Forge and later hauled pitchers of water on the battlefield at Monmouth. When her husband was wounded, she is said to have set down her jug and joined his gun crew, earning folk legend status as the cannon-firing "Molly Pitcher."

After petitioning to fight, free blacks were allowed to join the revolutionary army. Rhode Island even formed an African American regiment. But repeated proposals to arm southern slaves met with defeat. South Carolina and Virginia went so far as to move in the opposite direction, offering to give away slaves captured from Tory planters as a bonus to white recruits. Thus it is no surprise that thousands of enslaved people, especially in the South, risked their lives to escape to British lines.

The War at Sea

Even as the Americans' army grew into a respectable force, their lack of naval strength proved a constant disadvantage. As early as October 13, 1775, the Continental Congress had agreed to arm two vessels to prey on British supply ships on the Atlantic. In retrospect, the vote marked the birth of the American navy. At the time, however, many delegates still held out hope for reconciliation with Britain. Samuel Chase, a cautious lawyer from Maryland, thought a new navy would be large enough to provoke British resentment and retaliation but far too small to be effective. He objected that it was "the maddest Idea in the World to think of building an American Fleet."

Despite such objections, Congress promptly appointed a committee to acquire sailing craft for "protection and defense." Most of the 13 states built up their own small navies for local purposes, only adding to the confusion. The lack of central coordination proved deadly. When Massachusetts sent its ships "down east" along the Maine coast to challenge a Loyalist buildup at Castine in 1779, British vessels cornered the fleet at Penobscot Bay and crushed the enterprise.

Despite its strength, the British navy was stretched thinner as more European powers joined the fray: France in 1778, Spain in 1779, and Holland in 1780. The English feared possible invasion, and French corsairs harassed Britain's coastline, joined by American captains. One of these captains, a Scottish immigrant named John Paul Jones, arrived in European waters from America in early 1778, just as Franklin signed the pact with France. In April, Jones led a night raid on the port of Whitehaven in his native Scotland. He inflicted slight damage on the Irish Sea town, but the propaganda triumph of an American success in British waters proved huge. The brazen young captain won an even greater victory the next year off Flamborough Head on England's east coast. Jones and his crew—including men of 11 nationalities—were sailing an aged French ship named the *Bonhomme Richard* in tribute to Benjamin Franklin's "Poor Richard." In a fierce battle, they managed to board Britain's sleek new H.M.S. *Serapis* and capture the larger, heavily armed British frigate before their own vessel sank.

In all, the Continental Navy equipped more than 50 vessels and captured nearly 200 British craft as prizes. But these numbers pale in comparison to the activities of American privateers. More than a thousand private ship owners obtained licenses from Congress to seize enemy ships and divide the proceeds among themselves and their crew. With international commerce curtailed, shipowners and sailors were eager to try their luck at this tempting opportunity. Average pay aboard privateers was higher than on a government vessel, and discipline was less strict. In 1778 nearly 10,000 men were engaged in privateering aboard several hundred vessels. Their small, quick boats swarmed the Atlantic like troublesome gnats, frustrating England's mighty navy. According to one estimate, by war's end the British had surrendered 2000 ships, 12,000 men, and goods valued at £18 million. Moreover, because privateering drew merchant investors directly into the Patriot war effort, it helped bind the coastal elite more firmly to the American cause.

The Long Road to Yorktown

By July 1778, Clinton's British forces had returned to New York City, and their situation had not improved. Frustrated in New England and the middle tier of states, Clinton revived the southern strategy discussed at the beginning of the war. A southern plan offered numerous potential benefits. Because the region produced staple crops, it held more economic value for Britain than the North did. Less thickly settled than the North, the South was more vulnerable. In addition, it supposedly contained a wide array of Loyalists who would offer their support. The recently acquired colonies of East and West Florida had never rebelled, and the British army might win back Georgia and the Carolinas with a sufficient show of force. Success there would open up Virginia for reconquest.

Furthermore, the South's warm weather allowed longer campaigns and easier provisioning of troops. A lengthy growing season meant more fodder for the wagon horses and cavalry mounts so essential to any large military operation. The region's long Atlantic coastline, far from New England privateers, lay open to the British. Clinton knew that Washington's distant, land-based army would have trouble defending it. Moreover, nearly 500,000 enslaved African Americans posed a constant threat to Patriot planters and represented potential support for British invaders. Finally, the same whites who dreaded slave rebellion also feared war with Native Americans, as Jefferson had explained in the Declaration of Independence. So the possible use of Indian allies also entered Britain's strategic calculation.

Indian Warfare and Frontier Outposts

Most Native Americans in eastern North America remained loyal to the British during the Revolutionary War. Exceptions existed, such as the Oneida, Tuscarora, and Catawba, but Indians in many regions had long-standing grievances about the encroachments of colonial whites. In southern Appalachia, colonial land investors and settlers had defied the king's Proclamation

The Revolutionary War in the North

British
Patriots
British victories
Patriot victories

1 Arnold leads winter journey to Quebec, 1775

2 Montgomery fails to conquer Canada, 1775–1776

3 Knox hauls cannon from Ft. Ticonderoga, 1776

4 William Howe withdraws from Boston to Halifax, 1776

5 Howe brothers capture New York with huge force, 1776

6 Washington retreats, then re-crosses the Delaware, 1776–1777

7 William Howe sails from New York, moves on Philadelphia, 1777

8 Washington meets Howe at Brandywine and Germantown, 1777

9 Burgoyne tries to seize Hudson Valley from Canada , 1777

10 Arnold defeats British near Ft. Stanwix, 1777

11 Gates forces Burgoyne's surrender at Saratoga, 1777

12 Clinton retreats from Philadelphia to New York, 1778

13 Marching from Valley Forge, Washington wins at Monmouth, 1778

14 Brant/Butler attack Wyoming Valley, 1778; Cherry Valley, 1779

15 Sullivan attacks Iroquois villages, 1779

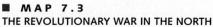

■ **M A P 7 . 3**
THE REVOLUTIONARY WAR IN THE NORTH

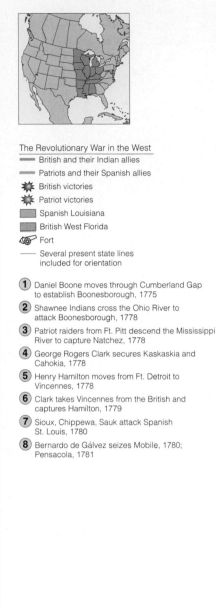

The Revolutionary War in the West

━━━━ British and their Indian allies
╌╌╌╌ Patriots and their Spanish allies
✦ British victories
✦ Patriot victories
▨ Spanish Louisiana
▨ British West Florida
🔫 Fort
───── Several present state lines
included for orientation

① Daniel Boone moves through Cumberland Gap to establish Boonesborough, 1775

② Shawnee Indians cross the Ohio River to attack Boonesborough, 1778

③ Patriot raiders from Ft. Pitt descend the Mississippi River to capture Natchez, 1778

④ George Rogers Clark secures Kaskaskia and Cahokia, 1778

⑤ Henry Hamilton moves from Ft. Detroit to Vincennes, 1778

⑥ Clark takes Vincennes from the British and captures Hamilton, 1779

⑦ Sioux, Chippewa, Sauk attack Spanish St. Louis, 1780

⑧ Bernardo de Gálvez seizes Mobile, 1780; Pensacola, 1781

■ **MAP 7.4**
THE REVOLUTIONARY WAR IN THE WEST

Line for more than a decade. At Sycamore Shoals on the Watauga River in 1775, North Carolina speculators led by Richard Henderson illegally purchased much of the Cherokees' territory. A young war chief named Dragging Canoe, defying his more conservative elders, vowed to turn the region into a "dark and bloody ground." True to his word, he laid siege to the new "Over-Mountain" Watauga settlement in July 1776. Whites struck back, organizing separate expeditions from four southern states. In all, 6000 troops pushed into the mountains, laying waste to Cherokee villages.

Meanwhile, Daniel Boone (an agent for Henderson) led settlers through Cumberland Gap in western Virginia to establish a fort on the Kentucky River at Boonesborough in 1775. By 1777, these pioneer families faced constant warfare against Indian adversaries who were fighting for their homelands. The Native Americans were also being urged on by Henry Harri-

■ The British used Fort Niagara (on the southwest edge of Lake Ontario, at the mouth of the Niagara River) to launch attacks on American settlements and to shelter Indian allies. During the harsh winter of 1779–1780, 5000 Iroquois refugees, made homeless by the scorched-earth campaign of General John Sullivan, camped near the fort in five feet of snow.

son, the British commandant at far-off Detroit. In one six-month span, Harrison, who became known as the Scalp Buyer, received 77 prisoners and 129 scalps from this frontier warfare.

Along the upper Ohio, the violence escalated, despite efforts by Indian elders to maintain neutrality. Not all deaths occurred in battle. Americans killed Shawnee leader Cornstalk and his son during a truce in 1777. The next year, they murdered the neutral Delaware leader, White Eyes, although they had recently hinted to him and other Native Americans in Ohio Country that the Indians might one day "form a state" and have "representation in Congress." Four years later, at the village of Gnadenhutten (south of modern-day Canton, Ohio), militia from Pennsylvania massacred 100 peaceful Delaware men, women, and children who had been converted to Christianity by missionaries of the Moravian church.

By then, conflict had also flared farther north, much of it involving Native Americans. Joseph Brant, a mixed-race Mohawk leader educated in New England and loyal to the British, pushed south from Fort Niagara on Lake Ontario. Joined by a Loyalist band under John Butler, Brant and his men attacked poorly guarded frontier settlements. First in the Wyoming Valley of northeastern Pennsylvania and later in New York's Cherry Valley, the raiders killed hundreds of settlers.

In the summer of 1779, American General John Sullivan, fresh from fighting the British in Rhode Island, received a new assignment: lead a punitive campaign to annihilate Indian towns as a reprisal for the Cherry Valley slayings. His revenge-minded army of more than 4000 marched into Iroquois Country, pushing aside resistance from Brant and Butler at Newtown (Elmira, New York). Sullivan's troops destroyed 40 villages of the four tribes in the Iroquois Confederacy most linked to the British cause: the Mohawk, Onondaga, Cayuga, and Seneca. They avoided towns of the two Iroquois groups sypathetic to the Americans—the Oneida and Tuscarora—but elsewhere they chopped down orchards, torched crops, burned 160,000 bushels of corn, and sent several thousand Indian refugees streaming toward Fort Niagara. Hunger and retaliatory raids haunted the region until the end of the war.

While the British were passing arms and supplies to the divided Iroquois Confederacy through Fort Niagara, they were also using several western posts to arm other Indian allies and seek an advantage in the interior. Soldiers at Fort Michilimackinac recruited Sioux, Chippewa, and Sauk warriors for an unsuccessful attack on Spanish-held St. Louis in 1780. At Fort Detroit, Harrison continued to equip war parties of Ottawa, Fox, and Miami Indians to attack American settlers migrating into the Ohio Valley.

■ In 1781, 7600 Spanish and French troops under Bernardo de Gálvez laid siege to Pensacola. The turning point came on May 8, when a Spanish shell struck the British powder magazine. The explosion left 100 dead or wounded (many of them Pennsylvania Loyalists), and the British promptly surrendered the port and all of West Florida.

In 1778, with support from his home state of Virginia, a young Patriot surveyor named George Rogers Clark organized a foray west to counter these raids and lend support to Spanish and French allies in the upper Mississippi Valley. He secured the settlements at Kaskaskia and Cahokia on the Mississippi River, and in February 1779 he led a grueling winter march to the fort at Vincennes in southern Indiana. In surprising that outpost on the Wabash River, Clark managed to capture Henry Harrison, but he failed to seize Detroit.

The Unpredictable War in the South

The rebel war effort beyond the Appalachian Mountains also expanded south. In 1778 a Patriot party setting out from Fort Pitt managed to descend the Ohio and Mississippi rivers unnoticed. The raiders captured Natchez on the Lower Mississippi and seized property in British West Florida. But it was the energetic governor of Spanish Louisiana, Bernardo de Gálvez, whose moves proved decisive. Living in New Orleans, Gálvez maintained a careful neutrality between the Americans and their British rivals through 1778. But when Spain allied with France and declared war on Britain the next year, the governor acted quickly to keep the British from gaining ground on the Gulf Coast.

Moving from west to east, Governor Gálvez drove the British from the Mississippi River in 1779, seized their fort at Mobile in 1780, and conquered Pensacola, the capital of British West Florida, in 1781. His plan to retake St. Augustine with American help came to nothing. Still, his troops had reasserted Spain's control over the entire Gulf Coast and protected Spanish interests in the Gulf of Mexico. The fall of Mobile and Pensacola also cut British supply lines to the southeastern interior. The move hurt Creeks and Cherokees, who depended on their ally's assistance. Without additional guns, knives, and powder, the Indians could offer little assistance in Britain's ambitious plan to win back the South and regain the upper hand in the war for eastern America. It was support the British could ill afford to lose.

Still, the crown's forces regained control of most of Georgia from the rebels in 1778. The next year, they blocked American and French efforts to retake Savannah. Early in 1780, British generals Clinton and Cornwallis ferried troops by sea from New York to South Carolina aboard more than a hundred ships. By May, this army had isolated Charleston and forced the capitulation of 5500 American troops. The surrender was the largest loss of American men and

The Revolutionary War in the South
- British and their Loyalist allies
- Patriots and their French allies
- ✹ British victories
- ✹ Patriot victories

1. Clinton and Cornwallis force surrender of Charleston, May 1780
2. Gates moves the American army to Camden, August 1780
3. Cornwallis bests Gates at Camden and moves North, August 1780
4. Americans defeat Ferguson at Kings Mountain, October 1780
5. Morgan meets British at Cowpens, defeats Tarleton, January 1781
6. Cornwallis pursues Greene's army across the Dan River, February 1781
7. Greene confronts Cornwallis at Guilford Courthouse, March 1781
8. After a retreat to Wilmington, Cornwallis moves to Virginia, April 1781
9. Washington moves south, pins Cornwallis at Yorktown, August 1781
10. De Grasse from West Indies, defeats the British fleet, September 1781

■ **MAP 7.5**
THE REVOLUTIONARY WAR IN THE SOUTH

weapons during the entire conflict. (Not until the Civil War—at Harpers Ferry, Virginia, in 1862—and World War II—at Bataan in the Philippines in 1942—were comparable numbers of U.S. Army soldiers obliged to lay down their arms.) For disappointed Patriots, the fall of Charleston nearly offset the triumph at Saratoga. One soldier wrote that the defeat delivered "a rude shock to the Independence of America."

A confident Clinton returned to New York, leaving Cornwallis in command in South Carolina. Throughout that summer, fierce fighting erupted across the state. Banastre Tarleton's green-coated British dragoons (mounted troops), along with their Loyalist supporters, went head to head against the guerrilla bands led by Thomas Sumter, Andrew Pickens, and Francis Marion. In June, Congress appointed Horatio Gates to take command of southern operations, and he hurried to the Carolinas with fresh troops.

On August 16, 1780, in a poorly calculated move, Gates's army confronted Cornwallis at the South Carolina garrison town of Camden, 120 miles north of Charleston. The Americans, short on rest, food, and leadership, suffered another huge defeat. The British killed or wounded eight hundred and took a thousand prisoners. Two days after the Camden disaster, as Gates fled north ahead of his troops, Tarleton's cavalry landed another blow. They surprised Sumter's band of 800 partisans at Fishing Creek near the Catawba River and took 300 prisoners. The dragoons inflicted 150 casualties and freed several hundred Loyalists and British regulars while suffering almost no losses themselves.

That September, as Washington absorbed word of the defeats at Camden and Fishing Creek, he received yet another "rude shock." Benedict Arnold—in command of West Point, the key outpost controlling the Hudson River—had plotted to defect and yield the post to the British. A gifted and admired leader in battle, Arnold was also brash, self-centered, and easily affronted. Troubled by his war wounds and passed over by Congress for promotion, Arnold felt increasingly alienated from the Patriot cause. His scheme was revealed by the American capture of his British contact, Major John André. The major was hanged as an enemy spy, but Arnold escaped and received command of British troops.

These setbacks troubled not only General Washington but also Congress. Its members stood firmly committed to maintaining civilian control over the American army. They appointed military leaders and supervised their funds, reviewing countless problems of the war effort on a daily basis. Apart from Arnold's treason, Congress rarely faced disloyalty among officers, but frustration and disobedience among enlisted men were more common. Early in 1780, soldiers from Massachusetts, New York, and Connecticut had mutinied in separate incidents. Members of the Pennsylvania and New Jersey Lines soon staged similar strikes over disputed terms of enlistment. After five years of war, a harried Congress also faced soaring inflation, scarce resources, and sinking citizen morale. Cornwallis had reason for optimism as he divided his troops and pressed into North Carolina in the fall of 1780. But the next 12 months saw a dramatic reversal in British fortunes.

That reversal began in October with a surprising Patriot victory in the southern backcountry. British major Patrick Ferguson had organized South Carolina Loyalists into a successful fighting unit. Cornwallis dispatched him and his troops toward the Blue Ridge Mountains in western Carolina to guard the army's flank and harry rebel supporters. Overconfident, Ferguson repeated Burgoyne's mistake by threatening disloyal mountain settlers with hangings and retribution. More than 800 frontier settlers rallied at Sycamore Shoals in the Watauga Valley and raced south to challenge the British. On October 6, at King's Mountain just below North Carolina's southern border, these sharpshooters surrounded the Loyalist troops and decimated the entire force, killing Ferguson and taking 700 prisoners. British casualties in the one-sided affair exceeded 300, whereas fewer than 90 "Over-Mountain Men" were killed or wounded.

The Final Campaign

A shrewd change in leadership followed the American victory at King's Mountain. Congress realized its mistake in appointing Gates to the southern command, and it turned to Washington to suggest a replacement. He selected Nathanael Greene, an experienced Rhode Islander who soon proved more than a match for Cornwallis. General Greene arrived in Charlotte, North Carolina, in December 1780, taking charge of a tattered army of 1600. The British, stung by their losses at King's Mountain, postponed designs on North Carolina. This gave the new commander precious weeks to reorganize his American force.

Greene used his time wisely. Earlier, he had served as the army's quartermaster general, overseeing supplies, and he quickly realized that his soldiers had pressing needs. He swiftly ordered one town to make shoes for his men, another to sew uniforms. He also dispatched scouts to explore possible river crossings and paths of retreat, necessary for the elusive "fugitive war" he planned to conduct. Shocked by the violence of partisan warfare and conscious of the need to win public support, he urged restraint on such experienced guerrilla fighters as Sumter and Marion while weaving them into his overall plans.

Going against traditional practice, Greene decided to divide his small army and send half his men into South Carolina under the seasoned Daniel Morgan to harass the British flank. "It makes the most of my inferior force," he explained, "for it compels my adversary to divide his, and holds him in doubt as to his own line of conduct." Cornwallis took the bait and dispatched Tarleton in pursuit. He caught up with Morgan at Hannah's Cowpens, west of King's Mountain, on January 17, 1781.

Louis Nicolas Van Blarenberghe, *The Storming of Yorktown in 1781,* 1784. Reunion des Musées Nationaux/Art Resource, NY

■ The joint American-French victory at the siege of Yorktown, Virginia, in October 1781 ended British hopes for preventing American independence. As Cornwallis's troops marched out to lay down their arms, a band played "The World Turned Upside Down." "Finally," Lafayette wrote proudly, "everything came together at once, and we had a sensational turn of events. . . .The play is over."

The outnumbered rebel militia lacked experience and discipline, but Morgan shrewdly turned this weakness to an advantage at the Battle of Cowpens. He stationed the militia units in front of his Continental forces with orders to fire two rounds and fall back. Sensing an enemy retreat, the British force of 1100 advanced too far too fast. Morgan's men promptly overwhelmed them. Tarleton managed to escape, but he left behind 100 dead, 800 prisoners, and most of his horses and ammunition. Morgan's force suffered only 148 casualties, mostly wounded militia. He rightly called the battle of Cowpens "a devil of a whipping."

Though frustrated, Cornwallis clung to the belief that "a successful battle may give us America." He discarded all excess baggage and pursued the rebel army 200 miles across North Carolina. Greene directed a speedy retreat over swollen rivers to the Virginia border, then doubled back to confront the weary British in the Battle of Guilford Courthouse on March 15. Although the American forces eventually withdrew from the field, Cornwallis sustained such heavy losses that he was forced to alter his plans.

The British retreated to the coast at Wilmington, North Carolina, and then marched north in early summer 1781 to Yorktown, Virginia. There, Cornwallis hoped to obtain reinforcements by sea, rally Loyalists in the Chesapeake region, and divide the rebelling colonies once and for all. The design's success hinged on continued naval superiority and timely support from General Clinton in New York. But Cornwallis could be assured of neither.

In mid-August, the French fleet in the Caribbean set out for Chesapeake Bay. It planned to spend eight weeks in American waters, assisting the combined French–American army, located near New York. "Employ me promptly and usefully," French admiral De Grasse urged, so that "time may be turned to profit." Suddenly Washington had access to impressive naval power. He seized his chance. He sent word south to Lafayette in Virginia to keep Cornwallis contained at Yorktown. Then, to hold Clinton's forces in New York, he ordered his men to make a show of building roads and baking ovens, as if preparing for a lengthy siege of the city. Behind this disguise, French and American soldiers slipped away, secretly marching south to lay a trap for the British army.

De Grasse reached Chesapeake Bay with two dozen ships at the end of August. On September 5, he repulsed a British fleet off the mouth of the bay, dashing Cornwallis's hopes for relief by sea. When 9000 Americans and 7800 French converged on Yorktown in late September, they outnumbered their 8000 opponents by more than two to one. The trap had been sprung, and the siege proved brief. Plagued by sickness and shortages of food and munitions, the British army surrendered on October 19, 1781. For Washington and his army, Yorktown was a stunning victory. Intermittent warfare continued for another year. But the Americans finally had powerful leverage to bargain for peace and force Britain to recognize their independence.

Winning the Peace

After Yorktown, the fighting in America gave way to diplomacy in Europe. Indeed, the final phase of the war played out in European courts. There, the maneuvering was almost as complicated and risky as it had been on the battlefield. As one representative, the American Congress dispatched Henry Laurens, its former president, to the Dutch Republic. The South Carolinian was to negotiate a loan and a commercial treaty with the United Province of the Netherlands, but the British captured Laurens at sea. They salvaged the incriminating documents Laurens tried to throw overboard and then locked him in the Tower of London. This left Benjamin Franklin, John Adams, and John Jay as the key American players. Often at odds, the three men nevertheless managed to achieve a final triumph that proved as unlikely and momentous as Washington's victory in Virginia. They did it, wrote the immodest Adams, "in spite of the malice of enemies, the finesse of Allies, and the mistakes of Congress."

For the British, the road to the peace table had been long and unpleasant. Early feelers about a negotiated settlement—from the Howes in 1776 and the Carlisle Commission in 1778—had not mentioned independence. But conditions changed drastically after Yorktown. Domestic unrest in Britain had already boiled into riots, and the expanded war was going poorly in India and the West Indies. "O God, it is all over!" Lord North muttered when he received the news of Cornwallis's defeat in Virginia. Within months, Sir Guy Carleton replaced Clinton in command of the remaining British forces in America, the hawkish Lord Germain stepped down from the Cabinet, and North resigned after 12 years as prime minister. Even the king spoke briefly of abdicating. But instead, he approved a new ministry more suited to the rising antiwar sentiment in Parliament. The Earl of Shelburne became prime minister in July 1782. Even before he assumed office, he had authorized peace discussions with his old acquaintance, Benjamin Franklin.

Benjamin West, *Signing of the Peace Treaty.* Courtesy, Winterthur Museum

■ The final American victory in the War of Independence came at the peace table, when negotiators John Jay, John Adams, and Benjamin Franklin won favorable terms in the 1783 Treaty of Paris. Benjamin West's unfinished painting also includes the absent Henry Laurens (rear) and Franklin's grandson (right), the delegation's secretary.

Franklin was in a difficult position. The crucial alliance he had negotiated with France stated that the Americans would not sign a separate peace with Britain. Moreover, Congress, grateful for vital French military and financial support, had instructed the American negotiators to defer to the wishes of Vergennes, the French foreign minister. The Americans did not realize that the minister's own agenda differed sharply from their own. Balancing the desire to reduce British power against the crippling costs of the war, Vergennes had already entertained thoughts of a truce that would leave London in control of all the territory it currently held in America. This consisted of Penobscot Bay in Maine (with its valuable supplies of naval timber), New York City, and parts of the lower South. Vergennes opposed the Americans' republican principles, and he resented their desire to expand their boundaries and gain the right to fish the Grand Banks off Newfoundland. He refused to treat the American diplomats as equal partners. To strengthen the French position, he also hoped to keep the weak new governments dependent on France whether the American states remained united or broke apart, as most European observers thought likely.

The American peace commission, though cautioned from home and belittled abroad, ultimately elected to chart its own course. The three commissioners fared surprisingly well in the treacherous waters of European diplomacy, starting with Franklin's first informal talks with the British. He laid out four "necessary" points, leading with the recognition of American independence. To this he added the removal of British troops, the right to fish in Newfoundland waters, and the revision of the Canadian border, which the Quebec Act of 1774 had pushed south to the Ohio River.

Franklin then noted some "desirable" items, no doubt intended to position the Americans for later bargaining. The British, he suggested, should consider paying an indemnity for war damages. In doing so, they would officially acknowledge their own blame for the war. Perhaps they should cede Canada to the United States as well. For their part, the British sought compensation for the American Loyalists who had been driven from their homes and the right to collect old debts that colonists had owed to British merchants before 1776.

After helping Washington at Yorktown, French admiral De Grasse had sailed back to the Caribbean to seize Great Britain's wealthiest colony, Jamaica. But British admiral George Rodney had intercepted his ships and taken De Grasse prisoner. Word of the naval victory strengthened Britain's negotiating hand and weakened France's position. Hoping to disrupt the American–French alliance and to reestablish profitable trade with their former colonies, the British negotiated preliminary peace terms with the Americans in November 1782. In return for independence, troop withdrawal, and fishing rights, the Americans agreed vaguely that their Congress would "recommend" that individual states approve compensation for confiscated Loyalist property.

On the Canadian boundary question, the Americans scored another success, but one that came at the expense of Indian nations. By giving up their bid for all of Canada, the negotiators persuaded Britain to relinquish the Ohio Valley and accept a northern boundary for the United States defined by the Great Lakes and the St. Lawrence River. In the west, the United States would reach to the Mississippi River, and Americans would gain free navigation on the waterway, despite Spanish opposition. In the south, the 31st parallel, above East and West Florida, would provide the American boundary.

The diplomats endorsed the final peace terms at Versailles, France, in September 1783. Amid all the other treaty terms, the British yielded East and West Florida to Spain. In the process, however, they made no mention of the Indians who had served as allies in the American conflict. Abandoned, the Native Americans had to confront their new situation alone. To end up "betrayed to our Enemies & divided between the Spaniards and the Americans is Cruel & Ungenerous," protested the Creek leader, Alexander McGillivray. His people had been "most Shamefully deserted."

Conclusion

The War for Independence that began at Lexington had lasted eight years. Like any lengthy armed struggle, it took a heavy toll on combatants and non-combatants alike. Personal survival itself was far from certain, as encounters with sickness and the enemy carried off enlisted men. American forces lost an estimated 25,000 soldiers over eight years. The number seems small in modern terms, but comparable losses in the present military service, as a proportion of the current United States population, would total more than 2 million people.

For those who avoided death, lesser dangers abounded. Separations were frequent, and uprooting from home became commonplace. Losses of property proved extensive, and indebtedness appeared to be widespread. Some, of course, managed to benefit from the precarious circumstances. During the war years, whether by determination, foresight, or simple good fortune, they expanded their wealth, gained their freedom, or enhanced their reputation. But other individuals and families, through lost opportunities, poor choices, or bad luck, suffered from the winds of war. Despite constant uncertainties at the individual level, a makeshift revolutionary army, learning as it marched, had forced the British to concede American independence.

As in all wars, some of the most decisive action occurred far from the battlefield. In London, weakness and inconsistency in the chain of command, combined with a lumbering bureaucracy and divided public sentiment, undermined the British war effort. In Europe, skillful American diplomats built the international alliances needed to secure victory and won peace terms that promised survival to the new confederation of states. Meanwhile, a flurry of constitution-writing unprecedented in history had launched more than a dozen newly independent states, and the Articles of Confederation, approved after long delay, had knit them together into a formal league with a common Congress. The new and difficult art of republican self-government remained a work in progress, with some of the most difficult and contentious choices still to come.

As the former slave Thomas Peters climbed aboard the *Joseph James* with his family and other Loyalists to leave New York in 1783, pressing problems still confronted all those who had had a stake in the conflict. Some of the white settlers, Indian allies, and African Americans who had taken the British side chose to withdraw altogether. They joined the massive evacuation engineered by royal ships from St. Augustine, Savannah, Charleston, and New York. But all who stayed did not celebrate for long. The fragile unity built on fighting a common enemy was soon to be strained to the limit, as new debates erupted over the meaning and direction of the unfinished revolution.

Loyalties fluctuated with the fortunes of war, and even those far from the fighting became entangled in the web of confrontations, debts, and reprisals that played out year after year. The story of Thomas Peters and his family serves to underscore the point that no one could predict clearly the ultimate outcome of protracted warfare in America.

Sites to Visit

The Saratoga National Historical Park

The National Park Service maintains a visitor center and has arranged a self-guided battlefield tour that includes the locations for the British and American camps during the crucial engagement of October 1777 at this park, which is located 10 miles south of Saratoga Springs, New York, on Route 50.

Brandywine Battlefield State Park

This park is located on Highway 202 west of Philadelphia, Pennsylvania, not far from the borders of Delaware and Maryland. (At nearby Chadds Ford, the Wyeth Museum celebrates three generations of one of America's great artistic families.)

The Continental Congress
memory.loc.gov/ammem/bdsds/bdsdhome.html

This Web site on the Continental Congress in the American Memory series of the Library of Congress contains materials dating from 1774.

Virginia Runaways Project
www.uvawise.edu/history/runaways/index.html

This digital database of runaway slave and servant advertisements from eighteenth-century Virginia newspapers contains full transcripts and images of all runaway ads placed in Virginia newspapers from 1736 to 1790, including those for slaves who responded to Lord Dunmore's proclamation.

The Cowpens National Battlefield
www.nps.gov/cowp/index.htm

The actual site of the battle where Daniel Morgan's troops defeated Banastre Tarleton's British forces (January 17, 1781) is located 10 miles west of Gafney, South Carolina, off Highway I–85. The battle was dramatized in Hollywood's film *The Patriot* (see www.patriotresource.com).

Spy Letters of the American Revolution
www.si.umich.edu/spies/index-timeline.html

This Web site, maintained by the Clements Library at the University of Michigan, contains 12 facsimiles and transcriptions of spy letters contained in the Sir Henry Clinton collection and provides some context for each letter.

Old Fort Niagara
www.oldfortniagara.org/

This New York State Historic Site overlooks Lake Ontario at the mouth of the Niagara River. Built by the French in 1727, the fort is located just off the Robert Moses Parkway, not far from Niagara Falls, at Youngstown, New York.

The Birth of the Navy of the United States
www.history.navy.mil/faqs/faq31–1.htm

Visit the Naval Historical Center Web site to learn about the history of the U.S. Navy.

For Further Reading

General

Colin G. Calloway, *The American Revolution in Indian Country: Crisis and Diversity in Native American Communities* (1995).

Edward Countryman, *The American Revolution* (1985).

Don Higginbotham, *The War of American Independence* (1971).

Sidney Kaplan and Emma Nogrady Kaplan, *The Black Presence in the Era of the American Revolution* (revised edition, 1989).

Piers Mackesy, *The War for America, 1775–1783* (1965).

Robert Middlekauff, *The Glorious Cause* (1982).

Mary Beth Norton, *Liberty's Daughters: The Revolutionary Experience of American Women, 1750–1800* (1980).

Ray Raphael, *A People's History of the American Revolution: How Common People Shaped the Fight for Independence* (2001).

Gordon S. Wood, *The Creation of the American Republic, 1776–1787* (1969).

Alfred F. Young, ed., *Beyond the American Revolution: Explorations in the History of American Radicalism* (1993).

Declaring Independence

Eric Foner, *Tom Paine and Revolutionary America* (1976).

Ira D. Gruber, *The Howe Brothers and the American Revolution* (1972).

Pauline Maier, *American Scripture: Making the Declaration of Independence* (1997).

Charles Patrick Neimeyer, *America Goes to War: A Social History of the Continental Army* (1996).

Richard A. Ryerson, *The Revolution Is Now Begun: The Radical Committees of Philadelphia, 1765–1776* (1978).

Hal T. Shelton, *General Richard Montgomery and the American Revolution* (1994).

"Victory or Death": Fighting for Survival

Wayne Bodle, *The Valley Forge Winter: Civilians and Soldiers at War* (2002).

R. Arthur Bowler, *Logistics and the Failure of the British Army in America, 1775–1783* (1975).

Stephen Conway, *The British Isles and the War of American Independence* (2000).

Sylvia R. Frey, *The British Soldier in America: A Social History of Military Life in the Revolutionary Period* (1981).

Richard M. Ketchum, *The Winter Soldiers* (1973).

Max M. Mintz, *The Generals of Saratoga: John Burgoyne and Horatio Gates* (1990).

Legitimate States, a Respectable Military

Willi: Paul Adams, The *First American Constitutions: Republican Ideology and the Making of the State Constitutions in the Revolutionary Era* (1980).

Elisha P. Douglass, *Rebels and Democrats: The Struggle for Equal Political Rights and Majority Rule During the American Revolution* (1955).

Jonathan R. Dull, *A Diplomatic History of the American Revolution* (1985).

James S. Leamon, *Revolution Down East: The War for American Independence in Maine* (1993).

Samuel Eliot Morison, *John Paul Jones: A Sailor's Biography* (1959).

The Long Road to Yorktown

Robert M. Calhoon, *The Loyalists in Revolutionary America, 1760–1781* (1973).

Barbara Graymont, The *Iroquois in the American Revolution* (1972).

Max M. Mintz, *Seeds of Empire: The American Revolutionary Conquest of the Iroquois* (1999).

Richard B. Morris, *The Peacemakers: The Great Powers and American Independence* (1965).

Steven Rosswurm, *Arms, Country, and Class: The Philadelphia Militia and the Lower Sort During the American Revolution* (1987).

J. Barton Starr, *Tories, Dons, and Rebels: The American Revolution in British West Florida* (1976).

Carl Van Doren, *Mutiny in January: The Story of a Crisis in the Continental Army* (1943).

Online Practice Test

Test your understanding of this chapter with interactive review quizzes at

www.ablongman.com/jonescreatedequal/chapter7

Additional Photo Credits

Page 219: Henry Gray, *The Morning After the Attack on Sullivan's Island, June 1776.* Gibbes Museum of Art/Carolina Art Association, 1907.002.0001

Page 221: Courtesy, The West Point Museum

Page 226: Library of Congress

Page 230: Collection of the Museum of Early Southern Decorative Arts; Winston-Salem, North Carolina

Page 232: The Bostonian Society

CHAPTER 8

New Beginnings: The 1780s

■ Jonathan Knight, c. 1797.

LUIS SALES SERVED AS A CATHOLIC MISSIONARY TO THE INDIANS ON THE PENINSULA OF Baja California from 1772 to 1790. His darkest times occurred in 1781. One fateful day, he recalled, "there entered the port of Loreto" a small vessel bringing families across the narrow Gulf of California "from Sonora, infected with the small-pox." Immediately, the sickness "spread like lightning through all the missions," causing "havoc which only those who have seen it can believe. The towns and missions were . . . deserted, and bodies were seen in the road." Some who had watched loved ones break out in sores and die painful deaths insisted on "throwing themselves into the sea at the onset of the disease." Others, in desperation and fear, "cast themselves into mudholes, others into fire, and still others set about burning the pustules with live coals." Many Indians crowded into caves, Sales remembered, and "when they noticed any infected with the disease," they "fled to another cave," deserting the sick and spreading the illness. Time and again, "the poor little children, abandoned beside the dead, died without help."

While Father Sales ministered to survivors, the dozen families who had unwittingly brought the disease moved north along the peninsula to Alta (or Upper) California. Their destination was the San Gabriel Mission, built ten years earlier. They finally reached the outpost in late summer, "arriving with some little children recently coming out with smallpox." Mission leaders immediately quarantined them in a separate camp. Still, during that autumn, the Spanish-speaking newcomers managed to establish a village named Our Lady of the Angels, the start of modern-day Los Angeles. A census that year showed that this frontier band of "recruits, colonists, and families" contained a variety of Indian, black, and Spanish adults with several dozen mixed-race children. On their journey from Sonora, they had unintentionally spread destruction in their wake.

The torment Sales described was only a tiny part of a far wider swath of destruction created by this deadly disease. Between 1775 and 1782—the exact years of the Revolutionary War—a huge smallpox epidemic ricocheted relentlessly across broad sections of North America. At times the epidemic entwined itself with the war, traveling on supply ships and moving with marching troops. In the Northeast, it struck during the siege of Boston and the attack on Quebec. In the South, it cut down hundreds of Virginia slaves who had escaped at the start of the war to join Governor Dunmore, when he promised emancipation to slaves who would desert their rebel masters and fight for Britain. The disease found additional victims during the British siege of Charleston, South Carolina, in 1780.

Like the wartime violence, smallpox erupted first in Massachusetts. But the devastating contagion spread far more widely than the destruction caused by the war. Whereas the American army remained "continental" in name only, the great smallpox epidemic proved

Smallpox was among the deadliest of all epidemic diseases until its eradication in 1979.

The spread of smallpox, 1775–1782

Known transmission route

Probable transmission route

Modern state and provincial boundaries
are provided for reference

■ **MAP 8.1**
**THE SPREAD OF SMALLPOX ACROSS NORTH AMERICA,
1775–1782** A great smallpox epidemic swept North America
during the Revolutionary era. In 1781 it moved up the Baja
Peninsula with settlers heading for San Gabriel, the Spanish
mission that became Los Angeles, California.

truly continental in scope. It soon gained a foothold in New Orleans, Mexico City, and even
the far-flung trading posts that dotted the Canadian interior. In 1781 the disease menaced
Virginia as French and American troops completed their successful campaign against the
British at Yorktown. At the same time, it ravaged Indian villages as far away as the Northwest Coast. Within another year, as the War of Independence ended in the East, the
transcontinental epidemic also drew to a close.

The contagion left a patchwork of destruction from the Atlantic to the Pacific. The smallpox losses were greatest among Native Americans, and few groups or regions remained untouched. British sea captain George Vancouver, probing the Northwest Coast near the head of Puget Sound in 1792, observed numerous skulls, ribs, and "other vestiges of the human body in many places promiscuously scattered about the beach." Vancouver's pilot, Peter Puget, pressed farther into the sound that is now named for him. There he found deserted villages that only a dozen years earlier had bustled with people. In its eight-year course, the fearsome virus took more than 130,000 North American lives, many times the total lost on battlefields during the Revolution. In different ways, these two events exerted a drastic and lasting impact on the continent and its people.

As the dual scourges of epidemic and war subsided, fresh problems confronted North America's inhabitants. Despite the successful bid for independence by England's mainland colonies, the question of which European powers would exert the most influence on various parts of the huge continent remained unresolved. British power ruled Canada; Spanish authority claimed much of the West; and in Paris, despite the approach of the French Revolution, some still dreamed of restoring the Mississippi Valley to the control of France. In the North Pacific, Russians sent by Empress Catherine the Great intruded on the Alaskan coast. And lucrative new trade with China was soon luring sea captains from several nations, including the United States, to the Northwest coast. Ships from Atlantic ports could barter for sea otter pelts near Puget Sound and then cross the Pacific to deliver this "soft gold" to the Chinese in exchange for tea and porcelain. In the fertile woodlands between the Appalachian Mountains and the Mississippi River, Indians whom Pontiac had sought to unify a generation earlier once again endured sudden transfers of their ancestral land between distant powers. But now the rapid incursion of American settlers added new urgency and desperation to their situation.

Farther east, inhabitants of the Atlantic seaboard faced an array of thorny problems after warfare and smallpox loosened their grip. Many black Americans had escaped from servitude, won their freedom through military service, or been freed by masters who saw a conflict between slavery and the Revolution's rhetoric of equality. But half a million people remained legally enslaved. During the Revolutionary War, they had seen that armed rebellion in the name of liberty could succeed, and they were potential allies for any European power seeking to disrupt the fragile new society.

In addition, members of the Confederation's Continental (or national) Congress in Philadelphia had a restless army to pay, a weak government to reform, and enormous war debts to confront. When they imposed unprecedented taxes to pay off war bonds accumulated by wealthy speculators, irate farmers and veterans protested that Congress was gouging "the Many" to enrich "the Few." As these dissenters—increasingly numerous and desperate—showed signs of success in pressuring state governments to provide debt relief and issue paper money, wealthy creditors reacted forcefully. Like-minded men maneuvered to create a new and stronger central government that could support their interests and override state-level economic measures that favored the common people. Sidestepping the existing government, they drafted a new constitution at a closed convention in Philadelphia in 1787, and they campaigned successfully for its ratification by 1788. The reins of power, which nearly slipped from the hands of established American leaders during the tumultuous 1770s, had been securely restored by the end of the 1780s, in the face of bitter and varied opposition.

Beating Swords into Plowshares

At first, in the wake of military victory over Britain, the short-term survival of the new United States of America seemed assured, thanks to years of intense fighting and skillful diplomacy. The former colonies had banded together under the Articles of Confederation, duly ratified in 1781, which placed specific governmental powers in the hands of an elected national legislature, or Continental Congress. But deeper questions persisted. Who would benefit most from independence, and who would chart the direction of the new republican experiment? Should power rest primarily with the victorious army, the wealthy merchants, or the artisans and farmers who had provided the backbone of the revolutionary movement? And should authority be consolidated in the hands of a well-educated, new national elite, or should it be widely dispersed, with local communities and regions empowered to manage their own affairs?

Equally important, what did the newly emerging cultural patterns mean for the fledgling society? In these postwar years, scientific, educational, and humanitarian undertakings flourished. Literary endeavors also prospered, and lending libraries sprang up. "At no time did Literature make so rapid a progress in America, as since the peace," boasted a Massachusetts periodical in 1785. "It must afford real pleasure to every son of science, that our swords are beaten into ploughshares, and that the torch of Learning now shines with such lustre in this western hemisphere." This Biblical reference of turning from war and swords to peacetime activities like plowing was particularly compelling to a nation that had endured nearly a decade of war.

Will the Army Seize Control?

After their triumph at Yorktown, Washington's men had moved north to press British forces to evacuate New York City. More than 10,000 American troops and 500 officers encamped at Newburgh, on the Hudson River. With victory at hand, the soldiers looked forward to returning to civilian life. But they were also eager to receive their pay, long overdue because the protracted war had exhausted public finances. Clearly, they could negotiate best for the promised wages while they were still together and still on a wartime footing. Their bargaining position would weaken sharply once peace arrived and they laid down their weapons. Officers were especially reluctant to disband without clear assurances of money and status. In 1780 they extracted from the Congress a promise of half pay for life, in imitation of the European model. In December 1782, with no sign of the money in sight, the disgruntled officers sent a delegation to Philadelphia to press their claims.

Within Congress, the men around financier Robert Morris, including James Wilson and Alexander Hamilton, wanted to bolster and centralize the Confederation's finances. To that end, they sought a new "continental impost"—a duty of 5 percent on imported goods—to raise money from the states. In the short run, revenue from the impost would help make the Confederation government solvent. But the measure would also strengthen that government in the long run, for the new income would allow it to assume responsibility for paying off state war debts. In turn, this economic commitment would tie the interests of wealthy citizens to the Confederation government's survival and success. Morris even threatened to resign his position as secretary of commerce if the "nationalists" did not get their way. Rumblings from the officer corps would help these politicians push through the impost measure, crucial to their long-term goals. So they quietly encouraged the military dissidents in Newburgh.

In late February 1783, anonymous petitions—penned by the staff of Washington's old rival, Horatio Gates—circulated among officers encamped at Newburgh. These inflammatory "addresses" suggested that officers should sit tight, neither fighting nor laying down their arms, until Congress guaranteed their future payments. If the government met their demands, they would be like "lambs," General Henry Knox wrote privately to a fellow general. But if not, they would become "tigers and wolves." Such phrases suggest the veiled

Demobilization: "Turned Adrift Like Old Worn-Out Horses"

Joseph Plumb Martin was born in western Massachusetts in 1760, and he took up arms in the Revolution before his sixteenth birthday. He served faithfully in the Continental Army and was encamped at West Point, New York, when peace finally arrived. Later, in a compelling narrative of his wartime experiences, he recalled the demobilization process from the perspective of a common soldier.

William Ranney, *Veterans of 1776 Returning from the War*, c. 1848. Dallas Museum of Art, The Museum League Fund, Special Contributors and General Acquisitions Fund

William Ranney painted *Revolutionary War Veterans Returning Home* in 1848, when the United States was at war with Mexico. The image offered a positive reminder of earlier American military success. But in reality, soldiers leaving the Continental Army in 1783 had little reason to laugh and sing.

[On April 19, 1783,] we had general orders read which satisfied the most skeptical, that the war was over and the prize won [after] eight tedious years. But the soldiers said but little about it; their chief thoughts were closely fixed upon their situation. . . . Starved, ragged and meager, not a cent to help themselves with, and no means or method in view to remedy or alleviate their condition. This was appalling in the extreme. . . .

At length, the eleventh day of June 1783, arrived. "The old man," our captain, came into the room, with his hands full of papers. . . . He then handed us our discharges, or rather furloughs, . . . permission to return home, but to return to the army again if required. This was policy in government; to discharge us absolutely in our present pitiful, forlorn condition, it was feared, might cause some difficulties. . . .

Some of the soldiers went off for home the same day that their fetters were knocked off; others stayed and got their final settlement certificates, which they sold to procure decent clothing and money. . . . I was among those. . . . I now bid a final farewell to the service. I had obtained my settlement certificates and sold some of them and purchased some decent clothing, and then set off from West Point. . . .

When those who engaged to serve during the war enlisted, they were promised a hundred acres of land, each. . . . When the country had drained the last drop of service it could screw out of the poor soldiers, they were turned adrift like old worn-out horses, and nothing said about land to pasture them upon. . . . Congress did, indeed, appropriate lands, . . . but no care was taken that the soldiers should get them. [Instead,] a pack of speculators . . . were driving about the country like so many evil spirits, endeavoring to pluck the last feather from the soldiers. The soldiers were ignorant of the ways and means to obtain their bounty lands. . . . It was, soldiers, look to yourselves; we want no more of you.

We were, also, promised six dollars and two thirds a month. . . . And what was six dollars and sixty-seven cents of this "Continental currency," as it was called, worth? It was scarcely enough to procure a man a dinner. . . . I received one month's pay in specie while on the march to Virginia, in the year 1781, and except that, I never received any pay worth the name while I belonged to the army. . . . It is provoking to think of it. The country was rigorous in exacting my compliance to *my* engagements . . . but equally careless in performing her contracts with me, and why so? One reason was that she had all the power in her own hands and I had none. Such things ought not to be.

After the war, Martin settled on the Maine frontier, and a speculator bought his right to 100 acres of bounty land in Ohio. In 1818, as a disabled laborer with a large family, he successfully petitioned Congress for a small pension to support the household. He died poor in 1850. ∎

Source: James Kirby Martin, ed., *Ordinary Courage: The Revolutionary War Adventures of Joseph Plumb Martin*, 2nd ed. (New York: Brandywine Press, 1999), pp. 159–164.

threat of a military takeover in order to impose stability after a turbulent revolution. The prospect of a military coup suited the unsettled circumstances (and a similar scenario would be played out by Napoleon Bonaparte in France a decade later). Some American officers clearly envisioned the prospect of using military might to assert and retain political power. Without approval from General Washington, the officers at Newburgh arranged a meeting to discuss their plight.

If the plotters hoped to draw Washington into the scheme, they were sorely disappointed. He did attend the officers' meeting on March 15, but he used his commanding presence to discredit the ill-advised plan. His eyes weakened by endless wartime correspondence, he drew a pair of spectacles from his pocket. Few had seen him wear glasses, and the gesture underscored the commander's years of dedication and sacrifice. He read a letter from Congress containing assurances of support, and he urged his officers not to take any actions that would undermine the honor they had earned. Finally, he agreed to draft a reasoned request to Congress, stressing the army's needs. His leadership prevailed, and the officers disavowed the "infamous propositions."

Within weeks, Congress offered assurances of back wages for the officers. However, promise of half pay for life met stiff opposition from congressmen who worried about its costliness. The plan was exchanged for a guarantee of full pay to officers for the next five years, and all parties accepted the compromise. In April 1783, word spread that preliminary articles of peace had been signed in Paris. By June most soldiers were headed home.

The Society of the Cincinnati

By quieting his officers, Washington had averted the threat of a military coup. The commander's strong stance against the suspected Newburgh conspiracy reminded his admirers of the story of Roman general Cincinnatus, well known to people at that time. In the early Roman Republic, the Senate called Cincinnatus from his farm to command an army against the Aequians. After defeating the invaders, he put down his sword and took up his plow again rather than seize power as a military ruler. His selfless action earned him the lasting respect of the Roman people. The familiar story of Cincinnatus appealed to Washington. At a crucial moment in the republic's earliest days, the American general had bravely urged fellow officers to respect the fragile principle of civilian control over the military.

Thomas Jefferson praised Washington's action. He wrote to him admiringly that "the moderation and virtue of a single character has probably prevented this revolution from being closed as most others have been by a subversion of that liberty it was intended to establish." Still, Jefferson and others worried that some military officers might yet meddle in politics while hiding behind the noble name of Cincinnatus. Their fears soon seemed confirmed. In May 1783, as demobilization got under way, General Knox announced formation of the Society of the Cincinnati. The new organization invoked the name of the famous Roman, in a plural form, to put its members in the best light. It was open only to officers in the Continental army at the war's end, plus former officers and invited honorary members.

Some onlookers believed that the "Cincinnati Club" was no more than a social fraternity for men united by their war experience. Benjamin Franklin assumed those joining the society had been drawn together simply by the lure of ceremony and recognition. Perhaps, he mused, these officers had "been too much struck with the Ribbands and Crosses they have seen . . . hanging to the buttonholes of Foreign Officers." But others sensed a more sinister purpose. After all, members contributed an entire month's salary to a charitable fund that resembled a political war chest. Also, the society's state chapters maintained contact with each other through newsletters concerning "the general union of the states." Most ominously, participants endorsed hereditary membership so that the eldest sons of Continental officers would join the society down through the generations.

For skeptics, the society appeared to plant the seeds of a self-perpetuating ruling class. In a scathing pamphlet titled *Considerations on the Society or Order of Cincinnati . . . with*

Remarks on Its Consequences to the Freedom and Happiness of the Republic, Judge Aedanus Burke of South Carolina protested that the organization revealed a "thirst for power" and created a "race of hereditary patricians, or nobility." Critics such as Burke argued that the society would spawn a separate aristocracy of the very kind Americans had fought to erase.

Jefferson and other friends of Washington, who was automatically a member, urged the general not to accept a leadership position in the new organization. Struck by this "violent and formidable" opposition, Washington suggested changes in the society, including doing away with the hereditary and honorary memberships. However, he never played a central role in the organization, and his well-publicized alterations were never implemented. The Cincinnati exerted influence as a pressure group before receding from politics in future generations.

Renaming the Landscape

The controversy over the Society of the Cincinnati represented part of a larger debate about the direction of postwar life. The victors in any revolutionary struggle must move quickly to solidify their success, heal internal differences, and fulfill bold promises. In the wake of the revolutionary war, many Americans—despite continuing disagreements—set out to build a national culture and a shared identity. Those who had fought or had endured hardship because of the war wanted to create a country that would justify their sacrifices and uphold the ideals of the revolution. Citizens of the new Confederation would strive to match all that they still admired about European culture and, at the same time, separate themselves from all that they distrusted or rejected. Like the Puritans before them, they aspired to provide new models for the Atlantic world.

One zealous professor went so far as to rewrite nursery rhymes to eliminate offending words.

They began with names. Everywhere, people christened new towns, counties, streets, and schools and renamed old ones. Just as citizens had stripped away royal statues and coats of arms at the beginning of the war, they replaced numerous British names, such as those of hated prewar governors. Dunmore County in Virginia, named after Lord Dunmore, received the Indian name *Shanando* (later spelled *Shenandoah*). Tryon County, New York, which had celebrated Governor William Tryon, became Montgomery County, after the American general who died at Quebec. A frontier town in what would become Vermont, named after Governor Thomas Hutchinson of Massachusetts, took its new name, Barre, from Isaac Barré, a parliamentary supporter of the American cause.

Political leaders rediscovered and popularized Christopher Columbus as well. Their reasoning was simple: For generations, the English had downplayed the explorer's importance as they contested Spanish claims in the Western Hemisphere. Now, American writers coined the ringing term *Columbia* for their land to stress its separation from Britain. In South Carolina, citizens named their new capital Columbia in 1786. That same year, in Philadelphia, an Irish immigrant named Mathew Carey launched an ambitious new periodical called *The Columbian Magazine.* Five years later, supporters of the proposed national capital christened it the District of Columbia. In New York City, King's College had been founded with a royal charter in 1754 and had served as an army hospital during the Revolutionary War. But when the school reopened in 1784 under local governance, it was called Columbia College (later Columbia University).

Most people in the new republic found any references to royalty distasteful. One zealous professor at Columbia College went so far as to rewrite nursery rhymes to eliminate offending words. Children should no longer hear that a pie filled with singing blackbirds appeared "before the king." The "dainty dish" would be "set before the Congress" instead. King Street in Boston quickly became State Street. Still, royal figures who had aided the revolution received their due. At the Falls of the Ohio River, settlers named their new town Louisville, honoring America's wartime alliance with King Louis XVI of France.

Farther up the Ohio River, in 1790, General Arthur St. Clair renamed a village near Licking Creek, calling it Cincinnati. He hoped to honor all his fellow officers in the controversial society and to invoke Cincinnatus, the Roman general. Such classical references cropped up everywhere. In 1789, for instance, citizens of Vanderheyden's Ferry on the Hudson River voted to rename their town Troy, New York, after the citadel that the Greeks captured in Homer's *Iliad.* "I find not the least resemblance," complained one newspaper editor, "between the old city of that name and this small village." (The trend of putting ancient names on small towns continued well into the nineteenth century. Settlers along the Mississippi River, known as "the Nile of America," invoked famous Egyptian cities when they laid out Cairo, Illinois; Memphis, Tennessee; and Alexandria, Louisiana.)

Of all the new names, those honoring individual war heroes became the most popular. Citizens hailed foreign supporters of the revolution—such as Lafayette, Pulaski, and Steuben—by using their names on streets and towns. They saluted American officers the same way. Washington's name was used most often, but those of Montgomery, Wayne, Greene, Lincoln, Mercer, Marion, and others popped up as well. North Carolina named one of its trans-Appalachian forts on the Cumberland River Nashborough, after General Francis Nash, who had died at the battle of Germantown. Citizens changed the fort's name to *Nashville* in 1784. Two years later, inhabitants of a site on the Tennessee River named their new town Knoxville in honor of General Henry Knox, who had become the Confederation's secretary of war the previous year.

An Independent Culture

New names were just part of the story. Many Americans felt that their whole language needed to be made more independent and accessible. Noah Webster, a schoolteacher who had fought against General Burgoyne, believed that "as an independent nation, our honor requires us to have a system of our own, in language as well as government." In his *American Spelling Book* (1783), Webster championed a simple, uniform written language that rejected English conventions. Words such as *colour* and *labour* lost their silent *u, theatre* became *theater,* and *plough* was shortened to *plow.* The New Englander followed this success with an influential grammar book and a popular reader. Webster went on to produce *An American Dictionary of the English Language* (1828) that incorporated 5000 new words, many of them reflecting Indian origins (*tomahawk*) and American nature (*rattlesnake*).

Webster also joined other reformers in lobbying state legislatures for copyright laws that would protect the literary works that poured from the pens of ambitious writers. Philip Freneau, a classmate of James Madison at Princeton, drafted a poem titled "The British Prison Ship" (1781), about his war experiences. Authors living near Hartford, known as the Connecticut Wits, made similar nationalistic contributions. Timothy Dwight, future president of Yale College, created a poetic allegory, "The Conquest of Canaan" (1785), and Joel Barlow composed an epic poem titled "The Vision of Columbus" (1787), heralding a bright future for citizens of the new nation.

> Each rustic here, that turns the furrow'd soil,
> The maid, the youth, that ply mechanic toil,
> In freedom nurst, in useful arts inured,
> Know their just claims, and see their rights secured.

Increasingly, the land itself captured the imagination of Americans. In 1784 a Connecticut silversmith engraved the first map of the new United States and a a recent Yale graduate, Jedidiah Morse, published *Geography Made Easy,* which went through 25 editions. (Five years later, Morse created *The American Geography* and earned his reputation as the "Father of American Geography.") In Pennsylvania, naturalist William Bartram distributed seeds

Charles Willson Peale, *Portrait of William Bartram.* Independence National Historical Park

■ When Pennsylvania botanist William Bartram explored the Southeast, Indians called him Pucpuggy—"the flower gatherer." Years later, Charles Willson Peale painted the naturalist holding a flower.

from an experimental garden that his father, Quaker botanist John Bartram, had developed beside the Schuylkill River. The younger Bartram also drafted a pioneering nature book about his travels throughout the Southeast. In nearby Philadelphia, versatile painter and patriot Charles Willson Peale launched a museum to promote interest in art and the natural world. He gathered specimens, mastered taxidermy, and originated the practice of displaying stuffed animals in a model of their natural habitat. "Sir," George Washington wrote to Peale from Mount Vernon, "you will receive by stage the body of my gold pheasant packed in wool." At Monticello, Thomas Jefferson also corresponded with Peale and continued to pursue his own fascination with the American landscape. He promoted exploration, tested new crops, and tried his hand at archaeology by excavating ancient Indian mounds.

In *Notes on the State of Virginia* (1785), Jefferson detailed his region's geography, society, and natural history. He also challenged the theories of famous French naturalist Comte de Buffon regarding the vitality of New World species. Buffon had declared, without first-hand knowledge, that America's weak soil and dubious climate prompted the inevitable degeneration of plants and animals, including people. Jefferson and others disagreed. Hector St. John de Crèvecoeur, a Frenchman who made his home in America, had already argued the opposite case. In 1782 he published *Letters from an American Farmer*. In the book's most famous essay, "What Is an American?" Crèvecoeur proclaimed that poor European immigrants became revitalized "in this great American asylum." "Every thing has tended to regenerate them," he wrote. "In Europe they . . . withered; and were mowed down by want, hunger, and war; but now, by the power of transplantation, like all other plants, they have taken root and flourished!"

The Natural History Museum, London

■ Exploring near the Altamaha River in Georgia, William Bartram and his father found "several curious shrubs, one bearing beautiful good fruit." They named it the Franklin tree after their scientist friend in Philadelphia, Benjamin Franklin. William drew a watercolor of the rare plant and saved seeds to protect the species.

According to Crèvecoeur, free people flourished in America not only because of "new laws" but also because of "a new mode of living, a new social system" that nurtured community growth. Crèvecoeur's argument had merit: Voluntary associations bent on improving local conditions sprang up everywhere. Of course, societies for bettering jails, assisting debtors, and building libraries had existed in port cities before independence. But a new generation revived many of these charities after the war and created new ones at an unprecedented rate. Earnest reformers launched more than 30 new benevolent organizations between 1783 and 1789. Some provided relief for the physically and mentally ill. Others offered aid to strangers and immigrants. Still others granted charity to the poor and disabled or lobbied to reform harsh penal codes.

In 1785 prominent New Yorkers John Jay and Alexander Hamilton joined like-minded citizens to form a Society for the Promotion of the Manumission of Slaves. Society members decried slavery as "disgraceful" and "shocking to humanity." And in Connecticut, citizens banded together to stop the abuse of liquor. Members of this early temperance organization protested that the state's residents consumed 400,000 gallons of rum annually and that communities paid dearly in both financial and moral terms. Meanwhile, the new Massachusetts Humane Society dedicated itself to assisting people in "suspended animation" between life and death, whether from drowning, drinking, heatstroke, or other causes. The society provided crude lifesaving equipment along waterfronts. It also constructed huts, stocked with food and firewood, to aid shipwreck survivors on isolated coastlines. Similar efforts to reform and improve the new nation sprang up everywhere. Amid such optimism, no sooner had the former British colonists disentangled themselves from the British Empire than they began to speak of shaping an expansive empire of their own.

Competing for Control of the Mississippi Valley

"It has ever been my hobby-horse," John Adams wrote in 1786, "to see rising in America an empire of liberty, and a prospect of two or three hundred millions of freemen, without one noble or one king among them. You say it is impossible. . . . I would still say, let us try the experiment." Westward expansion became a persistent American theme. But during the postwar decade, interest and activity centered mostly on the land just beyond the eastern mountains, territory reserved for Indians by the British until they ceded the lands to the United States at the end of the Revolution. There, countless tributaries of the Mississippi River flowed west from the Appalachian ridges toward the interior of the continent.

In the South in the 1780s, pioneer families searching for land pushed west along an old buffalo trail and Indian trading path. Passing through Cumberland Gap, where southwest Virginia now touches Kentucky, they spread out across parts of the lower Mississippi Valley, a region that eventually became known as the Old Southwest. These aspiring homesteaders promptly faced resistance from Native American inhabitants and their Spanish supporters. At the same time, north of the Ohio River, other American settlers were flocking to newly claimed lands that lay between the Allegheny Mountains and the Upper Mississippi, a vast, wooded expanse later remembered as the Old Northwest. They, too, met stiff opposition from Native Americans defending their homelands and from the Indians' British allies in neighboring Canada. By the time the Constitutional Convention met in Philadelphia in the summer of 1787, the Continental Congress of the existing Confederation government was busy revising an elaborate plan to draw this territory into the union.

Disputed Territory: The Old Southwest

For a generation, as part of wider reforms within its American empire, Spain had been rebuilding its position north of the Gulf of Mexico and east of Texas in the Old Southwest. The Spanish had acquired Louisiana from France in 1763 and had conquered West Florida. In a 1783 treaty, Britain gave back East Florida to the Spanish and agreed that Spain would retain West Florida as well. The Spanish occupied St. Augustine, Pensacola, New Orleans, and Natchez, not to mention St. Louis farther north. Because they controlled both banks of the lower Mississippi and dominated the gulf with their navy, the Spanish controlled who could use the huge river as an access route to the Atlantic. Mississippi Valley settlers knew that if they carried their produce downstream to New Orleans, they could then ship it to the West Indies and Atlantic ports more cheaply than they could haul bulky commodities east across the Appalachian Mountains. Besides, merchants in Louisiana paid for goods in Spanish silver, and settlers upriver needed the hard currency.

Since 1763, the Spanish had let British subjects navigate freely on the Mississippi, so trans-Appalachian fur traders had become accustomed to using this thoroughfare. And during the Revolutionary War, Spain's American allies had retained access to the river. But Spain was shocked when Britain, through its separate treaty with the United States in 1783, granted the Americans a generous southern boundary: the 31st parallel. The treaty terms also included the right of Americans to navigate the Mississippi.

Spain had good reason to claim that its West Florida province stretched north *above* 31 degrees at least to the mouth of the Yazoo River and perhaps as far as the Tennessee River. Moreover, the Spanish felt that they should be the only ones to decide whose boats had access to the Mississippi. To be sure, the Spanish in New Orleans had grown dependent on foreign produce arriving by river from the north. But they also feared American expansion into the Mississippi Valley. Spanish authorities debated whether to co-opt the newcomers and profit from their trade or resist settlers pushing from the east.

VIRGINIA

St. Louis

Lexington

Louisville

KENTUCKY
(1792)

Cumberland Gap

Cumberland R.

Nashville

TENNESSEE
(1796)

CHICKAMAUGA

Knoxville

French Broad

Holston R.

NORTH
CAROLINA

Running Water

Hiwassee R.

CHEROKEE

SOUTH
CAROLINA

Columbia

Savannah R.

Arkansas R.

Chickasaw
Bluffs (Memphis)

CHICKASAW

Tennessee R.

Yazoo R.

Mississippi R.

Augusta

CREEK

Chattahoochee R.

Ogeechee R.

Savannah

GEORGIA

Flint R.

St. Mary's R.

CHOCTAW

31° N latitude

Natchez

Red R.

Mobile

Pensacola

Baton Rouge

New Orleans

Apalachicola R.

SEMINOLE

St. Augustine

ATLANTIC
OCEAN

*Gulf of
Mexico*

Legend:
- Major Southeastern Indian groups
- Attempted state of Franklin
- Spanish boundary claim
- U.S. boundary set in 1783 treaty with England
- Spanish Louisiana, eastern boundary
- Spanish East Florida, northern boundary
- Spanish West Florida
- --- Natchez Trace

■ MAP 8.2

SOUTHERN LAND DEBATES AFTER 1783   Following the Revolution, competing forces collided in the trans-Appalachian South. The United States claimed land reaching the Mississippi River down to 31 degrees latitude, and the Spanish claimed territory north to the Tennessee River. Although major Indian tribes continued to possess much of the region, coastal states also claimed sweeping jurisdiction. In Georgia, for instance, settlement remained confined near the Savannah River, but the state sold speculators large tracts as far west as the Yazoo River.

For its part, the new Confederation had the force of numbers working to its advantage. The Proclamation Line of 1763 had dammed up colonial expansion for two decades. After the war, Americans migrated by the thousands to three existing centers of Anglo settlement in the Old Southwest. By 1785, 10,000 settlers clustered along the Holston, Watauga, and French Broad rivers above Knoxville. Nearly three times that many newcomers had already staked claims to the rich land south of the Ohio River between Lexington and Louisville. In addition, another 4000 were clearing farms along the Cumberland River around Nashville. These Americans took advantage of the fact that Spain had not negotiated an explicit boundary treaty of its own with the United States in 1783. As the flow of settlers increased, some talked aggressively about pushing even farther. They imagined establishing a foothold on the Mississippi at Chickasaw Bluffs (modern Memphis) or perhaps seizing Natchez or New Orleans.

American Claims and Indian Resistance

The weak Confederation government lacked power to constrain the westward push. And state governments, with little money to pay war veterans, had instead given them paper vouchers with which to claim frontier farmland. In the southern states, powerful land speculators pressed their legislatures to support expansion. Georgia, unlike many other states, had not relinquished its western lands to the Confederation. The state's so-called Yazoo claim embraced a region of 35 million acres. This vast expanse stretched west from the Chattahoochee River (Georgia's present boundary with Alabama) to the Mississippi River and from the lower border of modern-day Tennessee to the 31st parallel. "I look forward to a time, not very far distant," wrote Judge George Walton, when Georgia "will be settled and connected . . . from the shores of the Atlantic to the banks of the Mississippi." By 1789, Walton had been elected governor of the state, and the land business boomed. During his tenure, Walton signed warrants for huge tracts up to 50,000 acres, sometimes selling unusable or even nonexistent acreage.

Unlike Georgians, pioneers from Virginia and the Carolinas faced a rugged mountain barrier. But they still trekked west through Cumberland Gap, seeking land of their own or land that they could improve and then sell to later arrivals. In the decade after the war, back-woodsman Daniel Boone worked as a surveyor for these migrants in the trans-Appalachian region of Virginia that became Kentucky in 1792. He accumulated more than 20,000 acres of his own, only to lose much of it in litigation with other claimants. During that same decade, North Carolina issued more land patents than it had created during the entire colonial era, most of them deeds for homesteads west of the mountains. Some of North Carolina's western landholders tried to create their own separate jurisdiction, calling themselves residents of the mountain state of Franklin. Without recognition from the Confederation government, their venture soon failed. Instead, all of North Carolina's western territory—from the Appalachians to the Mississippi—became the state of Tennessee in 1796.

Native American southerners, living in all these lands, suddenly found themselves caught between the competing claims of Spain and the United States. Ravaged by the recent smallpox epidemic and the bitter war and utterly ignored during peace negotiations, they endured the increasingly aggressive acts of state legislatures and frontier settlers from the east. The Cherokees, Creeks, Choctaws, and Chickasaws—numbering roughly 40,000 people—all debated over which leaders and strategies to follow. Some responded to their new situation by selecting leaders with European-American ties. Among the Creeks, for example, Alexander McGillivray rose to prominence. The son of a wealthy Scottish trader and a Creek woman, he had been raised on his father's Georgia plantation before becoming the Creeks' spokesperson in 1782. The fact that he owned 50 slaves and kept a wine cellar may have boosted his bargaining power with Spanish and American officials. However, it also separated him from the needs and lives of those he represented.

The renegade Cherokee warrior Dragging Canoe, who had split with tribal elders before the Revolution broke out, offered a different approach. Hundreds of militant Indians, discouraged by the compromises of their leaders, had joined his band of guerrilla fighters known as the Chicamaugas. After Americans burned the Chicamauga encampments at Lookout Mountain in the closing days of the Revolutionary War, the

John Trumbull, *Hopthle Mico*, 1790. The Charles Allen Munn Collection, Fordham University Library, Bronx, New York (Catalog #3)

■ In 1790 American artist John Trumbull paused from painting scenes commemorating the Revolution in order to sketch members of a Creek Indian delegation visiting New York City from Georgia. In this picture of an important Native American orator, a medal presented by the American government is visible amid the ruffles of his shirt.

Indians erected five new villages nearby on the Tennessee River, including Dragging Canoe's headquarters at Running Water Town.

From this well-protected location—near where Alabama, Georgia, and Tennessee now meet—the Chicamaugas recruited allies and led forays to stop American encroachment. They drew aid from the Spanish when possible, sending delegations as far as St. Augustine. When Anglo frontiersmen murdered Old Tassel, a moderate Cherokee leader, during a truce in 1788, Indian support for the militant Chicamaugas increased. But Dragging Canoe died in 1792 before he could build a strong alliance with Indians north of the Ohio River. They, too, struggled with the steady incursions of newcomers and the disintegration of their way of life.

"We Are Now Masters": The Old Northwest

Like their neighbors in the South, most Native Americans in the North had sided with the British during the Revolutionary War. So Americans lost no time in claiming northern Indian domains ceded by Britain in the 1783 Treaty of Paris. "We are now Masters of this Island," General Philip Schuyler boasted to the Iroquois, "and can dispose of the Lands as we think proper." Britain refused to vacate western forts at Oswego, Niagara, Detroit, and Michilimackinac on the pretext that Americans still owed prewar debts to London merchants. Even so, the British could provide little material support to the Indians of the region, who felt betrayed by the terms of the Paris treaty.

American delegations moved quickly to draft treaties with the Iroquois and the Ohio Valley tribes. Delegates bluntly asserted the right of the new United States government to Indian lands. The Congress of this recently established Confederation government instructed these negotiators to deal with the Native Americans as dependents rather than equals, calling them children rather than brothers. The treaty makers even took hostages to force the Indians to accept their terms. Ordinary Americans sealed these claims with a surge of migration into western Pennsylvania and beyond. "The Americans . . . put us out of our lands," Indian leaders complained to the Spanish governor at St. Louis in 1784, "extending themselves like a plague of locusts in the territories of the Ohio River which we inhabit."

Clearly, the British and the Indians had lost the upper hand. However, Americans initially remained divided among themselves over who would control the region. One by one, the states of Massachusetts, New York, Connecticut, and Virginia ceded separate territorial claims—dating from their early colonial charters—to the Confederation government. However, Connecticut retained economic control over a "western reserve" of 4 million acres south of Lake Erie that it used to satisfy claims from the state's war veterans. Similarly, Virginia held onto land rights for an even larger "military district" to repay soldiers and war victims.

These western land acquisitions transformed the Confederation. For the first time, it became more than a league of states. With lands of its own to organize and oversee, the Confederation government took on attributes of a sovereign ruling body. As the number of cessions increased, Congress put Thomas Jefferson in charge of a committee to draft a plan to administer this national domain. Before he departed for Europe to replace Benjamin Franklin as the American minister to France, Jefferson drew up an orderly design for western land distribution.

This document became the basis for the Land Ordinance of 1785. Jefferson knew that in the South, where hired surveyors often staked out piecemeal claims on a first-come, first-served basis, the best property had gone to wealthy investors. Moreover, boundary litigation over odd-shaped and overlapping lots had proved endless. To avoid these complications, the 1785 ordinance called for surveyors to lay out a grid of adjoining townships, beginning at the point where the Ohio River flowed out of Pennsylvania. A township would contain 36 numbered sections, each 1 mile square (640 acres). This grid plan shaped all future American land policy and left a permanent mark on the country's landscape. As its most far-reaching innovation, the ordinance reserved the income from one valuable section near the heart of every township—square number 16—to support public education.

■ A sketch by Congressman Thomas Jefferson shows his proposal to divide the new interior territories into 14 states (with Number 7 to be named Saratoga after the crucial Revolutionary War victory). By suggesting numerous compact states, Jefferson hoped to maximize the Congressional voting power of western farmers. Others, eager to limit western power in Congress, pushed successfully for fewer, larger states.

But orderly surveying and public education were just parts of Jefferson's plan. Hoping to populate the region with self-sufficient yeomen farmers, he proposed that the government give away land in small parcels rather than sell it in large blocks that only wealthy speculators could afford. He envisioned self-government for these enterprising settlers, not colonial rule. For Jefferson, the more weight these independent farmers obtained in the American government the better, so he urged the rapid entry of numerous new territories into the union on an equal footing with the 13 original states. He suggested creating up to 14 small, rectangular districts in the west, with elaborate names such as Metropotamia. At least nine would be north of the Ohio River, and each could become a separate state with voting rights in Congress.

According to Jefferson's report "Government for the Western Territory," the first settlers to arrive in each district were to form their own temporary governments. And when the local population reached 20,000, residents could call a convention, frame a constitution, and send a delegate to Congress. When the district's population equaled the number of free inhabitants living in the smallest of the 13 original states, that district could enter the union if certain conditions were met. Each new state must agree to support a republican form of government, remain part of the Confederation, and accept a share of the federal debt. It must also agree to exclude slavery after 1800. Once Jefferson left for France, Congress accepted his report. However, it then modified the plan greatly. In the Land Ordinance of 1785, Congress removed his call for numerous districts, ignored his suggestion of ornate names, dismissed the notion of free land, and dropped the idea of ending slavery.

The Northwest Ordinance of 1787

Surveying the vast wilderness north of the Ohio River into neat geometric squares raised untold practical and diplomatic problems. The task would take years to complete. Almost immediately—and long before the initial ordinance could take hold—political shifts produced an entirely new law from Congress: the Northwest Ordinance of 1787. This law determining how territories north of the Ohio River would be governed contained a number of additional changes to Jefferson's original plan. For example, it reversed direction on the slave question once again, introducing an immediate prohibition of slavery north of the Ohio River. However, it made arrangements to deport fugitive slaves back to their owners in slaveholding states.

In various ways, the new ordinance proved less democratic than earlier versions. Congress cut the possible number of new states from the Northwest, specifying there could be only three to five new states. This move limited the potential political weight of the vast territory. In addition, the ordinance increased property requirements for citizens who wanted to vote or hold office. It also slowed the process by which new states could gain admission to the union. Eventually, Congress granted statehood to five new entities—Ohio (1803), Indiana (1816), Illinois (1818), Michigan (1837), and Wisconsin (1848)—but the process took more than half a century. Minnesota, part of which was also in the original cession from Britain, did not become a state until 1858.

Most members of Congress feared the prospect of democratic governance and local control in the Old Northwest, giving a strong voice to people with different regional interests. And they worried that aggression by settlers could spark expensive Indian wars. To retain control over the region, they provided for the appointment of territorial officials—a governor, a secretary, and three judges—instead of allowing elected governments. Even when territorial legislatures formed, the governor would have veto power over their actions. James Monroe, head of the committee that moved the bill through Congress, wrote candidly to Jefferson, "It is in effect to be a colonial gover[nme]nt similar to wh[at] prevailed in these States previous to the revolution."

These changes benefited eastern land speculators most, some of whom were members of Congress. They hoped to control these lands for profit. What they did not want was to see numerous western states emerge quickly to play a powerful role in the national government. In 1786, former army officers in New England, joined by five surveyors who had seen the promising region first-hand, organized the Ohio Company to buy up western land. They dispatched a clever Massachusetts minister named Manasseh Cutler to lobby Congress to sell a huge tract to the company at bargain rates. Cutler joined forces with congressional insiders associated with another venture, the Scioto Company. Together, they engineered a deal providing 1.5 million acres to the Ohio Company and another 5 million acres for the Scioto investors.

Whatever suspicious bargains surrounded congressional passage of the Northwest Ordinance of 1787, the new law still granted basic rights to western residents. These guarantees—following state bills of rights—included religious freedom, trial by jury, and access to common-law judicial proceedings. Most important, the western territories were assured of full entry into the union as equal states rather than receiving dependent status as permanent colonies. This system established an orderly method for bringing new regions of settlement into the union. The same process, first used when Vermont became the fourteenth state in 1791, remained in use as late as 1959, when the Pacific territories of Alaska and Hawaii received statehood.

Courtesy, Monroe County Historical Commission, Monroe, MI

■ Marie-Thérèse Lasselle (1735–1819) witnessed a generation of transitions in the Great Lakes region. She and her husband ran a trading post at Kekionga on the Maumee River (now Fort Wayne, Indiana). Long after the Revolutionary War drove them to Detroit, she created this self-portrait, using watercolor on embroidered silk.

■ MAP 8.3
NATIVE AMERICAN OHIO BEFORE 1785   For centuries, what is now Ohio was a land of Native American villages, set by rivers. Key eighteenth-century Indian towns and trails are shown here. (In 1781 whites massacred Christian Indians at the Moravian mission of Gnadenhutten.)

Creditors and Debtors

The end of the Revolutionary War brought widespread economic depression. The money spent by foreign armies for goods and services dried up, and the split with Britain disrupted established patterns of commerce. When peace returned, merchants and artisans scrambled to find new markets and to locate new routes of profitable trade. At the same time, those who had preserved their holdings or made money during the war snapped up foreign goods that had been scarce during the fighting. These purchases—whether for luxury goods or more necessary items—drained hard currency away from the states and increased the Confederation's debt.

Citizens everywhere felt the brunt of the postwar slump as prices dropped and the money supply shrank. As credit tightened, merchants called in their loans and unpaid bills. But the people who had taken on debts earlier, when higher prices prevailed, had more difficulty in paying them off. Families, especially poor artisans and subsistence farmers, suddenly faced the threat of foreclosure and loss of their property. They fought back in local elections, state legislatures, and even the streets. Violence broke out in state after state, from New Hamp-

■ **MAP 8.4**
SETTLERS' OHIO, AFTER 1785 Starting in 1785, the American government imposed a novel grid system on the territory northwest of the Ohio River. Rectangular property lines and geometric state boundaries laid out by surveyors later overlay the natural landscape of the American West.

shire to Georgia, as hard-pressed people, many of them veterans, decried fiscal policies that seemed to favor the moneyed classes. When armed conflict erupted in Massachusetts, wealthy merchants raised an army to suppress the revolt. They succeeded, but they feared similar conflicts in the future. After all, democratic forces had shown that they had the strength to win control in a number of the state legislatures. The Massachusetts rebellion therefore helped prompt a drastic effort to restructure and strengthen the national government through a special, closed-door convention in Philadelphia.

New Sources of Wealth

As diplomats finalized the Peace Treaty of 1783, the British government managed to fire one parting shot at the former colonies. To nurture Britain's maritime trade and punish New England shippers, it imposed restrictions on the Americans' trade with the British West Indies. The move barred American ships from a key portion of Britain's imperial commerce, forcing merchants to seek out new avenues of trade. In 1784 an American vessel entered the Baltic Sea and established trade relations with Russia. Meanwhile, the New England whaling towns of Nantucket and New Bedford rebuilt their war-ravaged fleets and stepped up their search for whales to provide oil for American lamps. Sea captains had no trouble finding sailors in need of work. Ship owners extended their reach in any direction where they sensed possible profits, even into the African slave trade and the remote China trade.

Early in 1783, a Savannah merchant named Joseph Clay commented that a "vast number" of slaves had fled Georgia and South Carolina during the war. As rice plantations renewed production, African workers were "exceeding scarce and in demand." Sensing a profit, foreign slave traders shipped 15,000 Africans to the two states by 1785. American captains moved to grab a share of the trade. The seaports of Bristol, Newport, and Providence in Rhode Island, as well as Boston and Salem in Massachusetts, all sent ships to the west African coast in hopes of renewing a trade that had been interrupted during the war. True, antislavery sentiment had increased with the idealism of the Revolution. And several states, including Massachusetts, Rhode Island, and even Virginia, had passed laws outlawing slave imports. But these developments did not prevent American sea captains from transporting Africans to the Spanish West Indies and to Georgia and South Carolina. "The Negro business is a great object with us," Clay reported in 1784. "It is to the Trade of this Country, as the Soul to the body."

Although American merchants had taken part in the African trade and other commerce for generations, their ships had rarely, if ever, ventured outside the Atlantic. That changed dramatically in the decade after Yorktown. John Ledyard, an American who had sailed with Captain Cook in the Pacific, convinced financier Robert Morris of the profits to be made by opening new trade routes to the Orient. The project would take an enormous investment—ten times the amount needed to send a ship to Europe—but the potential rewards were irresistible. "I am sending some Ships to China," Morris announced to John Jay, "in order to encourage others in the adventurous pursuits of Commerce." His first vessel, a former privateer renamed the *Empress of China*, left New York harbor for Canton by way of the Indian Ocean early in 1784. It carried almost 30 tons of ginseng root—242 casks procured from the mountains in the "back part of Virginia"—highly prized by the Chinese. The ship also carried 2600 furs, which the Chinese used to line fashionable winter clothing, and $20,000 in hard currency, a huge drain on New York's economy.

In six months, the American vessel reached Canton, China's outlet for foreign commerce. "The Chinese had never heard of us," one sailor noted, "but we introduced ourselves as a new Nation, gave them our history, with a description of our Country," and stressed the mutual advantages of trade, "which they appear perfectly to understand and wish." The Chinese called the strangers "the new people." They called their country "the flowery flag kingdom" because to them the stars on the American flag resembled blossoms. Business proved brisk, and in May 1785 the *Empress of China* returned to New York loaded with tea, chinaware, and silk. Morris and his partners raked in a hefty 20 percent return on their investment.

Other traders took notice. In 1787 the Browns, wealthy merchants in Providence, diverted their slave ship, the *General Washington*, from the African trade to the China tea trade. That same year, six Boston investors sent two vessels—the *Columbia* and the *Lady Washington*—around Cape Horn at the tip of South America to trade for furs on the American Northwest Coast. Within five years, their captains, Robert Gray and William Kendrick, had pioneered new Pacific routes for American ships.

Captain Gray traded cloth and iron goods for sea otter pelts with the Nootka Indians. Then he took the *Columbia* across the Pacific, pausing at the Hawaiian Islands for supplies. Reaching Canton in 1789, Gray found 70 foreign ships in the harbor, 14 of them American. He traded profitably and proceeded home through the Indian Ocean, making the *Columbia* the first American ship to circumnavigate the globe. Because Gray's voyage affirmed the rewards of trade along the Northwest Coast, a diplomatic controversy flared the following year at Nootka Sound, on the west side of Vancouver Island. Although Spain protested British and American trading activities in the area, Gray was back on the Northwest Coast by 1792. He entered a powerful stream—where the states of Washington and Oregon now meet—and named it the Columbia River, after his ship. When he planted the American flag at the mouth of this major

George Davidson, *Attacked at Juan de Fuca Straits*, c.1792. Oregon Historical Society, OrHi 85076

ATACKTED at JUAN, DE, FUCA, STRAITS.

■ This painting on glass shows Northwest Coast Indians menacing the American ship *Columbia* from their large war canoes. Captain Robert Gray was conducting trade for sea otter pelts to transport across the Pacific Ocean to China, where the soft fur was highly valued.

waterway, his action foreshadowed later territorial claims by the United States in the Oregon region. At the same time, Captain Kendrick, sailing in the *Lady Washington*, anchored off the Japanese island of Honshu, hoping to gain access for American trade. But Japan remained closed, and Kendrick's objective was not realized for another 62 years.

While American merchants probed for new markets from the Baltic to the Pacific, they also moved to strengthen their economic and political position at home. Peacetime brought forth a variety of ingenious schemes, many of which foundered in the troubled economy. But one practice attracted wide interest among the wealthiest people in town after town. Paying only a small fraction of the original value, they bought up a variety of loan certificates, paper notes, and wartime securities issued by state governments and the Continental Congress. Certificates issued to soldiers and officers at the end of the war rapidly became part of this speculative market as the original recipients sold their notes to prosperous speculators in return for ready cash. As a result, such holdings accumulated increasingly in the hands of the well-to-do. In Maryland, for example, the claims on $900,000 owed by the state became concentrated in the possession of only 318 people by 1790. Moreover, 16 of these people controlled more than half of the total value, and the 8 largest holders possessed 38 percent. As their speculative holdings increased, these few wealthy investors maneuvered to influence political events. They realized that the people who controlled the reins of power at the state and national levels would determine whether and how the various notes of credit might be redeemed. With this in mind, they purchased large quantities of these notes for a fraction of their face value. These men stood to reap enormous profits from any government that would pay interest on, and then buy back, all these paper arrangements at their original high value.

"Tumults in New England"

The few people who had acquired most of the paper securities wanted their holdings redeemed for hard money. But the majority of citizens, faced with rising debts amid an economic downturn, resented the heavy taxes needed to pay interest on the debt to these wealthy speculators. Favoring much easier credit, they urged their states to issue new paper money. This conflict was familiar from colonial times, when many merchants and planters, in debt to British firms, had chafed under Britain's tight fiscal policies. But the views of local elites had shifted when they gained control over their own state governments. They now wanted to limit paper money in ways that favored their new position as powerful creditors and holders of wartime certificates. Their opponents argued that issuing paper money could take the pressure off cash-strapped farmers and help retire enormous war debts. In seven states, these advocates of economic relief carried the day. State government presses put additional notes in circulation.

Local battles over debt, credit, and currency issues hit hardest in the Northeast for several reasons. During the war, Americans had foiled British plans to isolate and crush New England's rebellious colonists. Indeed, the region had prospered. Yankee farmers sold provisions to the Continental Army at hefty prices. French forces stationed at Newport in 1780 paid for food and firewood in gold coins. And throughout the war, numerous New England ships, known as privateers, fought with an eye on profit, hauling captured enemy vessels into local ports as prizes. In 1783, however, Britain's move to ban American ships from the British West Indies cut off the lucrative trade that New Englanders had created. For generations, these American captains had sold fish, grain, and lumber to the islands in exchange for hard currency. Sudden exclusion from Britain's Caribbean colonies dried up the flow of much-needed cash into New England and undermined the region's economy.

These changes had an immediate impact. In New Hampshire courts, debt cases rose six-fold from 1782 to 1785. Even if the debts themselves were not large, the heavy costs of traveling to court and paying high legal fees pushed thousands of families into insolvency. As long as the courts remained open, judges routinely ordered the seizure and sale of property. Embittered farmers watched as their horses, cows, wagons, and household goods disappeared in auction at low prices. Hard times often spark drastic responses, and New England's pot soon boiled over. Early in 1787, from his desk at Mount Vernon, Washington's secretary noted that the "tumults, insurrections, and *Rebellion* in New England have of late much engrossed the minds of the people here."

Newspaper accounts told of disturbing events in Rhode Island. There, rural politicians seeking relief for indebted farmers swept into power during the elections of April 1786. Their triumph freed the assembly from its longtime domination by rich Providence merchants. The newcomers, elected on their paper money platform, wasted no time in implementing their ballot box revolution. Their region had a withered economy, and the state government carried a burdensome war debt. To address these matters, assemblymen approved a huge outlay of paper money: £100,000. The assembly planned to distribute the legal tender among the towns and lend it to citizens on equitable terms. The revenue received back in taxes as the economy rebounded would then be used to pay off the state's debts and retire the paper currency. To ensure the plan's success, legislators declared the money as legal tender that all creditors had to accept as payment. And if any creditors refused to accept the paper money, debtors could deposit the funds with the county court. The judge would then advertise that the debt had been paid.

Many merchants closed their stores rather than accept payments in the new medium of exchange.

Not surprisingly, creditors and speculators resented Rhode Island's currency law. Moreover, they fumed at the new legislature's unwillingness to assume a share of the national debt and pay off wealthy bond holders, as other states had done. Without control over the legislature, these speculators feared they would be left holding all the continental securities they had acquired. They took swift action. Though heavily outnumbered, members of the moneyed class in Providence used their economic strength to fight back. Many merchants closed their stores rather than accept payments in the new medium of exchange. Some even left the state to avoid being forced to accept debt payments in paper money. When judges who favored the merchants' cause finally declared the new statute unconstitutional, creditors everywhere sighed with relief. Their newspapers condemned the "Rogue Island" currency law as a dire example of the dangers of democracy.

The Massachusetts Regulation

In Massachusetts and New Hampshire, unlike Rhode Island, wealthy merchants in coastal centers retained control over the new state assemblies. They therefore had the power to resist public pressure to generate more paper money. Such a policy might provide relief for an expanding backcountry population hit hard by the economic downturn and the scarcity of circulating currency, but it did not suit the interests of these creditors. Instead, it was the enforcement of debt collection by the courts that would best expand merchants' holdings and improve their standing in international trade. As in other states, a small contingent of wealthy speculators had bought up, at bargain rates, most of the public securities and certificates issued during the war. They anticipated enormous windfall profits if a government they controlled could redeem these notes, in gold and silver, at their full face value.

In New Hampshire, by 1785, securities valued at nearly £100,000 belonged to just 4.5 percent of the state's adult male population: 1120 men among approximately 25,000. A mere 3 percent of this group—34 men—controlled more than a third of this vast speculative investment. Most of these men had close ties to the prevailing government, situated in Exeter, near the coast. When farmers organized conventions to voice their economic grievances, merchants infiltrated and disrupted their meetings. In September 1786, 200 citizens, many of them armed war veterans, marched on Exeter to demand money reforms before conditions "drive us to a state of desperation." Officials organized cavalry units to confront the desperate citizens, arresting their leaders from the crowd "as a butcher would seize sheep in a flock." As soon as the state's governor, General John Sullivan, had suppressed the dissenters, he issued a proclamation forbidding further conventions. He then wrote to Massachusetts governor James Bowdoin, offering to help crush similar unrest in the neighboring state.

Early in 1786, the Commonwealth of Massachusetts had imposed a heavy direct tax

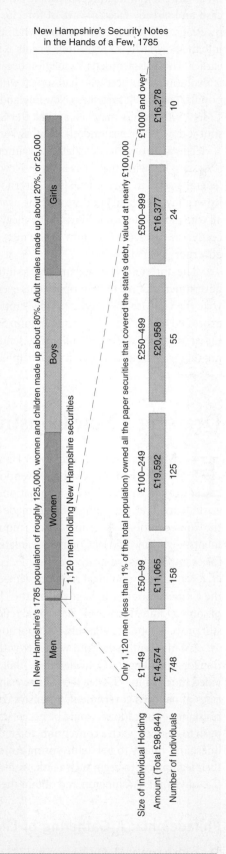

■ **FIGURE 8.1**
CONCENTRATION OF SECURITY NOTES IN THE HANDS OF A FEW: THE EXAMPLE OF NEW HAMPSHIRE IN 1785

on its citizenry, stipulating that people pay it in hard currency. Western farmers lacked sufficient cash and already faced a wave of foreclosures for debt. They protested the tax law at town meetings and county conventions. When their complaints fell on deaf ears, they took actions into their own hands, "regulating" events as the North Carolina Regulators had done two decades earlier. The Massachusetts Regulation became known as Shays's Rebellion when Daniel Shays, a revolutionary officer who had served with distinction under Lafayette, emerged as one of its popular leaders. At first, these New England Regulators focused on closing the courts. In August 1786, 1500 farmers marched against the Court of Common Pleas in Hampshire County and shut it down. The next month, another band closed the court in Worcester.

The confrontation escalated as winter set in. By January the next year, more than 1000 Shaysites, knowing that their allies in New Hampshire had been defeated, moved to seize the federal arsenal in Springfield. But Governor Bowdoin had mobilized an army, financed largely by wealthy merchants in Boston. This private militia overpowered the westerners and forced all who did not flee to sign an oath of allegiance. Disarmed but not silenced, the dissidents succeeded in defeating Bowdoin in the next election and extracting some relief from the new governor, John Hancock.

The unrest in New England played into the hands of those advocating a stronger national government. (Some of their opponents even suspected that ardent nationalists had helped provoke the violence specifically to rally support for their cause.) In a typical letter, Henry Knox expressed fear to his fellow general, John Sullivan, that "we are verging fast to anarchy." Writing in May 1787, he urged Sullivan to send delegates from New Hampshire to a crucial meeting that was about to begin in Philadelphia.

Drafting a New Constitution

Even before Yorktown, Alexander Hamilton, Washington's youthful Caribbean-born aide-de-camp, had proposed a convention to restructure the national government. Now he worked with another young nationalist, James Madison, and their energetic supporters to bring it about. Congress had made earnest efforts toward reform, but any changes to the Confederation's governing articles required approval from all 13 states. Thus, vital amendments—which would let Congress regulate commerce, raise revenue, and establish a judiciary, for example—proved nearly impossible. For some powerful leaders, especially merchants and creditors, a major political revision seemed in order. They were willing to alter the Articles of the Confederation, which governed the United States, or perhaps even scrap them, in favor of some modified structure that would reflect their worldview and serve their own interests yet still prove acceptable to a sufficient portion of the people.

"Many Gentlemen both within & without Congress," wrote Madison, desire a "Convention for amending the Confederation." Still, it would take impressive leadership—Madison provided much of it—to seize the initiative and then generate enough momentum to change the rules of national government. Extensive compromise, both between elite factions and toward resistant popular forces, would be necessary at every stage. After all, it would take an enormous push to engineer such a convention, to guide it to restructure the government along nationalist lines, and finally to persuade voting Americans to ratify the proposed changes and accept their legitimacy. To begin such a task, would-be reformers needed to recruit the enormous prestige of George Washington and obtain the acquiescence of a stymied Congress.

Philadelphia: A Gathering of Like-Minded Men

The path began at Mount Vernon in 1785 when Washington hosted commissioners appointed by Maryland and Virginia to resolve state boundary disputes regarding the Potomac River.

Charles Willson Peale, *N.W. View of the State House of Philadelphia, July 1778*. The Historical Society of Pennsylvania

■ In July 1787 *Columbian Magazine* published "A N.W. View of the State House in Philadelphia," drawn by Charles Willson Peale during the Revolutionary War. Once again, the country was in turmoil, and readers were eager for a glimpse of the place where delegates were meeting in secret session to alter the government.

During the gathering, these men (including James Madison) scheduled a broader meeting on Chesapeake trade for the next year at Annapolis, Maryland. They invited all the states to send representatives. Only 12 delegates from five states showed up at Annapolis in September 1786, but news of the serious unrest in New England prompted talk of a more extended meeting. Alexander Hamilton, as a representative from New York, persuaded the other delegates to call for a convention in Philadelphia the following May to discuss commerce and other matters. Madison won endorsement for the proposal from the Virginia legislature and then from Congress. Reform-minded congressmen, such as James Monroe, saw an opportunity to amend and improve the existing Confederation structure. But when the states sent delegates to Philadelphia the following spring, many of the appointees felt that amendments might not go far enough. They were open to the more sweeping changes that Madison and other nationalists had in mind. So the gathering called to consider commercial matters and propose improvements to the Articles of Confederation soon became a full-fledged Constitutional Convention, a private meeting to design and propose an entirely new structure for governing the United States.

Madison reached Philadelphia in early May 1787. He immediately began drafting plans for drastic change and lobbying delegates, some of whom came early to attend a secret gathering of the Society of the Cincinnati. On May 25, when representatives from seven states had arrived, they launched the convention and unanimously chose Washington as the presiding officer. Participants agreed that they would operate behind closed doors and each state delegation would have one vote. There would be no public discussion or official record of their proceedings. Soon, delegates from 12 states had joined the gathering. Only Rhode Island opted not to send representatives.

The 55 delegates had much in common. All were white, male, and well educated, and many already knew one another. These members of the national elite included 34 lawyers, 30 public creditors, and 27 members of the Society of the Cincinnati. More than a quarter of the participants owned slaves, and nearly a dozen had done personal business with financier Robert Morris of the Pennsylvania delegation. Not surprisingly, all seemed to agree that the contagion of liberty had spread too far. Indeed, Elbridge Gerry of Massachusetts called the current situation "an excess of democracy."

Specifically, these men feared recent legislation that state assemblies had adopted to assist hard-pressed citizens: laws that delayed tax collection, postponed debt payments, and issued paper money. Most delegates hoped to replace the existing Confederation structure with a national government capable of controlling finances and creating creditor-friendly fiscal policy. To be effective, they believed, a strengthened central government must have greater control over the states. Only Robert Yates and John Lansing of New York and Luther Martin of Maryland staunchly resisted expanding central power.

Many of the delegates, especially those from the large states, thought that the national legislature should be based on proportional representation according to the number of inhabitants rather than each state receiving equal weight regardless of its population. Also, most wanted to see the single-house (unicameral) Congress of the Confederation replaced by an upper and lower house that would reflect the views and values of different social classes. John Adams had helped create such a two-house (bicameral) system in the Massachusetts constitution, thereby limiting pure democracy and giving more political power to propertied interests. Besides calling for checks within the legislative branch itself, Adams had also laid out strong arguments for separating, and checking, the powers of each competing branch of government. For a sound and lasting government, Adams had argued in earlier essays, the legislative branch should be balanced by separate executive and judicial branches that are equally independent. Most delegates agreed with this novel system of checks and balances, intended to add stability and remove corruption.

Compromise and Consensus

The Philadelphia gathering, which lasted through the entire summer, would later be known as the Constitutional Convention of 1787. Even as a general consensus emerged within the small meeting, countless personal, practical, and philosophical differences persisted. Hamilton delivered a six-hour speech in which he staked out an extremely conservative position, no doubt intended to make other proposals look more moderate and therefore acceptable. He underscored "the imprudence of democracy" and stressed a natural separation between "the few and the many"—the "wealthy well born" and the "turbulent and changing" people. Hamilton's conservative oration called for the chief executive and the senators to be chosen indirectly, by elected representatives rather than by the people themselves, and he recommended that these high officials should serve for life. Such ideas undoubtedly appealed to many of his listeners, but all of the delegates knew that a majority of citizens would never accept such proposals. Pierce Butler of South Carolina, invoking ancient Greece, urged members to "follow the example of Solon, who gave the Athenians not the best government he could devise but the best they would receive."

This attentiveness of convention members to what the public would accept is illustrated by their approach to voting rights. Even delegates who wanted to limit the vote to property holders realized that various state constitutions, responding to popular pressure, had already distributed suffrage more broadly. Property ownership was no longer a universal voting requirement, and states varied on whether religion, race, or gender could determine eligibility. James Wilson of Pennsylvania, second only to Madison in working to build a practical nationalist majority in the convention, pointed out that "it would be very hard and disagreeable" for any person, once franchised, to give up the right to vote. Accordingly, the delegates proposed that in each state all those allowed to vote for the "most numerous branch of the state legislature" would also be permitted to cast ballots for members of the House of Representatives. But they shied away from accepting direct election for the Senate or the president, and they deferred suffrage matters to the states.

Time and again during the 16-week convention, these like-minded men showed their willingness to bargain and compromise. Lofty principles and rigid schemes often gave way to balancing and improvisation. The unlikely creation of the electoral college for selecting a president is one example. Delegates who differed over the length for the chief executive's term of office and right to run for reelection also disagreed on the best method of presidential selection. Some of them suggested that ordinary voters should elect him; others proposed that the state governors, or the national legislature, or even electors chosen by state legislators should choose the chief executive.

Finally, the aptly named Committee on Postponed Matters cobbled together an acceptable system: a gathering (or "college") of chosen electors from each state would cast votes for the presidency. This electoral college plan had little precedent, but it managed to balance competing interests. Under the scheme, state legislatures would set the manner for selecting electors. The least populous states would get a minimum of three electoral votes, and states with more people would choose more electors in proportion to their numbers, giving them added weight in the decision. The people could also participate in the voting process, though only if their state legislatures called for it. And if no candidate won a majority in the electoral college, the House of Representatives had the right to determine the president, with each state having one vote. The system was far from elegant or democratic, but it placated varied interests, and it won prompt approval.

Questions of Representation

As deliberations stretched across the long, hot summer of 1787, two central issues threatened to unravel the convention: political representation and slavery. Questions of representation pervaded almost every discussion, pitting large states such as Virginia, Pennsylvania, and Massachusetts against the less populated states. Madison's well-organized Virginians offered a comprehensive blueprint outlining a new national government that would have three separate branches. This design, called the "Virginia Plan," recommended a bicameral national legislature with proportional representation in each body. The House of Representatives would be chosen by popular election, the Senate by state legislators.

Madison's system clearly favored populous states. Not surprisingly, a coalition of small-state delegates led by William Paterson of New Jersey submitted an alternative "New Jersey Plan." This less sweeping revision built on the current Articles of Confederation. It called for a continuation of the existing unicameral legislature, in which each state received an equal vote. A committee chaired by Benjamin Franklin managed to break the impasse. The idea of an upper house, or Senate, would be retained, and each state, whatever its size, would hold two senate seats. Seats in the House of Representatives would be determined proportionally, according to the relative population of each state. Moreover, this lower house would have the power to initiate all bills dealing with finance and money matters.

> *As deliberations stretched across the long, hot summer of 1787, two central issues threatened to unravel the convention: political representation and slavery.*

To implement proportional representation in a fast-growing society, the delegates provided for a national census every 10 years. No European country had attempted a regular periodic headcount, so the census represented a radical innovation at the time. This in turn raised a thorny question. Should slaves—people enumerated in the census yet denied the rights of citizens—be counted in determining a state's proportional representation in the national government? Slaveholding states wanted their human property to count because that would give those states more representation. The convention resolved this dilemma in mid-July with

Equal Representation?

The ratified Constitution was an approved blueprint, not a finished house. In the name of "We, the people of the United States," the new plan affirmed citizen representation in government. The tradition had grown during generations of local self-rule in the colonies, and debate over the issue had sparked rebellion from British rule. Regular elections allowing the choice of "representative" public officials would be central to the new framework. But each state government held the right to decide how "the people" would be defined in election matters. And no one knew how the proposed federal court system might rule on these issues. Everywhere, concerned onlookers wondered how representation would work in the new republic.

After all, the majority of inhabitants found themselves excluded from the franchise on the basis of age, gender, or race. Status as a slave or servant, lack of sufficient property, military status, tax classification, criminal record, or length of residency could also be factors in denying the vote. But to many in the ruling elite, broadening the franchise appeared a dangerous proposition. "Democracy," Elbridge Gerry had told the Constitutional Convention, is "the worst . . . of all political evils." (Later, when he served as governor of Massachusetts, Gerry's name became associated with the art of drawing voting districts in strange shapes to assure political advantage, a practice known ever after as *gerrymandering*.)

Struggles over the right to vote have expanded the franchise and the

Voting districts linked together in strange ways for political advantage have been known as a "gerrymander" ever since 1812, when a cartoonist suggested that the arrangement designed by Elbridge Gerry to connect counties in Massachusetts resembled "a new species of Monster."

Courtesy, American Antiquarian Society

federal government's role in guaranteeing that right through amendments to the Constitution itself. After the bloody Civil War, the Fifteenth Amendment (1870) granted that a citizen's voting rights could not be "denied or abridged . . . on account of race, color, or previous condition of servitude" (gender was not mentioned), and it empowered Congress to enforce the article. But Congress shirked this assignment and tolerated new devices for black disfranchisement. Similarly, Congress failed to protect Native American voting rights, even after a 1924 act granted Indians the rights of citizenship. Meanwhile, women mounted a suffrage campaign of their own, leading to passage of the Nineteenth Amendment (1920), removing voting restrictions "on account of sex."

As enfranchisement expanded, so did the proliferation of devices to inhibit voting and limit its value. In the segregated South, poll taxes, literacy tests, and outright intimidation all

became tactics for preventing black voter registration and participation. So did racial gerrymandering. When Charles Gomillion, a sociologist at Tuskegee Institute, registered hundreds of black voters in Macon County, Alabama, during the 1950s, the white legislature fought back. It redrew the boundaries of the city of Tuskegee to exclude most black voters, "gerrymandering" them into adjacent precincts where their votes would count for little. In a landmark case (*Gomillion v. Lightfoot*, 1960), the Supreme Court ruled such redistricting unconstitutional. When Congress, pressured by the Civil Rights Movement, passed the Voting Rights Act of 1965, the idea of "one person, one vote" gained a legal foothold in the land. Each person should be able to register freely, cast a secret ballot, and have that vote tallied fairly. But in addition, one citizen's vote should *count* as much as another.

In one way, the framers of the Constitution anticipated the problem of uneven representation, for they mandated a new census every ten years. This headcount would allow state and federal legislators to reapportion representation every decade in a rapidly growing society, with courts overseeing the disputes. But in another way, the framers, through their electoral college system, created a time bomb of sorts. What would happen if a presidential candidate received the majority of the popular vote but only a minority of votes in the electoral college? Such an unlikely event occurred once in 1876, with chaotic results, and again in 2000. Both times, millions of voters suddenly realized that in selecting a president each ballot does not have equal weight. This ensures that the debate over how American leaders are selected will continue for years to come. ■

a "three-fifths" formula that Madison had proposed in earlier legislation. The odd recipe made every five enslaved people equivalent to three free people in apportionment matters.

In an ironic twist, the same week the Constitutional Convention delegates approved the notorious three-fifths clause, the existing government of the United States leaned in the opposite direction. Meeting in New York, members of th Confederation's Congress passed the Northwest Ordinance, which outlawed slavery in the new territory above the Ohio River. Because there was much contact between the two meetings, some scholars speculate that powerful Southerners agreed to give away the prospect of slavery north of the Ohio River in exchange for more support of slavery within the new plan taking shape in Philadelphia.

Slavery: The Deepest Dilemma

During the debate over the three-fifths clause, Madison commented that the greatest division in the United States "did not lie between the large & small States: it lay between the Northern & Southern," owing to "the effects of their having or not having slaves." This highly charged issue continued to simmer beneath the surface for most of the summer.

In late August, with most other matters resolved, delegates could no longer postpone questions surrounding slavery. Yet again, a committee deliberated, and a bargain was struck. But this time, hundreds of thousands of human lives were at stake. Planter delegates from Georgia and South Carolina refused to support any document that regulated the slave trade or curtailed slavery itself. And, they asserted, such a charter could never win acceptance at home. In part they were bluffing. In fact, constraints against slavery had wide popular appeal in the expanding backcountry of the Deep South, where independent farmers outnumbered planters, ministers questioned slavery, and pioneers wanted national support in confronting powerful Indians.

Yet few delegates challenged the proslavery posture, possibly because strong antislavery opinions could have prolonged or even deadlocked the convention. The weary delegates were eager to complete their work and fearful of unraveling their hard-won consensus. Rather than force the matter, even those who disapproved of slavery rushed to compromise. In doing so, they heaped a huge burden on generations of Americans to come. Southern delegates dropped their protests against giving Congress the power to regulate international shipping. In exchange, the framers approved a clause protecting the importation of slaves for at least 20 years. They also added a provision governing fugitive slaves that required the return of "any person held to service or labor." Through a calculated bargain, delegates had endorsed slavery and drawn the South into the union on terms that suited that region's leaders. The word *slave* never appeared in the finished document.

In early September, the convention members put the finishing touches on their proposal and prepared to present it to the public. Most still had qualms about the document they had created and wondered whether Americans would accept it. Winning state-by-state approval would involve an uphill battle, especially given the delegates' resistance to the idea of a bill of rights. George Mason, who had drawn up Virginia's Declaration of Rights 11 years earlier, reminded members that such a set of guarantees "would give great quiet to the people." But in the convention's closing days, fellow delegates voted down his suggestion overwhelmingly.

Without a bill of rights, Mason and Gerry refused to endorse the final document, along with Edmund Randolph of Virginia. Other delegates who

In a crucial decision, members of the Constitutional Convention elected to protect the slave trade and preserve slavery. One African American who had already taken matters in her own hands was Mumbet, a slave in Massachusetts and widow of a Revolutionary War soldier. In 1781 she sued for her freedom on the grounds that "all were born free and equal." Her court victory proved a landmark in New England. Proudly, she took the name Elizabeth Freeman.

dissented had already departed. Of the 74 delegates chosen at the convention's outset, 55 actually attended the proceedings, and only 39 agreed to sign the finished plan. These small numbers made it more important than ever to end on a note of unanimity. By polling the state delegations instead of individual delegates, the document's authors shrewdly hid the three dissenting votes. This allowed them to assert, in article VII, that their task—framing a new constitution for the United States—had been approved "by the unanimous consent of the States present" on September 17, 1787.

Ratification and the Bill of Rights

Having negotiated an alternative structure for a strengthened central government, committed nationalists now faced their most difficult task: winning public acceptance for a document that defied existing law. After all, the proposed constitution ignored the fact that the Articles of Confederation—the document governing the United States at the time—could be amended only with the approval of all 13 states. Instead, the text drafted in Philadelphia stated that ratification (acceptance through voting) by conventions in any nine states would make the new document take effect in those places. Moreover, the proposed ratification process left no room for partial approval or suggested revisions. Each state, if it wanted to enter the debate at all, had to accept or reject the proposed frame of government as offered.

■ In 1788 newspapers tracked ratification of the new "federal superstructure" state by state. Massachusetts ratified the proposed Constitution in March—apparently aided by the Hand of God! New Hampshire provided the "ninth and sufficient pillar" in June, followed by Virginia four days later.

(Both images) Courtesy, American Antiquarian Society

The Campaign for Ratification

The Confederation Congress had acquiesced in allowing the convention to occur in the first place. Most congressional representatives had expected the meeting to produce proposals for amending the current government, not discarding it. But now that the Philadelphia conclave had ended, the Congress sitting in New York City balked at endorsing the revolutionary document. To avoid a lengthy and troublesome debate, proponents of the new constitution urged Congress simply to receive the frame of government as a possible proposal and then transmit it to the states without an endorsement. Congress did so on September 28, 1787, and the document's advocates portrayed the unanimous vote as an expression of approval.

Supporters had no time to lose because Pennsylvania's assembly was set to adjourn on the next day. An early victory in that large and central state would be crucial in building momentum before an organized opposition developed. So they hired a courier to rush the congressional letter of transmittal from New York to Philadelphia. There, the assembly faction dominated by Robert Morris quickly moved to schedule a state ratifying convention. When opposition members saw that they could not defeat the motion on short notice, 19 of them walked out of the chamber, hoping to prevent a vote that would begin the ratification the process. But proponents dragged back two of them to have enough members for a legal vote. Over the next three months, towns and counties elected delegates, a convention met, and Pennsylvania voted to approve the new plan. Delaware had already approved unanimously on December 7, and New Jersey and Georgia promptly followed suit. By the end of January, Connecticut had also ratified. Other states had called elections and scheduled conventions. Only Rhode Island, which had not sent delegates to the drafting convention, refused to convene a meeting to debate ratification.

By seizing the initiative early, the proponents of the new framework shaped the terms of debate. The drafters, anything but a cross-section of society, worked to portray themselves as such. They noted that their document began with the ringing phrase, "We the people of the United States," a last-minute addition by Gouverneur Morris of New York. And Madison told the public that the text sprang from "*your* convention."

Most important, in a reversal of logic and contemporary usage, the nationalists who supported the new constitution took for themselves the respected name of *Federalists*. They gave their opponents, a diverse assortment of doubters and critics, the negative-sounding term *Anti-Federalists*. The Federalists then used their ties to elite leaders and influential editors to wage a media war for public support. They dashed off letters, prepared pamphlets, and published essays praising the proposed constitution.

The strongest advocacy came from the pens of Alexander Hamilton and James Madison. The two men composed 80 essays for the New York press under the pen name *Publius*. John Jay added five more, and in the spring of 1788 the collection appeared as a book titled *The Federalist*. In the most famous piece, "Number 10," Madison challenged the widely accepted idea that a republic must be small and compact to survive. Turning the proposition around, he argued that minority opinions would fare better in a large nation, where diverse competing interests would prevent a unified majority from exerting control.

Dividing and Conquering the Anti-Federalists

Opponents of the new plan found themselves on the defensive from the start. Many of them had supported some government change, and most conceded the presence of economic difficulties. But the Federalists' dire predictions of impending chaos struck them as exaggerated. "I deny that we are in immediate danger of anarchy," one Anti-Federalist writer protested.

Richard Henry Lee, president of the Confederation Congress, condemned the Federalists as a noisy "coalition of monarchy men, military men, aristocrats and drones." Other prominent figures joined him in opposition: George Clinton in New York; Luther Martin, Samuel

Chase, and William Paca in Maryland; and Patrick Henry, George Mason, and Benjamin Harrison in Virginia. Though not always sufficiently forceful or committed, such notables became the spokespeople for a far wider array of skeptics.

Many critics of the proposed constitution protested the plan's perceived threat to local political power. Despite Madison's reassurances in Federalist Number 10, they believed that local and state governments represented voters more fairly and responded to their needs and concerns more quickly than a distant national authority could. For some critics this belief expressed a radical democratic principle; for others it represented their firm provincial bias. In short, Anti-Federalists were too diverse to speak with a single voice. Their ranks included many subsistence farmers living at a distance from any navigable river or urban market. These self-sufficient yeomen were joined by numerous war veterans who saw their rights to direct influence in republican government diminished by the proposed system. A wide variety of indebted people also opposed ratification, on the grounds that a strong national government would favor the interests of bond holders and foreign creditors ahead of the economic well-being of ordinary people.

But if Anti-Federalists were numerous in the remote countryside, Federalists predominated in the coastal commercial centers. Using a variety of tactics, they pressed their advantages in the fight to control state ratifying conventions. They lured prominent Anti-Federalist delegates with hints of high office in the proposed national government. They also intimidated less prominent figures by ridiculing them as Shaysite extremists. Meanwhile, in state after state, they forged coalitions linking large commercial farmers living near towns and rivers with aspiring artisans and city-based entrepreneurs. Through intensive politicking, they garnered approval in Massachusetts in February 1788, but only by a thin margin (187 votes to 168 in the ratifying convention). This commitment from "the Bay State" helped to sway Maryland in April, South Carolina in May, and New Hampshire in June.

In July 1788 celebrations hailed the new Constitution. "Columbus" on horseback led New York City's parade, followed by artisan groups. The silk banner of the pewterers proclaimed that under the Federal Plan, "All Arts Shall Flourish in Columbia's Land, And All Her Sons Join as One Social Band."

The Federalists could now claim the nine states they said they needed to implement their plan, and the approved Constitution became the law of the land. But in Massachusetts, they had triumphed only by promising to add a bill of rights, giving explicit written protection for valued civil liberties. They had to make similar assurances during the summer to secure slim majorities in Virginia (89 to 79) and New York (30 to 27). North Carolinians had voted down the proposed frame of government at their first ratifying convention because it lacked a bill of rights. A second North Carolina convention, called in 1789, withheld approval until a bill of rights had actually been introduced into the first Federal Congress as proposed amendments to the Constitution. In 1790, Rhode Island narrowly voted approval for the new framework (34 to 32) rather than risk being left in economic and political isolation.

Adding a Bill of Rights

In a society consisting of almost 3 million people, the franchise remained a limited privilege, open primarily to white men with property. All told, only about 160,000 voters throughout the country took part in choosing representatives to the state ratifying conventions. And only about 100,000 of these people—less than 7 percent of the entire adult population—cast votes for delegates who supported the Constitution. Fully aware of these slim numbers, the Federalists knew they would have to fulfill their promise to incorporate a bill of rights. Madison, goaded by Jefferson from his post in Paris, promised Virginians that he would push for the inclusion of specific rights as amendments to the Constitution. In making this promise, he had several motives. First, he hoped to ensure his own election to the nation's new House of Representatives. Second, he wanted to stave off the prospect that discontented states would call a second national convention "for a reconsideration of the whole structure of government."

In compiling a list of protections, or bill of rights, Madison drew from scores of proposals for explicit amendments put forward by the state ratifying conventions. He selected those, mostly dealing with individual rights, that could pass a Federalist-dominated Congress and would not dilute any of the proposed new government's powers. He set aside suggestions for limiting the government's right to impose taxes, raise a standing army, or control the time and place of elections. True to his word, he pushed 12 less controversial statements through the Congress as constitutional amendments, despite congressional apathy and opposition. Within two years, three-fourths of the states ratified ten of these short but weighty pronouncements. Hence, the first ten amendments—the Bill of Rights—quickly became a permanent part of the U.S. Constitution.

Many of the protections provided by the Bill of Rights harked back to lessons learned in the colonists' earlier struggle with Parliament. The ten amendments guarded the right of the people to bear arms, limited government power to quarter troops in private homes, and banned unreasonable searches or seizures. They also guaranteed crucial legal safeguards by ensuring the right to trial by jury, outlawing excessive bail and fines, and prohibiting "cruel and unusual punishments." The First Amendment secured freedom of speech and of the press, protected people's right to assemble and petition, and prohibited Congress from meddling in the exercise of religion. By securing these freedoms, Madison engineered a final set of compromises that ensured the acceptance and longevity of the Constitution he had done so much to frame.

Conclusion

The War for Independence exhausted the new nation. Defeating the British and managing the difficult task of demobilization and reconstruction consumed American energy and resources in the 1780s. So did the new western domain, where Americans had to balance prospects for national expansion against the military threats posed by European empires and Native American groups that asserted old and competing claims in the region. Also, economic differences set aside during the war reemerged in the years after Yorktown, so questions of wealth and property loomed large. How should the public debt be handled? Should slavery and the African slave trade be allowed to continue?

Over all these matters hovered the basic issue of governance. Independence from Britain meant an end to monarchy for Americans. They were keenly aware that they were sailing in uncharted waters as they experimented with constitution-making at every level. Acceptance of the Articles of Confederation in 1781 was a major accomplishment, and all assumed that the structure would demand further revision and adjustment. However, few could foresee that it would be set aside for a more centralized federal design within eight years.

The fierce debate over ratification of the new constitution raised fresh uncertainties about the long-term survival of the union. Much hinged on selection of the first president for the newly constituted nation. Only a few years earlier, Madison—then a young representative serving in Philadelphia—had met George Washington as the general journeyed south toward Yorktown in 1781. Now the fellow Virginian, 19 years Madison's senior, was the overwhelming favorite to become the first chief executive of the new republic.

Sites to Visit

Washington's Newburgh Headquarters

For 16 months in 1782–1783, the farmhouse of Jonathan Hasbrouck served as Washington's headquarters in Newburgh, New York, 12 miles north of West Point. The state of New York purchased the stone building on Lafayette Street in 1850 and opened it as the first publicly operated historic site in the United States.

Fraunces Tavern

Here, at 54 Pearl Street near the tip of Manhattan, Washington bid farewell to his officers in 1783. From 1785 to 1787, while New York served as the capitol city, the building held the departments of foreign affairs, the treasury, and war. Now it houses a museum with exhibits relating to the eighteenth century.

Mount Vernon

www.mountvernon.org/

During the nineteenth century, concerned women rallied to preserve Mount Vernon, George Washington's estate on the Potomac River. It is still maintained by the Mount Vernon Ladies' Association. If you cannot visit the plantation itself, eight miles south of Alexandria, Virginia, you can visit the Web site.

Independence National Historical Park in Philadelphia

Covering 45 acres and containing 20 buildings, this site includes Independence Hall, where the Constitutional Convention met in the summer of 1787. The Visitor Center is at Third and Walnut Streets. On the Market–Frankfurt Subway, use the 5th St. and Market station.

The Natchez Trace Parkway

Running 444 miles from Natchez, Mississippi, to the outskirts of Nashville, Tennessee, this one-time Chickasaw Indian trail became a pathway for boatmen returning north after floating their goods down the Mississippi. It is now a scenic road maintained by the National Park Service.

Congress and the Constitution

memory.loc.gov/ammem/bdsds/bdsdhome.html

The Continental Congress and the Constitutional Convention are the subjects of a rich Web site created by the Library of Congress in its American Memory series.

James Madison: His Legacy

www.jmu.edu/madison/madison.htm

The James Madison Center at James Madison University in Virginia maintains this Web site, which provides ready access to materials on Madison's life and interests, along with links to numerous documents and Web sites.

Historic Bartram's Garden

www.ushistory.org/tour/index.html

This Web site is part of LibertyNet's Virtual Tour of Historic Philadelphia. The garden itself, located at 54th Street and Lindbergh Boulevard, is run by the John Bartram Association, named for William's botanist father. Visit http://www.bartramtrail.org/ to learn more about backpacking Bartram's Trail through the South.

For Further Reading

General

Merrill Jensen, *The New Nation: A History of the United States During the Confederation, 1781–1789* (1948).

Richard B. Morris, *The Forging of the Union, 1781–1789* (1987).

Kenneth Silverman, *A Cultural History of the American Revolution* (1976).

Larry E. Tise, *The American Counterrevolution: A Retreat from Liberty, 1783–1800* (1998).

Gordon S. Wood, *The Creation of the American Republic, 1776–1787* (1969).

Beating Swords into Plowshares

Elizabeth A. Fenn, *Pox Americana: The Great Smallpox Epidemic of 1775–82* (2001).

Richard H. Kohn, *Eagle and Sword: The Federalists and the Creation of the Military Establishment in America, 1783–1802* (1975).

Henry F. May, *The Enlightenment in America* (1976).

George R. Stewart, *Names on the Land*, 4th ed. (1982).

Competing for Control of the Mississippi Valley

Gregory Evans Dowd, *A Spirited Resistance: The North American Indian Struggle for Unity, 1745–1815* (1992).

R. Douglas Hurt, *The Ohio Frontier: Crucible of the Old Northwest, 1720–1830* (1996).

Peter S. Onuf, *Statehood and Union: A History of the Northwest Ordinance* (1987).

John Sugden, *Blue Jacket: Warrior of the Shawnees* (2000).

Arthur Preston Whitaker, *The Spanish American Frontier, 1783–1795* (1927, reprinted 1969).

Creditors and Debtors

E. James Ferguson, *The Power of the Purse: A History of American Public Finance, 1776–1790* (1961).

Jackson Turner Main, *The Anti-Federalists: Critics of the Constitution, 1781–1788* (1961).

Edmund S. Morgan, *Inventing the People: The Rise of Popular Sovereignty in England and America* (1988).

David P. Szatmary, *Shays' Rebellion: The Making of an Agrarian Insurrection* (1980).

Drafting a New Constitution

Charles A. Beard, *An Economic Interpretation of the Constitution of the United States* (1913).

Donald A. Grinde, Jr., and Bruce E. Johansen, *Exemplar of Liberty: Native America and the Evolution of Democracy* (1991).

Leonard W. Levy and Dennis J. Mahoney, eds., *The Framing and Ratification of the Constitution* (1987).

John P. Kaminski, ed., *A Necessary Evil? Slavery and the Debate Over the Constitution* (1995).

Jack N. Rakove, *Original Meanings: Politics and Ideas in the Making of the Constitution* (1996).

Ratification and the Bill of Rights

Akhil Reed Amar, *The Bill of Rights: Creation and Reconstruction* (1998).

Saul Cornell, *The Other Founders: Anti-Federalism and the Dissenting Tradition in America, 1788–1828* (1999).

Michael Kammen, *A Machine That Would Go by Itself: The Constitution in American Culture* (1986).

Robert A. Rutland, *The Ordeal of the Constitution: The Antifederalists and the Ratification Struggle of 1787–1788* (1966).

Garry Wills, *Explaining America: The Federalist* (1981).

Online Practice Test

Test your understanding of this chapter with interactive review quizzes at

www.ablongman.com/jonescreatedequal/chapter8

Additional Photo Credits

Page 255: CORBIS
Page 260 (bottom): The American Numismatic Society
Page 263: The Natural History Museum, London
Page 281: Susan Anne Livingston Ridley Sedgwick, *Elizabeth "Mumbet" Freeman*, 1842. Courtesy of the Massachusetts Historical Society (MHS image #0028)
Page 284: Collection of The New-York Historical Society
Page 285: Abby Aldrich Rockefeller Folk Art Center, Williamsburg, VA

Revolutionary Legacies, 1789–1803

Joshua Johnson, *Portrait of a Cleric*, c. 1805–1810. Bowdoin College Museum of Art, Brunswick, Maine (Acc. #1963.490). Museum Purchase, George Otis Hamlin Fund

■ *Portrait of a Cleric*, c. 1805–1810 by Joshua Johnson

THE AMERICAN REVOLUTION DESTROYED ONE INDIAN CONFEDERATION AND LED TO THE creation of another. The Six Nations of the Iroquois Confederacy—which consisted of the Seneca, Cayuga, Oneida, and Mohawk nations of present-day New York state had suffered greatly during the war. Then, in the late 1780s, some tribal members migrated westward and northward, away from their ruined fields and still smoldering villages. Regrouping in Detroit, they sought to forge a new political alliance, this time with other Indians living along the Ohio River and in the Great Lakes region. Mohawk leader Joseph Brant (born Thayendanegea) urged the Algonquians, Shawnees, Delawares, Miamis, and Weas, among others, to join in common purpose, to resist U.S. territorial aggression, even as each group retained its separate identity. Together, he claimed, western Indians could "eat out of one bowl with one spoon." Unity would bring strength, he explained: "Whilst we remain disunited, every inconvenience attends us. The Interest of any one Nation should be the Interests of us all, the welfare of the one should be the welfare of all the others."

The European Americans were determined to rid themselves of the persistent military threat posed by Indian and British forces in the Northwest Territory and so launched a concerted campaign against Indians in the area that is present-day Ohio, Indiana, and Michigan. Under the leadership of Miami chief Little Turtle (Michikinikwa), and with support from the British, this Ohio Confederacy held off the advances of the American army. In August of 1794 the forces of General "Mad" Anthony Wayne overwhelmed those of Little Turtle. The Ohio confederation of Indians lay in ruins until a new generation of leaders arose.

Artist Gilbert Stuart painted this portrait of Mohawk leader Joseph Brant, born Thayendanegea, in 1786.

The Ohio Confederacy offers some intriguing parallels to the coalition of colonies during the Revolution and to the union of the states afterward. Before the Revolution, Benjamin Franklin had marveled at the cohesion of the Six Nations (the precursor of the Confederacy), drawing inspiration from the Indians' example. He noted, "If Six Nations of Ignorant savages" could create a union, then 13 colonies led by white men should be able to do so also. Patterns of leadership in the Confederacy were in some ways similar to those of the Patriots. Joseph Brant, in his call for unity, was the Thomas Jefferson—the political theorist—of the Confederacy. Little Turtle was its George Washington, a leader skilled in both political negotiation and military warfare.

Soon after the war, Brant pointed to lessons that the Indians learned from the United States in creating the Ohio Confederacy: with political unity came military strength. Indians, like the colonists, sought to overcome regional and cultural differences among themselves. In both cases, disparate groups found common ground in their fight against a common enemy—Great Britain in the case of the thirteen colonies, the United States in the case of the Ohio Confederacy.

Indians and European Americans soon discovered that neither the Ohio Confederation nor the new United States could function as completely independent political entities. In the early 1790s the Indians relied heavily on the British for guns and artillery. And until 1815, the United States found itself mired in European conflicts, its trade and domestic politics shaped by ongoing wars between France and Britain.

From 1775 to 1800, the Great Lakes region, or Northwest Territory west of the Appalachian Mountains and east of the Mississippi River, was a vast middle ground, where Indian villagers coexisted with British traders and French trappers. The cultures of these groups intermingled. For example, Brant had visited England in the mid-1770s, and he had been educated at a Christian school in Connecticut, so he was comfortable with certain European and American customs related to dress and diet. After the Revolution, the incursion of European American settlers into this "middle ground" disrupted Native hunting practices. Squatters from the East did not want only to cultivate the land; they wanted to own it. Violence escalated in an endless cycle of raids and retaliation. The U.S. citizens who settled in the area that is today Michigan, Indiana, Ohio, and Kentucky—the trans-Appalachian West—were the vanguard of the new, expanding republic. At the same time, they drew the army of the infant nation into a costly, bloody war.

One U.S. official labeled these European American migrants "white savages," suggesting that they would make more trouble for the country than the "tawny ones" would. Indeed, the Revolution had spawned a number of new groups who would challenge colonial ideas about race, gender, wealth, and standing in the community. White settlers were being compared to Indians in the Northwest Territory. In New England and the Upper South, another new class—free people of color—struggled to assert their rights. Throughout the colonies, some women maintained a high degree of political engagement; New Jersey even granted well-to-do women the right to vote, if only for a brief period. Artisans also sought to wield new political clout. "White savages," free blacks, women voters, artisan–politicians—they all revealed both the social tensions mounting in the new republic and the promise it offered to these same groups.

> *The Revolution had spawned a number of new groups who would challenge colonial ideas about race, gender, wealth, and standing in the community.*

The country's natural landscape and resources, as well as its sheer size, shaped both economic and political development. Leaders continued to disagree over whether such a huge country could remain a unified republic of well-informed voters. James Madison argued that a large population dispersed over a wide area would prevent any single group from tyrannizing smaller and diverse groups. Regional economic activity—cotton cultivation in the South and commercial development in the North—demonstrated the young nation's potential as a producer of goods. Also, the country's physical expanse allowed people to leave their homes in the East, migrate, regroup, and begin life anew in the West. Geographic mobility remained a hallmark of the American experience.

The first census of the United States, conducted in 1790, tallied 4 million people. Of this number, 750,000 were black. People of various ethnicities clustered together in pockets throughout the states. German-born people accounted for one-third of all Pennsylvanians, and almost one-fifth of New York residents were Dutch. Numbers of Northerners and Southerners were about equal. However, ethnic and regional differences proved less significant in shaping the emerging two-party system than the persistent split between urban-based merchants and rural interests such as southern planters. Moreover, policy differences between these wealthy propertied white men—proponents of a strong federal government versus supporters of states' rights and local authority—could not account for all the domestic turmoil that rocked the young republic in its early years. The Revolution unleashed enormous creative energy as some people, unfettered by restrictions imposed by the Crown, pursued new economic opportunities. In contrast, many artisans and small farmers continued to stagger under a burden of debt and new federal taxes. For them, the Revolution was a betrayal of their vision for America.

The impulse for association so evident in the U.S. union of states and in the Indians' Ohio Confederacy permeated everyday American life. In effect, ordinary people put into practice the grand theories of the Revolution. Exhorting their brothers and sisters to join in religious fellowship, revivalists formed new spiritual communities. Reform groups wrote constitutions for themselves in an effort to commit their principles to paper. Temperance advocates joined together and called on men and women to cast off the tyranny of drink; the reformed drunkard was considered as noble as the patriot.

Most dramatically, opponents of slavery kept alive the rhetoric and the ideals of the Revolution. In 1800 Gabriel, an enslaved blacksmith in Richmond, Virginia, plotted a rebellion to seize the city. His actions gave voice to the egalitarian principles articulated in Philadelphia in 1776 and then in Saint-Domingue in 1791, when slaves had staged a bloody revolt against their French masters. (In 1804 they renamed the country Haiti.) Gabriel's rebels used the words of the Founding Fathers to justify their actions, rallying around the cry, "Death or Liberty." One even compared himself to George Washington in his struggle to "obtain the liberty of [his] countrymen." Gabriel's plans to kill all whites except abolitionists failed when informants betrayed him to Richmond authorities. Yet Gabriel's rebellion, even though unsuccessful, is indicative of the struggle of almost all Americans, regardless of creed or color, wrestling with the legacy of the Revolution.

Competing Political Visions in the New Nation

In the first two decades of the life of the new nation, domestic politics remained entwined in relations with the great European powers. For all their bold talk of freedom and liberty, the heirs of the Revolution continued to formulate public policies based upon the models offered by Great Britain and France specifically. Some Americans found much to admire in British traditions of social order and stability, traditions shaped by a strong central authority in the form of a monarchy. Other Americans derived inspiration from the French Revolution, which began in 1789; they believed that, for all its bloody excesses, the revolution represented an ideal of true democracy, an ideal at odds with entrenched privilege in the form of monarchies and aristocracies. The British model appealed to Federalists, supporters of a strong central government. In contrast, the French model appealed to Anti-Federalists, soon to be called Democratic-Republicans, supporters of the rights of the states and of the active participation of ordinary citizens in politics. These divergent views shaped both foreign and domestic policy in the 1790s.

Within this contentious atmosphere, George Washington assumed the presidency in 1789, backed by the unanimous endorsement of the Electoral College. Even today, he has the distinction of being the only president in U.S. history to be elected unanimously. The early days of his administration provided some evidence that even his political foes shared his core beliefs. Support for Washington appeared to be widespread: When the new president traveled from his home in Virginia to the capitol in New York, cheering throngs of citizens lined the route, and parades of artisans marked celebrations in the largest towns.

Neither the ratification of the Constitution nor Washington's election silenced the continuing debate over civil liberties and the nature of the national government. Responding to the concerns of the Anti-Federalists, Congress quickly passed ten amendments, collectively called the Bill of Rights, to the Constitution. Ratified by the necessary number of states in 1791, the

J.I. Morton, *Washington's Reception By The Ladies On The Bridge At Trenton, NJ, April 1789: On His Way To New York To Be Inaugurated First President Of The United States, 1845. Museum of the City of New York, The Harry T. Peters Collection (56.300.847)*

WASHINGTON'S RECEPTION BY THE LADIES, ON PASSING THE BRIDGE AT TRENTON, N.J. APRIL 1789, ON HIS WAY TO NEW YORK TO BE INAUGURATED FIRST PRESIDENT OF THE UNITED STATES.

■ Founders of the new nation identified citizenship with economic independence. By this definition, women, children, slaves, and others dependent on property owners could not become citizens. However, drawing on their privileged status, white women sought to carve out a place for themselves in the young republic. This scene shows the women and girls of Trenton, New Jersey, greeting the newly elected president George Washington en route to his inauguration in New York City, the temporary capital. The girls sang as he passed by, "Virgins fair and Matrons grave,/Those thy conquering Arms did save."

amendments were intended to protect white men from the power of government, whether local, state, or national. The Judiciary Act of 1789 established a national, federal court system that included a five-member Supreme Court and the office of attorney general, charged with enforcing the nation's laws. The new republic was taking shape as the founders had hoped. It would be a nation of laws, with the executive, legislative, and judicial branches of government checking one another's power.

Like other political leaders of the time, Washington believed that ideological differences between political leaders should never become institutionalized in the form of separate political parties. These leaders believed politicians should debate issues freely among themselves, without being bound by partisan loyalty to one view or political candidate over another. However, by the late 1790s, the intense rivalry between Alexander Hamilton, Washington's secretary of the treasury, and Thomas Jefferson, his secretary of state, had produced a two-party system that proved remarkably durable. Representing two competing political visions, Hamilton and his supporters (known as Federalists) and Jefferson and his supporters (called Democratic-Republicans) disagreed on foreign diplomacy and domestic economic policies. Hamilton advocated a strong central government that would promote commerce and manufacturing. In contrast, Jefferson favored states' rights bolstered by small, independent farmers who would serve as the nation's moral and political center. These opposing viewpoints represented a continuation of the debate over the proper role of government, a debate that had shaped the Constitution. The Democratic-Republicans were the political heirs of the Anti-Federalists, and the Federalists continued to support the power of the federal government.

In 1792 Washington ran for and won a second term, although his rivals for office (his own vice president, John Adams, and New York governor George Clinton) all lacked party designations in the contest. Four years later, Washington declined to run for a third term. His successor was John Adams, an unabashed Federalist who rankled Jefferson and other more egalitarian-minded citizens. Between 1789 and 1800, the clash between the Federalists and the Democratic-Republicans reverberated on the high seas, in Indian country, and in the halls of Congress.

Federalism and Democratic-Republicanism in Action

In 1793, France and England went to war over territorial claims in Europe and the West Indies. At the outbreak of the war, President Washington issued a Neutrality Proclamation. The United States, he declared, would remain on the sidelines of the conflict. Nevertheless, the two combatants drew the new country into the struggle, and few Americans could resisit taking sides.

In the 1790s many Americans followed closely the dramatic events unfolding in France. At first, U.S. support for that country's revolution was widespread; by imposing constitutional constraints on their king, Louis XVI, the French seemed to be engaged in a heroic struggle, much like that of the Patriots of 1776 who had challenged the absolute power of the English crown. However, in 1792, French revolutionaries beheaded the king and launched what came to be known as the Reign of Terror, executing aristocrats and presumed opponents of the revolution— wealthy people tied to the monarchy through kin ties and economic interests.

In the United States, public opinion toward the revolution shifted in response to the Reign of Terror. Many Americans abhorred the carnage. In their eyes, the blood-soaked Place de la Concorde in Paris, where heads rolled off the guillotine platform and into baskets with the rhythmic precision of drumbeats, represented the end of order and humanity. Federalist politicians hoped to take advantage of these views, claiming that the bloody excesses of the French Revolution represented an argument in favor of a moderate and stable central government for the United States, one like that of Great Britain.

Tensions between France and the United States took a turn for the worse when France's first envoy to the United States, Citizen Edmund Genet, ignored the Neutrality Proclamation and tried to enlist American support for French designs on Spanish Florida and British Canada. Genet was eager to raise an army among Americans who lived on the borders of these territories. The French thought they would find support among men who hoped to free the Mississippi River from Spanish control and open it to U.S. commercial interests.

Nor did Britain endear itself to its former American subjects during these years. Pursuing French military forces in 1793, the British navy seized 300 American merchant ships plying the West Indian seas, forcing American sailors into service. In a practice known as impressment, British sea captains boarded American ships and captured sailors at gunpoint. England claimed that it was simply reclaiming its own sailors, who had deserted from the Royal Navy in response to U.S. captains who offered them higher wages. Meanwhile, along the United States' northern border, British officials were supplying the Indians of the Ohio Confederacy with guns, alcohol, and encouragement in their fight against the Americans. Nevertheless, Alexander Hamilton and the Federalists continued to proclaim their support of Britain against France. These proponents of strong central government feared that the French would aid and encourage violent anti-Federalist tendencies, such as those that had motivated Shays's Rebellion in 1786. Thomas Jefferson and other Democratic-Republicans condemned the French Reign of Terror but admired the French spirit embodied in their motto: *egalité* and *fraternité* (equality and brotherhood).

> *As secretary of the treasury, Hamilton took bold steps to advance the commercial interests of the new nation.*

As secretary of the treasury, Hamilton took bold steps to advance the commercial interests of the new nation. Hamilton wanted the wealthy to invest in American rather than European manufacturing enterprises. He believed that if government promoted a robust economy that benefited successful businesspeople and investors, then, eventually, the poorest people would prosper as well. For example, tariffs protecting domestic manufacturers would provide employment to artisans. In 1789, Hamilton persuaded Congress to enact the first U.S. tariff on imported goods to encourage home manufactures and to raise money for the treasury. (Between 1790 and 1860, the tariff yielded two-thirds of the national government's income.)

Hamilton also sought to strengthen the federal government through monetary policy. At his prodding, in 1790 Congress agreed to fund the national debt—that is, to assume responsibility for repaying the government's creditors and for paying the interest on it (a total of $54 million). It also assumed responsibility for debts that the individual states had incurred during the Revolution. To pay for all this, federal officials stepped up debt collection and imposed new taxes on individuals. In 1791 Congress also issued a 20-year charter to the first Bank of the United States. Hamilton had argued that this institution, modeled after the Bank of England, would help stimulate the economy by circulating surplus funds held by the government. He intended that the bank would serve the interests of urban-oriented manufacturers.

In his "Report on the Subject of Manufactures" (1791), Hamilton argued that factories stimulated economic growth. They used labor-saving machinery, promoted foreign emigration, and freed the United States from dependence on European-made goods in times of war, he pointed out. They also spurred a demand for consumer products and furnished "greater scope for the diversity of talents and dispositions which discriminate men from each other." Hamilton also advocated the employment of poor women and children in factories. He especially admired the way British employers hired women and children in their own textile mills.

Ralph Earl, *Elijah Boardman.* The Metropolitan Museum of Art. Bequest of Susan W. Tyler, 1979. (1979.395)

■ **Elijah Boardman of New Milford, Connecticut, poses at his desk in 1789. The portrait highlights Boardman's success as a merchant. His business prospered because wealthy Americans wanted to dress fashionably, as he did, with his ruffled sleeves, silk stockings, and fancy shoe buckles. In the background are some of the colorful, luxurious fabrics he sold. By the late eighteenth century, New England merchants were at the center of a thriving worldwide exchange of goods between Europe, the United States, and China. Their profits helped to finance the country's industrial revolution.**

An advocate of agricultural interests and the power of individual states, Jefferson disagreed with Hamilton on all these issues. Jefferson bitterly opposed the Bank of the United States, arguing that only the states could issue charters for financial institutions. He favored a lower tariff, arguing that high-priced imports hurt farmers and other small consumers. More generally, Jefferson objected to the idea that fiscal policy should serve as a tool for nation building. The leader of the Democratic-Republicans believed that the government should not interfere in the lives of its citizens by imposing higher taxes on individual households or on imported goods. He was not interested in extending government aid to manufacturers or other businesses. According to Jefferson, governments, like individuals, should exercise restraint in their spending and should avoid accumulating debt. Hamilton and Jefferson's opposing views of government shaped the American political party system for generations to come.

Planting the Seeds of Industry

When the "Report on the Subject of Manufactures" came out, in 1791, New England was already moving in the direction that Hamilton advocated. That same year, Samuel Slater, a 21-year-old English inventor, arrived in the United States. With financial support from Moses Brown, a wealthy merchant of Providence, Rhode Island, Slater constructed the first cotton thread spinning machine on American soil. To launch his Steam Cotton Manufacturing Company, Slater hired seven boys and two girls (between ages 7 and 12) to operate the machinery.

Nevertheless, during the late eighteenth century, most manufacturing took place in individual households. For example, working in sheds called ten footers (so called because of their length), master shoemakers employed journeymen (skilled workers) and apprentices (young boys learning the trade) as well as their own wives and children. Throughout New England and the Mid-Atlantic, families processed wheat, pork, hides, and cheese and made soap, candles, and leather. From 1800 to 1810, Philadelphia textile factories turned out 65,000 yards of cloth annually, but households in the region produced nearly four times that much. These small home-based producers shared similar values with yeoman (small property-owning) farmers; both groups prized property ownership and the independence of their households.

In 1793 Massachusetts-born Eli Whitney invented the cotton gin. This machine gave a tremendous boost to both the southern plantation system and the fledgling northern industrial system. By quickly removing the seeds from cotton balls and cleaning other impurities from raw cotton, the cotton gin fostered the emergence of a new cotton economy. Planters rushed to meet the nearly insatiable demand for cotton from mill owners in both England and New England. Southern slaveholders expanded their holdings into Alabama and Mississippi, where fresh, fertile lands beckoned. Between 1793 and 1815, annual cotton production soared from 3 million to 93 million pounds.

In the 1790s undeniable signs of an emerging manufacturing economy appeared, especially along the "fall line," the region where the Piedmont's hills meet the broad coastal plain. Stretching from New England to New York, New Jersey, and Pennsylvania, this area had all the ingredients for an American Industrial Revolution: water power from rushing rivers, a faltering agricultural economy that western producers would soon eclipse, capital from successful merchants, and a dense population to serve as both workers and consumers.

Many people marveled at U.S. energy, productivity, and diversity. Especially in the North, the sounds of industry attested to American ingenuity and ambition. On a visit to the United States in 1794, an Englishman named Henry Wansey found Boston "a very flourishing place, full of business and activity." Its docks groaned under "casks of sugar and rice, bags of cotton and wool, pipe staves, lumber, iron bars, bags of nails, and, in short, every article of commerce." The Boston Duck and Sail Cloth Manufactory, an imposing structure 180 feet long and two stories high, employed as many as 400 people. Boston and its environs also boasted distilleries and factories that turned out wallpaper, nails, woolen goods, carpets, and paper. Sawmills and flour mills dotted the countryside. Throughout the North, silversmiths, booksellers, hairdressers, and makers of toys, fine carriages, and furniture, among others, produced luxury goods and provided a variety of services.

Yet Wansey also saw evidence of labor problems to come. The expanding American economy yielded many jobs preferable to those of factory and domestic work, prompting high rates of labor turnover. In New York City, textile artisans brought over from Lancashire, England, proved unreliable. They left the factories at the first opportunity, eager to buy land of their own and thus "arrive at independence." And in Newark, New Jersey, wealthy women had trouble retaining domestic servants. Poorer women were eager to take advantage of economic opportunities that did not require them to wait on their social betters hand and foot. They resented the deference demanded of them in the domestic-employer relationship. When their employees "stipulated that they shall sit at table [and dine] with their masters and mistresses," the mistresses were horrified at this breach of social etiquette.

By the mid-1790s Hamilton and his supporters were praising the regional economic growth and specialization that protective tariffs nourished. In the South, the growing reliance

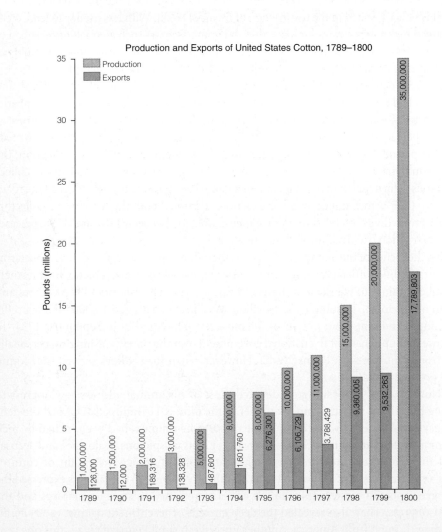

Production and Exports of United States Cotton, 1789–1800

■ **FIGURE 9.1**
EXPORTS OF UNITED STATES COTTON, 1784–1800

Sources: Stuart Brucey, *Cotton and the Growth of the American Economy, 1790–1860* (1967), pp. 14–15; Timothy Pitkin, *A Statistical View of the Commerce of the United States of America* (1835), p. 111.

■ This logo advertises the Hampshire machine. A precursor of the canal lock, the machine consisted of a pulley that carried a canal barge in a cart up an inclined plane. Invented in 1795, it was used on the Connecticut River in western Massachusetts. However, it proved too cumbersome in the long run. Most canals used locks, sections closed off with gates so that the water level could be raised or lowered.

on slaves for cotton, the newly crowned king of crops, further accelerated that growth. Tar, pitch, and turpentine produced in North Carolina, tobacco from Virginia and the Carolinas, and wheat grown in the Mid-Atlantic states, revealed the richness of the new nation's natural resources. Freed from colonial restrictions, the New England shipbuilding industry thrived, constructing masts, boards, planks, and barrels from the forests of Maine and New Hampshire. Miners extracted iron from the land; mariners pulled fish from the sea. Innovations in transportation facilitated growth. Since the Revolution, construction had begun on 11 canals. In addition, the Lancaster Turnpike, a 62-mile road, connected Philadelphia to its outlying areas. Privately financed by stockholders, the venture yielded a profit of 15 percent annually (because of tolls) for its investors and furthered settlement of the western part of the Mid-Atlantic region.

Echoes of the American Revolution in the Countryside

Despite Hamilton's optimism about the economy, Washington's administration faced violent resistance to its policies from certain quarters. In the West, American soldiers suffered a series of humiliating defeats in battles with Indians until they finally subdued Little Turtle and his warriors at the Battle of Fallen Timbers in 1794. That same year, farmers and grain distillers in southwestern Pennsylvania refused to pay their federal taxes, prompting Washington to send militiamen to quell the protest. Known as the Whiskey Rebellion, this uprising was sparked by the new 7-cents-a-gallon tax on whiskey. It was the culmination of a lengthy rural protest against Hamilton's "hard money" policy. By favoring hard currency (coinage) over the more plentiful paper money, this policy resulted in the constriction of financial credit. With less money to lend, creditors charged high interest rates for loans they did grant. Debtors such as small farmers had to repay loans when money was even scarcer than when they borrowed it. This meant they could not pay their taxes or repay their loans; as a result, many faced foreclosure on their property.

Until 1787, debtor-farmers in the Pennsylvania counties of Westmoreland, Bedford, and Huntingdon had managed to protect their holdings against seizure by winning the sympathy and support of local tax commissioners, juries, and judges. In some of these counties, as many as 43 percent of all taxable landowners were in danger of losing their property to creditors in the period 1782–1792. But by providing for a federal system of tax collection, the Constitution bypassed sympathetic local officials. Enraged by the new, efficient tax collection methods, which meant they would lose their land, Pennsylvania farmers blocked the roads leading into their communities. Road obstructions disrupted both the work of tax collectors and court proceedings intended to enforce their authority. Between 1787 and 1795, 62 cases of road obstruction occurred throughout the state.

Using the tactics of the Stamp Tax rioters a generation earlier, western Pennsylvania farmers also attacked the officials charged with collecting the whiskey tax. The tax hurt farmers who distilled grain into whisky and shipped it east for sale. They set fire to their offices and ran them out of town. To subdue the rebellion, Washington gathered 13,000 men from the states' militias and sent them to four of the most resistant counties in September 1794. To underscore the supremacy of the national government over the states, Washington personally led the troops into western Pennsylvania. However, when the soldiers arrived they found that the protesters had dispersed.

In November 1794 Washington devoted most of his annual address to Congress to defending his actions as commander-in-chief of the militia. He indirectly charged the defiant Pennsylvania distillers with treason. The protests, he claimed, had been incited by men who demonstrated "an ignorance or perversion of facts, suspicions, jealousies and accusations of the whole government." Yet Washington failed to gauge the extent of country dwellers' economic distress. By defying federal authority so openly, the farmers expressed the general grievances of westerners who felt underrepresented in state legislatures and the halls of Congress. They also revealed the deep current of resentment against the Federalists running through rural America. Another uprising in rural Pennsylvania—this one cen-

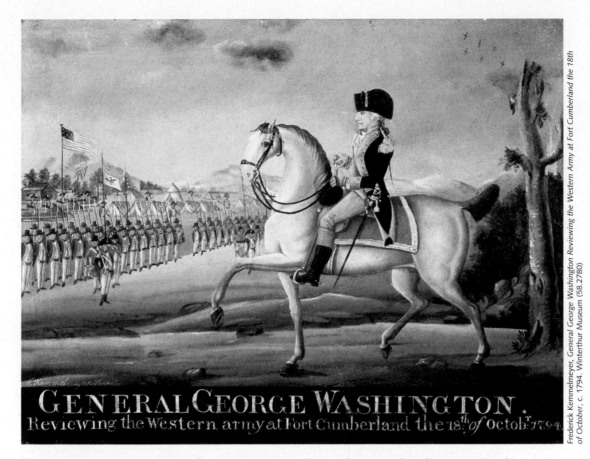

■ This 1794 painting seemingly evokes the American Revolution, when General Washington reviewed American troops. However, in this scene, President Washington is surveying some of the 13,000 state militiamen he commanded in an effort to suppress the Whiskey Rebellion in western Pennsylvania. Farmers objected to the new government tax on whiskey. With cries of "Liberty and No Excise," the protesters harassed federal tax collectors, reminiscent of anti–Stamp Act demonstrations three decades before. The Whiskey Rebellion melted away quickly. Critics objected to Washington's willingness to use such a huge force against the protesters.

tered in the southeastern part of the state in 1799—violently affirmed popular opposition to federal taxes. Protesters charged that "Congress and the government" intended to "rob the people" and reduce them to the status of European peasants, "poor as snakes." Yet, like the Whiskey Rebellion, these civil disturbances sputtered and then failed, leaving the authority of the federal government intact.

Securing Peace Abroad, Suppressing Dissent at Home

In 1795 the president sent Chief Justice John Jay to England to negotiate a key treaty. The negotiations were intended to address the problems of British forts in the Northwest, American debts owed to British creditors, British seizure of American ships and sailors in the West Indies, and the right of individual Americans to trade freely with European belligerents in wartime. Jay obtained a treaty but failed to extract meaningful compromises from England. Pro-British in his political leanings, he found it difficult to press that country for concessions. He was also hampered by the fact that Hamilton—in an effort to thwart the treaty—had supplied the British with secrets related to Jay's bargaining strategy.

In the treaty that bore his name and that the Senate eventually ratified, England grudgingly agreed to evacuate its northern forts and to stop seizing American ships. More ominously, Jay acquiesced to English demands that individual Americans pay the debts they had owed to English creditors since before the Revolution. The Americans believed that their victory in the war exempted them from longstanding financial obligation to their English creditors. The Democratic-Republicans took alarm at these developments. In their view, the new agreement humiliated all Americans and threatened southern planters in particular.

TABLE 9-1		
The Election of 1796		
Candidate	Political Party	Electoral Vote
John Adams	Federalist	71
Thomas Jefferson	Democrat-Republican	68
Thomas Pinckney	Federalist	59
Aaron Burr	Democrat-Republican	30

Western agricultural interests gained as a result of the Pinckney Treaty of 1795, negotiated by American diplomat Thomas Pinckney. The formal name of the agreement was the Treaty of San Lorenzo. Under this agreement, Spain allowed the United States to navigate the Mississippi River freely and to land goods at New Orleans free of taxes for three years. Yet this measure hardly placated the Democratic-Republicans, still smarting over what they considered Jay's humiliating treaty with the British.

With their eye on the next presidential election, the Democratic-Republicans began a vigorous campaign in favor of their own candidate, Thomas Jefferson. They contrasted Jefferson, the friend of the small farmer, with the Federalists' choice, Massachusetts's John Adams, advocate of a strong central government run by the well-educated and the well-born. Jefferson's party expressed particular dismay over Washington's haste to crush the rebellious Pennsylvania farmers in 1794 and over Jay's Treaty. Yet, backed by the New England states, Adams won the election, though narrowly. Because he received the second largest number of electoral votes—68 to Adams's 71—Jefferson became the new vice president according to the terms of the Constitution then in effect (Article II, Section I).

In his farewell address, printed in newspapers but not delivered in person, Washington reviewed his years in office. Most memorably, he warned against the "insidious wiles of foreign influence" and against alliances with foreign powers that could compromise America's independence and economic well-being. "Europe has a set of primary interests which to us have none or a very remote relation," he wrote. "Why, by interweaving our destiny with that of any part of Europe, entangle our peace and prosperity in the toils of European ambition, rivalship, interest, humor, caprice?"

Nevertheless, upon assuming the presidency in 1797, Adams found that European powers still had a hold on American domestic and foreign relations. France began to seize American merchant vessels (300 of them by mid–1797) in retaliation for what it saw as favoritism toward England in Jay's Treaty. In October of that year, the new president sent John Marshall and Elbridge Gerry to join the U.S. ambassador to France, Charles Pinckney, to negotiate a new treaty with France. However, French intermediaries (referred to only as X, Y, and Z in the Americans' dispatches) demanded that the three U.S. commissioners arrange for a loan of $12 million to France and pay a $250,000 bribe. Only then would the envoys be allowed to speak to the foreign minister, Charles Talleyrand. The sentiments of the American public, outraged at the idea of paying a bribe and willing to defend their new nation against all aggressors, were captured in the cry, "Millions for defense, but not one cent for tribute." Adams called the commissioners home.

In the next two years, tensions escalated on both the domestic and international stage. Federalists throughout the country called for war against France, and the Adams administration sought to shore up the country's military forces by creating a navy and the Marine Corps. Hoping to rid U.S. coastal waters of French "pirates," ships that were seizing American vessels, in May 1798 Congress authorized American ships to seize "armed vessels under authority or pretense of authority from the Republic of France." Over the next two years, the undeclared so-called Quasi War pitted the American navy against its French counterpart.

The major players in this drama—Adams, Talleyrand, and his successor, Napoleon—were all determined to avoid outright war. They succeeded. The two nations signed a treaty, called the Convention of 1800, in Paris. This agreement dissolved the Franco-American Alliance

PROPERTY PROTECTED. a la Francoise.

■ In 1798 Americans reacted indignantly to news that France had demanded a bribe and a large loan before its ambassadors would agree to meet with American envoys. In this political cartoon, America is portrayed as an innocent young woman assaulted by French diplomats. The incident precipitated an undeclared war on the high seas, called the Quasi War, between the two countries.

that the two nations had created during the Revolution, provided restitution for American shippers damaged by French aggressors, and secured a permanent peace between the United States and France. French privateers and naval vessels were removed from the U.S. coastline.

Conflicts continued to simmer on the domestic front. Soon after Adams's inauguration, the Federalist-dominated Congress moved to suppress the rising chorus of dissent among rural people, Democratic-Republican leaders, and newspaper editors. Such dissent, they charged, amounted to sedition—an act of insurrection against the government. Foreign influences were whipping up disloyalty among the populace and endangering the security of the new nation, the Federalists claimed. To eradicate this perceived threat, Congress passed the Alien and Sedition Acts in 1798. These new laws made it more difficult for immigrants to become resident aliens, gave the president the power to deport or imprison aliens, and branded as traitors any people (U.S. citizens included) who "unlawfully combine or conspire together, with intent to oppose any measure or measures of the government of the United States."

Even though the Alien and Sedition Acts were unconstitutional—they violated the First Amendment's guarantee of freedom of speech—the Federalist-dominated Supreme Court upheld them. Consequently, Democratic-Republicans were by definition guilty of treason, for they advocated policies and supported candidates opposed by the Federalists, the party in power.

Ten newspaper editors were convicted, and many others charged and jailed, under the Sedition Act. Their convictions suggested the increasing influence of newspapers as conduits of information and as shapers of strong political opinion. Between 1790 and 1810, the number of newspapers in the country ballooned from 90 to 370. But editors were not the only targets of the new laws against sedition. Some Democratic-Republican lawmakers also spent time in jail because their speech offended their partisan rivals. Matthew Lyon, a congressman, went to prison for suggesting that President Adams showed "unbounded thirst for ridiculous pomp, foolish adulation, and selfish avarice."

In 1798 and 1799 the state legislatures of Kentucky and Virginia issued a series of resolutions condemning the Alien and Sedition Acts. Outraged at what they saw as the Federalists' blatant power grab, the two legislatures proposed that individual states had the right to declare such measures "void and of no force." Thomas Jefferson (for Kentucky) and James Madison (for Virginia) wrote the actual resolutions. In declaring that states could essentially nullify federal laws, the two Founding Fathers unwittingly laid the theoretical framework for Southerners to ignore congressional authority in the future.

Civil Liberties Under Siege During Wartime and Other National Crises

Passed by Congress in 1798, the Alien and Sedition Acts severely curtailed freedom of speech among immigrants and native-born Americans alike. Supporters of these measures feared that the nation would soon be embroiled in a war with France and that all critics of the Federalist government, including Democratic-Republicans, must be silenced. During several other periods in American history, government officials have advocated the suspension of civil liberties on the grounds of national security. Immigrants and political radicals have proved especially vulnerable to these measures in times of crisis.

Soon after the outbreak of Civil War, in April 1861, President Abraham Lincoln suspended the writ of habeas corpus (that is, he denied arrested persons the right to petition for their freedom in federal court) in the states of Pennsylvania, Delaware, and Maryland and in the District of Columbia. Military authorities had the power to arrest people suspected of aiding the Confederacy and to detain suspects indefinitely without formally charging them with a crime. Two years later Lincoln extended the suspension to all other states under Union control.

During World War I, Congress passed the Entry and Departure Controls Act. The law made it easier for government officials to target noncitizens "whose presence was deemed contrary to public safety." During the Red Scare of 1919–1920, some Americans feared that the recent Russian Revolution would inspire the spread of communism in the United States. Officials cited the act in their attempts to deport thousands of immigrants, many of whom were labor and political radicals.

The outbreak of war with Japan in 1941 led President Franklin D. Roosevelt to sign Executive Order 9066. This measure resulted in the relocation of more than 110,000 West Coast Japanese immigrants and Japanese American citizens to internment camps. In two different cases, *Hirabayashi v. United States* and *Korematsu v. United States,* the Supreme Court upheld the government's position. However, in 1988 Congress awarded restitution payments of $20,000 to each of 60,000 surviving internees.

After World War II, tensions surrounding the Cold War led to suppression of the rights of U.S. communists and other people suspected of disloyalty toward the United States. Under the Internal Security Act of 1950, communists had to register with the government. Many other Americans lost their jobs because they expressed, or were charged with expressing, views critical of U.S. policies on any number of subjects, including civil rights and foreign affairs.

During the Vietnam War in the late 1960s and early 1970s, President Richard Nixon's administration sought to suppress antiwar sentiment in the United States. High-ranking officials, including Attorney General John Mitchell and Federal Bureau of Investigation head J. Edgar Hoover, monitored

People of Color: New Freedoms, New Struggles

In the late eighteenth century, North American elites demonstrated an emerging preoccupation with matters of race as a means of categorizing people and distinguishing groups from each other. Spanish officials in colonial New Mexico conducted a 1790 census that divided the population into a variety of groups based on ethnicity: Spanish, Indian, Mestizo (Spanish and Mexican Indian), *coyote* (Spanish and New Mexican Indian), mulatto (a person of African plus Spanish or Indian heritage), *genízaro* (children of acculturated Indians), and *color quebrado* and *lobo* (both designating some form of mixed-race parentage). In the United States, a 1790 naturalization law limited naturalized U.S. citizenship to "free white persons," thereby belying the oft-heard claim that all men were equal under the law.

The crosscurrents of the revolutionary legacy showed themselves most obviously in the status of African Americans after the war. To some extent, people's fate depended on where they lived and labored. Soon after the United States won its independence from England, all the northern states lay the groundwork for the abolition of slavery. In the Upper South, citing the egalitarian principles of the Revolution, some planters also freed their enslaved workers. But overall, economics rather than principles influenced these decisions. The North and Upper South had

Convicted leaders of the American Communist Party.

possession of a false driver's license or passport.

In response to the terrorist acts of September 11, 2001, President George W. Bush proposed that foreign nationals accused of terrorism be tried by military tribunals. Constitutional rules of evidence would not apply in these special courts. Meanwhile, the Justice Department enacted new guidelines allowing officials to eavesdrop on people in federal custody and to listen in on conversations between these prisoners and their lawyers. In October 2001 Congress passed the U.S.A. Patriot Act of 2001. This act expanded the government's authority to monitor and destroy terrorists' sources of funding, to wiretap and engage in other forms of surveillance activity, and to detain immigrants suspected of terrorism.

Americans who applaud these measures argue that "the Constitution is not a suicide pact" and that stringent measures are needed to protect the security of the United States and its citizens. Critics counter that the suspension of legal rights in the name of national security might eventually erode civil liberties for all Americans. ■

the activities of, and kept secret files on, antiwar activists.

In the late twentieth century, the rise of terrorist activity around the world resulted in several laws designed to detect and apprehend people suspected of such activity. The 1978 Foreign Intelligence Act, and its expansion in 1994, authorized electronic wiretapping and eavesdropping and covert physical searches in the effort to collect information related to terrorism. In 1996 Congress passed the Antiterrorism and Effective Death Penalty Act, which targeted immigration offenses, including

been accustomed to using bound workers of all kinds, including white indentured servants, youthful apprentices, and slaves. With changes in the economy, owners of grist mills and other enterprises now wanted paid labor. Paid laborers offered a flexible workforce; they could be hired and fired at a moment's notice.

Even free African Americans faced an uphill struggle in their efforts to achieve political rights and economic well-being. Free people of color found their employment options limited as white men competed with them for jobs and political representation. When they emerged from bondage, freed people created educational and religious institutions that affirmed their sense of community and shared heritage. However, chronic underemployment and persistent white prejudice, sanctioned by law, condemned many black men and women to poverty. Lacking full citizenship rights, they saw the Revolution as an unfulfilled promise rather than a glorious achievement.

Blacks in the North

For many northern blacks, the Revolution continued to resonate in their memories and their hopes. Gad Asher, seized from his home on the western coast of Africa around 1750, had been forced to work as a slave for a ship carpenter in East Guilford, New Jersey. During the Revolution, Asher had served as a soldier in his master's place. His owner promised him the money he would earn as a Continental soldier. Yet when Asher came home after the war, his master reneged on the promise. Eventually, Asher managed to earn enough money on his own to buy his freedom. In 1785 he and his wife had a son, Jeremiah. The youngster loved to hear his father and two other African American veterans talk of the "motives which had prompted them to 'endure hardness'" while fighting the British. Recalled Jeremiah many years later,

> I was so accustomed to hear these men talk, until I almost fancied to myself that I had more rights than any white man in the town. Such were the lessons taught me by the old black soldiers of the Revolution. Thus, my first ideas of the right of the colored man to life, liberty, and the pursuit of happiness, were received from these old veterans and champions for liberty.

Between 1790 and 1804, all the northern states abolished slavery. Some, such as New York and New Jersey, did so gradually, stipulating that the children of slaves must serve a period of time (as long as 28 years in certain states) before they could gain their freedom. In 1800, over 36,500 blacks in the North were still enslaved, and some 47,000 were free. Pennsylvania did not liberate its last slave until 1847. Yet throughout the North, blacks—whether enslaved or free— were only a small percentage of the total population, ranging from less than 1 percent in Vermont to almost 8 percent in New Jersey. Most black men worked as farm hands or manual laborers, most black women as domestic servants or laundresses. Nevertheless, some whites saw black men as rivals for their jobs and as a threat to the well-being of the white population.

At both the state and national levels, most free blacks lacked basic citizenship rights. In 1792, two years after Congress limited naturalization to white aliens, it restricted the militia to white men. State legislatures in New England and the Mid-Atlantic region imposed various other restrictions on free people of color. These measures limited blacks' right to vote, serve on juries, and move from place to place. Rectifying an "oversight" in their state constitutions, New Jersey and Connecticut later took special pains to disfranchise African American men. Massachusetts offered free blacks the most rights, including the right to vote (for men) and the right of blacks and whites to intermarry.

As slaves, blacks had served in a variety of skilled capacities in the North. Yet as free people, they faced mounting pressures in trying to live independently. Certain jobs, such as those with the federal postal service, remained closed to them by law. And municipal authorities refused to grant them licenses to ply their trades, such as wagon driving. Lacking the means to buy tools and equipment and the ability to attract white customers, many black artisans had to take menial jobs.

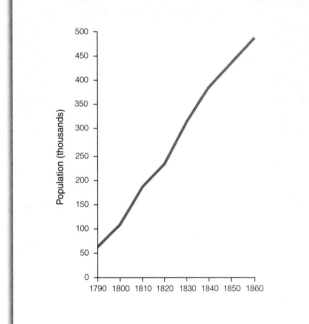

■ **FIGURE 9.2**
FREE BLACKS AS A PERCENTAGE OF TOTAL POPULATION IN SELECTED SOCIETIES
Source: The New York Public Library African American Desk Reference, p. 38.

Blacks' experiences in New York City are an apt example. In 1790 the free black population in that city amounted to about 1000 people; ten years later that number had more than tripled. In 1800 about 38 percent of male free heads of household in New York made their living as artisans. By 1810 that number had fallen to 29 percent, and it continued to drop in the years that followed. Increasingly, free black men took jobs as laborers, sailors, and domestic servants, and black women worked mostly as domestic servants and laundresses.

Still, free blacks in the North set about creating their own households and institutions. They moved out of the garrets and back rooms in houses owned by whites and set up housekeeping on their own. In Boston in 1790, one in three blacks lived outside white households;

Richard Alsop, *Cuffey near him. . .grasps his hand!* 1807. Engraving. Library Company of Philadelphia (Acc. #Am 1807 Als, 7487.O)

■ Massachusetts Governor John Hancock sponsored a celebration for Boston blacks in 1793. This picture appeared in a local periodical, *American Mercury*, accompanied by a satirical poem. The poet ridiculed blacks and the "motley scenes" they produced: "loud to anarchy their voices raise." New England blacks felt the tension between their newly won freedom and old forms of prejudice and subordination that endured after emancipation. Often isolated from each other in the workplace, they appreciated the opportunity to come together, enjoy each others' company, and, in this case, to dance, in the poet's words, "to the sweet Tune of Freedom born anew."

30 years later, eight in ten did so. In response to efforts of white Methodists to segregate church seating, Philadelphia black leaders formed the Free African Society in 1787. The first independent black church in the North, St. Thomas Protestant Episcopal Church, was founded in Philadelphia in the early 1790s. Absalom Jones, an African American preacher, headed the new church. In 1794 the Bethel African Methodist Episcopal Church, a branch of the Methodist denomination, was dedicated.

Black people also continued to celebrate their own festivals, some of which originated in the colonial period: Pinkster (based on the Jewish and Christian celebration of Pentecost) in New York and Training Day, Negro Election Day, and Coronation Day in New England. Usually conducted in late spring or early summer, these events featured parades in which black people came together to strut their finery, play drums and other African musical instruments, and proclaim their identity as a free people. In Massachusetts, blacks celebrated "Negro Election Day" by choosing their own "governors" and "judges," unofficial but influential community leaders (often African-born). In Providence, slaves and free people of color joined with small numbers of Narraganset Indians in Negro Election Day celebrations. The festivals gave men and women alike an opportunity to escape the confines of the workplace, even if only for a short time, and eat, drink, and dance with other people of color.

Manumissions in the South

In 1782 the Virginia state legislature lifted a 59-year-old ban on manumission, a process by which owners released selected people from bondage. Over the next ten years, approximately 10,000 Virginia slaves gained their freedom through manumission. Some planters believed

■ An anonymous artist captured this scene, probably in the slave quarters of a South Carolina plantation, in 1800. It is unknown what kind of entertainment or celebration the musicians and dancers are engaged in. The two men on the right are playing musical instruments of west African origin: a banjo and a *quaqua,* or skin-covered gourd used as a drum. On large lowcountry plantations especially, Africans and their descendants preserved traditional musical forms and social rituals.

The Old Plantation, c. 1790–1800. Abby Aldrich Rockefeller Folk Art Museum. Colonial Williamsburg Foundation, Williamsburg, VA

that the Revolution was the will of God, and they came to believe that slavery violated their religious principles. Some, taking to heart the rhetoric of the Revolution, objected to the glaring contradiction between the ideal of liberty and the reality of bondage. In 1802 a Maryland woman freed her slaves because, she said, the institution went against "the inalienable Rights of Mankind."

In the Upper South, especially, private manumissions dramatically increased the free black population. There, the emergence of a more diversified economy, including craft shops and grist mills, had lowered slave prices and encouraged abolitionist sentiment among some lawmakers, clergy, and slave owners. Between 1790 and 1810, the free black population in Baltimore increased from around 325 to over 5600.

Virginia planters George Washington and Robert Carter were unusual in terms of the numbers of slaves they manumitted (several hundred) and their efforts to ease the transition to freedom for people who possessed neither land nor financial resources. Providing for manumission in his will, Washington arranged apprenticeships for younger freed blacks and pensions for aged ones. In 1792 Carter granted his older slaves small plots of land. In general, however, newly emancipated men and women had difficulty finding employment as free workers. Nor was their freedom guaranteed: the 1782 Virginia manumission law provided that black debtors could be returned to slavery. The next year, Maryland went out of its way to stipulate that manumitted blacks were not "entitled to the rights of free men" except in their ability to own property. In southern cities, free people of color had to compete with both whites and enslaved laborers for work. The latter group, especially, formed a pool of cheap labor that limited the economic opportunities of all free workers, white and black alike.

Not all southern blacks achieved freedom through manumission. Some slaves, inspired by the growing community of free people of color in their midst and by the example of the black revolutionaries in the Caribbean island of Saint-Domingue in 1791, freed themselves. They ran away, heading for the anonymity of a nearby town or a haven such as Philadelphia or New York. Despite the growth in the free black population, the number of slaves actually increased in the Upper South, from over 520,000 in 1790 to almost 650,000 in 1810. In the South, slavery proved to be an extraordinarily durable institution.

Continuity and Change in the West

Later generations of Americans claimed that the western fringe of European American settlement—the ever-receding frontier—was the most American of all places. There, it was said, with a great deal of hard work, the rugged sons and daughters of the Revolution and their descendants could carve a living out of the land and prosper independently of landlords and creditors. Yet this image was more fantasy than reality. In certain key respects, western communities tended to duplicate their eastern counterparts. The opening of federal lands proved a boon for speculators, who extended credit to homesteaders and profited from the sale of small land parcels. Charged high prices for their purchases and forced to buy expensive supplies transported across the Appalachians, some settlers rapidly sank into debt. Westerners, like their eastern counterparts, needed money and business savvy—and in some cases political connections—to succeed.

Many native-born men and women and German and Scots-Irish immigrants who followed the Shenandoah Valley south brought with them, or bought, enslaved workers to toil on river docks and in cotton fields. The late-eighteenth-century trans-Appalachian West (modern-day Ohio, Indiana, Kentucky, and Tennessee) thus offered few African Americans a fresh start. Even in the Northwest Territory, where slavery was prohibited by law, African Americans faced the same kind of prejudice that shaped social relations in the East. Rather, than extend the bounds of liberty, western settlement solidified ideas about white supremacy.

From the Canadian border to Georgia, the trans-Appalachian West had become a cultural battlefield. European Americans warred against Indians, but Indian leaders also disagreed bitterly with one another about how to respond. Should they defend their hunting grounds to the last man, woman, and child? Seek refuge elsewhere? Capitulate completely to an alien culture? Or embrace some combination of these alternatives? The true history of the West during this period reveals the dangers of generalizing about "Americans," "Indians," and "foreigners." Yet one generalization does hold true: the abundance of natural resources and the vastness of the land, combined with the clash of cultures and the prevalence of armed men of all backgrounds, made life particularly dangerous in the borderlands.

Indians Wars in the Great Lakes Region

Many Indians residing in the Northwest Territory in the 1790s were refugees from the East, victims of the Revolutionary War. As they resettled in villages, they managed to retain some elements of their cultural identity. These groups included the Ottawas, Ojibways, Wyandots, Algonquians, Delawares, and what remained of the Iroquois Confederacy. They also included peoples who had long occupied the area that today is called the Great Lakes region and the Upper Midwest (Map 9.1): the Miamis, Weas, Piankashaws, Potawatomis, Menominees, Kickapoos, Illinois, Peorias, Kaskaskias, Fox, Winnebagos, Sauks, and Shawnees.

In the seven years immediately after the Revolution, thousands died in Indian–white clashes in this region. What caused this violence? By encouraging European Americans to stake their claim to the area, the Northwest Ordinance inflamed passions on both sides: whites' determination to occupy and own the land and Indians' equal determination to resist this incursion. In 1790, under orders from President Washington, Brigadier General Josiah Hamar led a force of about 1500 men into the Maumee River Valley in the northwest corner of modern-day Ohio. Orchestrating two ambushes in September, Miami chief Little Turtle and his men killed 183 of Hamar's troops, driving the general back in disgrace. The next year, Washington chose another officer, General Arthur St. Clair, to resume the fight. St. Clair's men met Little Turtle's warriors in November near the upper Wabash River and slightly south of the site of Hamar's defeat. During this engagement, 600 whites died.

Washington tried once more to find a commander equal to Little Turtle. This time he chose General Anthony Wayne, a Revolutionary War hero dubbed "Mad Anthony" for his

■ MAP 9.1

THE NORTHWEST TERRITORY After the Revolution, the Northwest Territory became a battleground. Indians—both long-term residents and newcomers—as well as European American squatters and speculators vied for control of the land. The Northwest Ordinance of 1787 provided for territorial governments before an area could apply for statehood. The present-day states of Ohio, Indiana, Michigan, Illinois, and Wisconsin were carved out of the Northwest Territory. All had gained statehood by 1848, but only after almost sixty years of bloodshed between Indians and U.S. troops in the region.

bold recklessness. Wayne mobilized a force of 3000 men and constructed a string of new forts as well. Alarmed by this new offensive, Little Turtle urged his warriors and the Ohio Confederacy to make peace. Instead, they chose a new leader, a warrior named Turkey Foot. When the anticipated encounter came in August 1794, at the British Fort Miami on the Maumee River (near the western shore of Lake Erie), the Indians found themselves surrounded. They sought refuge in the fort, but the British would not let them enter, refusing to become involved in a wider war with the Americans. Hundreds of Indians perished as Wayne's forces closed in.

The withdrawal of British support helped to doom the Ohio Confederacy, which was less a union of Indians than a lopsided alliance between Indians and their British benefactors. On August 3, 1795, 1100 Indian leaders met at Fort Greenville (in western Ohio) and ceded to the United States a vast tract of Indian land: all of present day Ohio and most of Indiana. Little Turtle helped negotiate the agreement.

Indian Acculturation in the West

Various Indian groups differed in their responses to the European Americans who settled among them or attempted to persuade—or force—them to "acculturate" by adopting the customs and habits of whites. According to European Americans, men farm and herd sheep and cattle; women milk cows, keep chickens, tend the garden, spin thread, and weave cloth. However, in the "middle ground" throughout the West, newly arrived settlers and indigenous peoples traded foodways, folk remedies, and styles of dress. Even Joseph Brant and Little Turtle picked and chose among European American (and, in Brant's case, English) cultural

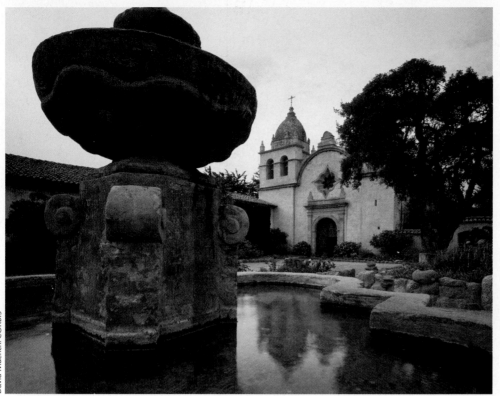

David Muench/CORBIS

■ Mission San Carlos Borromeo in Carmel, California. In the foreground is the mission's central courtyard. In the background is the *ranchería,* where Indians lived. In this and other missions along the California coast, Indians maintained separate residences in traditional-style dwellings. Even Indians who worked and prayed at the missions attempted to preserve their own customs related to clothing, food, and kinship and family relations.

traits. Little Turtle drank tea and coffee, kept cows, and shunned leather breeches in favor of white men's clothing. The fact that his wife made butter suggested that she was skilled in the ways of European American homemakers. Little Turtle himself appealed to Quaker missionaries to help the Miamis adapt to stock raising and the plow. The white population was advancing "like oil on a blanket," he pointed out, and the Indians were disappearing "like snow before the sun."

Adopting some habits of European Americans—for example, liquor consumption—amounted to self-destruction. On the "middle ground," alcohol was a prized trade item. Moreover, European Americans and Indians often used it to lubricate political negotiations and cultural rituals. Yet conflicts over liquor, and tensions vented under the influence of liquor, became increasingly common—and deadly. Some Indian leaders, such as Joseph Brant and Little Turtle, who came to view the drinking of alcohol as a full-blown crisis among their people, believed that Indians must reject the white man's bottle if they were to survive. Others placed their priorities elsewhere and continued to indulge in alcohol. In 1799 Seneca leader Handsome Lake (Skanyadariyoh) emerged from an alcohol-induced coma to proclaim *Gai'wiio,* or Good Message. This message urged Indians to accept certain elements of whites' culture (stock tending and individual homes) while retaining traditional rituals and languages.

But liquor was not the only crisis facing the Indians, as the experience of the Five Civilized Tribes in the southeastern United States revealed. This group included the Cherokee, Chickasaws, Chocktaws, Creeks, and Seminoles. The migration of whites into their hunting grounds had depleted their game supply and devastated their crop fields. After the Revolution, the Cherokees appealed to the federal government for aid. Some of the other groups, unable to hunt for food, took up agriculture. Men, using plows, replaced women, who had relied on hoes. Protestant missionaries encouraged Indian women to learn to spin thread and weave cloth.

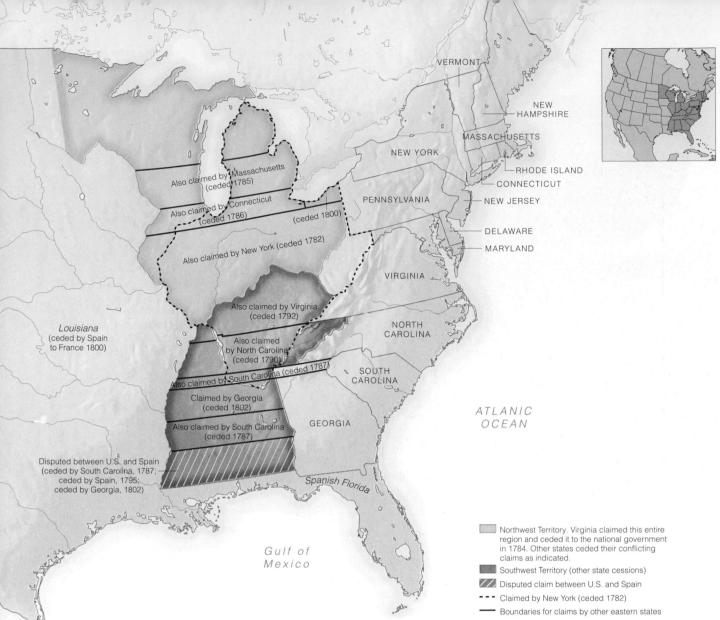

VERMONT

NEW HAMPSHIRE

MASSACHUSETTS

NEW YORK

RHODE ISLAND

CONNECTICUT

PENNSYLVANIA

NEW JERSEY

DELAWARE

MARYLAND

VIRGINIA

NORTH CAROLINA

SOUTH CAROLINA

GEORGIA

ATLANTIC OCEAN

Also claimed by Massachusetts (ceded 1785)

Also claimed by Connecticut (ceded 1786)

(ceded 1800)

Also claimed by New York (ceded 1782)

Louisiana (ceded by Spain to France 1800)

Also claimed by Virginia (ceded 1792)

Also claimed by North Carolina (ceded 1790)

Also claimed by South Carolina (ceded 1787)

Claimed by Georgia (ceded 1802)

Also claimed by South Carolina (ceded 1787)

Disputed between U.S. and Spain (ceded by South Carolina, 1787; ceded by Spain, 1795; ceded by Georgia, 1802)

Spanish Florida

Gulf of Mexico

Northwest Territory. Virginia claimed this entire region and ceded it to the national government in 1784. Other states ceded their conflicting claims as indicated.

Southwest Territory (other state cessions)

Disputed claim between U.S. and Spain

- - - Claimed by New York (ceded 1782)

—— Boundaries for claims by other eastern states

■ **MAP 9.2**
WESTERN LAND CLAIMS OF THE STATES   Several of the original thirteen colonies, including Massachusetts, Connecticut, New York, Virginia, South Carolina, North Carolina, and Georgia claimed land west of the Appalachian mountains. By 1802, these states had ceded their western lands to the federal government. The Land Ordinance of 1785 provided that this expanse be auctioned off in parcels no less than 640 acres each, with a minimum price of one dollar per acre—too expensive for many family homesteaders, thus opening the way for investors to purchase and profit. Hoping to raise money through land sales, the federal government did not object to speculation.

The southeastern groups only gradually accepted the idea of keeping livestock, for they retained cultural scruples against eating certain kinds of animals. The Cherokees, for example, believed that people would assume the characteristics of the animals they ate, so they discouraged the consumption of pork and other pig products. Yet in 1796, when a federal Indian agent toured Creek country, he noted signs of "civilization": black slaves (most of them runaways from southern plantations) hard at work in the fields and fences that protected crops from cattle and other beasts. The willingness of members of the Five Civilized tribes to accommodate themselves to European American law and divisions of labor allowed them to stay in their homeland and retain key elements of their cultural identity. Later generations of southwestern Indian leaders challenged this strategy of accommodation.

In southwest and far west borderland areas, Spanish officials met with mixed success in their attempts to convert Indians to Christianity and encourage them to engage in sedentary farming. For example, between 1772 and 1804, Spanish priests established five missions among the Chumash, hunter-gatherers living in permanent villages along the California coast. When large numbers of the Indians moved to these settlements, they forfeited their traditional kin and trade networks, and their distinctive culture began to fade. Birth rates plummeted due to disruptions in family life (more women than men lived in the missions), and mortality rates increased dramatically as the Spanish introduced new diseases.

In contrast, along the Texas Gulf Coast, the Spanish made little headway in their efforts to bring the Karankawas Indians into the missions. Members of this nomadic tribe arrived at the mission gates only when their own food reserves were low; in essence, the Karankawas simply included the missions in their seasonal migrations between the Gulf Coast and the coastal prairie.

Land Speculation and Slavery

The West was not necessarily a place of boundless economic opportunity for all people who settled there. When Americans poured into the trans-Appalachian West after the Revolution, they often carried alcohol and guns, staples of trade among all groups. These items proved a lethal mix, injecting violence into commercial and diplomatic relations among a variety of cultural groups. Moreover, land speculators sought to make large profits from family homesteaders forced to buy property at inflated prices. And too, many European American migrants brought their slaves west in a bid for economic self-sufficiency or profit-making, or both. For all these reasons, in several respects the West soon came to resemble society on the eastern seaboard, with its hierarchies based on class, ethnicity, and race.

Eager investors and creditors thwarted many homesteaders' quest for cheap land. Post-Revolutionary-era schemes such as the Ohio Company of Associates foreshadowed the significance of land speculation in shaping patterns of settlement and property ownership in the West. With backing from wealthy investors, the Ohio Company quickly bought up tracts of land and then sold parcels to family farmers at inflated rates. A similar venture was initiated in Georgia in 1795, when speculators bribed state legislators for the right to resell huge tracts to the west of the state, land that the state did not even own. The state legislature passed the so-called Yazoo Act (named for a Georgia river) because of these bribes. The act resulted in the defrauding of thousands of buyers, whose land titles were worthless.

By protecting slavery and opening up new territory to European America settlement, the new nation condemned southern blacks to a kind of legal bondage that stood in stark contrast to revolutionary principles. Many settlers relied on slave labor. By the late eighteenth century, Kentucky slaves numbered 40,000—more than 18 percent of the state's total population. In isolated settlements, where farmers owned just one or two slaves, African Americans faced a kind of loneliness unknown on large plantations in the East. In 1793, near Newport, Kentucky, slaves Moses and Humphrey informed their master, James Taylor, that "there are no colored people here, we have no women to wash for us, on Sundays we stalk about without being able to talk to anyone." Where white planters embraced new kinds of opportunity in the new territories, their slaves experienced backbreaking toil unrelieved by companionship or family ties.

Patterns of land use directly affected the spread of slavery into the West. Despite eastern planters' use of European soil conservation techniques (crop rotation, use of manure as fertilizer), many of them had to contend with depleted soil in the Upper South. Generations of tobacco growers had worn out the land, depriving it of nutrients. As a result, many growers

Courtesy, Museo de America, Madrid. Photo by Iris Engstrand

■ In 1791, an artist made this sketch of the wife of a Spanish soldier stationed at the presidio, or military garrison, in Monterey, California. Many elite Spaniards in the Americas went to great lengths to dress like their European counterparts. This woman is wearing the elegant dress, elaborate jewelry, and dainty shoes that befit her status. One eighteenth-century resident of New Mexico wrote that, despite the hot climate, European Americans "will go up to their ears in debt simply to satisfy their pride in putting on a grand appearance." However, most *nuevomexicanos* adopted some elements of Indian-style clothing, such as practical leather moccasins and garments made of buckskin and coarse woolens.

were forced to abandon tobacco. Some of them moved west into Indian lands (Mississippi Territory) to cultivate cotton. The scarcity of labor motivated slave owners to push workers to the limits of their endurance. Slaves prepared the ground for cultivation, rooted out tree stumps, and cleared brush. Then slaves followed the rhythms of the cotton-growing season: planting in the spring, hoeing in the summer, and harvesting in the fall. Slaves on cotton plantations worked in gangs under the sharp eye of a white overseer or black driver. Men, women, and children labored as human hoeing machines, growing as much cotton as quickly as possible. In contrast, slaves who worked in rice fields were organized under the task system: each day, once they completed a certain amount of field work, they were allowed to devote time to cultivating their own gardens and tending their own chickens. Whether working on a gang or task system, blacks and Indian captives of war remained vulnerable to certain Indian tribes such as the Cherokee, which actively practiced slavery.

Even many free people of color found a less than hospitable welcome in the West. In 1802 delegates to the first Ohio territorial convention moved to restrict blacks' economic and political opportunities, even though fewer than 400 were living in Ohio at the time. One proposal read that "no negro or mulatto shall ever be eligible to hold any office, civil or military, or give oath in any court of justice against a white person." Although slavery was outlawed in Ohio and other territories, blacks still lacked the right to vote. Soon after Ohio became a state in 1803, the legislature took steps to prevent the in-migration of free blacks altogether.

Several other Midwestern territories and states followed Ohio's example. In 1803 the territorial legislature of Indiana passed a "black law" prohibiting blacks or Indians from testifying in court against white people. Black families in the Northwest were also vulnerable to kidnapping: some white men seized free blacks and sold them as slaves to plantation owners in the South. Moreover, whites took advantage of poor blacks by "indenturing" their children. Under this arrangement, a white man or woman controlled the labor of a black youth for a stipulated number of years. In Indiana, terms of indenture for any black person could last as long as 90 years.

Shifting Social Identities in the Post-Revolutionary Era

The nation's founders had argued for an egalitarian society, one in which people prospered according to their talents and ambition. Of course, their definition of egalitarianism encompassed only white men. Still, it was a revolutionary idea and led to challenges of social hierarchies after the Revolution. These hierarchies included institutions such as the patriarchal (male-headed) family, established Protestant denominations, power systems based on social standing, and ideas about race and gender. Several writers applauded these leveling tendencies. They argued that authority of all kinds—fathers over families, clergy over congregations, political leaders over citizens—was suspect and counter to revolutionary ideas. Ordinary men and women penned letters to local newspapers, glorifying common laborers and questioning the claim to power of "the marchent, phesition [physician] the lawyer and divine [minister] and all the literary walkes of life, the Jutical & Executive oficeers & all the rich who live without bodily labour." This letter writer's creative spelling suggests that even people lacking in formal education felt free to voice their opinions on political issues of the day.

In the early nineteenth century, voluntary reform organizations multiplied across the nation, transforming the professions, the religious landscape, slavery, the rights of women, and a host of other American institutions. In the years immediately after the Revolution, both the possibilities and limitations of reform became clear. Some groups—for example, white working men—sought to advance their own self-interest without showing much concern for the plight of African American laborers. In other cases, people banded together to target the behavior of a specific group: drunkards, slave owners, the irreligious, or prostitutes. These moral reform groups welcomed diversity among members, as long as new converts supported the cause.

The Search for Common Ground

As people embraced a common cause with like-minded others, a variety of groups emerged. Manumission and temperance societies had appeared during the Revolution. Other kinds of associations sprang up and multiplied after the war. For example, in southwestern Pennsylvania, tax resisters formed the Mingo Creek Society. The organization offered mediation services for citizens who felt "harassed with suits from justices and courts, and wished a less expensive tribunal." In New York, 15 women formed the Society for the Relief of Poor Widows and Small Children. Often, free people of color in the North and South created new churches designated as "African," a testament to a shared heritage that predated their transportation to America and enslavement.

Americans redefined the family to accommodate new circumstances and ideas. Some whites who chose to live in Indian villages (known as white Indians) felt they had found new families. Wrote Mary Jemison, a captive and then willing member of the Senecas, "It was my happy lot to be accepted for adoption." She described her initiation ceremony in these terms: "I was received by the two squaws to supply the place of their brother in the family; and I was ever considered and treated by them as a real sister, the same as though I had been born of their mother."

In some instances the family metaphor extended to religious ties. Members of Baptist and Methodist congregations referred to themselves as brothers and sisters. They called their preachers "elder brother" or, in some places in the South, "Daddy." The Shakers, a sect founded by Englishwoman Ann Lee in the 1770s, forbade sexual intercourse between male and female members. In this group, the church itself replaced traditional family relationships.

Shaker Village at Harrodsburg, KY

■ Men and women participate in a Shaker worship service in New Lebanon, New York. The formal name of the church was the United Society of Believers in Christ's Second Appearance. The group's more familiar name derived from their peculiar worship style, which involved trembling and shaking. Founded in 1787, the New Lebanon community was the church's largest. Members of the group reconfigured traditional family relations. They forbade marriage but, like several other Protestant denominations, encouraged congregants to call each other brothers and sisters.

Artisan–Politicians and the Plight of Post-Revolutionary Workers

In the decades after the Revolution, residents of port cities along the eastern seaboard grew accustomed to public parades marking special occasions: a visit from George Washington, the ratification of the Constitution, the Fourth of July. Most of these parades consisted of groups of artisans marching together, carrying the banners of their respective occupations. As one example, the bricklayers' flag declared, "Both Buildings and Rulers Are the Works of Our Hands."

Proud of their role in the Sons of Liberty and other revolutionary organizations, bricklayers—along with tanners, carpenters, glassblowers, weavers, and other groups of artisans—proclaimed themselves the proud citizens of the new nation. In some respects, these groups resembled the guilds of Europe: members of one craft united and caring for one another in mutual obligation. In other respects, American worker organizations were unique, for they built on a distinct revolutionary heritage that stressed the equality of all (white) freeborn men. Master artisans in several cities—including Boston, Albany, Providence, Portsmouth, Charleston, Savannah, and New York—created organizations called the General Society of Mechanics and Tradesmen that brought together skilled workers from a variety of fields. The proliferation of newspapers let these artisans participate in a new, more open public forum. Such participation in turn helped gain them influence within local politics. In some towns, as many as 85 percent of adult men owned property of some kind and thus were eligible to vote. Indeed, artisans' organizations soon became quasi-political groups, extending their reach in ways that pre-Revolutionary trades-based associations had not.

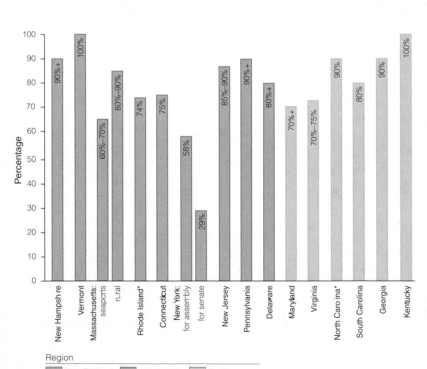

■ **FIGURE 9.3**
PERCENTAGE OF WHITE MEN ELIGIBLE TO VOTE IN THE UNITED STATES, 1792

Source: Robert J. Dinkin, *Voting in Revolutionary America: A Study of Elections in the Original Thirteen States, 1776–1789* (1982), pp. 36–39.

New Bedford Whaling Museum (#803)

■ After the Revolution and well into the early nineteenth century, African Americans, both enslaved and free, served as sailors in disproportionate numbers. This picture suggests the dangers faced by all men who labored on whaling ships. By the 1790s, American whalers were searching for sperm whales as far away as the South Pacific. These whales were the source of several prized substances, including sperm oil (a fuel), spermaceti (used to make candles), and ambergris (an ingredient in expensive perfumes). During the heyday of the sperm whale industry, American fleets were killing 10,000 whales annually.

Still, these organizations exhibited their own brand of elitism. Although commerce flourished in the 1790s, not all members of the laboring classes prospered. Journeymen in particular faced an uncertain future. In Philadelphia in the 1790s, half of the journeymen shoemakers eventually established their own shops, but only 10 percent of their tailor counterparts managed to do so. Dockworkers and other kinds of laborers struggled to find year-round employment. Meanwhile, more and more free men of color were drawn to sailing. Although they had little chance to rise within the ranks of a ship's command, they accepted the seafaring life because it was the steadiest work they could find.

As the country expanded and developed methods and systems of transport, the canal worker replaced the skilled artisan as the typical laborer. The diggers who constructed the canals of the early 1790s included men from all walks of life: part-time farmers, indentured servants, slaves, and white transients. Moving around in search of work, they led an unsettled existence that contrasted greatly with the more predictable life of urban artisans.

The plight of menial laborers (in the countryside and the cities) suggests the ironies that accompanied the decline of indentured servitude and the rise of the "free laborer." To be sure, master artisans attained a degree of economic independence that many other workers did not. But for men and women who lacked skills, money, and wealthy patrons,

A Sailmaker Discusses "Means for the Preservation of Public Liberty" on the Fourth of July, 1797

*U*rban skilled artisans (also called mechanics) played a significant role in the American fight for independence. In the years after the conflict, many artisans remained active in politics. They believed that the success of the new nation depended on the ability of its citizens to remain informed about and engaged in the political process.

In a speech delivered on July 4, 1797, a New York sailmaker, George James Warner, warned that citizens must strive to preserve the hard-won gains of the Revolution.

We must guard as a most valuable privilege, the freedom and rights of election. WHEREVER the wealthy by the influence of riches, are enabled to direct the choice of public officers, *there* the downfall of liberty cannot be very remote. It is our own fault if an influence so dangerous, has become in any measure prevalent among us. It would not be the case if the people did not consent to become the dupes of design. It is because tradesmen, mechanics, and the industrious classes of society consider themselves of TOO LITTLE CONSEQUENCE to the body politic that *any thing* belonging to the system of oppression at all obtains. We ought to spurn from us with disdain, the individual who would not solicit our vote, from motives of personal consideration. He ought not to be listened to, who would *demand* it as the price of friendship, or who would *expect* it from regard to his superior riches. It too often happens that men only capable of attracting public notice by an ostentatious display of their wealth, are deemed best qualified to protect the rights of the people, and consequently receive their suffrages; while our choice ought only to be directed to men of TALENTS and VIRTUE whatever their situation in life might be. The *possession* of riches is not necessarily accompanied by superior understanding or goodness of heart. On the contrary, the experience of ages confirms this opinion, that a state of mediocrity is more favorable to them both.

If, instead of improving on it original plan, our government, at any future period, should be irresistibly impelled in an unalterable course toward despotism, the dividing line between the *rich* and the *poor* will be distinctly marked, and the *latter* will be found in a state of vassallage [slavery] and dependence on the former.

Be it your care then, my fellow-citizens, to guard with unceasing vigilance against the growth of this evil; assume the native dignity of your character and maintain with a modest but determined spirit, the liberty of opinion. Suffer no one to DICTATE imperiously what line of conduct you are to pursue; but at the same time let no one be sacrificed at the alter of public vengeance, for a candid and liberal expression of his sentiments. . . .

We must endeavor to acquaint ourselves with the political situation and relative interests of our country. Without this information, we shall either be unable to form an accurate opinion on our own, or often become the dupes of the designing. The PUBLIC PRINTS naturally present themselves as the vehicles of this necessary knowledge. Those conducted in a spirit of liberality, yet alto-

freedom often meant financial insecurity and, in some cases, reliance on public or private charity. Those who did find work usually had the kinds of jobs that came with the booming economy of the late eighteenth century: moving goods from one place to another, building new structures, and providing personal services for the merchants who profited from all this commercial activity. In the coming years, trade associations for skilled white artisans would take pains to distance themselves from workers whom post-Revolutionary prosperity had left behind.

"Republican Mothers" and Other Well-Off Women

Some well-educated women in the United States read English writer Mary Wollstonecraft's *Vindication of the Rights of Women* published in England and in the United States in 1792. In that manifesto, Wollstonecraft argued that young men and women should receive the same

The New York City Mechanics' Society was founded in 1785 and incorporated in 1792. The society included many different kinds of artisans. In addition to representing the interests of skilled artisans, it served as a mutual aid association, lending money to members and distributing charity to the poor. This certificate of membership combines the traditional symbol of arts and crafts, the arm and hammer, with images of American patriotism (the eagle in the center foreground) and prosperity (waterways and fields on the left, urban townhouses on the left). Children are prominently featured here. In 1820 the General Society opened a school for the children of its members, and began offering classes to women in 1821.

gether consonant to the principles on which our revolution was achieved, should employ the public attention and meet its decided support. It will be found, that a JUST and EQUAL GOVERNMENT will ever derive additional stability, as the PEOPLE obtain a more general knowledge of its principles and operations. The result is, that every

sincere friend to our NATIONAL CONSTITUTION, ought sedulously to promote the dissemination of this knowledge, as a barrier to the risings of sedition, as well as to the encroachments of arbitrary power.

In his speech, Warner also called for "the practice of all the moral virtues" *and the education of children "as to the*

RIGHTS which they possess, and the DUTIES which they owe society." Warner himself became active in New York's Democratic-Republican party. ■

Source: George James Warner, *Means for the Preservation of Public Liberty* (New York, 1797); reprinted in Howard B. Rock, *The New York City Artisan, 1789–1825* (Albany: State University of New York Press, 1989), pp. 6–11.

kind of education. She objected to a special female curriculum that exclusively emphasized skills such as needlepoint and musical accomplishments; this "false system of education," she charged, left women "in a state of perpetual childhood."

In 1801 an anonymous "American Lady" published an essay titled "A Second Vindication of the Rights of Women." In it, she claimed that "a good kitchen woman [that is, a household drudge], very seldom makes a desirable wife, to a man of any refinement." The anonymous "American Lady" and others who shared her opinion celebrated a new kind of woman—the "Republican mother"—who provided cultured companionship for her husband and reared her children to be virtuous, responsible members of society. This image of womanhood led to a new notion: that well-off women should dedicate themselves to tending the home fires rather than aspiring to a more public role in business or politics.

Prior to the Revolution, women tended to bear many children, since additional hands were needed to labor in the fields. The decline in white women's fertility rates after the Revolution suggested that the economy had shifted. Factory managers and bookkeepers did not need to rely on the paid labor of their offspring. And some women could now buy products their grandmothers had made at home. In particular, a small but influential group of well-to-do women in the cities were shedding their roles as producers of candles, soap, and textiles. Instead, they became consumers of these staples and of luxury goods, and they managed household servants. As "Republican mothers," these women participated in the public life of the new nation as the guardians of the home and the socializers of children.

But the idea of the "Republican mother" also suggested a more radical notion. If such a woman wanted to earn the respect accorded all intelligent human beings, she must strive for an education equal to that of men's. In the 1790s a number of academies for "young ladies" opened in New England, including Sarah Peirce's in Litchfield, Connecticut, and Susanna Rowson's in Medford, Massachusetts. Many female academies catered to boarders, students living away from home. These schools offered courses in such "womanly pursuits" as needlework, etiquette, and music. But many also offered a classical curriculum consisting of mathematics, foreign languages, and geography. This system of study encouraged young women to think for themselves. In this respect, female academies challenged the view that women were intellectually inferior to and necessarily dependent on men.

Some elite women—like the anonymous "American Lady" and Alice Izard of Charleston, South Carolina—did not share this more radical viewpoint. For example, in opposition to Woll-

■ James Peale completed this painting of his family in 1795. Peale came from a distinguished family of artists. The picture represents the ideal of post-Revolutionary citizenship and family life. Husband and wife are both featured prominently, although their roles differ. The husband represents the household in the public, political sphere. The wife, a devoted mother, is responsible for preparing the children to be virtuous citizens of the new republic. Growing up in a well-to-do home, these playful children are exempt from the hard labor associated with childhood in the colonial period and, in the 1790s, still characteristic of childhood among enslaved, rural, and poor families.

Analectic Magazine, November, 1802. Photo courtesy The New York Public Library

■ With the Revolution came a heightened awareness of the significance of women's education. Private academies offered instruction to elite young women. This engraving, titled *Return from a Boarding School,* appeared in the November 1802 issue of *Analectic Magazine*. The fashionably dressed student, on the right, sits at the piano and greets visitors while her father, on the left with her mother, agonizes over the tuition bill. The shovel, washtub, and broom indicate that the parents are hard-working, simple people. Yet the parlor, with its birdcage, furniture, and carpets, suggests that the household values both prosperity and sociability.

stonecraft's argument in favor of equal education for young men and women, Izard expressed disgust with notions of female equality. "It is not by being educated with Boys, or imitating the manners of Men that we shall become more worthy beings," she proclaimed. Women need not attain public glory, she wrote, to gain "domestic honor and true praise."

Alice Izard was not alone in her beliefs. After the Revolution, many American women, even those of modest means, eagerly read advice manuals written by both native and foreign-born authors. These manuals stressed the importance of good manners over formal education. And even graduates of the new female academies often renounced aspirations to public life once they married and assumed household responsibilities. Wrote Eliza Southgate Bowne, a defender of women's education, "I believe I must give up all pretension to *profundity,* for I am much more at home in my female character."

Other women were more sympathetic to Wollstonecraft's arguments regarding women's equality with men. As the author of a series of essays on women's rights such as "On the Equality of the Sexes," published in *Massachusetts Magazine* in 1790, Judith Sargent Murray was the intellectual heir of Abigail Adams. With a notable lack of success, Adams had urged her husband, John, to secure married women's property rights in the Constitution. By arguing for the inherent equality of men and women, Murray echoed Wollstonecraft and laid the groundwork for the women's rights movement to come. The white women of means who came of age after the Revolution keenly felt the ties that bound them together, even as those ties limited their participation in the public sphere, especially after the wartime emergency had passed.

A Loss of Political Influence: The Fate of Nonelite Women

The Revolution gave elite white women a rationale for speaking out in the realm of politics. Yet the war had a very different impact on other groups of women. For example, among the Cherokees, the introduction of a European American division of labor lessened women's customary political influence as leaders and diplomats. European Americans believed that only men should serve in positions of authority, and so Cherokee women felt pressured to refrain from taking part in political negotiations and to subordinate themselves to men. In 1787 one Cherokee leader (called a War Woman, or Beloved Woman) wrote to Benjamin Franklin. She was confident in her own ability to participate in postwar Indian–white negotiations. Out of respect for Franklin, and in the diplomatic tradition of her people, she enclosed in the letter some of the same tobacco used in the peace pipes of Cherokee warriors. She lectured Franklin, "I am in hopes that if you Rightly consider that woman is the mother of All—and the woman does not pull Children out of Trees or Stumps nor out of old Logs, but out of their [women's] Bodies, so that they [men] ought to mind what a woman says."

By the end of the century, only men had the power to negotiate treaties and land transactions. Still, some women managed to resist this new arrangement. Nancy Ward, the "Beloved Woman of Chota," participated in a treaty conference in Hopewell, South Carolina, in 1785. Speaking as the "mother of Cherokee warriors," she became a powerful person in her own right, not just because of her ties to male leaders. In the early nineteenth century she mobilized other Cherokee women, and together they spoke out forcefully against the practice of selling Cherokee lands to whites.

In the West, Indian women registered the brunt of ongoing conflicts between their own people and European American settlers. In New Mexico, female Indian captives from Plains tribes (such as the Apache, Comanche, and Kiowa) became *indios servientes* in Hispanic households. In some cases their masters set them to work tending sheep, an occupation that had been reserved for men in traditional native cultures. In the East, Native American women dispossessed of their land pieced together a meager existence. For example, in Natick, Massachusetts, women turned to weaving and peddling baskets and brooms, while their men scrounged for wage labor. Many Indian women, such as Hannah Freeman, a Lenape woman in rural Pennsylvania, depended on white farmers for seasonal work. Born in southeastern Pennsylvania 1731, Freeman spent her lifetime moving or being moved from Pennsylvania to New Jersey to Delaware and back again as her family sought refuge from whites and struggled to make a living. By the 1790s, she was an itinerant laborer; her biographer noted that "she has been moving from place to place making baskets &c and staying longest where best used but never was hired or recd wages except for baskets." In 1800 she entered the Chester County Poorhouse, where she died two years later.

Commercial development, combined with race and gender discrimination, offered only modest possibilities for many impoverished women and women of color.

For some Americans, the postwar years brought unprecedented opportunities to buy, sell, and trade. However, commercial development, combined with race and gender discrimination, offered only modest possibilities for many impoverished women and women of color. Like other free blacks, Chloe Spear of Boston "worked early and late" at a number of jobs, such as laundering and ironing clothes. Eventually, she managed to purchase her own home. In Rhode Island, Elleanor Eldrige started her work career at age ten in 1795. Thereafter, she worked as a domestic servant, spinner, weaver, dairymaid, and nurse. She finally went into business, first as a soapboiler and then as a wallpaperer and house painter. However, like many free blacks, Eldrige remained vulnerable to the machinations of white men who tried to defraud her of her hard-won earnings.

Some white women also felt the effects of fluctuations in the market economy. In Philadelphia in the mid-1790s, two former servants—Polly Nugent (married to a blacksmith who had just lost his job) and Grace Biddle (newly widowed)—had to plead for assistance from their former mistress, Elizabeth Drinker. The city's "Bettering House" for indigent people housed men and women, blacks and whites. Many women had neither the resources nor the opportunities to improve their lot after the Revolution.

The Election of 1800: Revolution or Reversal?

The campaign of 1800 pitted Thomas Jefferson and his vice-presidential running mate, Aaron Burr, against the incumbent, John Adams, and his vice-presidential nominee, Charles Pinckney. Certain elements of the campaign were predictable. The Democratic-Republicans blasted Alexander Hamilton's economic policies and the Adams administration's military buildup. Jefferson's party also condemned the Alien and Sedition Acts' effect of silencing Adams's political opponents. For their part, the Federalists portrayed Jefferson as a godless supporter of the French Revolution. They also charged that he had fathered children by one of his slaves, Sally Hemings. (Two centuries later, DNA evidence suggested that this charge might be true.)

Jefferson prevailed in the 1800 election, but his victory did not come easily. The electoral college allowed delegates to vote separately for president and vice president, and as a result Jefferson tied with Burr. Each man received 73 votes. Then the decision went to the House of Representatives, which was dominated by Federalists. After a series of tied votes, Jefferson finally gained a majority. His selection in February 1801 marked the orderly transfer of power from the Federalists to the Democratic-Republicans, a peaceful revolution in American politics.

TABLE 9-2		
The Election of 1800		
Candidate	**Political Party**	**Electoral Vote**
Thomas Jefferson	Democrat-Republican	73
Aaron Burr	Democrat-Republican	73
John Adams	Federalist	65
Charles C. Pinckney	Federalist	64

As chief executive, Jefferson did little to change the direction of the country. Aware of his razor-thin victory, he retained many Federalist appointees. And his eagerness to expand the boundaries of the United States—which culminated in the Louisiana Purchase of 1803—solidified the Hamiltonian principles that favored commerce and trade over agrarian values.

The Enigmatic Thomas Jefferson

Who was Thomas Jefferson? In 1800 Jefferson, the presidential candidate, wrote, "I have sworn upon the altar of God eternal hostility against every form of tyranny over the mind of man." Yet Jefferson's own views on ordinary people were less heroic. Specifically, his support for slavery and the assimilation of Indians provided justification for whites' violent assault on both groups in the early nineteenth century.

Many Americans know Jefferson as the author of the Declaration of Independence. But he also sought to justify slavery as a central institution in the new republic. In his *Notes on the State of Virginia* (1785), Jefferson searched for a rationale to exclude nonwhite men from the new body politic. His stereotypical views of all blacks (for example, he believed they lacked imagination and intelligence) suggested what we today would call scientific racism.

Jefferson wrote much about the noble calling of the yeoman farmer. Yet he assigned the task of tilling the soil on his own estate (Monticello, near Charlottesville, Virginia) to his enslaved workers. When he did acknowledge the abolitionist sentiment, he warned of a possible race war between aggrieved blacks and their white masters. Such a war, he said, would "produce convulsions, [and] probably never end but in the extermination of one or the other race."

The president's views on Indians also did nothing to reverse the course of aggression in the West. He believed that land ownership created the stable institutions necessary for civilized behavior. He told the Delawares,

> When once you have property, you will want laws and magistrates to protect your property and persons, and to punish those among you who commit crimes. You will find that our laws are good for this purpose. You will wish to live under them; you will unite yourselves with us, join in our great councils, and form one people with us, and we shall all be Americans. You will mix with us by marriage. Your blood will run in our veins and will spread with us over this great island.

Yet the system of private property, and the violent methods that whites used to enforce it, spelled the destruction of traditional Indian ways of life. Jefferson's views on assimilation sounded idealistic. But in practical terms, they paved the way for seizures of Indian lands and the forced migrations that removed the Five Civilized Tribes from their homelands in the nineteenth century. Though committed to a political union of disparate states, Jefferson despised what he considered to be racial differences between groups of people.

It is tempting to excuse Jefferson's racist beliefs by saying he merely reflected his time. But in fact, a significant number of Jefferson's contemporaries were voicing their misgivings about slavery. While Jefferson acknowledged their arguments, he did not share their beliefs. A citizen of a trans-Atlantic "republic of ideas," he corresponded with political thinkers—from John Adams to the Marquis de Lafayette—who understood the inherent tension between freedom for whites and slavery for blacks. Obviously, Jefferson knew that some of the northern states (Massachusetts and Vermont among them) had written constitutions that incorporated the sentiments of the Declaration of Independence. These states had interpreted the document in ways that justified the abolition of slavery. Moreover, a notable number of Jefferson's wealthy Virginia compatriots (including George Washington) had chosen to free their slaves, either by their own hand or through provisions of their wills, to practice in their own households what they preached to British tyrants.

Jefferson lived in an age when revolutionary enthusiasm was sweeping the western world. Challenges to slavery had rocked Europe; France outlawed the practice in 1794, although Napoleon later reinstated it. Abolition had also transformed the Western Hemisphere with the successful rebellion of the Saint-Domingue slaves in 1791. The United States provided the political theory and rhetoric to inspire abolitionists around the globe, but within the new nation, the debate over the institution of slavery continued to rage. The southern states, in particular, took decisive steps to solidify the institution within their own boundaries.

Protecting and Expanding the National Interest: Jefferson's Administration to 1803

As president, Jefferson reconsidered his original vision of the United States: a compact country in which citizens freely pursued modest agrarian interests without interference from the national government or distractions from overseas conflicts. Indeed, during his years in office, the federal government moved toward increasing its own power.

In early 1801, just before Jefferson assumed the presidency, the Federalist-dominated Congress had strengthened the national court system by passing the Judiciary Act of 1801. The act created 16 circuit (regional) courts, with a judge for each, and bolstered support staff for the judicial branch in general. President Adams appointed these judges (so-called midnight judges because they were appointed right before Jefferson took office). Before stepping down,

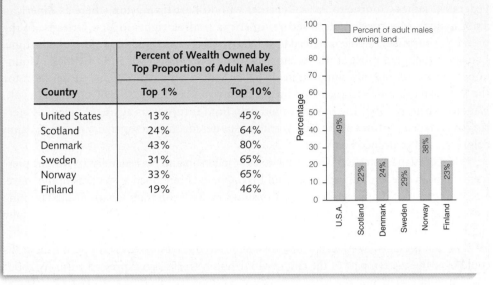

Country	Percent of Wealth Owned by Top Proportion of Adult Males	
	Top 1%	Top 10%
United States	13%	45%
Scotland	24%	64%
Denmark	43%	80%
Sweden	31%	65%
Norway	33%	65%
Finland	19%	46%

■ **FIGURE 9.4**
DISTRIBUTION OF WEALTH IN THE UNITED STATES AND EUROPE, 1798

Source: Lee Soltow, *Distribution of Wealth and Income in the United States in 1798* (1989), p. 238.

Adams had also appointed Secretary of State John Marshall as chief justice of the Supreme Court. Adams's last-minute acts had long-term consequences.

Marshall remained on the bench for 34 years. He presided over the court when it rendered its landmark *Marbury v. Madison* decision in 1803, which established the judiciary's right to declare acts of both the executive and legislative branches unconstitutional. When Jefferson assumed the presidency, the actual document listing Adams's choices for "midnight judges" had not yet been finalized. Jefferson ordered the new secretary of state, James Madison, to withhold the appointments. One of the nominated judges, William Marbury, petitioned the Supreme Court to force Madison to approve Adams's appointments to the bench. The Court refused to do so, arguing that the basis of Marbury's suit, Section 13 of the Judiciary Act of 1789, was unconstitutional. With this decision, the Court thereby established the principle of judicial review—the notion that the justices could invalidate any state or congressional statute they deemed unconstitutional. Chief Justice Marshall declared, "It is emphatically the province and duty of the judicial department to say what the law is."

In the realm of international affairs, Jefferson asserted his own authority. Challenges from foreign powers prompted the Democratic-Republican president to take bold steps to protect U.S. economic and political interests abroad and along its own borders. In 1801 Jefferson's administration launched a war against pirates in North Africa when Tripoli (modern-day Libya) demanded ransom money for kidnapped American sailors. (Together, the North African kingdoms of Tunis, Tripoli, Algeria, and Morocco were known as the "Barbary States." The war against Tripoli, which spanned four years, revealed the extent of U.S. trade interests even at this early point in the nation's history. The United States signed a peace treaty with Tripoli in 1805 and paid $60,000 for the release of the American captives. The plight of these captives, many of whom had been enslaved, transfixed whites at home. For the first time, whites contemplated a form of slavery that confounded traditional notions of skin color and legal status.

At the beginning of the nineteenth century, the European powers continued their operations in the territory west of the United States. In 1801 Napoleon persuaded the King of Spain to secretly cede the trans-Mississippi region called Louisiana to France. Retaining control of New Orleans, Spain denied Americans the right to use that city as a depository for goods awaiting shipment. In 1803 Jefferson sent his fellow Virginian, and prominent Anti-Federalist, James Monroe to Paris. Together with Robert Livingston (there as American ambassador), Monroe set out to secure American trading rights to New Orleans. To the president's surprise, Napoleon agreed to sell the whole area to the United States. At the time, Louisiana included most of the territory between the Mississippi and the Rocky Mountains—a total of 828,000 square miles. The United States agreed to pay $15 million for the Louisiana Purchase. Frustrated by his inability to quell the Saint-Domingue revolt, Napoleon believed that the money would help fund future wars against England. Referring to his failed ventures in the New World, he sputtered, "Damn sugar, damn coffee, damn colonies. . . . I renounce Louisiana."

The Louisiana Purchase reversed the roles of Jefferson and his Federalist rivals. The president advocated territorial expansion, but his opponents remained suspicious of the move. Devoted to a strict interpretation of the Constitution, Jefferson traditionally favored limiting federal authority. Yet he sought to justify the purchase by pointing out that it would finally rid the area of European influence. He proposed shifting Indians from the Mississippi Territory (part of present-day Alabama and Mississippi) to the West so that European Americans could have the eastern part of the country to themselves. He also expressed curiosity about the geography and natural resources of the new acquisition. For their part, the Federalists feared

■ **MAP 9.3**

THE BARBARY STATES   The Barbary states included the small kingdoms of Morocco, Algeria, Tunis, and Tripoli in northern Africa. Before the Revolution, Great Britain paid the states protection money each year; in return, Barbary pirates agreed not to loot British ships or capture their sailors for ransom. This arrangement covered the ships of the American colonies as well. After the Revolution, the Barbary states dealt directly with the United States. Tripoli insisted that the United States pay more money. President Jefferson refused. The ensuing U.S.–Tripoli war ended in 1805; the treaty signed that year freed the U.S. of protection payments.

that Louisiana would benefit mainly agrarian interests and eventually dilute New England's long-standing political influence and power. They suspected Jefferson of attempting to expand the influence of his own political party.

Neither the Democratic-Republicans nor the Federalists expressed much concern about the fate of the many Indian and Spanish-speaking inhabitants of Louisiana. All these peoples became residents, if not citizens, of the United States when the Senate approved the purchase in October 1803.

Conclusion

In his first inaugural address, Jefferson spoke about partisan politics. He cautioned, "Every difference of opinion is not a difference of principle." Indeed, Jefferson felt that partisan conflicts obscured a broad, common ground uniting all leaders of the new republic: "We have called by different names brethren of the same principle. We are all Republicans, we are all Federalists." Jefferson was suggesting that all political leaders shared essentially the same views about the role of government and the importance of economic opportunity for ordinary people. Most office holders, regardless of party affiliation, remained committed to the "pursuit of happiness," which they defined as the right to own private property. These leaders also expressed suspicion of groups that professed religious beliefs that lay outside the mainstream of Protestantism or liberal Deism (a general belief in God without ties to a particular religious denomination). They considered slavery not a moral issue, but a political issue that individual states must address. They united behind the idea that women, as well as black and Indian men, should have no formal voice in governing the nation.

Despite these common principles shared by many political leaders in the post-Revolutionary period, this era saw the rise of two opposing camps—those favoring local control and those supporting federal authority. Many people defined political interests in "either-or" terms: either the French system of political equality *or* the British monarchy; either the individual states *or* the federal government; either the farm *or* the factory. Such thinking promoted a narrow view of the United States, a society of great economic and ethnic diversity. For example, certainly the country was large and prosperous enough to accommodate the views of people who believed that both manufacturing and farming were crucial for national growth and development, or who believed that the states and the federal government could share power in a way that enhanced the rights and well-being of all citizens. Yet the machinery of government ran most efficiently on a two-party system. A candidate's political victory depended on his winning more votes than his opponent, and the electoral system provided no avenues for different groups to share power. This system made it extremely difficult for people who had no place in it to find their own political voice and claim the Revolutionary legacy as their own.

At the same time, the new nation gave white men opportunities practically unknown in the rest of the world. Regardless of their background, many white men could aspire to own property and to participate in the political process. The federal government supported economic growth by facilitating territorial expansion, technological innovation, and the protection of private property. As much for the prosperity it promoted as for the noble ideas it nourished, the Revolution continued to inspire liberation movements within the United States and throughout the world.

Sites to Visit

Thomas Jefferson
www.pbs.org/jefferson/

This site is the companion to the Public Broadcasting System series on Jefferson. The site includes material on how people understand Jefferson today.

Archiving Early America
earlyamerica.com

Old newspapers provide a window into issues of the past. This site includes the Keigwin and Matthews collection of early newspapers.

Alexander Hamilton
odur.let.rug.nl/~usa/B/hamilton/hamilxx.htm

This site, from a Hypertext of American History, examines Hamilton's life and influence in the United States during the early national period.

The XYZ Affair
gi.grolier.com/presidents/aae/side/xyzaffr.html

This site examines the XYZ affair.

The Whiskey Rebellion
www.whiskeyrebellion.org

This site devoted to the 1794 Whiskey Rebellion includes a narrative of events and a timeline.

Native Languages of the Americas
www.geocities.com/bigorrin/miam.htm

This site provides information on the language of the Miami and Illinois Indians, a dialect of the same Algonquian language spoken in Indiana and later in Oklahoma.

The Avalon Project at the Yale Law School
www.yale.edu/lawweb/avalon/quasi.htm

This site explores the Quasi War between the United States and France.

The Marshall Cases
odur.let.rug.nl~usa/D/1801-1825/marshallcases/marxx.htm

John Marshall, and the cases he heard, shaped the form and function of the judicial system in the United States.

National Museum of the American Indian
www.si.edu/nmai

The Smithsonian Institution maintains this site, which provides information about the museum that is dedicated to the history and culture of Native Americans.

For Further Reading

General Works

Joyce Appleby, *Inheriting the Revolution: The First Generation of Americans* (2000).

Joseph J. Ellis, *Founding Brothers: The Revolutionary Generation* (2000).

Lester D. Langley, *The Americas in the Age of Revolution: 1750–1850* (1996).

Philip Morgan, *Slave Counterpoint: Black Culture in the Eighteenth-Century Chesapeake and Lowcountry* (1998).

Richard White, *The Middle Ground: Indians, Empires, and Republics in the Great Lakes Region, 1650–1815* (1991).

Competing Political Visions in the New Nation

Joyce Appleby, *Capitalism and the New Social Order: The Republican Vision of the 1790s* (1984).

Terry Bouton, "A Road Closed: Rural Insurgency in Post-Independence Pennsylvania," *Journal of American History* 87 (Dec. 2000):855–887.

Albert Bowman, *The Struggle for Neutrality: Franco-American Diplomacy During the Federalist Era* (1974).

John Hoadley, *Origins of American Political Parties, 1789–1803* (1986).

James Roger Sharp, *American Politics in the Early Republic: The New Nation in Crisis* (1995).

James Morton Smith, *Freedom's Fetters: The Alien and Sedition Laws and American Civil Liberties* (1956).

People of Color: New Freedoms, New Struggles

Ira Berlin, *Slaves Without Masters: The Free Negro in the Antebellum South* (1981).

Graham R. Hodges, *Root and Branch: African-Americans in New York and East Jersey, 1613–1863* (1999).

James O. Horton and Lois Horton, *In Hope of Liberty: Culture, Community, and Protest Among Northern Free Blacks, 1700–1860* (1997).

Leon Litwack, *North of Slavery: The Negro in the Free States, 1790–1860* (1961).

Shane White and Graham White, *Stylin': African-American Expressive Culture from Its Beginnings to the Zoot Suit* (1998).

Continuity and Change in the West

Henry W. Bowden, *American Indians and Christian Missions: Studies in Cultural Change* (1981).

Gregory Evans Dowd, *A Spirited Resistance: The North American Indian Struggle for Unity, 1745–1815* (1992).

R. David Edmunds, *Tecumseh and the Quest for Indian Leadership* (1984).

Robert V. Hine and John Mack Faragher, *The American West: A New Interpretive History* (2000).

Reginald Horsman, *Expansion and American Indian Policy, 1783–1812* (1992).

Dorothy V. Jones, *License for Empire: Colonialism by Treaty in Early America* (1982).

James P. Ronda, *Lewis and Clark Among the Indians* (1984).

Shifting Social Identities in the Post-Revolutionary Era

Nathan O. Hatch, *The Democratization of American Christianity* (1989).

Jacqueline Jones, *American Work: Four Centuries of Black and White Labor* (1998).

Linda Kerber, *Women of the Republic: Intellect and Ideology in Revolutionary America* (1980).

William G. McLaughlin, *Cherokee Renascence in the New Republic* (1986).

Billy G. Smith, *The "Lower Sort": Philadelphia's Laboring People, 1750–1800* (1990).

The Election of 1800: Revolution or Reversal?

Doron Ben-Atar and Barbara B. Oberg, eds., *Federalists Reconsidered* (1998).

David B. Davis, *The Problem of Slavery in the Age of Revolution, 1770–1823* (1975).

Joseph J. Ellis, *American Sphinx: The Character of Thomas Jefferson* (1996).

Peter S. Onuf, *Jefferson's Empire: The Language of American Nationhood* (2000).

Anthony F. C. Wallace, *Jefferson and the Indians: The Tragic Fate of the First Americans* (1999).

Additional Photo Credits

Page 289: Gilbert Stuart, *Joseph Brant*, 1786. Fenimore Art Museum, Cooperstown, New York (N-199.61).
 Photo by Richard Walker. Fenimore Art Museum, Cooperstown, New York (N-199.61).
Page 291: Courtesy, Janice L. and David Frent
Page 295: The National Archives
Page 296: Courtesy, American Canal and Transportation Center
Page 306: The Ohio Historical Society
Page 312: Shaker Village of Pleasant Hill, Harrodsburg, KY

PART FOUR

Expanding the Boundaries of Freedom and Slavery, 1803–1848

IN THE FIRST HALF OF THE NINETEENTH CENTURY, FEW IF ANY NATIONS ON earth could rival the United States' remarkable record of growth. At its founding, the country consisted of 4 million people living in 13 states that hugged the eastern seaboard of North America. By the mid-nineteenth century, the nation's population had grown to 22.5 million people as a result of reproduction, foreign immigration, and the conquest of indigenous and Spanish-speaking peoples. Because of a mix of diplomatic pressure and military aggression, dramatic geographic expansion accompanied the burgeoning population growth. By 1850 the country sprawled the breadth of the continent to the Pacific Ocean.

Territorial expansion, economic growth, and increasing ethnic diversity profoundly shaped American politics in the first half of the nineteenth century. Innovations in transportation (the steamboat), communication (the telegraph), and the production of crops and textiles (reapers and mechanical looms) allowed Americans to move materials, people, and information more quickly and to produce food and goods more efficiently. Meanwhile, the immigration of large numbers of western Europeans, the rapid expansion of the free black population, and the conquest of Spanish-speaking peoples in the Southwest in 1848 challenged the United States' view of itself as an exclusively Anglo-Protestant nation.

Some citizens declared that the United States had a God-given duty and God-given right to expand its borders in opposition to the British and Russians in the Northwest and in opposition to Spain and later Mexico in the South and Southwest. Thus, territorial expansion brought the United States into conflict with other countries and groups that claimed the land. America's victory in the War of 1812 secured the nation's Great Lakes border and at the same time proved that American soldiers and sailors were the equal of England's seasoned fighting forces. In 1823, fearful that European powers would take advantage of independence movements in Latin America, the United States issued the Monroe Doctrine, stating that the era of colonization of the Americas was over.

Nevertheless, Indian tribes continued to resist the incursion of European Americans who believed that land was a commodity to be wrested from native peoples and then bought and sold. In the southern part of the country, the Five Civilized Tribes and other Native American groups occupied territory coveted by both gold seekers and cotton growers. Many American voters demanded that their political leaders work to expand the nation's boundaries through a variety of means: treaty, negotiation, or military force.

Andrew Jackson, who assumed the presidency in 1828, seemed a fitting symbol and a representative politician of the age. Determined to expand the power of the executive branch of government, Jackson claimed to represent the interests of ordinary people in his political battles against the Second Bank of the United States and the Supreme Court and in his forceful removal of Indian tribes from the Southeast to Indian Territory (present-day Oklahoma). Like other politicians of the time, Jackson conceived of citizenship as a system of rights and privileges for white men only.

Still, European Americans trumpeted the arrival of a new era of egalitarianism. Western settlers laid claim to political power, and suffrage restrictions based on property ownership crumbled in the wake of egalitarian legislation and rhetoric. Americans were restless, moving out west and back east again, around the countryside, and in and out of cities. Believing that people could and should work together to reform society, many created reform associations, embraced new religious beliefs, and joined political parties. New forms of association yielded new kinds of communities in an era characterized by great geographic mobility.

At the same time, two distinct power systems coalesced to ensure that certain groups would monopolize the political and economic life of the country. In the South, cotton planters launched an aggressive defense of the institution of slavery. In the North, an emerging class system extended the differences between the political influence and material well-being of factory owners and machine operatives.

For the country, therefore, growth brought great promise and great peril. Abolitionists, associations of working people, nativists (people hostile to immigrants), women's rights advocates, and a variety of other groups proclaimed their agendas for social change. Most significantly, by 1848 it was becoming more difficult for national legislators to resolve the question of whether to allow slavery in the territories. As passions rose, few could imagine a political compromise that would satisfy abolitionists and proslavery advocates alike. As mid-century approached, more and more Americans seemed prepared to express their convictions—or their prejudices and resentment—through violent means.

1826	American Society for the Promotion of Temperance founded
1827	Workingmen's Party founded in Philadelphia
1828	*Cherokee Phoenix* begins publication
1829	Gold discovered on Cherokee lands in Georgia
1831	Nat Turner leads slave rebellion in Virginia William Lloyd Garrison publishes *The Liberator*
1832	Nullification crisis *Worcester v. Georgia* Jackson vetoes Second Bank of the United States Black Hawk War
1833	Great Britain abolishes slavery National Road completed
1834	Cyrus McCormick patents reaper First strike at Lowell mills Whig Party organized
1835	Alexis de Tocqueville, *Democracy in America* Texas revolts against Mexico
1836	Congress passes gag rule on antislavery petitions Republic of Texas founded
1837	Panic of 1837 John Deere invents steel plow
1838	Pennsylvania revokes black male suffrage Cherokee removal begins; Trail of Tears
1840	Liberty Party founded
1841	John Tyler assumes presidency after death of William Henry Harrison Supreme Court rules in favor of *Amistad* Africans
1844	Mormon leader Joseph Smith killed by mob in Nauvoo, Illinois
1845	Irish potato famine Frederick Douglass, *Narrative of the Life of Frederick Douglass* Texas becomes twenty-eighth state
1846	Great Britain cedes southern part of Oregon Country to United States Mexican–American War begins
1847	United States wins battles of Buena Vista, Vera Cruz, Mexico City Capture of San Patricio soldiers, Battle of Churubusco
1848	Treaty of Guadalupe Hidalgo ends Mexican–American War Women's Rights convention in Seneca Falls, New York Popular revolutions sweep Europe

CHAPTER 10

Defending and Expanding the New Nation, 1803–1818

John Lewis Krimmel, *Night Life in Philadelphia—an Oyster Barrow in front of the Chestnut Street Theater,* c.1811–1813. The Metropolitan Museum of Art, Rogers Fund, 1942 (42.95.18). Photograph ©1982 The Metropolitan Museum of Art

■ *Night Life in Philadelphia: An Oyster Barrow in Front of the Chestnut Street Theater, 1811–12.*

I N EARLY NOVEMBER 1804 A GROUP OF SOLDIERS WORKED FEVERISHLY TO CONSTRUCT A rough military garrison on the north bank of the Missouri River, near several Mandan Indian villages and what is today Washburn, North Dakota. The soldiers knew they had to work quickly. Within a month, winter would descend on the Northern Great Plains, and the temperature would plummet. In fact, not long after Fort Mandan was completed, the temperature registered at 45 degrees Fahrenheit below zero.

The garrison provided shelter for an expedition party led by Meriwether Lewis and William Clark. Both captains in the U.S. Army, Lewis and Clark had been commissioned by President Thomas Jefferson to explore the upper reaches of the newly acquired Louisiana Territory, which had doubled the size of the country. With the ultimate goal of reaching what is today Oregon, their party spent the winter at Fort Mandan and joined the buffalo hunts and nightly dances sponsored by their hosts, the Mandan Indians. Between November 1804 and March 1805, Lewis and Clark also found time to record their observations on all manner of things natural and cultural. In their journals and their letters to President Jefferson, they described the language of the Hidatsa Indians and the beadwork of the Arikaras, the medicinal prop- erties of native plants, and the contours of the Missouri River. In a ship- ment prepared for the president, they included deer horns, pumice stones, the pelt of a white weasel, and an assortment of live animals. (Sadly, only a magpie and a prairie dog survived the journey to Washington, D.C.)

Lewis and Clark's trek took 28 months to complete and covered 8000 miles. Along the way, the two men assured the Indians they met that their expedition's purpose was purely scientific. However, Jefferson had also commissioned them to chart a waterway passage to the North- west. The president hoped to divert the profitable fur trade away from Canada and into the hands of Americans by locating a river connecting the Northwest directly to eastern U.S. markets. Jefferson also instructed Lewis and Clark to initiate negotiations with various Indian groups, to pave the way for miners and ranchers to move into the area.

Captain Meriwether Lewis posed in Indian dress for this watercolor completed in 1807 by French artist C. B. J. Févret de Saint-Mémin.

Throughout their journey, Lewis and Clark expressed awe of the magnifi- cence of the land—its physical beauty and its commercial potential. While camped at Fort Mandan, Lewis described the Missouri: "This immence river so far as we have yet ascended waters one of the fairest portions of the globe, nor do I believe that there is in the universe a similar extent of country, equally fertile, well watered, and intersected by such a number of navigable streams." When the expedition's official report was published in 1814, it caused a sensation. Americans swelled with pride at the bounteous expanse called the Upper Louisiana.

Lewis and Clark's party consisted of a diverse group of people, including British and Irish enlisted men, and Lewis's African American slave, York. At Fort Mandan, the group picked up Toussaint Charbonneau, a French Canadian, and his 15-year-old wife, Sacajawea,

The Lewis and Clark expedition to the Pacific

——— Pittsburgh to Camp Wood, 1803

——— Camp Wood to Pacific and return, 1804–1805

▪▪▪ Continental Divide

⚙ Fort 🏠 Camp

Lewis and Clark returned east from the Pacific to St. Louis by slightly different routes in 1806

Present state names and boundaries provided for orientation

■ **MAP 10.1**

LEWIS AND CLARK This map, showing the route of the Lewis and Clark expedition, suggests the importance of interior waterways in facilitating travel and exploration in the West. Spain feared, rightly, that the Americans would use western rivers to establish trade links with the Indians and thereby challenge Spain's northern border with the United States.

Source: From Stephen Ambrose, *Undaunted Courage.*

a Shoshone Indian. The explorers came to rely on Sacajawea's skills as an interpreter. And because women never traveled with Indian war parties, Sacajawea's presence reassured suspicious Native Americans that the goal of the expedition was peaceful. White men were fond of boasting that "they were great warriors, and a powerful people, who, if exasperated, could crush all the nations of the earth." Indians heard these threats frequently and so were not inclined to look kindly upon an expedition of white men.

Lewis and Clark failed in their mission to locate a commercial route across the Rocky Mountains; the terrain proved too rugged. However, by sponsoring this and other major exploration parties, the federal government signaled its intention to help European Americans settle the West. The expedition also revealed that control of western waterways would be crucial to America's attempt to explore the interior of the continent and to establish trading relations with the Indians. The exploitation of waterways and water power proved a key component in the new nation's economic growth and development. In sum, the Lewis and Clark expedition yielded information that furthered westward migration, commercial development, and scientific knowledge about the western landscape.

During the first two decades of the nineteenth century, the United States faced a number of challenges from within and outside its borders, challenges that had long-lasting political and economic effects. Indians in general were a persistent threat to the new nation. Indeed, in the Great Lakes region, various tribes maintained political and military alliances with Great Britain. Nevertheless, in this period the United States successfully met its most severe test to date: a war with England that raged from 1812 to 1815. The effects of this so-called Second

American Revolution were far-reaching. The conflict eliminated the British from the Northwest once and for all. Its military heroes, including Andrew Jackson and William Henry Harrison, went on to illustrious political careers. The war also spurred industrialization and stimulated commerce. In the South, the cotton plantation system began to shape the political and economic life of the entire region.

Some Europeans who visited the United States during these years criticized Americans for their crudeness and their lack of accomplishment in literature, architecture, road building, and manners. Yet after the War of 1812, American patriotism soared. The country now stretched from New Orleans to the Canadian border—an enormous expanse blessed with rich natural resources. Its military leaders were the equal of, if not superior to, the finest European officers. However, some Americans began to see a threat to their sense of themselves as a unique people. That threat—the expansion of human bondage—would come not from the outside but from within their own borders.

The British Menace

Inthe election of 1804, Democratic-Republican Thomas Jefferson and his vice-presidential running mate, George Clinton, a former governor of New York, easily bested their Federalist opponents, Charles C. Pinckney and Rufus King. Jefferson had gained widespread favor among the voters through the Louisiana Purchase. And his decision to repeal the federal excise tax on whiskey that had so angered farmers in the West secured his popularity. On the eve of his second term, he no doubt imagined himself examining the specimens and reading the reports that Lewis and Clark sent back from the West. Yet the ongoing squabbling between France and England and the increasing aggression of the British navy toward American sailors demanded his attention.

Developments overseas preoccupied Jefferson during his second term in office. England and France continued to challenge each other as the reigning powers of Europe. In 1805 the British navy, under the command of Lord Nelson, defeated the French and Spanish fleets in the Battle of Trafalgar off the coast of Spain. That same year, France reveled in its own triumph on land when Napoleon conquered the Austrian and Russian armies at the Battle of Austerlitz. Supreme on the seas, England in 1806 passed the Orders in Council, which specified that any country that wanted to ship goods to France must first send them to a British port and pay taxes on them. Many Americans believed that England's policies amounted to acts of military and economic aggression against the United States.

William Clark, *Eulachon (T. Pacificus)*, 1806, Voorhis Journal #2. William Clark Papers, Missouri Historical Society Archives

■ **Lewis and Clark were not only explorers; they were also pioneering naturalists committed to gathering, recording, and studying plants and animal life in the West. William Clark drew this sketch of a eulachon, also called a candlefish, as part of his journal entry for February 25, 1806. Pacific Indians dried the oily fish and used it as a torch.**

TABLE 10-1		
The Election of 1804		
Candidate	**Political Party**	**Electoral Vote**
Thomas Jefferson	Democratic-Republican	162
Charles C. Pinckney	Federalist	14

The Embargo of 1807

Not content to control trade across the Atlantic as decreed by the 1806 Orders in Council, the British also seized sailors from American ships, claiming that these men were British seamen who had been lured away from their own vessels by American captains promising them higher wages. In some cases these claims were probably true. However, U.S. political leaders charged that an estimated 6000 U.S. citizens had been seized by the British navy between 1808 and 1811, including an unknown number of African Americans, many of whom were working as mariners. Seafaring appealed to free men of color because it paid good wages. In the early

THE IMPRESSMENT OF AN

American Sailor Boy,

SUNG ON BOARD THE BRITISH PRISON SHIP CROWN PRINCE, THE FOURTH OF JULY, 1814
BY A NUMBER OF THE AMERICAN PRISONERS.

THE youthful sailor mounts the bark,
  And bids each weeping friend adieu :
Fair blows the gale, the canvass swells :
  Slow sinks the uplands from his view.

Three mornings, from his ocean bed,
  Resplendent beams the God of day :
The fourth. high looming in the mist,
  A war-ship's floating banners play.

Her yawl is launch'd ; light o'er the deep,
  Too kind, she wafts a ruffian band :
Her blue track lengthens to the bark,
  And soon on deck the miscreants stand.

  Around they throw the baleful glance :
  Suspense holds mute the anxious crew—
Who is their prey ? poor sailor boy !
  The baleful glance is fix'd on you.

Nay. why that useless scrip unfold ?
  They damn'd the " lying yankee scrawl,"
Torn from thine hand, it strews the wave—
  They force thee trembling to the yawl.

Sick was thine heart as from the deck,
  The hand of friendship wav d farewell ;
Mad was thy brain, as far behind,
  In the grey mist thy vessel fell.

One hope, yet, to thy bosom clung,
  The captain mercy might impart ;

Vain was that hope, which bade thee look,
  For mercy in a Pirate's heart.

What woes can man on man inflict,
  When malice joins with uncheck'd power ;
Such woes, unpitied and unknown,
  For many a month the sailor bore !

Oft gem'd his eye the bursting tear,
  As mem'ry linger'd on past joy ;
As oft they flung the cruel jeer,
  And damn'd the " chicken liver'd boy."

When sick at heart, with " hope defer'd,"
  Kind sleep his wasting form embrac'd,
Some ready minion ply'd the lash,
  And the lov'd dream of freedom chas'd.

Fast to an end his miseries drew :
  The deadly hectic flush'd his cheek :
On his pale brow the cold dew hung,
  He sigh'd, and sunk upon the deck !

The sailor's woes drew forth no sigh ;
  No hand would close the sailor's eye :
Remorseless, his pale corse they gave,
  Unshrouded to the friendly wave.

And as he sunk beneath the tide,
  A hellish shout arose ;
Exultingly the demons cried,
  " So fare all Albion's Rebel Foes !"

■ This poem was published in the United States during the War of 1812 to highlight the plight of American sailors pressed into service by British sea captains. The poem tells the story of a young lad ripped from his shipmates and subjected to scorn and abuse by British sailors. After he dies, his corpse is thrown into the ocean. His tormentors exclaim, "So fare all Albion's [England's] Rebel Foes!"

nineteenth century, black mariners' pay equaled that of their white counterparts. And in this line of work, a man's skill, not the color of his skin, determined the nature of his job. With limited economic opportunities on shore, black sailors accepted the danger and long absences from home. However, neither black nor white sailors had bargained for enforced service in His Majesty's Royal Navy.

Seizure, or impressment, reminded Americans of their pre–Revolutionary War days, when British "press gangs" prowled the docks of American port cities and seized colonial merchant sailors. In 1807 the tensions over this practice erupted into violence. Just ten miles off the shore of Virginia, the American ship *Chesapeake* came under attack from a British vessel. British naval officers claimed that the Americans were harboring four British deserters. In the ensuing exchange of cannon fire, 3 Americans were killed and 18 wounded. Jefferson demanded that England leave American sailors and ships alone, but he was rebuffed.

In 1807 President Jefferson decided to place an embargo on all exports to the European powers in an effort to force those nations to respect the rights of Americans on the high seas. The move aroused intense opposition in Federalist-dominated New England, where the regional economy depended heavily on foreign trade. The Embargo Act passed by Congress halted the shipment of goods from the United States to Europe. Because Europe—including England—relied heavily on American grain and timber, Jefferson hoped that the move would force England to respect American independence. The president saw this measure as preferable to either war or capitulation to England, but the New England states, which were particularly hard hit by the embargo, saw the matter quite differently. As the effects of the embargo took hold, the New England grain growers saw the markets for their products dry up, and the ship-building industry, which made heavy use of timber, ground to a standstill. Southern tobacco and cotton planters faced similar hardship because of the embargo. By 1808 some of them had joined with Northerners to circumvent the embargo by moving their goods through Canada and then to Europe.

> *The embargo seemed only to intensify, not lessen, tensions between England and the United States.*

Yet Jefferson held his course. He prodded Congress to enforce the unpopular act, but his efforts provoked a backlash. Ordinary citizens compared him to George III, and New England politicians threatened to take their states out of the union. Despite all the uproar, the embargo did benefit Americans in some ways. Specifically, it encouraged New Englanders to rely more on goods produced locally and less on foreign imports. Jefferson had advocated a policy that had an unanticipated effect: it promoted industrialization at home. At the same time, the embargo seemed only to intensify, not lessen, tensions between England and the United States.

On the Brink of War

Both the Federalists and the Democratic-Republicans suffered a blow to their leadership in 1804. That year, the Federalist party lost one of its original leaders with the death of Alexander Hamilton at the hand of his rival, Aaron Burr. Both successful New York attorneys, the two men had risen together through the political ranks in the 1780s and 1790s. Burr served as Jefferson's running mate in the election of 1800; four years later he ran for governor of New York. Incensed by a report that Hamilton had claimed he was "a dangerous man, and one who ought not to be trusted with the reins of government," as well as "still more despicable rumors," Burr challenged his antagonist to a pistol duel in Weehawken, New Jersey, in July 1804. (Many European American men, especially in the South, considered dueling a means to preserve their honor in response to a perceived insult leveled at them or at a family member.) As the combatants faced off, Burr fired at Hamilton. Mortally wounded, Hamilton died the next day. As a result, Burr's political career lay in ruins. In 1807 he stood trial for treason, charged with conspiring to create an empire for himself out of the territory Spain held west of the Mississippi. Acquitted of the charges, he nevertheless fled the United States for Europe.

Jefferson declined to run for a third presidential term in 1808, and he left office in March 1809 upon the inauguration of the new president, James Madison. Soon after Madison took office, Congress repealed the embargo and replaced it with the Non-Intercourse Act, which eased the complete ban on exports to Europe. This measure permitted American exporters to ship their goods to all European countries except for France and England, still at war with one another. New Englanders opposed even this limited embargo.

Meanwhile, the Federalists' influence in Congress was waning. The partisan division within Congress—the Federalists, with their emphasis on a strong national government, against the localist Democratic-Republicans—gradually eased. That division had emerged in response to the ratification of the Constitution and debates over the direction of the new nation. By 1810 a new split had emerged—between young, hotheaded representatives from the West and their more conservative seniors from the eastern seaboard. The western group, or "war hawks," called on the nation to revive its former glory. Americans must uphold U.S. honor, they declared, by opposing European, especially British, claims to military dominance. The war hawks also yearned to vanquish the Indians who impeded settlement of the area west of the Mississippi.

In 1810 Congress passed legislation called Macon's Bill No. 2. Under its provisions, if either France or England agreed to resume trade with the United States, then the Americans would resume trade with that country and refuse to trade with the other. France's emperor Napoleon seized this offer to reestablish economic ties with the United States. Outraged, England began to contemplate war not only with its arch enemy, France, but also with the upstart United States. The new nation had positioned itself directly in the middle of a conflict between the two major European powers.

Looking eastward, the war hawks saw an England determined to defile the honor of their young nation. Looking westward, these same men saw an equally threatening menace: the rise of an ominous Indian resistance movement that blended military strength with native spirituality. The movement was led by Shawnee brothers Tecumseh and Tenskwatawa. Tenskwatawa (also known as the Prophet) claimed that he had a vision in which he received a message from the world's creator. In the Prophet's words, the creator stated that European Americans "grew from the scum of the great water, when it was troubled by an evil spirit and the froth was driven into the woods by a strong east wind." The Prophet declared to other Indians, "They are numerous, but I hate them. They are unjust; they have taken away your lands, which were not made for them."

In 1808 the two brothers founded Prophet's Town in Indiana. They envisioned a sovereign Indian state and the preservation of Native American culture. Tenskwatawa spoke of a time and place where Indians would reject alcohol and scorn "the food of whites" as well as the "wealth and ornaments" of commercial trade. Tecumseh set out to deliver the message to as many Indian groups as possible, traveling the broad swath of territory from Florida to Canada.

In his journey south, Tecumseh found the Creek nation in Muskogee Territory particularly receptive to his message of Indian solidarity. By that time the Creeks had lost millions of acres of land to the Americans. Tecumseh deputized a relative, Seekaboo, to remain with the Creeks and instruct them in the religion of Tenskwatawa. He could not know that, within a few years, Tenskwatawa's message would spark armed conflict between the Creeks and American troops.

Library of Congress

■ This lithograph of the Prophet (Tenskwatawa) was based on an 1824 painting of the Shawnee mystic and holy man. Early in life, he suffered an accident with bows and arrows, losing his right eye. He and his older brother Tecumseh called on all Indians to resist the encroachment of their lands by whites and to renounce the way of life followed by whites, including the use of liquor. After the Indians' defeat at the Battle of Tippecanoe in 1811, the Prophet retreated to Canada. He returned to the United States in 1826. By that time he no longer wielded influence as a leader of the Shawnees.

Meanwhile, in 1809, the territorial governor of Indiana, William Henry Harrison, plied a group of Indian leaders with liquor, then got them to agree to sell 3 million acres to the U.S. government for just $7600. Upon hearing of the deal, Tecumseh decried a new form of American aggression: "treaties" between U.S. officials and Indians who lacked the authority to sell their people's homeland. "All red men," Tecumseh proclaimed, "[must] unite in claiming a common and equal right in the land, as it was at first, and should be yet; for it never was divided, but belongs to all, for the use of each."

In November 1811 Harrison led 1000 U.S. soldiers in an advance on Prophet's Town. But before they could reach the settlement, several hundred Shawnees under the command

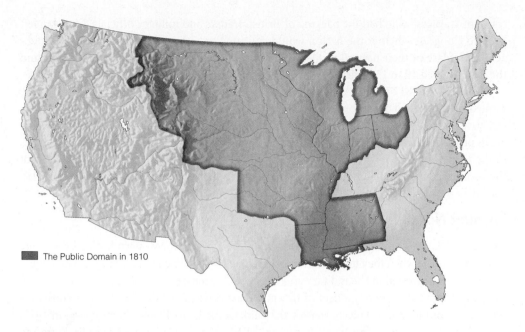

■ **MAP 10.2**

THE PUBLIC DOMAIN IN 1810   This map indicates the expanse of western lands owned by the U.S. government in 1810, after the Louisiana Purchase. American war veterans received land warrants in return for military service in the Revolutionary War and the War of 1812. A warrant entitled the bearer to settle a specific number of acres of unoccupied lands. Warrants could be transferred, sold, and traded like stocks and bonds. After the War of 1812, the government issued 29,186 land warrants for a total of 4.8 million acres.

Source: After Charles O. Paulin, *Atlas of Historical Geography* (Washington, DC), Plate 57.

of Tenskwatawa attacked their camp on the Tippecanoe River. The Indians suffered a sound defeat, and Harrison burned Prophet's Town to the ground. A Potawatomi chief, Shabonee, who fought at the Battle of Tippecanoe, later recalled the false sense of superiority that had inspired the Indians' doomed attack on Harrison and his men. According to Shabonee, the Indians believed, "the white soldiers are not warriors. Their hands are soft. Their faces are white. One half of them are calico [fabric] peddlers. The other half can only shoot squirrels." Warriors or not, the Americans had a distinct advantage over the Indians: better guns. Clearly, military technology, not just determination, would shape the western conflict.

The War of 1812

The defeat of the Shawnees at Tippecanoe only inflamed western war hawks' passions and stiffened their resolve to break the back of Indian resistance altogether. But to achieve this goal, the United States would have to invade Canada and eliminate the British arms suppliers who had been trading with the Indians. Claiming the mantle of patriotism, western and southern members of the House of Representatives agitated for a war that would eliminate both the British threat on the high seas and the Canada-based Indian–British alliance. These Americans wanted a war that would win for them a true independence once and for all. "On to Canada! On to Canada!" became the rallying cry of the war hawks.

In a secret message sent to Congress on June 1, 1812, President Madison listed Americans' many grievances against England: the British Navy's seizure of American citizens, the blockades of American goods, and continued conflict "on one of our extensive frontiers," the result of "savages" who had the backing of British traders and military officials. Madison left it up to Congress whether the nation would continue to endure these indignities or would act "in defense of their natural rights." Seventeen days later, the House voted 79 to 49 and the Senate voted 19 to 13 to declare war on England and, by extension, the western Indians.

The War of 1812 united Americans behind a banner of national expansion. But, at the same time, it exposed dangerous divisions between regions of the country and between political viewpoints. Many New Englanders saw the conflict as a plot by Virginia Democratic-Republicans primarily to aid France in opposition to England and to add agrarian (that is, slave) states to the Union. In an ironic twist, the New England Federalists—usually staunch defenders of the national government—argued that states should control their own commerce and militias.

Pushing North

Although the Americans were better armed and organized than the western Indians, they were at a disadvantage when they took on the soldiers and sailors of the British Empire. The United States had not invested in the military and thus was ill-prepared for all-out war. The American navy consisted of merely a fleet of tiny gunboats constructed during the cost-conscious Jefferson administration. The charter for the Bank of the United States had expired in 1811, depriving the country of a vital source of financial credit. Suffering from a drop in tax revenues as a result of the embargo on foreign trade, the nation lacked the funds to train and equip the regular army and the state militias. Nevertheless, in the fall of 1812, the Americans launched an ambitious three-pronged attack against Canada, striking from Niagara, Detroit, and Lake Champlain. All three attempts failed miserably.

Lacking united, enthusiastic support on the home front, the Americans' offensive got off to a bad start. Yet some people, even in Federalist New England, believed that all Americans should support the war, regardless of the potential outcome. Writing from a Federalist stronghold in December 1812, Abigail Adams (the wife of former president John Adams) acknowledged to a correspondent that her home state of Massachusetts "had much to complain of" because the war had severely disrupted trade. However, she added, "that cannot justify [Massachusetts] in paralyzing the arm of Government [that is, opposing federal trade policies], when raised for her defense and that of the nation." She warned against "a house divided against itself," which she believed could be the nation's undoing.

In the West, the British moved to take advantage of divisions on American soil. They cemented their long-standing alliance with the Indians, who possessed both military prowess and an abiding hatred of the land-hungry Americans. In late 1812, Tecumseh (who had accepted a commission as a brigadier general in the British army) and British General Isaac Brock captured Detroit. Indians also participated in England's successful raid on Fort Dearborn (Chicago). In at least two cases, when U.S. soldiers marched into Canada, they lost their advantage when state militia members refused to cross the border. Leaders of these militias claimed that their sole purpose was to defend their states from attack, not invade foreign territory.

BIG DICK AT THE 'MERMAID'S RETREAT.' SEE CHAPTER II.

Courtesy, Dartmouth University Library

■ In 1815 approximately 6000 American prisoners of war were confined to Britain's dank Dartmoor Prison in Devonshire, England. Many of them were African Americans, who represented one-fifth of all sailors who fought in the war. Among that group was Richard Crafus. An imposing man, Crafus earned the title "King Dick" by serving as the leader of the central barracks at Dartmoor, where blacks were held. He strolled through the cell block, carrying a large club and settling disputes between the prisoners.

■ **MAP 10.3**

THE NORTHERN FRONT, WAR OF 1812   Much of the fighting of the War of 1812 centered in the Great Lakes region. It was there, the war hawks charged, that the British were inciting Indians to attack American settlements. Conducted in 1812 and 1813, the campaign against Canada was supposed to eliminate the British threat and, some Americans hoped, win Canadian territory for the United States.

Yet the Americans scored some notable successes in 1813. That September, Commodore Oliver H. Perry defeated a British fleet on Lake Erie. Exhilarated, he declared, "We have met the enemy and they are ours." But Perry's victory came at a steep price. Shortly before the engagement, about a third of all the officers and men in the American fleet had fallen victim to a typhus epidemic. Then the battle started. By the end of the day, of the 100 men who had reported for duty that morning, 21 were dead and more than 60 wounded.

Perry's hard-won victory forced the British back into Canada, over Tecumseh's objections. General William Henry Harrison followed in hot pursuit. British Colonel Henry Proctor marched his troops to eastern Ontario, leaving Tecumseh to try holding the Americans at bay. At the Battle of the Thames (that October), Harrison defeated the Indians. Many perished, Tecumseh among them. A group of Kentucky soldiers skinned what they mistakenly believed to be his corpse. His body was never found.

Later that autumn, an American campaign against Montreal failed. The Americans trudged back into New York state, the British close behind them. Flush with their victory in Montreal, the British captured Fort Niagara and set Buffalo and other nearby towns aflame.

By mid–1814, the English had also crushed Napoleon. This success freed up 15,000 British troops, who promptly sailed for North America. Still, in July 1814 the Americans, under the leadership of Major General Jacob Brown and Brigadier General Winfield Scott, managed to defeat the British at the Battle of Chippewa, across the Niagara River from Buffalo. But by the end that year, the Americans had withdrawn to their own territory and relinquished their goal of invading and conquering Canada. The arrival of fresh British troops forced the Americans to defend their own soil.

Fighting on Many Fronts

For the Americans, the most humiliating episode of the war came with the British attack on the nation's capital. On August 24, 1814, the British army, backed by the Royal Navy, sailed into Chesapeake Bay. At the Battle of Bladensburg, Maryland, they scattered the American troops they encountered. The Redcoats then advanced to Washington, where they torched the Capitol building and the White House, causing extensive damage to both structures.

The *Baltimore Patriot* carried an eyewitness account of the confusion surrounding the spectacle. Residents of the capital city had received word that the British were advancing. On Sunday, August 21, public officials frantically packed up their books and papers. Private citizens, also gathered up their furniture and other belongings and left town. By Tuesday, the city stood nearly empty. As a ragtag American force succumbed to the British, President Madison "retired from the mortifying scene, and left the city on horseback." His aides and some military officers accompanied him. As it turned out, he escaped just in the nick of time: by Wednesday flames had engulfed not only the capitol but also Monroe's residence. Disorganized, hungry, and hot, the American troops had put up scant resistance. The eyewitness reported, "Our army may with truth be said to have been beaten by fatigue, before they saw the enemy."

Yet the Americans rallied and pursued the British and overtook them in battle in Baltimore. (This victory inspired an observer, Francis Scott Key, to write "The Star Spangled Banner" as he watched "the bombs bursting in air" over Baltimore's Fort McHenry.) The Americans scored another crucial victory in September, when U.S. naval commander Thomas McDonough crushed the British fleet on Lake Champlain near Plattsburgh, New York.

In the Southeast, Tecumseh's message of Indian unity had resonated with particular force among Native Americans once the war broke out. Some Cherokees and Choctaws cast their lot with the United States. However, a minority of Creeks were emboldened by Tenskwatawa's message, "War now. War forever. War upon the living. War upon the dead; dig up their corpses from the grave; our country must give no rest to a white man's bones." By 1813, a group of warriors called Red Sticks (for their scarlet-painted weapons) stood ready to do battle with the Americans. Yet they faced opposition from some of their own people, the White Sticks, who counseled peace. The Red Sticks finally decided to attack Fort Mims (in what is now Alabama). In response, Andrew Jackson, leader of the Tennessee militia, received a commission as major general. His mission was to retaliate against the Indians.

Jackson had a history as a speculator in Indian lands in Mississippi Territory. Even in a country where anti-Indian sentiment ran high, his views were extreme. He called Native Americans "savage bloodhounds" and "blood thirsty barbarians." After the attack on Fort Mims, he vowed, "I must destroy those deluded victims doomed to distruction by their own restless and savage conduct." He boasted about collecting the scalps of all his Indian victims.

Jackson's 3500 troops laid waste to Creek territory. Regiments of Cherokee, Choctaw, and Chickasaw Indians, as well as White Sticks, helped them. During a monumental battle in March 1814,

Gilbert Stuart, *George Washington*. White House Collection, Courtesy, White House Historical Association (21)

■ **Dolly Madison, wife of the president, helped to rescue this famous painting of George Washington by artist Gilbert Stuart when the British invaded Washington in August 1814. The full-length portrait hung in what was then called the President's House. She later wrote a friend that the British attack had rendered her "so unfeminine as to be free from fear." She had hoped to remain in the mansion "if I could have had a cannon through every window, but alas! Those who should have placed them there, fled."**

Library of Congress

■ This engraving, published in 1814, depicts the bombardment of Fort McHenry by British warships in September of that year. When he witnessed the battle, Francis Scott Key, a Washington lawyer, was aboard a prisoner exchange boat in Baltimore Harbor. He was seeking release of a friend captured by the British. After penning the poem "The Star Spangled Banner," Key set the words to music, using the tune of a popular English drinking song. Congress declared the song the national anthem in 1931.

more than three-quarters of the 1000 defending Red Sticks and a number of Indian women and children died at Horseshoe Band (in modern-day Alabama). Jackson survived the battle thanks to the intervention of a Cherokee soldier. Some American soldiers took their victory to a brutal extreme; they flayed the corpses of their victims and made horse bridles out of their skin.

Yet Jackson insisted on praising his soldiers as a civilizing force. They were only reclaiming the land from a band of savages, he explained. In a postbattle speech to the men under his command, he declared,

> In their places a new generation [of Indians] will arise who know their duties better. The weapons of warfare will be exchanged for the utensils of husbandry; and the wilderness which now withers in sterility and seems to mourn the desolation which overspreads it, will blossom as the rose, and become the nursery of the arts.

In the Treaty of Horseshoe Bend that followed the massacre, the Americans forced the Creek Nation to give up 23 million acres. The remnants of the Red Sticks fled to the swamps of Florida. There they eventually regrouped in the company of fugitive slaves, as Seminoles (from the Spanish *cimarrones,* or runaway slaves).

Jackson next marched to New Orleans to confront the British. Knowing he would be facing some of Europe's finest soldiers, he assembled 7000 men, U.S. soldiers and militiamen from the states of Louisiana, Kentucky, and Tennessee. Two Kentucky regiments consisted of free Negro volunteers, about 400 men in total. The Battle of New Orleans, fought on January 8,

■ A scene from the Battle of New Orleans.

1815, began with a ferocious assault by British soldiers. But within just half an hour, 2000 of them lay dead or wounded. The Americans lost only 70. They had vanquished the army of Europe's greatest military power.

An Uncertain Victory

American and British negotiators had signed a peace agreement that ended the war two weeks before "Old Hickory" defeated the British in New Orleans. (Jackson received his nickname when one of his soldiers called him "tough as hickory.") Later, many Americans associated Andrew Jackson with the war's decisive battle and most glorious victory. The Battle of New Orleans might have been a glorious victory for the Americans, but it was hardly the decisive battle of the war.

In the fall of 1814 Madison had decided to end the war. He dispatched John Quincy Adams, son of former president John Adams, to the Belgian city of Ghent to start negotiations. Representative Henry Clay and three other American envoys accompanied Adams. At first, English representatives to the meeting made two demands. The Americans, they said, must agree to the creation of an Indian territory in the upper Great Lakes region. They must also cede much of the state of Maine to England. The Americans refused, and the negotiations dragged on.

In the meantime, the New England states had grown increasingly impatient with what they called "Mr. Madison's war." As with the embargo, they saw the effort as a mistake and a threat to their regional commercial interests. In December 1814, Massachusetts, Connecticut, Rhode Island, New Hampshire, and Vermont sent delegates to a gathering in Hartford, Connecticut, to consider a course of action. The delegates demanded that the federal government give their states financial aid to compensate for the revenue they had lost as a result of disrupted trade. Some delegates even hinted that their states wanted to secede from the union. Although most delegates shied away from the idea, the majority of them apparently wanted to leave that possibility open.

Back in Ghent, the British had reversed their initial position by late December. They had lost recent battles in upper New York and in Baltimore and, as always, were still worried about new threats from France. They dropped their demands for territory and for an Indian buffer state in the upper Midwest. They also agreed to an armistice that, in essence, represented a draw: both combatants would retain the same territory they had possessed when the war began. The British made no concessions to the Americans' demands that they stop impressing American sailors and supplying the western Indians with arms or that they revoke the Orders in Council. Still, most U.S. citizens considered the war a great victory for the United States. After 1815, the Americans and the British never again met each other across a battlefield as enemies.

Some of the American soldiers and sailors who had survived the conflict paid a high price. For example, Benjamin F. Palmer was an American sailor imprisoned in an English jail from 1813 to 1815. There he subsisted on meager rations and witnessed unspeakable cruelties, including the murder of inmates by guards. In all probability, the Treaty of Ghent did not change Palmer's views of the British soldiers' "Brutal & Savage Barbarity." In total, 6000 American combatants had died or suffered wounds in the war. Yet survivors felt that they and their dead fellows had preserved the nation's honor.

Many Indians saw matters quite differently. For them, the War of 1812 had only stiffened white settlers' determination to take native peoples' land. Andrew Jackson, the Indian-hater and Indian-killer, would aggressively pursue a national political career. And so, the Battle of Horseshoe Bend signaled not only a continuation of bloodshed but also a terrifying sign of things to come. American nationalism came at the expense of vast Indian homelands and thousands of lives on both sides.

The "Era of Good Feelings"?

In 1816 the Democratic-Republicans nominated James Monroe for president, to run against Federalist candidate Rufus King. Although Monroe only narrowly won his party's endorsement, he soundly defeated King in the general election. Monroe benefited from several developments that had mortally wounded the Federalist party: the War of 1812 victory, presided over by a Democratic-Republican chief executive; the New England Federalists' flirtation with secession (and treason) during the war years; and the strong nationalist tendencies of both the Jefferson and Madison administrations, which had stolen the Federalists' thunder.

Addressing Congress in December 1817, Monroe expressed optimism about the state of the nation. The country's boundaries were secure, and the Indians had little choice but to retreat farther and farther west. The president predicted that, shortly, "Indian hostilities, if they do not altogether cease, will henceforth lose their terror." Equally inspiring, the Americans had once again defied the British Empire and won. Two treaties with Britain—the Rush–Bagot of 1817 and the Convention of 1818—set the U.S.–Canadian border at the 49th parallel and provided that the two countries would jointly occupy Oregon Territory for ten years.

Monroe called on Congress to acknowledge "the vast extent of territory within the United States [and] the great amount and value of its productions" and to facilitate the construction of roads and canals. It was this "happy situation of the United States," in Monroe's words, that ushered in what some historians called "The Era of Good Feelings." Although voters continued to disagree over some issues of the day—such as the national bank, sectionalism, and internal improvements—they did not necessarily express those disagreements in the form of bitter partisan wrangling. In any case, the term "good feelings" can be applied only to a

TABLE 10-2		
The Election of 1816		
Candidate	**Political Party**	**Electoral Vote**
James Monroe	Democratic-Republican	183
Rufus King	Federalist	34

Benjamin Hawkins and the Creek Indians, c. 1805. Greenville County Museum of Art, South Carolina

■ Southeastern Indians varied widely in their willingness to adopt European American ways. Some argued that the best way to preserve their community and remain on the land of their forebears was to accommodate themselves to white practices of trade, textile production, and farming. This 1805 painting shows Benjamin Hawkins, a government Indian agent, at a Creek settlement near Macon, Georgia. Hawkins expresses evident satisfaction with the Indians' neat cabins, well-tended fields, flocks of sheep, and bountiful harvest of vegetables.

narrow group of enfranchised citizens, men who shared common beliefs about territorial expansion and economic development.

The War of 1812 yielded little in the way of material gains for the United States or concessions from England. Yet it permanently reshaped American social, political, and economic life. The nation exploited the vulnerable southeastern Indians and hastened their removal from their homeland. Many veterans of the war gained land grants, military glory, and political influence in return for their sacrifices. Although the war had disrupted foreign trade, it also gave home manufacturers a tremendous boost. The textile industry spearheaded a revolution in industry. And a new class of workers—factory operatives (machine tenders)—emerged to symbolize both the promise and the hazards of technological innovation.

Praise and Respect for Veterans After the War

American veterans of the War of 1812 won the praise of a grateful nation. Even the British expressed a grudging respect for Americans' fighting abilities. One British naval officer admitted, "I don't like Americans; I never did, and never shall like them." He further declared that he had "no wish to eat with them, drink with them, deal with them, or consort with them in any way." But, he said, he would rather not fight with them either, for they were "an enemy so brave, determined, and alert, and in every way so worthy of one's steel, as they have always proved." To reward veterans for their service, Congress offered them 160-acre plots of land in the territory between the Illinois and Mississippi rivers. These grants did much to encourage families to emigrate west and establish homesteads.

Cherokee Women Petition Against Further Land Sales to Whites in 1817

In traditional Cherokee society, men took responsibility for foreign affairs while women focused on domestic matters, leading to a roughly equal division of labor. However, European American diplomats, military officials, and traders dealt primarily with Indian men. As a result, beginning in the eighteenth century, Cherokee women's traditional influence was eroding within their own communities. In this new world, Indian warriors wielded significant power.

Nevertheless, Cherokee women insisted on presenting their views during the crisis of 1817–1819, when men of the group were deciding whether to cede land to U.S. authorities and move west. The following petition was supported by Nancy Ward, a Cherokee War Woman. This honorific title was bestowed on women who accompanied and attended to the needs of war parties. Ward had supported the colonists' cause during the American Revolution.

Wilma Mankiller, Cherokee Chief

Peter Turnley/CORBIS

Amovey [Tennessee] in Council 2nd May 1817

The Cherokee Ladys now being present at the meeting of the Chiefs and warriors in council have thought it their duties as mothers to address their beloved Chiefs and warriors now assembled.

Our beloved children and head men of the Cherokee nation we address you warriors in council we have raised all of you on the land which we now have, which God gave to us to inhabit and raise provisions we know that our country has once been extensive but by repeated sales has become circumscribed to a small tract, and [we] never have thought it our duty to interfere in the disposition of it till now, if a father or mother was to sell all their lands which they had to depend on which their children had to raise their living on which would indeed be bad and to be removed to another country we do not wish to go to an unknown country [to] which we have understood some of our children wish to go over the Mississippi but this act of our children would be like destroying your mothers. Your mothers your sisters ask and beg of you not to part with any more of our lands, we say ours[. Y]ou are our descendants and take pity on our request, but keep it for our growing children for it was the good will of our creator to place us here and you know our father the great president [James Monroe], will not allow his white children to take our country away for if it was not they would not ask you to put your hands to paper for it would be impossible to remove us all for as soon as one child is raised, we have others in our arms for such is our situation and will consider our circumstance.

Therefore children don't part with any more of our lands but continue on it and enlarge your farms and cultivate and raise corn and cotton and we your mothers and sisters will make clothing for you which our father the president has recommended to us all we don't charge anybody for selling any lands, but we have heard such intentions of our children but your talks become true at last and it was our desire to forewarn you all not to part with our lands.

Nancy Ward to her children[:] warriors to take pity and listen to the talks of your sisters, although I am very old yet cannot but pity the situation in which you will hear of their minds. I have great many grand children which I wish they do well on our land.

In addition to Nancy Ward, 12 Cherokee women signed the petition. Their names suggest the varying degrees of assimilation to white ways on the part of Cherokees in general. Petitioners included Cun, o, ah and Widow Woman Holder, as well as Jenny McIntosh and Mrs. Nancy Fields.

It is unclear what effect, if any, this petition had on Cherokee male leaders. The Cherokee nation did halt land cessions to whites between 1819 and 1835. ■

Source: Cherokee Women to Cherokee Council, May 2, 1817, series 1, Andrew Jackson Presidential Papers, Library of Congress Manuscripts Division, Washington, D.C. Reprinted in Nancy F. Cott, Jeanne Boydston, Ann Braude, Lori Ginzberg, and Molly Ladd-Taylor, eds., *Root of Bitterness: Documents of the Social History of American Women* (Boston: Northeastern University Press, 1996), pp. 177–178.

Some military heroes of the war parlayed their success into impressive political careers. Andrew Jackson won election to the presidency in 1824, William Henry Harrison, in 1840. Winfield Scott served in a war against Mexico in 1848 and ran for president in 1852.

But European American veterans were not the only ones to gain status and influence within their own communities as a result of the conflict. A Cherokee leader named the Ridge also earned the gratitude of American officials for his contributions to the war effort. (His original Indian name, Kah-nung-da-tla-geh, means "the Man Who Walks on the Mountaintop.") The Ridge accepted the government's attempts to press the Cherokees to adopt European American ways. When the Ridge married a Cherokee woman named Susanna Wickett in the early 1790s, the couple settled in a log cabin (in northwest Georgia) rather than in a traditional Cherokee dwelling made of hardened clay daubed onto a wooden frame. During the war against the Red Sticks, the Ridge served under Andrew Jackson and earned the title of major. For the rest of his life, the Cherokee leader was known as Major Ridge. His wife devoted herself to tending an orchard, keeping a garden, and sewing clothes, tasks traditionally performed by European American but not Native American women. Eventually, the family prospered and bought African American slaves. They eventually became Christians as well.

The Ridge's battlefield experiences earned him the respect of other Cherokees who embraced the "civilization" program that missionaries and government officials promoted. At the same time, the Ridge vehemently resisted U.S. officials' attempts to persuade the Cherokee to give up their lands to whites and move west. Emerging as a leader of the Cherokee nation after the War of 1812, he criticized members of his group who had abandoned their lands in favor of a new life in the West. He declared, "I scorn this movement of a few men to unsettle the nation, and trifle with our attachment to the land of our forefathers." The Ridge believed that his people should adopt some elements of white culture but should also hold fast to their native lands in opposition to white settlers and politicians.

This cartoon, c. 1810, reveals two sides to the western emigration question. On the right, a well-dressed Easterner sets out for Ohio. He encounters a dejected, ragged migrant returning home. The men's horses tell a larger story about the failed dreams and hardship endured by many western emigrants. In the caption the artist cautions travelers on "the impropriety and folly of emigrating" from New England to the "Western Wilderness."

Courtesy, American Antiquarian Society

A Thriving Economy

The Embargo of 1807 and the War of 1812 stimulated home manufactures—especially the production of cloth and other goods in private households and factories. Home manufacturing resulted in a significant shift in the national economy—from reliance on imported goods to the production of those goods at home. The experiences of one rural Massachusetts family demonstrate the impact this shift had on individuals. Before the war, Lucy Kellogg and her sister worked at home, braiding straw hats to be sold at market. The war ruined their straw business, since economic hardship among New Englanders meant fewer people could afford to buy hats. In response, the sisters invested in cotton looms, which they used to make cloth. They secured cotton thread from the Massachusetts factories that had sprung up during the war to compensate for the lack of English textile imports. The Kellogg sisters found a ready market for their shirts, gingham dresses, and bed tickings. Still, their family was restless, moving briefly to New Hampshire but then returning to Worcester, where they resumed farming.

The end of the war saw up an upsurge in this kind of internal migration. New Englanders, especially, pushed west in search of new opportunities. Between 1800 and 1820, the population of Ohio grew from 45,000 to 581,000. Nevertheless, some emigrants expressed disillusion with the hardships and rigors of western life. Clearing the land of trees and then living in an isolated cabin did not appeal to everyone. John Stillman Wright initially sold his New York State farm in 1818 and settled in Ohio with high hopes. Later, he published *Letters from the West*, which recounted "the cruel disappointment and vain regret, which so many thousands are now enduring."

New means of transportation—and new means to fund them—facilitated the movement of goods, people, and ideas from the East to the West (and, in some cases, back again). Indeed, riding in stagecoaches, wagons, and boats and on horseback, Americans seemed to be on the move constantly. In 1807 an entrepreneur named Robert Fulton piloted the *Clermont,* a new kind of boat powered by steam, up the Hudson River from New York City. Within a few years, such vessels were plying the western waterways: the Columbia, Sacramento, Colorado, and Mississippi rivers and their tributaries. Steamboats traveled up river, against the current, ten times faster than keelboats, which had to be pushed, pulled, or hauled by men or mules.

New improvements in land transportation also stimulated economic growth. The profits that the Philadelphia and Lancaster Turnpike raked in by charging travelers tolls inspired other local private corporations to invest in roads. By 1810 several thousand such corporations were building roads up and down the East Coast. Funding came from a variety of sources, both public and private. Philadelphia textile mill owners financed transportation links with the city's hinterland (rural areas to the west) to bring their goods to the largest number of customers. Individual cities also invested in routes westward. The state of Virginia authorized a board of public works to expend funds for roads and other internal improvements. Western politicians flexed their political muscle in 1806 by securing congressional authorization for the building of the Cumberland (later National) Road, which snaked through the Allegheny Mountains and ended at the Ohio River.

> *New improvements in land transportation also stimulated economic growth.*

The acceleration of commerce in the West, combined with the disruption in trade from Europe that had come with the embargo and war, stimulated manufacturing throughout the United States. Philadelphia's growth proved particularly dazzling. During the War of 1812, the city's craft producers did not have to worry about foreign competition. Local merchant-financiers, who otherwise might have been pouring their money into trade ventures, began to invest in manufacturing. As early as 1808, the city's new factories had compensated for the glass, chemicals, shot, soap, lead, and earthenware that no longer flooded in from England. Philadelphia soon took the lead in production of all kinds, whether carried out in factories, artisans' shops, or private homes. Metalworking, ale brewing, and leather production counted among the array of thriving industries that made Philadelphia the nation's top industrial city in 1815.

Still, in 1820, about two-thirds of all Philadelphia workers labored in small shops employing fewer than six people. Only 10 percent were employed in establishments larger than nine people. Moreover, because of an influx of English and Irish immigrants in the late eighteenth century, the city never developed a mechanized textile industry along the lines of New England's. Many of these newcomers were skilled textile workers; they continued to work in small shops rather than tend machines in large factories like New England textile workers.

Transformations in the Workplace

Even the earliest stages of the industrial revolution transformed the way people lived and worked. Some crafts—for example, the production of leather, barrels, soap, candles, and newspapers—expanded from small shops with skilled artisans into larger establishments with unskilled wage earners. In these cases, production was reorganized; now wage earners under the supervision of a boss replaced apprentices and journeymen who had formerly worked alongside a master artisan. These workers performed a single task many times a day instead of using their specialized skills to see a production process through to completion.

While skilled artisans were alarmed at the prospect of being reduced to mere "hands" tending machines, the sons and daughters of many New England farmers eagerly took new jobs in the mills. They appreciated the opportunity to escape close family supervision, to live on their own, and to earn cash wages. Some farm hands and manual laborers considered factory work, no matter how grueling and ill-paid, preferable to plowing fields, digging ditches, and

Revolutions in Transportation

The introduction of commercial steamboat service in 1807 marked a new era in seafaring transportation. Until that time, improving the speed of ships involved adding more sails while still relying on windpower. With the invention of the steam-powered boat, shippers were no longer at the mercy of the wind and the currents.

Over the generations, American prosperity has depended on moving things—whether barrels of flour, new computers, or people—over long and short distances. New forms of power such as steam, electricity, and gasoline, combined with innovations in technology and engineering, produced revolutions in transportation.

The first railroads also relied on steam engines; they challenged wagons and horses as the most efficient means of moving across land. During the Civil War, northern and southern armies used railroads to move men, weapons, and supplies to battlefields. This task was complicated by the South's lack of a standard railroad gauge, (that is, a uniform track size) necessitating unloading goods from one train and loading them onto another.

By the end of the nineteenth century, five transcontinental railroad lines spanned the entire breadth of the United States. During this time, two specific innovations transformed rail travel and transport. The Pullman sleeping car allowed passengers to travel long distances in comfort. Refrigerated cars allowed farmers to ship fresh vegetables, fruits, and meat to distant markets and consumers.

In the 1880s the first streetcars ran on electric power. Gasoline-powered engines propelled automobiles (developed in the 1890s) and airplanes, inaugurated by the first successful flight of brothers Orville and Wilbur Wright in 1903. By the 1920s, automobiles were the chief means of passenger transportation, and trucks rivaled trains as means of shipping foodstuffs and manufactured goods. Commercial airline service began in the 1950s. In the late twentieth century, shippers introduced a system called containerization, a form of transportation linking land, sea, and water. Containers of uniform size could be loaded onto ships, trucks, or trains, facilitating the international trade necessary to a global economy.

Various means of conveyance relied on new developments in engineering. Locks adjusted the water level of canals that were integral to freight transportation in the eastern United States in the first half of the nineteenth century. Crucial to the westward migration of thousands of Americans during that period were interstate roads. Costing $6.82 million, the gravel-paved Great National Pike stretched from Cumberland, Maryland, to Vandalia, Illinois. Begun in 1806, it took 34 years to complete. The first transcontinental railroad, finished in 1869, was an engineering marvel, with trestles spanning deep chasms, tracks running alongside rivers, and tunnels burrowing through mountains.

hauling lumber. Chauncey Jerome, a young Connecticut man, lamented that few opportunities were open to him in rural areas: "There being no manufacturing of any account in the country, the poor boys were obliged to let themselves to the farmers, and it was extremely difficult to find a place where they would treat a poor boy like a human being."

New England rapidly became the center of mechanized textile production in the United States. By the late eighteenth century, Boston shippers were making handsome profits by supplying Alta Californio (the area north of San Diego, encompassing present-day California, Nevada, and parts of Arizona and Utah) with cloth, shoes, and tools, selling Western otter pelts in China, and returning home laden with Chinese porcelains and silks. These profits financed New England's mechanized textile industry. By 1813, 76 cotton mills housing a total of over 51,000 spindles had cropped up within the vicinity of Providence, Rhode Island.

Faced with a shortage of adult men (many were moving west), New England mill owners sought other local sources of labor. The Rhode Island system of production had relied on child spinners working in small mills. This system gave way to the Lowell model, based in Waltham and Lowell, Massachusetts, which brought young women from the surrounding countryside to work in gigantic mills. Many of the women were eager to earn cash wages and to escape the routine of farm life. Still, New England mill owners realized that they had to reas-

Modern transportation containers

Beginning in 1900, the largest cities constructed systems of underground tunnels for streetcars. Between 1900 and 1930, states and counties paved 700,000 miles of roads and highways. The Federal Aid Highway Act of 1956 established the interstate highway system. By the end of the twentieth century, the total highway mileage in the United States was 4 million miles, with about 46,000 of that number part of the interstate system. By this time almost 200,000 miles of pipeline carried various fuels and gases from Alaska to the continental United States and within and between states.

In 2000, approximately 125 million cars, 70 million trucks, 700,000 buses, and 200,000 aircraft were in use in the United States. The proliferation of vehicles put tremendous strains of the environment. Environmental regulations increased fuel efficiency, especially for newer vehicles; between 1970 and 2000, average miles per gallon on cars increased from 13.5 miles to 21.3 miles. In the early twenty-first century, the United States accounts for one-fourth of all fossil fuel emissions in the world. These emissions increase pollution in American cities and greenhouse gases worldwide.

In early 2002, President George W. Bush's administration announced a shift in federal policy, from a quest for ever-more fossil-fuel–efficient cars to the development of vehicles powered by hydrogen-based fuel cells. However, scientists predicted that this particular revolution in transportation was still decades in the future. ∎

sure Yankee parents that their daughters would find the factories to be safe, attractive places to work. Mill owners offered the young women housing in dormitory-like boardinghouses staffed by older women, called matrons, who looked after them.

Some New Englanders were unsettled by the social changes that accompanied these new ways of working. Factories encouraged parents to put their children to work rather than sending them to school. The new production system also widened the economic inequality between owners and wage hands. Colonial communities, where men and women, rich and poor, had worked together in the fields, gave way to mill towns. There, the wives of owners lived lives of privilege and leisure compared with the women who toiled at looms or spindles all day.

Nevertheless, New England had not yet developed what might be called a factory working class. Many people went back and forth between farm and factory, depending on their own fortunes and inclinations. Some workers were neither suited for nor inclined to work in or around the mills; they quit or were fired. One account in the contract books of the Pomfret Manufacturing Company in Massachusetts revealed that a 14-year-old girl named Sukey Blois was hired on May 7, 1807. The details of her hiring are followed by the words, "Quit May 10."

These transformations in the workplace and in social relations disturbed some white laborers in particular. They feared for their own status as freeborn, proud sons (and grandsons) of

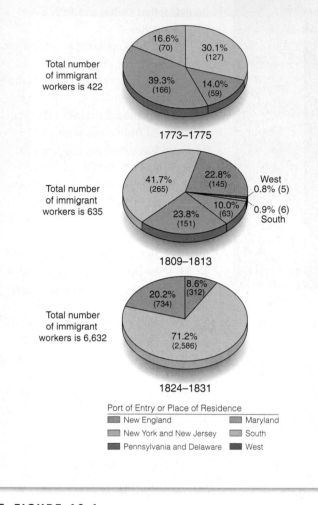

■ FIGURE 10.1
**GEOGRAPHIC LOCATIONS OF BRITISH IMMIGRANT
TEXTILE WORKERS, 1770s–1831**

Source: David J. Jeremy, *Transatlantic Industrial Revolution: Diffusion of Cotton
Power-Loom Weaving Technology* (Cambridge, MA: MIT Press, 1981), p. 156.

the Revolution. To them, the factory represented a loss of independence; they were becoming mere "hands" to tend machines. In 1806 striking Philadelphia shoemakers charged, "The name of freedom is but a shadow." The court ruled that by joining together to withhold their labor from their employer, these workers were guilty of conspiring to raise their own wages.

Some whites went so far as to claim that they were "wage slaves." No longer in charge of their own work lives, they felt condemned to long hours and low pay. The contrast between the ideal of household independence—a father and husband who owned property and could provide comfortably for his family—and the reality of men, women, and children working for pitiful wages in a noisy, dirty factory was profoundly demeaning to these men. They claimed that toiling for puny wages was not all that different from laboring as slaves.

Black men and women continued to suffer the stigma of slavery. Regardless of legal status, all blacks were descendants of slaves. This stigma determined the jobs for which blacks were hired and the pay they received. The 7500 free blacks who lived in New York City in 1810 were about only 8 percent of the city's total population. But they made up fully 84 percent of all black people in the city (the rest were enslaved children who would not gain their freedom until they became adults). They struggled to earn a living, and they had limited employment options. One job that was open to them was the dangerous, dirty work of cleaning chimneys. Black men served as master chimney sweeps and employed youths of their own race as assistants and apprentices. In an attempt to control the sweeps, the New York City Council tried to insist that they purchase expensive licenses to ply their trade. In response, a group of master chimney sweeps decried a double standard; resenting what they considered unreasonably high licensing fees, they declared that they wanted to be treated "in the same manner as you have thought proper to do in respect to Cartmen, porter, measurer &c." Realizing that they had to protect themselves, they established their own mutual aid society, the United Society of Chimney Sweeps. Some members asserted their equality with white men of the city by noting that they too had "served in the revolutionary war & some of them received wounds." Their efforts proved short-lived, however. Eventually, the use of machinery eroded black men's monopoly on this kind of work. Most black men could not afford to purchase the machines, which eliminated the need for skilled labor.

Chimney sweeps plied their trade by walking the streets and calling out loudly, "Sweep O! Sweep O!" to potential customers. In 1816 the New York City Common Council moved again to restrict the sweeps' work. The council outlawed "crying aloud or singing in the public streets." Those who persisted, council members warned, would be deprived of their licenses. In other cities as well, municipal officials, backed by white laborers, sought to regulate the behavior of black men who worked outdoors, whether it was pulling carts, cleaning streets, peddling goods, or emptying chamberpots. Whites claimed that black outside workers were noisy and disorderly. These complaints revealed the hypocrisy of white people, who relegated blacks to the most disagreeable jobs and then criticized these workers for not pursuing other (better) kinds of work.

In the coming years, some white workers embraced the cause of temperance as a means of distancing themselves from poor people in general and poor blacks in particular. White men's own sober behavior, they claimed, was far superior to that of the rowdy poor, especially black men and women who had to make their living by working outdoors, singing and "crying" for customers—practices that whites linked to drunken, disorderly behavior. White men in cities increasingly associated productive labor with inside work performed by people who practiced punctuality, thrift, and sobriety. Poor people of both races remained vulnerable to the charge of vagrancy. According to an observer in the New York *Independent Mechanic* in 1811, vagrants "infest our streets, by day, shocking the delicacy of our females, and disgusting the feelings of everyone, who is not as debased as the wretches themselves."

Industrialization was not confined to New England; the southern states encouraged the development of textile mills as well. Yet in the South, industrialization had different social consequences. By 1816, England had begun to dump its accumulated stores of textiles in the United States, selling them at bargain rates and putting hundreds of American mills out of business. Some New England factory owners moved their operations to the South, hoping to find cheaper land and labor. The southern mills used white wage hands, enslaved workers, or a combination of the two.

Many owners of southern industrial establishments sought to piece together their labor forces on the basis of the availability of different kinds of labor: enslaved and free, black and white, male and female, young and old. Thus, ironworks, gold and coal mines, brickworks, hemp factories, salt-processing plants, and lumber, railroad, and canal camps often employed men of both races, enslaved and free. In southern cities, white artisans concerned about losing their livelihood protested the use of skilled slave labor. But their complaints fell on deaf ears. Most members of city councils and regulatory boards owned slaves themselves, and they had no intention of giving up their enslaved workers so that white artisans could find jobs.

Southern industry always reflected developments in the plantation economy. For example, when cotton prices rose, slave owners kept their slaves working in the fields. Thus, planters discouraged any kind of large-scale manufacturing that might disrupt the agrarian society they had built so carefully over so many years.

However, in 1816 neither southern nor northern congressmen foresaw that the differences between their two regions would intensify over the coming years. That year Congress debated whether to impose a tariff on foreign goods. The proposed tax would require importers of such goods to pay duties of 20 to 25 percent of the value of the total. A young representative from South Carolina, John C. Calhoun, spoke in favor of the tariff bill. The South, he explained, might someday have to rely heavily on manufacturing. Calhoun, therefore, was open to a tariff that would raise the price of goods manufactured in the United States. In contrast, Representative Daniel Webster of New Hampshire opposed the measure. The tariff, he said, would further harm the New England shipping industry by dampening foreign trade altogether. The Tariff of 1816 passed and became law. Within a few years these two men reversed their positions on the tariff as the North became more rigidly associated with manufacturing and the South with staple crop agriculture.

(Both images) Courtesy, American Antiquarian Society

■ In the early nineteenth century, many skilled artisans worried that economic growth and development would erode their independence. They sought to portray themselves as upright and virtuous citizens and, by extension, superior to poor people who lacked either self-discipline or steady employment. These engravings feature sayings from Benjamin Franklin published in *Poor Richard Illustrated: Lessons for the Young and Old on Industry, Temperance, Frugality &c.*

The Rise of the Cotton Plantation Economy

The growth and spread of the cotton economy redefined the institution of slavery, the southern political system, and, ultimately, all of American history. With the invention of the cotton gin and the acquisition of the Louisiana Territory, cotton production boomed, and with it the enslaved population. About 700,000 slaves resided in the United States in 1790; just two decades later, that figure had jumped to 1.1 million. In 1790 plantations produced 3000 bales (about 300 pounds each) of cotton; 20 years later, that number hit 178,000. On the eve of the Civil War, in 1860, the southern states were growing 4 million bales of cotton. Behind these figures lay a human drama of immense proportions.

Beginning in 1808, the United States outlawed the importation of new slaves. However, the astounding profitability of cotton heightened the demand for slave labor. Although South Carolina had banned its own trans-Atlantic slave trade in 1787 (that is, outlawed the importation of slaves into the state), the state reopened the trade in 1803. Between those years, annual exports of cotton had risen from less than 10,000 pounds to more than 6 million. Between 1803 and the imposition of the national ban five years later, South Carolina imported 35,000 Africans. (This number far exceeded the number of slave importations in any other five-year period in the state's history.) However, other states began to rely on the domestic slave trade—the forced migration of slaves from the upper South to the lower South.

The institution of slavery was marked by sharp regional variations. Between 1800 and 1820, those variations reflected the impact of cotton cultivation on local economies. At the same time, the contours of an African American culture emerged. This culture had certain characteristics regardless of place, such as strong ties that bound nuclear and extended family members, rich oral and musical traditions heavily influenced by West African customs, and individual and collective resistance to slavery. White people as a group understood little of this culture; they viewed black people primarily as workers who would never become citizens. As U.S. military strength and nationalistic pride grew, southern planters imposed a harsher, more regimented system of slavery on the black population. The tension between the rhetoric of freedom and the reality of slavery shaped southern—and American—life for the next four decades.

Regional Economies of the South

Throughout the South, shifts in production methods transformed the demographic and economic make-up of specific regions. For example, by the early nineteenth century, the Chesapeake tobacco economy had declined as a result of worn-out lands and falling prices. In its place arose a more diversified economy based on crafts, the cultivation of corn and wheat, and the milling of flour and wheat. Owners put enslaved men to work making barrels and horseshoes while their wives, sisters, and daughters labored as spinners, weavers, dairymaids, personal servants, and livestock tenders.

The lower South states of Georgia and South Carolina also saw their economies change during this period. The indigo export business never recovered from the Revolution, when it was outlawed by the Continental Congress to deprive foreign countries of the prized dye. European customers now had to turn to Louisiana and Central America for indigo. In contrast, the lowcountry (coastal) South Carolina rice economy recovered and flourished after the war. Technical advances in tidal rice production boosted the size of rice holdings, and ambitious planters bought up the land of neighboring small farmers. In a particularly rich rice district, All Saints Parish, one out of two slaves lived on a plantation with more than a hundred slaves in 1790; 30 years later, four out of five lived on such large establishments. In these areas, the plantation owners themselves often lived elsewhere, and black people constituted almost the entire population.

Adding to the wealth of South Carolina was the rapid development of cotton cultivation, especially in the state's interior, away from the coast. In 1810 fully half of the state's population lived away from the coast. There, prosperous cotton planters began to rival their

Francis Guy, *Perry Hall Slave Quarters with Field Hands at Work*, c.1805. The Maryland Historical Society, Baltimore, Maryland (86.33)

■ This painting (c. 1805) by Francis Guy is titled *Perry Hall Slave Quarters with Field Hands at Work.* Enslaved workers, organized in a gang, cultivate tobacco on a Chesapeake plantation. After the turn of the century, the center of the plantation staple crop economy moved south and west. The Chesapeake region of Maryland and Virginia developed a more diversified economy than that of the rich cotton lands of Alabama and Louisiana.

lowcountry rice-growing counterparts in social status and political influence. Meanwhile, Charleston's population grew more diverse, as refugees from Saint-Domingue (current-day Haiti) arrived in the 1790s and as the free black population grew.

Southern slaveholders supported territorial expansion because they understood that a thriving staple-crop economy relied on the cultivation of fresh lands. Cotton planters rushed into the Louisiana Territory after 1803. They accelerated an economic process that had begun in the late eighteenth century: the replacement of a frontier exchange economy with plantation agriculture. (Sugar dominated the New Orleans region; cotton, the rest of the Lower Mississippi valley.) No longer able to serve as traders in this frontier territory, slaves remained confined to their masters' estates. Their owners forbade them to sell or buy goods and to own firearms. By 1800, slaves in lower Louisiana were producing 4.5 million pounds of sugar annually and more than 18,000 bales of cotton.

The reaches of the Lower Mississippi took on an increasingly multicultural flavor. A strong Spanish influence persisted as a vestige of colonial days. French-speaking planter–refugees and their slaves from revolutionary Saint-Domingue came to New Orleans while the city was still in French hands (1800 to 1803). Between 1787 and 1803, nearly 3000 slaves arrived to be sold in New Orleans—some imported clandestinely from Africa, others bought from the Spanish in West Florida, still others transported from the Chesapeake region. In 1803 and afterward, American planters began to import even larger numbers of slaves from the North. Slave owners who settled in Natchez, on the banks of the Mississippi River, grew cotton—and grew rich.

Black Family Life and Labor

Between 1790 and 1861, approximately 400,000 Africans were imported into the territory that became the United States. Yet by 1860, the black population had grown to more than 4 million—a tenfold increase in 160 years. These numbers suggest a tremendous rate of natural increase. Some planters continued to buy slaves brought into the country illegally after 1808. But most of the increase stemmed from births. The preferences of both slaveowners and slaves account for this development. Unlike their Latin American and West Indian counterparts who preferred to work large numbers of male slaves to death, southern planters encouraged black women to bear many children. At the same time, enslaved African Americans valued the family as a social unit; family ties provided support and solace for a people deprived of fundamental human rights. Even under harsh conditions, black people fell in love, married (albeit informally, without the sanction of law), had children, and reared families. Despite the lack of protection from local, state, and national authorities, the slave family proved to be a remarkably resilient institution.

The stability of individual slave families depended on several factors, including the size and age of the plantation and the fortunes and life cycle of the slaveowner's family. Very large or long-established plantations had more two-parent slave families compared to small or newer holdings, which tended to have more unrelated people. Slave families were broken up when whites died and their "property" bequeathed to heirs. Slaves might also be sold or presented to other family members as gifts. For example, a slaveowner might present a slave to a son or daughter getting married and setting up a new household. In these instances, whites' family ties came at the expense of blacks' family ties. Ultimately, slaveowners prized the natural increase of their workers but had little respect for the family feeling that black people nourished within their own communities.

Enslaved African Americans valued the family as a social unit [providing] support and solace for a people deprived of fundamental human rights.

Still, enslaved men and women struggled to retain some control over their own lives. Slaves tended to be exogamous—that is, they married outside their circle of cousins and other close relatives. To keep from being sold, slave girls at times felt compelled to demonstrate their fertility to their owners. Many of them had their first child with an enslaved man in their late teens, then entered stable marriages later. Mothers and fathers often named their children after a parent or grandparent. On the Good Hope Plantation in Orangeburg, South Carolina, five slave children were born between 1804 and 1819. Flora and Clarinda were each named for their mother's mother, Sambo for his mother's father, and Primus and July for their fathers.

Many slave families suffered disruption in response to the growing demand for slaves in the fresh cotton lands of Alabama and Mississippi. The forced migration from upper South to lower South necessarily severed kin ties, but slaves often reconstituted those ties in the form of symbolic kin relationships. For example, families adopted new, single members of the slave community, and the children called these newcomers "Aunt" or "Uncle." Slaves throughout the South tended to have large families, and they preferred to live in units consisting of two parents with children. However, they adapted their household structures to the available housing. On the Oakland Plantation in West Feliciana Parish, Louisiana, the slave quarters consisted of 15 cabins that housed various forms of families. In 1811, four married couples and their children lived alone, but other cabins consisted of single people, a married couple only, or households of extended family and adopted kin. Established in 1809, this plantation had fewer nuclear families than long-established rice plantations in South Carolina did, for example.

After the Civil War, southern blacks combined their work and family lives by laboring within their families in the fields. Under slavery, however, owners showed little or no inclination to take family relationships into account when they parceled out work assignments to men, women, and children. Rather, those assignments, and the conditions under which slaves performed them, reflected the size and crops of a particular plantation. An estimated 75 percent of antebellum slaves worked primarily as field hands. On large plantations the division of labor could be quite specialized. Men served as skilled carpenters, blacksmiths, and barrelmakers, and women worked as cooks, laundresses, nursemaids, and personal maids.

Rice slaves continued to work under the task system. Each day, after they completed a specific assigned task, they spent their time as they chose, within limits. The women washed clothes and cleaned the living quarters. The men hunted and fished. Both men and women visited friends and worked in their own gardens. Slaves jealously guarded their limited forms of freedom. One white man in Georgia described a slave who had completed his appointed task for the day: "His master feels no right to call on him," leaving him "the remainder of the day to work in his own corn field."

Even in the cotton-growing regions, where blacks labored under the regimented gang system, slaves tried to work for themselves in the little free time they had on Saturday afternoons and Sunday. In Louisiana, one white observer noted that the slave man returning to his living quarters after a long, hot day in the fields "does not lose his time. He goes to work at a bit of the land which he has planted with provisions for his own use, while his companion, if he has one, busies herself in preparing some for him, herself, and their children." Family members who grew or accumulated a modest surplus—of corn, eggs, vegetables—in some cases could sell their wares in a nearby market or to slaves on another plantation.

Some slaves appropriated goods from their master's storeroom and barn and sold or traded them to other slaves or to poor whites. This kind of labor benefited individual slaves and their families. These transactions often took place under the cover of darkness. Planters complained of slaves who stole their cattle, hogs, chickens, sacks full of cotton, farm equipment, and stores of ham and flour. In 1806 planters in lowcountry South Carolina, along the Combahee River, railed against a problem that would grow worse in the coming years: "pedling boats which frequent the river . . . for the purpose of trading with The Negroe Slaves, to the very great loss of the Owners, and Corruption of such slaves." Thus slaves' various forms of labor fell into at least three categories: work performed at the behest of and directly under the supervision of whites, labor performed by and for family members within the slaves' living quarters, and the sale (or sometimes clandestine exchange) of goods with masters, other slaves, and poor whites.

Resistance to Slavery

In 1817 the New Orleans City Council decreed that slaves could sing and dance at a stipulated place—Congo Square—every Sunday afternoon. Thereafter, a variety of groups came together to make music. These groups included recent émigrés from Saint-Domingue and slaves

John Antrobus, *Plantation Burial*, c.1860. The Historic New Orleans Collection, accession no. 1960.46

■ British artist John Antrobus titled his 1860 painting *Plantation Burial*. Held at night, after the workday, slave funerals provided an opportunity for the community—including slaves from nearby plantations—to come together in mourning. Planters remained suspicious of such gatherings, which were marked by African musical forms and religious rituals. Whites feared that slaves would conspire under the cover of darkness.

newly imported from Africa; slaves from neighboring plantations, in town for the day; and free people of color (Creoles), who often blended Spanish and French classical music traditions. One eyewitness declared that the Congo Square musicians "have their own national music, consisting for the most part of a long kind of narrow drum of various size." In towns and on plantations throughout the South, black people drew from West African musical styles, using drums as well as banjolike instruments, gourd rattles, and mandolins. From Congo Square and other southern places flowed the roots of several uniquely American musical styles: the blues, gospel, ragtime, jazz, swing, and rock 'n' roll.

In their artistic expression, dress, hairstyles, and language, slaves sought to preserve their cultural uniqueness and create an existence that slaveholders could not touch. In the South Carolina lowcountry, slaves spoke Gullah. Originally a pidgin—a blend of words and grammatical structures from West African languages and English—Gullah later developed into a more formal Creole language. Slaves throughout the United States also mixed West African religious beliefs with Christianity. Nevertheless, they showed little interest in some of the essential features of European American Protestantism, including the concept of original sin and the possibility of eternal damnation in the afterlife. Many West African groups believed in a close relationship between the natural and supernatural worlds. In slave quarters, spiritual leaders not only preached a Christianity of equality but also told fortunes and warned away "haunts" (spirits of the dead).

In gatherings of many kinds, enslaved Americans affirmed their bonds with one another and their resistance to bondage. For example, funerals provided opportunities for music and expressions of group solidarity. The rich oral tradition that characterized slave life preserved collective memories of Africa and the lore of individual families and kin networks.

Black resistance to slavery took many forms. Slaves might work carelessly in an effort to resist a master's or mistress's demands. During the course of their workday, some slaves broke hoes and other farm implements. A cook might burn the biscuits, thus spoiling a special dinner party for her mistress. Striking out more directly, the African-influenced "conjurer"—often a woman who had a knowledge of plants and herbs—could wreak havoc on a white family by concocting poisons or encouraging disruptive behavior among slaves.

Slaves also stole goods from their masters and at times stole themselves by running away. (This practice was more common among young, unmarried men than among those who had family obligations.) Some slaves revolted. In St. Charles and St. John the Baptist parishes in Louisiana, an 1811 revolt of 400 slaves cost two whites their lives and left several plantations in flames. Under the leadership of a free man of color, Charles Deslondes, the original group acquired new members as they marched toward New Orleans. U.S. troops cut their advance short, killing 66 of them. In the Southeast in 1817 and 1818, 400 to 600 runaway slaves converged on the swamps of central Florida, uniting with Indian refugees from the Red Stick War. Together, they raided Georgia plantations until Andrew Jackson and his soldiers halted them in April 1818.

To justify their own behavior, masters and mistresses created a number of myths about the black people they exploited. Whites had a vested interest in believing that their slaves felt gratitude toward them. Skilled in the so-called deference ritual, some slaves hid their true feelings and acted submissively in the presence of white people. Owners and overseers alike interpreted this behavior as a sign of black contentment.

Yet most whites understood that danger could lurk beneath the surface of the most accommodating slave. Therefore, the prevailing stereotypes of black men and women encom-

100 DOLLS. REWARD.

RAN AWAY

From me, on Saturday, the 19th inst.,

Negro Boy Robert Porter,

aged 19; heavy, stoutly made; dark chesnut complexion; rather sullen countenance, with a down look; face large; head low on the shoulders. I believe he entered the City of Washington on Sunday evening, 20th inst. He has changed his dress probably, except his boots, which were new and heavy.

I will give $50 if taken and secured in the District of Columbia, or $100 if taken north of the District, and secured in each case and delivered before the reward shall be good.

Dr. J. W. THOMAS.

Pomunky P. O., Charles Co., Md.

Chicago Historical Society, ICHi-22005

■ From colonial times through the abolition of slavery in 1865, runaways were a persistent problem for slaveholders. This advertisement was published in the Centerville, Maryland, *Times and Eastern-Shore Public Advertiser.* Typically, the owner describes the runaways in terms of their height, skin color, and other distinguishing characteristics. For example, Sam supposedly rolls his eyes "when spoken to." Runaways tended to be young men. This group of four, three men and a woman, probably had to go their separate ways, eventually, to avoid detection.

passed two caricatures: "Sambo" and "Mammy" were childlike and grateful, and "Nat" and "Jezebel" were surly, cunning, dangerous, and unpredictable. One Kentucky slave, Susan, was described by a planter in 1822 as "the biggest devil that ever lived." Susan reportedly poisoned a stud horse and set a stable on fire, causing $1500 worth of damage, after managing to escape from handcuffs.

Although some planters boasted of their fatherly solicitude for their slaves, in fact, slaveowners harbored deep fears about the men and women they held in bondage. These fears explain the barbaric punishments that some owners inflicted on men, women, and children. Whip-wielding overseers made pregnant women lie down in a trench in the fields, presumably so that the lash would not harm the fetus. Even in "respectable" southern families, slave owners branded, mutilated, and beat enslaved workers for resisting discipline or to deliver a warning to other potentially defiant slaves. In the slave South, American cries of freedom, equality, opportunity, and the blessings of citizenship rang hollow.

Conclusion

In the first two decades of the nineteenth century, striking historical developments stirred the spirit of American nationalism. The Louisiana Purchase magnified the natural wealth of the young nation, and the federal government encouraged citizens to exploit that wealth through trade and settlement. Both the Embargo of 1807 and the War of 1812 freed the country from the British menace in the West and on the high seas. The war also bolstered the American economy by stimulating technological innovation and the growth of manufacturing. Territorial expansion combined with economic development created new jobs for a burgeoning population. Unlike the rigidly class-conscious nations of Europe, America seemed to offer limitless possibilities—at least for propertied white men, the only people entitled to the full rights of citizenship.

Southern cotton planters and northern factory owners derived their newfound prosperity from very different sources: staple crop agriculture on one hand and the emerging industrial system on the other. At the same time, these two groups had much in common. As they expanded their operations, whether sprawling plantations or gigantic mill complexes,

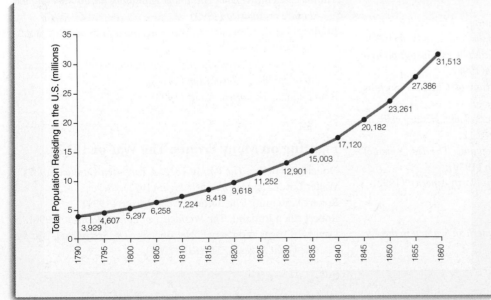

■ **FIGURE 10.2**
ESTIMATED POPULATION OF THE UNITED STATES, 1790–1860

Source: *Historical Statistics of the United States*, p. 7.

they displaced smaller landowners and raised land prices. Members of both elite groups proved restless entrepreneurs, eager to move around to find the freshest lands and the cheapest labor. Their personal wealth and their political power set them apart from the people under them— the slaves and wage earners—who produced that wealth. And both the southern "lords of the lash" and the northern "lords of the loom" depended on large numbers of slaves to grow cotton. Thus, the fluffy white fiber of the cotton boll is perhaps a most fitting symbol of the emerging American economy. Producing and processing it yielded tangible benefits for a few and created a new, harsher world of work for many.

Sites to Visit

The Lewis and Clark Expedition
www.cp.duluth.mn.us/~tmcs/lewsclrk1.htm

This site offers assorted materials treating the expedition that explored the Louisiana Territory.

The Barbary Treaties
www.yale.edu/lawweb/avalon/diplomacy/barbary

This site includes the texts of treaties between the United States and the Barbary states, 1786–1816.

Documents from the War of 1812
www.yale.edu/lawweb/avalon/diplomacy/britian/br1814m.htm

This site includes important documents from the War of 1812.

Whole Cloth: Discovering Science and Technology Through American Textile History
www.si.edu/lemelson/centerpieces/whole_cloth/

The Jerome and Dorothy Lemelson Center for the Study of Invention and Innovation and Society for the History of Technology assembled this site. It includes excellent activities and sources related to early American manufacturing and industry.

Indian Affairs: Laws and Treaties
www.library.okstate.edu/kappler/

This digitized text at Oklahoma State University includes preremoval treaties with the Five Civilized Tribes and other groups.

For Further Reading

General

Stephen E. Ambrose, *Undaunted Courage: Meriwether Lewis, Thomas Jefferson, and the Opening of the American West* (1996).

Joanne P. Melish, *Disowning Slavery: Gradual Emancipation and "Race" in New England, 1780–1860* (1998).

Theda Perdue, *Slavery and the Evolution of Cherokee Society, 1540–1866* (1979).

Carroll Pursell, *The Machine in America: A Social History of Technology* (1995).

Howard B. Rock, *Artisans of the New Republic: The Tradesmen of New York City in the Age of Jefferson* (1979).

Donald J. Weber, *The Spanish Frontier in North America* (1992).

The British Menace

W. Jeffrey Bolster, *Black Jacks: African-American Seamen in the Age of Sail* (1997).

Thomas J. Fleming, *Duel: Alexander Hamilton, Aaron Burr and the Future of America* (1999).

Bradford Perkins, *Prologue to War: England and the United States, 1805–1812* (1961).

Burton Spivak, *Jefferson's English Crisis: Commerce, Embargo, and the Republican Revolution* (1974).

John Sugden, *Tecumseh: A Life* (1998).

Fighting on Many Fronts: The War of 1812

Donald R. Hickey, *The War of 1812: A Forgotten Conflict* (1989).

Walter Lord, *The Dawn's Early Light* (1972).

Robert V. Remini, *The Battle of New Orleans* (1999).

Robert Allen Rutland, *The Presidency of James Madison* (1990).

David C. Skaggs and Larry L. Nelson, eds., *The Sixty Years' War for the Great Lakes, 1754–1814* (2001).

The "Era of Good Feelings"?

James H. Broussard, *The Southern Federalists, 1800–1816* (1979).

Theda Perdue, *Cherokee Women: Gender and Culture Change, 1700–1835* (1998).

Kirkpatrick Sale, *The Fire of His Genius: Robert Fulton and the American Dream* (2001).

Ronald Schultz, *The Republic of Labor: Philadelphia Artisans and the Politics of Class, 1720–1830* (1993).

Cynthia Shelton, *The Mills of Manayunk: Industrialization and Social Conflict in the Philadelphia Region, 1787–1837* (1986).

George Rogers Taylor, *The Transportation Revolution, 1815–1860* (1951).

The Rise of the Cotton Plantation Economy

Eugene D. Genovese, *Roll, Jordan, Roll: The World the Slaves Made* (1976).

Charles W. Joyner, *Down by the Riverside: A South Carolina Slave Community* (1984).

Ann Patton Malone, *Sweet Chariot: Slave Family and Household Structure in Nineteenth-Century Louisiana* (1992).

Michael Mullin, *Africa in America: Slave Acculturation and Resistance in the American South and British Caribbean* (1992).

Jeffrey Robert Young, *Domesticating Slavery: The Master Class in Georgia and South Carolina, 1670–1837* (1999).

Online Practice Test

Test your understanding of this chapter with interactive review quizzes at

www.ablongman.com/jonescreatedequal/chapter10

CHAPTER

11

Expanding Westward: Society and Politics in the "Age of the Common Man," 1819–1832

Smithsonian Institution, American Art Museum/Art Resource, NY

■ "Woman Who Strikes Many," Blackfeet, 1832.

CAMPAIGNING FOR POLITICAL OFFICE IN TENNESSEE IN THE 1820S WAS NOT AN ACTIVITY for the faint of heart. Candidates competed against each other in squirrel hunts, the loser footing the bill for the barbecue that followed. A round of speechmaking often was capped by several rounds of whiskey drinking enjoyed by candidates and supporters alike. Into this boisterous arena stepped a man unrivaled as a campaigner. David Crockett ran successfully for several offices, including local justice of the peace in 1818, state legislator in 1821 and 1823, and U.S. congressman in 1827, 1829, and 1833. The plainspoken Crockett knew how to play to a crowd and rattle a rival. He bragged about his skill as a bear hunter and ridiculed the fancy dress of his opponents. He condemned closed-door political caucuses (small groups of party insiders who hand-picked candidates) and praised grassroots democracy. Crockett claimed he could out-shoot, out-drink, and out-debate anyone who opposed him. If his opponent lied about him, why, then, he would lie about himself: "Yes fellow citizens, I can run faster, walk longer, leap higher, speak better, and tell more and bigger lies than my competitor, and all his friends, any day of his life." Crockett's blend of political theater and folksy backwoods banter earned him the allegiance of voters like him—men who, though having little formal education, understood the challenges of carving a homestead out of the dense thickets of western Tennessee.

John Gadsby Chapman painted this portrait of David Crockett in 1834.

Crockett's raucous brand of campaigning appealed to Westerners, that is, at this point in history, European Americans living just west of the Appalachian Mountains. His social betters might sniff that he was a rough, ignorant man—in the words of one Tennessee political insider, "more in his proper place, when hunting a Bear in the cane Brake, than he will be in the Capital." But newspaper reporters and defeated opponents alike grew to respect his ability to champion ordinary farmers. As a politician, Crockett spoke for debtors, squatters, and militia veterans of the Revolutionary War. He scorned the well-born in favor of men who could shoot down and skin a wolf.

During the 1820s, European American settlers in the trans-Appalachian West transformed the style and substance of American politics. Beginning with Kentucky in 1792, western states began to relax or abolish property requirements for adult male voters. Even the English that Americans spoke changed. New words introduced into the political vocabulary reflected the rough-hewn, woodsman quality of western electioneering: candidates hit the campaign trail, giving stump speeches along the way. They supported their party's platform with its planks (positions on the issues). As legislators, they voted for pork-barrel projects that would benefit their constituents at home. Emphasizing his modest origins, David Crockett became widely known as Davy Crockett. (It is hard to imagine anyone calling the Sage of Monticello Tommy Jefferson.)

These developments reflected the movement of European Americans westward. In 1790, 100,000 Americans (not including Indians) lived west of the Appalachian

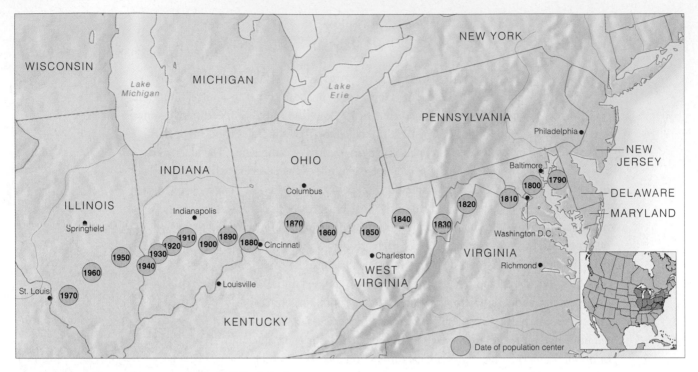

■ **MAP 11.1**

THE CENTER OF POPULATION MOVES WEST, 1790–1970 In 1830 most European Americans still lived along the eastern seaboard. Yet the statistical center of the country had shifted dramatically westward as settlers moved across the trans-Appalachian West. Migrants from the South sought out the fresh cotton lands of Alabama and Mississippi, while New Englanders created new communities in the Upper Midwest. Migration to areas such as Wisconsin and Georgia was contingent on the removal of Indians from those areas, either by treaty or by military force.

Mountains; half a century later that number had increased to 7 million, or about 4 out of 10 Americans.

Western settlers attacked what they considered to be centralized, eastern-based institutions of wealth and privilege. They scorned a six-person Supreme Court that could overturn the laws of Congress and the individual states; the privately held Second Bank of the United States, which, its critics charged, enriched its own board of directors at the expense of indebted farmers; and federally sponsored internal improvements, such as turnpikes and canals, which, many western homesteaders believed, served the interests of well-connected merchants and financiers.

Western voters rejoiced with the 1828 election of Andrew Jackson to the presidency; here, they claimed, was a man who would battle eastern financiers and at the same time support white settlers' claims to Indian lands in the West. Jackson held out the promise that ordinary men would have a political voice and access to expanding economic opportunities. Indeed, during these years, voter participation in presidential elections soared, from 25 percent of eligible voters in 1824 to 50 percent in 1828.

During his two terms in office (1828–1836), Andrew Jackson so dominated the American political landscape that historians have called him the symbol of an age and the representative man of his time. Born in humble circumstances, orphaned at age 14, Jackson achieved public acclaim as a lawyer, a military officer, and, finally, president. In promoting a strong central government, and the authority of the chief executive in particular, he fought against foreign military forces (the British in the War of 1812) and Native Americans, and he clashed with southern states' rights advocates. Jackson backed up his vision with the use of violence and, at times, contempt for the law. Nevertheless, Jackson's view appealed strongly to workers and small farmers, men who resented what they called entrenched eastern privilege in politics and the economy.

Yet democracy had its limits during this period, for most people could not vote. Native Americans remained barred from even the rudiments of formal citizenship. White married women, who could neither own property nor vote, found themselves second-class citizens. Almost all free people of color, whether in the North, South, or Midwest, likewise lacked basic rights—to vote, serve on juries, or send their children to public school.

Further complicating this age was the rise of social classes. Acquiring great economic and political significance, the class system seemed to mock the idea of equality. The outlines of this system appeared in the 1820s in the Northeast, where business and factory managers received salaries, not hourly wages, and their wives were full-time homemakers and mothers. New forms of popular literature, such as the *Ladies Magazine,* published in Boston, glorified the middle-class family, especially the pious wife and mother who held moral sway over it.

The "age of the common man" was thus rife with irony. Jackson himself embodied many apparent contradictions. An Indian-fighter, he adopted a young Indian boy as his ward. A foe of privilege, he was a slave owner. A self-professed champion of farmers and artisans, he expressed contempt for their representatives in Congress. He also took steps to expand the power of the executive branch. The 1820s in general revealed these larger contradictions as national leaders pursued a more democratic form of politics on one hand and supported a system based on class and racial differences on the other. The resulting tensions shaped American society and politics in the third decade of the nineteenth century.

The Politics Behind Western Expansion

As the United States gained new territory through negotiation and conquest and people moved west, the nation felt the impact. Western debtors' economic distress echoed in eastern centers of finance. Congressional debates over whether Missouri should be admitted to the Union as a slave or free state sent shock waves throughout the country. Of the political conflict over the fate of slavery in the territories, the elderly Thomas Jefferson wrote, "This momentous question, like a firebell in the night, awakened and filled me with terror. I considered it at once as the death knell of the Union."

As new states were carved out of the west, gaining national influence in Congress, traditional methods of choosing candidates and the old political parties of Democratic-Republicans and Federalists came under fire. Parties began to choose their presidential nominees in conventions, not in caucuses of legislators. Rejecting practices that favored the wealthy, more and more states abolished the requirement that would-be voters and office holders had to own property. "The people must be heard!" became a rallying cry.

However, the opening of the West to European American settlement, which invigorated white men's democracy, also sowed seeds of economic and political conflict. Settlers made their way not through empty territory but through Native American homelands. Once in the West, most of these settlers faced the same kinds of conflicts that increasingly preoccupied Easterners, especially those between masters and slaves and debtors and creditors.

The Missouri Compromise

In 1819 the United States consisted of 22 states. Slavery was legal in half of them. Late that year, the territory of Missouri applied for statehood. This move set off panic in both the North and South because a twenty-third state was bound to upset the delicate balance of senators

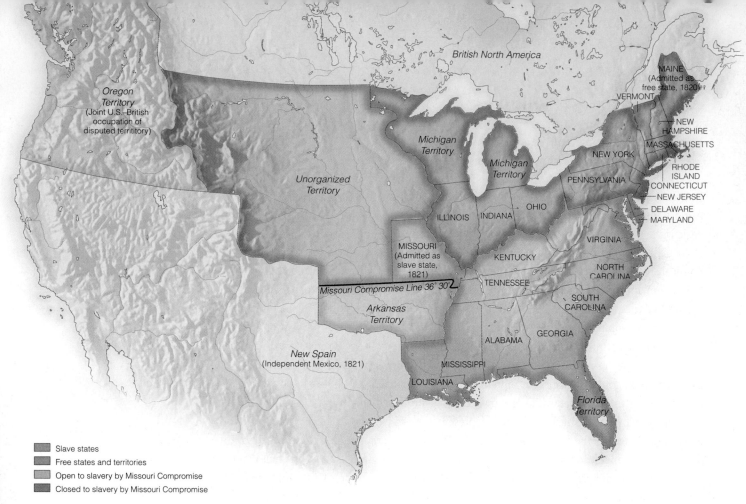

Slave states

Free states and territories

Open to slavery by Missouri Compromise

Closed to slavery by Missouri Compromise

■ **MAP 11.2**

THE MISSOURI COMPROMISE   Missouri applied for statehood in 1819, threatening the balance between 11 free and 11 slave states. According to a compromise hammered out in Congress, Missouri was admitted as a slave state, and Maine, formerly part of Massachusetts, was admitted as a free state. Slavery was banned above the 36°30′ parallel.

between slave and free states. Representative James Tallmadge of New York proposed a compromise: no slaves would be imported into Missouri in the future, and the new state would gradually emancipate the enslaved men and women living within its borders. The Tallmadge Amendment was defeated in the House as Southerners resisted this blatant attempt to limit the spread of slavery. The debate over the future of Missouri occupied Congress from December 1819 to March 1820.

In the Senate, Rufus King of New York claimed that Congress had the ultimate authority to set laws governing slavery. However, his colleague William Pinckney of Maryland retorted that new states possessed the same rights as the original 13; that is, they could choose whether to allow slavery. Maine's application for admission to the Union suggested a way out of the impasse. Speaker of the House of Representatives Henry Clay of Kentucky proposed a plan calling for Missouri to join the Union as a slave state. At the same time, Maine, originally part of Massachusetts, would become the twenty-fourth state and be designated a free one. In the future, slavery would be prohibited from all Louisiana Purchase lands north of latitude 36°30′, an area that included all territory north of present-day Missouri and Kansas. The House and the Senate finally approved the compromise, which maintained the balance between the number of slave and free states.

The day Congress sealed the compromise, Secretary of State John Quincy Adams walked home from the Capitol with Senator John C. Calhoun of South Carolina. The two men engaged in a muted but intense debate over slavery. Calhoun claimed that the institution "was the best guarantee to equality among the whites." Slavery, he asserted, demonstrated that all white men were equal to one another and superior to all blacks. Unnerved by Calhoun's comments,

Adams concluded that the debate over Missouri had "betrayed the secret of [Southerners'] souls." By reserving backbreaking toil for blacks, wealthy planters fancied themselves aristocratic lords of the manor. Adams confided in his diary that night, "They look down upon the simplicity of a Yankee's manners, because he has no habits of overbearing like theirs and cannot treat negroes like dogs."

Adams acknowledged that the compromise had kept the number of slave and free states in balance. Still, he reflected, slavery "taints the very sources of moral principle." Would it not have been better to confront the issue squarely and amend the Constitution in favor of free labor in all new states admitted to the Union? Adams feared that the North-South conflicts over the issues might someday imperil the nation itself. He concluded ominously, "If the Union must be dissolved, slavery is precisely the question upon which it ought to break." Five years later, Adams won the presidency of the United States. Elected separately by the voters, his vice president was none other than John C. Calhoun. Over the next four years, the two men managed to maintain an uneasy political alliance.

Ways West

Through land grants and government financing of new methods of transportation, Congress encouraged European American migrants to push their way west and south. The Land Act of 1820 enabled westerners to buy a minimum 80 acres at a price of $1.25 an acre in cash—even in those days, a bargain homestead. Built with the help of government legal and financial aid, new roads and canals, steamboats, and, after the early 1830s, railroads facilitated migration. Between 1820 and 1860, the number of steamboats plying the Mississippi River jumped from 60 to more than 1000. Canals linked western producers to eastern consumers of grains and cattle and connected western consumers to eastern producers of manufactured goods. Shipping costs and times between Buffalo and New York shrank. Cities such as Rochester and Syracuse, New York, and Cincinnati, Ohio, flourished because of their geographic position along waterways.

Americans took a variety of routes West. One route was taken in the 1820s by desperate planters moving out of the exhausted lands of the Upper South (the states of Virginia and Maryland), the Carolinas, and Georgia, westward into Alabama, Arkansas, Louisiana, and Mississippi. This migration across the Appalachian Mountains furthered the nationalist idea of the "expansion of liberty and freedom," a view held by many white men regardless of political affiliation. Yet it also spread slavery. The sight of slave "coffles"—groups of men, women, and children bound together in chains, hobbling down a city street or a country road— became increasingly common in this western region. In 1821 Virginia, North Carolina, South Carolina, and Georgia had produced two-thirds of the nation's cotton crop; the rest came from recently settled areas. Just a dozen years later the proportions shifted: Tennessee, Louisiana, Alabama, Mississippi, and Florida together produced two-thirds of all cotton, and the remaining one third came from older areas. The race to riches in the western portions of the South went to planters who had the most slaves and the most money to drain swamps and build the levees needed to hold back springtime river flooding. Soon a new planter elite—men and women who presided over vast slave holdings and lorded over their poor-white neighbors—dominated the lower Mississippi Valley.

European Americans also migrated across the border into Mexican territory. In 1821 Spain approved the application of a U.S. citizen, Moses Austin, to settle 300 American families on 200,000 fertile acres along the Colorado and Brazos river bottoms in southeastern Texas. Austin died soon after, but his son Stephen carried on his legacy. Within two years, the younger Austin had received permission (now from the government of newly independent Mexico) to bring in another 100 families. These settlers, together with squatters, numbered about 1500 people. Although the Mexican constitution prohibited slavery, some of the newcomers brought their slaves with them, and some free people of color came on their own. All these migrants from the United States called themselves Texians to distinguish themselves from the *Tejanos,* or Spanish-speaking

■ MAP 11.3

PRINCIPAL CANALS BUILT BY 1860 Many canals were expensive ventures and, in some cases, engineering nightmares. The Erie Canal had a competitive advantage because it snaked through the Mohawk Valley, the only major level pass through the mountain chain that stretched from Canada to Georgia. In contrast, the Pennsylvania Main Line Canal, which ran from Harrisburg to Pittsburgh, used a combination of inclined planes and steam engines in ten separate locations to haul boats up and down the Allegheny Mountains.

residents of the region. These newly arrived Texians agreed to adopt the Catholic faith and become citizens of Mexico. Eager for settlers to improve the land, Mexican authorities made it clear they would welcome new settlers "from hell itself," in the words of one official.

By late 1821 Mexico's independence had nullified the trade embargo that Spain had imposed on Mexico and on cities to the north, including Santa Fe and Albuquerque in New Mexico Territory. Ambitious people of all stripes rushed into New Mexico, including European American merchants who brought ready-made cloth (in the process displacing Hispanic and Native American textile producers), U.S. soldiers who claimed "God-given rights of conquest," and mountain men intent on harvesting animal pelts from the New Mexico Rocky Mountains.

In the 1820s, 900 additional families sponsored by Austin arrived in Texas. They were followed by 3000 squatters. This mass migration raised well-founded fears among Mexican officials that they would lose authority over the American newcomers within their borders.

The Panic of 1819 and the Plight of Western Debtors

In 1819 a financial panic swept across the nation, followed by an economic depression. The Second Bank of the United States played a major role in triggering this economic downturn, which came to be called the Panic of 1819. Granted a twenty-year charter by Congress

HAULING THE WHOLE WEEKS PICKING

■ The rich bottomlands of the Mississippi Delta proved ideal for growing cotton. After the forced removal of the Five Civilized Tribes from the Old Southwest, slave owners established expansive plantations in the delta. This scene, painted in 1842 by artist William Henry Brown, shows a group of slaves bringing in "the whole weeks picking" of cotton on the Vick plantation near Vicksburg, Mississippi.

William Henry Brown, *Hauling the Whole Weeks Picking*, 1842. The Historic New Orleans Collection, (1975.93.1 & 1975.93.2)

in 1816, the Bank resembled its predecessor, seeking to regulate the national economy through loans to state and local banks. In 1819 the Bank clamped down on small, local "wildcat" banks, which had extended credit to many people who could not repay their loans. Many homesteaders were not self-sufficient farmers but producers of staple crops or proprietors of small enterprises. They relied on credit from banks and local private lenders. As a result, the Bank's crackdown on wildcat banks had a devastating impact on western households. Debtors unable to meet their obligations had their mortgages foreclosed, their homes seized, and their crops and equipment confiscated. Ruined by the Panic of 1819, many western farmers developed an abiding hatred of the Bank of the United States and a deep resentment of eastern financiers.

Davy Crockett's own family history suggests the plight of families dependent on bank credit to create homesteads out of western territory. The son of a propertyless squatter, Crockett had an intense fear of debt. Although he campaigned as a hunter and a farmer, he had built several enterprises on land he leased or owned on Shoal Creek in south central Tennessee: a water-powered grist mill, a gunpowder factory (worked by slaves), an iron ore mine, and a liquor distillery. For each venture, he had to borrow money from local creditors. Spending much of his time away from home, Crockett relied on his wife, Elizabeth, and his children to manage these businesses. (He had nine children by Elizabeth and three by his first wife, Polly, who died in 1815.)

The depression of 1819 cut off Crockett's sources of credit, and in 1822 a flash flood swept away his grist mill and powder factory. Without milled grain, the distillery could no longer operate. Creditors immediately set upon the family, demanding payment of their debts. The Crocketts were fortunate enough to own land they could sell, using the proceeds to repay their debts. Nevertheless, they decided to move further west, to a remote area on the banks of the Obion River in northwest Tennessee. There they started over. Crockett described the area as a "complete wilderness" (although he noted that it was also "full of Indians who were hunting"). The region still showed the effects of an earthquake that had occurred in 1811. With its downed trees and thick brambles, the fissure-riddled landscape presented challenges to

■ **MAP 11.4**

MEXICO'S FAR NORTHERN FRONTIER IN 1822   This map shows Mexico's far northern frontier in 1822. When Moses Austin died suddenly in 1821, the task of supervising the settlement of in-migrants from the United States fell to his son Stephen. The Mexican government authorized the younger Austin to act as empresario of the settlement. He was responsible for the legal and economic regulations governing the settlements clustered at the lower reaches of the Colorado and Brazos rivers.

the farmers who ventured there. Once again, Crockett needed bank loans, this time to buy flour and seed for cotton.

Many western settlers engaged in the same sort of cycle: borrowing to improve their land, then selling out and moving on. Unable to pay their debts, the least fortunate among them were thrown in jail. In several states, politicians urged the abolition of debtors' prison. They pointed out that jailing people who owed money did little to ensure that the debt would be repaid. New York state legislators passed such a law in 1831 in response to a group of well-to-do petitioners who argued that debtors' prison was "useless to the creditor   oppressive to the debtor—injurious to both."

Crockett advocated a system that would allow local sheriffs to buy debtors' property at bankruptcy auctions and then sell it back to the former owners. He denounced the bankers and other creditors, men who "had gone up one side of a creek and down another, *like a coon,* and pretended to grant the poor people great favors" in making them loans that the moneylenders knew they could not afford to repay. Then these creditors demanded their money and wiped out families, taking their land and livestock. Too often, according to Crockett, the backwoods farmer was burdened by debt and vulnerable to depressions and scheming creditors alike.

The Panic of 1819 caused widespread economic distress. Small farmers who lost their land through foreclosure could not produce crops for the eastern market, contributing to the rise in the price of food. Deprived of credit, small shopkeepers also felt the effects of the depression.

With rising unemployment, consumers could not afford to buy cloth, and as the demand for cotton fell, southern plantation owners, too, felt the contraction. Within a few years Andrew Jackson would capitalize on the fears and resentments of working men, farmers, planters, and tradesmen, as he championed the "common man" in opposition to what debtors called the "eastern monied interests." In doing so he would transform the two-party system.

The Monroe Doctrine

James Monroe won reelection easily in 1820. The depression did not affect his popularity. He also benefited from the disorganization of his opponents and from the demise of the Federalist party. Congressman John Randolph of Virginia suggested that the voters were unanimous on only one issue: their indifference to Monroe. As it turned out, the president's 231–1 victory in the Electoral College was the last chapter in the so-called Era of Good Feelings.

On the international front, Monroe's second term opened on a tense note. Foreign nations had started claiming land or promoting their own interests near U.S. borders. The United States remained especially wary of the Spanish presence on its southern and western borders. In 1818, President Monroe authorized General Andrew Jackson to broaden his assault on the Seminole Indians—a group composed of Native Americans and runaway slaves—in Florida. For the past two years, U.S. troops had pursued fugitive slaves into Spanish-held Florida. Now Jackson and his men seized the Spanish fort at Pensacola and claimed all of western Florida for the United States. The United States demanded that Spain either suppress the Seminole population or sell all of east Florida to the United States. With the Transcontinental Treaty of 1819, Spain gave up its right to both Florida and Oregon (although Britain and Russia still claimed land in Oregon). In 1822 General Jackson became the first governor of Florida Territory.

In 1821 the czar of Russia forbade non-Russians from entering the territory north of the fifty-first parallel and the open sea 100 miles off the coast of what is now Canada and Alaska. The Russians had established trading posts up and down that coast, some almost as far south as San Francisco Bay. Meanwhile, the crowned heads of Europe were cracking down on popular rebellions (in Italy in 1821 and Spain in 1823). Rumors circulated that these monarchs were planning new invasions of Latin America.

TABLE 11-1		
The Election of 1820		
Candidate	**Political Party**	**Electoral Vote**
James Monroe	Democratic-Republican	231
John Quincy Adams	Democratic-Republican	1

Fearful of an alliance between Russia, Prussia, Austria, Spain, and France, President Monroe and Secretary of State John Quincy Adams formulated a policy that became a landmark in American diplomatic history. Adams rejected a British proposal that Great Britain and the United States join forces to oppose a further Spanish encroachment in Latin America. He convinced Monroe that the United States must stand alone against the European powers—Spain in the South and Russia in the Northwest—if it hoped to protect its own interests in the Western Hemisphere. In his annual message to Congress in December 1823, the president declared that the era of Europe's colonization of the Americas had ceased. Henceforth, he said, foreign nations would not be allowed to intervene in the Western Hemisphere.

The United States conceived the so-called Monroe Doctrine as a self-defense measure aimed specifically at Russia, Spain, and Britain. With the Russo-American Treaty of 1824, Russia agreed to pull back its claims to the area north of 54°40′, the southern tip of the present-day Alaska panhandle. However, the United States did not have the naval power to back up the Monroe Doctrine with force.

In its earliest form, the doctrine was more a statement of principle than a blueprint for action. The United States sought to discourage European powers from political or military meddling in the Western Hemisphere. The doctrine would have greater international significance in the late nineteenth century, when the United States developed the military might to enforce it.

The Strange Career of the Monroe Doctrine

What U.S. president was responsible for relocating several hundred suspected Taliban and Al Qaeda terrorists from Afghanistan to Cuba in early 2002? President George W. Bush had ultimate authority for the decision, of course; he claimed that intelligence officers needed to interrogate the men in a secure U.S. military installation, away from war-torn Afghanistan. Yet indirectly, at least, the detainees found themselves in steel cages on the shores of Guantanamo Bay because President James Monroe had announced his famous doctrine to the world almost 180 years before.

At the time, Monroe and his secretary of state, John Quincy Adams, saw threats to U.S. economic interests and national security. Both Russia and Great Britain were making territorial claims in the Northwest, in what was called Oregon Country. To the south of the United States, a number of Spanish colonies had won, or were about to win, their independence: Chile in 1818, Mexico in 1821, Brazil in 1822, and Venezuela in 1824. The Monroe administration hoped to convince Spain, France, and Portugal not to take advantage of this unstable situation.

However, over the years, the purpose of the doctrine shifted from trying to keep the European powers from recolonizing any part of the Americas to justifying U.S. territorial acquisition and attempts to police and intervene in the domestic affairs of Latin American countries. For example, Presidents Tyler and Polk cited the doctrine to further the nation's continental expansion, including the conquest of Texas and California. In the mid–1890s, Secretary of State Richard Olney justified the U.S. decision to intervene in a border dispute between Britain and Venezuela by proclaiming, "Today the United States is practically sovereign on this continent and its fiat is law . . . its infinite resources combined with its isolated position render it master of the situation and practically invulnerable as against any or all other powers."

The American victory over Spain in the War of 1898 gave policymakers an opportunity to gain influence over Cuban domestic matters. The Platt Amendment to the Cuban–American Treaty of 1903 restricted the freedom of the newly independent Cuban government. Under pressure from the United States, Cuba incorporated into its constitution provisions that barred a foreign power (other than the United States) from intervening in Cuban political and economic affairs and gave the United States the right to buy or lease sites for naval installations (including the site at Guantanamo Bay). In 1934 President Franklin D. Roosevelt nullified most provisions of the Platt Amendment, but the United States retained its right to the base at Guantanamo. This decision was part of U.S. actions to claim small but geographically critical land holdings around the globe to use for military purposes: imperial claims to Guam, Hawaii, and the Philippines in addition to the base in Cuba, for example.

Theodore Roosevelt devised his famous policy called the Roosevelt Corollary to justify military intervention into Central American countries that

Andrew Jackson's Rise to Power

The election of 1824 provided a striking contrast to the bland affair four years earlier. In 1824 the field of presidential nominees was crowded, suggesting a party system in disarray. In the spirit of openness, secretive congressional caucuses no longer nominated presidential candidates. Instead, a number of states backed their "favorite sons" in the presidential race. Although all the candidates called themselves "Democratic-Republicans," the label meant little more than the fact that most politicians sought to distance themselves from the outmoded "Federalist" label, which hearkened back to the post-Revolutionary period, rather than pointing forward to the nation's new challenges. Secretary of State John Quincy Adams threw his hat in the ring. Other nominees included Representative Henry Clay of Kentucky and Andrew Jackson, now a senator from Tennessee. Jackson received the highest number of electoral votes (99), but no candidate achieved a majority. As a result, the election went to the House of Representatives. The Twelfth Amendment to the Constitution, adopted in 1804, provided for separate electoral balloting for the office of vice president, and John C. Calhoun won that vote.

Clay withdrew from the race. He had promised Jackson his support but then endorsed Adams, whom the House subsequently elected. When Adams named Clay secretary of state,

AFP/CORBIS

Guantanamo Bay with Al-Qaeda prisoners

communist nation. Presidents John F. Kennedy and Ronald Reagan cited the Monroe Doctrine in pushing Congress to authorize the use of force against the spread of communism in Latin America. Yet by 1989 President George Bush felt no need to justify his administration's action in Panama, when U.S. troops forcibly seized dictator Manuel Noriega and returned him to the United States to stand trial on charges of drug smuggling.

Over the generations, the Monroe Doctrine has proved a flexible policy, providing justification for almost any action the United States deemed necessary to its self-interest, broadly defined. Detaining Al Qaeda members at the Guantanamo naval station, for example, allows U.S. authorities to hold them securely, without the dangers of keeping them on American soil, where democratic traditions and constitutional rules might complicate the situation. This state of affairs exemplifies both the strength and the weakness of the Monroe Doctrine; the United States controls a small piece of Cuba, but the communist regime there stubbornly endures. ∎

were indebted to American banks or businesses. Under Roosevelt's Big Stick policy, U.S. marines landed in Nicaragua in 1912 and remained in the country until 1933. The stated purpose of the occupation was to make certain that Nicaragua paid off its debts to U.S. banks. A guerrilla group led by General Augusto Cesar Sandino led an armed resistance against the American troops. In the mid–1970s, members of a resistance movement fighting the repressive Somoza regime in Nicaragua called themselves Sandinistas in honor of the general, who was killed by Nicaraguan government troops in 1934.

As a result of the revolution led by Fidel Castro in 1959, Cuba became a

---

Jackson's supporters cried foul. The election, they charged, amounted to nothing more than a corrupt deal between two political insiders.

Haunted by these charges, Adams served his four-year term under a cloud of public distrust. A member of a respected New England family and the son of former president John Adams, the new chief executive had served with distinction in Monroe's cabinet. Still, Adams proved ill suited to the rough-and-tumble world of what came to be called the New Democracy. Adams held strong political views; he advocated a greater federal role in internal improvements and public education, a variation on Henry Clay's "American System," a set of policies which promoted a national bank, public funding of canals and turnpikes, and a high tariff to protect domestic manufactures.

Adams's party, which called itself the National Republicans, faced a formidable challenge in the election of 1828. Having seethed for four long years, Andrew Jackson's

TABLE 11-2			
The Election of 1824			
Candidate	Political Party	Popular Vote	Electoral Vote
John Quincy Adams	Democratic-Republican	108,740	84
Andrew Jackson	Democratic-Republican	153,544	99
William H. Crawford	Democratic-Republican	46,618	41
Henry Clay	Democratic-Republican	47,136	37

Library of Congress

■ Some commentators disapproved of what they considered the excessively lively inauguration gala for President Jackson in 1829. One described the affair this way: "On their arrival at the White House, the motley crowd clamored for refreshments and soon drained the barrels of punch, which had been prepared, in drinking to the health of the new Chief Magistrate. A great deal of glassware was broken, and the East Room was filled with a noisy mob."

supporters (the Democratic-Republicans) now urged "the people" to reclaim the White House. The campaign was a nasty one. Jackson's opponents attacked his personal morality and that of his wife and his mother. Jackson's supporters countered with the charge that Adams himself was corrupt and that he and his cronies must be swept from office. At campaign rallies, Jacksonians waved about brooms to signal their disgust with the current administration.

By the time of the 1828 election, the Democratic-Republicans and their rivals had developed sophisticated national organizations. They sponsored local entertainments such as parades and barbecues. These gatherings brought out the vote and cultivated party loyalty. With the decline of state laws regulating voter qualifications, ordinary people in the South and the West cast ballots for the first time. The "Hero of the Battle of New Orleans" won a stunning victory, accumulating a record 647,292 popular votes. His supporters hailed the well-to-do slaveholder as the president of the "common" (meaning white) man.

In office, Jackson tightened his party's grip on power by introducing a national political spoils system. Through this process, successful candidates rewarded their supporters with jobs and tossed their rivals out of appointed offices. The spoils system let the Democratic-Republicans—now called the Democrats—build a nationwide political machine. Not surprisingly, it also provided fertile ground for corruption.

TABLE 11-3

The Election of 1828

Candidate	Political Party	Popular Vote	Electoral Vote
Andrew Jackson	Democratic	647,292	178
John Quincy Adams	National Republican	508,064	83

Federal Authority and Its Opponents

When Americans defeated the British in the War of 1812, they ensured the physical security of the new nation. However, the war's end left a crucial question unanswered: what role would federal authority play in a republic of states? During Andrew Jackson's tenure, Congress, the chief executive, and the Supreme Court all jockeyed for influence over one another and over the states. To be sure, some groups, such as the Cherokee nation, challenged federal power. But these efforts failed against the sheer determination of Andrew Jackson. During his term in office, Jackson claimed a broad popular mandate, the authority the people gave him to act, in his effort to increase the power of the presidency.

At the same time, militant southern sectionalists regarded the growth of federal executive and judicial power with alarm. If the president could impose a high tariff on the states and if the Supreme Court could deny the states the authority to govern Indians within their own borders, might not high-handed federal officials someday also threaten the South's system of slavery?

Judicial Federalism and the Limits of Law

In a series of notable cases, the Supreme Court, under the leadership of Chief Justice John Marshall, sought to limit states' power to control people and resources within their own boundaries. In *McCulloch v. Maryland* (1819), the Court supported Congress's decision to grant the Second Bank of the United States a 20-year charter. The state of Maryland had imposed a high tax on notes issued by the bank. Declaring that "the power to tax involves the power to destroy," the Supreme Court ruled the state's action unconstitutional. The court justices held that, although the original Constitution did not mention a national bank, Congress retained the authority to create such an institution. This fact implied that Congress also had the power to preserve it. This decision relied on what came to be called a "loose construction" of the Constitution to justify "implied powers" of the government. Under a "loose" construction, or interpretation, of the Constitution, the federal government reserved for itself forms of authority not explicitly stated in the Constitution. Similarly, in deciding *Cohens v. Virginia* (1821), the Court limited the power of individual states. The Cohens had been convicted of illegally selling lottery tickets. The Supreme Court upheld their conviction but also asserted its own authority to review state legislation that affected the federal government's powers.

In 1832 a case involving the rights of the Cherokee nation brought the Court head to head with President Jackson's own brand of federal muscle-flexing. With the expansion of cotton cultivation into upland Georgia in the early nineteenth century, white residents of that state increasingly resented the presence of their Cherokee neighbors.

At the same time, some Cherokees worked and worshipped in ways similar to European Americans: they cultivated farmland, converted to Christianity, and established a formal legal code. A census authorized by the Cherokee Nation in 1828 enumerated the population and provided evidence of the group's conformity to whites' ways. For example, the 2600 residents of Georgia's Coosewaytee District owned a total of 295 slaves, 2944 black cattle, 1207 horses, 4965 swine, 113 looms, 397 spinning wheels, 461 plows, and several sawmills, grist mills, and blacksmith shops. Two missionary schools had a total of 21 Cherokee pupils. On July 4, 1827, Cherokee leaders met in convention to devise a republican constitution. In the grand tradition of the Patriots of 1776, the group proclaimed itself a sovereign nation, responsible for its own affairs and free of the dictates of individual states.

By the late 1820s certain white people, including the president, were calling for the removal of the Cherokee from the Southeast. The 1829 discovery of gold in the Georgia hills brought 10,000 white miners to Cherokee territory in a gold rush that the Indians called the "Great Intrusion." Whites, it seemed, were less interested in Indian assimilation and religious conversion than they were in the riches to be extracted from Indian land. President Jackson saw the very existence of the Cherokee nation as an affront to his authority and a hindrance to Georgia's economic well-being. He resented the fact that the Cherokee considered themselves a sovereign nation, independent of the U.S. president. Jackson also feared that the Cherokee would prevent whites from mining or farming land within Indian borders. Jackson, in fact, favored removing all Indians from the Southeast to make way for whites. He declared that Georgia should be rid of "a few thousand savages" so that "towns and prosperous

	Census of 1809	Census of 1824	Percent of Change 1809–1824
Cherokee Population	12,395	16,060	30%
Negro slaves	583	1,277	119
Whites	314	215	-29
Schools	5	18	260
Students	94	314	234
Gristmills	13	36	177%
Sawmills	3	13	333
Blacksmith shops	—	62	—
Stores	—	9	—
Tanyards	—	2	—
Powder mills	1	1	—
Looms	429	762	78%
Spinning wheels	1,572	2,486	58
Wagons	30	172	473
Plows	567	2,923	416
Threshing machines	—	1	—
Horses	6,519	7,683	18%
Cattle	19,165	22,531	18
Swine	19,778	46,732	136
Sheep	1,037	2,566	147
Goats	—	430	—

■ **FIGURE 11.1**
CHEROKEE NATION INTERCENSUS CHANGES, 1809–1824

Source: Douglas C. Wilms, "Cherokee Land Use in Georgia Before Removal," in William L. Anderson, ed., *Cherokee Removal: Before and After* (Athens: University of Georgia Press).

farms" could develop there. In 1830, with the president's backing, Congress passed the Indian Removal Act. The Act provided for "an exchange of lands with the Indians residing in any of the states or territories, and for their removal west of the river Mississippi."

Outraged by this naked land grab, the Cherokee Nation refused to sign the removal treaties specified by Congress as part of the Indian Removal Act. In a petition to Congress in 1830, members of the group declared, "We wish to remain on the land of our fathers. We have a perfect and original right to claim this, without interruption or molestation." In a message to his own people in 1831, Cherokee leader John Ross invoked the promise of President Jackson himself. Ross noted that the president had claimed two years earlier that "*so far as we had rights we should be protected in them.*"

Citing both the treaties that guaranteed them a right to the land and the "laws of the United States made in pursuance of treaties," the Cherokee Nation appealed to the Supreme Court. In an effort to protect their land titles, the Indian nation had first tried to take its case to Georgia courts, but Georgia refused to allow it to press its claim. The Georgia legislature maintained that it had authority over all the Indians living within the state's borders, and that the Cherokee nation lacked jurisdiction over its own people.

The Cherokee hoped that the Supreme Court would support their position that they were an independent entity, not bound by the laws of Georgia. In a set of cases—*Cherokee Nation v. Georgia* (1831) and *Worcester v. Georgia* (1832)—the Court agreed that Georgia's

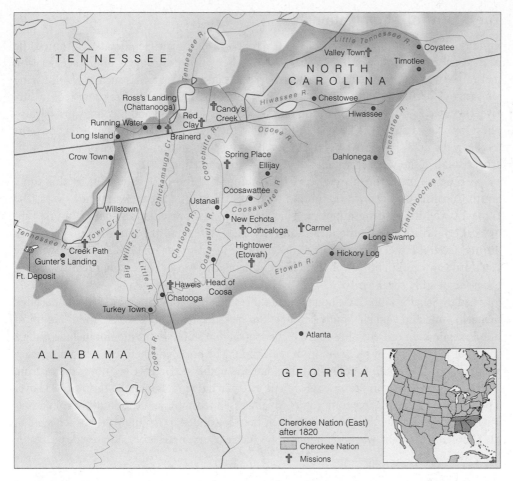

■ **MAP 11.5**

THE CHEROKEE NATION AFTER 1820   This map shows the Cherokee nation on the eve of removal to Indian Territory (present-day Oklahoma). The discovery of gold in the region sparked a constitutional battle over control of Cherokee land. In 1832 the Supreme Court ruled that the federal government had ultimate authority over Indian nations. The state of Georgia ignored the ruling and sought to enforce its own laws in Cherokee territory.

authority did not extend to the Cherokee Nation. The Court proclaimed that Indian self-governing bodies were "domestic dependent nations" under the authority of the U.S. government, not the individual states. Under this ruling, Georgia lacked the authority to force Indians from their land. More generally, the states must defer to the federal government in issues related to the welfare and governance of the Indians. Governor Wilson Lumpkin of Georgia rejected these Supreme Court rulings. In 1832 he declared, "It is due to the sovereign character of every State of the Union to maintain its territorial rights and policy over its own population." Jackson, too, ignored the Court's display of judicial authority. Of the *Worcester* decision, Jackson declared, "John Marshall has made his decision. Now let him enforce it."

Some of the president's own supporters protested his determination to deprive landowners—even Indian landowners—of their personal property. Davy Crockett announced that he was voting his conscience and opposing Jackson's Indian removal policy. Declared Crockett, "I believed it was a wicked, unjust measure, and that I should go against it, let the cost to myself be what it might." Nevertheless, in 1832 the president sent troops to Georgia to begin forcing the Indians out of their homeland.

The "Tariff of Abominations"

Besides engineering the removal of the Cherokees, Jacksonian Democrats continued the post–War of 1812 policy of high tariffs. In 1828 they pushed through Congress legislation that raised fees on imported manufactured products and raw materials such as wool. Facing a disastrous decline in cotton prices after the Panic of 1819, Southerners protested: to survive, they had to both sell their cotton on the open world market and buy high-priced supplies from New England or Europe. In their view, the higher the tariff on English goods, the less likely the English were to continue to purchase their cotton from southern planters. Southerners dubbed the 1828 legislation the "Tariff of Abominations."

A renewal of the tariff four years later moderated the 1828 rates. But by this time, South Carolina politicians were in no mood to sit back and accept what they saw as the arrogant wielding of federal power. They drew on past precedents in developing a theory called nullification—the idea that individual states had the authority to reject, or nullify, federal laws. The Virginia and Kentucky Resolutions of 1798 and 1799 and the Hartford Convention of New England states during the War of 1812 had previously raised the issue of state sovereignty.

Led by Senator John C. Calhoun, the nullifiers met in a convention in 1832 and declared the tariff "null and void" in South Carolina. But Jackson struck back swiftly. In his Nullification Proclamation of December 10, 1832, he argued that states' rights did not include nullification of federal laws or secession from the Union. The president then sent a token military and naval force to South Carolina to intimidate the nullifiers. Henry Clay, now senator from Kentucky, brokered a compromise agreement: a 10 percent reduction in the Tariff of 1832 over a period of eight years. This compromise finally eased tensions, and the South Carolina nullifiers retreated for the time being. However, they continued to maintain "that each state of the Union has the right, whenever it may deem such a course necessary . . . to secede peaceably from the Union."

The "Monster Bank"

The repository of federal funds ($10 million), the Bank of the United States in the 1830s had 30 branches and controlled the money supply by dictating how state banks should repay their loans: in paper notes or in currency. After the expiration of the charter of the first Bank of the United States in 1818, Americans relied on a combination of state bank notes and on coins minted by the individual states as well as by foreign countries. Congress attempted to relieve the chaotic money and state-banking system by chartering a Second Bank of the United States in 1816. As a central (though privately held) institution, the bank also aided economic growth and development by extending loans to commercial enterprises.

In 1832, Jackson vetoed a bill that would have renewed the charter of the Second Bank of the United States, which was due to expire in 1836. Somewhat contradictorily, Jackson claimed to represent the interests of small lenders such as farmers, but he also advocated hard money (currency in the form of gold or silver, not paper or credit extended by banks). Traditionally, small lenders objected to hard money policies, which kept the supply of currency low and interest rates for borrowers high. Jackson also objected to the bank's work as a large commercial institution. For example, he blamed the bank for precipitating the Panic and Depression of 1819 by withholding credit from small banks, causing them to recall their loans and, in some cases, fail.

José Agustin de Escudero Describes New Mexico as a Land of Opportunity, 1827

In the early nineteenth century, many people believed that the West afforded abundant economic opportunities for those willing to work hard. However, in most areas of the trans-Appalachian West, farming was a risky venture. Farmers needed cash or credit to hire hands—or to buy slaves—to clear dense underbrush and make other improvements on the land. Floods and droughts could wipe out a year's hard work and ruin even the most industrious family.

Nevertheless, certain frontier livelihoods did not take large investments in labor or equipment. In 1827, José Agustin de Escudero, a lawyer from the Mexico state of Chihuahua, visited the northern reaches of his country and reported on the partido system of sheep raising in the colony of New Mexico. He reported that the quality and expanse of the land meant that young men of modest means could prosper after a few years without securing large loans.

It can be asserted that there were no paupers in New Mexico at that time, nor could there be any. At the same time, there were no large-scale stockmen who could pay wages or make any expenditure whatever in order to preserve and increase their wealth in this branch of agriculture. A poor man, upon reaching the age when one generally starts a family, would go to a rich stockman and offer to help him take care of one or more herds of sheep. These flocks were composed of *a thousand* ewes and *ten* breeding rams, which were never separated from the herd as is the practice of stock raisers in other countries. Consequently, in each flock, not a single day would go by without the birth of two or three lambs, which the shepherd would put with the ewe and force the female to suckle without the difficulties which he would have had with a larger number of offspring. The shepherd would give the owner ten or twenty per cent of these sheep and an equal amount of wool, as a sort of interest, thus preserving the capital intact.

From the moment he received the flock, the shepherd entered into a contract in regard to the future increase, even with his own overseer. As a matter of fact, he usually contracted it at the current market price, two reales per head [an advance from the stockman], the future increase to be delivered in small numbers over a period of time. With this sum, which the shepherd had in advance, he could construct a house, and take in other persons to help him care for and shear the sheep, which was done with a knife instead of shears. The milk and sometimes the meat from the said sheep provided him sustenance; the wool was spun by his own family into blankets, stockings, etc., which could also be marketed, providing an income. Thus the wealth of the shepherd would increase until the day he became, like his overseer, the owner of a herd. He, in turn, would let out his herds to others after the manner in which he obtained his first sheep and made his fortune. Consequently, even in the homes of the poorest New Mexicans, there is never a dearth of sufficient means to satisfy the necessities of life and even to afford the comfort and luxuries of the wealthiest class in the country.

José de Escudero was a visitor to, not a resident of, New Mexico. It is possible that he oversimplified the partido shepherds' self-sufficiency in this region. Soon after winning its independence from Spain, Mexico opened New Mexico to U.S. traders. By the mid–1820s, traders were leading mule trains along the Santa Fe Trail, which ran from Franklin, Missouri, to Santa Fe, New Mexico. In his account here, de Escudero indirectly highlights the roles of wives and mothers (as spinners and weavers of cloth) in preserving the economic independence of the shepherds' households.

Nevertheless, de Escudero's observations suggest that a combination of factors, including the nature of the landscape itself (in this case suitable for sheep grazing) and the amount of initial capital necessary to the enterprise (in this case a minimal amount of cash), were crucial elements in providing young men and their families with economic opportunities on the frontier. ■

Library of Congress

Merino sheep.

Source: H. Bailey Carroll and J. Villasana Haggard, trans. and ed., *Three New Mexico Chronicles* (Albuquerque, 1942): 41–42.

Engraving by Amos Doolittle, from Jeremy Cross, The True Masonic Chart (New Haven, Conn., 1819). Courtesy of Scottish Rite Museum of Our National Heritage, Library, 14.I, C951,1820a. Photography: Van Gorden-Williams Library John Miller Documents.

■ Many political leaders in the New Republic, including George Washington, were members of the Masons, a fraternal order. The Masons drew their members from a cross-section of the male, primarily urban population, including merchants, artisans, and sailors. The order relied on secret rituals and on symbols such as those in this engraving, which appeared mysterious and threatening to outsiders. In 1831 the Anti-Masonic party became the first party to select its presidential candidate at a convention, where it also adopted a party platform.

TABLE 11-4

The Election of 1832

Candidate	Political Party	Popular Vote	Electoral Vote
Andrew Jackson	Democratic	687,502	219
Henry Clay	National Republican	530,189	49
John Floyd	Independent		11
William Wirt	Anti-Masonic	33,108	7

Jackson condemned the bank as a "monster" intent on devouring hardworking people and enriching a few eastern financiers. In his veto message to Congress, he denounced the bank as an instrument of privilege, one that granted favors to the well-born and well-connected. He fumed, "The humble members of society—the farmers, mechanics, and laborers—who have neither the time nor the means of securing like favors to themselves, have a right to complain of the injustice of their Government."

By vetoing the bank bill, Jackson angered members of Congress and his own cabinet. They had urged him to recharter the bank because they believed the credit system was necessary for economic progress and expansion. Convinced that Jackson had overextended his reach, his opponents seized on the issue as a sign of the chief executive's political vulnerability. Harboring presidential ambitions himself, Henry Clay was certain that the bank controversy would prove Jackson's downfall.

However, Clay, the "Great Compromiser," badly miscalculated. Congress upheld Jackson's veto of the Bank (the Bank closed when its chapter expired in 1836). Nominated for president by the National Republicans in 1832, Clay drew support from merchants who had benefited from Bank of the United States loans and from the sizable contingent of Jackson-haters. Yet a new player, the Anti-Masonic party, entered the fray and complicated matters for Clay, as it drew some of the anti-Jackson sentiment away from him. This group accused the Masons, a secret fraternal order, of subverting American democratic values. Jackson himself was a member of the Masons, prompting the new party to call into question the president's devotion to the "common man."

The Anti-Masonic party gained some favor in New England and the Mid-Atlantic states, where rumors flew about the Masons' secret rituals and alleged clandestine political influence. Still, Jackson won in a landslide against Clay. The president carried not only his stronghold, the West, but also the South and substantial parts of New York, Pennsylvania, and New England. The Anti-Masonic candidate, William Wirt, won only Vermont.

While in office, Jackson used his veto power a total of 12 times. All his predecessors *combined* had used it just 10 times. When his opponents finally formed a political party in 1834, they called themselves Whigs, after the English antimonarchist party. In choosing this name, their intention was to ridicule "King Andrew." In the words of the states' rights advocates, Jackson's high-handed manner was "rather an appeal to the loyalty of subjects, than to the patriotism of citizens." The Whigs opposed the man who had built up the power of the presidency in defiance of Congress and the Supreme Court.

Real People in the "Age of the Common Man"

Universal white manhood suffrage set a new standard for political involvement in the United States. Now, white men could vote and run for office regardless of their class or religion. However, as the voting public expanded, those excluded from it charged that white men's rights came at their expense. White men had the freedom to move west and settle the land because Indians lost their own claim to the land. White men could buy and sell slaves because African American men and women lacked the power to control their own work and keep their families together. White men pursued their careers and stations in the public sphere because women were restricted to the domestic sphere. Together, Indians, blacks, and white women constituted about 70 percent of the American population in the 1820s. Thus, in the "age of the common man," less than one-third of the adult population had the right to vote.

In the early 1830s, a wealthy Frenchman named Alexis de Tocqueville visited the United States and wrote about the contradictions he saw. In his book *Democracy in America* (published in 1835), de Tocqueville noted that the United States lacked the rigid hierarchy of class privilege that characterized European nations. However, he also noted some sore spots in American democratic values and practices. He commented on the plight of groups deprived of the right to vote, whose lack of freedom stood out starkly in the otherwise egalitarian society of the United States. He sympathized with the southeastern Indians uprooted from their homelands. He raised the possibility that conflicts between blacks and whites might eventually lead to bloodshed. He even contrasted the situation of young unmarried white women, who seemed so free-spirited, with that of wives, who appeared cautious and dull. He concluded, "In America a woman loses her independence forever in the bonds of matrimony." In other words, de Tocqueville saw America for what it was: a blend of freedom and slavery, of independence and dependence.

Wards, Workers, and Warriors: Native Americans

Population growth in the United States—and on the borderlands between the United States and Mexican territory—put pressure on Indian societies. Yet different cultural groups responded in different ways to this pressure. Some, like the Cherokees, conformed to European American ways and became sedentary farmers. Others were forced to work for whites. Still others either waged war on white settlements and military forces or retreated further and further from European American settlements in the hope of avoiding clashes with the intruders.

Nevertheless, prominent whites continued to denigrate the humanity of all Indians. In the 1820s Henry Clay claimed that Indians were "essentially

■ This photo of the Fairmont Waterworks in Philadelphia shows the effects of Greek architecture on American public buildings in the early nineteenth century. Designed by Frederick C. Graff, the waterworks were completed in 1822. Numerous banks, colleges, commercial buildings, and large private homes built during this period were designed in the Greek Revival style. The United States saw itself as the embodiment of democracy, a form of government characteristic of some early Greek city-states.

Richard T. Nowitz/CORBIS

inferior to the Anglo-Saxon race . . . and their disappearance from the human family will be no great loss to the world." In 1828 the House of Representatives Committee on Indian Affairs surveyed the Indians of the South and concluded that "an Indian cannot work" and that all Indians were lazy and notable for their "thirst for spirituous liquours." According to the committee, when European settlers depleted reserves of wildlife, Indians as a group would cease to exist.

Members of the Cherokee Nation bitterly denounced these assertions. "The Cherokees do not live upon the chase [for game]," they pointed out. Neither did the Creeks, Choctaws, Chickasaws, and Seminoles—the other members of the Five Civilized Tribes, so called for their varying degrees of conformity to white people's ways.

Charting a middle course between the Indian and European American worlds was Sequoyah, the son of a white Virginia trader–soldier and a Cherokee woman. A veteran of Andrew Jackson's campaign against the Creeks in 1813–1814, Sequoyah moved to Arkansas in 1818, part of an early Cherokee migration west. In 1821 he finished a Cherokee syllabary (a written language consisting of syllables and letters, in contrast to pictures, or pictographs). The product of a dozen years' work, the syllabary consisted of 86 characters. In 1828 the *Cherokee Phoenix,* a newspaper based on the new writing system, began publication in New Echota, Georgia.

Sequoyah's written language enabled the increasingly dispersed Cherokee Indians to remain in touch with each other on their own terms. At the same time, numerous Indian cultural groups lost their struggle to retain even modest control over their destinies. In some areas of the continent, smallpox continued to ravage native populations. In other regions, Indians became wards of, or dependent on, whites, living with and working for white families. Other groups, living close to whites, adopted their trading practices. In Spanish California, the Muquelmne Miwoks in the San Joaquin delta made a living by stealing and then selling the horses of Mexican settlers.

In other parts of California, Spanish missionaries conquered Indian groups, converted them to Christianity, and then forced them to work in the missions. In missions up and down the California coast, Indians worked as weavers, tanners, shoemakers, bricklayers, carpenters, blacksmiths, and other artisans. Some herded cattle and raised horses. Indian women cooked for the mission, cleaned, and spun wool. They wove cloth and sewed garments.

The Newberry Library, Chicago

■ Artist Charles Bird King painted this portrait of Sequoyah while the Indian leader was in Washington, D.C., in 1828. Government officials honored him for developing a written form of the Cherokee language. He is wearing a medal presented to him by the Cherokee nation in 1825. He later settled permanently in Sallisaw, in what is today Sequoyah County, Oklahoma.

Nevertheless, even Indians living in or near missions resisted the cultural change imposed by the intruders. Catholic missionaries complained that Indian women such as those of the Chumash refused to learn Spanish. But by abandoning their native tongue, these women would have lost much—positions of influence within their own religious community—and gained little because positions of authority were dominated by Spanish-speaking men. The refusal among some Indians to assimilate completely signaled persistent, deep-seated conflicts between native groups and incoming settlers. In 1824 a revolt among hundreds of newly converted Indians at the mission *La Purisima Concepción* north of Santa Barbara revealed a rising militancy among native peoples.

After the War of 1812, the U.S. government had rewarded some military veterans with land grants in the Old Northwest. Federal agents tried to clear the way for these new settlers—farmers as well as miners with their eye on the rich lead deposits in northern Illinois and southern Wisconsin—by ousting Indians from the area. Overwhelmed by the number of whites, some Indian groups such as the Peorias and Kaskaskias gave up their lands to the interlopers. However, the Kickapoos along the Wabash and Illinois rivers, together with the Winnebagos, Sauks, and Fox, took a stand against the white intrusion. In 1826 and 1827 the Winnebagos attacked white families and boat pilots living near Prairie du Chien, Wisconsin. Two years later, the Sauk chief Black Hawk (known to Indians as Ma-ka-tai-me-she-kia-kiak) assembled a coalition of Fox, Winnebagos, Kickapoos, and

Potawatomis. Emboldened by the prospect of aid from British Canada, they clashed with federal troops and raided farmers' homesteads and miners' camps.

In August 1832 a force of 1300 U.S. soldiers and volunteers struck back, attacking an encampment of Indians on the Bad Axe River in western Wisconsin. The soldiers killed 300 Indian men, women, and children. The massacre, the decisive point of what came to be called the Black Hawk War, marked the end of armed Indian resistance north of the Ohio River and east of the Mississippi. If the United States did not have justice on its side, it at least had superior military might. In the courts and on the battlefield, Indian cultures were under siege.

Slaves and Free People of Color

In 1820 the U.S. population included 1.5 million slaves. A decade later that figure had grown to 2 million, almost entirely from natural increase. In the same ten-year period, the number of free blacks increased from 99,281 to 137,529 in the North as a result of emancipation. The figure rose from 134,223 to 182,070 in the South. The large free black population in the Upper South was scattered in rural areas, whereas the small numbers of their Lower South counterparts were concentrated in the cities.

Overall, however, the proportion of free blacks within the southern population declined. True, some masters freed their slaves, and some slaves managed to run away or buy their freedom. The free population also grew by natural means. But within the South, whites perceived free blacks as an unwelcome and dangerous presence, especially given the possibility that they would conspire with slaves to spark a rebellion. For these reasons some states began to outlaw private manumissions (the practice of individual owners freeing their slaves) and to force free blacks to leave the state altogether.

One free black who inspired such fears was Denmark Vesey. Born on the Danish-controlled Island of Saint Thomas in 1767, Vesey was a literate carpenter as well as a religious leader. In 1799 he won $1500 in a Charleston lottery and used some of the money to buy his freedom. In the summer of 1822, a Charleston, South Carolina, court claimed to have unearthed evidence of a "diabolical plot" hatched by Vesey together with plantation slaves from the surrounding area. The judges charged that Vesey and his coconspirators aimed "to trample on all laws, human and divine; to riot in blood, outrage, and rapine . . . and conflagration, and to introduce anarchy and confusion in their most horrid form."

The judges' claims provide a laundry list of whites' fears about free men of color. In their account of the testimony, they suggested that Vesey drew inspiration from the Saint Domingue slave revolt that freeman Toussaint L'Ouverture had led in 1791. They claimed Vesey closely followed congressional debates during the Missouri Compromise crisis of 1819 and 1820. They implicated members of Charleston's African Methodist Episcopal Church, an independent body founded in 1818, which whites believed provided fertile ground for black insurrectionists. Finally, the judges took note of one witness who claimed that, "even whilst walking through the streets in the company with another, he [Vesey] was not idle; for if his companion bowed to a white person he would rebuke him, and observe that all men were born equal." Notions of freedom and equality had explosive potential in the slave South.

Yet the historical record strongly suggests that no plot ever existed. Black "witnesses" who feared for their own lives provided inconsistent and contradictory testimony to a panel of judges. Authorities never located any material evidence of a plan, such as stockpiles of weapons. Under fire from other Charleston elites for rushing to judgment, the judges redoubled their efforts to embellish vague rumors of black discontent into a tale of a well-orchestrated uprising and to implicate growing numbers of black people. As a result of the testimony of several slaves, 35 black men were hanged and another 18 exiled outside the United States. Of those executed, Vesey and 23 other men said nothing to support even the vaguest charges of the court.

The uncovering of the Vesey "plot" prompted whites throughout the South to crack down on meetings, religious or otherwise, among slaves and free people of color. In Charleston, a new white group calling itself the South Carolina Association sought to restrict the movements of free blacks and return fugitive slaves to their owners. The city's African Methodist Episcopal Church was shut down and its preacher, Moses Brown, hounded out of South Carolina.

In the North, some blacks were granted the right to vote after emancipation in the late eighteenth century; however, many of those voting rights were lost in the early nineteenth century. New Jersey (in 1807), Connecticut (1818), New York (1821), and Pennsylvania (1838) all revoked the legislation that had let black men cast ballots. In several instances, the political party in power feared that black voters would swing the election to their opponents. Free northern blacks continued to suffer under a number of legal restrictions. Most were not citizens and therefore perceived themselves as oppressed like the slaves in the South.

A new group of black leaders in the urban North began to link their fate to that of their enslaved brothers and sisters in the South. In Boston, North Carolina–born David Walker published his fiery *Walker's Appeal to the Coloured Citizens of the World* in 1829. Walker called for all blacks to integrate fully into American society, shunning racial segregation whether initiated by whites or by blacks themselves. Reminding his listeners of the horrors of the slave trade, he declared that black people were ready to die for freedom: "I give it as a fact, let twelve black men get well armed for battle, and they will kill and put to flight fifty whites." Walker ended by quoting the Declaration of Independence. Whites, he argued, had demonstrated more cruelty and tyranny toward blacks than Great Britain had ever shown toward the colonies.

Also in Boston, Maria Stewart, a charismatic black preacher, became the first American-born woman (of any background) to lecture in public. In 1832 and 1833 she delivered a series of stirring addresses. She argued that free blacks in the North were not much better off than enslaved blacks in the South. "Knowledge is power," she exhorted her audience, urging them to pursue education on their own.

Northern black leaders disagreed among themselves on the issues of integration and black separatism—for example, whether blacks should create their own schools or press for inclusion in the public educational system. A few leaders favored leaving the country altogether, believing that black people would never find peace and freedom in the United States. Founded by whites in New Jersey in 1817, the American Colonization Society (ACS) paid for black Americans to settle Monrovia (later Liberia) on the west coast of Africa. The group claimed that foreign colonization would bring American blacks "unspeakable blessings." The ACS drew support from a variety of groups: whites in the Upper South who wanted to free their slaves but believed that black and white people could not live in the same country and some slaves and free people of color convinced that colonization would give them a fresh start. A small number of American-born blacks settled in Liberia. However, most black activists rejected colonization. They had been born on American soil, and their forebears had been buried there. Maria Stewart declared, "But before I go [to Africa] the bayonet shall pierce me through."

Northern black leaders disagreed among themselves on the issues of integration and black separatism.

Northern whites sought to control black people and their movements. Outspoken black men and women such as Walker and Stewart alarmed northern whites who feared that if blacks could claim decent jobs, white people would lose their own jobs. African Americans who worked outdoors as wagon drivers, peddlers, and street sweepers were taunted and in some cases attacked by whites who demanded deference from blacks in public. In October 1824 a mob of white men invaded a black neighborhood in Providence, Rhode Island. They terrorized its residents, destroyed buildings, and left the place "almost entirely in ruins." The catalyst for the riot had come the previous day, when a group of blacks had refused to yield the inside of the sidewalk—a cleaner place to walk—to white passersby. These blacks were arrested, but a jury found the defendants not guilty. Noting the unabashed racism of white Northerners and the unwillingness of white Southerners to acknowledge the terrible consequences of slavery,

Alexis de Tocqueville wrote, "There is something more frightening about the silence of the South than about the North's noisy fears."

The South's silence was broken in 1831 when white Southerners took steps to reinforce the institution of slavery, using both violent and legal means. That year Nat Turner, an enslaved preacher and mystic, led a slave revolt in Southampton, Virginia. In the 1820s the young Turner had looked skyward and had seen visions of "white spirits and black spirits engaged in battle . . . and blood flowed in streams." Turner believed that he had received divine instructions to lead other slaves to freedom, to "arise and prepare myself, and slay my enemies with their own weapons." In August he and a group of followers that eventually numbered 80 moved through the countryside, killing whites wherever they could find them. Ultimately, nearly 60 whites died at the hands of Turner's rebels. Turner himself managed to evade capture for more than two months. After he was captured, he was tried, convicted, and sentenced to death. A white man named Thomas Gray interviewed Turner in his jail cell and recorded his "confessions" before he was hanged.

> *In the early nineteenth century, work was becoming increasingly identified as labor that earned cash wages.*

Published in 1832 by Gray, *The Confessions of Nat Turner* reached a large, horrified audience in the white South. According to Gray, Turner said that he had exhibited "uncommon intelligence" when he was a child. As a young man, he had received inspiration from the Bible, especially the passage "Seek ye the kingdom of Heaven and all things shall be added unto you." Perhaps most disturbing of all, Turner reported that, since 1830, he had been a slave of "Mr. Joseph Travis, who was to me a kind master, and placed the greatest confidence in me; in fact, I had no cause to complain of his treatment to me." Turner's "confessions" suggested the subversive potential of slaves who were literate and Christian and those who were treated kindly by their masters and mistresses.

After the Turner revolt, a wave of white hysteria swept the South. In Virginia near where the killings had occurred, whites assaulted blacks with unbridled fury. The Virginia legislature seized the occasion to defeat various antislavery proposals. Thereafter, all the slave states moved to strengthen the institution of slavery. For all practical purposes, public debate over slavery ceased.

Legal and Economic Dependence: The Plight of Women

In the political and economic realms, the egalitarian impulse rarely affected the status of women in a legal or practical sense. Regardless of where they lived, enslaved women and Indian women had almost no rights under either U.S. or Spanish law. Still, legal systems in the United States and the Spanish borderlands differed in their treatment of women. In the United States, most of the constraints that white married women had experienced in the colonial period still applied in the 1820s. A husband controlled the property that his wife brought to the marriage, and he had legal authority over their children. Indeed, the wife was considered her husband's possession. She had no right to make a contract, keep money she earned, or vote, run for office, or serve on a jury. In contrast, in the Spanish Southwest, married women could own land and conduct business on their own. At the same time, however, husbands, fathers, and local priests continued to exert much influence over the lives of these women.

European American women's economic subordination served as a rationale for their political inferiority. The "common man" concept rested on the assumption that only men could ensure American economic growth and well-being. According to this view, men had the largest stake in society because only they owned property. That stake made them responsible citizens.

Yet women contributed to the economy in myriad ways. Although few women earned cash wages in the 1820s, almost all adult women worked. In the colonial period, society had highly valued women's labor in the fields, the garden, and the kitchen. However, in the early nineteenth century, work was becoming increasingly identified as labor that earned cash wages. This attitude proved particularly common in the Northeast, where increasing numbers of workers labored under the supervision of a boss. As this belief took root, men began valuing women's contributions to the household economy less and less. If women did not earn money, many men asked, did they really work at all?

In these years, well-off women in the northeastern and mid-Atlantic states began to think of themselves as consumers and not producers of goods. They relied more and more on store-bought cloth and household supplies. Some could also afford to hire servants to perform housework for them. Privileged women gradually stopped thinking of their responsibilities as making goods or processing and preparing food. Rather, their main tasks were to manage servants and create a comfortable home for their husbands and children. They saw their labor as necessary to the well-being of their families, even if their compensation came in the form of emotional satisfaction rather than cash.

■ The plight of needlewomen became representative of the hazards faced by female workers in the new urban commercial economy of the late eighteenth and early nineteenth centuries. Many women worked at home, sewing garments that they returned to a "jobber" for payment. The labor, often performed by candlelight in ill-lighted tenements, was tedious and ill-paid. Laundry work also took up much of women's time.

In contrast, women in other parts of the country continued to engage in the same forms of household industry that had characterized the colonial period. In Spanish settlements, women played a central role in household production. They made all of their family's clothes by carding, spinning, and weaving the wool from sheep. They tanned cowhides and ground blue corn to make tortillas, or *atole*. They produced their own candles and soap, and they plastered the walls of the home.

In the Spanish mission of San Gabriel, California, the widow Eulalia Pérez cooked, sewed, ministered to the ill, and instructed children in reading and writing. As housekeeper, Pérez kept the keys to the mission storehouse. She also distributed supplies to the Indians and the *vaqueros* (cowboys) who lived in the mission. She supervised Indian servants as well as soap makers, wine pressers, and olive oil producers.

At Mission San Diego, Apolonaria Lorenzana worked as a healer and cared for the church sacristy and priestly vestments. Lorenzana devoted her life to such labors, from the time she arrived in Monterey as a child of seven (in 1800) until her death in the late nineteenth century. Although the priests tried to restrict her to administering the mission hospital, she took pride in her nursing abilities, "even though Father Sánchez had told me not to do it myself, but to have it done, and only to be present so that the servant girls would do it well."

Indian women also engaged in a variety of essential tasks. Sioux and Mandan women, though of a social rank inferior to men, performed a great deal of manual labor in their own villages. They dressed buffalo skins that the men later sold to traders. They collected water and wood, cooked, dried meat and fruit, and cultivated maize (corn), pumpkins, and squash with hoes made from the shoulderblades of elk. These women worked collectively within a network of households rather than individually within nuclear families.

In many communities, women, regardless of ethnicity, were paid in kind for their work—that is, they received food and shelter but not money. Nevertheless, some women did work for cash wages during this era. New England women and children, for example, were the vanguard of factory wage-earners in the early manufacturing system. In Massachusetts in 1820 women and children constituted almost a third of all manufacturing workers. In the largest textile factories, they made up fully 80 percent of the workforce.

The business of textile manufacturing took the tasks of spinning thread and weaving cloth out of the home, where such tasks often were performed by unpaid, unmarried daughters, and relocated those tasks in factories, where the same workers received wages. The famous "Lowell mill girls" are an apt example. Young, unmarried white women from New Hampshire, Vermont, and Massachusetts, these workers moved to the new company town of Lowell, Massachusetts, to take jobs as textile machine operatives. In New England, thousands of young men had migrated west, tipping the sex ratio in favor of women and creating a reserve of female laborers. But to attract young women to factory work, mill owners had to reassure them (and their parents) that they would be safe and well cared for away from home. To that end, they established boarding houses where employees could live together under the supervision of a matron—an older woman who served as their mother-away-from-home.

Company towns set rules shaping employees' living conditions as well as their working conditions. In the early 1830s, a posted list of "Rules and Regulations" covered many aspects of the lives of the young women living at the Poignaud and Plant boardinghouse at Lancaster, Massachusetts. The list told the women how to enter the building (quietly, and then hang up "their bonnet, shawl, coat, etc. etc. in the entry") and where to sit at the dinner table (the two workers with greatest seniority were to take their places at the head of the table). Despite these rules, many young women valued the friendships they made with their coworkers and the money they made in the mills. Some of these women sent their wages back home so that their fathers could pay off the mortgage or their brothers could attend school.

> *The new delineation between men's and women's work and workplaces intensified the drive for women's education begun after the Revolution.*

But not all women wage-earners labored in large mills. In New York City, single women, wives, and widows toiled as needleworkers in their homes. Impoverished, sewing in tiny attics by the dim light of candles, these women were at the mercy of jobbers—merchants who parceled out cuffs, collars, and shirt fronts that the women finished. Other urban women worked as street vendors, selling produce, or as cooks, nursemaids, or laundresses.

The new delineation between men's and women's work and workplaces intensified the drive for women's education begun after the Revolution. If well-to-do women were to assume domestic responsibilities while their husbands worked outside the home, then women must receive their own unique form of schooling, or so the reasoning went. Most ordinary women received little in the way of formal education. Yet elite young women had expanded educational opportunities, beginning in the early nineteenth century. Emma Willard founded a female academy in Troy, New York, in 1821, and Catharine Beecher established the Hartford (Connecticut) Female Seminary two years later. For the most part, these schools catered to the daughters of wealthy families, young women who would never have to work in a factory to survive. Hailed as a means to prepare young women to serve as wives and mothers, the schools taught geography, foreign languages, mathematics, science, and philosophy, as well as the "female" pursuits of embroidery and music.

Out of this curriculum designed especially for women emerged women's rights activists, women who keenly felt both the potential of their own intelligence and the degrading nature of their social situation. Elizabeth Cady, an 1832 graduate of the Troy Female Seminary, later went on to marry Henry B. Stanton and bear seven children. But by the 1840s she strode onto the national stage as a tireless advocate of women's political and economic rights.

Ties That Bound a Growing Population

The Founding Fathers had disagreed among themselves about whether democracy could still thrive in a large nation, where news necessarily traveled slowly and people remained isolated from their neighbors. However, by the 1820s few Americans doubted that the nation could grow and still preserve its democratic character. In fact, westward expansion seemed to promote democracy. Now, more ordinary white men than ever participated in the political process.

At the same time, population growth and migration patterns disrupted old bonds of community. When people left their place of birth, they often severed ties with their family and

■ The Rev. John Atwood and family reading the Bible, 1845.

original community. New forms of social cohesion arose to replace these traditional ties. By the 1830s, for example, the national party system of Democrats and Whigs claimed the allegiances of white men from all sections of the country. Indeed, when one English visitor to New York state observed the "furious acrimony of party spirit," he suggested that Americans cared more for the trappings of partisan loyalty—"the spirit of electioneering"—than for ideas themselves.

In addition, new religions sought to make sense of changing political and economic landscape. High literacy rates among the population created a new community of readers, a dispersed audience for periodicals as well as for a new, uniquely American literature. Finally, opinionmakers used the printed word to spread new ideas and values across regional boundaries. These ideas, such as glorification of male ambition, helped knit together far-flung segments of the population, men and women who began to speak of an "American character."

New Visions of Religious Faith

New forms of religious faith arose in response to turbulent times. During the Indian Wars in the Old Northwest, a Winnebago prophet named White Cloud helped Black Hawk create a coalition of Winnebagos, Potawatomies, Kickapoos, Sauks, and Fox Indians. A mystic and medicine man, White Cloud preached against the white man and exhorted his followers to defend their way of life, an Indian way that knew no tribal boundaries. White Cloud, the religious leader, and Black Hawk, the military leader, surrendered together to federal troops on August 27, 1832, signifying the spiritual component in the Indians' militant resistance to whites. Through the rest of the nineteenth century, a number of Indian groups found inspiration, and in some cases common ground, in the teachings of Indian religious leaders.

New religious enthusiasms took hold in other parts of the country as well. In the late 1820s and early 1830s, the Second Great Awakening swept western New York. The fervor of religious revivals so heated the region that people began to call it "the Burned-Over District." Hordes of people of various Protestant denominations attended week-long prayer meetings, sat together on the "anxious bench" for sinners, and listened, transfixed, as new converts told of their path to righteousness.

What explains this wave of religious enthusiasm? A major factor was a clergyman named Charles Grandison Finney who managed to tap into the wellspring of hope and anxiety of the time. A former lawyer, Finney preached that people were moral free agents, fully capable of deciding between right and wrong and doing good in the world. Finney's message had great appeal during this period of rapid social, economic, and technological change. In New England and New York, for example, canals were bringing new kinds of goods to rural areas and longtime residents were departing for the Midwest. Traditional social relationships seemed threatened.

Finney believed that people could control their own destinies and that they should work through earthly institutions to do it. In one sermon, he declared, "The church must take the right ground in regard to politics. . . . The time has come that Christians must vote for honest men." Of course, not all Christians agreed on what constituted the "right ground" in politics. But Finney sought to link the life of the spirit with political and reform efforts, and many men and women responded enthusiastically.

Throughout the country, religious institutions also grappled with questions about slavery. As the fear of possible black uprisings spread, white clergy in the South began to turn away from their former willingness to convert anyone. Instead, they began seeking respectability in

Laurie Platt Winfrey, Inc

■ The long-lived religious revival called the Second Great Awakening swept through the United States in the 1820s and 1830s. Charles Grandison Finney, an itinerant preacher, helped lead the movement. He urged listeners to consider themselves "moral free agents" with control over their own destinies. Services conducted outdoors, called "camp meetings," provided settings for mass audiences to engage in emotional release and personal testimonials of newly found faith.

the eyes of the well-to-do, slave-owning class. Incorporating masculine imagery into their sermons, they used the language of militant patriotism to distance themselves from the white women, slaves, and free people of color in their congregations. At a western revival in 1824, one itinerant Methodist minister described his military service in the War of 1812; he had helped to vanquish not only the British but also "the merciless savages of the forest, and to secure and perpetuate the liberties secured to us by our forefathers." These preachers strove to reinforce the power of husband over wife, parent over child, and master over slave, relations that defined the typical plantation household.

Elsewhere, some church leaders sought to purge Christianity of what they saw as its too-worldly nature and to revive the primitive church that Jesus and his disciples had established. On April 6, 1830, a young farmer named Joseph Smith, Jr., founded the Church of Jesus Christ of Latter-Day Saints (also called the Mormons) in Fayette, New York. Smith said that, in a vision, he had received the text of a holy book originally written by a Native American historian more than 1400 years earlier. Transcribed from tablets presented to him by an angel named Moroni, the text was called the *Book of Mormon*. Together with the Old and New Testaments, it formed the basis of a new faith. Over the next few years, the Mormon Church grew rapidly, claiming 8000 members by the mid-1830s. However, the young church also aroused intense hostility among mainstream Protestant denominations that regarded the new group's theology and textual inspiration with suspicion. It was almost impossible for religious institutions to escape the worldly realm of politics and social fragmentation.

Literate and Literary America

In 1828 a young widow named Sarah Hale broke new ground for women. She became the first woman to edit an American periodical when she accepted responsibility for editing the *Ladies Magazine,* published in Boston. Once a hatmaker but now a published poet and novelist, Hale aimed "to make females better acquainted with their duties and privileges" through the articles in her magazine. Between 1825 and 1850, thousands of other magazines cropped up and then disappeared, the product of a growing audience of literate (and literary) city-dwellers. But the *Ladies Magazine,* later renamed *Godey's Lady's Book,* lived an uncommonly long life under Hale's editorial guidance.

The *Ladies Magazine* appealed primarily to well-off white wives and mothers in the Northeast, the South, and the West. They identified with its message promoting motherhood and the virtues of piety and self-sacrifice. The *Ladies Magazine* and other publications portrayed women as especially devout and thus powerful: men might claim as their domain "the government and the glory of the world," wrote Hale in 1832, "but nevertheless, what man shall become depends upon the secret, silent influence of women." That influence, Hale and other men and women like her believed, derived from women's roles as nurturers and caretakers.

Indeed, many of the poems and short stories published in the *Ladies Magazine* and other women's periodicals came under the category of sentimental literature. Such writing was calculated to appeal to readers' emotions, rather than their intellect, as their titles reveal: "Burial of a Motherless Infant," "The Blind Mother and Her Children," and "The Harp of the Maniac Maiden" (about a young girl's descent into insanity).

Just as sentimental fiction and poetry attracted a large readership among women, a number of male writers staked their claim to emerging American literature. Washington Irving, James Fenimore Cooper, and William Cullen Bryant all explored regional histories and landscapes in their works. In *Rip Van Winkle* (1819) and the *Legend of Sleepy Hollow* (1820), Irving wrote about the legends of upstate New York. Cooper explored the western New York middle ground contested by the British, Americans, French, and Indians in the late eighteenth century in such works as *The Spy* (1821) and *Last of the Mohicans* (1826). Bryant, inspired by the sight of the Illinois plains in 1832, penned "The Prairies." This praise-song to the vast plains described them as beautiful and "quick with life" ("The graceful deer/Bounds to the woods at my approach"). As the vanguard of a new generation of male American authors, these writers began a literary "American Renaissance."

Along with this new American literary tradition, small towns across the nation began publishing newspapers to educate, inform, and entertain readers. News stories about national elections and legislation, about foreign monarchs and conflicts, reached log cabins in the West as well as elegant townhouses in Boston and Philadelphia. Wrote Washington Irving in 1820, "Over no nation does the press hold a more absolute control than over the people of America, for the universal education of the poorest classes makes every individual a reader."

Newspapers, books, and magazines promoted a set of values that writers claimed described an enduring American character. The ideal American supposedly was ambitious—ready to seize opportunity wherever it could be found—and at the same time devoted to home and family. In fact, these values strongly resembled those adopted by the British middle classes at the same time. Indeed, the United States spawned its own brand of middle-class sensibility called Victorianism, after the English queen who reigned from 1837 to 1901.

Four core values defined early American Victorianism. First, the Victorians believed in the significance of the individual. People should be judged on the basis of their character, not on the circumstances of their birth. This belief, however, generally applied only to white men. Second, individuals should have the freedom to advance as far as their talents and ambition took them; no person should claim advantages over others by virtue of a noble title or aristocratic lineage. Third, work was intrinsically noble, whether performed by a canal digger wielding a pick-axe or a merchant using a quill pen. All people, regardless of their trade, deserved to reap the fruits of their labor. Finally, men and women occupied separate but complementary spheres. American society could be orderly and stable only if men could find a haven from the heartless world of work in their own homes. There, wives tended the hearth and infused the household with their love, self-sacrifice, and religious devotion.

Victorians often saw work as an individualistic endeavor, with men, women, and children earning wages for the number of hours they worked or for each task they performed. However, not all groups embraced Victorian attitudes. The Sioux and Mandan, among other Indian tribes, favored a communal way of life that valued community over the individual. Likewise, Spanish-speaking settlers of tight-knit adobe pueblos prized the close cooperation of men and women: *compadres* (godfathers) with *comadres* (godmothers). These settlers lived their lives according to the seasonal rhythms of agriculture and stock-raising.

In the South, slaveholders straddled both positions. They idealized both profit-seeking individualism and a traditional way of life based on community ties. These white men and women eagerly raked in the financial gains that flowed from their control over staple crop agriculture. Yet in their public pronouncements, they scorned the exclusive pursuit of profit. They held their loyalties to family, kin, and community above the crass emphasis on cash that Yankees espoused. As conflicts between Indians and whites revealed, differences in values were far more than theoretical abstractions. Ultimately, they could wreak death and destruction, as northerners and southerners soon discovered.

Freed from the arduous household labor required of the colonial housewife, the idealized mother of the nineteenth-century emerging middle classes devoted herself to providing religious instruction to her children. This mother, portrayed in *Godey's Lady's Book,* teaches her daughter to pray. The well-appointed bedroom suggests a life of physical comfort and ease.

Conclusion

Western settlement infused American politics with raw energy in the 1820s. Andrew Jackson was the first in a long line of presidents who boasted of their humble origins and furthered their careers by denouncing what they called the privileges enjoyed by wealthy Easterners. The western impulse for grassroots politicking shaped in political reforms, such as those that gave voters more power in nominating candidates for office and electing members of the Electoral College. The challenges faced by western settlers in establishing homesteads and paying their debts emerged as national, not purely local issues. Through the sheer force of his personality, Andrew Jackson exemplified these dramatic changes in the political landscape. Almost single-handedly, he extended the limits of executive power and remade the American party system in the process.

However, the contradictions in Jacksonian politics became glaring in the coming years. As the nation expanded its borders and diversified its economy, distinctions between social classes sharpened. The country also staked its claim to foreign territory, using violence to advance democratic values. Meanwhile, the North and South eyed each other with increasing distrust. And the contrast between those who moved from place to place voluntarily and those who were forced to move became even more dramatic.

Sites to Visit

The Second Bank of the United States, 1816–1936
odur.let.rug.nl/~usa/E/usbank/bank04.htm

The political conflict surrounding the Second Bank of the United States contributed to the rise of the Whig party.

The Erie Canal
www.syracuse.com/features/eriecanal

This site presents the Erie Canal as "the super highway of pre–Civil War America."

The Cherokee Nation
www.cherokee.org/culture/history.asp

This is the official Web site of the Cherokee Nation based in Talequah, Oklahoma.

Commerce on the Prairie
www.ukans.edu/carrie/kancoll/books/gregg/contents.htm

This University of Kansas site includes information on life and commerce on the frontier between the United States and Mexico.

Pioneering the Upper Midwest: Books from Michigan, Minnesota, and Wisconsin, ca. 1820–1910
memory.loc.gov/ammem/umhtml/umhome.html

This Library of Congress site looks at first-person accounts, biographies, promotional literature, ethnographic and antiquarian texts, colonial archival documents, and other works from the seventeenth to early twentieth century. It covers many topics and issues related to Americans and the settlement of the Upper Midwest.

The Settlement of African Americans in Liberia
www.loc.gov./exhibits/african/perstor.html

This site contains images and text relating to the colonization movement sponsored by the American Colonization Society.

African American Women Writers from the Nineteenth Century
digital.nypl.org.schomburg/writers_aa19/toc.html

The New York Public Library–Schomburg Center for Research in Black Culture site contains texts of nineteenth-century African American literature by women.

For Further Reading

General

Stuart R. Blumin, *The Emergence of the Middle Class: Social Experience in the American City, 1760–1900* (1989).

Daniel Feller, *The Jacksonian Promise: America, 1815–1840* (1995).

D. W. Meinig, *The Shaping of America: A Geographical Perspective on 500 Years of History. Vol. 2: Continental America, 1800–1867* (1993).

Melvyn Stokes and Stephen Conway, eds., *The Market Revolution in America: Social, Political, and Religious Expressions, 1800–1880* (1996).

Anthony F. C. Wallace, *The Long, Bitter Trail: Andrew Jackson and the Indians* (1993).

David J. Weber, *The Spanish Frontier in North America* (1992).

The Politics Behind Western Expansion

William J. Cooper, *The South and the Politics of Slavery, 1828–1856* (1978).

James W. Covington, *The Seminoles of Florida* (1993).

Mark Derr, *The Frontiersman: The Real Life and Many Legends of Davy Crockett* (1993).

Ernest R. May, *The Making of the Monroe Doctrine* (1976).

Timothy Matovina, *Tejano Religion and Ethnicity: San Antonio, 1821–1860* (1995).

Ronald E. Shaw, *Canals for a Nation: The Canal Era in the United States, 1790–1860* (1990).

Federal Authority and Its Opponents

William W. Freehling, *Prelude to Civil War: The Nullification Controversy in South Carolina, 1816–1836* (1966).

Michael D. Green, *The Politics of Indian Removal: Creek Government and Society in Crisis* (1982).

Michael F. Holt, *Political Parties and American Political Development from the Age of Jackson to the Age of Lincoln* (1992).

Lawrence Frederick Kohl, *The Politics of Individualism: Parties and the American Character in the Jacksonian Era* (1989).

Marvin Meyers, *The Jacksonian Persuasion: Politics and Belief* (1968).

Robert V. Remini, *Andrew Jackson and His Indian Wars* (2001).

Real People in the "Age of the Common Man"

Virginia Marie Bouvier, *Women and the Conquest of California, 1542–1840: Codes of Silence* (2001).

Thomas Dublin, *Transforming Women's Work: New England Lives in the Industrial Revolution* (1994).

Albert L. Hurtado, *Intimate Frontiers: Sex, Culture and Gender in California* (1999).

Jack Larkin, *The Reshaping of Everyday Life, 1790–1840* (1988).

Walter Licht, *Industrial America: The Nineteenth Century* (1995).

David Walker, *David Walker's Appeal, in Four Articles* (1965 ed.).

Julie Winch, *Philadelphia's Black Elite: Activism, Accommodation, and the Struggle for Autonomy, 1787–1848* (1988).

Ties That Bound a Growing Population

Jeanne Boydston, *Home and Work: Housework, Wages, and the Ideology of Labor in the Early Republic* (1990).

Richard L. Bushman, *Joseph Smith and the Beginnings of Mormonism* (1984).

Charles Hambrick-Stowe, *Charles Grandison Finney and the Spirit of American Evangelism* (1996).

Nathan O. Hatch, *The Democratization of American Christianity* (1989).

Christine L. Heyrman, *Southern Cross: The Beginnings of the Bible Belt* (1997).

Paul E. Johnson, *A Shopkeeper's Millennium: Society and Revivals in Rochester, New York, 1815–1837* (1978).

Walter Bern Michaels and Donald E. Pease, eds., *The American Renaissance Reconsidered* (1985).

Online Practice Test

Test your understanding of this chapter with interactive review quizzes at

www.ablongman.com/jonescreatedequal/chapter11

Peoples in Motion, 1832–1848

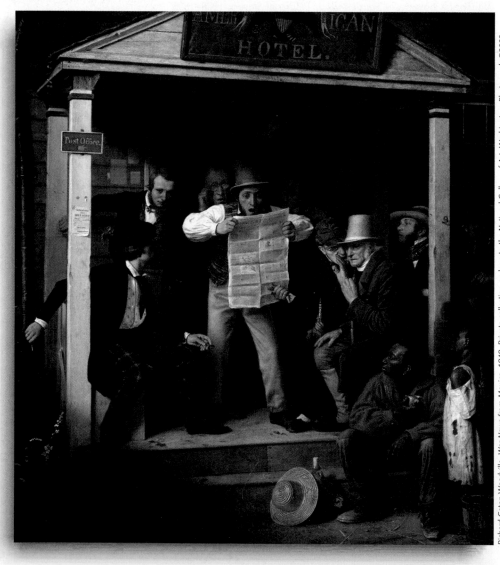

Richard Caton Woodville, *War News from Mexico*, 1848. Private collection on loan to the National Gallery of Art, Washington. Photograph ©2002 Board of Trustees, National Gallery of Art, Washington

■ Richard Caton Woodville's *War News from Mexico*, 1848.

IN THE SPRING OF 1847 JANNICKE SAEHLE LEFT HER HOME IN BERGEN, A CITY ON THE western coast of Norway, and boarded a ship bound for New York City. From New York, the young woman traveled by steamship up the Hudson River to Albany. There she boarded a train to Milwaukee, Wisconsin. Although arduous, the journey had its pleasures. Piloted by a charming captain, the steamship resembled, in Saehle's words, "a complete house four stories high, and very elegantly furnished, with beautiful rugs everywhere." On the train, the passengers enjoyed each other's company as well as "the noteworthy sights that we rushed past." By the summer Saehle was living with and working as a domestic servant for a Norwegian family, the Torjersens, in Koshkonong in southeastern Wisconsin. Founded in 1840, Koshkonong was a rapidly growing settlement of Norwegian immigrants farming the fertile prairie.

Jannicke Saehle was eager to make a new life for herself in the United States. For just a few months of service in the Torjersen household, she received the harvest of 3 acres of wheat for three years. In the fall she found a job washing and ironing at a tavern in Madison. For the first five weeks she earned a dollar a week. Then she received a raise of $.25 a week, with the promise of another raise, and relief from washing, at the end of the winter. Although she could not speak English, she was pleased to "enjoy the best treatment" from the tavern owners and patrons. However, she hoped to leave the tavern and work as a domestic servant for a local family, the Morisons. Saehle believed this new position would be comfortable; with the Morisons she could "live more peacefully and have a room by myself."

Norwegian immigrants to the United States, 1880s.

In September 1847, Jannicke Saehle wrote of her good fortune in America in a letter to her family back in Norway. She described "the superabundance of food" in the Torjersen home. On his 40-acre farm Torjersen kept swine and produced "tremendous amounts" of wheat, potatoes, beans, cabbage, cucumbers, onions, and many other kinds of vegetables. At the Madison tavern she had "food and drink in abundance" and dined on the same fare served to the guests: for breakfast, "chicken, mutton [lamb], beef or pork, warm or cold wheat bread, butter, white cheese, eggs, or small pancakes, the best coffee, tea, cream and sugar." For supper she feasted on "warm biscuits, and several kinds of cold wheat bread, cold meats, bacon, cakes, preserved apples, plums, and berries, which are eaten with cream, and tea and coffee." Saehle felt heartbroken to see excess food thrown to the chickens and pigs, for, she wrote, "I think of my dear ones in Bergen, who like so many others must at this time lack the necessaries of life."

During the 1840s, more than 13,000 immigrants from Norway, Sweden, and Denmark arrived in the United States, a sixfold increase over the number of Scandinavians who had

Deutsches Ledermuseum

■ Plains Indians developed new art forms in response to the westward movement of European American trappers, missionaries, and settlers. Native artists used picture writing to describe violent encounters between Indians and intruders. They etched pictures on sandstone or painted them on cliffs or clothing. These battle pictographs, painted on a Cheyenne buffalo robe c. 1845, bear similarities to other images produced by Flathead artists. Scholars believe that these drawings formed a language understood by a variety of Indian groups from Canada to the American Southwest.

arrived the decade before. This migration continued to increase over the course of the nineteenth century. In the 1880s, more than 655,000 Scandinavians, fleeing poverty and military conflict, came to America. Many traveled to Wisconsin and Minnesota, where they farmed small homesteads and found the cold winter climate similar to that of their homeland.

In the rural upper Midwest, clashes between Indians and white settlers shaped the experiences of many immigrants. Newcomers to Minnesota, especially, did not fare well; there the great Sioux uprising of 1862 resulted in the deaths of hundreds of Indians and immigrant settlers, Swedes and Norwegians prominent among them. However, by the late 1840s, settlers in Wisconsin such as Jannicke Saehle had little reason to fear the Indians whose ancestral lands they occupied; the U.S. army's destruction of a band of Sauk Indians under the leadership of Black Hawk in 1832 had opened up much of the area to whites.

In the 1830s and 1840s, patterns of settlement and employment among immigrant groups varied widely in the United States. For example, most Irish immigrants lacked the resources to move much farther west than the eastern seaboard ports where they landed. In contrast, many Germans arrived with enough money to buy farmland in the Midwest or take up a trade in eastern cities. Nevertheless, Norwegian immigrants had much in common with other groups that came to the United States in these years. Many relied for jobs and housing on compatriots who had already arrived. The newcomers found employment in expanding regional economies. Communities of immigrants built their own religious institutions and mutual aid societies.

In the 1830s and 1840s, the United States was home to many peoples in motion. Groups of Indians in the Southeast and Midwest and slaves in the upper South were forced at gunpoint to move from one region of the country to another. From western Europe came poor and persecuted groups drawn to the United States by the demand for labor and the promise of religious and political freedom. Some Americans eagerly pulled up stakes and moved to nearby cities or towns in search of better jobs. Migrants with enough resources made the long journey across the Sonoran Desert in the Southwest or to the Oregon Territory in the Northwest.

Population movements and economic change generated new forms of community and group identity. Some immigrants and migrants left behind old identities and created new ones for themselves in their new homes. In their native lands, many newcomers to the United States had lived and labored as peasants under the control of aristocratic landlords. Now in America these immigrants worked as wage earners or as small farmers. Urban workers founded the National Trades Union, an organization that tried to help laboring people wield political influence. Women and men who believed in their power to change society banded together for any number of causes—including those that challenged basic institu-

■ **MAP 12.1**
WESTERN TRAILS   This map shows the major trails
followed by western emigrants in the nineteenth century.
Settlers endured long and dangerous journeys. For example, beginning at
Independence, Missouri, and stretching to Portland, Oregon, the Overland Trail
was 2000 miles long. Covering the entire trail could take four to six months. Wagon trains had to
traverse rocky terrain, scale mountains, and ford rivers. Along the way, outposts such as Fort Laramie and
Fort Hall gave travelers a chance to refresh their supplies, rest their livestock, and repair their wagons.
Though resentful of such incursions, Indians rarely attacked large wagon trains.

tions such as the nuclear family, slavery, and white supremacy. Some reformers established
new communities based on alternative notions of marriage and child-rearing.

Partisan politics also entered a new era. By 1836, the so-called Second Party system had
emerged, as Jacksonian Democrats squared off against the Whigs on familiar issues including
tariffs and new systems of transportation. A coalition of anti-Jackson forces, the Whigs, sought
to craft an economic program that would appeal to the largest number of voters. Less concerned with the purity of their ideas than with success at the ballot box, the Whigs saw their
policies as a means to winning elections and not necessarily as ends in themselves.

The choices offered by the Whigs and Democrats failed to represent what many groups
saw as their pressing political and economic interests. Many Americans turned to violence to
advance or defend their causes. The deep-seated resentments or lofty aspirations among various ethnic and religious groups and social classes provoked bloodshed. Urban mobs vented
their wrath against African Americans, abolitionists, and Irish immigrants and other
Catholics. The government itself sponsored violence, which peaked in the late 1830s with the
forced removal of southeastern Indians to the West, and again in the late 1840s, when the
United States wrested a vast expanse of land from Mexico. Indeed, within the larger society,
physical force seemed to be an acceptable means of resolving disputes; tellingly, politicians of
all persuasions followed Andrew Jackson's lead and staked their claim to national leadership
on the basis of their records as soldiers, military officers, and Indian-killers.

Although industrial machines such as locomotives and textile looms grew more sophisticated in these years, farming remained the primary occupation for many people. However, when the land refused to yield crops, millions of people had to move on—from the blighted potato fields of Ireland, the rocky soil of New England, or the worn-out fields of the cotton South. In search of new economic opportunities, some people moved into lands belonging to other people. In the territory occupied by native Spanish speakers in Texas or by Indians in the Southeast, people stood ready to fight—and die—for the land.

Mass Migrations

When foreign visitors called Americans a "restless" people, they were referring to patterns of both immigration and migration within the country. Between 1830 and 1850, 2.3 million immigrants entered the United States, up from a total of 152,000 during the two previous decades. In the 1840s, 1.7 million immigrants arrived (in 1850 the country's total population stood at 27 million people). Most newcomers came from Ireland, Germany, England, Scotland, and Scandinavia. In the United States itself, individuals and families moved around the country with almost dizzying speed in search of better jobs. They migrated from rural to urban areas, from one city to another, out west and then back to the east. In Boston, in any one year, about a third of the population left the city to find a new home elsewhere. In the late 1840s, almost half of all urban residents moved within a 12-month period. For the country as a whole, an estimated one family in five moved every year, and on average every family moved once every five years. Many westward migrants had enough money to move overland and buy a homestead once they arrived in Wisconsin or Oregon. However, much of the population turnover in urban areas stemmed from landless people's relentless quest for higher wages and cheaper places to rent.

Some people moved because other people forced them to—under the crack of a whip and in manacles. Slave traders in the Upper South transported thousands of slaves to the Lower South for sale "on the block." Indians underwent the equivalent of a middle passage (the horrific slave ship voyages between Africa and the Americas) when U.S. soldiers forced them to walk from their homelands in the southeast to Indian Territory (now the state of Oklahoma).

Europeans marveled at Americans' apparent willingness to search out new opportunities. But to some Americans, moving meant the death of dreams and the loss of hope for a better life.

Newcomers from Western Europe

By the early nineteenth century, life had become more precarious than ever for the long-suffering people of Ireland. Over the generations, small farm plots had been subdivided among heirs to the point that most holdings consisted of less than 15 acres each. At the same time, the population of Ireland had grown exponentially—to more than 4 million people in 1800. England treated Ireland like a colony that existed purely for the economic gain of the mother country (or, in the eyes of the Irish, an occupying power). A series of English laws and policies mandated that farmers export most of the island's grain and cattle, leaving the impoverished people to subsist mainly on a diet of potatoes. Then, beginning in 1845, a blight devastated the potato crop. In the next five years, 1 million people died and another million fled to the United States. The great Irish migration had begun.

Increasing numbers of poor Irish had settled in the United States before the potato famine of the mid–1840s. In the 1820s, about 50,000 such immigrants arrived; the following decade saw a spike in numbers to more than 200,000. Yet a more dramatic increase was yet to come. As the 1840s and 1850s unfolded, 1.7 million Irish men, women, and children emigrated to the United States. This exodus continued over the next century as more than 4.5 million Irish arrived. Many immigrants were single women who found work as servants and sent money back to Ireland. As Margaret McCarthy wrote in a letter to her parents back home in County

Population Change in Ireland, 1841–1851

Percentage of change per county

+9 -20
0   -25
-13

Arable Land in Ireland, 1841

Percentage per county

80
50
30

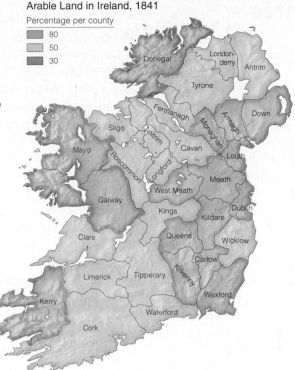

■ MAP 12.2
POPULATION CHANGE IN IRELAND, 1841–1851 During the famine of the late 1840s, some counties in Ireland lost more than one-quarter of their population to out-migration. However, emigration rates in some of the very poorest counties were not always high. People there were too poor to pay for passage to the United States. The county of Kerry, in the country's southwestern corner, is an example.

Pauperism in Ireland, 1847–1851

More than 50% of population pauper for over 1 year by Poor Law Union

Cork, in 1850, the newcomers embraced "this plentyful Country where no man or woman ever Hungerd or ever will and where you will not be Seen Naked."

By the 1870s, the Irish constituted fully 20 percent of the population of New York City, 14 percent of Philadelphia, and 22 percent of Boston (the "hub of Gaelic America"). The newcomers quickly formed mutual aid associations and other community organizations. In cities across America, the Sisters of Mercy, a Roman Catholic order founded in Dublin, established homes to provide lodging for single women and day nurseries for the children of working mothers.

Most Irish immigrants lacked the resources to move much farther west than the eastern seaport cities where they landed, and they soon realized that their struggle against poverty, discrimination, and religious persecution would not end in the United States. The arrival of large numbers of Irish immigrants in the 1830s threatened the jobs of native-born Protestants, who reacted with resentment and violence. Employers posted signs outside their doors reading "No Irish Need Apply." Despised for their Roman Catholicism and their supposed "clannishness," the Irish competed with African Americans for the low-paying jobs at the bottom of the economic ladder. At times, anti-Irish sentiment reached violent extremes. In 1834 a mob destroyed the Ursuline convent

Diasporas

Almost all of the Irish men, women, and children who emigrated from their homeland in the nineteenth century came to the United States. In this respect, the Irish exodus was somewhat unusual. Over the last four and a half centuries, many peoples have participated in transoceanic mass migrations. Yet most of those migrations have been characterized by a scattering of peoples to different countries. Since its beginnings, the United States has been a major host, but not the only one, to immigrants as well as forced migrants.

When specific ethnic or cultural groups disperse from one place to many different places, they produce a diaspora. Originally, the word *Diaspora* (with a capital *D*) referred to the dispersal of Jewish communities out of Palestine and into Europe and Africa 2000 years ago. Now scholars use the term more generally to refer to many kinds of population dispersals in the past and today. These migrations are the result of two historical phenomena. The first is an emerging world economy with its intense demand for labor, especially in the mining, agricultural, and industrial sectors. The second phenomenon is the desire among specific peoples to flee poverty and persecution and to seek out land, jobs, and religious and political freedom elsewhere.

The African diaspora reveals the effects of a forced migration. Between 1500 and 1850 slave traders transported 12 million Africans to the Western Hemisphere. An estimated one-tenth of that number died during the Middle Passage. Of the survivors, 10 million were taken to the Caribbean or Latin America and fewer than 450,000 to the area that is now the United States. Yet by 1865, the U.S. African American population accounted for 30 percent of all people of African descent in the Western Hemisphere. Why? American slaveholders encouraged their slaves to have families. In addition, cotton cultivation in the United States was not as unhealthful as other kinds of work performed by slaves elsewhere in the hemisphere. Thus, African Americans had higher fertility rates and lower mortality rates than their counterparts to the south.

Over the generations, voluntary migration to the United States has taken place among other mass population movements around the world. Many of the groups that arrived in the United States between 1880 and 1920, such as Italians, Russian Jews, and Germans, also sent immigrants to other parts of the world. In the twentieth century, political and religious conflict in their homeland propelled Greek emigrants to many different countries. They settled in New York, Philadelphia, Chicago, Los Angeles, and San Francisco, but others migrated to such diverse places as Dakar, Senegal; Kinshasa, Zaire; Addis Ababa, Ethiopia; and Sydney and Melbourne, Australia. Their modern dispersal was similar to that of Lebanese emigrants, who went not only to the United States but also to Latin America, Africa, and Australia.

In some cases, governments have encouraged their citizens to search widely for work to increase the flow of cash into their own countries. When China began to trade with the rest of the world in 1845, that country sponsored a mass out-migration among men. Those men were supposed to work abroad temporarily and send their earnings home. The Chinese who arrived in the United States in the mid-nineteenth century were part of a larger mass migration that sent 400,000 men also to Canada, Australia, and New Zealand. Between 1845 and 1900, 1.5 million Chinese went to Southeast Asia (Indonesia, Thailand, Vietnam, Malaysia, and Singapore) to work in the mines or the fields. Another half million went to Peru, Cuba, and Chile. Chinese workers in all these countries tried to save to send money back home to their families.

In the early twentieth century, officials on the island of Okinawa, part of Japan, took note of their faltering agricultural economy. They encouraged able-bodied young people to find employment elsewhere and send their wages to families back home. Beginning in 1900, Okinawa immigrants arrived in Hawaii to work on sugar plantations. Over the next decades other Okinawans moved to California to labor in the fruit and vegetable fields and to the Philippines to grow Manila hemp. Others went to Canada, Brazil, Argentina, Bolivia, Mexico, Cuba, Paraguay, and the islands of Micronesia.

In the 1980s, the Ferdinand Marcos government in the Philippines made a series of agreements with other countries to accept Filipino workers. Marcos saw the wages the migrants sent home as a means to boost the national economy. However, by that time, the worldwide demand for male workers in the

in Charlestown, near Boston, after terrifying the women and children residents and ransacking the building. In 1837 a group of Boston City Guards (a fraternal order) assaulted the Montgomery Guards, the first Irish military company in the city. (Local military companies often functioned as social groups for men of all ages.) The attackers accused the immigrants of lacking patriotism because they had created a group based on ethnic loyalties.

■ **MAP 12.3**
THE GRAND MIGRATION The Grand Migration of Jews out of Europe lasted from 1880 to 1914. This map shows that, while significant numbers of Jewish emigrants were coming to the United States, some were going to Mexico, Argentina, and South Africa.

The "Grand Migration," 1880–1914

- Very heavy emigration
- Heavy Jewish immigration
- Significant Jewish immigration
- Significant emigration
- ● Gateways of migration

maritime and oil industries had declined. As a result, the Philippines sent mainly women workers abroad, to the United States, Hong Kong, and Europe. Most of these immigrant women worked in domestic service. Their wages were the greatest source of foreign money in the Philippine economy. However, this diaspora had severe consequences for domestic life in the Philippines, where the absence of so many wives and mothers severely disrupted the family. Diasporas profoundly affect home countries as well as host countries. ■

Nevertheless, by the 1850s, the Irish had gained a measure of influence. They filled many high positions in the U.S. Catholic church and became active in the Democratic party. They claimed that their white skin entitled them to distance themselves from blacks and lay claim to full American citizenship. More than one hundred years later, the election of the first Catholic president of the United States—John Fitzgerald Kennedy of Boston, a descendant of famine-era immigrants on both his mother's and father's side of the family—became a milestone in the Irish rise to political power.

The hardship endured by the Irish in the early nineteenth century mirrored the political and economic distress of many other people living in Europe at the time. The Revolutions of 1848 stemmed from a rising nationalist fervor among Germans, Italians, Czechs, and Hungarians against the Austrian Empire. Popular uprisings in France, Germany, and parts of Italy struck out against monarchy and called for constitutional government. In England and Germany, new textile factories could not accommodate all the urban workers who sought jobs. Europeans in rural areas also fell on particularly hard times. Dramatic population increases made food scarce, and the Industrial Revolution put artisans out of work. In an effort to bolster their power, wealthy landholders consolidated their estates from the holdings of peasant farmers. In the process, the demand for farm labor decreased, pushing many people off the countryside.

Between 1831 and 1850, more than half a million Germans arrived in the United States. Those numbers exploded in the next few decades. An uprising against the authoritarian Prussian state had failed in 1848, and German intellectuals, farmers, and workers alike fled across the ocean. Like Scandinavian immigrants, many Germans settled in the Midwest. Some had responded to the promises of railroad land and recruiting offices scattered through Europe. These offices promised transportation subsidies and low-interest loans to immigrants who bought land from the railroads—land the railroads had purchased from the federal government on generous terms.

> *Between 1831 and 1850, more than half a million Germans arrived in the United States.*

The stories of the Stille and Krumme families paint a compelling picture of many German immigrants' experience during this period. Wilhelm Stille came to Ohio in the mid–1830s. In letters home, he praised the vitality of the local German immigrant community, the bountiful soil, and the "feel for freedom" that infused even the most recent newcomers. Over the next few years Stille worked at a variety of jobs in a steam mill and a distillery and for a merchant. Scraping together some money, he started his own trading business. He traveled as far away as New Orleans and South America with flour, potatoes, string beans, cabbage, onions, and apples. Then Stille married a young woman newly arrived from Switzerland. Together the couple tried their hand at farming.

Meanwhile, Wilhelm's sister Wilhelmina, who had accompanied him to America, married another German immigrant, Wilhelm Krumme. Wilhelmina missed her mother and felt guilty about leaving her. But, she assured her mother, "I'm much better off here than with you, that's because you can live in peace over here." Wilhelmina's husband worked on the National Road, crushing rocks, and the couple received money sent from their families in Europe. Still, in the early 1840s a national depression hit them hard: "These are bad times now, there's not much work and if you work the pay is not good." In 1841 Wilhelmina gave birth to a son, but she died of tuberculosis a few months later. Within a year, Wilhelm remarried, again to a German-born woman. In a letter to his relatives back home, he explained that he had almost had to give his son up for adoption; it was that difficult for him to work and provide for the boy at the same time. Both hardship and opportunity defined life in a new land.

The Slave Trade

Between 1800 and 1860, the average price of slaves quadrupled, revealing a growing demand for bound labor. The slave market responded accordingly. In the last three decades before the Civil War, approximately 670,000 people were bought and sold. As many as one out of every ten slave children in the Upper South was sold to the Lower South (many to cotton planters) between 1820 and 1860. Slave households in Virginia bore the brunt of these forced separations. There, an estimated three quarters of the people sold never saw their spouse, parents, or children again.

Owners sold slaves for a variety of reasons. Some they considered poor workers or too "uppity." Occasionally, a mistress decided to rid herself of the sight of a slave woman whom her husband had sexually abused. Selling slaves also generated ready cash for masters who wanted to build a new house, divide an estate, or settle a debt. Moses Grandy, for example,

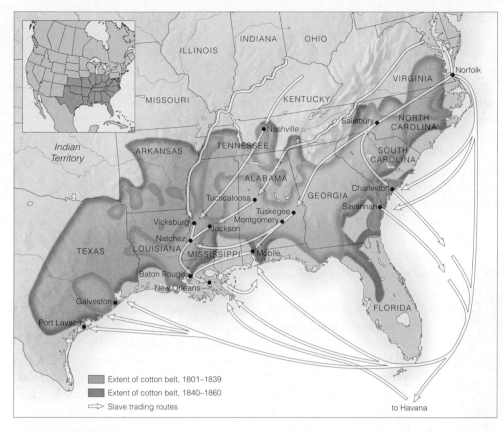

■ MAP 12.4

EXPANSION OF THE COTTON BELT AND SLAVE TRADING ROUTES, 1801–1860   This map shows the spread of cotton cultivation and routes followed by traders in transporting slaves from the upper South to the new plantations of the Southwest. After Texas won its independence from Mexico in 1836, the new republic legalized slavery. Many white landowners believed that they could not grow cotton without the use of slave labor.

was sold because his master, who had failed to pay his mortgage, needed the cash. A later sale separated Grandy from his wife: standing on a sidewalk one day, he saw his wife in chains, in a coffle passing by. He recalled the scene in his autobiography, *Narrative of the Life of Moses Grandy, Late a Slave in the United States of America* (1844):

> Mr. Rogerson was with them on his horse, armed with pistols. I said to him. "For God's sake, have you bought my wife?" He said he had; when I asked him what she had done, he said she had done nothing, but that her master wanted money. He drew out a pistol and said that if I went near the wagon where she was, he would shoot me. I asked for leave to shake hands with her which he refused, but said I might stand at a distance and talk with her. My heart was so full that I could say very little. . . . I have never seen or heard from her from that day to this. I loved her as I love my life.

The slave trade became big business. Many wealthy traders made regular trips between the Upper and Lower South. Owners of slaves who worked in the sawmills and grist mills of Virginia and Maryland realized they could profit handsomely by selling blacks to cotton planters in Mississippi and Alabama. A large slave trade establishment such as Franklin and Armfield, for example, had operations in Alexandria, Virginia (where slaves languished in pens until traders could ship them south), in Natchez, Mississippi, and in New Orleans, Louisiana. The pace of buying and selling picked up in late fall, after slaves had harvested grains and tobacco in the upper South and cotton in the lower South. Traders transported men, women, and children by boat down the eastern seaboard or down the Mississippi River or chained and forced them to walk as much as 20 miles a day for seven or eight weeks at a time in the chill autumn air. Eventually, slaves stood on the block in the markets of New Orleans, Natchez, Charleston, and Savannah, where white men inspected them for health, strength, and compliance.

The European American slave owners who had moved to Texas in the 1820s took their slaves with them. When Mexico abolished slavery in 1829, some European American masters freed their slaves but then forced them to sign lifelong contracts that kept them in a state akin to bondage. Nevertheless, some free people of color—men such as John Bird—saw Texas as a place of opportunity. He had brought his family to Texas from Virginia because he hoped that they "would be received as citizens and entitled as such to land."

Indeed, during this period, voluntary migrations of African Americans formed the counterpoint of the slave trade as runaways and free people of color made their way out of the old slave states. An estimated 50,000 enslaved workers tried to escape each year, but few made it to the North and freedom.

Some southern free people of color headed to northern cities. By 1850, more than half of all Boston blacks had been born outside Massachusetts. Of those migrants, about one-third had been born in the South, most in Virginia, Maryland, and the District of Columbia. Slave runaways who lived in fear of their safety and their lives eluded census takers, but by midcentury as many as 600 fugitives lived in Boston.

Regardless of their place of origin, many migrants took up residence with other blacks, who helped ease the newcomers' transition to city life. These boarding arrangements strengthened ties between the enslaved and the free communities. For example, when authorities arrested the runaway George Latimer in Boston in 1842, free blacks in that city took immediate action. They posted signs condemning the police as "human kidnappers." Some tried to wrench him physically from his captors. Still others sponsored protest meetings in the local African Baptist Church and made common cause with white lawyers sympathetic to abolitionism. Finally a group of blacks and whites raised enough money to buy Latimer from his owner and free him. Out of this campaign came a 150-pound antislavery petition containing the names of thousands of Massachusetts citizens. The petition, ignored by Congress, called for legislation forbidding the complicity of state officials in apprehending fugitive slaves.

Meanwhile, throughout the urban North, whites began eyeing blacks' jobs. Irish immigrants in particular desperately sought work. Skilled black workers found it increasingly difficult to ply their trades as cooks, hotel and boat stewards, porters, brickmakers, and barbers. In 1838, 656 black artisans in Philadelphia reported that they had to abandon their work because white customers would no longer patronize them. White factory owners in Philadelphia preferred white laborers. In that same city, a bustling site of machine shops and textile factories, almost no blacks did industrial labor of any kind. Shut out of ship-caulking work in New Bedford, Massachusetts, fugitive slave Frederick Douglass warned of the consequences of an economic system that condemned all blacks to lowly, ill-paid labor, "Men are not valued in this country, or in any country, for what they *are;* they are valued for what they can do." Douglass understood that whites would judge blacks on the basis of their jobs as menial laborers and not on the basis of their rights as American citizens. These judgments, he predicted, would lead to further discrimination and hardship among blacks.

Born a slave in Maryland in 1818, Frederick Douglass became a leading abolitionist speaker, editor, and activist. Not content to condemn southern slaveholders exclusively, he also criticized northern employers for not hiring blacks. Trained as a ship caulker, Douglass faced job discrimination in the shipyards of New Bedford, Massachusetts, where he and his wife, Anna, settled soon after he escaped slavery and they moved north (in 1838).

Trails of Tears

In 1835 President Andrew Jackson made a puzzling declaration. The removal of eastern Indian groups to Indian Territory, he said, would ensure their "physical comfort," "political advancement," and "moral improvement." Rarely have a chief executive's words contrasted so starkly with reality.

Throughout the 1830s, the U.S. government pursued the policy of removing Indians from the Southeast by treaty or by force. The 1832 Treaty of Payne's Landing, negotiated by the

Seminole Indians and James Gadsden, a representative of Secretary of War Lewis Cass, aimed to force the Seminoles out of Florida and into Indian Territory (present-day Oklahoma). The federal government promised to give individual Indians cash, plus blankets for the men and dresses for the women, in exchange for their lands. Government authorities also hoped to recapture the large number of runaway slaves who had sought refuge in Seminole villages, deep in the swamps of central Florida.

Three years later, many of the Indians had departed for the West. But a small number withdrew deeper into the Everglades and held their ground. They were led by a young man named Osceola, who with his followers waged a guerrilla war (based on ambush tactics rather than traditional conventions of European American warfare) against U.S. troops. Accustomed to meeting the enemy on a battleground, U.S. army troops failed to dislodge significant numbers of Indians who had hidden themselves in the swamps. Referring to the twin military goals of removing the Indians and capturing runaway slaves, General Thomas S. Jesup expressed his frustration with the military operation: "We have committed the error of attempting to remove them when their lands were not required for agricultural purposes, when the greater portion of their country was an unexplored wilderness, the interior of which we were as ignorant of as the interior of China." Osceola's resistance, called the Second Seminole War, dragged on for seven years. Eventually, the government forced 3000 Seminoles to move west, but not until it had spent $20 million, and 1500 U.S. soldiers had lost their lives.

The Choctaws of the southern Alabama–Mississippi region, the Chickasaws directly to the north of them, and the Creeks in central Georgia and Alabama suffered the same fate in the 1830s. The Creeks remained bitterly divided among themselves on the issue of removal. Creek leader Eneah Emothla organized a violent resistance movement against government soldiers. Emothla's actions gave the government a pretext for forcibly relocating 15,000 of his people, more than a fifth of whom died as a result of the operation.

The threat of removal also provoked intense conflict within the Cherokee Nation. Cherokee Indians, Major Ridge, his son John Ridge, and Elias Boudinot, leaders of the so-called Treaty Party, urged their people to give up their homeland and rebuild their nation in the West. John Ross and others like him opposed the Ridges and Boudinot. The Cherokees must remain in Georgia at all costs, Ross insisted. He claimed that he spoke for a majority of Cherokees. To silence him, the U.S. government threw him in prison. Then it concluded negotiations with the Treaty Party, which agreed to sell Cherokee land to the federal government for $5 million. Elias Boudinot said, "We can die, but the great Cherokee Nation will be saved." Within a few years, the Ridges and Boudinot died at the hands of anti–Treaty Party Cherokee assassins.

The Cherokee Elias Boudinot was educated at missionary schools in North Carolina and Connecticut. As editor of the *Cherokee Phoenix,* Boudinot clashed with Principal Chief John Ross on the issue of forced removal to the West. Ross believed that the paper's editorial policy should reflect the official Cherokee position on the matter. Boudinot resigned in protest. In 1835, Boudinot, with his cousin John Ridge, and Major Ridge, defied Ross and other leaders and signed the Treaty of New Echota. Although the treaty did not have the approval of the Cherokee Nation, it paved the way for the Trail of Tears, 1838–1839.

In 1838 General Winfield Scott, with 7000 troops under his command, began rounding up the citizens of the Cherokee Nation. U.S. troops held men, women, and children in concentration camps before forcing them to march west. During the period from 1838 to 1839, nearly 16,000 Indians began a journey that they called the Trail on Which We Cried. Four thousand of them died of malnutrition and disease in the course of the 116-day forced march. U.S. troops confiscated or destroyed the material basis of Cherokee culture: sawmills, cotton gins, barns, homes, spinning wheels, meetinghouses, flocks, herds, and the printing press used to publish the *Cherokee Phoenix.*

Rebecca Neugin later recalled the arrival of army troops at her house. "My father wanted to fight," she said, "but my mother told him that the soldiers would kill him if we did and we surrendered without a fight. They drove us out of our house to join other prisoners in a stockade." The soldiers let Rebecca's mother take a few cooking utensils with her; the family lost everything else. Still, Neugin's family remained

■ MAP 12.5

INDIAN REMOVAL This map shows the routes of forced migration of the Five Civilized Tribes in the 1830s. By the 1870s, several groups of Plains Indians, including the Cheyenne, Arapaho, Comanche, and Kiowa, had joined them in Indian Territory (present-day Oklahoma).

Indian removal, 1829–1840

☐ Indian tribes' home territories

■ Land granted to Indians west of the Mississippi River

1830 —— Date and route of removal

intact. Many others did not. A soldier who participated in the operation saw children "separated from their parents and driven into the stockade with the sky for a blanket and the earth for a pillow."

U.S. officials claimed that troops had carried out the removal with "great judgment and humanity." However, an internal government report completed in 1841 revealed that the United States had reneged on even its most basic treaty promises. "Bribery, perjury, and forgery, short weights, issues of spoiled meat and grain, and every conceivable subterfuge was employed by designing white men." Many government agents seized goods such as blankets and food intended for Indians and sold these goods for profit. Military authorities suppressed the report, and the public never saw it.

Migrants in the West

For many native-born migrants seeking a new life west of the Mississippi, the road proved neither smooth nor easy. For example, the Mormon community moved west, seeking refuge from religious persecution. The founder of the church, Joseph Smith, had aroused the anger of his neighbors in Nauvoo, Illinois. They took alarm at the Nauvoo Legion, a military company formed to defend the Mormon community. They also heard rumors (for the most part true) that Smith and other Mormon leaders engaged in plural marriage. Through this practice the Mormon Church granted men permission to marry more than one wife.

TABLE 12-1

Outfitting a Party of Four for the Overland Trail

Area	Item	Amount	Unit Cost ($)	Cost ($)	Weight (lb.)
Transport	Wagon	1	90.00	90.00	
	Oxen	4 yoke	50.00/yoke	200.00	
	Gear		100.00	100.00	
Food	Flour	600 lb.	2.00/100 lb.	12.00	600
	Biscuit	120 lb.	3.00/100 lb.	3.60	120
	Bacon	400 lb.	5.00/100 lb.	20.00	400
	Coffee	60 lb.	7.00/100 lb.	4.20	60
	Tea	4 lb.	50.00/100 lb.	2.00	4
	Sugar	100 lb.	10.00/100 lb.	10.00	100
	Lard	200 lb.	6.00/100 lb.	12.00	200
	Beans	200 lb.	8.00/100 lb.	16.00	200
	Dried fruit	120 lb.	24.00/100 lb.	28.80	120
	Salt	40 lb.	4.00/100 lb.	1.60	40
	Pepper	8 lb.	4.00/100 lb.	.32	8
	Saleratus	8 lb.	4.00/100 lb.	.32	8
	Whiskey	1 keg	5.00/keg	5.00	25
Goods	Rifle	1	30.00	30.00	10
	Pistols	2	15.00	30.00	10
	Powder	5 lb.	.25/lb.	1.25	5
	Lead	15 lb.	.04/lb.	.60	15
	Shot	10 lb.	.10/lb.	1.00	10
	Matches			1.00	1
	Cooking utensils			20.00	25
	Candles and soap	65 lb.	From home	from home	65
	Bedding	60 lb.	From home	from home	60
	Sewing kit	10 lb.	From home	from home	10
	Essential tools			from home	20
	Clothing			from home	100
			Totals	$589.69	2216

In 1844 the Nauvoo Legion destroyed the printing press owned by a group of rebellious church members who objected to what they considered Smith's authoritarian tactics. Civil authorities charged Smith and his brother Hyrum with the destruction of private property and arrested and jailed the two men in the nearby town of Carthage. In June 1844 an angry mob of non-Mormons broke into the jail and lynched the brothers.

By 1847, Brigham Young, who had inherited the mantle of leadership from Smith, determined that the Mormons could not remain in Illinois. Migrants, some of them pushing handcarts loaded with personal belongings, set out for the West. Several thousand settled at the base of the Wasatch Mountains on the edge of the Great Salt Basin, in what is present-day Utah. By 1852, 10,000 Mormons lived in Salt Lake City. With their large numbers and church-inspired discipline, the community prospered. They created an effective irrigation system and turned the desert into a thriving agricultural community.

The Mormons had not settled an uninhabited wilderness. Around Salt Lake, Canadian trappers, Paiute Indians, and Spanish speakers from New Mexico crossed paths, some to hunt, others to gather roots and berries, herd sheep, or trade captives. A variety of cultural groups mingled with and reacted to one another in diverse ways, from intermarriage to savage brutality. Here, one might hear the sounds of a Mexican's guitar, the song of a man half-Mohawk and "half American Scotch," or the lament of an Indian woman taken captive and forcibly separated from her children.

Scotts Bluff National Monument, Nebraska. United States Department of the Interior, National Park Service

■ This picture of the Whitman mission at Waiilatpu, Oregon, in 1845, shows the missionaries' house on the left, a mill in the background, a blacksmith shop in the right center, and a gathering place for worshippers on the far right. By this time the Whitmans had turned their attention from converting Indians to preaching to European American emigrants recently arrived from the East.

A Christmas dinner celebrated near Great Salt Lake around this time revealed the multi-cultural mix of western life. The guests included Osborne Russell (a European American trader), a Frenchman married to a Flathead woman, and various other intermarried Cree, Snake, and Nez Percé Indians. The group feasted on the meat of elk and deer, a flour pudding, cakes, and strong coffee. After the meal, the women cleared the table. The men smoked pipes and then went outside and conducted target practice with their guns.

Other European Americans also migrated to the Northwest during this period. Protestant missionaries initially settled Oregon beginning in 1834. But in contrast to the Mormons, these northwestern colonists found themselves in the midst of hostile Native Americans. One young doctor and his wife from western New York, Marcus and Narcissa Whitman, established a mission near present-day Walla Walla, Washington. There they encountered the Cayuse Indians and what Narcissa Whitman called "the thick darkness of heathenism." Deciding that white settlers offered a more fertile field for converts, the Whitmans encouraged emigrants from the East to move to Oregon. More than a thousand did so during the "Great Migration" of 1843.

The U.S. government aided this westward movement when it commissioned its Topographical Corps of Engineers to survey the Oregon Trail. That task fell to an expedition headed by John Charles Frémont, educated in mathematics and engineering. From 1843 to 1844, members of Frémont's expedition, including several Indian scouts and fur trappers, took precise measurements of the terrain using barometers and field telescopes.

Their final report had immense practical value for the emigrants, for it mapped the way west and provided crucial information about pasture, sources of water, and climate. In addition to detailing plant and animal life, the *Report of the Exploring Expeditions to the Rocky Mountains* described a middle ground where "well-dressed" Indians spoke fluent Spanish, where whites employed Indian labor to grow their wheat and irrigate their fields, and where German immigrants were following a variety of "agricultural pursuits."

The Oregon settlements founded by missionaries were fragile affairs. Discouraged and overwhelmed by homesickness, Narcissa Whitman eagerly awaited copies of the latest *Mothers' Magazine* sent to her by female relatives in the East. After 1843, the influx of newcomers brought her some consolation but also brought outbreaks of measles, to which the Native Americans had no immunity. An ensuing epidemic among the Cayuse claimed many lives. In 1847, blaming the missionaries for the deaths of their people, several Indians attacked the Whitman mission, killing 12 whites, including Narcissa and Marcus Whitman.

New Places, New Identities

The Midwest and the borderlands between U.S. and Spanish territories were meeting places for many different cultures. Leaving established communities behind, some migrants challenged rigid definitions of who was black, Indian, Hispanic, or European American. Moving from one place to another enabled—or forced—people to adopt new individual and group identities.

People who fell into one racial category in the east sometimes acquired new identities in the west. Some people classified as "black" in the south became "white" outside the region. In 1831, George and Eliza Gilliam decided to leave their home in Virginia and make a new life for themselves in western Pennsylvania. Eliza died in 1838, and George remarried nine years later. He prospered over the course of his lifetime. He worked as a doctor and druggist and invested in and sold real estate. George and his second wife, Frances, eventually moved to Illinois, and the couple finally settled in Missouri. Several of the Gilliam children attended college in Ohio. In 1870, the census listed the value of his estate at $95,000 (the equivalent of $2 million dollars today).

For George Gilliam and his family, the move west produced an American success story. Yet this migration story was unusual in at least two respects. First, the Gilliams left behind a large amount of property, including slaves, when they moved from Virginia in 1831. Second, in leaving Virginia, they became white.

George Gilliam was the son of a white father and a black mother. Although he and his first wife Eliza were very light-skinned, the commonwealth of Virginia classified them both legally as black. Beginning their married life near Petersburg, they were well aware of Virginia's tightening restrictions on free people of color; black men could not vote or enter certain professions such as the law or the ministry. Convicted of a crime, even free blacks could be sold into slavery and sent south. The year the Gilliams left Virginia, the state legislature enacted an additional law making it illegal to teach black children, whether slave or free, to read and write. Though connected by blood to several elite white families, the Gilliams faced at best an uncertain future in Virginia, where local officials knew who they were and who their parents were. In contrast, the public records in their new home states of Pennsylvania, Illinois, and Missouri listed family members as white. Outside the slave South, the Gilliams managed to reinvent themselves and embrace opportunities sought by many other Americans in this era of migration.

Leaving established communities behind, some migrants challenged rigid definitions of who was black, Indian, Hispanic, or European American.

Throughout the West, migrants forged new identities as a matter of course. For example, many people straddled more than one culture in the western borderlands. In 1828 Mexican military officer Jose Maria Sanchez described the *Tejano* settlers (Spanish-speaking natives of Mexico) he met in the province of Tejas (Texas): "Accustomed to the continued trade with the North Americans, they have adopted their customs and habits, and one may say truly that they are not Mexican except by birth, for they even speak Spanish with a marked incorrectness."

In other provinces of northern Mexico, European American Protestant traders and travelers mingled with native Spanish speakers. For example, in Santa Fe, New Mexico, Gertrudis Barceló owned a saloon that served as a meeting site for people of many cultures. There European American men could attend a nighttime fandango (dance), play monte (a card game), listen to Spanish music, and socialize with native Spanish speakers. A center of politics, business, and social life, the saloon broke down barriers based on religion, language, and even preconceived notions of personal morality as men and women came to gamble, drink, and carouse.

In some cases new relationships led to marriage and, ultimately, the creation of households that blended Catholic and Protestant, Spanish and European American cultures.

In parts of the West, traditional social identities yielded to new ones, based less on a single language or ethnicity than on a blend of cultures and new ways of making a living from the land. The 1830s and 1840s marked the height of the Rocky Mountain fur trade. The trade could generate huge profits for the eastern merchants who controlled it; for example, the Rocky Mountain Fur Company sold 168 packs of beaver pelts for $85,000 in 1832—more than $1 million today. However, individual trappers fared more modestly. They ranged freely across national boundaries and cultures, going wherever the bison, bear, and beaver took them. These men demonstrated a legendary ability to navigate among Spanish, French, European American, and Native American communities. Westerners coined new terms to describe the people representative of new kinds of cultural identity within trading communities. Some white men became "white Indians," and the children they had with Indian women were called "métis" (mixed bloods). William Sherley "Old Bill" Williams, a convert to the religion of the Osage Indians of the southeastern Plains, was not unusual in the ways he crossed cultural boundaries. He married an Osage woman, and when she died, he wed a New Mexican widow. His third wife was a Ute woman. Williams's life story suggests the ways that Indian and Hispanic women could serve as cultural mediators between native peoples and European American traders.

A Multitude of Voices in the National Political Arena

The increasing diversity of the American population, combined with specialized regional economies, heightened tensions within and between different groups and sections of the country. The Second Party system, which replaced the Federalist–Anti-Federalist rivalry of the early nineteenth century, was characterized by intense competition between the Jacksonian Democrats and anti-Jackson Whigs. But this new system could not accommodate the old or new conflicts based on race, religion, ethnicity, regional loyalties, and political beliefs. Social and cultural disputes spilled out of the courthouse and the legislative hall and into the streets. Public demonstrations ran the gamut from noisy parades to bloody clashes. During these displays, resentments between ethnic and religious groups, arguments over political issues, and opposition to reformers often blended together.

Specific interests—the white laboring classes, abolitionists, southern slave owners, and nativists (people hostile to immigrants)—sought to find their own political voices. Yet as national parties, the Democrats and Whigs refrained from facing, head-on, controversial issues such as slavery. Deprived of what they considered effective representation on the national level, some Americans grew increasingly frustrated by their own lack of political clout. Their grievances set off a full-blown political crisis and led to party realignment once again in the 1850s.

Whigs, Workers, and the Panic of 1837

Ill with tuberculosis, Andrew Jackson did not run for a third term in 1836. The Democrats nominated Jackson's vice president and friend Martin Van Buren for president. As his running mate, they chose Col. Richard M. Johnson, the self-proclaimed killer of Tecumseh. The Jackson-haters, led by Senator Henry Clay and other Congressmen formed a political party called the Whigs. They drew their support from several groups: advocates of Clay's American System, states' rights southerners opposed to Jackson's heavy-handed use of national power, and merchants and factory owners in favor of the Second Bank of the United States. Evangelical Protestants from the middle classes also joined the anti-Jackson forces; they objected to his rhetoric stressing class differences because they believed that individual religious conviction, not a group's material status, should shape politics and society. Still somewhat disorganized, these allied groups fielded three candidates: Hugh White of Tennessee, Senator Daniel Webster of Massachusetts, and General William Henry Harrison of Indiana. Benefiting from the Whigs' disarray, Van Buren narrowly won the popular vote but swept the Electoral College.

In northeastern cities, political candidates of all persuasions began to court the allegiance of workers aligned with a new trade union movement. Urban traders and laborers had become a political force in their own right. The spread of the factory system threatened the livelihoods of artisans in a number of trades. Immigration increased workers' anxieties. People worried about making a living tended to favor the Democratic Party, which spoke against class privilege and the wealthy. In the late 1820s and early 1830s, a variety of trade organizations had formed to advance the interests of skilled workers (the "producing classes," they called themselves). These unions pressed for a ten-hour workday, the abolition of paper money (so that workers would receive their wages in hard currency rather than bank notes) and debtors' prisons, and higher wages. In some cities, though representing only a minority of workers, these unions fielded their own candidates through Workingmen's Parties. In other places, workers counted on the Democrats to advance their interests at the polls. However, once in office, politicians often were indifferent to the demands of urban laboring people.

In some cases, journeymen protesting long hours and low wages took their grievances to the streets. In New York City in 1834, groups of sailors, bakers, shoemakers, carpet weavers, locksmiths, stonecutters, and hatters staged boisterous work stoppages. In October of that same year, the stonecutters turned their fury on a building under construction. They smashed windows and caused much damage until "a strong posse of watchmen" made them disperse.

The founding of the National Trades Union (NTU) in 1834 made workers more politically visible. The union represented workers as diverse as jewelers, butchers, bookbinders, and factory workers. In Philadelphia in the early 1830s, for example, the local NTU organization, called the General Trades Union, consisted of 50 trade societies and supported a number of successful strikes. Both Whigs and Democrats professed allegiance to the union, but neither party went out of its way to represent the interests of workers over other groups, such as farmers and bookkeepers.

But even larger troubles loomed for the trade union movement. In the course of his term, Van Buren had to grapple with the effects of a major depression, the Panic of 1837. Brought on by overspeculation—in canals, turnpikes, railroads, and slaves—the panic deepened when large grain crops failed in the West. British creditors worsened matters when they recalled loans they had made to American customers.

The depression, which lasted until the early 1840s, devastated the NTU and its constituent organizations. Up to one-third of all Americans lost their jobs when businesses failed. Those fortunate enough to keep their jobs were in no position to press for higher wages. Not until the Civil War era did members of the laboring classes recapture political momentum at the national level.

TABLE 12-2			
The Election of 1836			
Candidate	Political Party	Popular Vote	Electoral Vote
Martin Van Buren	Democratic	765,483	170
William Henry Harrison	Whig	739,795	73
Hugh L. White	Whig		26
Daniel Webster	Whig		14
W.P. Magnum	Independent		11

Max Rosenthal, *Henry Clay.* The National Portrait Gallery, Smithsonian Institution

■ Henry Clay had a distinguished career as statesman and politician for more than four decades. He was President John Quincy Adams's secretary of state. He served as speaker of the House of Representatives for a longer term than anyone else in the nineteenth century. He represented Kentucky in the Senate. A prominent Whig leader, he promoted "the American System" of tariffs and federal subsidies for transportation projects. By 1840, members of both parties were boasting of their (supposed) humble origins. Here Clay is portrayed as the "Old Coon" because the Whigs had adopted the raccoon as their symbol for the election of 1840.

Suppression of Antislavery Sentiment

In 1831 a Boston journalist named William Lloyd Garrison launched *The Liberator,* a newspaper dedicated to "immediate emancipation" of all slaves. Two years later, a group of 60 blacks and whites formed the American Anti-Slavery Society (AA-SS). That same year, Great Britain had abolished slavery in the West Indies. This move encouraged like-minded Americans eager to cooperate with their British counterparts to abolish slavery everywhere. In the United States, the abolitionist movement enlisted the energies of a dedicated group of people who believed not only that slavery was immoral but also that the federal government must take immediate steps to destroy this "peculiar institution."

The position of the AA-SS was clear: "the slaves ought instantly to be set free, and brought under protection of law." The *Declaration of Sentiments of the American Anti-Slavery Society* strongly condemned southern slaveholders and supporters of African American colonization. Indeed, it criticized the latter group for encouraging American blacks to move to Africa—in the words of the AA-SS, a "delusive, cruel and dangerous" scheme. A well-organized movement, the society sponsored an aggressive campaign against slavery, gathering hundreds of names on antislavery petitions to present to Congress. The group also distributed antislavery literature throughout the North.

The society drew moral and financial support from northern communities of free people of color as well as from white women and men. All the supporters showed a great deal of courage within a larger American society indifferent to the issue of slavery. Activists such as Maria Stewart and David Walker had laid the foundation for the abolitionist movement. Well-to-do black leaders, including Henry Highland Garnet, Charles Lenox Remond, and his sister Sarah Parker Remond, spoke out on behalf of southern blacks in chains. Fugitive slaves, including Frederick Douglass, Solomon Northup, and William and Ellen Craft, electrified northern abolitionist audiences with their first-hand accounts of the brutality of slavery and of their own daring escapes from bondage.

The American Anti-Slavery Society sponsored an aggressive campaign against slavery, gathering hundreds of names on antislavery petitions, to present to Congress.

Douglass's autobiography, *Narrative of the Life of Frederick Douglass* (1845), immediately gained an enthusiastic audience among abolitionists on both sides of the Atlantic. Within five years of its publication the book had sold 30,000 copies. An American tale of determination and self-education, the *Narrative* is also a literary classic. In one passage Douglass describes standing on the banks of the Chesapeake Bay, watching sailboats "robed in purest white" skimming along the water:

> I have often, in the deep stillness of a summer's Sabbath, stood all alone along the lofty banks of that noble bay, and traced, with saddened heart and tearful eye, the countless number of sails moving off to the mighty ocean. The sight of these always affected me powerfully. My thoughts would compel utterance; and there with no audience but the Almighty, I would pour out my soul's complaint.

Large and charismatic, Douglass had a compelling speaking style. He soon became a much-sought-after abolitionist speaker in the Northeast, the Midwest, and England.

A few white women also became active in the abolitionist cause. Sarah and Angelina Grimké, for example, left the household of their slave-owning father in Charleston, South Carolina, and moved to Philadelphia. The Grimké sisters spoke before groups composed of men and women, blacks and whites in the North, an act offensive to many other whites. They were struck by what they considered the similar legal constraints of slaves and white women. White men considered both groups to be unworthy of citizenship rights, childlike in their demeanor, well-suited for domestic service, and inherently unintelligent. Also in the North, local associations, such as the Female Antislavery Society of Andover, Massachusetts, mobilized women who then fired off letters to the *Liberator* and other publications. In these letters, they urged other women to respond to "the sighs, the groans, the deathlike struggles of scourged sisters in the South. . . . We feel that woman has a place in this God-like work."

Such activities provoked outrage not only from southern slave owners but also from anti-abolitionists and their allies in Congress—in other words, most northern whites. In Washington, D.C., the House of Representatives imposed a gag rule on antislavery petitions, forbidding them to be read aloud or entered into the public record. Supporters of slavery also resorted to violence. In 1834 a mob of whites attacked a school for young women of color operated by a white teacher, Prudence Crandall, near New Haven, Connecticut. A local paper charged that the school was fostering "levelling [egalitarian] principles, and intermarriage between whites and blacks." The next year in Boston a different mob attacked the *Liberator* founder, William Lloyd Garrison himself, tying a rope around him and parading him through the streets of that city while onlookers jeered. In 1837 in Alton, Illinois, a group of whites murdered outspoken abolitionist Rev. Elijah P. Lovejoy. Hounded out of Missouri because of his antislavery pronouncements, Lovejoy had moved directly across the river to Alton, in free-state Illinois, where he published the *Alton Observer* and organized the Illinois Anti-Slavery Society. The mob had destroyed his printing press before turning on Lovejoy. After the killing, Garrison and others hailed Lovejoy as a martyr.

Throughout the North, anti-abolitionist mobs voiced the fears of whites who believed that every black man who had a job took one from a white man. Antiblack riots broke out in New York City, Philadelphia, and Cincinnati in 1834, and again in Philadelphia in 1842. White workers attacked blacks so often in the 1830s and 1840s that bricks became known as "Irish confetti" because of the way immigrants used them as weapons.

Still, these dramatic episodes had little noticeable impact on the two major political parties. In 1840 the Democrats renominated Van Buren, although many people blamed him

The Library Company of Philadelphia (1835—7/P.8658)

■ The artist titled this print "**New Method of Assorting the Mail, as Practised by Southern Slave-Holders.**" In July 1835, a proslavery mob broke into the U.S. post office in Charleston, South Carolina, and burned abolitionist literature. The sign on the side of the building offers a "Reward for Tappan." The brothers Arthur and Lewis Tappan were wealthy New York City merchants who funded abolitionist activities. Southern slaveholders hoped to stem the north–south flow of abolitionist literature, which took the form of sermons, pamphlets, periodicals, and resolutions.

for the depression. Eager to find a candidate as popular as Andrew Jackson, the Whigs selected William Henry Harrison; his supporters called him "Old Tippecanoe" in recognition of his defeat of Indians at the battle of the same name in 1811. As Harrison's running mate the Whigs chose John Tyler, who had been both governor of and a senator from Virginia. To counter their reputation as well-heeled aristocrats, which in fact they were, the Whigs promoted Harrison as a simple, humble man living in a log cabin and drinking hard cider. They rallied around the slogan "Tippecanoe and Tyler Too."

The election of 1840 represented the triumph of style over substance in political electioneering as the two major parties ignored the growing controversy over slavery. That year abolitionists meeting in Albany, New York, founded a new party, the Liberty Party, dedicated to eradicating slavery. Although it garnered only 7000 votes for its candidate, James G. Birney, in the general election, the party soon gained the ability to swing local elections in favor of antislavery candidates. Still, Whigs and Democrats dominated the campaign of 1840. The two major parties were well organized and evenly matched. They used symbols, songs, and imagery in innovative ways to build party loyalty. Sloganeering substituted for meaningful discussion of the issues of the day.

TABLE 12-3			
The Election of 1840			
Candidate	Political Party	Popular Vote	Electoral Vote
William Henry Harrison	Whig	1,274,624	234
Martin Van Buren	Democratic	1,127,781	60
James G. Birney	Liberty	7,069	

By this time, the Whigs had gained strong support among wealthy southern planters, who worried that Van Buren would not protect their interests in slavery. Harrison won the election, but he contracted pneumonia at his inauguration and died within one month of taking office. Ridiculed as "His Accidency," Tyler assumed the presidency and soon lost his core constituency, Whigs who favored a strong central government, by vetoing bills for both a national bank and higher tariffs. The new president represented members of the Whig party who were ardent supporters of states' rights. As a result, he proved a poor standard-bearer for the numerous nationalist-minded Whigs. Tyler learned a hard lesson: that members of his own party were a loose coalition of groups with varying views on a range of issues rather than a unified party bound to a single idea or principle.

Abolitionists could claim few victories, either real or symbolic, during these years. However, they did take heart from the *Amistad* case. In 1839 Spanish slave traders attempted to transport 53 illegally purchased Africans to Havana, Cuba, on a ship named *Amistad*. En route to Havana, the Africans, under the leadership of a young man named Cinqué, rebelled, killed the captain, and took over the ship. Soon after, U.S. authorities captured the ship off the coast of Long Island. President Van Buren wanted to send the blacks to Cuba. However, a federal district court judge in Hartford, Connecticut, ruled that because the African slave trade had been illegal since 1808, the Africans had been wrongfully enslaved. The U.S. government appealed the case to the Supreme Court.

To publicize the *Amistad* case, abolitionists produced a play, "The Black Schooner or the Private Slaver '*Amistad*.'" To raise funds, Philadelphia black leader Robert Purvis paid to have Cinqué's portrait painted; then antislavery activists sold copies for $1 each. In 1841 former president John Quincy Adams argued the Africans' case before the high court. The court ruled in their favor. Of the original 53 men, women, and children, 35 had survived the ordeal (the rest died), and they returned to Africa. Slavery advocates and abolitionists alike pondered the question: Could the law be used to dismantle slavery?

Nativists as a Political Force

Among the active players on the political scene were the nativists, who opposed immigration and immigrants. The immigrants who came to the United States were a varied group in terms

Unknown Artist, *La Amistad*, c.1840. New Haven Colony Historical Society, New Haven, CT (#1972.1)

■ Abolitionists hailed the eventual freeing of the *Amistad* captives as one of their few successes in the fight against slavery before the Civil War. This picture shows the Spanish slave ship, commandeered by the captives under the leadership of Cinqué, anchored off Culloden Point, Long Island, in 1839. Initially charged with the murder of the ship's captain, the Africans were held in New Haven, Connecticut, until a U.S. Supreme Court ruling led to their release and return to Africa in 1842.

of their jobs, religion, and culture. Some farmed homesteads in Michigan, and others worked in northeastern factories. But to nativists, these distinctions made little difference: all immigrants were foreigners and thus unwelcome. Some nativists were also temperance advocates calling for the prohibition of alcohol; they objected to the Irish drinking in taverns and the Germans drinking in their *Biergarten*. Protestants worried that large numbers of Catholic immigrants would be loyal to the pope in Rome, the head of the Catholic Church, and thus undermine American democracy. Members of the working classes, black and white, feared the loss of their jobs to desperate newcomers who would accept low, "starvation" wages. But nativists objected just as much when immigrants kept to themselves— in their Catholic schools or in their German *Turnverein* (gymnastics clubs). They also complained when immigrants participated in U.S. politics as individual voters and members of influential voting blocs.

Samuel F. B. Morse, the artist and inventor, was among the most vocal nativists. In the early 1840s he ceased painting portraits and turned his creative energies to developing a form of long-distance electric communication. Congress financed construction of the first telegraph line, which ran from Washington to Baltimore. In May 1844, Morse sent a message in code, "What hath God wrought!" and the modern telegraph was born. The precursor of all later communication innovations, the telegraph revolutionized the spread of information and tied the country together.

Morse was convinced that Catholic immigrants in particular (mostly the Irish) were a grave threat to American democracy. In his book *Imminent Dangers to the Free Institutions of the*

■ Nicolino Calyo's **Street Cries: The Butcher**, c. 1840–1844.

Nicolino Calyo, Street Cries: The Butcher, c. 1840–44. Museum of the City of New York. Gift of Mrs. Francis P. Garvan in memory of Mr. and Mrs. Francis P. Garvan (55.6.22)

United States (1835), Morse charged that Catholics favored "monarchical power" over republican governments. Catholicism was like a cancer, he wrote, "We find it spreading itself into every nook and corner of the land; churches, chapels, colleges, nunneries and convents are springing up as if by magic every where." In his fears, Morse expressed nostalgia for a simpler past, even as his technical ingenuity paved the way for the modern world.

In 1844, an openly nativist political organization, the American Republican Party, made substantial gains in New York, Philadelphia, and Boston. The party elected six of its candidates to Congress and dozens of others to local political offices. In 1849, nativists founded the Order of the Star-Spangled Banner. Also called the Know-Nothing Party, the group got its name by cautioning its members to profess ignorance when asked about its existence. The Know-Nothings drew their support from a broad spectrum of the native-born population, including Whigs who saw immigrants as the backbone of the Democratic party. Native-born Democrats who shared that view also supported the Know-Nothings.

Anti-Catholic prejudices in particular helped to justify territorial expansion. Many U.S. Protestants believed the government was justified in siezing the land of Spanish-speaking Catholics in the West. They claimed religious and cultural superiority over Hispanics. As Protestant explorers, traders, and travelers reported on their experiences in the Southwest, they condemned what they called the region's "ignorant, priest ridden peasantry," in the words of one writer for *Harper's Magazine.* They also disdained Hispanic material culture: adobe houses revealed "the power of mud," suggested one European American. Albert Pike, a native New Englander, called the Santa Fe region "bleak, black, and barren." Other Protestants disdained what they considered "a people infatuated with the passion" for gambling. Protestant stereotypes of Mexican Roman Catholics set the stage for the U.S. conquest of northern Mexico in the late 1840s. However, not just in the West, but all over the continent, nativists' ideas had violent consequences.

In the 1830s and 1840s, violence in the form of military action or urban riots pitting anti-abolitionists against abolitionists, workers against employers, or nativists against immigrants constituted a widespread form of political expression. However, the opposing sides in some riots were not nearly so clear-cut. For example, with the demise of the Philadelphia General Trades Union, the laboring classes fell to fighting among themselves, venting their ethnic and religious differences. In May 1844, in the Philadelphia suburb of Kensington, Irish Catholic immigrant cloth weavers and native-born Protestant artisans brawled in the streets for four days. Protestant artisans came together to urge temperance, protest the increasing prominence of Irish politicians in the Democratic Party, and advocate the use of the King James Version of the Bible in the public schools. Catholic clergy disapproved of that translation, which, they claimed, public school teachers imposed on Catholic school children with the aid of taxpayers' dollars. The May riot, fueled by the emergence of the nativist American Republican Party, left several native-born workers dead and the Irish workers' churches and homes in shambles. Thus, ethnic animosity, anti-Catholicism, and nativism, as well as the temperance cause (widely associated with pre–Civil War reform) blended to produce often violent conflict.

The Library Company of Philadelphia (59541.D)

■ Taken on May 9, 1844, this daguerreotype is one of the first American photographs to record an urban civil disturbance. A crowd gathers outside Philadelphia's Girard Bank, at the corner of Third and Dock streets. At the time, soldiers called in to quell the riot were occupying the bank. Called the Bible Riots, the clash between Protestant and Catholic workers revealed tensions arising from nativism, temperance activism, and the use of the Protestant version of the Bible in the public schools.

Reform Impulses

In August 1841 writer Lydia Maria Child recorded a striking scene in New York City: a march sponsored by the Washington Society, a temperance group, was snaking its way through the streets. The procession stretched for 2 miles and consisted of representatives from "all classes and trades." The marchers carried banners depicting streams and rivers (the pure water favored over liquor) and poignant scenes of the grateful wives and children of reformed drunkards. Stirred by the martial sounds of trumpets and drums, Child wrote that the music was "the voice of resistance to evil." She added, "Glory to resistance! for through its agency men become angels."

Inspired by Charles Grandison Finney's faith in the "perfectibility" of human beings and heartened by the rapid pace of technological progress, many Americans set about trying to "make angels out of men," in Child's words. In the process, various reform associations targeted personal habits such as dress and diet, conventional beliefs about sexuality and the status of women, and institutions such as schools, churches, and slavery. Their efforts often brought women out of the home and into public life. Marches and meetings also led to encounters between different cultural groups: Christian missionaries and non-Christians, rich and poor, native-born and immigrants. Yet not all Americans shared the reformers' zeal. Even those who did rarely agreed about the appropriate means to transform society.

Public Education

In the eyes of some Americans, a growing nation needed new forms of tax-supported schooling. As families moved from one area of the country to another, public education advocates pointed out, children should be able to pick up in one school where they had left off in another. Members of a growing middle class wanted to provide their children with schooling beyond basic literacy instruction (reading and writing skills) and had the resources to do so. Factory owners, for their part, supported education that would produce a self-motivated, disciplined labor force.

Horace Mann, a Massachusetts state legislator and lawyer, was one of the most prominent educational reformers. In 1837 Mann became secretary of the first state board of education. He stressed the notion of a common school system available to all boys and girls regardless of class or ethnicity. In his annual report of 1848, he noted, "Education, then, beyond all other devices of human origin, is the great equalizer of the conditions of men—the balance-wheel of the social machinery." In an increasingly diverse nation, schooling promoted the acquisition of basic knowledge and skills. But it also provided instruction in what Mann and others called American values: hard work, punctuality, and sobriety.

How exactly would educators teach reading and writing skills and moral values? The dictionary of Connecticut's Noah Webster (published in 1828) and the McGuffey's *Reader* series, first published in 1836, provided a way. In his books, William H. McGuffey, a college professor and Presbyterian minister, combined lessons in reading with lessons in moral behavior: "Beautiful feet are they that go/Swiftly to lighten another's woe." Over the next 20 years, the McGuffey series sold more than 7 million copies.

By the 1840s, public school systems attended by white children had cropped up across the North and the Midwest. Urban districts, using tax revenues to support schools, sought to educate as many pupils as possible. These districts pioneered in grading classrooms, imposing uniform standards for curricula and teachers' qualifications, and regimenting pupils to make schooling more "efficient." Toward that end, local school boards eagerly tapped into the energies of women as teachers. School officials claimed that women were naturally nurturing and could serve as "mothers away from home" for small children.

■ Artist Albertis Browere titled this 1844 painting *Mrs. McCormick's General Store.* These barefoot boys are getting into trouble. Reformers advocated universal, compulsory schooling as one way to rid street corners of young mischief makers. Had these youngsters lived in the country, they probably would have been working in the fields.

Furthermore, schools could pay women only a fraction of what men earned. Between the 1830s and 1840s, the number of female schoolteachers in Massachusetts jumped more than 150 percent.

In 1846 writer and educator Catharine Beecher urged unmarried women to devote themselves to teaching. That year, she created a Board of National Popular Education, which sent New England teachers to the Midwest. By 1847 she had enlisted the services of 70 young Protestant women to serve as teacher–missionaries in Illinois, Indiana, Iowa, Wisconsin, Michigan, Tennessee, and Kentucky. Beecher expected these young women to endure hardship cheerfully. Many tried to do so. Dutifully reporting from her new home in what she described as "a newly organized county," one teacher wrote, "I came expecting to make sacrifices, and suffer privations." She found her pupils to be "ragged and dirty in the extreme" and unschooled in proper classroom decorum.

Other forms of education also multiplied. Lyceums—informal lectures offered by speakers who traveled from place to place—attracted hordes of adults regardless of their formal education. By the mid–1830s, approximately 3000 local lecture associations, mostly in New England and the Midwest, were sponsoring such series. In addition, local agricultural fairs offered informal practical instruction to rural people.

Despite the lofty goals of Mann and other reformers, public schooling did not offer a "common" experience for all American children.

The number of colleges more than doubled (46 to 119) between 1830 and 1850. Founded in 1837, Mount Holyoke, a college for women in Massachusetts, and Oberlin in Ohio, which accepted black men as well as women of both races, were unusual for their liberal admission policies. Most colleges were supported by a specific religious denomination or cultural group. In Indian Territory, for example, the Cherokee National Council founded the Cherokee Female Seminary in 1851. With a classical curriculum similar to that of Mount Holyoke, the school was intended for the daughters of wealthy, assimilated Cherokees.

In an ironic twist, innovations in education heightened differences in status. Despite the lofty goals of Mann and other reformers, public schooling did not offer a "common" experience for all American children. Almost exclusively, northern white children benefited from public school systems. Slightly more than one-third of all white children attended school in 1830; twenty years later, the ratio had increased to more than one half. In northern cities, these proportions were considerably higher; there reformers were able to provide elementary-school instruction for relatively large numbers of white children, both immigrant and native-born.

By contrast, few black children had the opportunity to attend public schools. In the South, slave children were forbidden by law to learn to read and write. Recalled one former slave many years later, "dey [owners] didn't teach 'em nothin' but wuk [work]." By the 1830s, schools for even the children of free people of color had to meet in secret. In the North, many black households needed the labor of children to survive, resulting in black school-attendance rates well below those of whites. Throughout the Northeast and Midwest, black children remained at the mercy of local officials, who decided whether they could attend the schools their parents' tax dollars helped to support.

In the late 1840s, Benjamin Roberts, a black man, launched a series of lawsuits against the Boston School Committee on behalf of his five-year-old daughter Sarah. Roberts demanded that the city's schools be integrated. The abolitionist-politician Charles Sumner argued the Roberts case before the state's highest court, but lost. However, in 1855, the Massachusetts legislature would outlaw segregated schools.

All over the country, education remained an intensely grassroots affair, belying the reformers' call for uniform systems. Local communities raised money for the teacher's salary, built the schoolhouse, and provided wood to heat the building. Southern states did not develop uniform public education systems until the late nineteenth century. Lacking local, popular support for tax-supported schooling, poor white children remained illiterate, while wealthy parents hired tutors for their own children or sent them to private academies.

Formal training for professionals also changed during this period. New state licensing and certification standards meant that people preparing to become physicians and lawyers must receive specialized training. As these professions came to insist on formal educational standards for practitioners, some women lost some of their traditional roles such as midwifery and healing. By the 1830s, almost all states required that doctors be licensed. The only way to attain such a license was to attend medical school, and these schools still excluded women. In regions of the country where medical schools appeared, the self-taught midwife gradually yielded to the formally educated male physician. In contrast, in rural communities of black and white Southerners, Native Americans, and Hispanics, women continued to practice time-honored ways of midwifery and healing.

Alternative Visions of Social Life

The crosscurrents of reform showed up most clearly in debates about sexuality, the family, and the proper role of women. For example, reformer Sylvester Graham argued that even husbands and wives must monitor their sexual activity. Sexual excess between husband and wife, he claimed, caused ills ranging from headaches, chills, and impaired vision, to loss of memory, epilepsy, insanity, and "disorders of the liver and kidneys." Graham also promoted a diet of special crackers made of wheat flour (now called Graham crackers) and fruit (in place of alcohol and meat) in addition to a regimen of plain living reinforced with cold showers.

The crosscurrents of reform showed up most clearly in debates about sexuality, the family, and the proper role of women.

Other reformers disagreed with Graham's notion that people must repress their sexuality to lead a good and healthy life. Defying conventional standards of morality, sponsors of a number of experimental communities discouraged marriage-based monogamy (a legal commitment between a man and a woman to engage in sexual relations only with each other) and made child-rearing the responsibility of the entire community rather than just the child's parents. These communities were communitarian—seeking to break down exclusive relations between husband and wife, parent and child, employer and employee—in an effort to advance the well-being of the whole group, and not just individuals within it. These communities were also utopian, seeking to forge new kinds of social relationships that would, in the eyes of the reformers, serve as a model for the larger society.

Many of these communities explicitly challenged mainstream views related to property ownership and the system of wage labor as well as rules governing relations between the sexes. The Scottish industrialist and socialist Robert Owen founded New Harmony in Indiana in 1825 basing his experiment on principles of "cooperative labor." In 1826 Owen released his "Declaration of Mental Independence, " which condemned private property, organized religion, and marriage. By this time, 900 persons had joined the New Harmony order.

The community at Nashoba, Tennessee, was more radical still, at least in theory. In 1825 a Scottish immigrant and heiress named Frances Wright established the settlement a few miles from Memphis, on land that the U.S. government had seized from the Chickasaws. A liberal thinker on many issues such as slavery and the roles of women, Wright wanted to prepare slaves for a life of freedom. Inspired by Owen, she embraced his program. Yet Nashoba, isolated in the Tennessee swamps, was an unhealthy site for everyone, white and black, young and old. The slaves resented the labor the community required of them before they could gain their freedom. Outsiders recoiled at what they considered the loose morality of the experiment, especially Wright's apparent approval of interracial sexual relations. Newspapers denounced her as a "voluptuous preacher of licentiousness," intent on converting the whole world "into a universal brothel." When Nashoba collapsed in the late 1820s, Wright joined the Owenites in New Harmony. She later moved to New York City, where she became a public lecturer, speaking out on behalf of workers and against the legal subordination of women.

Several other prominent communitarian experiments that challenged conventional marital relations were vehemently criticized, and participants were sometimes physically attacked by their neighbors. Salt Lake City Mormons, who practiced plural marriage, continued to meet intense hostility from outsiders.

Another group, the Oneida Community, founded in upstate New York near Utica in 1848 by John Humphrey Noyes, went even further than the Mormons in advocating an alternative to monogamy. At its peak, Oneida consisted of 300 members who endorsed the founder's notion of "complex marriage," meaning communal sexual unions and community-regulated parent–child relations. Charges of adultery eventually forced Noyes to flee the country and seek refuge in Canada.

Numerous moral reforms overlapped with and reinforced each other. For example, women's rights advocates often supported temperance. Husbands who drank, they pointed out, were more likely to abuse their wives and children. Sarah and Angelina Grimké gained prominence as both abolitionists and advocates for women's rights. They also followed Sylvester Graham's program, and for a short time they sported "bloomers" (loose fitting pants, popularized by dress reformer Amelia Bloomer) in place of cumbersome dresses.

Abolitionism and women's rights reinforced each other and spawned overlapping political movements in Europe as well as in the United States. Beginning in the 1820s, European women reformers began challenging a host of institutions, including slavery, capitalism, and the nuclear family. By the late 1840s, abolitionism, socialism, and utopianism helped inspire the European revolutions of 1848.

In the United States, women's rights advocates made some progress independent of the abolitionist movement. For instance, in 1839, Mississippi passed the nation's first Married Women's Property Law. The ruling was intended to protect the fortunes of the married daughters of wealthy planters. In 1848 both New York and Pennsylvania passed legislation giving married women control over any real property (land) or personal property they brought to marriage. But the organized women's rights movement drew its greatest inspiration from the abolitionist cause.

Elizabeth Cady Stanton, who played an active role in a local Female Anti-Slavery Society, is an apt example. Together with other American women, Cady Stanton attended the 1840 World Anti-Slavery Convention in London. Male leaders of the British and Foreign Anti-Slavery Society relegated the women delegates to a balcony and excluded them from the formal deliberations. Eight years later, Cady Stanton worked with Lucretia Mott, a Quaker minister; Susan B. Anthony, a young women's rights activist; and other similarly inclined men and women to organize a women's rights convention at Seneca Falls, New York.

Massachusetts resident Margaret Fuller explored many reform impulses of the day during her brief life (1810–1850), Educated in the classics by her father at home (in Cambridge), in the 1830s she embraced a new intellectual sensibility called Transcendentalism. Fuller cultivated friendships with two other famous Transcendentalists living in the Boston area: Ralph Waldo Emerson and Henry David Thoreau. Transcendentalists believed in the primacy of the spirit and the essential harmony between people and the natural world. They took their inspiration from European Romantics, who celebrated the beauty of nature in art, music, and literature. Transcendentalists also encouraged engagement with the world: in Emerson's words, "I will not shut myself out of this globe of action, and transplant an oak into a flower-pot." In 1840, Fuller began editing *The Dial*, the transcendentalist movement's magazine.

Margaret Fuller was one of the foremost American intellectuals of the antebellum period. Throughout her life she remained conscious of an inner struggle between her passionate self, desiring an active life, and her intellectual self, wanting to engage in study and debate with other scholars. She explored Transcendentalism, feminism, social reform, and finally the revolutionary fervor of Italian nationalism.

In the early 1840s, Fuller sponsored study groups among her female neighbors in Boston. By pondering questions such as "What is beauty?" and "What is truth?" the groups sought to discover the "connection between nature and the affections of the soul." Fuller also lent her moral support to a Transcendentalist community named Brook Farm, in West Roxbury, Massachusetts. There, men and women shared equally in the home chores and fieldwork. However, most members preferred thinking to laboring, and the venture failed in 1846.

Around this time, Fuller published *Woman in the Nineteenth Century*, one of the first feminist essays written by an American. "I would have Woman lay aside all thought, such as she habitually cherishes, of being led and taught by men," wrote Fuller. She then embraced the role of investigative journalist, writing about the plight of slaves, Indians, and imprisoned women for the New York *Tribune*. In 1847, the newspaper sent her to Italy to report on the Italian unification movement. Returning home in 1850, Fuller; her new husband, Italian revolutionary Giavanni Angelo, Marchese d'Ossoli; and their son drowned off the shore of Fire Island, New York, when their ship sank. In just two decades of her adult life, Margaret Fuller had embraced a spectrum of social ideas, from reformist to revolutionary.

The United States Extends Its Reach

In the mid–1840s, the editor of the *New York Morning News* declared that the United States had a "manifest destiny" to "overspread the continent" and claim the "desert wastes." Those inhabiting the "desert wastes"—Mexican settlers and a variety of Indian groups—apparently would have little say in the matter. The term *manifest destiny* soon became a catchall phrase, justifying American efforts not only to conquer new territory but also to seek out new markets for its goods across the oceans. With its growing population and increasingly specialized regional economies, the country strove to expand both geographically and economically.

International political developments and technological innovations led to expanded opportunites for trading. In 1846 Britain repealed its exclusionary Corn Laws, which had protected its own agricultural markets from foreign competition. As a result, farmers in the U.S. Midwest had fresh incentive to produce wheat for export. The invention of the clipper ship, which ushered in "the golden age of American shipping," also helped in the expansion of global trade. Narrow-bodied vessels, topped with large sails on towering masts, the new ships "clipped off" the miles. American merchants used them to import tea from China and wool from Australia. Investors from the eastern United States financed trading companies that marketed antelope skins, beaver pelts, and cured beef to places as far away as Cuba. They eyed Asian ports hungrily, an impulse that would result in U.S. seizure of Pacific island naval waystations in the late nineteenth century.

Within the United States, many groups advocated the expansion of the country's borders. Among all American exports to foreign countries, cotton was king, accounting for half of the total goods shipped after 1840. Southern planters and northern merchants alike made huge profits from the cotton trade. In 1840 English textile manufacturers depended on the fiber, and the American South produced about three-quarters of their supply. No wonder then that southern slave owners were eager to extend their land holdings into Texas. They were joined in that hope by residents of the western states, men such as Davy Crockett, hoping to press into the fresh lands of the far West and Southwest. Little did they know that their interest would evetually lead to all-out war.

The Lone Star Republic

In the early 1830s, the Mexican government grew alarmed by the growing number of American emigrants to Texas. Worried that the settlers would refuse to pledge allegiance to Mexico, that country closed the Texas border to further in-migration. By 1835 only one out of every eight residents of Texas was a *Tejano* (that is, a native Spanish speaker); the rest, numbering 30,000, hailed from the United States. The U.S.-born Texians, together with some prominent *Tejanos,* had become increasingly well armed and militant. They organized volunteer patrols to attack Indian settlements. These forces became the precursor of the Texas Rangers, a statewide organization of law enforcement officers.

In 1836 the Texians decided to press for independence from Mexico. Only by becoming a separate nation, they believed, could they trade freely with the United States, establish their own schools, and collect and spend their own taxes. The pro-independence Texians included Davy Crockett. He had lost his congressional race in 1835, partly because of his opposition to Jackson's Indian removal policies. Crockett moved to Texas in late 1835; he hoped to revitalize his political career there and also find work as a land agent.

In early February 1836, Crockett and the other armed Texians retreated to a Spanish mission in San Antonio called the Alamo. The next month, a military force led by Antonio López de Santa Anna, president of the Republic of Mexico and a general in the army, battled them for 13 days. All 187 Texians died at the hands of Santa Anna and his men (the Mexican leader lost 600 of his own troops). Historians disagree on whether the Alamo defenders died fighting or were executed by Mexican soldiers.

In April a force of Texians and their *Tejano* allies, including military leader Juan Seguin, surprised Santa Anna and his men at the San Jacinto River and killed another 600 of them. The victors captured Santa Anna and declared themselves a new nation.

Sam Houston, former U.S. congressman from Tennessee and commander-in-chief of the Texian army, became president of the Republic of Texas (also called the Lone Star Republic) in 1837. Some *Tejanos* who objected to Mexican high-handedness joined in supporting the new republic. They resented restrictions imposed by Mexico limiting trade between the Mexican states and the United States. For these reasons a number of prominent *Tejano* leaders, including Jose Antonio Navarro, Francisco Ruiz, and Lorenzo de Zavala, signed their names to the Texas Declaration of Independence. De Zavala became vice president of the new republic.

In New Mexico and other northern territories of Mexico, many Spanish speakers had long felt abandoned by the Mexican government, which had made no provisions for their self-government and, as in the case of Texas, inhibited trade relations with the United States. In 1835 one New Mexico newspaper editorialized, "The rain of brute force has been replaced by reason. We can be sure that Americans will not take the land by bullets. Their weapons are their industry, their liberty, and their independence. Mexico has left us in a deplorable state, a deplorable darkness." Although other Mexican provinces protested the way they were treated by the government, Texas was the only Mexican state to launch a successful rebellion against Mexico.

Texas's independence raised the fears of U.S. abolitionists and blacks living in the new republic. In contrast to Mexico, which had abolished slavery in 1829, Texas approved a constitution that not only legalized slavery but also prohibited free blacks from living in the country. Greenbury Logan, a black man who owned a farm near Austin, petitioned to stay. He wrote, "Every privilege dear to a free man is taken away." But vigilantes forced him to leave. They also forced out many *Tejanos.* Among them was Juan Seguin, who had helped defeat Santa Anna at the Battle of San Jacinto and was now the mayor of San Antonio. Not until 1981 did another *Tejano,* Henry Cisneros, hold the office of mayor of the city of San Antonio.

The Election of 1844

As an independent republic, Texas became a hotly contested political issue in the United States. During the election of 1844, politicians began to debate whether the United States should annex Texas. Van Buren was outspoken in his opposition to the idea. As a result,

TABLE 12-4			
The Election of 1844			
Candidate	Political Party	Popular Vote	Electoral Vote
James K. Polk	Democratic	1,338,464	170
Henry Clay	Whig	1,300,097	105
James G. Birney	Liberty	62,300	

Courtesy, Oberlin College Archives

■ In the mid–1840s, the Liberty Party moved this big tent around the country, holding their meetings and conventions in it. Charles G. Finney had used the tent for his religious revivals the decade before. Above the tent flew a banner that read "Holiness to the Lord." Some critics objected to the party's "mixing up" of religion and politics. Responded one party member, "Mix them, and mix them, and keep mixing, until they ceased to be mixed, and politics became religion and religion, politics."

the frankly expansionist Democrats spurned the former president as a candidate and nominated James K. Polk of Tennessee. They called for "the reannexation of Texas" and the "reoccupation of Oregon." Their rallying cry became "54°40′ or Fight," a reference to their desire to own the area (expressed in terms of its longitude and latitude coordinates) claimed by the British in present-day Canada south of Alaska and west of the Continental Divide. Kentucky congressman Henry Clay received the Whig nomination after he announced he was against the annexation of Texas. But under pressure from southerners, he later changed his mind, to the disgust of party leaders.

Neither the Democrats nor the Whigs had shown an interest in addressing the issue of slavery directly in the last presidential election. Yet in 1844 the controversy over the annexation of Texas made it impossible for the two parties to ignore the growing controversy over bound labor. Under the banner of the young Liberty Party, some abolitionists charged that territorial expansion would mean the continued growth and prosperity of the slave system; they pointed to the public pronouncements of southern planters, who were outspoken in their desire to expand their slaveholdings into the fertile lands of Texas. In 1844 the Liberty Party once again nominated James G. Birney as its presidential candidate.

The Liberty Party revealed a major split within the abolitionist movement in general. One faction within that movement was represented by the prominent abolitionist William Lloyd Garrison, editor of the *Liberator* and a founder of the American Anti-Slavery Society. Garrison had alienated his conservative supporters with several controversial principles. Specifically, he believed that women had a right to participate equally in the abolitionist movement with men. He also saw all political institutions and parties as inherently corrupt, since they upheld the U.S. Constitution, a document Garrison believed legitimized slavery. Another abolitionist faction was represented by members of the Liberty Party, men who believed that political action, far more than moral suasion (appealing to people's sense of justice and humanity) would halt the spread of slavery. By upholding abolitionism but rejecting Garrison's views, Liberty men claimed that slavery was ultimately a political issue, one that should rightfully claim the attention of all political parties.

For their part, Democrats and Whigs believed, correctly, that most voters would ignore slavery when they cast their ballots. Thus members of both parties tried to silence both sides of the slavery debate. They turned a deaf ear to the proslavery advocates on one hand and squelched northern abolitionist opinion by ignoring petitions to Congress on the other. In the end, Polk won the election. The expansionists had elected one of their most ardent champions to the highest office in the land.

Still, Polk was not interested in going to war with Great Britain over the vast territory of Oregon. In 1846 the two countries reached a compromise. Britain would accept the 49th parallel as the border between Canada and the United States and retain the disputed islands off the coast of Vancouver. The United States settled for one-half of its original claim to Oregon. Therefore, it was free to turn its full attention to extending its southern and western borders.

War with Mexico

Texas leaders wanted to become part of the United States. In 1845, as one of his last acts as president, Tyler invited Texas to become the twenty-eighth state. He also understood

Joseph Vollmering, The U.S. Naval Expedition Under Comore. M.C. Perry, Ascending the Tuspan River, 1848. Amon Carter Museum, Forth Worth, Texas (1976.33.2)

■ This painting shows the U.S. Navy going up the Tuxpan River in Mexico during the U.S.–Mexican War. Located on the Gulf coast halfway between Vera Cruz and Tampico, Tuxpan was the last significant Mexican port to be seized by U.S. forces by the spring of 1847. Commodore M. C. Perry assembled a formidable force of Marines and infantry to take over the town on April 19, 1847.

that annexing Texas was a way to goad Mexico into open hostilities; Mexico had warned the United States that such a move would mean war. A joint resolution of both houses of Congress confirmed Texas statehood in December of 1845.

The boundaries between Mexico and the new state of Texas remained in dispute. Mexico recognized the Nueces River as the boundary for Texas. In contrast, Texians and U.S. politicians envisioned the boundary hundreds of miles to the west at the Rio Grande. Complicating matters further, the new president, James K. Polk, had sent an envoy, John Slidell, to purchase California and a disputed section of Texas from Mexico. Mexico refused the deal. Nevertheless, around this time, Polk wrote in his diary that if he could not acquire all of New Mexico and California through diplomatic negotiation, he was determined to obtain them by force. The stage was set for war.

Armed conflict broke out in January 1846. U.S. troops, under the command of General Zachary Taylor (a veteran of wars against Tecumseh, the Seminoles, and Black Hawk), clashed with a Mexican force near the mouth of the Rio Grande near Matamoros. Taylor had deliberately moved his troops across the Nueces River into disputed territory; his intention was to provoke an armed response from Mexico. A skirmish ensued, 11 Americans were killed, and Taylor pulled back. Polk used this military action as justification for a declaration of war against Mexico. The president declared, "American blood has been shed on American soil."

Not all Americans supported the war. Transcendentalists and others objected to what they saw as a naked land grab. Refusing to pay taxes for what he considered a war to expand slavery, Henry David Thoreau went to jail. He explained his actions in an essay, "Civil Disobedience," published in 1848. He wrote, "It is not desirable to cultivate a respect for the law, so much as for the right. The only obligation which I have a right to assume is to do at any time what I think right."

Nativists also objected to the war, fearing that the United States would have to assimilate thousands of Indians and Spanish-speaking Roman Catholics. Some members of Congress also condemned Polk's "act of aggression." A newly elected U.S. Representative from Illinois named Abraham Lincoln, together with a few other legislators, sponsored a series of resolutions. The "Spot Resolutions" demanded that Polk specify the exact spot where bloodshed had occurred.

The Wilmot Proviso declared that "neither slavery nor involuntary servitude shall ever exist" in territories the United States acquired from Mexico.

Predictably, opponents of slavery were among Polk's most outspoken critics. Soon after the outbreak of war, Representative David Wilmot of Pennsylvania attached an amendment to a bill appropriating money for the war. Called the Wilmot Proviso, the measure declared that "neither slavery nor involuntary servitude shall ever exist" in territories the United States acquired from Mexico. Though a member of the Democratic party, Wilmot spoke primarily as a white Northerner; he wanted to preserve the West for "the sons of toil of my own race and color." Wilmot's views show how racial prejudice and antislavery sentiment coexisted in the minds of many white Northerners. The House approved the Proviso, but the Senate did not. Abandoning party loyalty, southern Democrats claimed that Congress had no right to deprive slaveholders of their private property anywhere in the nation.

Meanwhile, Polk launched a three-pronged campaign against Mexico. He sent Taylor into northern Mexico and ordered General Stephen Watts Kearny into New Mexico and then into California. Following the third directive of the campaign, General-in-Chief of the U.S. Army Winfield Scott coordinated an amphibious landing of 10,000 soldiers at Vera Cruz, on the Gulf of Mexico coast. Marching west, Scott's men followed in the footsteps of the Spanish conquistadors of the sixteenth century. Mexican forces tried to defend their homeland using guerrilla tactics. But U.S. soldiers overcame them by terrorizing civilians. Scott acknowledged that the men under his command had "committed atrocities to make Heaven weep and

■ MAP 12.6

THE U.S.–MEXICAN WAR During the U.S.–Mexican War, American troops marched deep into the interior of Mexico. General Winfield Scott raised the American flag over Mexico City on September 14, 1847. The treaty that concluded the war was named after the village of Guadalupe Hidalgo, a few miles north of the Mexican capital. The U.S. army withdrew the last of its troops from foreign soil in July 1848.

every American of Christian morals blush for his country. . . . Murder, robbery and rape of mothers and daughters in the presence of tied-up males of the families."

Along the way, at the Battle of Churubusco in August 1847, U.S. forces encountered a battalion of Irish immigrants who had originally served with the United States but were now fighting for Mexico. The San Patricio Battalion (Patrick's Company) consisted primarily of Irish-born men who had deserted from the U.S. army and defected to Mexico. Some had recoiled at the atrocities committed by U.S. troops on Mexicans; others wanted to ally with Catholic Mexico in opposition to Protestant America. Court martial

Senator John C. Calhoun Warns Against Incorporating Mexico into the United States

*I*n January 1848, Senator John C. Calhoun delivered a speech, addressing his remarks to President Polk and to his fellow lawmakers. He urged them to resist calls to incorporate all of a conquered Mexico into the United States. Calhoun favored the spread of slavery into new territories. However, here he expresses the fear that residents of Mexico were incapable of becoming suitable U.S. citizens for "racial" reasons.

It is without example or precedent, either to hold Mexico as a province, or to incorporate her into our union. No example of such a line of policy can be found. We have conquered many of the neighboring tribes of Indians, but we never thought of holding them in subjection—never of incorporating them into our Union. They have either been left as an independent people amongst us, or been driven into the forests.

I know further, sir, that we have never dreamt of incorporating into our Union any but the Caucasian race—the free white race. To incorporate Mexico, would be the first instance of the kind of incorporating an Indian race; for more than half of the Mexicans are Indians, and the other half is composed chiefly of mixed tribes. I protest such a union as that! . . .

Sir, it is a remarkable fact, that in the whole history of man, as far as my knowledge extends, there is no instance whatever of any civilized colored races being found equal to the establishment of free popular government, although by far the largest portion of the human family is composed of these races. . . . Are we to associate with ourselves as equals, companions, and fellow-citizens, the Indians and mixed race of Mexico? Sir, I should consider such a thing as fatal to our institutions.

Calhoun then moves on to another theme. He disputes the notion that Mexico can begin as a territory and then work its way up to statehood, following the standards Congress set for other western territories.

You can establish a Territorial Government for every State in Mexico, and there are some twenty of them. You can appoint governors, judges, and magistrates. You can give the people a subordinate government, allowing them to legislate for themselves, whilst you defray the cost. So far as the law goes, the thing is done. There is no analogy between this and our Territorial Governments. Our Territories are only an offset of our own people, or foreigners from the same regions from which we came. They are small in number. They are incapable of forming a government. It would be inconvenient for them to sustain a government, if it were formed; and they are very much obliged to the United States for undertaking the trouble, knowing that, on the attainment of their majority—when they come to

trials of captured San Patricio soldiers resulted in death sentences for 70 of them. Heeding formal protests from the archbishop of Mexico and the British ambassador of Mexico, General Scott pardoned 50 of the men because of their young age or because they could prove they had not fought willingly with the Mexicans. Yet Mexico continued recruiting San Patricio soldiers for the duration of the war. In all, more than 4800 Irish-born soldiers served in the U.S. army during the U.S.–Mexican War. Of that number, about 4 percent ended up fighting for the Mexicans.

In September 1847 Mexico City surrendered, and the war ended. Mexico had been in no shape to resist superior U.S. firepower. The United States paid for Scott's victory with 13,000 lives and $100 million. The Mexicans lost 20,000 lives.

In the Treaty of Guadalupe Hidalgo (approved by the Senate in 1848) Mexico agreed to give up its claims to Texas. The United States gained all of Texas and half of the territory of Mexico: the area west of Texas, comprising present-day New Mexico, Arizona, and California. Male residents of areas formerly held by Mexico were given one year to decide whether to stay in the United States and become citizens or return to Mexico. They were also entitled to retain their titles to the land, a provision that proved difficult to enforce in the face of European American land hunger.

The U.S. government paid Mexico $18,250,000. Of that amount, $15 million was designated as payment for land lost; the rest was restitution to U.S. citizens who might bring claims against

Portrait of John C. Calhoun by Charles Bird King, c. 1818–1825.

manhood—at twenty-one—they will be introduced to an equality with all other members of the Union. It is entirely different with Mexico. You have no need of armies to keep your Territories in subjection. But when you incorporate Mexico, you must have powerful armies to keep them in subjection. You may call it annexation, but it is a forced annexation, which is a contradiction in terms, according to my conception. You will be involved, in one word, in all the evils which I attribute to holding Mexico as a province. In fact, it will be but a Provincial Government, under the name of a Territorial Government. How long will that last? How long will it be before Mexico will be capable of incorporation into our Union? Why, if we judge from the examples before us, it will be a very long time. Ireland has been held in subjection by England for seven or eight hundred years, and yet still remains hostile, although her people are of kindred race with the conquerors. A few French Canadians on this continent yet maintain the attitude of hostile people; and never will the time come, in my opinion, Mr. President, that these Mexicans will be reconciled to your authority. . . . Of all nations of the earth they are the most pertinacious—have the highest sense of nationality—hold out the longest, and often even with the least prospect of effecting their object. On this subject also I have conversed with officers of the army, and they all entertain the same opinion, that these people are now hostile, and will continue so. . . .

We make a great mistake, sir, when we suppose that all people are capable of self-government. We are anxious to force free government on all; and I see that it has been urged in a very respectable quarter, that it is the mission of this country to spread civil and religious liberty over all the world, and especially this continent. It is a great mistake. None but people advanced to a very high state of moral and intellectual improvement are capable, in a civilized state, of maintaining free government; and amongst those who are so purified, very few, indeed, have had the good fortune of forming a constitution capable of endurance.

Calhoun also warns that "these twenty-odd Mexican States" would eventually have power in Congress. He asks his listeners whether they would want their own states "governed by" these peoples. ■

Source: Clyde A. Milner, ed., *Major Problems in the History of the American West: Documents and Essays* (1989), pp. 219–221.

Mexico for damaged or destroyed property during the war. Americans had conflicting views of the treaty. Abolitionists saw it as a blood-drenched gift from American taxpayers to slaveholders. Others argued that Polk had squandered a rare opportunity to seize all of Mexico.

Conclusion

In the 1830s and 1840s, mass population movements affected almost every aspect of American life. Immigrants from western Europe helped to swell the nation's labor force in midwestern farming communities and eastern cities. The arrival of the Roman Catholic Irish provoked a backlash among native-born Protestants and spawned a nativist political movement. Reformers in the United States and Europe went back and forth across the Atlantic, exchanging ideas related to women's rights, abolitionism, and utopian communities. As European Americans pushed the boundaries of the country west and south, they clashed with Indians and with foreign powers that claimed those lands as their own. Thus migration and immigration had profound consequences for American politics, economy, ideas, and society.

Most striking was the restlessness among land-hungry slave owners and antislavery forces alike. The war with Mexico in general and the clash over the Wilmot Proviso in particular opened a new chapter in the debate over slavery. In considering the Proviso, Congressmen gave up their party loyalties as Democrats or Whigs and began to think of themselves as Southerners and Northerners. When Wilmot proclaimed that he wanted to preserve the West for his "own color," he revealed that even antislavery Northerners did not necessarily embrace black people as equals. When Southerners indicated that even the vast expanse of Texas would not satisfy their desire for land, they revealed that the conflict over slavery was far from over. In fact, that conflict was about to enter a new and ominous stage.

Sites to Visit

The American Whig Party, 1834–1856
odur.let.rug.nl/~usa/E/uswhig/whigsxx.htm

This site explores the rise and fall of the anti-Jackson Whig Party.

The Alexis de Tocqueville Tour: Exploring Democracy in America
wwww.tocqueville.org/

Text and images are part of this companion site to C-SPAN's recent programming on de Tocqueville.

America's First Look into the Camera: Daguerreotype Portraits and Views, 1839–1862
memory.loc.gov/ammem/daghtml/daghome.html

The Library of Congress's daguerreotype collection consists of more than 650 photographs from the 1839–1864 period. The collection includes portraits, architectural views, and some street scenes.

Important Black Abolitionists
www.loc.gov/exhibits/african/influ.html

This Library of Congress exhibit includes pictures and text related to African American abolitionists.

On the Trail in Kansas
www.ukans.edu/carrie/kancoll/galtrl.htm

This Kansas collection site provides primary sources and images related to the Oregon Trail and European Americans' early movement westward.

The Era of the Mountain Men
www.xmission.com/~drudy/amm.html

This site includes private correspondence from early settlers in the area west of the Mississippi River.

Exploring *Amistad*
amistad.mysticseaport.org/main/welcome.html

The Mystic Seaport Museum in Mystic, Connecticut, maintains this site, which includes collections of historical documents related to the slave revolt aboard the *Amistad* and the trial that followed.

The Trail of Tears
www.americanwest.com/pages/indians.htm

A site on the forced migration of Cherokees from their home in the Southeast to Indian Territory.

The American Presidency: A Glorious Burden
americanhistory.si.edu/presidency/index.html

The Smithsonian Institution maintains this site on American presidents.

"Been Here So Long": Selections from the WPA American Slave Narratives
newdeal.feri.org/asn/index.htm

A site devoted to the interviews of former slaves conducted in the late 1930s.

The Roberts Case and the Efforts to Desegregate Boston Schools
www.sjchs-history.org

This site explores the legal challenge to racial segregation in Boston's schools during the late 1840s.

The Mexican–American War Memorial
sunsite.dcaa.unam.mx/revistas/1847

Images and text explore the causes, course, and outcome of the Mexican–American War.

For Further Reading

General

Michael Holt, *The Rise and Fall of the American Whig Party: Jacksonian Politics and the Onset of the Civil War* (1999).

Michael Morrison, *Slavery and the American West: The Eclipse of Manifest Destiny and the Coming of the Civil War* (1997).

Mary P. Ryan, *The Cradle of the Middle Class: The Family in Oneida County, New York, 1790–1865* (1983).

Charles G. Sellers, *The Market Revolution: Jacksonian America, 1815–1846* (1991).

Edward H. Spicer, *Cycles of Conquest: The Impact of Spain, Mexico, and the United States on the Indians of the Southwest, 1533–1960* (1962).

Harry L. Watson, *Liberty and Power: The Politics of Jacksonian America* (1990).

David J. Weber, *The Spanish Frontier in North America* (1992).

Mass Migrations

Jennifer S. H. Brown, *Strangers in Blood: Fur Trade Company Families in Indian Country* (1980).

Kathleen Neils Conzen, *Immigrant Milwaukee, 1836–1860: Accommodation and Community in a Frontier City* (1976).

Frederick Douglass, *The Narrative of the Life of Frederick Douglass, An American Slave* (1845).

John Ehle, *Trail of Tears: The Rise and Fall of the Cherokee Nation* (1988).

John Mack Faragher, *Women and Men on the Overland Trail* (1979).

Walter Johnson, *Soul by Soul: the Inside of the Antebellum Slave Market* (1999).

Philip J. Schwarz, *Migrants Against Slavery: Virginians and the Nation* (2001).

A Multitude of Voices in the National Political Arena

Donald B. Cole, *Martin Van Buren and the American Political System* (1984).

Paul A. Gilje, *The Road to Mobocracy: Popular Disorder in New York City, 1763–1834* (1987).

Daniel Walker Howe, *The Political Culture of the American Whigs* (1979).

Lawrence F. Kohl, *The Politics of Individualism: Parties and the American Character in the Jacksonian Era* (1989).

Richard P. McCormick, *The Second American Party System: Party Formation in the Jacksonian Era* (1966).

David R. Roediger, *The Wages of Whiteness: Race and the Making of the American Working Class* (rev. ed., 1999).

Reform Impulses

Charles Capper, *Margaret Fuller: An American Romantic Life* (1992).

Jed Dannenbaum, *Drink and Disorder: Temperance Reform in Cincinnati from the Washington Revival to the Women's Christian Temperance Union* (1984).

Michael D. Fellman, *The Unbounded Frame: Freedom and Community in Nineteenth-Century America Utopianism* (1969).

Howard Jones, *Mutiny on the Amistad: The Saga of a Slave Revolt and Its Impact on American Abolition, Law, and Diplomacy* (1987).

Carl Kaestle, *Pillars of the Republic: Common Schools and American Society, 1780–1860* (1983).

Henry Mayer, *All on Fire: William Lloyd Garrison and the Abolition of Slavery* (1998).

Shirley J. Yee, *Black Women Abolitionists: A Study in Activism, 1828–1860* (1992).

The United States Extends Its Reach

Arnoldo De León, *The Tejano Community, 1836–1900* (1982).

Richard Griswold Del Castillo, *The Treaty of Guadalupe Hidalgo: A Legacy of Conflict* (1990).

Robert W. Johannsen, *To the Halls of the Montezumas: The Mexican War in the American Imagination* (1985).

David Alan Johnson, *Founding the Far West: California, Oregon, and Nevada, 1840–1890* (1992).

Paul D. Lack, *The Texas Revolutionary Experience: A Political and Social History, 1835–1836* (1992).

Ramón Ruiz, ed., *The Mexican War: Was It Manifest Destiny?* (1963).

Online Practice Test

Test your understanding of this chapter with interactive review quizzes at

www.ablongman.com/jonescreatedequal/chapter12

1848	Gold is discovered in California.

	Women's Rights Convention, Seneca Falls, New York. Free Soil Party is founded.
1849	"Forty-Niners" migrate to California.
1850	Clayton–Bulwer Treaty. Compromise of 1850; Fugitive Slave Law.
1851	Fort Laramie Treaty. Indiana Constitution bars in-migration of African Americans.
1852	American (Nativist) party is founded. Abolitionists free fugitive slave Shadrach. Harriet Beecher Stowe, *Uncle Tom's Cabin*.

125,000 SETS. 270,000 VOLUMES SOLD.

UNCLE TOM'S CABIN

FOR SALE HERE.

The Greatest Book of the Age.

1853	Gadsden Purchase. Matthew Perry's fleet enters Tokyo Harbor.
1854	Kansas–Nebraska Act. Republican party is founded. Cyrus McCormick patents mechanical reaper. Henry David Thoreau, *Walden*.
1855	William Walker captures Granada, Nicaragua. Pottowatamie Creek massacre. Walt Whitman, *Leaves of Grass*.
1856	Lecompton (Kansas) Constitution.
1857	*Dred Scott* Supreme Court Case. George Fitzhugh, *Cannibals All*.
1858	Lincoln–Douglas debates.
1859	Harpers Ferry raid. Harriet Wilson, *Our Nig*. Cortina's War in Texas.

1860	South Carolina secedes from Union.
1861	Confederate States of America is formed. Civil War begins. U.S. Sanitary Commission is founded.
1862	Minnesota (Santee) Sioux uprising. Congress passes Homestead, Morrill, and Pacific Railroad acts. Battle of Antietam.
1863	Emancipation Proclamation. Richmond Bread Riots. Battle of Gettysburg. Northern antidraft riots. Lincoln delivers Gettysburg Address.

PART FIVE

Disunion and Reunion

THE CIVIL WAR WAS THE COUNTRY'S GREATEST POLITICAL AND MORAL crisis. By 1860 the two-party system could no longer contain the dispute between proslavery and antislavery forces. That dispute centered on the fate of slavery in new territories to the west. Several dramatic developments—the secession of southern states from the union, the formation of the Confederate States of America, and a Confederate attack on a federal fort in Charleston Harbor—precipitated all-out war. In the spring of 1861 few people could have anticipated that the conflict would drag on for four long years and claim more than 600,000 lives.

The Second Party System, based on divisions between Whigs and Democrats, unraveled in the 1850s. Both parties represented coalitions of groups that expressed cultural, not sectional, sensibilities. Yet a series of events led to a realignment of parties into northern and southern camps. Many Northerners chafed under the Fugitive Slave Act of 1850, which required that all citizens assist law enforcement agents in retrieving runaway slaves for their owners. The founding of the Republican party in 1854 gave a political voice to Northerners hoping to preserve the western territories for family farmers who would not have to compete for land and labor with large slaveholders. In 1857 the Supreme Court ruled that black people had no rights that any court was bound to respect. Violent conflicts between proslavery and antislavery forces in Kansas and a failed raid by abolitionists on Harpers Ferry, Virginia (in 1859), revealed that legislators' resolutions and maneuverings were insufficient to stave off bloodshed.

In pursuing a militant nationalism, Confederates hoped to compensate for their relative weakness in terms of population and industrial capacity compared with the North. They believed that they could use a large, docile black labor force to grow food and serve as a support system for the army. They anticipated that European nations, dependent on southern cotton, would extend them diplomatic recognition and that white civilians would rally to the defense of their homeland no matter what the price in money or blood. Confederates also believed that western Indians would gladly assist them in their cause against a hated U.S. army and that brilliant southern generals could outstrategize a huge, lumbering invading army indefinitely. On all these counts they miscalculated, but their miscalculations were revealed gradually.

During the war, white Southerners had to contend with two major unanticipated consequences of the conflict. First, war mobilization efforts across the South necessitated the centralization of government and economic policymaking. Principled states' rights supporters opposed these efforts. Second, slaves and free blacks alike proved traitorous to the Confederate cause. In myriad ways—running away from their owners and spying for the enemy, slowing their work pace in the fields, and fighting for the Union army—black people served as combatants in the war. They fought for their families and their freedom and for a country that would grant them full citizenship rights. In the North, only in late 1862 did President Abraham Lincoln announce that the United States aimed to destroy slavery, but violent antidraft, antiblack riots in several cities showed that the northern population was deeply divided over emancipation.

Soon after the end of the war, in April 1865, congressional Republicans began to challenge President Andrew Johnson's plan for reconstructing the South; they considered it too lenient toward the former Confederate states. In 1867 these political leaders had enough votes to enact their own plan, calling for the enfranchisement of black men in the South, the reorganization of southern state governments under leadership loyal to the Union, and the enactment of a labor contract system between southern landowners and black laborers.

Members of the Republican party backed a strong Union, a federal system in which the central government would ensure that individual men could pursue their own self-interest in the marketplace of goods and ideas. Yet the Civil War era exposed the limits of the Republican vision. The Plains Indians sought not citizenship but freedom from federal interference altogether. Women and working people challenged various components of the Republican ideal, with its emphasis on unbridled individualism and federal subsidies of business. African Americans aspired to own property, vote, and send their children to school, just as other nineteenth-century Americans did. They wanted to farm their own land and care for their own families free from white intrusion. Yet congressional Republicans did not enact large-scale land redistribution programs; most felt that once the rebels were subdued and slavery abolished, their duty was done.

Civil strife persisted into the postwar period. Union generals turned from quelling the southern rebellion to putting down armed resistance among the Plains Indians. Former rebels formed vigilante groups to attack black voters and their allies in the South. By the early 1870s most Northerners had lost interest in the welfare of the former slaves and acquiesced as former Confederates reclaimed state governments. The last occupying forces withdrew from the South in 1877. In welding the country together as a single economic and political unit, the Republicans had triumphed. However, white Southerners retained control over their local social and political affairs. The revolution to secure African American civil rights was stalled for nearly 100 years.

1864 Fort Pillow massacre of African American (Union) soldiers.
Sand Creek (Colorado) massacre.
Sherman's March to the Sea.

1865 Freedmen's Bureau is formed.
Confederacy is defeated.
Lincoln is assassinated; Andrew Johnson becomes president.
Thirteenth Amendment is ratified.

1866 Civil Rights Act of 1866.
National Labor Union is founded.
Equal Rights Association is founded.
Ku Klux Klan is organized.
Congress approves Fourteenth Amendment.

1867 National Grange is founded.
U.S. purchases Alaska from Russia.
Reconstruction Act of 1867.

1868 Johnson is impeached and acquitted.
U.S.–China Burlingame Treaty.
Colored Labor Union is founded.
Fourteenth Amendment is ratified

1869 Congress approves Fifteenth Amendment.
Transcontinental Railroad is completed.
National Woman Suffrage Association and American Woman Suffrage Association are formed.
Knights of Labor is founded.

1870 Fifteenth Amendment is ratified.

1871 Ku Klux Klan Act.

1872 Apex Mining Act of 1872.
Congress creates Yellowstone National Park.
Susan B. Anthony attempts to vote.
Crédit Moblier scandal.

1873 Timber Culture Act.
Onset of depression.

1874 Freedman's Savings Bank fails.

1875 Civil Rights Act.
Resumption Act.
Whiskey Ring is exposed.

1876 Battle of Little Big Horn.
Contested presidential election between Rutherford B. Hayes and Samuel J. Tilden.

1877 Compromise of 1877.
California Workingmen's Party is formed.
Great Railroad Strike.

The Crisis over Slavery, 1848–1860

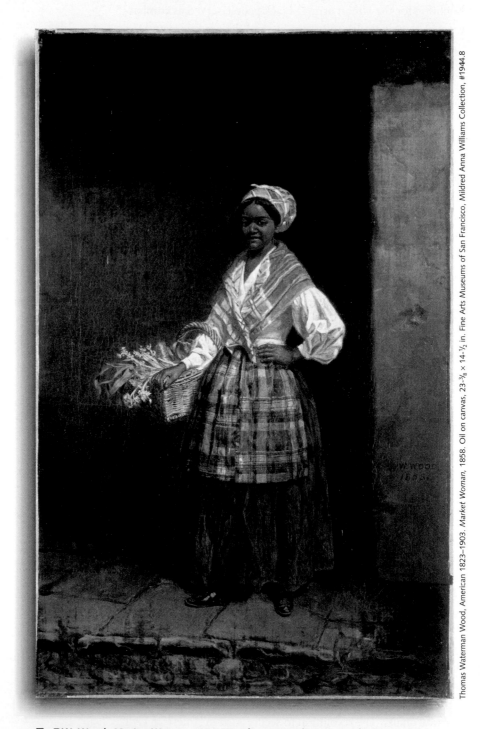

Thomas Waterman Wood, American 1823–1903. *Market Woman*, 1858. Oil on canvas, 23-³/₈ × 14-¹/₂ in. Fine Arts Museums of San Francisco, Mildred Anna Williams Collection, #1944.8

■ T.W. Wood, *Market Woman*, 1858. Wood's portrait depicts an African American woman going about one of her daily chores—going to market.

O N JANUARY 24, 1848, HENRY WILLIAM BIGLER TOOK A BREAK FROM BUILDING A sawmill for John Sutter in California's Sacramento Valley and penned in his pocket diary, "This day some kind of mettle was found . . . that looks like goald."

GOLD! News of the discovery at Sutter's mill spread like wildfire. By 1849 immigrants from all over the world and migrants from all over the United States had begun to pour into the foothills of the Sierra Nevada Mountains. Dubbed "the Forty-Niners," they had journeyed westward across the mountains, from the tenements of New York City and the great plantations of Mississippi; north from Mexico; and over the oceans, from western Europe, China, and South America. Equipping themselves with simple mining tools, the Forty-Niners began to dig for buried treasure, determined to stake a claim and make a fortune. And so they sang:

I'll scrape the mountains clean, my boys,
I'll drain the rivers dry,
A pocket full of rocks bring home,
So brothers, don't you cry!

During the Gold Rush years of 1848 to 1859, various cultural groups were thrown in close proximity to each other. Men from Belgium, France, Germany, Scotland, Chile, and Long Island learned to appreciate flour and corn tortillas (*tortillas de harina* and *tortillas de maiz*) and beef cooked in chile, staples of the Mexican diet. The disproportionate number of men permitted small numbers of women to challenge European American gender conventions. A gold miner might take a break from washing his clothes, straighten his aching back, and watch a Mexican woman and her daughter, well mounted on their horses, rounding up a herd of near-wild cattle. An-Choi, a Chinese immigrant woman, earned a tidy sum by opening a brothel

Chinese and European American miners pan for gold in the Auburn Ravine in California in 1852.

that catered to gold miners. Biddy Mason, an enslaved woman, successfully sued for her freedom and became the first African American homesteader in Los Angeles.

California came to be part of the United States as a result of the U.S.-Mexican War. In the 1848 Treaty of Guadalupe Hidalgo, Mexico agreed to hand over territory stretching from Texas northwest to California. As a result, the United States obtained a vast expanse of land—almost 530,000 square miles—called the Mexican Cession.

In addition to the land, the nation added to its population large numbers of men, women, and children already living in the area—13,000 Spanish speakers and 100,000 Indians (all former Mexican citizens) in California alone. After 1848 many new settlers streamed into California, and the migrants pressed for statehood, granted in 1850. By that year 90,000 new European American settlers lived in the state. Prominent among the Forty-Niners were Chinese immigrants—20,026 had arrived in California by 1852. Within two decades their numbers would swell to 50,000. From the American South came both free and enslaved African Americans; between 1850 and 1852, the California black population more than tripled from almost 700 people to over 2200. Rapid growth meant that, soon after the beginning of the Gold Rush, California had surpassed the minimum population necessary for statehood—60,000 people.

California became a state in 1850, but only after a bitter Congressional debate over the extension of slavery. The resulting Compromise of 1850 included several provisions bearing on the issue of slavery: California would be admitted as a free state; slave-trading would be outlawed in the District of Columbia; carved out of the Mexican Cession, the Utah and New Mexico territories could decide for themselves whether or not to legalize slavery. Finally, a new, harsh, fugitive slave law provided for the capture and return of slaves who found their way to free states in the north or west, including California. Though called a compromise, in fact these provisions inflamed the passions on both sides of the slavery debate—abolitionists in the North and slaveowners in the South.

Despite California's status as a free state, the principle of free labor was often violated. For example, in 1850 the state enacted a law with the misleading title, "An Act for the Government and Protection of the Indians," which provided for the indenture or apprenticeship of Indian children to white men for indeterminate periods of time. The law also allowed for the hiring out, to the highest bidder, of adult Indians deemed guilty of vagrancy. Indians in the region belonged to the Uto-Aztecan, Hokan, Penutian, Yukian, and Athabascan language families. Nevertheless, European Americans ignored these distinctions and called all Indians by the contemptuous term "Diggers," denounced them as lazy and uncivilized, and denied them the rights accorded American citizens.

Though a free state, California also enacted discriminatory legislation against African Americans. The state's Fugitive Slave Law of 1852 decreed that, regardless of his or her current status, a black person who entered the state as a slave and thereafter attempted to remain on free soil was a fugitive slave. That year, three African American gold miners, Robert Perkins, Carter Perkins, and Sandy Perkins, all former slaves who had been freed by their owner, were arrested under the law and ordered re-enslaved in their native Mississippi. Moreover, some European Americans continued to hold people against their will illegally. Thomas Shearon, a quartz-mining entrepreneur from Nashville, Tennessee, defied the state constitution by using slave labor in the vicinity of San Francisco.

Other California labor systems revealed that the principle of free labor was not carried out in practice. Chinese immigrants to California entered the country organized in companies, or district associations, indebted to merchants for their transportation and bound to work for an employer until the debt was repaid. Fearing competition from cheap labor, alarmed European Americans labeled these Asian workers "coolies" (i.e., enslaved laborers). By 1852 the Chinese in California (almost all of them men) had been pushed out of mining as a result of the discriminatory Foreign Miners Tax, a measure leveled with special force against both Chinese and Mexican miners.

Although the Treaty of Guadalupe Hidalgo guaranteed U.S. citizenship rights to Mexicans, those rights were not enforced under the law. Many Mexicans found them-

Courtesy, Bancroft Library, University of California, Berkeley

■ This pair of cartoons, titled "What We Want in California," suggests that migrants from the East hoped to reestablish a middle-class ideal in their new home. Above, an Indian family watches the arrival of a train from New York. Below, a European American family relaxes in a well-appointed parlor.

nerable to violence and land dispossession perpetrated by the growing European American majority. Delegates to California's constitutional convention in 1849 stipulated that only white *Californios* (descendants of the original Spanish colonists) were entitled to vote, over the objections of the 8 *Californios* among the 48 delegates in attendance. The majority of delegates also approved a measure prohibiting Indians and blacks from testifying against white people in court.

At mid-century the legal, economic, and cultural tensions among different groups in California mirrored tensions within the country as a whole. Rapid population growth, the coming together of many different cultures, and dramatic economic changes all fueled the conflict over slavery. The controversy surrounding California statehood revealed that awkward and unjust Congressional "compromises" would satisfy neither side in a debate that was becoming increasingly strident and even violent. All over the nation, in the pages of the popular press, on the streets of Boston, in the cotton fields of Alabama, no less than in the courts of California, Americans gradually united around a radical proposition: that the question of whether or not human beings could be held as private property was an issue on which there could be no compromise.

Regional Economies and Conflicts

It is tempting to view the decade of the 1850s with an eye toward the impending firestorm of 1861. However, in the early 1850s, few Americans could have anticipated the Civil War. At mid-century the United States was going through a period of rapid transition. New developments such as railroads, the factory system, and more efficient farm equipment led to significant changes in regional economies and began to give shape to an emerging national economy. Annexation of land in the Southwest and West and the conquest of Indians on the Plains produced dramatic social upheavals for Native Americans in those regions. Meanwhile, Americans continued to wrestle with the role of slavery in this rapidly changing society.

Native American Economies Transformed

On the Plains, Indians confronted wrenching transformations in their way of life. Forced to relocate from the Southeast to Indian Territory (present-day Oklahoma), the Five Southern ("Civilized") Tribes, the Cherokee, Choctaw, Creek, Chickasaw, and Seminole, grappled with the task of rebuilding their political institutions. By the 1850s the Cherokees had established a new capital at Tahlequah, along with public schools. They published a Cherokee newspaper (the *Advocate*) and created a flourishing print culture in their own language.

To the north and west of Indian Territory, Plains Indian tribes such as the Sioux, Kiowahs, and Arapaho exploited the horse, which had been introduced by Europeans in the Southwest in the seventeenth century. By raiding, trading, and breeding, these groups increased their stock of horses, which they used to hunt bison and transport their lodges and food from site to site. With abundant food and the means to trade with whites, these groups prospered for a brief period in the mid-nineteenth century. Their beadwork and animal skin painting exemplified the artistic vitality of their cultures.

In the 1850s U.S. officials negotiated treaties with various Plains Indian groups to enable European Americans to move west without fear of attack. Most settlers were bent on heading straight for California or the Northwest, traversing the Plains, which they called the Great American Desert in the mistaken belief that the absence of trees there demonstrated the infertility of the soil. The Fort Laramie Treaty of 1851 and the Treaty of Fort Atkinson three years later provided that the government could build roads and establish forts along western trails and that, in return, Indians would be compensated with supplies and food for their loss of hunting rights in the region. A young Cheyenne woman, Iron Teeth, recalled "the government presents" to her people in these terms: "We were given beef, but we did not care for this kind of meat. Great piles of bacon were stacked upon the prairies and distributed to us, but we used it only to make fires or to grease robes for tanning." She and her family sought out other items from government trading posts: "brass kettles, coffee-pots, curve-bladed butcher knives, boxes of black and white thread."

Thus as whites moved west in large numbers to "scrape the mountains clean and drain the rivers dry," they overran the fragile settlements of Indians and disregarded U.S. treaties and tribal boundaries. Taking leave of the Fort Laramie conclave of 1851, Cut Nose of the Arapaho had declared, "I will go home satisfied. I will sleep sound, and not have to watch my horses in the night, or be afraid for my women and children. We have to live on these streams and in the hills, and I would be glad if the whites would pick out a place for themselves and not come into our grounds." But within a generation, the Plains Indians were beseiged by the technology, weaponry, and sheer numbers of newcomers heading west.

Land Conflicts in the Southwest

In the mid-nineteenth century the United States gained control over a vast expanse of land, provoking legal and political conflicts over the rights and labor of the people who lived there, both natives and newcomers. Under the terms of the Treaty of Guadalupe Hidalgo, Mexico ceded not only California but also the province of New Mexico, territory that included the present-day states of New Mexico, Arizona, Utah, Nevada, and southern Colorado. In 1853 the United States bought an additional tract of land from Mexico, 55,000 acres located in the area south of the Gila River (in present-day New Mexico and Arizona). Overseen by the U.S. secretary of war, a Mississippi planter named Jefferson Davis, the agreement was called the Gadsden Purchase (after James Gadsden, a railroad promoter and one of the American negotiators).

The presence of so many Mexicans in this region prompted fears that any new state carved from the territory would remain under political control of Spanish speakers. European Americans charged that Mexicans were "not Americans, but 'Greaser' persons ignorant of our laws, manners, customs, language, and institutions," and consequently "unfit for statehood." New Mexico did not become a state until 1912.

The outcome of the U.S.-Mexican War—the U.S. seizure of present-day Texas and the area west of it—intensified rather than lessened conflicts over the land. Newly arrived European Americans battled native *Tejanos* (people of Mexican origin or descent) for political and economic supremacy. White migrants from the southern United States brought their slaves with them to the region, claiming that the institution of slavery was crucial for commercial development. With their irrigated fields, Mexican and Indian farmers had already demonstrated that crops could grow in the Southwest, suggesting that the slave system could also flourish there. German immigrants came to central and east Texas, founding towns with German names such as Fredericksburg, Weimar, and Schulenburg. During the 1850s, commercial farming continued to replace subsistence homesteading as the cattle industry spread and the railroads penetrated the region. Although European Americans monopolized the courts and regional political institutions, *Tejanos* retained cultural influence throughout Texas, dominating the cuisine and styles of music and architecture.

U.S. courts tended to disregard the land titles held by *Californios* and *Tejanos*. In the early 1850s California authorities battled Mexican social bandits such as Joaquin Murrieta, who, with his men, raided European American settlements. Murrieta and others argued that they were justified in stealing from privileged European Americans who, they claimed, disregarded the lives and property of Mexicans. In 1859 in the Rio Grande Valley of Texas, tensions between the *Tejano* majority and groups of European American law enforcement officers called the Texas Rangers

©1995-2001 Denver Public Library, Colorado Historical Society and Denver Art Museum

■ Dwellings of U.S. residents varied greatly depending on regional cultures. The Pueblo Indians of the Southwest took their name from the multilevel, rectangular, flat-roof clay houses where they lived. (*Pueblo* is the Spanish word for "village.") These structures have receding terraces connected by wooden ladders. In the forefront of this pueblo in Taos (present-day New Mexico) are clay beehive ovens. Farmers, hunters, and gatherers, the Pueblo Indians became residents of the United States as a result of the Treaty of Guadalupe Hidalgo in 1848.

erupted into full-scale warfare. Juan Cortina, who had fought on the side of Mexico during the Mexican War, orchestrated attacks on European Americans and their property in the vicinity of Brownsville. U.S. retaliation led to Cortina's War, pitting the Mexican leader against a young U.S. colonel, Robert E. Lee. Cortina himself became a hero to *Tejanos*. "You have been robbed of your property, incarcerated, chased, murdered, and hunted like wild beasts," he declared; "to me is entrusted the work of breaking the chains of your slavery."

Ethnic and Economic Diversity in the Midwest

The Yankee Strip (named for the northeasterners who migrated there) ran through northern Ohio, Indiana, and Illinois and encompassed the entire states of Michigan, Wisconsin, and Minnesota. Here migrants from New England settled and established public schools and Congregational churches. Immigrants from western Europe also made a home in this region—the Germans, Belgians, and Swiss in Wisconsin, the Scandinavians in Minnesota. At times cultural conflict wracked even the smallest rural settlements. In some Wisconsin villages, equally matched numbers of Yankees and Germans contended for control over the local public schools, with the group in power posting notices for school board elections in its own language, hoping that its rivals would not show up at the polls. Yankees complained that the Scandinavian farmers put their wives to work in the fields and that Germans took their children with them to *Biergarten* (places where beer was served).

The lower Midwest, including the southern portions of Ohio, Indiana, and Illinois, retained strong cultural ties to the southern states. In this region, many settlers had migrated from the South. Though residing in free states, they maintained broad support for the institution of slavery. In some cases they outnumbered their Yankee counterparts and managed to shape the legal system in a way that reflected a distinct antiblack bias. For example, Indiana's state constitution, approved in 1851, prohibited black migrants from making contracts with whites, testifying in trials that involved whites, voting, and entering the state.

Most rural midwestern households followed the seasonal rhythms characteristic of traditional systems of agriculture. However, by the mid-nineteenth century family farming had become dependent on expensive machinery and hostage to the national and international grain markets. John Deere's steel plow (invented in 1837) and Cyrus McCormick's horse-drawn mechanical reaper (patented in 1854) boosted levels of grain production. Yet these devices also required farmers to invest an ever-greater proportion of their profits in technology and in labor provided by hired hands. In Titibawassee, Michigan, an immigrant recently arrived from Germany bought land and eastern-made farm machinery, noting proudly that his new steam engine (purchased at a cost of $2135) "has 10 horse power and is arranged so that the power can be used in two ways so that if grinding grain does not pay, I will saw wood." Improved agricultural efficiency meant that the Midwest, both upper and lower, was fast becoming the breadbasket of the nation.

Regional Economies of the South

At mid-century the South Atlantic states encompassed a number of regional economies. Bolstered by the high price of cotton on the world market, slave plantations prospered in the Black Belt, a wide swath of fertile soil stretching west from Georgia. In many areas of the South, planters concentrated their money and energy on cotton, diverting slaves from nonagricultural labor to toil in the fields. During the 1850s, enslaved Virginia sawmill laborers, South Carolina skilled artisans, and Georgia textile mill operatives all found themselves reduced to the status of cotton hands. In some cases, white laborers took their places in mills and workshops. In other parts of the South, slaves combined field work with nonagricultural work. For example, on expansive low-country South Carolina rice plantations, slaves worked in the fields, but they also processed the raw material, preparing it for market.

Even modest farmers shared with the great planters a southern way of life that prized the supremacy of whites over blacks.

Increasingly, northern critics described the South as a land of economic extremes, with wealthy planters enjoying their white-columned mansions while degraded blacks slaved obediently in the fields. The reality was more complicated. Even among whites, there were huge variations in material conditions and daily experiences. A large amount of wealth in land and slaves was concentrated among a small percentage of the white population, and many non-slaveholding whites were tenant farmers, leasing their land, mules, and implements from wealthy planters. In some areas as many as one of five farms was operated by tenant farmers.

At the same time, about half the total southern white population consisted of yeoman farmers, families that owned an average of 50 acres and produced most of what they consumed themselves, with the occasional help of a hired hand (a leased slave or a wage-earning white person). In upcountry Georgia and South Carolina, yeoman farmers maintained local economies that were little affected by the cotton culture of the great planters in the Black Belt. These families grew what they needed: corn for themselves and their livestock and small amounts of cotton that the women spun, wove, and then sewed into clothing. Men and women alike labored in neighborhood networks of exchange, trading farm produce such as milk and eggs for services such as shoemaking and blacksmithing. Nevertheless, even modest farmers shared with the great planters a southern way of life that prized the independence of white households and the supremacy of whites over blacks.

The institution of slavery discouraged immigrants from moving to the rural South in large numbers. German artisans realized that slave labor would undercut their own wages, and Scandinavian farmers understood that they could not compete with large planters in terms of landowning or slave owning. However, the ethnic diversity of southern port cities offered a

Harper's Weekly, January 5, 1867

■ This wood engraving from *Harper's Weekly* suggests the specialized nature of rice cultivation in the low country of South Carolina and Georgia. Rice growers used complex systems of dikes, ditches, and floodgates to grow the grain and threshing mills to process it. Masters assigned their enslaved workers daily tasks; after completing those tasks, men and women could spend time raising crops or tending livestock for their own use.

striking contrast to the countryside, where native-born Protestants predominated. In 1860, 54 percent of all skilled workers and 69 percent of unskilled workers in Mobile, Alabama, were immigrants. On assignment from the *New York Times* in the 1850s, journalist Frederick Law Olmsted noted that in New Orleans, German and Irish workers labored shoulder-to-shoulder with slave artisans, and although white immigrants "were rapidly displacing the slaves in all sorts of work," it was still possible to glimpse an "Irishman waiting on negro masons."

Throughout the slave states, black people continued to challenge the underpinnings of white supremacy. On the backroads of the plantation counties, late at night, poor workers of both races colluded to deprive the planter elite of their ill-gotten gain. Slaves swapped hams pilfered from smokehouses and bags of cotton lifted from storehouses for cash and goods offered by landless whites. In the vicinity of Augusta, Georgia, planters formed the Savannah River Anti-Slave Traffick Association in response to "the extensive and growing traffick unlawfully carried on with slaves by white persons and chiefly by Retailers of Spiritous Liquors."

Southern blacks were a diverse group. In the cities, planters allowed highly skilled slaves to hire themselves out and keep part of the money they earned for themselves. In their pride of craft and in their relative freedom to come and go as they pleased, these people inhabited a world that was neither completely slave nor completely free. Located primarily in the upper South and in the largest towns, communities composed of free people of color supported churches and clandestine schools, mocking the white notion that all black people possessed a childlike temperament and were incapable of caring for themselves. During the 1850s, the population of Virginia's free people of color increased from 54,333 to 58,042; in North Carolina the number increased from 27,463 to 30,463. The reality of southern society was not captured by the simple picture of white prosperity and black enslavement. Not all black people were enslaved field hands, and not all whites were privileged landowners. The widespread mythology masked a more complicated social reality.

A Free Labor Ideology in the North

In reaction to the southern slave system, the rural areas of the Northeast and Mid-Atlantic spawned a potent free labor ideology, which held that workers should reap what they sow, unfettered by legal systems of slavery and indentured servitude. Free labor advocates glorified the family farmer, the sturdy landowner of modest means, the husband and father who labored according to the dictates of the season and owed his soul—and his vote and the land he tilled—to no master. Nevertheless, the reality that sustained this ideal was eroding in the North during the 1850s.

More and more northerners were earning wages by working for bosses, rather than tilling their own land. Faced with competition from Midwestern farmers and burdened by unfavorable growing conditions imposed by rocky soil and a long winter, New Englanders were migrating to nearby towns and mill villages and to the West. By 1860 the region's textile and shoemaking industries were largely mechanized. From New Hampshire to Rhode Island, growing numbers of water-powered factories perched along the fall line, where rivers spilled swiftly out of the foothills and into the coastal plain. The all-white factory workforce included men and women, adults and children, Irish Catholics and native-born Protestants, failed farmers and young men and women eager to leave the uncertain, hardscrabble life of the countryside for the promise of the mill towns.

And yet the process of industrialization was an uneven one. For example, rural shoemaking workers labored at home, producing shoes for merchant capitalists who provided the raw materials and paid them by the piece. In contrast, in the huge new shoe factories of Lynn, Massachusetts, one worker at a Singer sewing machine (adopted by the John Woolredge Company for shoemaking) achieved the same output as 11 people doing the same task by hand in their homes. In the seaport cities, wage earning had become the norm, although many men and women continued to toil in the hope that they might eventually work for themselves. Thus the seamstress aspired to own a dress shop, the hotel waiter a tavern, the journeyman carpenter a small business.

In New York, Boston, Cincinnati, and elsewhere, large numbers of Irish newcomers successfully challenged small numbers of black workers for jobs at the lowest echelons of the labor force. In 1853 fugitive slave Frederick Douglass noted with dismay, "White men are becoming house-servants, cooks and stewards on vessels—at hotels. They are becoming porters, stevedores, hod-carriers, brickmakers, whitewashers and barbers, so that blacks can scarcely find the means of subsistence." Stung by the contempt of Yankee Protestants, impoverished Irish Catholics sought to assert their equality through race. They distanced themselves from African Americans by claiming a white skin as a badge of privilege over the former slaves, a badge of equality with the native born.

Maine textile workers, with their shuttles, pose for a formal portrait around 1860. Although women factory workers developed a collective identity distinct from that of middle-class wives, most young, native-born women eventually married and withdrew from the paid labor force. Many male factory workers were skeptical that women could or should play an effective role in labor organizations such as unions. Nevertheless, women workers in a number of industries, including textiles and shoes, formed labor organizations in the antebellum period.

Although Northerners in general contrasted themselves to the "backward slave South," their region of the country retained elements of unfree labor systems. New Jersey did not emancipate the last of its slaves officially until 1846, and throughout the North, vestiges of slavery lingered through the mid-nineteenth century. As a group of disproportionately poor people, blacks in New England, the Mid-Atlantic, and the Midwest were vulnerable to labor exploitation, including indentured servitude and a system of "apprenticeship" whereby black children were taken from their parents and forced to work for whites. In Delaware, an African American charged with a petty crime could be "disposed as a servant" by court authorities to the highest bidder for a term of seven years.

Many nonslave workers did not receive pay for their labors. As is the case today, wives and mothers throughout the country performed almost all of their work in the home without monetary compensation, although the measure of a white man was rendered more and more in cash terms. On farms and in textile mills such as those of Pawtucket, Rhode Island, children played a key role in the livelihood of individual households but received little or nothing in cash wages. Some members of the white working classes began to condemn "wage slavery," a system that deprived them of what they considered a fair reward for their labors and left them at the mercy of merchant capitalists and factory bosses. These workers charged that they were paid so little by employers, their plight was similar to that of black slaves in the South.

Different regions developed specialized economies. In turn, these regions relied on each other for the production of staple crops and manufactured goods. The result was a national economy. Southern slaves produced the cotton processed in New England textile mills. Midwestern farmers grew the grain that fed eastern consumers. California Forty-Niners discovered the gold that expanded the national currency supply. Yet these patterns of economic interdependence were insufficient to resolve the persistent political question: Which groups of people are entitled to American citizenship, with all the rights and privileges that the term implies?

Individualism Vs. Group Identity

Throughout the country, racist ideas and practices began to exert greater force. People were defined ever more strongly on the basis of their nationality, language, religion, and skin color. They were more and more limited in their legal status and the jobs they could obtain. Degrading images of legally vulnerable groups—blacks, Chinese, Hispanos—became a part of popular culture, in the songs people sang and the pictures they saw in books and magazines. Through these means, native-born Americans of British stock sought to distance themselves from people of color and from immigrants.

Paradoxically, some writers also began to highlight the idea of American individualism during this time. Such authors extolled what they considered to be the universal qualities embedded in American nationhood. They believed that the United States consisted not of distinctive and competing groups, but of a collection of individuals, all bent on pursuing their own self-interest, variously defined. They believed that the "representative" American was ambitious and acquisitive, eager to make more money and buy new things.

Yet not everyone could afford to embrace this optimistic form of individualism. Many who were marginalized found emotional support, and in some cases even political power, in a strong group identity. For example, on the Plains, the Sioux Indians resisted the idea that United States officials could carve up territory and sell land to individual farmers at the expense of a people that pursued the buffalo across artificial political boundaries. During negotiations at Fort Laramie in 1851, Black Hawk, a leader of the Oglala

TABLE 13-1

Nativity of Residents of the Boston Area, 1860

Country of Birth	Middlesex County	Norfolk County	Suffolk County
United States	166,126	83,693	125,439
England	4,273	2,494	4,472
Ireland	38,098	19,138	48,095
Scotland	1,272	607	1,440
Wales	28	34	61
Germany	629	1,159	1,290
France	187	133	397
Spain	39	9	59
Portugal	19	62	38
Belgium	5	6	19
Holland	67	17	177
Turkey	4	1	6
Italy	29	26	258
Austria	24	21	44
Switzerland	28	55	125
Russia	4	4	38
Norway	28	11	68
Denmark	26	18	97
Sweden	98	41	259
Prussia	150	103	744
Sardinia	1	1	64
Greece	3	3	10
China	9	5	4
Asia	19	13	29
Africa	----	2	20
British America	4,784	1,563	7,503
Mexico	6	1	2
South America	24	18	44
West Indies	59	27	149
Sandwich Islands	15	9	10
Atlantic Islands	39	5	260
Bavaria	33	246	250
Baden	73	331	663
Europe[a]	133	6	165
Hesse	14	32	107
Nassau	----	4	18
Poland	----	2	78
Wurttemberg	16	38	142
Australia	1	----	10
Pacific Islands	1	7	8
Other countries	----	5	38
Total foreign	50,238	26,257	67,261
Total population	216,354	109,950	192,700

[a] Not specified.

Source: Oscar Handlin, *Boston's Immigrants* (New York: Atheneum, 1972), p. 245.

Sioux, condemned the whites with his understatement, "You have split my land and I don't like it." In contrast to the Plains Indians, who wanted no role in American politics, African Americans and white women strove for full citizenship rights. These groups looked forward to the day when each person was accorded the same rights and was free to pursue his or her own talents and ambitions.

Putting into Practice Ideas of Social Inferiority

Everywhere, European American men sought to achieve or preserve the most stable, well-paying, and appealing jobs for themselves. By promoting ideas related to the inferiority of African Americans, Hispanos, and immigrants, white men could justify barring these groups from the rights of citizenship and landownership as well as from nonmenial kinds of employment. In Texas, Mexican leader Juan Cortina condemned Anglo interlopers whose "brimful of laws" facilitated the seizure of *Tejanos'* land by U.S. law enforcement agents and the courts. In California, U.S. officials justified the exclusion of blacks, Indians, Chinese, and the poorest Mexicans from citizenship rights by claiming that members of these groups were nonwhite or, in the words of one state judge writing in 1854, "not of white blood." (Of course, the concept of "white blood" has no scientific basis because the different blood types—A, B, AB, and O—are found among all peoples.)

The precarious social status of various groups was revealed in patterns of their work.

The precarious social status of various groups was revealed in patterns of their work. In California, white men pursued opportunities on farms and in factories while increasing numbers of Chinese men labored as laundrymen and domestic servants. Indians toiled as field hands under white supervision. In rural Texas, Anglos established plantations and ranches while more and more Mexicans worked as *vaqueros* (cowboys), shepherds, sidewalk vendors, and freighters. In Massachusetts mill towns, white men and women served as the forefront of an industrial labor force while many African Americans of both sexes and all ages were confined to work in kitchens and outdoors as sweepers, cart drivers, and hawkers of goods.

Despite the divergent regional economies that shaped them, emerging ideologies of racial inferiority were strikingly similar. European Americans persisted in focusing on physical appearances, and they stereotyped all Chinese, Mexicans, and African Americans as promiscuous, crafty, "degraded," and intellectually inferior to whites. They characterized these groups as "cheap labor" who got by with little money: the Chinese supposedly could subsist on rice, Mexicans on beans and *tortillas,* blacks on the "fatback" of the pig. Such prejudices, in places as diverse as Boston, San Antonio, and San Francisco, prevented many people of color from reaching the limits of their own talents in mid–nineteenth-century America.

"A Teeming Nation"—America in Literature

Ideas about ethnic and racial difference coexisted with notions of American individualism, which stressed forms of universal equality. The variety of voices that gave expression to the national ideals of personal striving and ambition suggested the growth, energy, and vitality of the United States in the 1850s. In the Northeast, writers such as Ralph Waldo Emerson, Henry David Thoreau, Herman Melville, and Walt Whitman each crafted a unique writing style. At the same time, these men promoted a robust sensibility attuned to the challenges posed by the rigors of both the external world of natural beauty and the inner world of the spirit.

Some forms of literature offered an explicit critique of American materialism, with its love of things. According to Emerson, people were too concerned about material possessions; as he put it, things were "in the saddle," riding everyone. During the 1850s, Thoreau's work became more explicitly focused on nature. In his book *Walden* (1854), he described swimming in the Massachusetts pond of the same name: "In such transparent and seemingly bottomless water, reflecting the clouds, I seemed to be floating through the air as in a balloon." An apprecia-

George Caleb Bingham, *Raftsmen Playing Cards*, 1847. The Saint Louis Art Museum, Ezra H. Linley Fund

■ Just as American writers explored questions of national identity, American artists portrayed everyday scenes related to the vitality of American enterprise and democracy. This painting, **Raftsmen Playing Cards** (1847), was one from George Caleb Bingham's series of pictures of Missouri rivermen. A contemporary observer speculated that the youth on the right is "a mean and cunning scamp, probably the black sheep of a good family, and a sort of vagabond idler." Large rivers such as the Missouri and Mississippi remained powerful symbols of freedom in the American imagination.

tion of the wonders of nature—wonders that could be felt and tasted, as well as seen—amounted to a powerful force of democratization; anyone and everyone could participate. In turn, Thoreau actively supported the abolition of slavery; his love of nature formed the foundation of his belief in the universal dignity of all people in general and the cause of freedom for black people in particular.

In contrast, other writers celebrated busy-ness, whether in the field or workshop. In the introduction to his book of poetry titled *Leaves of Grass* (1855), Walt Whitman captured the restlessness of a people on the move: "Here is not merely a nation but a teeming nation of nations. Here is action untied from strings necessarily blind to particulars and details magnificently moving in vast masses." To Whitman, the expansiveness of the American landscape mirrored the American soul, "the largeness and generosity of the spirit of the citizen." His sensuous "Song of Myself" constituted an anthem for all Americans poised, gloriously diverse in their individuality (and their sexuality), to exploit the infinite possibilities of both body and spirit: "I dote on myself, there is a lot of me and all so luscious."

Challenges to Individualism

Many men and women remained skeptical of—and, in some cases, totally estranged from—the wondrous possibilities inherent in Whitman's phrase, "Me, Me going in for my chances." In northern cities, individualism spawned the kind of creative genius necessary for technological innovation and dynamic economic change, but it had little meaning for Native Americans

Professor Howe on the Subordination of Women

Antebellum southern elites prized what they called "natural" hierarchical social relations: the authority of fathers and husbands over daughters and wives, parents over children, rich over poor, and whites over blacks. According to slaveholders, clergy, and scholars, these relationships provided social stability and ensured that the weak and dependent would receive care from the rich and powerful. In July 1850, George Howe, professor of biblical literature at the Theological Seminary at Columbia, South Carolina, addressed the graduating class of a private women's academy. Howe suggested that the roles of women (elite white women) were enduring and never-changing.

The Endowments, Position and Education of Woman. An Address Delivered Before the Hemans and Sigourney Societies of the Female High School at Limestone Springs

The duties of life to all human beings are arduous, its objects are noble—each stage of its progress is preparatory to some other stage, and the whole a preparation to an interminable existence, upon which, in one sense, we are hereafter to enter, and in another, have already entered. Others may slightly regard the employments, trials and joys of the school girl. I am disposed to put on them a higher value. Our wives, sisters, and our mothers were in the same position yesterday. You will occupy a like [position] with them tomorrow. Whatever of virtue, of patient endurance, of poignant suffering, of useful labor, of noble impulse, of generous endeavor, of influence exerted on society for its good, has been exhibited in their example, in a few short years we shall see exhibited also in yours.

To woman, . . . there must be ascribed . . . acuteness in her powers of perception, . . . instincts . . . and emotions. When these are powerfully excited there is a wonderful vigor and determination of will, and a ready discovery of expedients to accomplish her wishes. She has readier sympathies, her fountain of tears is nearer the surface, but her emotions may not be so constant and permanent as those of man. She has greater readiness and tact, purer and more noble and unselfish desires and impulses, and a higher degree of veneration for the virtuous and exalted, and when she has found the way of truth, a heart more constant and more susceptible to all those influences which come from above. To the gentleness and quiet of her nature, to its affection and sympathy, that religion which pronounces its benediction on the peace-makers and the merciful, which recommends to them the ornament of a meek and quiet spirit, which, in the sight of the Lord, is of a great price, addresses itself with more force and greater attraction than it addresses man. Born to lean upon others,

in the West, most of whom were desperately seeking a collective response to new threats in the form of cattle ranchers and the U.S. Cavalry. On the Great Plains, groups such as the Mandan and Pawnee performed ceremonies and rituals that celebrated kinship and village life above the individual.

African Americans in the North forged a strong sense of group identity. Though they rejected notions of white people's "racial" superiority, blacks had little choice but to think of themselves as a group separate and distinct from whites. Their sense of group solidarity was manifested in everyday life and in political rhetoric and action. In northern cities, blacks took in boarders and joined mutual-aid societies in order to affirm the collective interests of the larger black community. In contrast, well-to-do whites were increasingly emphasizing the sanctity of the nuclear family, composed solely of parents and children. Black leaders criticized the racist laws and ideas that affected the lives of black men, women, and children. For example, the charismatic Boston preacher Maria Stewart denounced the twin evils of racial and gender prejudice for condemning all black women to a life of menial labor: "How long shall the fair daughters of Africa be compelled to bury their minds and talents beneath a load of iron pots and kettles? The [white] Americans have practised nothing but head-work these 200 years, and we have done their drudgery."

Some groups of women embraced a collective identity of womanhood, although the definition of that identity took several forms. For example, in the North, writers such as Catharine Beecher articulated a vision of female self-sacrifice fueled by family obligations and emotional relationships. Beecher declared that self-sacrifice formed the "grand law of the sys-rather than to stand independently by herself, and to confide in an arm stronger than hers, her mind turns more readily to the higher power which brought her into being . . . .

Providence, then, and her own endowments mark out the proper province of woman. In some cases she may strive for the mastery, but to rule with the hand of power was never designed for her. When she thus unsexes herself she is despised and detested by man and woman alike. England's Queen Victoria at the present moment, if not more feared, is far more beloved in the quiet of her domestic life, than Elizabeth was, the most feared of her female Sovereigns.

Howe ends his address by drawing an implicit comparison between the South and the North. Like many Southerners, he associated the North with labor radicalism, abolitionism, and challenges to the "natural" position of women.

When women go about haranguing promiscuous assemblies of men, lecturing in public, either on infidelity or religion, on slavery, on war or peace—when they meet together in conventions and pass resolutions on grave questions of State—when they set themselves up to manufacture a public opinion for their own advantage and exaltation—when they meet together in organized bodies and pass resolutions about the "rights of woman," and claim for her a voice and a vote in the appoint-

Louisa McCord was the member of an elite slaveholding family in South Carolina. She was an ardent supporter of slavery. Though an accomplished essayist herself, she believed that white women should remain subordinate to their fathers and husbands. In 1856 she wrote, "The positions of women and children are in truth as essentially states of bondage as any other, the differences being in degree, not kind." She added that the "true definition of slavery" thus "applies equally to the position of women in the most civilized and enlightened countries."

ment of civil rulers, and in the government, whether of Church or State, she is stepping forth from her rightful sphere and becomes disgusting and unlovely, just in proportion as she assumes to be a man. ∎

Source: George Howe, *The Endowments, Position and Education of Woman. An Address Delivered Before the Hemans and Sigourney Societies of the Female High School at Limestone Springs,* July 23, 1850 (Columbia, SC: I.C. Morgan, 1850), pp. 5, 9, 10–11.

tem" by which women should live their lives. Through poetry, short stories, and novels for popular audiences, other women writers posited an alternative to the world of masculine daring and individualism.

Informed by religious devotion and sustained by labors of love in the home, this female world offered an alternative to the individualism necessary to profit-seeking, whether on the family farm or in the bank or textile mill. As consumers of store-bought food and goods, antebellum housewives believed they were deprived of the satisfactions supposedly enjoyed by their grandmothers and associated with maintaining a colonial household—churning butter, spinning flax, making candles, and weaving cloth. Yet middle-class women believed they could take pride in rearing virtuous citizens and caring for overworked husbands. Sarah Willis Parton (Fanny Fern) cautioned her readers in a series of sketches published in 1853 (*Fern Leaves from Fanny's Portfolio*) that marriage is "the hardest way on earth of getting a living. You never know when your work is done."

Well-to-do white women in the Northeast yearned to be productive and useful although they stood outside the cash-based market economy. Nevertheless, other groups of women cherished different kinds of aspirations. Organizers of the country's first conference devoted to the status of women, the Seneca Falls Convention held in upstate New York in 1848, derived inspiration from the abolitionist movement and protested the efforts of white men to exclude women from formal participation in it. Elizabeth Cady Stanton and Lucretia Mott recalled the humiliation they felt when they found themselves relegated to a women's gallery at the World Anti-Slavery Convention in London in 1840. In their demands for women's rights they

Bettmann/CORBIS

■ Isabella Baumfree was born into slavery in New York State in 1797. Thirty years later she escaped from bondage and became a preacher. In 1843 she changed her name to Sojourner Truth. A powerful orator, she spoke on behalf of abolitionism and urged white women's-rights activists to embrace the cause of enslaved women. Truth sold small cards, called *cartes de visite,* to support herself. On this card, a portrait taken in 1864, she notes that she must sell her image ("the Shadow") to make a living.

linked the plight of the slave with the plight of free women, arguing that white men exploited and denigrated members of both groups. Stanton, Mott, and others received crucial support from African American leaders such as Sojourner Truth and Frederick Douglass.

Delegates to Seneca Falls (including Douglass) approved a document called the "Declaration of Sentiments," modeled after the Declaration of Independence: "When in the course of human events . . . . We hold these truths to be self-evident: that all men and women are created equal." This group of women thus claimed for themselves a revolutionary heritage and all the rights and privileges of citizenship: to own property in their own names, to vote, to attend schools of higher learning, and to participate "in the various trades, professions, and commerce." In the process they expressed at least an implied kinship with the freedom fighters of France, Italy, and Germany who also launched struggles for self-determination during the fateful year of 1848.

Many women, including enslaved workers throughout the South and hard-pressed needleworkers toiling in cramped New York City tenements, could not devote themselves full time to the care of hearth and home, nor could they aspire to a career of public agitation. In her autobiographical novel, *Our Nig; or, Sketches from the Life of a Free Black, in a Two-Story White House, North* (1859), Harriet Wilson wrote bitterly of the fate of women such as her mother, a woman "early deprived of parental guardianship, far removed from relatives . . . left to guide her tiny boat over life's surges alone and inexperienced." Like the book's main character, Alfrado, Wilson herself had suffered at the hands of tyrannical white women employers, but at the end of the story Alfrado achieves a measure of dignity and independence for herself by setting up a small business. She thus offered an explicit challenge to both the arrogance of propertied white men and the homebound sentimentality of wealthy white women.

In sum, there was no single, transcendent American identity in the mid-nineteenth century. And yet, critiques of the dominant culture could at times uphold its lofty ideals while condemning everyday reality. In his 1852 speech "The Meaning of July Fourth for the Negro," delivered in Rochester, New York, Frederick Douglass took the country to task for failing to live up to the principles embodied in the Declaration of Independence: "Stand by those principles," he exhorted his listeners, "at whatever cost." His words foreshadowed a great war.

The Paradox of Southern Political Power

Slavery needed to expand to survive. Decades of intensive cultivation were exhausting the cotton fields in the South. The planter elite was counting on the admission of new territories as slave states to preserve their threatened power in Congress. To slave owners, northern-sponsored efforts to block their expansion amounted to a death sentence for all that the white South held dear. In defense of the slave system, the white South had to mount a strong offense or die.

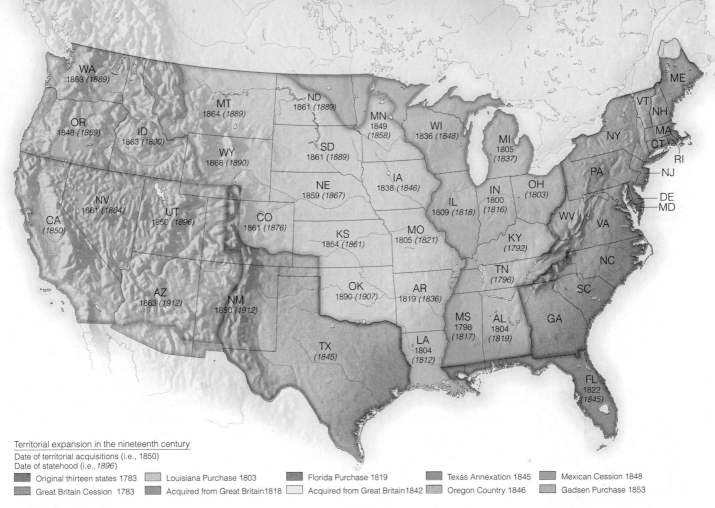

Territorial expansion in the nineteenth century

Date of territorial acquisitions (i.e., 1850)
Date of statehood (i.e., *1896*)

Original thirteen states 1783	Louisiana Purchase 1803	Florida Purchase 1819	Texas Annexation 1845	Mexican Cession 1848
Great Britain Cession 1783	Acquired from Great Britain 1818	Acquired from Great Britain 1842	Oregon Country 1846	Gadsen Purchase 1853

■ **MAP 13.1**

TERRITORIAL EXPANSION IN THE NINETEENTH CENTURY As a result of the Mexican War (1846–1848),
the United States won the territory west of Texas by conquest. In 1853, James Gadsden, U.S. ambassador to
Mexico, received congressional approval to pay Mexico $15 million for 55,000 square miles in present-day
southern Arizona and New Mexico. That year marked the end of U.S. continental expansion.

In the early 1850s, proslavery forces maintained firm control over all branches of the
federal government. Nevertheless, southern planters felt increasingly defensive as the country expanded westward. In 1850 a writer for *DeBow's Review,* a mouthpiece for the planter class,
offered a peculiar combination of bravado and anxiety. Boasting of the South's agricultural
capacity and resources so integral to "the welfare of humanity at large," the writer nonetheless claimed that the region's "undisturbed progress" depended on "a firm adherence to the
compromises of the constitution" and warned against "the abolition excitement," which would
necessarily upset the delicate balance between slave and free states.

Gradually, this tension between southern strength and southern fears led to the fraying
and then unraveling of the Jacksonian American party system, which had relied on a truce
maintained between Whigs and Democrats on the issue of slavery. A new party, the Republicans, fused the democratic idealism and economic self-interest of native-born Northerners
in such a powerful way that white Southerners believed that the institution of slavery was in
danger of succumbing to the Yankee onslaught. And so a clash of ideas gradually slipped out
of the confines of the polling place and into the realm of armed conflict.

The Party System in Disarray

In 1848, eight years after the appearance of the antislavery Liberty party, cracks in the second two-
party system (which pitted the Whigs against the Democrats) intensified with the founding of
the Free-Soil party. Free-Soilers challenged the prevailing notion that the Whigs and Democrats

could continue to smooth over the question of slavery in the territories with a variety of patchwork policies and piecemeal compromises. The Free-Soil platform promoted a forthright no-slavery-in-the-territories policy and favored the Wilmot Proviso (introduced in Congress in 1846), which would have banned slavery from all land acquired as a result of the Mexican War. In the presidential election of 1848, the Free-Soil party nominated former President Martin Van Buren, Democrat of New York. At the same time, Free-Soilers extended their appeal to the Whig party by supporting federal aid for internal improvements, free western homesteads for settlers, and protective tariffs for northern manufacturers.

TABLE 13-2			
The Election of 1848			
Candidate	Political Party	Popular Vote	Electoral Vote
Zachary Taylor	Whig	1,360,967	163
Lewis Cass	Democratic	1,222,342	127
Martin Van Buren	Free-Soil	291,263	----

Nevertheless, the two major parties persisted in avoidance politics. The Democrats chose General Lewis Cass as their standard-bearer, a man known as the "father of popular sovereignty" because he favored allowing citizens of new states to decide for themselves whether to permit slavery within their borders. The Whigs put forth General Zachary Taylor, although the Louisiana slaveholder and Mexican War veteran had never held elected office. Still, Taylor managed to parlay his military record into a close win in the fall of 1848. Slaveholders were concerned by the support that the Free-Soiler Van Buren had garnered among Democrats in New York State. He had drawn enough votes from the Democrats to allow the Whig Taylor to capture the election, and Northerners in general were demonstrating dissatisfaction with both the Whigs and the Democrats.

In 1849 Southerners confronted a disturbing reality. Although slave owners controlled the presidency and the Supreme Court and outnumbered the North in the House of Representatives, the North maintained the upper hand in the Senate. Moreover, California's application for statehood in 1849 raised the specter of an unbalanced federal system consisting of 16 free states and 15 slave states. And the abolitionist threat appeared in other guises as well: the territories of Utah and New Mexico apparently preparing to ban slavery once they became states, abolitionists clamoring for the immediate emancipation of all slaves, and black men and women, including former slave Harriet Tubman, working with abolitionists in the upper South and the North to facilitate the escape of slaves through a network of safe stops called the Underground Railroad. The "railroad" consisted of northerners, white and black, who sheltered fugitives from southern slavery in their flight to the North or, in some instances, to Canada.

The Compromise of 1850

Against this backdrop of sectional controversy, Congress debated the terms under which California would enter the Union in 1850. In their physical demeanor, the three principals in the Senate debate revealed that the effort to placate those on both sides of the slavery question was on the verge of exhaustion. John C. Calhoun, dying of tuberculosis, argued that the North must concede that the South had the right to its own property, regardless of whether that property took the form of land or human beings. Together, the frail Henry Clay, age 73, and Daniel Webster, 68 years old and racked with disease, sought to wring concessions from both sides.

A young Democratic senator from Illinois, Stephen Douglas, helped to cobble together a complicated agreement that proved workable enough in the short run but only prolonged the showdown over slavery. Under the Compromise of 1850, California would enter the Union as a free state that year. New Mexico and Utah would eventually submit the slavery question to voters and thus put the idea of popular sovereignty to a practical test. The federal government would abolish the slave trade in Washington, D.C. (a move that did not affect the status of slaves already living there), and shore up the Fugitive Slave law of 1793 with a new, harsher measure.

The Fugitive Slave Law of 1850 essentially did away with the notion of the North as free territory, for it required local and federal law enforcement agents to retrieve runaways no matter where they sought refuge in the United States. Blacks were denied a trial or the right to testify on their own behalf. Fugitive slave commissioners earned $10 for each runaway they returned to a claimant. By compelling ordinary citizens to aid in the capture of alleged fugitives, the law brought the issue of slavery to the doorstep of northern whites. In the fall of 1850, Millard Fillmore, who had assumed the presidency in July of that year after Taylor died in office, signed the bill.

TABLE 13-3			
The Election of 1852			
Candidate	Political Party	Popular Vote	Electoral Vote
Franklin Pierce	Democratic	1,607,510	254
Winfield Scott	Whig	1,386,942	42
John P. Hale	Free-Soil	155,210	----

Despite these dramatic events, the presidential campaign of 1852 was a lackluster affair. The Democrats nominated an unknown lawyer, Franklin Pierce. Although he hailed from New Hampshire, Pierce supported slavery. The Whigs turned their back on President Fillmore and chose as their nominee General Winfield Scott, who had gained fame during the Mexican War of 1848. Yet the Whigs split into regional factions during the election; Northerners resented Scott's support of the Fugitive Slave Law, and Southerners doubted Scott's devotion to slavery. This split foreshadowed the end of national political parties and the emergence of regional parties, an ominous development indeed.

Expansionism and Political Upheaval

The interests of southern planters affected not only domestic politics, but debates and policies related to foreign affairs as well. Even as Congress was heatedly discussing the Compromise of 1850, Southerners were contemplating ways to extend their reach across and even beyond the continental United States. They wanted to find new fresh, fertile lands for cotton cultivation, and, they hoped, to incorporate those lands into the United States. Such expansion would also help to bolster the political power of slaveowners in Congress by someday adding new slave states to the Union.

In 1850 the United States and Great Britain signed the Clayton–Bulwer Treaty, agreeing that neither country would seek to control the rights to any canal spanning the Panama–Nicaragua isthmus. In 1848 President Polk had made a gesture to buy Cuba from Spain, an offer that was rebuffed but one that did not discourage two privately financed expeditions of proslavery Americans from making forays into Cuba in an effort to seize the island by force on behalf of the United States. In 1854 the American ambassadors to Great Britain, France, and Spain met in Ostend, Belgium, and issued a statement declaring that, if Spain would not sell Cuba, the United States would be justified in taking control of the island. According to the Americans, the Monroe Doctrine gave license to the United States to rid the western Hemisphere of European colonial powers. Noting that two of the three ambassadors hailed from slave states, abolitionists charged that the Ostend Manifesto was just one more ploy to extend the power of slaveholders throughout the northern hemisphere.

In 1855 a young proslavery American adventurer, Tennessee-born William Walker, gathered a band of 58 mercenaries and managed to capture Granada, Nicaragua. Declaring himself president of Nicaragua, Walker encouraged the institution of slavery and won U.S. recognition for his regime in 1856. Walker was driven out of the country a year later, but his arrogance and bold move helped to set the stage for the Nicaraguan anti-American movement that would resurface in the twentieth century.

Political maneuvering and military might combined to advance the march of European Americans across the American continent, fueling popular notions of "manifest destiny," as if expansion were preordained by God and not furthered by rifles and bayonets. In 1853, Congress authorized the Gadsden Purchase, 30 million acres of land within the present-day states of New Mexico and Arizona. But, at least in a commercial sense, expansion failed to stop at the edge of the continental United States. Americans saw the Pacific Ocean as a trade route and East Asia as a trading partner. Commodore Matthew Perry commanded a fleet of U.S. Navy ships that steamed into Tokyo Harbor. The treaty Perry helped arrange with Japan in 1854 protected American whaling ships, sailors, and merchants in that part of the world and opened the door to an increase in trade later in the century.

By the mid-1850s the uniting of the continent into what would eventually become the 48 contiguous states was a source of sectional tension as well as national pride. Fewer and fewer Northerners supported what they considered proslavery charades, so-called legislative compromises. And the territory of Nebraska, poised on the brink of statehood, forced national lawmakers to confront again the political problem of the expansion of slavery. Once more Senator Douglas from Illinois stepped in to fill the breach left by the dying generation of great compromisers. Committed to the idea of a transcontinental railroad traversing the Nebraska Territory, Douglas adhered to the traditional (if increasingly unlikely) goal of mutual accommodation between North and South, free and slave states, but he believed that such accommodation demanded a constant process of negotiation and flexibility on both sides. Thus he argued that the gigantic territory be split into two new states, Kansas and Nebraska, whose respective voters would decide the issue of slavery for themselves. His proposal necessitated that part of the Missouri Compromise of 1820, the part that forbade slavery above the 36–30 line, would have to be repealed.

The Kansas–Nebraska Act became law in 1854. The Act enraged northern Free-Soilers, forced to watch the dismantling of the 1820 agreement. They became convinced that what they called the Slave Power Conspiracy would stop at nothing until slavery overran the entire nation. The measure also had a profound effect on the Plains Indians, for it deprived them of fully one-half the land they had been granted by treaty. Specifically, the act wrought havoc on the lives of Ponca, Pawnee, Arapaho, and Cheyenne on the southern and central plains. European American settlers poured into the region, provoking Indian attacks. In September 1855, 600 American troops staged a retaliatory raid against an Indian village, Blue Water, in Nebraska, killing 85 Sioux and leading to an escalation in violence between Indians and settlers in the area. Among the young warriors involved in these battles was Crazy Horse, who became a famous leader of the Sioux in the coming years.

In their impatience with the two major parties, Free-Soilers were not alone in the early 1850s. The American party, founded in 1852, departed from the bland consensus embodied by the Whigs and Democrats and built its movement on nativism—the belief that Americans must rule America—in the North and South. The party explicitly condemned the growing political influence of immigrants, especially Roman Catholics. It derived its nickname, the Know-Nothings, from members' habit of claiming "I know nothing" when asked about their organization. With its ranks filled with former Whigs, the party tapped into a deep wellspring of resentment against immigrants on the part of urban, native-born workers as well as Protestant farmers anxious about retaining their influence in public affairs. Candidates for office who appealed to Irish voters ran the risk of incurring the Know-Nothing charge that Catholic priests were in league with "the worst class of American politicians, designing demagogues, selfish office-seekers, and bad men, calling themselves Democrats and 'Old Line Whigs'!" During the early 1850s, the Know-Nothings revealed that anxiety over immigration was not limited to northeastern cities; the loosely organized party was responsible for bloody clashes—native born against newcomer—in Baltimore, Louisville, St. Louis, and New Orleans.

The Republican Alliance

The rapid rise of the Know-Nothings further indicated that voters had grown disillusioned with the two-party system. Confirmation of that fact appeared on March 20, 1854, in the small town of Ripon, Wisconsin, when a group of disaffected Whigs created a new party called the Republicans. One core idea informed the party: that slavery must not be allowed to spread into the western territories. From this base the Republicans built an organization so powerful that it would capture the presidency within six years.

The genius of the Republican party resided in its ability to create and maintain an alliance between groups with vastly different goals. Now forced by the Fugitive Slave Act of 1850 to serve

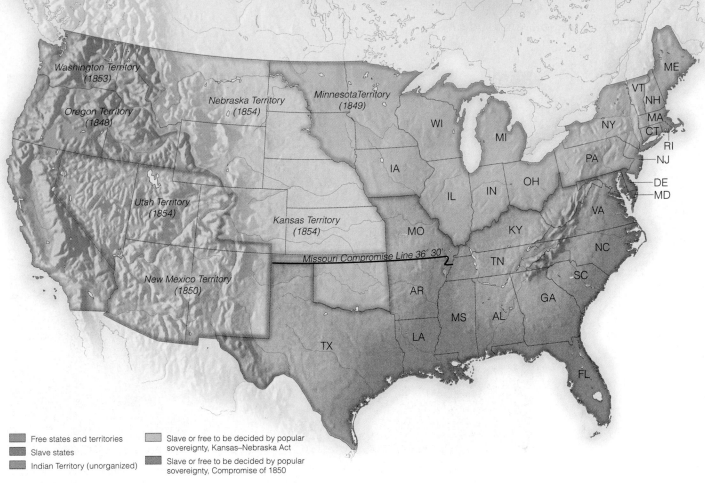

Free states and territories

Slave states

Indian Territory (unorganized)

Slave or free to be decided by popular sovereignty, Kansas–Nebraska Act

Slave or free to be decided by popular sovereignty, Compromise of 1850

■ **MAP 13.2**

THE KANSAS–NEBRASKA ACT, 1854 Stephen A. Douglas, senator from Illinois, proposed the Kansas–Nebraska Act of 1854. Douglas hoped to ensure that any transcontinental railroad route would run through Illinois and benefit his constituents. To secure southern support for the measure, proponents of the bill repealed the Missouri Compromise of 1850. As a result of the act, settlers displaced many Plains Indians from their lands. In the mid–1850s, the territory of Kansas became engulfed in an internal civil war that pitted supporters of slavery against abolitionists.

slaveholders (by returning runaway slaves to them) and fearful of the potential of slaveholding Southerners to capture their party, some northern Democrats cast their lot with the Republicans. From the ranks of antislavery men—the long-suffering adherents of the Liberty and Free-Soil parties—came another wing of the Republicans. These party members openly proclaimed their belief in the power of the federal government to halt the relentless march of slavery and ensure that, throughout the land, free soil would be tilled by free labor, free men and women.

Yet antislavery Republicans were by no means unified on major issues apart from the extension of slavery. Many Northerners were willing to tolerate slavery as long as it could be confined to the southern states; they cared little or nothing for the rights of black people, slave or free. And in fact, in the Midwest, Republicans saw no contradiction in calling for the end of slavery in one breath and for the end of black migration to the area in the next. Likewise, members of various northern white working classes feared the encroachment of slavery into the free states. These white men believed that, given the chance, black people would gladly abandon the South in favor of economic opportunities in the North. As job competitors, blacks would force whites to work for less money than they were accustomed to, or would push whites out of jobs altogether—at least those were the fears of white men who sought to block all blacks from moving north. For these reasons white Republicans could dislike slavery as an institution and at the same time approve of the discriminatory legislation that limited the economic and geographical mobility of black people.

George Caleb Bingham, *County Election*, 1851–1852. The Saint Louis Art Museum, Gift of Bank of America

■ In addition to his river scenes, George Caleb Bingham painted a series of pictures celebrating local politics. Titled *County Election,* this piece was completed in 1851–1852. Bingham had lost a campaign to become a congressional representative from Missouri in 1846. This scene suggests that election day is an opportunity for the men of the county to come together and eat and drink, swap information, and close deals.

Many northern merchants supported the Republicans' claims for the power of the federal government above that of the states. Still, some of the wealthiest and most influential in the cities of Philadelphia and New York maintained overtly racist views and retained cultural ties with southern slaveholders. Juxtaposed to these groups of whites were northern blacks, like those in Boston who in 1856 offered only limited support for the new party: "We do not pledge ourselves to go further with the Republicans than the Republicans will go with us," they vowed.

From the ranks of the newly formed Illinois state Republican party emerged a formidable leader capable of bringing all of these factions together. Born in 1809 in Kentucky, Abraham Lincoln came from a modest background and followed a checkered path into Illinois Whig politics: from youthful plowhand and log-splitter, to local postmaster and county surveyor, and finally self-taught lawyer and member of the state legislature (1834–1842). Although his 6-foot 4-inch frame and humble background drew ridicule from wealthy people—a Philadelphia lawyer described him as "a tall rawly boned, ungainly back woodsman, with coarse, ill-fitting clothing"—Lincoln made good use of his oratorical gifts and political ambition in promoting the principles of free soil.

The presidential election of 1856 revealed the full dimension of the national political crisis. The Democrats nominated James Buchanan, a "dough-face" (i.e., proslavery Northerner) from Pennsylvania, with John Breckinridge of Tennessee as his running mate. In their platform they took pains to extol the virtue of sectional compromise on the slavery issue, by this time a very unpopular position. Meanwhile, the enfeebled Whigs could do little but stand by helplessly and declare as their "fundamental article of political faith, an absolute necessity for avoiding geographical parties," another plank decidedly out of favor with a growing number of voters. The Know-Nothings cast their lot with former President Millard Fillmore. They offered voters little more than the ringing declaration that only "*native*-born citizens should be selected for all state, federal, and municipal offices of government employment, in preference to all others."

Drawing on former members of the Free-Soil and Whig parties, respectively, the Republicans nominated John C. Frémont of California for president and William Dayton of New Jersey for vice president. Their platform stated in no uncertain terms the party's opposition to the extension of slavery, as well as Republican support for a transcontinental railroad and other federally sponsored internal improvements such as roads and harbors. The document also included the bold, noble rhetoric—in favor of "the blessings of liberty" and against "tyrannical and unconstitutional laws"—that would be the hallmark of the Republican party in the decade to come.

Despite his nickname "Old Fogy," Democratic candidate James Buchanan won the election. Nevertheless, the fact that the Republican Frémont carried 11 of the 16 northern states boded well for the Republican party and ill for the slaveholders' union. In Illinois, Frémont had benefited from the tireless campaigning of Abraham Lincoln, who electrified ever-growing crowds of people with the declaration that "the Union must be preserved in the purity of its principles as well as in the integrity of its territorial parts."

TABLE 13-4			
The Election of 1856			
Candidate	Political Party	Popular Vote	Electoral Vote
James Buchanan	Democratic	1,832,955	174
John C. Frémont	Republican	1,339,932	114
Millard Fillmore	American	871,731	8

The Deepening Conflict over Slavery

Only a small subset of Americans—adult white men—participated directly in the formation of new political parties that set the terms for congressional debates over territorial expansion and slavery. Nevertheless, during the 1850s, increasing numbers of ordinary people were drawn into the escalating conflict over the South's "peculiar institution" as some Northerners mounted concerted challenges, violent as well as peaceful, to the Fugitive Slave Law. The western territory of Kansas became a bloody battleground as abolitionists and proslavery forces fought for control of the new state government.

Sites of struggle over the slavery issue included the streets of Boston, the Supreme Court of the United States, political rallies in Illinois, and a federal arsenal in Harpers Ferry, Virginia. No longer would the opposing sides confine their disagreements to congressional debates over the admission of new states. Nor would words be the only weapons. The country was rushing headlong into nationwide armed conflict.

The Rising Tide of Violence

The Fugitive Slave Law of 1850 caused fear and alarm among many Northerners. In response to the measure, some African Americans, hiding in northern cities, fled to Canada, often with the aid of conductors on the Underground Railroad. In the summer of 1854 the National Emigration Convention of Colored Peoples drew more than 100 black leaders to Cleveland, where they debated the merits of migration to Canada, the West Indies, Central and South America, or Liberia in Africa.

Abolitionists, white and black, made dramatic rescue attempts on behalf of men and women sought by their self-proclaimed southern owners. In Boston in 1851, a waiter named Shadrach Minkins (he called himself Frederick Jenkins) was seized at work and charged with running away from a Virginia slaveholder. During a court hearing to determine the merits of the case, a group of blacks stormed in, disarmed the startled authorities, and, in the words of a sympathetic observer, "with a dexterity worthy of the Roman gladiators, snatched the trembling prey of the slavehunters, and conveyed him in triumph to the streets of Boston." Shadrach Minkins found safety in Montreal, Canada, and a Boston jury refused to convict his lawyers, who had been accused of masterminding his escape. The spectacular public rescue of Minkins, and other such attempts, both successful and unsuccessful, throughout the North, brought the issue of slavery into the realm of public performance in northern towns and cities.

In Cincinnati, Ohio, a group of African American men met to press demands for equal rights and to declare that "we sympathize deeply with the man *Shadrach* of Boston, who fled from the American Fiery Furnace, to its contrast—the snows of Canada." Throughout the North, African American conventions responded to the slavecatchers' provocation, providing a forum not only for leaders such as Frederick Douglass of New York and John M. Langston of Ohio but also for barbers, farmers, and other workers.

Black women remained conspicuous for their absence from these formal conventions. Delegates to the meeting in Troy, New York, in 1855 cast out the lone woman in attendance, Barbery Anna Stewart; several men objected to her presence "on the ground that this is not a Woman's Rights Convention." Nevertheless, black and white women working together became prominent supporters of the abolitionist cause. Though unable to vote, they made public speeches and petitioned politicians, and they coordinated local boycotts of products made by slave labor.

Gradually, the war of words over slavery cascaded out of small-circulation abolitionist periodicals and into the consciousness of a nation. In particular, author Harriet Beecher Stowe managed to wed politics and sentiment in a most compelling way. Her novel *Uncle Tom's Cabin* (1852) sold more than 300,000 copies within 10 months and a million copies over the next seven years. The book, originally serialized in a magazine, *The National Era,* introduced large numbers of Northerners to the sufferings of an enslaved couple, Eliza and George. Slavery's greatest crime, in Stowe's eyes, was the forced severance of family ties between husbands and wives, parents and children.

Southern slaveholders were outraged at Stowe's attempt to portray their way of life as an unmitigated evil; a South Carolina slave-holding woman, Louisa McCord, wrote "We proclaim it [slavery], on the contrary, a Godlike dispensation, a providential caring for the weak, and a refuge for the portionless." Another Southerner, George Fitzhugh, took this argument to its logical conclusion. In his book *Cannibals All! Or, Slaves Without Masters* (1857), Fitzhugh claimed that civil society demanded the enslavement of the masses, whether white or black: "Some were born with saddles on their backs, and others booted and spurred to ride them—and the riding does them good." Fitzhugh also argued that slaves, whom he claimed were cared for by benevolent planters, were better off than northern factory workers, whom he asserted were exploited and neglected by indifferent employers.

A roving reporter for the *New York Times,* Frederick Law Olmsted, expressed in journalistic terms what Stowe had described in her novel: cruel aristocrats lording over plantations operated by degraded slaves and non-slaveholding whites mired in sloth, ignorance, and poverty. Olmsted seemed most concerned about effects of slavery on whites; in one of his dispatches he quoted a Louisiana planter, who believed that the institution's "influence on the character of the whites was what was most deplorable." Thus in the 1850s the issue of slavery became a staple of both mainstream periodicals and the best-seller list. Few people could ignore the controversy.

As increasing numbers of Americans read the starkly drawn images of the South produced by northern printing presses, the territory of Kansas was becoming engulfed in a regional civil war. Proslavery settlers, aided and abetted by their compatriots (called Border Ruffians) from Missouri, installed their own territorial government at Shawnee Mission in 1855. Opposing these proslavery settlers were the Free-Soilers, some of whom had organized into abolitionist groups, such as the New England Emigrant Aid Company, and armed themselves with rifles. Antislavery groups called the guns Beecher's Bibles, after Brooklyn's Reverend Henry Ward Beecher, Harriet Beecher Stowe's brother and a fundraiser for abolitionist forces in Kansas.

Systems of Unfree Labor

The controversy over slavery ultimately precipitated the Civil War, the bloodiest conflict in the nation's history. Yet the abolition of slavery (with the ratification of the Thirteenth Amendment in 1865) did not eradicate forms of coerced labor. Indeed, systems of unfree labor—in which individuals are forced to work without compensation and for the benefit of someone else—have characterized the whole sweep of American history.

In the seventeenth century, most tobacco field workers in the Chesapeake region were indentured servants. These young men and women received passage from Europe to the colonies. In return, they bound themselves to a master for a stipulated amount of time (usually seven years). Apprentices, children and young people, labored for a master artisan until they reached age 21.

Beginning in the late seventeenth century, the institution of slavery spread throughout the colonies. This system, which depended on the labor of Africans and their descendants, differed in crucial ways from indentured servitude and apprenticeship. Slaves remained slaves for life, and they had no rights under law. Children took the status of their enslaved mother.

States outside the South had emancipated their slaves by the mid-nineteenth century. However, forms of bound labor persisted. In some Mid-Atlantic and New England small towns, local officials sold the labor of impoverished men, women, and children to the highest bidder, thereby relieving taxpayers of the expense of supporting them. Poor people confined to workhouses were forced to toil at many different kinds of jobs,

Shackled inmates work to clear brush along a highway near Prattville, Alabama. A 1996 settlement prevented the state from shackling inmates together on a "chain gang," but shackling of individual convict laborers was still permissible.

such as growing crops, spinning thread, weaving cloth, and producing handicrafts. In some cases, ship captains kidnapped sailors and forced them to work for no pay on long voyages. Indian and African American children remained at risk as labor-hungry whites forcibly "apprenticed" them with the aid of the courts.

By the late nineteenth century, peonage characterized the southern staple crop economy as well as the rural extractive sector (logging, sawmills, turpentine production, and mining). Held against their will, sharecroppers and railroad workers alike labored in isolated rural areas where law enforcement agents were few and far between. The outlawing of peonage in 1911 failed to end this practice.

The southern states also pioneered in the use of convict labor, a means of channeling petty criminals (and random, innocent young African American

men) into the rough and dangerous work of building roads through swamps and digging coal out of the earth. Convict labor officials often demonstrated a reckless disregard for human life. Unlike slave owners, prison officials and the private individuals who leased convicts had few incentives to treat these workers in a humane way.

In the early twenty-first century, coerced labor persists. Some illegal immigrants continue to indenture themselves to smugglers and remain indebted to these smugglers for many years. Prisoners perform a variety of tasks for private companies, including entering data into computers and taking hotel reservations by phone. American labor unions publicize the fact that some products consumed in this country have been manufactured by unfree workers abroad, such as prisoners in China and child laborers in Pakistan and Vietnam. ■

AP/Wide World Photos

This dangerous situation soon gave way to terrorism and insurrection on both sides. In 1855, in retaliation for a proslavery raid on the "Free-Soil" town of Lawrence, Kansas, an Ohio abolitionist named John Brown, together with his four sons and two other men, hacked to death five proslavery men at Pottowatamie Creek. The massacre only strengthened the resolve of proslavery advocates, who in the next year drew up a constitution for Kansas, which effectively nullified the principle of popular sovereignty over the issue of slavery. Called the Lecompton Constitution, the document decreed that voters might approve or reject slavery, but even if they chose to reject it, any slaves already in the state would remain slaves under the force of law. By throwing his support behind the Lecompton Constitution, President Buchanan alienated northern members of his own party, and the Democrats descended into north–south factionalism.

The spilling of blood over slavery was not confined to the Kansas frontier. In 1856 Senator Charles Sumner of Massachusetts, an outspoken abolitionist, delivered a speech on the floor of the United States Senate condemning "The Crime Against Kansas" (the Lecompton Constitution) and the men who perpetrated it, men he characterized as "hirelings picked from the drunken spew and vomit of an uneasy civilization," men who (like his own colleague Senator Butler of South Carolina) loved slavery the way that degenerates loved their prostitutes. Shortly after this speech, Congressman Preston S. Brooks of South Carolina, a relative of Senator Butler, leapt to the defense of the white South and attacked Sumner on the floor of the Senate, beating him into unconsciousness with a cane. This was "southern chivalry" and "southern honor," fumed an outraged northern press: a defenseless man beaten almost to death by a bully armed with a club. Soon, "Bleeding Kansas" became a rallying cry for abolitionists everywhere. They contemplated the necessity of defending themselves and their interests in the courtrooms of New England and the small towns of the West no less than in Congress.

The *Dred Scott* Decision

Across the street from the Capitol, proceedings in the Supreme Court were more civil but no less explosive. In 1857 a former slave named Dred Scott sued in federal court, claiming that he was a citizen of Missouri and a free man. Scott maintained that he had become free once his master had taken him onto free soil (the state of Illinois and the territory of Wisconsin). In the case of *Dred Scott v. Sanford* (1857), the court ruled that even residence on free soil did not render a slave a free person, for, regardless of their status, black people had "no rights which the white man was bound to respect." With this single decision, then, Chief Justice Roger B. Taney and the Court threw off the hard-won balance between slave and free states. In effect, the Court declared unconstitutional the Compromise of 1820, which had banned slavery in the region north of Missouri's southern boundary, because, the justices held, slave owners could not be deprived of their property without due process. This decision threatened the precarious freedom of the South's quarter million free people of color and extended the reach of slavery into the northern states.

Most white people residing outside the South never read the Court's ruling, but if they had, they probably would have agreed with the justices' claim that, since the earliest days of the Republic, blacks "had been regarded as beings of an inferior order, and altogether unfit to associate with the white race, either in social or political relations." At the same time, northern opinion makers warned that the decision made Northerners complicit in the slave system. Of the "slave power," the *Cincinnati Daily Commercial* thundered, "It has marched over and annihilated the boundaries of the states. We are now one great homogeneous slaveholding community." Convening in Philadelphia, black leaders expressed the hope that white Northerners would condemn the Scott decision and "make common cause with us . . . and striking for impartial liberty, they will join with us in our efforts to recover the long lost boon of freedom."

Even nonabolitionists had good reason to fear the long-term implications of the ruling, for it suggested that the institution of slavery was about to spill out of the confines of the southern states and into the rest of the country. Free white men and women feared competing with slaves in the workplace, whether in the West or East. In 1857 a depression hit the northeastern and midwestern states, as the discovery of California gold produced inflation in the East.

Businesses failed and debtors had a difficult time repaying their creditors. In New England, shoe-makers responded to these economic pressures, and to the labor-saving machinery installed by their employers, by banding together and forming a union. Members of the new organization, called the Knights of St. Crispin, believed their future looked bleak. They reasoned that they would not be able to seek new economic opportunities out West if that part of the country were dominated by southern planters and cheap slave labor. Like other members of the northern laboring classes, the shoemakers also feared a mass migration of blacks out of the South and into the North. As a result, national unions such as the ones formed by bookbinders and printers in 1850 began to take precautionary measures by barring free people of color from apprenticeship positions and from certain workplaces altogether.

The Lincoln–Douglas Debates

Against this backdrop of economic turmoil and political conflict, the congressional elections of 1858 assumed great significance. In particular, the Senate contest in Illinois pitted

■ The election of 1858 pitted Stephen A. Douglas, Democratic senator from Illinois, against his Republican challenger, a lawyer named Abraham Lincoln. The debates between the two candidates revealed the increasing divisiveness of the slavery question. Douglas maintained that compromise on the issue was still possible; he argued that the European American men residing in territories should decide the question for themselves. Although Lincoln lost this election, he articulated a view that was rapidly gaining support throughout the North: the idea that slavery must not be allowed to spread outside the South.

Library of Congress

Library of Congress

incumbent Stephen A. Douglas against challenger Abraham Lincoln. In a series of seven public debates, the two men debated the political conflict over slavery as it had been shaped during the tumultuous decade after the Mexican War. Though no friend of the abolitionists, Douglas was quickly falling from favor within the Democratic party; the Supreme Court had nullified his proposal for popular sovereignty in the territories, and he had parted ways from his southern brethren when he denounced Kansas's Lecompton Constitution. Yet in the last debate between Lincoln and Douglas, held in Alton on October 15, 1858, Douglas declared, "I care more for the great principle of self-government, the right of the people to rule, than I do for all the negroes in Christendom."

Lincoln ridiculed the doctrine of popular sovereignty, which he maintained was as thin as the "soup that was made by boiling the shadow of a pigeon that had starved to death." He had no desire to root out slavery in the South, but, "I have said, and I repeat, my wish is that the further spread of [slavery] may be arrested, and that it may be placed where the public mind shall rest in the belief that it is in the course of ultimate extinction." According to a reporter present, this last remark provoked great applause. And this was no minor confrontation between two candidates; it is estimated that in six of the seven debates the two men spoke before crowds exceeding 10,000 people each. Lincoln lost the election (in which blacks were not allowed to vote as a matter of Illinois law), but, more significantly, he won the loyalty of Republicans all over the North and put the white South on notice that the days of compromise were over. Meanwhile, with the admission as free states of Minnesota in 1858 and Oregon in 1859, Congress began to reflect a distinct antislavery bias.

Harpers Ferry and the Presidential Election of 1860

On a Sunday night in October 1859, John Brown and 19 other men (including at least five African Americans) launched a daring attack on the federal arsenal in Harpers Ferry, Virginia. They had received guns and moral support from some of the North's leading abolitionists, and their plan was to raid the arsenal and distribute firearms to slaves in the surrounding area, thereby inciting a general rebellion that, they hoped, would engulf the rest of the South. The Virginia militia cornered Brown and his men, but not before the insurrectionist had killed seven people (including a free man of color) and injured ten others. Within two days a U.S. Marine force, commanded by Lieutenant Colonel Robert E. Lee, had captured Brown and his surviving followers.

Two weeks later Brown stood in a Virginia courtroom and declared that his intention indeed had been "to free the slaves." Brown was convicted of several charges: treason against the United States for his raid on the federal arsenal, murder, and inciting an insurrection. On December 2, 1859, before being led to the gallows, Brown handed a scrap of paper to one of his guards: "I John Brown am now quite *certain* that the crimes of this *guilty land: will* never be purged *away:* but with Blood." Brown failed as the instigator of a slave rebellion, but he succeeded as a prophet.

The raid on Harpers Ferry cast a shadow over the party conventions held in the summer of 1860. By then it was apparent that the national party system had all but disintegrated. Southerners in effect seceded from the Democratic party by walking out of their Charleston

The Ohio Historical Society

■ Augustus Washington, son of a former slave, took this picture of John Brown in 1846, 13 years before the raid on Harpers Ferry, Virginia. A pioneer daguerreotypist, Washington operated a successful studio in Hartford, Connecticut. After the passage of the Fugitive Slave Law in 1850, Washington emigrated with his family to Liberia, an African settlement for American freeborn blacks and former slaves, founded as a republic in 1847.

convention rather than supporting Stephen Douglas as candidate for president. Within a few weeks, representatives of both the northern and the southern wings of the party reconvened in separate conventions in Baltimore; Northerners gave the nod to Douglas and Southerners chose as their standard-bearer John C. Breckinridge, a proponent of extending slavery into the territories and annexing Cuba. Representing the thoroughly discredited strategy of compromise was the candidate of the Constitutional Union party, John Bell of Tennessee.

In Chicago, the Republicans lined up behind the moderate Abraham Lincoln and agreed on a platform that had something for everybody, including measures to boost economic growth (as promoted by Henry Clay's American System earlier in the century): a proposed protective tariff, a transcontinental railroad, internal improvements, and free homesteads for western farmers. The Republicans renounced the Know-Nothings. Lincoln himself had taken the lead in admonishing Republicans who sought to curtail the voting rights of European immigrants, such as the Germans and Scandinavians. Lecturing members of his own

TABLE 13-5

The Election of 1860

Candidate	Political Party	Popular Vote	Electoral Vote
Abraham Lincoln	Republican	1,865,593	180
Stephen A. Douglas	Democratic	1,382,713	12
John C. Breckinridge	Democratic	848,356	72
John Bell	Constitutional Union	592,906	39

TABLE 13-6

U.S. Population, by Nativity and Race, for Regions, 1830–1860

Year	Total	White Total	White Native	White Foreign Born	Negro Total	Negro Slave	Other Races
Northeast							
1860	10,594,268	10,438,028	8,419,243	2,018,785	156,001	18	239
1850	8,626,851	8,477,089	7,153,512	1,323,577	149,762	236	----
1840	6,761,082	6,618,758	----	----	142,324	765	----
1830	5,542,381	5,417,167	----	----	125,214	2,780	----
Midwest							
1860	9,096,716	8,899,969	7,357,376	1,542,593	184,239	114,948	12,508
1850	5,403,595	5,267,988	4,617,913	650,075	135,607	87,422	----
1840	3,351,542	3,262,195	----	----	89,347	58,604	----
1830	1,610,473	1,568,930	----	----	41,543	25,879	----
South							
1860	11,133,861	7,033,973	6,642,201	391,772	4,097,111	3,838,765	2,277
1850	8,982,612	5,630,414	5,390,314	240,100	3,352,198	3,116,629	----
1840	6,950,729	4,308,752	----	----	2,641,977	2,427,986	----
1830	5,707,848	3,545,963	----	----	2,161,885	1,980,384	----
West							
1860	618,976	550,567	406,964	143,603	4,479	29	63,930
1850	178,818	177,577	150,794	26,783	1,241	26	----
1840	----	----	----	----	----	----	----
1830	----	----	----	----	----	----	----

Source: Historical Statistics of the United States from Colonial Times to 1957 (Washington, D.C.: U.S. Department of Commerce, 1960) pp. 11–12.

party in Massachusetts, he declared, "I have some little notoriety for commiserating the oppressed condition of the negro, and I should be strangely inconsistent if I could favor any project for curtailing the existing rights of white men, even though born in different lands, and speaking different languages from myself."

Yet Republicans held out little hope for other groups demanding the rights and protection that flowed from American citizenship. Spanish-speaking residents of California, Chinese immigrants, free people of color throughout the North, Indian tribes from North Carolina to the northwestern states, the wives and daughters of men all over the country—these groups were not included in the Republicans' grand design for a country based on the principles of free labor.

Abraham Lincoln was elected president in 1860, although he received support from only 40 percent of the men who cast ballots. Lincoln won the Electoral College, and he also received a majority of votes. However, ten southern states had refused to list him on the ballot; in that region of the country he received almost no votes. Stephen Douglas won almost 30 percent of the popular vote; together, Douglas and Breckenridge outpolled Lincoln (2.2 million votes to 1.85 million). Nevertheless, the new president had swept New England, New York, Pennsylvania, and the upper Midwest. Regional (northern and southern) interests took precedence over national political parties.

Lincoln and his party represented the antislavery sentiments of northern family farmers. The South took heed of this dramatic shift in the national political landscape. By the end of 1860 South Carolina had seceded from the Union, and the nation headed toward war.

Conclusion

During the 1850s, Americans on both sides of the slavery issue began to voice their opinions, and their frustrations, in ever more dramatic ways. Ultimately, these deep feelings led to war. People all over the country came to feel that the debate over slavery had relevance to their lives. In the slave states, black workers remained yoked to a system that denied their humanity and mocked the integrity of their families. In the nonslave states, free people of color understood that northern racial prejudice was but a variation of the slaveholders' theme of domination. New England farm families looking to move west were convinced that western homesteads would not improve their economic security if these homesteads were surrounded by plantations cultivated by large numbers of enslaved workers. Although they expressed little regard for the rights of blacks, enslaved or free, the northern laboring classes feared that the expansion of slavery into the western territories would limit their own economic opportunities; whether shoemakers, wagon drivers, or seamstresses, they could not possibly compete with bound workers in the labor market. The Republicans drew inspiration from the anxieties of all these groups, and the party's platform beckoned toward a future full of hope, a future that would fulfill the long-thwarted promise of the young country as a "republic of equal rights, where the title of manhood is the title to citizenship."

In contrast, southern whites of various classes agreed on a rallying cry that stressed independence from Yankee interlopers and freedom from federal interference. Yet this uni-

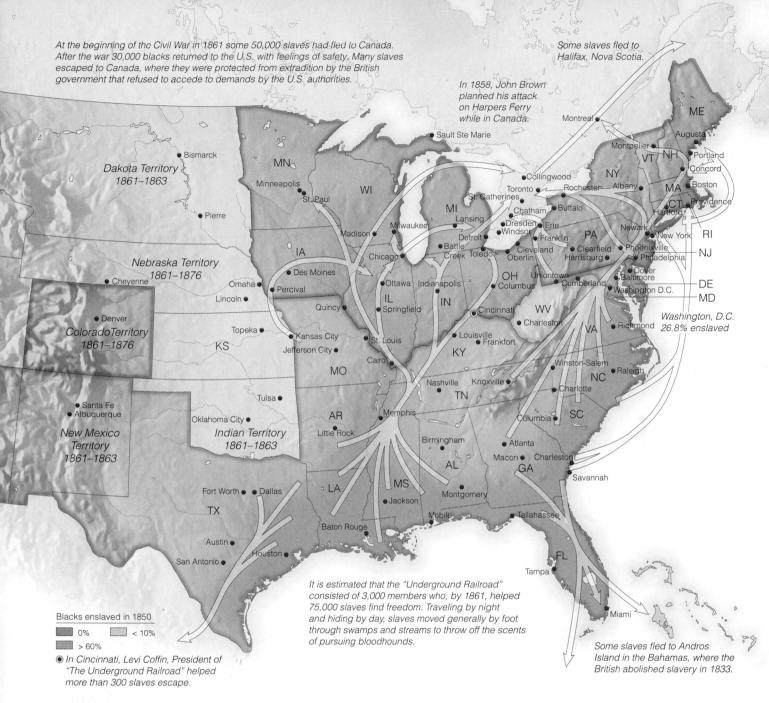

At the beginning of the Civil War in 1861 some 50,000 slaves had fled to Canada. After the war 30,000 blacks returned to the U.S. with feelings of safety. Many slaves escaped to Canada, where they were protected from extradition by the British government that refused to accede to demands by the U.S. authorities.

Some slaves fled to Halifax, Nova Scotia.

In 1858, John Brown planned his attack on Harpers Ferry while in Canada.

Washington, D.C. 26.8% enslaved

It is estimated that the "Underground Railroad" consisted of 3,000 members who, by 1861, helped 75,000 slaves find freedom. Traveling by night and hiding by day, slaves moved generally by foot through swamps and streams to throw off the scents of pursuing bloodhounds.

Some slaves fled to Andros Island in the Bahamas, where the British abolished slavery in 1833.

Blacks enslaved in 1850

0%   < 10%
> 60%

⊙ In Cincinnati, Levi Coffin, President of "The Underground Railroad" helped more than 300 slaves escape.

■ MAP 13.3

THE UNDERGROUND RAILROAD   The Underground Railroad consisted of a network of people who helped fugitives in their escape from slavery en route to the North or Canada. An escaped slave named Harriet Tubman made an estimated 19 separate trips south to help an estimated 300 slaves escape to freedom. Like Tubman, most "conductors" on the Underground Railroad were blacks, many of them free men and women living in the North.

fying rhetoric carried different meanings for different groups of southerners. The owners of large plantations were desperate to preserve their enslaved labor forces, and also hungry for fresh lands and renewed political power; these men scrambled to maintain their own privileges in the face of growing northern influence in Congress. Nonslaveholding farmers sought to produce all household necessities themselves and remain independent of the worldwide cotton market economy so crucial to the wealth of slave masters and mistresses. Yet almost all southern whites, rich and poor, stood allied, determined to take up arms to protect their households and their distinctive "southern way of life."

On the eve of the Civil War, complex forces roiled an ethnically diverse society. Ultimately the North and South marched into combat, each side united enough to mobilize huge armies. However, wartime strains would expose the fault lines in the free labor coalition as well as in the slaveholders' republic.

Sites to Visit

Secession Era Editorial Project
history.furman.edu/~benson/docs/
> Furman University is digitizing editorials about the secession crisis and already includes scores of them on this site.

John Brown trial links
www.law.umkc/edu/faculty/projecs/ftrials/Brown.html
> For information about the John Brown trial, this site provides a list of excellent links.

Abraham Lincoln and Slavery
odur.let.nl/~usa/H/1990/ch5_p6.html
> This site discusses Lincoln's views and actions concerning slavery, especially the Lincoln–Douglas debate.

The Compromise of 1850 and the Fugitive Slave Act
www.pbs.org/wgbh/aia/part4
> From the series on Africans in America, an analysis of the Compromise of 1850 and the effect of the Fugitive Slave Act on black Americans.

The 1850s: An Increasingly Divided Union
nac.gmu/mmts/50proto.html
> A tutorial skill development site of the Multi-Media Thinking Skills project that focuses on events in the 1850s leading to the Civil War.

Words and Deeds in American History
leweb2.loc.gov/ammem/mcchtml/corhome.html
> A Library of Congress site containing links to Frederick Douglass; the Compromise of 1850; speeches by John C. Calhoun, Daniel Webster, and Henry Clay; and other topics from the Civil War era.

Harriet Beecher Stowe and Uncle Tom's Cabin
xroads.virginia.edu/~HYPER/STOWE/stowe.html
> This site provides both text and descriptions of Stowe's important books and information about the author's life.

For Further Reading

General Works

Eric Foner, *Free Labor, Free Soil, Free Men: The Ideology of the Republican Party Before the Civil War* (1970).

William W. Freehling, *The Road to Disunion* (1990).

Robert V. Hine and John Mack Faragher, *The American West: A New Interpretive History* (2000).

James Oliver Horton and Lois E. Horton, *In Hope of Liberty: Culture, Community and Protest Among Northern Free Blacks, 1700–1860* (1997).

Nancy Isenberg, *Sex and Citizenship in Antebellum America* (1998).

Regional Economies and Conflicts

Joan Cashin, *A Family Venture: Men and Women on the Southern Frontier* (1991).

Christopher Clark, *The Roots of Rural Capitalism: Western Massachusetts, 1780–1860* (1990).

Steven Hahn, *The Roots of Southern Populism: Yeoman Farmers and the Transformation of the Georgia Upcountry, 1850–1890* (1983).

Albert Hurtado, *Indian Survival on the California Frontier* (1988).

Susan Lee Johnson, *Roaring Camp: The Social World of the California Gold Rush* (2000).

John D. Majewski, *A House Dividing: Economic Development in Pennsylvania and Virginia Before the Civil War* (2000).

David Montejano, *Anglos and Mexicans in the Making of Texas, 1836–1986* (1987).

Shifting Collective Identities

Tomás Almaguer, *Racial Faultlines: The Historical Origins of White Supremacy in California* (1994).

Bonnie S. Anderson, *Joyous Greetings: The First International Women's Movement, 1830–1860* (2000).

Mary H. Blewett, *Men, Women, and Work: Class, Gender, and Protest in the New England Shoe Industry, 1780–1910* (1988).

Yong Chen, *Chinese San Francisco, 1850–1943: A Trans-Pacific Community* (2000).

Frances Levine, *Our Prayers Are in This Place: Pecos Pueblo Identity over the Centuries* (1999).

David Roediger, *The Wages of Whiteness: Race and the Making of the American Working Class* (1991).

The Paradox of Southern Political Power

Avery O. Craven, *The Growth of Southern Nationalism, 1848–1861* (1953).

Lacy K. Ford, *Origins of Southern Radicalism: The South Carolina Upcountry, 1800–1860* (1988).

Robert E. May, *The Southern Dream of a Caribbean Empire, 1854–1861* (1973).

Stephanie McCurry, *Masters of Small Worlds: Yeoman Households, Gender Relations, and the Political Culture of the Antebellum South Carolina Low Country* (1995).

Leonard Richards, *The Slave Power: The Free North and Southern Domination, 1780–1860* (2000).

The Deepening Conflict over Slavery

David Herbert Donald, *Lincoln* (1995).

William E. Gienapp, *The Origins of the Republican Party, 1852–1856* (1987).

Michael F. Holt, *The Rise and Fall of the American Whig Party: Jacksonian Politics and the Onset of the Civil War* (1999).

Stephen Oates, *To Purge This Land with Blood: A Biography of John Brown* (1984).

Manisha Sinha, *The Counterrevolution of Slavery: Politics and Ideology in Antebellum South Carolina* (2000).

Albert J. Von Frank, *The Trials of Anthony Burns: Freedom and Slavery in Emerson's Boston* (1998).

Online Practice Test

Test your understanding of this chapter with interactive review quizzes at

www.ablongman.com/jonescreatedequal/chapter13

Additional Photo Credits

Page 431: California History Section, California State Library, Photograph Collection. Mines & Mining: Gold: Scenes from Dag. #3 *Head of Auburn Ravine*, Neg. #912
Page 432: Michael Freeman/CORBIS
Page 438: American Textile History Museum, Lowell, Massachusetts
Page 443: Georgia Historical Society, Savannah, Georgia, D.M. Wright Papers, #1277, Box 36, Folder 286
Page 446: Courtesy, Janice L. and David Frent
Page 452: Harriet Beecher Stowe Center, Hartford, CT

"To Fight to Gain a Country": The Civil War

Winslow Homer, Young Union Soldier: Separate Study of a Soldier Giving Water to a Wounded Companion, 1861. Cooper-Hewitt, National Design Museum, Smithsonian Institution. Gift of Charles Savage Homer, Jr. (1912-12-110). Photo by Ken Pelka

■ Winslow Homer's painting *Young Union Soldier: Separate Study of a Soldier Giving Water to a Wounded Companion*, 1861.

PENSACOLA, FLORIDA, WAS THE SITE OF A DRAMATIC COURT MARTIAL TRIAL IN April 1862, when five men were charged with treasonous acts against the Confederate States of America. "Possessed of information well calculated to aid the enemy," and thus capable of "giving intelligence" to the enemy, the defendants had endangered the security of Confederate troops stationed in the area, according to the chief prosecutor. At the conclusion of the three-day hearing, the court convicted the men and ordered that two of them, alleged ringleaders, be hanged. Later, the presiding officer claimed that "high Military Necessity" had mandated the swift trial and stern verdict: coastal communities were engulfed in a "general stampede" as planters tried to move slaves and livestock out of the way of the encroaching Union army. According to the officer, at stake in this trial was the very fate of the would-be new nation.

By 1862, Confederate leaders knew full well that the war for southern independence would be a hard and long one. Indeed, the Pensacola court martial provided striking evidence of the political and military challenges faced by southern nationalists, for all of the defendants—George, Robert, Stephen, Peter, and William—were runaway slaves. The specific charges lodged against them read, "That the said slaves are intelligent beings possessing the faculties of Conveying information which would prove useful to the enemy and detrimental to the Confederate States." Clearly, these five men were combatants in the war, as threatening to the well-being of the Confederacy as any Yankee sharpshooter in a blue uniform. The charges also suggest that the Confederates were forced to repudiate elements of their own proslavery beliefs, which held that black people were childlike and servile, incapable of acting on their own, and grateful for the guidance and protection of southern whites.

Sgt. F. L. Baldwin, a Union soldier, poses with an American flag as a backdrop.

The Pensacola slaves were assigned a defense lawyer, who attempted to show that they had not actually encountered any Union soldiers and so had had no opportunity to divulge information related to Confederate troop movement. Technically, then, they were not guilty of spying. In court, however, the accused men did admit that, ever since President Abraham Lincoln had taken office in early 1861, three white men in the vicinity (a whiskey seller, an employee of the slaves' master, and a shingle maker) had been encouraging them to seek their freedom behind Union lines.

Prosecuting officers believed that "strong measures" were needed to prevent the nefarious activities of "spys whether white or black." These officials therefore were unprepared for the firestorm of criticism that followed the announcement of the verdict. The owner of the slaves, General Jackson Morton, expressed outrage that two of his men were marked for summary execution. In a formal complaint to Confederate authorities, Morton denounced the hearing as "vulgar and improper." By the time the controversy faded, an impressive array of Confederate military officers (from sentinels to a lieutenant, a captain, a colonel, a major

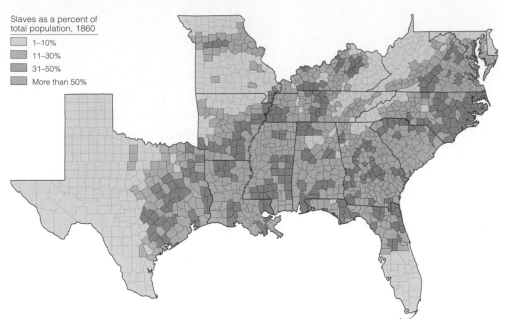

Slaves as a percent of
total population, 1860

- 1–10%
- 11–30%
- 31–50%
- More than 50%

■ **MAP 14.1**

SLAVERY IN THE UNITED STATES, 1860   In the South, the areas of the greatest concentration of slaves were also the areas of greatest support for the Confederacy. During the war, the Appalachian mountain region and the Upper Piedmont—the area between the mountains and the broad coastal plain—were home to people loyal to the Union and to people who became increasingly disaffected with Confederate policies as the war dragged on.

general, and a general) had had to justify their actions in convening the trial. The Confederate adjutant and inspector general took time out from more pressing matters to review the case for the secretary of war. In the words of one Confederate official, "The sacrosanctity of slave property in this war has operated most injuriously to the Confederacy."

Though at a distinct disadvantage compared to the North in terms of troops and materiel, the white South managed to fight on for four long bloody years. Early on, politicians hailed slaves as a tremendous asset, an immense, easily managed labor force that would grow food and dig trenches. Instead, African American men and women became freedom fighters, a source of subversion in the heart of the Confederacy. In October 1862, in response to the crisis of wartime slave management, the Confederate Congress passed a measure that exempted from military service one white man for every 20 slaves on a plantation. Many slave owners used this law to shield themselves or their sons from combat duty. In turn, the Twenty-Negro Law inflamed resentment among non–slave-owning, small farmers who charged that this rich man's war was actually a poor man's fight. Even within the ranks of the elite, conflicts over military strategy and national mobilization policies hobbled the Confederate effort. Many slaveholding women gradually came to see the sacrifice of their husbands, brothers, and sons as too high a price to pay for southern independence.

As defenders of slavery, the Confederates cast themselves as rebels in an age when the principle of individual rights was gaining ground. The citizens of France, Germany, and Italy were agitating on behalf of modern, democratic nation-states, and systems of serfdom and slavery throughout Europe and the Western Hemisphere were under siege. By early 1865, leading southern politicians and strategists had initiated a public debate over the possibility of offering slaves their liberty in return for military service. In acknowledging that African American men might serve as effective soldiers (as 179,000 of them had demonstrated in the Union army), the Confederates tolled their own death knell. White Southerners were fighting for their own nation, but African Americans were fighting to gain their own country as well.

The Republican conduct of the war revealed the party's long-range, guiding principles. Yet not all non-Southerners embraced the party's brand of nationalism. Several groups objected to a strong federal government, one that would weld the country together geographically as well as economically. The Lincoln administration met bitter resistance from Indian tribes as diverse as the Santee Sioux of Minnesota, the Cheyenne of Colorado, and the Navajo and Apaches of the Southwest. In northeastern cities, Irish immigrants battled federal draft agents and attacked black women, men, and children, their supposed competitors in the workplace. The Civil War, then, was less a "brothers' war" between the white farmers of the North and South exclusively and more a conflict that pitted diverse groups against each other over the issues of slavery, territorial expansion, federal power, and local control. Yet by the end of the war in April 1865, for the time being at least, the Republican vision of a union forged in blood had prevailed, at the cost of more than 600,000 lives.

Mobilization for War, 1861–1862

On December 20, 1860, less than eight weeks after Abraham Lincoln was elected president of the United States, South Carolina seceded from the Union, determined, in the words of its own Declaration of Independence, to "resume her separate and equal place among nations." By February 1, 1861, Mississippi, Florida, Alabama, Georgia, Louisiana, and Texas (all states dependent on slave-based staple crop agriculture) had also withdrawn from the United States of America. Three days later, representatives of the seven states met in Montgomery, Alabama, and formed the Confederate States of America. They also adopted a new constitution for their new nation. Though modeled after that of the United States, this document invoked the power of "sovereign and independent states" instead of "we, the people."

Delegates to the Montgomery convention elected as their president Jefferson Davis, a wealthy Mississippi planter with an impressive record of public service. Davis was a graduate of West Point, a veteran of the Mexican War, and a former United States congressman and senator. He had also held the position of secretary of war in the Franklin Pierce administration. Chosen vice president was a former Whig from Georgia, Alexander H. Stephens. In devising a cabinet, Davis bypassed some well-known radical secessionists—"fire eaters" such as William Lowndes Yancey (of Alabama) and Robert Barnwell Rhett, Jr. (of South Carolina)— on the assumption that the builders of a new nation would need skills different from the destroyers of an old one.

The Secession Impulse

In some respects, the Civil War seems difficult to explain, for the two sides shared a great deal. Most of the people North and South were English-speaking Protestants with deep roots in the culture of the British Isles. Together they celebrated a revolutionary heritage, paying homage to George Washington and the other Founding Fathers.

Why then was the white South, especially the slave South, so fearful of Abraham Lincoln? Although Lincoln enjoyed a broad Electoral College victory—180 votes to 123 for his opponents combined—the popular vote margin was slim. Six out of ten Americans cast their ballots for a candidate other than Lincoln in the 1860 presidential election. Together, Stephen A. Douglas and John C. Breckinridge polled 366,484 more votes than did the lanky lawyer from Illinois. Lincoln received no votes from the Deep South (he was not on the ballot in those states),

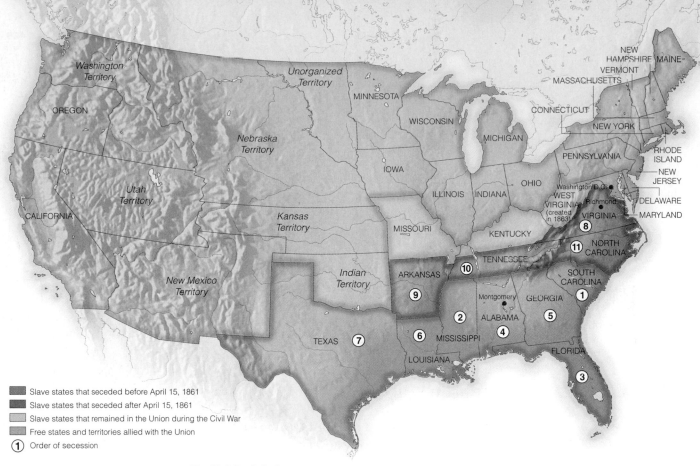

Legend:
- Slave states that seceded before April 15, 1861
- Slave states that seceded after April 15, 1861
- Slave states that remained in the Union during the Civil War
- Free states and territories allied with the Union
- (1) Order of secession

■ **MAP 14.2**

THE SECESSION OF SOUTHERN STATES, 1860–1861 The southern states seceded from the Union in stages, beginning with South Carolina in December 1860. Founded on February 4, 1861, the Confederate States of America initially consisted of only that state and six Deep South states. The four upper South states of Virginia, Arkansas, Tennessee, and North Carolina did not leave the Union until mid-April, when Lincoln called for 75,000 troops to put down the civil rebellion. The slave states of Delaware, Maryland, Kentucky, and Missouri remained in the Union, but each of those states was bitterly divided between Unionists and Confederate sympathizers.

and five upper South states gave him only 4 percent of his popular vote total (and those came mostly from German immigrants in or near St. Louis). The Republicans failed to capture either the House of Representatives or the Senate, and the Supreme Court remained within the southern camp, with five of its nine justices determined to protect the institution of slavery.

Political support for Lincoln thus appeared slim, and he did not seem likely to invoke his authority to move against slavery. He had made it clear that, as president, he would possess neither the authority nor the desire to disturb slavery as it existed in the South. However, he summed up his philosophy before the secession crisis this way: "As I would not be a *slave*, so I would not be a *master*. This expresses my idea of democracy. Whatever differs from this . . . is not democracy."

Not surprisingly, then, southern elites felt threatened by Lincoln in particular and the Republicans in general, pointing to the new president's oft-repeated promise to halt the march of slavery into the western territories. Although he was in no position to achieve this goal by executive order, Lincoln did have the power to expand the Republican base in the South by dispensing patronage jobs to a small group of homegrown abolitionists. He could also make appointments to the Supreme Court as openings became available. The Republican party was not a majority party; it was a sectional party in that its power was all in the North and the Upper Midwest. Ominously for the South, this sectional party had managed to seize control of the executive branch of government. The antebellum balance of power between slave and free states had tipped decisively in favor of the North.

466

Slaveowners reasoned that it was only a matter of time before the North—what some southern whites called the Anti–Slave Power Conspiracy—spread its tentacles all over the South. According to this view, John Brown's 1859 raid on the federal arsenal at Harpers Ferry, Virginia, was just the first in a series of planned attacks on the slave South. Moreover, some Southerners feared that the swearing in of (what they saw as) the ugly, uncouth new president would encourage the growth of any number of northern evils, from labor unionism and women's rights to free love and dress reform (promoted by the infamous "Bloomer women," who wore pants instead of skirts). Submission to "Black Republicans" would bring the South only humiliation and degradation.

Two last-ditch efforts at compromise failed to avert a constitutional crisis. In December 1860, as South Carolina was seceding and other states were preparing to join it, neither northern Republicans nor lower South Democrats showed any interest in a series of proposed constitutional amendments that would have severely curtailed the federal government's ability to restrict the interstate slave trade or the spread of slavery. Called the Crittenden Compromise (after its sponsor, Senator John J. Crittenden, a Whig from Kentucky), this package of proposed amendments was defeated in the Senate on January 16, 1861. A peace conference, organized by the Virginia legislature and assembled in February, revised the Crittenden Compromise, but key players were missing: the seven Confederate states and five northern states. Congress rejected the conference's recommendations at the end of February. By this time many Americans, radicals and moderates, Northerners and Southerners, were in no mood to compromise on the issue of slavery, especially its extension into the Western territories.

Lincoln was faced with the task of cobbling together a cabinet composed of representatives of his Republican coalition. Shrewdly, he named four party leaders who had challenged him for the presidential nomination the previous year (William H. Seward as secretary of state, Edward Bates as attorney general, Simon Cameron as secretary of war, and Salmon P. Chase as secretary of the treasury). He appointed Montgomery Blair (from strategically located Maryland) as postmaster general. In his inaugural address of March 4, Lincoln appealed to the South to refrain from any drastic action, invoking the historic bonds of nationhood, the "mystic chords of memory, stretching from every battle-field, and patriot grave, to every living heart and hearthstone."

In his inaugural address of March 4, Lincoln appealed to the South to refrain from any drastic action.

For the most part Lincoln's plea for unity fell on deaf ears. However, among the Southerners who initially resisted the secessionists' call to arms was the West Point graduate and Mexican War veteran Robert E. Lee of Virginia. As late as January 1861, Lee maintained that the framers of our Constitution would never have "exhausted so much labor, wisdom, and forbearance in its formation" if they had intended the Union to be so easily dismantled. Later, after Virginia seceded, Lee cast his lot with the Confederacy: "I cannot raise my hand against my birthplace, my home, my children," he declared. By his home Lee meant the Commonwealth of Virginia, not the collection of disaffected states.

Indeed, in early April, the Confederacy was a rhetorical powerhouse, full of blustering firebrands. But it was also a poor excuse for an independent nation, with only one-third of the U.S. population and almost no industrial capacity. Over the next few weeks, as the seven Confederate states attempted to coax the upper South to join their revolution, Lincoln emerged as an unwitting ally in their effort.

Located in Charleston Harbor, Fort Sumter was one of two Union forts in southern territory, and in the spring of 1861 it was badly in need of supplies. On April 12, Lincoln took the high moral ground by sending provisions but not troops to the fort. The Confederates found the move provocative nonetheless and began firing on the fort. After a 33-hour Confederate bombardment, the heavily damaged fort surrendered without a fight. In response, many white Southerners, such as Mary Boykin Chesnut, the wife of a high Confederate official, cheered and embraced the "pomp and circumstance of glorious war."

Alabama Secession Convention Occupations			
Occupation of Delegate	Cooperationists	Secessionists	Total
Farmer or Planter	20	118	38
Lawyer	10	22	32
Physician	2	3	5
Merchant	2	2	4
Farmer-Lawyer	3	1	4
Clergyman	3	1	4
Teacher	2	—	2
Judge	—	2	2
Sheriff	—	1	1
Manufacturer	1	—	1
Cotton factor	—	1	1
Factor-Merchant	1	—	1
Farmer-Manufacturer	1	—	1
Farmer-Merchant	—	1	1
Unknown	1	2	3
Total	46	54	100

Alabama Secession Convention Property Holding*			
Value of Property Held by Delegate	Cooperationists	Secessionists	Total
Real Property			
Less than $10,000	31	20	51
$10,000–$24,999	8	17	25
$25,000–$49,999	4	9	13
$50,000–$99,999	1	4	5
$100,000 and above	1	2	3
Total	45	52	97
Personal Property			
Less than $10,000	19	6	25
$10,000–$24,999	12	10	22
$25,000–$49,999	8	14	22
$50,000–$99,999	5	13	18
$100,000–$199,999	—	7	7
$200,000 and above	1	2	3
Total	45	52	97

*Three delegates not found in manuscript census; hence, 97 rather than 100 is the total here.

■ **FIGURE 14.1**
DELEGATES TO THE ALABAMA SECESSION CONVENTION

Three days after the capture of Fort Sumter, Lincoln (anticipating a conflict no longer than 90 days) called for 75,000 northern volunteers to quell a civil uprising "too powerful to be suppressed by the ordinary course of judicial proceedings." By the end of the month he had ordered a blockade of southern seaports. Condemning these moves as acts of "northern aggression," the upper South, including Virginia (deprived of its western part, which now formed a new state called West Virginia), Tennessee, Arkansas, and North Carolina all seceded from the Union by May 20. Grateful for the newfound loyalty of Virginia and eager to appropriate the Trede-gar Iron Works (in Richmond), the Confederacy moved its capital from the down-at-the-heels Montgomery to the elegant Richmond on May 11.

The process by which the southern states left the Union foreshadowed the political rifts the new nation faced in the horrific years to come. With the exception of Tennessee, which placed the secession question before its state legislators, all of the states elected delegates to special secession conventions; acting separately, each of these bodies ultimately ratified an ordinance of secession. Some white Southerners (especially Union sympathizers called Unionists) refused to vote for convention delegates at all, considering the whole enterprise illegal. Other voters supported delegates who initially favored cooperating with other southern states in the hope that the South could broker some compromise on slavery with the North, but then later, in the heat of the moment, changed their minds and voted to secede. Most of the delegates to the North Carolina secession convention were slave owners, hardly a representative group from that state of yeomen. During the war, poor Southerners would charge that wealthy slave owners protected their own economic interests while ignoring those of ordinary people. Moreover, a core of Unionists would prove active traitors to the Confederate cause.

Only Texas, Virginia, and Tennessee submitted their ordinances directly to the voters for approval, and although secession gained overwhelming approval in all three cases, it was not clear that those victories represented the will of the people. Moreover, certain segments of the southern population early demonstrated that they would withhold their support from the Confederacy; yeoman farmers in the upcountry, Louisiana sugar planters dependent on world markets for their product, and people in the hill country of east Tennessee all voted for Unionist delegates to their respective state conventions. The Border States of Missouri, Kentucky, Maryland, and Delaware remained within the Union, but among their residents were many outspoken people who openly sympathized with the South.

Commissioners from individual states helped to coordinate the secession process and justify the collective decision to leave the United States. As a group, the commissioners maintained that northern Republicans intended to dishonor and degrade southern white men. The commissioners highlighted slavery as the cause of secession, maintaining that Lincoln's election threatened to provoke a rebellion among the slaves and thus destroy a way of life for all southern white men and women. Stephen Hale, Alabama's commissioner to Kentucky, declared that the Republicans' "new theory of government" was a direct attack on southern property rights. A Republican administration, he declared, would lead to "all the horrors of a San Domingo servile insurrection." Southern whites, Hale maintained, were in danger of losing not only their slaves but also their lives. This overheated rhetoric paved the way to war.

Preparing to Fight

Poised to battle each other, the South and the North faced similar challenges. Both sides had to inspire—or force—large numbers of men to fight. Both had to produce massive amounts of cannon, ammunition, and food. And both had to devise military strategies that would, they hoped, ensure victory. In early 1861 white Southerners were boasting of the stockpiles of cotton that, if needed, would serve as leverage for military support, diplomatic recognition, and financial assistance from the great European powers. Plantations brimming with hogs and corn, it was hoped, would sustain both masters and slaves, in contrast to the North, where cotton mills would lie idle and workers would soon descend to poverty and starvation.

In defense of secession, white Southerners emulated the rhetoric of 1776—high tariffs on imported manufactured goods were latter-day taxes imposed without representation—and thus drew inspiration from the

Courtesy, The Museum of the Confederacy, Richmond Virginia

This picture shows three Confederate surgeons, along with their African American servant, at the hospital in Lynchburg, Virginia. Confederate officials used enslaved men and women in a variety of capacities—as menial laborers, cooks, and laundresses in army camps, aides in hospitals, railroad hands, and industrial laborers.

■ The Confederacy impressed large numbers of enslaved men and women into service. Black men worked on trains and on railroad maintenance crews. This photo shows a Georgia train roundhouse destroyed by General William T. Sherman's men on their march to the sea in late 1864. By forcing slaves to work far from home and in nonagricultural jobs, Confederate officials unwittingly contributed to the dismantling of slavery, a system that depended on controlling large numbers of blacks on plantations.

creation of the nation they now sought to dismantle. At the same time, however, Vice President Stephens acknowledged the revolutionary nature of the Confederacy. Repudiating the words of a famous Virginian, Thomas Jefferson, who had declared equality among men to be a "self-evident truth," Stephens boldly asserted, "Our new government is founded upon exactly the opposite idea; its foundations are laid, its cornerstone rests, upon the great truth that the negro is not equal to the white man; that slavery . . . is his natural and normal condition."

From the beginning of the war, Confederates aimed for a strategy calculated to draw on their strengths. They would fight a purely defensive war, a war of "annihilation," by overwhelming Union armies that ventured into Confederate territory. Small units of troops would be deployed around the South's 6000-mile border (a "dispersed defensive" tactic). Seasoned officers such as Robert E. Lee and Thomas J. Jackson would lead the charge to crush the Yankees. Finally, the South could command 3 million black people (a third of its total population of 9 million), all of whom, it was assumed, would do the bidding of planters and military men. Whereas the North would have to conquer the South to preserve the Union, the Confederacy would only have to survive to win its independence. White Southerners likened themselves to the Patriots of the American Revolution, boldly waging a defensive war against an arrogant, powerful enemy.

At first, the North was inclined to think little past the numbers: in 1860, it possessed 90 percent of the manufacturing capacity and three-quarters of the 30,000 railroad miles in the United States. Its population, 22 million, dwarfed that of the South. More than 1 million Northerners were employed in factories and workshops, compared to 110,000 Southerners. The North retained control of the (admittedly less than formidable) U.S. Navy and all other resources of the federal government, including a bureaucratic infrastructure to facilitate troop deployment and communication. Its diversified economy yielded grain as well as textiles; it could not only mobilize a large army but count on feeding it as well.

Early on, the North had a plan, but one that could hardly be dignified by the term *strategy*. It would defend its own territory from southern attack and target Confederate leaders, under the assumption that latent Union sentiment in the South would arise to smash the rebellion before it went too far. Union gunboats positioned along the East Coast and up and down the Mississippi River would seal off the Confederacy from foreign supply lines (the so-called Anaconda Plan proposed by General-in-Chief Winfield Scott in the summer of 1861). The North would also launch a political offensive calculated to undermine Confederate sympathizers by bolstering Unionist sentiment everywhere. For example, from the beginning of the war, Lincoln made clear that he would continue to appeal to slaveholders loyal to the Union, whether those slaveholders lived in the Border States or deep in the heart of the Confederacy.

Northerners also invoked a Revolutionary heritage to justify their cause. However, they downplayed the issue of unjust taxation and instead stressed the glories of the Union—in Lincoln's words, "the last, best hope of mankind" in an age of kings and emperors. In an address to the nation on July 4, 1861, the president declared that the nation preceded—and thus created—the Union. He maintained that no person should be enslaved to another person and that all people must have equal opportunities to succeed in life, regardless of their background or skin color. The war, he argued, was "essentially a people's contest": its purpose was "to lift artificial weights from all shoulders . . . to afford all an unfettered start, and a fair chance in the race for life." Northerners as a whole found these words uplifting. In contrast, Confederates urged white Southerners to die so that other people would remain enslaved. This message, however, lost its appeal among nonelite Southerners over the coming months and years.

Barriers to Southern Mobilization

On July 21, 1861, at Manassas Junction (Bull Run), about 30 miles southwest of Washington, D.C., Union and Confederate forces encountered each other on the field of battle for the first time. This was the fight that earned Thomas "Stonewall" Jackson his nickname and burnished his reputation, for Union troops skirmished briefly with the enemy and then turned and fled back to the capital, disgraced. In the coming weeks, Northerners gave up the idea that the effort to suppress the rebels would be an easy one, and Lincoln began to reorganize the country's officer corps and fortify its armies. Contrary to the expectations of the women who had accompanied the Union forces out of the nation's capital, planning to lunch while they observed the first battle of the war, this fight was no picnic, military or otherwise.

To win this initial victory, the Confederates had relied on the massing of several huge forces: those of Generals Joseph Johnston and P. G. T. Beauregard, as well as Stonewall Jackson. Consequently, southern military strategists decided they must continue to defend southern territory while going on the offensive against the Yankees (the "offensive-defensive" strategy was used for the duration of the conflict). In other matters, however, the South learned life-and-death lessons more slowly. Only gradually did the central paradox of the Confederate nation become abundantly clear: that a country

Harper's Weekly, May 4, 1861

■ This drawing, titled "The House-Tops of Charleston during the Bombardment of Sumter," appeared in the May 4, 1861, issue of *Harper's Weekly,* about three weeks after the event. Many Confederate women sent their husbands and sons into battle with great displays of patriotism. However, those parades and parties often masked deep fears. Noted one woman of her husband's departure, "It has always been my lot to be obliged to shut up my griefs in my own breast."

A Virginia Slaveholder Objects to the Impressment of Slaves

During the Civil War, some southern slave owners bitterly resisted Confederate slave impressment policies. On December 4, 1861, John B. Spiece, an Albemarle County, Virginia, slaveholder and lawyer, wrote to the Confederate attorney general and protested government policy.

Dr Sir, Although a stranger to you, yet in consequence of the excitement and distress in this section of the country, in reference to a certain matter; I am constrained to address you, not merely on my own account; but on behalf of a large number of most respectable citizens.. . .

A practice has prevailed for some considerable time in *this* section of the country of impressing into service of the confederate army, the horses wagons and *slaves* belonging to the people.

The "Press masters" will go to their houses, and drag of their property to Just Such an extent as they choose; until it has not only created great excitement and distress; but bids fair to produce wide spread ruin. And I am told that these "Press masters" are paid by the Government the enormous price of *two dollars and fifty cents for each team with they impress;*—hence their anxiety and untiring exertions to increase the number;—thus making thirty or forly dollars pr day—

While I do not controvert the right of the Government to impress into its service *wagons and teams;* yet I do controvert the right to impress *Slaves*—It does seem to me that no one can be impress'd into military service of any kind, unless he is subject to military duty: because this whole business is relating to the Army, and is purely a military matter.—

The people in this section of the country are much attached to their slaves, and treat them in a humane manner—consequently they are exceedingly pained at having them dragged off at this inclement season of the year, and exposed to the severe weather in the mountains of north western Virginia.. . . . Some have already died, and others have returned home afflicted with Typhoid fever, which has spread through the family to a most fatal and alarming extent.—

I am a practicing lawyer myself, but these "Press masters" will hear nothing from any one residing amongst the people.—

Therefore Sir, in consequence of the distress produced by the causes before mentioned, I am constrained to write to you; requesting you if you please, to give your opinion upon the questions involved.

To wit—If a man's wagon and team should be impress'd into Service, can his slave be impress'd to drive the said team—

Secondly—If a man has neither wagon or team can his slave be impress'd to drive some other team (*some* of the "Press masters" yield this *last* point, whilst others do not, and contend that they can impress just as many slaves as they choose from any plantation, taking all the negro men if they think proper.)—

---

founded on an agrarian ideal of "states' rights" needed to industrialize its economy and centralize its government operations to defeat the Union.

The first weeks of the war revealed that the South would pursue its antebellum aims of conquering western territory for slavery. An early victory of Texas forces over Union troops in New Mexico led to the formation of what slaveholders in that region called the Confederate Territory of Arizona. Over the next year the Confederates launched successful assaults on the cities of Albuquerque and Santa Fe, in present-day New Mexico. However, southern troops amounted to little more than a band of plunderers; in Rio Abajo, for example, farmers and ranchers switched their allegiance to the Union after the rebels raided their homesteads.

Deprived of money raised from customs duties (the blockade brought a halt to established patterns of overseas trade), the Confederacy relied on floating bonds ($400 million worth), raising taxes, and a 10 percent tax on farm produce. The Confederate Treasury printed money at a furious rate ($1 billion over the course of the conflict), but its value declined precipitously; near the end of the war one Confederate dollar was worth only 1.6 cents.

Raising a volunteer army and impressing slave labor (forcing slaves to labor for the military) met with stiff resistance from various quarters of southern society. For yeoman farm families, long defensive of the independence of their own households, Confederate mobilization efforts came as a rude shock. Antebellum Southerners believed that white fathers should pro-

Stockpile of rails at Alexandria, Virginia

Some few of the people have not been able to sow their grain this fall:—and there is deep dissatisfaction amongst the people—therefore I deem it proper and expedient that the authorities should know it—

Spiece goes on to cite the laws of the Commonwealth of Virginia, as amended in 1860, "by which it seems there is no power to impress Slaves." In the absence of Confederate congressional legislation to that effect, he argues, government authorities

lack the legal right to take slaves from their owners. Spiece concludes his letter by suggesting that in taking slaves far from their homes, Confederate authorities were endangering the security of the would-be-new nation.

There is also a serious evil in impressing slaves for the service in North western Virginia:—whilst there they get to talking with *Union men* in disguise, and by that means learn the original cause of the difficulty between North & South: then return home and inform other negroes:—not long since one of my neighbors negro men went to his master, and desired to let him go again to the north western army—adding "I wish you to let me go further than I went before["]—I have the honor to be most respectfully your Obt Servt.

It is unknown whether Confederate officials responded to Spiece's letter. ■

Source: Ira Berlin, Barbara J. Fields, Thavolia Glymph, Joseph P. Reidy, and Leslie S. Rowland, eds., *Freedom: A Documentary History of Emancipation, 1861–1867,* Series 1, Vol. 1, *The Destruction of Slavery* (1985), pp. 782–783.

tect and retain control over their dependents at all times. In August 1861, the attorney general of Virginia reluctantly informed the Confederate secretary of war that the residents of Shenandoah County, with a white population of 12,800, were balking at the call for 10 percent of its population in volunteers. Likewise, resentful of the impressment of the few slaves from their area, farmers in Randolph County, Alabama, pointed to the sacrifices of their own women and children, "industriously engaged on their farms," their necks reddened by the sun, while in the city wealthy whites (and their slaves) went about business as usual.

Some masters stood on principle in their efforts to keep their enslaved men and women out of the clutches of Confederate "press agents." Planters also expressed a well-founded fear that slaves impressed for a wide range of tasks, whether saltmaking or chopping trees or tending brick kilns, were difficult to control now that plantation discipline had been loosened. All over the South, white men resisted the idea that they must relinquish their slaves to the Confederacy to preserve the institution of slavery.

The Confederate call for volunteers failed to produce the number of soldiers (and menial laborers) needed to fight the Union, and so in March 1862 Davis received congressional authorization to implement a military conscription law (all men between ages 18 and 35 were called up for three years of service), the first draft on the North American continent. (By September the upper age had been raised to 45.) The law also exempted certain kinds of workers, such as railroad employees, schoolteachers, miners, and druggists, and allowed the buying of

Carl G. von Iwonski, *Block House, New Braunfels*. Yanaguana Society Collection. Daughters of the Republic of Texas Library

■ Farmer's cabin, Block House, New Braunfels, Texas.

"substitutes" by draftees who could afford the $300 price for them. This last type of exemption allowed wealthy men to pay someone to fight in their place.

These provisions provoked anger not only among ordinary citizens but also among principled states' rights advocates such as governors Joseph Brown of Georgia and Zebulon Vance of North Carolina. Brown exempted large numbers of men from the draft, claiming that the Confederacy posed a greater threat to states' rights than did the Union. On January 1, 1862, 209,852 southern men were present for duty. Yet the northern force was more than twice as large, with 527,204.

In Confederate encampments, antebellum identities gave way to wartime necessity. Reduced to the status of menial laborers, washing their own clothes and cooking their own meals, digging trenches and hauling wood, some sons from elite families felt demeaned by their new responsibilities. Soon after the war began, Colonel Jonathan A. Winston complained to the commander of the Confederate post at Yorktown, Virginia, that his men were "laboring in the unloading of Ships"—a poor use of their time, he thought, and a job better suited to slaves. However, there were too few blacks in the immediate area to meet all the needs of the army and the needs of the white soldiers themselves. For the purposes of war, white men must serve other white men.

Indians and Immigrants in the Service of the Confederacy

Just as the Confederates failed in their attempt to use fully the labor of enslaved workers, so they failed to reap much gain from the vaunted military prowess of Indians, especially those in Indian Territory (present-day Oklahoma). In 1861, southern military officials appealed to the Cherokees and the other Five Tribes for support, promising them arms and protection from

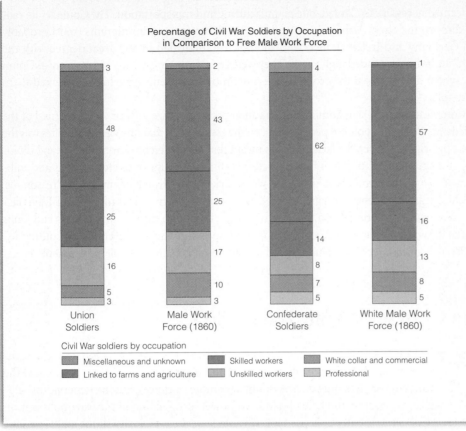

Percentage of Civil War Soldiers by Occupation
in Comparison to Free Male Work Force

Union Soldiers
3
48
25
16
5
3

Male Work Force (1860)
2
43
25
17
10
3

Confederate Soldiers
4
62
14
8
7
5

White Male Work Force (1860)
1
57
16
13
8
5

Civil War soldiers by occupation
■ Miscellaneous and unknown   ■ Skilled workers   ■ White collar and commercial
■ Linked to farms and agriculture   ■ Unskilled workers   ■ Professional

■ **FIGURE 14.2**
OCCUPATIONAL CATEGORIES
OF UNION AND CONFEDERATE
SOLDIERS

Union forces in return. Only gradually and reluctantly did Cherokee leader John Ross commit his men to the Confederacy: "We are in the situation of a man standing alone upon a low naked spot of ground, with the water rising all around him."

More devoted to the Confederate cause was Stand Watie, the brother of Elias Boudinot (one of the Cherokee leaders to have signed the original removal treaty). Backed by many Cherokee slaveholders, Stand Watie proceeded to mobilize what he called the "United Nations of Indians" as a fighting force on behalf of the Confederacy. Among those responding to the call to arms were Chocktaw and Chickasaw men, who formed Company E of the 21st Mississippi Regiment, "the Indian Brigade."

Although Indian Territory was considered of great strategic value to the Confederacy, southern military officials at times expressed frustration with the traditional battle tactics of Indian warriors. They were unused to military encounters that pitted long, straight rows of men on foot against each other. At the Battle of Elkhorn Tavern (Pea Ridge) in March 1862, Indian troops abandoned the battlefield in the face of cannon fire, leading their commander, Albert Pike, to demand that in the future they be "allowed to fight in their own fashion" rather than "face artillery and steady infantry on open ground." Yet most Confederate generals, like George Washington during the Seven Years' War, measured Indians by European American standards of what made a "proper" soldier on the battlefield. In the summer of 1862 the Confederacy lost its advantage in Confederate territory; the Cherokee and Creek were divided in their loyalties, with some joining Union forces and all "undisciplined . . . [and] not very reliable." By this time, the Comanche and Kiowa, resentful of the Confederacy's broken promises (guns and money diverted from them), had joined Union troops and were threatening to invade Texas.

Stand Watie

Even on the southern home front, ethnic loyalties among white men could disrupt services deemed necessary to Confederate manufacturing and transportation. The Confederate railroad director in Selma, Alabama, contended with a labor force of immigrants (most probably from Germany and Ireland), men who "do not feel identified in any great degree with the South" and who demanded high wages. They were constantly threatening to run away to Union lines, where they believed they could make more money and enjoy the luxuries denied them in war-torn Alabama.

Complicating the Davis administration's attempts to mobilize for war was the refusal of the Confederates to form a political party system, on the assumption that unity among whites was the highest priority. However, the lack of parties meant that real differences over military and diplomatic strategy were reduced to infighting between shifting groups of elected officials and military men. Davis and members of his cabinet were quick to label dissent of any kind as treasonous, squelching legitimate debate on significant issues. In wartime Richmond, pro- and anti-Davis factions were made and unmade on the basis of rumor, innuendo, and the friendships and feuds between the wives of officers and politicians. In this respect the white South clung to an outmoded identity as a collection of individuals bound to yield to no person, party, or government.

The Course of War, 1862–1863

When the time came to marshal resources in the service of the national state, Northerners were at a distinct advantage over the states' rights men who dominated the Confederacy. Not only did the Union have more resources, but the Republicans' support for the centralization and consolidation of power also facilitated the war-mobilization process. In Congress, the Republicans took advantage of their majority status and expanded federal programs in the realm of the economy, education, and land use. However, like Davis, Lincoln encountered vehement opposition to his wartime policies. Meanwhile, on the battlefield, Union losses were mounting. The United States confronted an uncertain fate.

■ Ulysses Grant

■ William Sherman

Library of Congress

Library of Congress

■ Robert E. Lee

■ Stonewall Jackson

The Republicans' War

Worried about disloyalty in the vicinity of the nation's capital, on April 27, 1861, Lincoln gave General Winfield Scott the power to suspend the writ of habeas corpus (a legal doctrine designed to protect the rights of people arrested) in Baltimore. By the end of the year, this policy, which allowed the incarceration of people not yet charged with a crime, was being applied in almost all of the loyal United States. Chief among those targeted were people suspected of interfering with war mobilization of men and supplies. Democrats stepped up their opposition to the president, denouncing him as a tyrant and a dictator. Meanwhile, from the other side of the political spectrum, abolitionists expressed their frustration with the administration's conciliatory policy toward the South in general and toward Unionist slaveholders in particular. Claimed Frederick Douglass, "Sound policy, not less than humanity, demands the instant liberation of every slave in the rebel states." Yet Lincoln persisted in appealing to masters' loyalty to the Union, declaring that his objective was "to save the Union, and . . . neither to save or destroy slavery."

Wartime manufacturing and commerce proved to be a boon to enterprising Northerners. Manufacturers made new use of forms of technology (Singer sewing machines to produce uniforms for soldiers, McCormick reapers to harvest grain for soldiers and civilians alike). In Cleveland, a young commission-house operator named John D. Rockefeller was earning enough money to hire a substitute to serve in the army for him. In the middle of the war he shifted his business from trading grain, fish, water, lime, plaster, and salt to refining the crude oil (used in kerosene lamps) recently discovered in western Pennsylvania.

War profiteers were not unique to the North. In 1862 the *Southern Cultivator,* a magazine published in Augusta, Georgia, ran an article titled "Enemies at Home," denouncing the "vile crew of speculators" who were selling everything from corn to cloth at exorbitant prices. However, Republicans saw nothing wrong in enhancing one's fortunes and at the same time contributing to the Union cause. Later recalling his rise to wealth and his effort to bring a bright, clean illuminant to the masses, Rockefeller melded morality with economic self-interest in a revealing and classic Republican way: "Let the good work go on. We must ever remember we are refining oil for the poor man and he must have it cheap and good."

The Republicans' willingness to centralize wartime operations led in 1861 to the formation of the U.S. Sanitary Commission, which recruited physicians, trained nurses, raised money, solicited donations, and conducted inspections of Union camps on the front. During the war, as many as 20,000 white and black women served as nurses, cooks, and laundresses in Union military hospitals. Black women worked primarily in the latter two categories. Appointed superintendent of nurses, Dorothea Dix (an advocate of reform on behalf of the mentally ill during the antebellum period) oversaw a force of 3000 white, mostly middle-class, women nurses. These women served as professional caretakers, often over the objections of skeptical male physicians.

The Republicans believed that the federal government should actively promote economic growth and educational opportunity. Not surprisingly, then, the war deepened the Republicans' determination to enact measures that had previously been thwarted by Democratic presidents and Congresses. In July 1862, the Republicans pushed through an "Act to Secure Homesteads to Actual Settlers on the Public Domain," which granted 160 acres of western land to each settler who lived on and made improvements to the land for five years. Congress also passed the Morrill Act, which created a system of land grant colleges. (Many of these colleges eventually became major public universities, including Colorado State University, Kansas State University, and Utah State University.) Also approved in 1862, the Pacific Railroad Act appropriated to the Union Pacific and the Central Pacific Railroads a 400-foot right-of-way along the Platte River route of the Oregon Trail and lent them $16,000 to $48,000 (depending on the terrain) per mile.

> *Union military strategy reflected a prewar Republican indifference to the rights and welfare of both northern and southern blacks.*

During the first year and a half of war, Union military strategy reflected a prewar Republican indifference to the rights and welfare of both northern and southern blacks. In September 1861 Lincoln revoked a directive released by General John Frémont that would have authorized the seizure of property and the emancipation of slaves owned by Confederates in the state of Missouri. The president feared that such a policy would alienate slaveholders who were considering switching their allegiance to the Union. Later that fall, the capture of Port Royal, South Carolina, gave license to Union soldiers to treat blacks as "contraband of war," the term implying that former southern slaves were now under the control of not southern but northern masters. The policy was an ambiguous one; it denied slaveholders their human property, but failed to recognize blacks as free people with rights.

As Union forces pushed deeper into Confederate territory, U.S. officers devised their own methods for dealing with the institution of slavery. By early 1862, the North had set its sights on the Mississippi River valley, hoping to bisect the Confederacy and cut off supplies and men bound from Texas, Arkansas, and Louisiana to the eastern seaboard. In February General Ulysses S. Grant captured Fort Henry and Fort Donelson on the Tennessee and Cumberland Rivers, the Union's first major victory of the war, and in April New Orleans fell to Admiral David Farragut. In New Orleans, General Benjamin Butler attempted to retain the loyalty of Unionist slaveholders by returning runaway slaves to them. This policy was not always greeted with enthusiasm within Union ranks. A Massachusetts soldier, restless under the command of an officer sympathetic to "slave catching brutes," vowed, "I never will be instrumental in returning a slave to his master in any way shape or manner."

Butler also inflamed local Confederates with his "Woman Order" of May 15, 1862, which held that any woman caught insulting a Union soldier should be considered a prostitute and treated as such. As far away as the British House of Commons, members of Parliament condemned the "infamous" conduct of Butler toward what they considered respectable American ladies.

The Ravages of War: The Summer of 1862

In the summer of 1862, the South suffered a hemorrhaging of its slave population, as the movement of Union troops up and down the eastern seaboard opened the floodgates to runaways. In August a group of Liberty County, Georgia, planters claimed that 20,000 slaves (worth $12 to $15 million) had absconded from coastal plantations, many of them holding "the position of Traitors, since they go over to the enemy & afford him aid and comfort" by providing information and erecting fortifications.

Yet over the course of the summer the Confederacy persevered on the battlefield, aided by the failure of Union armies to press their advantage. In June General George McClellan was turned back on the outskirts of Richmond, convincing Lincoln not only of the incompetence of his chief general but also of the value of a less forgiving approach toward the South. In July, intending to pursue a more aggressive strategy against the massive southern military force, Lincoln brought back the boastful General John Pope from the western campaign ("where we have always seen the backs of our enemies") to command the 50,000-man Army of the Potomac.

The second battle of Manassas in late August pitted Pope and the ridiculed "Tardy" George McClellan against Lee and Jackson. (Among Jackson's footsoldiers in that battle were New Orleans's Pelican Company F, a veritable "congress of nations" including native speakers of German, French, and Spanish.) Within five days the Union force had suffered 16,000 casualties (out of 65,000 men), whereas 10,000 men in Lee's smaller force of 55,000 had been killed or wounded.

The summer of 1862 highlighted the difficulties faced by both sides in fighting a war during warm weather (when roads were passable) in the southern swamps and lowlands. More deadly than bullets and cannon to troops were diseases, especially diarrhea, dysentery, typhoid, pneumonia, and malaria. These killers affected major campaigns, including the failed Union attempt to capture Vicksburg in July. Languishing in the swamps near Richmond, one Union soldier wrote in his diary, "The Army is full of sick men."

In September, Lincoln sent Pope back west to battle on another front. Republican policies related to western homesteads and railroads, combined with a general Union lust for territory, were having a devastating impact on western Indian tribes. The Santee Sioux of Minnesota resented the encroachment of white settlers and the failure of the federal government to make good on pledges of annuity payments and food. Said one white trader, "So far as I am concerned, if they are hungry let them eat grass or their own dung." That particular

Minnesota Historical Society (Neg. #36339)

■ This lithograph, published in 1883, shows the execution of 38 Minnesota Sioux at Mankato, Minnesota, on December 26, 1862. A crowd of European Americans gathers to watch the hangings. Men with wagons are ready to cart away the corpses. During August 1862, all of southern Minnesota had been engulfed in conflict between the Sioux and rural homesteaders. After the suppression of the uprising, U.S. officials forced the surviving Sioux into reservations in present-day South Dakota.

■ MAP 14.3

MESCALERO APACHES BATTLE CONFEDERATES, CENTRAL NEW MEXICO, 1861   The Confederates
hoped to conquer all of the Southwest for slavery. In the summer of 1861, a force led by Colonel John R.
Baylor invaded the Mesilla Valley in New Mexico Territory. The Southerners scored a series of notable
successes until defeated at La Glorieta Pass, a battle called the Gettysburg of the West, in March 1862.
Besieged by Apache and Navajo Indians, the Confederates retreated from New Mexico.

Library of Congress

■ The bodies of soldiers lie where they fell on September 17, 1862, the single day that claimed the largest number of lives in the Civil War. Like many other battles of the war, this one was shaped by the physical features of the battlefield itself, with soldiers on both sides seeking cover in small groves of trees and behind rocks, road ruts, and fences made of stone and wood.

comment helped ignite an uprising among the Sioux, who killed 500 whites before the Minnesota state militia quashed the rebellion at Wood Lake in the fall of 1862. The 38 Indian insurgents hanged by the U.S. Army in December 1862 constituted the largest mass execution in American history.

In other parts of the country the Yankee war against the Confederates spilled over into savage campaigns against Indian tribes. General James H. Carleton routed the Texas Confederates, who had been occupying New Mexico and Arizona, and then provided what he called a "wholesome lesson" to the Mescalero Apache and Navajo who had been menacing Spanish American "placitas" (communities) in the area. Sending his troops out to locate the Mescaleros, Carleton ordered, "The men are to be slain whenever and wherever they can be found. Their women and children are to be taken prisoner." Union soldiers captured Apache leader Mangas Colorado and later murdered him (although he had surrendered under a white flag). The Mescaleros were forced to accept reservation status at Bosque Redondo in the Pecos River Valley. Meanwhile, Colonel Kit Carson conducted a campaign of terrorism against the Navajos, burning *hogans* and seizing crops and livestock, claiming that "wild Indians could be tamed." Many of the survivors undertook the "Long Walk" to Bosque Redondo, a forced march reminiscent of the Cherokees' Trail of Tears a generation before.

In the East, on the banks of Antietam Creek, in northern Virginia, on September 17, the bloodiest single day of the war claimed 20,000 lives and resulted in a Union victory, although it was a dubious victory indeed. Part of the battle took place in a 30-acre cornfield, where Confederates had hidden themselves. Observing the tips of southerners' bayonets glistening in the sunlight, General Joseph Hooker and his men mowed them down with firepower "as the grass falls before the scythe," in the words of a newspaper reporter present at the slaughter. The corpses mingled among the cornstalks presented a grisly sight. Nevertheless, Hooker recalled of the encounter, "The conduct of my troops was sublime, and the occasion almost lifted me to the skies, and its memories will ever remain near me."

To journalists and soldiers alike, battles could offer stirring sights of long rows of uniformed men arrayed against each other, their arms at the ready, regimental flags unfurled in the wind. Yet for the women of Shepardstown, Maryland, left to clean up after the Antietam slaughter, there was no talk of the glory of war, only a frantic, round-the-clock effort to feed the Confederates and bind their wounds. Surveying the battlefield wreckage, one observer, Maria Blunt, lamented the carnage: the dead but also men "without arms, with one leg, with bandaged sides and backs; men in ambulances, wagons, carts, wheelbarrows, men carried on stretchers or supported on the shoulder of some self-denying comrade."

Maria Blunt was not alone in challenging gender conventions that decreed that nursing the wounded and comforting the dying in wartime was too grue-some a task for a woman. All over the South white women established tempo-rary hospitals in barns, private homes, and churches and mourned each human sacrifice to the cause: "A mother—a wife—a sister had loved him." In the sum-mer of 1862, Richmond contained 21,000 wounded Confederates, some of them attended by Sally Louisa Tompkins, commissioned a captain in the Con-federate army to facilitate the work of her infirmary.

The extraordinarily high casualty rate in the war stemmed from several factors. Confederates and Federals alike fought with new kinds of weapons (rifles and sharpshooters accurate at up to 1000 yards) while troops massed in old-style (that is, close) formation. Soft minie balls punctured and lodged in limbs, leading to high rates of amputation that in turn fostered deadly infec-tions. One Alabama soldier observed in 1862, "I believe the Doctors kills more than they cour [cure]." In fact, twice as many Civil War soldiers died of disease and infec-tion as were killed in combat.

Kate Cumming of Mobile, Alabama, earned the gratitude of the Confederacy for her work as a hospital matron during the war. Before and during the Civil War, many people believed that respectable women should not work in hospitals. Physicians claimed that women were likely to faint at the sight of blood and that they were not strong enough to turn patients over in their beds. Yet as the war progressed, more and more northern and southern women defied these stereotypes and served in hospitals as nurses, administrators, and comforters of the ill and dying. Noted Cumming soon after she first entered a hospital, "The foul air from this mass of human beings at first made me giddy and sick, but I soon got over it." Still, in southern hospitals, soldiers and enslaved workers handled much of the direct patient care.

The Emancipation Proclamation

Appalled by the loss of life but heartened by the immediate outcome of Anti-etam, Lincoln took a bold step. In September he announced that on January 1, 1863, he would proclaim all slaves in Confederate territory free. The word-ing of the Emancipation Proclamation itself suggested that Lincoln intended to bolster northern morale by infusing the conflict with moral purpose and at the same time to further the Union's interests on the battleground by encour-aging Southern blacks to join the U.S. army: "And upon this act, sincerely believed to be an act of justice, warranted by the Constitution, upon military necessity, I invoke the considerate judgment of mankind, and the gracious favor of almighty God." The measure left slavery intact in the loyal Border States and in all territory conquered by the Union. Consequently, nearly 1 million black people were excluded from its provisions. Skeptical of the ability of blacks and whites to live together, Lincoln remained committed to the colonization of freed blacks outside the United States (in Central America or the West Indies).

In the congressional elections of 1862, the Democrats picked up strength in New York, Pennsylvania, and Ohio and carried Illinois. The lower Midwest in general harbored large num-bers of Democrats who opposed the war (especially now that it was an "abolition war") and called for peace with the South; these so-called Copperheads disrupted Union enlistments and encouraged military desertions.

As the death toll climbed higher and higher, dissent in the North continued to grow. The Emancipation Proclamation electrified abolitionists, but the war effort was taking its toll among the laboring classes. Especially aggrieved were the working people who paid higher taxes (rel-ative to those paid by the wealthy) to keep the war machine running, and the dockworkers and others who lost their livelihoods when trade with foreign countries ceased. Their resent-ment boiled over in the summer of 1863.

Persistent Obstacles to the Confederacy's Grand Strategy

From the beginning of the war, the North's effort to blockade 3500 miles of southern coast-line met with fierce resistance on the high seas. The South made up in resourcefulness what it lacked in a navy, relying for supplies on swift steamers manned by privateers (British arms smuggled onto remote southern beaches could bring up to 700 percent in profits). Seemingly invincible Confederate ships such as the ironclad *Merrimack* and the well-fortified British-built warships *Alabama* and *Florida* prowled the southeastern seaboard, sinking Union vessels and protecting the blockade runners. Nevertheless, by December 1861, Union forces had established beachheads in Confederate territory up and down the East Coast.

In November 1861 Union naval forces intercepted a British packet ship, the *Trent*, and seized two Confederate diplomats, James Mason and John Slidell, who were en route to London and Paris, where they planned to plead the South's case in a bid to gain diplomatic recognition. To avoid a rift with England, Lincoln and Secretary of State William H. Seward released the two men. In the process Mason and Slidell lost whatever influence they might have had with European governments, and Lincoln enjoyed the praise of the British public for his moderation in handling the so-called *Trent* affair.

More generally, Confederate hopes for diplomatic recognition foundered on the shoals of European politics and economics, in England and in the Western Hemisphere. English textile mills drew on their own immense prewar stockpiles of raw cotton and sought out new sources of fiber in Egypt and elsewhere. Also, English workers flexed their political muscle in a successful effort to forestall recognition of the slaveholders' nation. Textile workers in particular did not want to compete with slave-produced material manufactured in an independent Confederacy.

Early in the war the Confederates recognized the strategic importance of Mexico, both as a trade route for supplies and as a means of access to ports. (Moreover, an estimated 2500 Hispanics fought for the South, among them the Cuban-born Loreta Janeta Velásquez, who disguised herself as a man and joined the Confederate army under the name of Lt. Harry T. Buford.) In approaching Mexican President Benito Juarez for aid in late 1861, Confederate envoy John T. Pickett discovered that, although Mexicans still smarted from their defeat on their own land 13 years before, the Juarez administration remained an ally of the United States. Another Confederate agent, Juan A. Quintero, did manage to win a trade agreement with the governor of a northern Mexican state, Santiago Vidaurri of Nuevo León.

By the summer of 1862, Britain and France were inclined to mediate peace in favor of Confederate independence, for the two powers assumed that the South's impressive

Massachusetts Commandery, Military Order of the Loyal Legion and the U.S. Army Military History Institute

■ Union ships moored at Hilton Head, South Carolina.

victories in Virginia and Tennessee signaled a quick end to the war. Nevertheless, the Confederacy's autumn setbacks of Antietam and Perryville (in Kentucky), combined with ennobling rhetoric of the soon-to-be-announced Emancipation Proclamation, proved that the Union was still very much alive, and the diplomatic recognition the white South so desperately craved remained elusive.

The Other War: African American Struggles for Liberation

From the onset of military hostilities, African Americans, regardless of whether they lived in the North or the South, perceived the Civil War as a fight for freedom. Although they allied themselves with Union forces, they also recognized the limitations of Union policy in ending slavery. Therefore, blacks throughout the northern and southern states were forced to take action to free themselves as individuals, families, and communities. Twenty-year-old Charlie Reason recalled his daring escape from a Maryland slave master and his decision to join the famous 54th Massachusetts Infantry composed of black soldiers: "I came to fight *not* for my country, I never had any, but to gain one." Soon after the 54th's assault on Fort Wagner (outside Charleston Harbor) in July 1863, Reason died of an infection contracted when one of his legs had to be amputated. In countless ways, black people throughout the South fought to gain a country on their own terms.

Enemies Within the Confederacy

In late 1863 a U.S. gunboat picked up 13 black fugitives off the coast of Georgia. Included in the group were the leader, Cain, as well as Bella and her 6-year-old son, Romeo; Lizzie and her four children (ages 5 months to 12 years); and Sallie with four children ranging in age from 7 months to 11 years. Within a few weeks Cain had returned to the mainland to rescue his kinfolk, including Grace and her five children, Grace's son-in-law, Charlie, and her four grandchildren. These groups of self-liberated slaves were like countless others; their ranks were dominated by women and children, for many black men were either "refugeed" farther inland by their masters (to keep them out of the clutches of the Yankees) or fighting in the Union army.

Like the Revolutionaries of 1776, slaveholding whites were shocked when they could not always count on the loyalty of "petted" domestics. Soon after the war began, South Carolina's Mary Boykin Chesnut had expressed unease about the enigmatic behavior of one of her trusted house slaves, Laurence, asking herself of all her slaves, "Are they stolidly stupid or wiser than we are, silent and strong, biding their time?" A few months later Chesnut's cousin was murdered while sleeping, bludgeoned by a candlestick; the cousin's slaves William and Rhody were charged with the crime. Of her own mulatto servant, one of Chesnut's women friends remarked, "For the life of me, I cannot make up my mind. Does she mean to take care of me—or to murder me?" Now rising to the surface, such fears put whites on alert, guarding against enemies in their midst.

Courtesy, Stowe-Day Foundation, Hartford, CT

■ Laura Towne and three of her pupils pose for a picture on Saint Helena Island, South Carolina, in 1866. A native of Pennsylvania, Towne traveled to the South Carolina Sea Islands in April 1862, soon after they were occupied by Union forces. She and her companion and fellow teacher Ellen Murray represented the hundreds of idealistic northern women who volunteered to teach southern black people of all ages during and after the Civil War. Declared Towne on her arrival in the South, "We've come to do antislavery work, and we think it noble work and mean to do it earnestly."

■ All over the South, black people watched and waited for opportunities to claim their own freedom. The movement of Union troops into an area often prompted slaves to flee from the plantation. Individuals and extended families sought safety behind Union lines or in nearby towns or cities or began the quest for long-lost loved ones.

Yet no single white man or woman could halt the tide of freedom. Given the chance to steal away at night or walk away boldly in broad daylight, black men, women, and children left their masters and mistresses, seeking safety and paid labor behind Union lines. Throughout the South, black people waited and watched for an opportunity to flee from plantations, their actions depending on the movement of northern troops and the disarray of the plantations they lived on. In July 1862, the Union's Second Confiscation Act provided that the slaves of rebel masters "shall be deemed captives of war and shall be forever free," prompting Union generals to begin employing runaway male slaves as manual laborers. Consequently, military authorities often turned away women, children, older adults, and the disabled, leaving them vulnerable to spiteful masters and mistresses. For black men pressed into Union military and menial labor service, and for their families still languishing on plantations, "freedom" came at a high price indeed.

The Ongoing Fight Against Prejudice in the North and South

In the North, the Emancipation Proclamation spurred the enlistment of black men in the Union army and navy. The proclamation itself allowed for such recruitment. Furthermore, many black men felt inspired to join U.S. forces since the Lincoln administration had declared the conflict a war for abolition. Eventually, about 33,000 northern blacks enlisted, following the lead of their brothers-in-arms from the South. For example, in October 1862, Massachusetts's Colonel Thomas Wentworth Higginson organized a black regiment on the South Carolina Sea Islands, noting that the First South Carolina Volunteers (unlike their northern white counterparts) were "fighting for their homes and families." The subsequent formation of the famous 54th Massachusetts regiment infuriated southern military leaders, many of whom refused to recognize black men as soldiers at all.

Chicago Historical Society, ICHi-0774

■ Many southern black men first experienced freedom as soldiers for the Union army. They embraced the rituals of Civil War–era manhood, including shouldering arms and participating in military dress parades. Organized early in 1864, the Second US Regiment, Battery A, shown here, served garrison duty at Nashville and in Middle Tennessee. The black troops helped win the Battle of Nashville (December 15–16, 1864) for the Union by holding a Confederate corps at bay on the right while General George H. Thomas led his force of 40,000 against the Confederates on the left.

For black northern soldiers, military service opened up a wider world; some learned to read and write in camp, and almost all felt the satisfaction of contributing to a war that they defined in stark terms of freedom versus slavery. They wore their uniforms proudly. However, Northern wartime policies toward black men as enlisted men and toward black people as laborers revealed that the former slaves (as well as free people of color in the North) would continue to fight prejudice on many fronts.

Some northern whites approved recruiting blacks, reasoning that for each black man killed in battle, one white man would be spared. Until late in the war, black soldiers were systematically denied opportunities to advance through the ranks and were paid less than whites. Although they showed loyalty to the cause in disproportionate numbers compared with white men, most blacks found themselves barred from taking up arms at all, relegated to fatigue work deemed dangerous and degrading to whites. They intended to labor for the Union, but, in the words of a black soldier from New York, "Instead of the musket it is the spade and the Whelbarrow and the Axe cuting in one of the horable swamps in Louisiana stinking and misery." For each white Union soldier killed or mortally wounded, two died of disease; the ratio for blacks was one to ten.

Many northern military strategists and ordinary enlisted men showed indifference at best, contempt at worst, for the desire of black fugitives to locate lost loved ones and begin to labor on their own behalf. In the course of the war, Union experiments with free black labor—on the South Carolina Sea Islands under the direction of northern missionaries, and in Louisiana, under the direction of generals Nathaniel Banks and Benjamin Butler—emphasized converting the former slaves into staple crop wage workers under the supervision of Yankees. Some of these whites, in their eagerness to establish "order" in former Confederate territory, saw blacks only as exploitable labor—if not cannon fodder, then hands to dig ditches and grow cotton.

Many southern blacks later recalled grateful first encounters with Yankee soldiers, men who brought them the news of their freedom. But others recalled harsh treatment at the hands of the blue-coated invaders. For example, Union soldiers seized the goods that Nancy Johnson and her husband, Boson Johnson (he was "a good Union man during the war," noted his wife), had spent a lifetime accumulating as slaves on a rice plantation in Canoochie Creek, Georgia: one mare, 625 pounds of bacon, 60 pounds of lard, 12 bushels of corn, 8 bushels of rice, 7 meat hogs, 11 stock hogs, and 25 chickens.

For many blacks, the war brought a mixture of joy and fear. In her book *Reminiscences of My Life in Camp* (published in 1902), former slave Susie King Taylor recalled the heady, dangerous days of 1862, when she fled from Savannah and found refuge behind Union lines off the coast of Georgia. There she met and married Edward Taylor, and together they (along with her uncles and cousins) joined the First South Carolina Volunteers (later known as the 33rd United States Colored Cavalry). The soldiers received no pay for the first 18 months of their service, and even in camp they remained vulnerable to Confederate snipers and bushwhackers. Yet Taylor gained a great deal of satisfaction from conducting a school for black children on St. Simon's Island and performing a whole host of tasks for the fighting men, from cleaning rifles to washing clothes and tending the ill. She understood that her own contributions to the war effort showed "what sacrifices we can make for our liberty and rights."

Battle Fronts and Home Fronts in 1863

In 1863 the North abandoned the strategy of conciliation in favor of an effort to destroy the huge southern armies and deprive the Confederacy of its slave labor force. By this time the war was causing a tremendous hardship among ordinary white folk in the South. Meanwhile, Lincoln found himself caught between African American freedom fighters who resented the poor treatment they received from many white commanders and white Northerners who took their opposition to the war in general and the military draft in particular to the streets. Deprivation at home and the mounting casualty rates on the battlefields were reshaping the fabric of American society, North and South.

Disaffection in the Confederacy

The Civil War assaulted Southerners' senses and their land. Before the war, slave owners and their allies often contrasted the supposed tranquility of their rural society with the rude, boisterous noisiness of the North. According to this view, the South was a peaceful place of contented slaves toiling in the fields, whereas the North was the site of workers striking, women clamoring for the vote, and eccentric reformers delivering streetcorner harangues.

The war exploded on the southern landscape with ferocious force, and the rumble of huge armies on the march shook southern society to its foundations. For the first time many Southerners smelled the acrid odor of gunpowder and the stench of rotting bodies. They heard the booms of near and distant cannon and the mournful sounds of church bells tolling for the dead. They saw giant encampments of soldiers cover what used to be cotton fields and black people where they were not supposed to be: on the road, fleeing from their masters. Some people lived on diets of onions and berries in the absence of harvests of corn and rice. Seemingly overnight, both armies constructed gorge-spanning train trestles and huge riverside docks and warehouses, all in preparation for conflict. As soldiers withdrew from the battlefield, they left behind a scarred and blood-spattered land, cornfields mowed down, fires smoldering in their wake.

These sights and sounds were especially distressing to Southerners who objected to the war as a matter of principle or because of its disastrous effects on their own households. Scattered throughout the South were communities resistant to the policies of what many ordinary whites considered the Richmond elite—the leaders of the Confederacy. In western North Carolina a group calling themselves Heroes of America declared their loyalty to the Union. In northern Alabama, the "Free State of Jones [County]" raised troops for the Yankee army.

Throughout the rural South, army deserters were welcomed home by their impoverished wives and children; it is estimated that during much of the war, as many as one-third of all Confederate soldiers were absent without leave at any particular time.

The antebellum South had celebrated individual households as the foundation of a slave-holders' republic, but now women took the lead in putting the interests of their own families above those of the Confederacy. A letter from "Your Mary" addressed to "Dear Edward" in the service recounted their son's crying the night before: "'O mamma! I am so hungry.' And Lucy, Edward, your darling Lucy; she never complains, but she is growing thinner and thinner every day. And before God, Edward, unless you come home, we must die."

Indeed, all over the South, groups of poor women resisted the dictates of the Davis administration, wealthy men and women who flaunted an extravagant wartime lifestyle of lavish dinners and parties. Women from Virginia to Alabama protested a Confederate 10 percent "tax-in-kind" on produce grown by farmers and the food shortages that reached crisis proportions. In April 1863 several hundred Richmond women, many of them wives of Tredegar Iron Works employees, armed themselves with knives, hatchets, and pistols and ransacked stores in search of food: "Bread! Bread! Our children are starving while the rich roll in wealth." An enraged President Davis told the rioters that he would give them five minutes to disperse before ordering troops to fire on them; the women went home. In their desperation they had highlighted the contradiction between the increasingly efficient process of Confederate industrialization and the increasingly inefficient process of providing basic necessities to people on the home front.

> *During much of the war, as many as one-third of all Confederate soldiers were absent without leave at any particular time.*

Whereas some white women resisted the Confederacy, others leaped to the fore to provide essential goods and services to the beleaguered new nation. Virginia's Belle Boyd kept track of Union troop movements and served as a spy for Confederate armies. Poor women took jobs as textile factory workers, and their better-educated sisters found employment as clerks for the Confederate bureaucracy. Slaveholding women busied themselves running plantations, rolling bandages, and knitting socks for soldiers. In Augusta, Georgia, the Ladies Aid Society sewed garments for the troops, and the Augusta Purveying Association provided subsidized food for the poor. Still, many women felt their labors were in vain. Of the Confederacy's stalled progress, Georgia's Gertrude Thomas noted, "Valuable lives lost and nothing accomplished."

The Tide Turns Against the South

In the fall of 1862 Lincoln replaced General McClellan with General Ambrose E. Burnside. In December, at a major battle at Fredericksburg, Virginia, the general's blundering produced what was called Burnside's Slaughter Pen: 13,000 northern casualties, many fallen in a small area near a stone wall. One survivor described the scene: corpses "swollen to twice their natural size, black as Negroes in most cases." The ground was littered with "one without a head, . . . one without a legs, yonder a head and legs without a trunk . . . with fragments of shell sticking in oozing brain, with bullet holes all over the puffed limbs."

As the northern public tried to come to terms with these losses, Lincoln replaced Burnside with General Joseph ("Fighting Joe") Hooker. In early May 1863, Lee and Jackson encountered Hooker at Chancellorsville, Virginia; the battle left Hooker reeling, but it also claimed the life of Jackson, mistakenly shot by his own men on May 2 in the early evening twilight. The South had lost one of its most ardent champions.

Lee decided to press his advantage by invading Pennsylvania and, it was hoped, encouraging northern Peace Democrats and impressing the foreign powers. The ensuing clash at Gettysburg was a turning point in the war. Drawn by reports of a cache of much-needed shoes, Confederate armies converged on the town, in the south-central part of the state and across the border from Maryland. Union forces pursued. In a three-day battle that began on July 1, the

Gettysburg, July 1–3, 1863

▢ Confederate positions ⇨ Confederate attacks
▢ Roads
▬ Union positions

■ MAP 14.4
THE BATTLE OF GETTYSBURG, JULY 1–3, 1863 The three-day battle of Gettysburg was a turning point in the war. This map shows that Confederate soldiers made repeated assaults on Union lines. Lee's confidence in this strategy was misplaced, and some of his own staff recognized it. Recalled General James Longstreet of the third day of fighting, "My heart was heavy. I could see the desperate and hopeless nature of the charge and the hopeless slaughter it would cause. . . . That day at Gettysburg was one of the saddest of my life."

92,000 men under the command of General George G. Meade were arrayed against the 76,000 troops of Robert E. Lee.

Gettysburg later came to represent the bloody consequences of a war fought by men with modern weapons under commanders with a premodern military sensibility. On the last day of the battle, the men under Major General George Pickett moved slowly into formation, passing along the way hastily dug graves and the fragments of bodies blown to bits the day before. At 3 P.M. a mile-wide formation of 15,000 men gave the rebel yell and charged three-quarters of a mile across an open field to do battle with Union troops well fortified behind stone walls. Within half an hour Pickett had lost two-thirds of his soldiers and all 13 of his colonels. The battle's three-day toll was equally staggering: 23,000 Union and 28,000 Confederate soldiers wounded or killed. Fully one-third of Lee's army was dead or wounded.

What made men of both sides fight on under these conditions? Some remained devoted to a cause. Others cared less about the Confederacy or the Union and more about proving their

Civil Disorders During Wartime

Throughout American history, fighting a war has both exacerbated old social tensions and created new ones. In mobilizing for combat, groups of Americans expressed their resentment toward other groups and clashed with each other over the allocation of food, housing, and jobs. People who dissented against the war effort found themselves branded as traitors and hounded by law enforcement authorities. Wartime civil disorders thus reveal political faultlines in a society that seeks to present a united front against an enemy.

The American Revolution pitted not just Patriots against the British but also whites against enslaved blacks, whites against Indians, Patriots against Loyalists, and large Hudson Valley landowners against their tenants. In 1779 the New York state legislature sponsored an armed invasion of the territory occupied by the Iroquois Confederacy, leading to the destruction of that group's villages and crops. In the Hudson Valley, New England interior, and port towns of Massachusetts, groups of women confronted merchants, demanded an end to price gouging, and then seized the staples they needed to feed their families.

During the War of 1812, political disagreements between Democratic-Republicans and Federalists spilled over into bloodshed. In Baltimore, Republican mobs, enraged by the antiwar policies of a leading Federalist newspaper, attacked several of their political foes, three of whom died. A fourth, Revolutionary War hero Henry (Light Horse Harry) Lee, later died from his injuries.

Both the North and the South had to contend with violence on their respective home fronts during the Civil War. In April 1863, in the Confederate capital of Richmond, a crowd of several hundred women appealed to the Virginia governor for relief from high food prices. Rebuffed, they looted bakeries and other kinds of stores as well. President Jefferson Davis intervened and threatened the women with violence if they did not disperse. A few weeks later, riots broke out in the North as white laborers, many of them Irish immigrants, protested the new Union draft law of July 1. In New York City, workers turned their wrath on African Americans, leaving more than 100 people dead.

Civil disorders during World War I revealed the contradiction between mobilizing for a modern war—a war to "make the world safe for democracy," in the words of President Woodrow Wilson—on the one hand and maintaining racial segregation on the other. At Camp Logan near Houston, Texas, in 1917, African American soldiers protested segregationist policies. In the ensuing melee, 20 people were killed and 100 arrested. Nineteen black soldiers were convicted and later hanged. In the summer of 1919, 26 clashes between blacks and whites broke out in cities all over the nation. Black people sought to exercise their rights as free citizens. Whites were determined to maintain racial segregation and white supremacy at all costs. The bloodiest

manhood and upholding their family's honor. Still others sought to memorialize comrades slain in battle or to conform to standards of discipline drilled into them. A survivor of Pickett's charge downplayed his own courage: "Instead of burning to avenge the insults of our country, families and altars and firesides . . . the thought is . . . *Oh*, if I could just come out of this charge safely how thankful *would I be!*"

The Union victory at Gettysburg on July 3 brought rejoicing in the North. The next day General Ulysses S. Grant captured Vicksburg on the Mississippi River, a move that earned him the rank of lieutenant general (conferred by Congress). Within a year he assumed the position of supreme commander of the Union armies.

Civil Unrest in the North

Yet not all segments of northern society joined in the celebration. Even principled supporters of the Union war effort were growing weary of high taxes and inflated consumer prices, not to mention the sacrifices of thousands of husbands, sons, and brothers. In May, federal soldiers had arrested the defiant and outspoken Copperhead Clement Vallandigham at his home in Dayton, Ohio. Subsequently convicted of treason (he had declared the conflict "a war for the freedom of blacks and the enslavement of whites"), Vallandigham was banished to the South.

Thomas S. England/TimePix

U.S. domestic uprisings during Vietnam war

riot was in Chicago, where 38 people were killed.

In World War II, blacks in Harlem launched a civil rebellion in 1943 in response to systematic discrimination in the defense industry. Elsewhere, white mobs attacked people of color who did not conform to traditional standards of submissiveness and deference. In June 1943, white soldiers in Los Angeles beat black and Mexican American youth, especially those wearing the zoot suits that were fashionable among urban Chicanos then. That same year, Detroit whites and blacks battled each other over limited housing space and job opportunities. The riots left 34 dead and 675 injured and resulted in 1 million hours of lost defense work.

Between 1965 and 1973, opposition to the Vietnam War precipitated violent encounters between demonstrators and police. In the summer of 1968 in Chicago, protesters sought to disrupt the Democratic National Convention. Under orders from Mayor Richard Daley, police attacked the demonstrators with tear gas and billy clubs. In the two-year period from 1969 to 1970, radical student groups carried out or attempted 174 campus bombings of Reserve Office Training Corps offices, launching a violent campaign in protest of government war policies.

In the fall of 2001, in response to the attacks on the World Trade Center and the Pentagon, the United States began to wage an aggressive war against terrorists in Afghanistan and elsewhere in the world. Americans overwhelmingly supported this effort and, for the most part, the tactics used to fight it. Protests against specific Bush administration policies, such as the decision to use military tribunals to try certain people accused of terrorism, took the form of legal challenges, candlelight vigils, and newspaper opinion editorial pieces, not bloody riots in the streets. ∎

Following a military draft imposed on July 1, the northern white working classes erupted. Enraged at the wealthy who could buy substitutes, resentful of the Lincoln administration's high-handed tactics, and determined not to fight on behalf of their African American competitors in the workplace, laborers in New York City, Hartford, Troy, Newark, and Boston (many of them Irish) went on a rampage. The New York City riot of July 11–15 was especially savage as white men directed their wrath against black men, women, and children. Members of the mob burned the Colored Orphan Asylum to the ground and then mutilated their victims.

A total of 105 people died before five Union troops were brought in to quell the violence. The regiments from Pennsylvania and New York were fresh from the Gettysburg battlefield; now they trained their weapons on citizens of New York City. In response to the rioting and to discourage other men from resisting the draft elsewhere, the federal government deployed 20,000 troops to New York. On August 19, the draft resumed.

The Desperate South

Meanwhile, the South had to contend not only with dissent and disaffection at home but also with the stunning battle and territorial losses it suffered at Gettysburg and Vicksburg. On August 21, Jefferson Davis proclaimed a day of "fasting, humiliation and prayer." Throughout the

Occupation	Failed to Report	Exempted for Cause	Commuted or Hired Substitue	Held to Service
Unskilled Laborer	25%	45%	24%	6%
Skilled Laborer	25%	44%	22%	9%
Farmer and Farm Laborer	16%	34%	31%	19%
Merchant, Manufacturer, Banker, Broker	23%	46%	29%	2%
Clerk	26%	48%	24%	2%
Professional	16%	49%	29%	6%

■ FIGURE 14.3
OHIO MEN DRAFTED FOR MILITARY SERVICE WHO REPORTED FOR DUTY OR HIRED SUBSTITUTES

faltering Confederacy white clergy exhorted their congregations to pray for God's mercy. Gone were the confident declarations that "God is on our side"; in their place were the self-doubts of generals and the wails of widows and fatherless children.

Even as Davis was invoking the name of the Almighty, 450 rebels under the command of William Clarke Quantrill were destroying the town of Lawrence, Kansas (long a hotbed of abolitionist sentiment), and killing 150 of its inhabitants. With the exception of Quantrill and John Singleton Mosby (whose squads of men roamed northern Virginia attacking Union posts and troops in 1863), Confederate military leaders shunned guerrilla warfare, preferring to meet the enemy on a field of honor. The desperate Quantrill raid on Lawrence demonstrated that the Confederate cause was, if not lost, then losing in the late summer of 1863.

Before the year was out Davis faced other setbacks as well. In January the French army occupied Mexico City, and the next year Mexican elites, with the aid of the French Emperor Napoleon III, placed Austrian Archduke Maximilian on the throne. With Mexico as part of the French Empire, Napoleon III hoped to use the country as a pawn in his scheme to spread his influence throughout Europe. Still, Grant's successes at Missionary Ridge and Lookout Mountain, in Tennessee, caused both France and England to draw back from offering overt support to the Confederacy in the form of sales of navy warships or diplomatic recognition. The Confederate president had long counted on securing the support of the great European powers; now those hopes were dashed.

Dedicating the national cemetery at Gettysburg on November 19, 1863, Lincoln delivered a short address that affirmed the nation's "new birth of freedom" and its commitment that "the government of the people, by the people, for the people, shall not perish from the earth." Meanwhile, Grant, the hero of Vicksburg, was poised at the border of northern Georgia, ready to push south to the sea and cut in half what was left of the Confederacy.

The Prolonged Defeat of the Confederacy, 1864–1865

By 1864 northern generals, with Lincoln's blessing, had decided to fight a "hard war" against their tenacious enemy. Union troops were authorized to live off the land (denying southern civilians the necessities of life in the process), to seize livestock and other supplies indiscriminately, and to burn everything that the Confederates might find useful. The purposes of this strategy were twofold: to harm irreparably (what was left of) Confederate morale and to facilitate the movement of northern troops through hostile territory. If north-

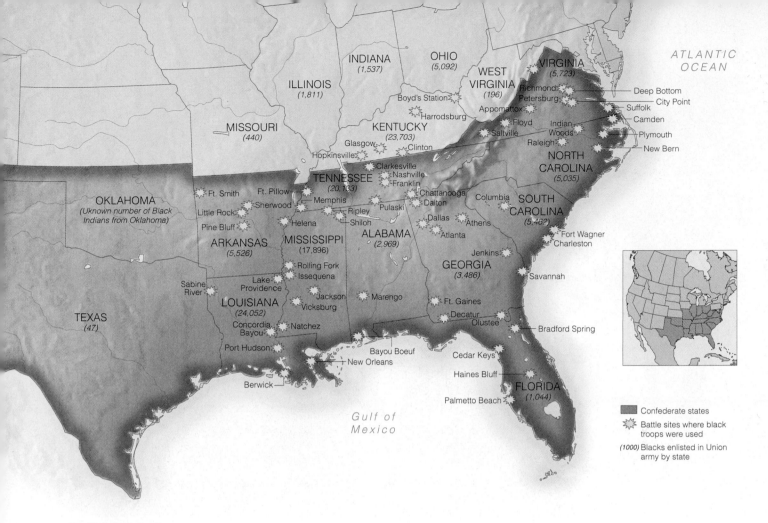

INDIANA (1,537)
OHIO (5,092)
ILLINOIS (1,811)
WEST VIRGINIA (196)
VIRGINIA (5,723)
ATLANTIC OCEAN
Boyd's Station
Harrodsburg
Richmond
Petersburg
Appomattox
Deep Bottom
City Point
Suffolk
Camden
Plymouth
New Bern
MISSOURI (440)
KENTUCKY (23,703)
Floyd
Saltville
Indian Woods
Raleigh
Glasgow
Clinton
Hopkinsville
Clarksville
Nashville
Franklin
NORTH CAROLINA (5,035)
OKLAHOMA (Uknown number of Black Indians from Oklahoma)
Ft. Smith
Ft. Pillow
Sherwood
Memphis
Ripley
Pulaski
Chattanooga
Dalton
Columbia
SOUTH CAROLINA (5,462)
Little Rock
Pine Bluff
Helena
Shiloh
Dallas
Athens
Atlanta
Fort Wagner
Charleston
ARKANSAS (5,526)
MISSISSIPPI (17,896)
ALABAMA (2,969)
Jenkins
Rolling Fork
Issequena
GEORGIA (3,486)
Savannah
Sabine River
Lake Providence
Jackson
Vicksburg
Marengo
Ft. Gaines
LOUISIANA (24,052)
Decatur
Olustee
Bradford Spring
TEXAS (47)
Concordia Bayou
Natchez
Port Hudson
Bayou Boeuf
New Orleans
Cedar Keys
Berwick
Haines Bluff
FLORIDA (1,044)
Palmetto Beach
Gulf of Mexico

Confederate states
Battle sites where black troops were used
(1000) Blacks enlisted in Union army by state

■ MAP 14.5

AFRICAN AMERICANS IN CIVIL WAR BATTLES, 1863–1865   Confederates killed African American soldiers captured in battle at Fort Wagner in Charleston Harbor (1863), the Union garrison of Fort Pillow on the Mississippi River (1864), and Petersburg, Virginia (1864), among other battles. By the end of the war, black men had fought in more than 200 battles. Their performance in combat no doubt contributed to the Confederate decision to arm slaves as soldiers in the last few weeks of the war.

ern troops could sever the area west of Georgia from the Confederacy and take Richmond and destroy its surrounding armies, the Union would be safe at last.

White Men's "Hard War" Toward African Americans and Indians

The policy of "hard war" should not be confused with total war, characterized by state-approved terrorism against civilians. However, Confederate policies toward black soldiers and Union policies toward Indian insurgents in the West did show elements of total war against particular segments of the population. In April 1864 Confederate General Nathan Bedford Forrest destroyed Fort Pillow, a Union garrison on the Mississippi River. After surrendering, black soldiers were systematically murdered. Wounded survivors were bayoneted or burned to death. Among southern generals, conventions of war (providing for the detention and exchange of prisoners of war) did not apply to African American soldiers.

Nor were Indian combatants and civilians accorded even the minimal respect shown to most white fighting men. In the early fall of 1864, a group of Cheyenne and Arapaho were camped along Sand Creek in the southeastern corner of Colorado. Black Kettle, a chief of the Cheyenne, had received promises from Union Col. John M. Chivington and others stationed at Camp Weld in Denver that the two sides would remain at peace with each other. Therefore, on the morning of November 29, 1864, when Black Kettle saw Chivington leading a Colorado volunteer militia toward his settlement, he waved a white flag and stood his ground.

Colorado Historical Society (WPA-834; 10025492)

■ In September 1864, the Indian chiefs Black Kettle and White Antelope, with other Cheyenne and Arapaho leaders, met with Colonel John M. Chivington at Camp Weld, Colorado. The purpose of the meeting was to secure a truce between the Indians and European Americans in the area. Two months later, Chivington attacked an encampment of these Indians on the banks of Sand Creek, about 100 miles southeast of Denver.

Chivington did not come in peace. That day he and his men massacred 125 to 160 Indians, mostly women, children, and old people, returning later to mutilate the bodies. In response, the Sioux, Arapaho, and Cheyenne launched their own campaigns on the white migrants traveling the South and North Platte trails. Chivington declared that it was "right and honorable" to use any means to kill Indians, including children ("nits make lice," he said). Captain Silas Soule, who rode with Chivington but refrained from killing innocent civilians on principle, later testified against the colonel during a military investigation in early 1865; walking on the streets of Denver one day, Soule was murdered by a Chivington supporter.

"Father Abraham"

Lincoln's wartime policies consisted of a calculated indifference toward the life and liberties of Native Americans on one hand and a noble defense of the principles of democratic government among white men on the other. The election of 1864 proceeded without major incident, although Lincoln himself faced some opposition within his own party. Together with his new running mate, a former slave owner from Tennessee named Andrew Johnson, Lincoln benefited from a string of preelection victories won for him by Admiral David G. Farragut at Mobile, Alabama, and by General Philip Sheridan in Virginia's Shenandoah Valley. As a result, he defeated the Democratic nominee, his own former general, George McClellan, who managed to garner 45 percent of the popular vote. One of the keys to Lincoln's success was the "peace platform" that the Democrats had drafted at their convention the summer before;

support among Union soldiers for "Little Mac" dropped precipitously as a result, and Lincoln won three-quarters of the army's vote.

Despite his limited military experience, Lincoln possessed a strategic sense superior to that of many of his generals. He played down his own military experience, making light of his minor part in the Black Hawk War of 1832; in that conflict, he reminisced, he had engaged in

TABLE 14-1			
The Election of 1864			
Candidate	Political Party	Popular Vote	Electoral Vote
Abraham Lincoln	Republican	2,213,655	212*
George B. McClellan	Democratic	1,805,237	21

*Eleven secessionist states did not participate.

"charges upon wild onions . . . [and] bloody struggles with the Musquetoes." However, he cared deeply about ordinary soldiers and talked with them whenever he had the opportunity. In return, Union troops gave "Father Abraham" their loyalty on the battlefield and, especially during the election of 1864, at the ballot box.

The Last Days of the Confederacy

Meanwhile, the transformation of the Confederacy—from a loose collection of agrarian states to a centralized war machine—was almost complete, and so the Confederacy itself, as a republic of slaveholders, was doomed. In September 1864 Lee, anxious for troops, had convinced Secretary of War James A. Seddon to impress 20,000 slave men and all free men of color and to organize them into military-like units. By December, only 1200 had been put to work and 800 had run away.

Some slaveholders were acknowledging the "mechanical genius" of their slaves, an argument against pressing them into Confederate service as manual laborers, but an implicit argument in favor of their use as soldiers. If black men were intelligent beings, then they could become disciplined military troops, so this (new) Confederate reasoning held. In January 1865 Lee admitted that the fate of the Confederacy depended on black labor, not only as skilled artisans but as soldiers as well. He noted that the best way to attract men to any "service which imposes peculiar hardships and privations" was to ensure that they had a personal interest in the outcome: "Such an interest we can give our negroes by giving immediate freedom to all who enlist, and freedom at the end of the war to the families of those who discharge their duties faithfully (whether they survive or not), together with the privilege of residing at the South." The South had shifted its cause from the preservation of slavery to the preservation of the Confederacy, with or without slavery.

Union General William Tecumseh Sherman's forces overtook Atlanta in September 1864 and swept southeast toward the coast, living off the land and denying Confederate soldiers and civilians alike food and supplies along the way. En route to Savannah, Sherman's men liberated Andersonville Prison, a 26-square-acre Confederate camp that held 33,000 prisoners in the summer of 1864. Unable to feed their own armies and so unwilling to commit large supplies of food to the prison, the Confederate commander, Henry Wirz, stood by while 13,000 died of starvation, disease, and exposure. (Wirz was the only Confederate officer to be tried, convicted, and executed for war crimes by the U.S. government.) Among the freed prisoners was Payson Wolfe, who had served with Michigan's Company K, an all-Indian company of sharpshooters. Wolfe returned home to Michigan but never fully recovered from the time he spent at Andersonville.

Northerners expressed outrage over Andersonville. However, considering conditions at Bosque Redondo, New Mexico, their denunciations had the ring of hypocrisy. This settlement was an internment camp for Apache and Navajo survivors of the campaign initiated against them in 1862; by spring of 1864 some 10,000 people were confined there, an estimated quarter of whom died before they were allowed to return home in 1868.

After presenting Lincoln with the "Christmas gift" of Savannah in December, Sherman took his 60,000 troops north, slogging through swamps and rain-soaked terrain to confront

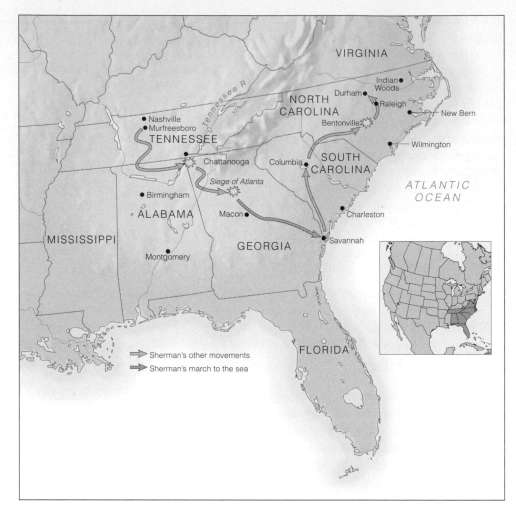

■ MAP 14.6

SHERMAN'S MARCH TO THE SEA, 1864–1865   General William T. Sherman's famous march to the sea marked the final phase of the Union effort to divide and conquer the Confederacy. Sherman's men burned Atlanta to the ground in September 1864. In late December they made their triumphant entry into the city of Savannah. Sherman followed a policy of "hard war" in these final months of the war; he ordered his troops to seize from civilians any food and livestock they could use and to destroy everything else, whether rail lines, houses, or barns. White Southerners expressed outrage over these tactics. Still, Sherman never systematically attacked civilians, a characteristic of the Union's "total war" against Native American peoples in the West.

the original secessionists. Later, he recalled with satisfaction, "My aim then was to whip the rebels, to humble their pride, to follow them to their inmost recesses, and make them fear and dread us." By mid-February, the state capital, Columbia, was in flames. African American troops were among the triumphant occupiers of the charred city.

In his second inaugural address, delivered March 4, 1865, Lincoln declared that the Almighty had rendered final judgment on the abomination that was slavery. The president vowed that the North would persevere "until all the wealth piled by the bondsman's two hundred and fifty years of unrequited toil shall be sunk, and until every drop of blood drawn with the lash shall be paid by another drawn with the sword."

By early April, Grant had overpowered Lee's army in Petersburg, Virginia. Withdrawing, Lee sent a telegram to Davis, who was attending church in Richmond, warning him that the fall of the Confederate capital was imminent. Davis and almost all other whites fled the city. Arriving in Richmond on April 3, only hours after the city had been abandoned, was the commander-in-chief of the Union army, Abraham Lincoln. Lincoln calmly walked the streets of the smoldering city (set afire by departing Confederates), flanked by a group of ten sailors. Throngs of black people greeted the president, exclaiming, "Glory to God! Glory! Glory! Glory!" When a black man kneeled to thank Lincoln, the president said, "Don't kneel to me. That is not right. You must kneel to God only, and thank Him for the liberty you will enjoy hereafter."

On April 9, Lee and his demoralized and depleted army of 35,000 men found themselves outnumbered by Grant and Meade, and Lee surrendered his sword at Appomattox Courthouse in northern Virginia. Lee had rejected a plea by one of his men that the army disband and continue to fight a guerrilla war in the woods and hills. The general predicted that such a force "would become mere bands of marauders," destroying the countryside and with it what was left of the fabric of southern society.

Union officials ensured rebel soldiers protection from future prosecution (for treason) and allowed the cavalry to keep their horses for use in spring planting. These policies were remarkably lenient treatment for traitors. Indeed, a sight on the day of the Confederate surrender suggested that Northerners would pay the defeated Confederates grudging respect. The ragtag members of the so-called Stonewall Brigade, men who had entered the war with Stonewall Jackson four years before, came forward to lay down their arms. In recognition, the Union army gave them a salute of honor, one group of fighting men acknowledging the bravery of another. However, this scene set the stage for the not-too-distant future, when the North and South reaffirmed their ties based on a shared "whiteness" in opposition to African Americans.

Watching a comedy with his wife, Mary, at Ford's Theater in Washington on the night of April 14, Lincoln was one of the last casualties of the war. Shot by John Wilkes Booth, a Confederate loyalist fearful that the president was bent on advancing "nigger citizenship," Lincoln lingered through the night but died the next morning. Booth himself was caught and shot within a matter of days. Of the departed president, Secretary of State Seward said, "Now he belongs to the ages."

Conclusion

Rather than asking why the South lost the Civil War, we might wonder why it took the North four years to win it. Despite all the political dissent and social conflict in the white South, despite the crumbling of the institution of slavery and the lack of support from the European powers, the Confederacy was able to mobilize huge armies under the command of brilliant tacticians such as Lee and Jackson. The war was fought on the battlefield by regiments of soldiers, not on the sea by navies or in the countryside by guerrillas. Therefore, as long as Confederate generals could deploy troops and outwit their foes during brief but monumental clashes, the Confederacy could survive to fight another day. The South had as its immediate goal the slaughter of as many Yankees as possible. Meanwhile, the North staggered under the weight of mobilizing large numbers of men in enemy territory and supplying those men with the necessary resources far from home.

In terms of lives lost (620,000), the Civil War was by far the costliest in the nation's history. (The death toll among American military personnel in the Revolution was 26,000; in World War I, 116,000; in World War II, 400,000; in Vietnam, 58,000.) At the end of the war, the Union was preserved and slavery was destroyed. Yet, in their quest for true freedom, African Americans soon learned that military hostilities were but one phase of a wider war, a war to define the nature of American citizenship and its promise of liberty and equality. Thus April 1865 marked not so much a final judgment as a transition to new battlefields.

Sites to Visit

The Valley of the Shadow: Living the Civil War
Pennsylvania and Virginia
jefferson.village.virginia.edu/vshadow/vshadow.html
> This project tells the histories of two communities on either side of the Mason–Dixon line during the Civil War. It includes narrative and an electronic archive of sources.

The Civil War in Charleston, South Carolina
www.awod.com/gallery/probono/cwchas/cwlayout.html
> This site covers the history of the Civil War in and around Charleston.

Abraham Lincoln Association
www.alincolnassoc.com/
> This site includes digital versions of Lincoln's papers.

United States Civil War Center
www.cwc.lsu.edu/
> Maintained by Louisiana State University, this site aims to promote the study of the Civil War by making available "all appropriate private and public data" related to the conflict.

Civil War Women
scriptorium.lib.duke.edu/collections/civil-war-women.html
> This Duke University library site includes original documents, links, and biographical information about several women and their lives during the Civil War.

Library of Congress Civil War Documents
and Photographs
memory.loc.gov/ammem/
> This Library of Congress site includes a wealth of texts and images related to the history of the Civil War.

Civil War Timeline
www.historyplace.com/civilwar/index.html
> This site offers a comprehensive Civil War timeline that includes photographs.

National Civil War Association
www.ncwa.org/
> This site documents the activities of one of the many Civil War reenactment organizations in the United States.

For Further Reading

General

David Herbert Donald, *Lincoln* (1995).

Edward Hagerman, *The American Civil War and the Origins of Modern Warfare* (1988).

Herman Hattaway and Archer Jones, *How the North Won: A Military History of the Civil War* (1980).

James M. McPherson, *Battle Cry of Freedom: The Civil War Era* (1988).

Reid Mitchell, *Civil War Soldiers: Their Expectations and Experiences* (1988).

Clarence Mohr, *On the Threshold of Freedom: Masters and Slaves in Civil War Georgia* (1986).

Mobilization for War, 1861–1862

Gabor Borit, ed., *Lincoln's Generals* (1994).

Drew Gilpin Faust, *The Creation of Southern Nationalism: Ideology and Identity in the Civil War South* (1988).

Joseph L. Harsh, *Confederate Tide Rising: Robert E. Lee and the Making of Southern Strategy, 1861–62* (1998).

Wilfrid Knight, *Red Fox: Stand Watie and the Confederate Indian Nations During the Civil War Years in Indian Territory* (1988).

Alan Nolan, *Lee Considered: General Robert E. Lee and Civil War History* (1991).

George Rable, *The Confederate Republic: A Revolution Against Politics* (1994).

Ralph Wooster, *The Secession Conventions of the South* (1962).

The Course of War, 1862–1864

Stephen Ash, *When the Invaders Came: Conflict and Chaos in the Occupied South, 1861–1865* (1996).

Howard Jones, *The Union in Peril: The Crisis over British Intervention in the Civil War* (1992).

Elizabeth Leonard, *All the Daring of the Soldier: Women of the Civil War Armies* (1999).

Heather Cox Richardson, *The Greatest Nation on Earth: Republican Economic Policies During the Civil War* (1997).

Stephen Sears, *Landscape Turned Red: The Battle of Antietam* (1983).

Emory Thomas, *The Confederacy as a Revolutionary Experience* (1991).

Lee Ann Whites, *The Civil War as a Crisis in Gender: Augusta, Georgia, 1860–1890* (1995).

The Third War: African American Struggles for Liberation

Ira Berlin et al., *Freedom: A Documentary History of Emancipation: Series 1, Vol. I: The Destruction of Slavery; Series 2: The Black Military Experience* (1982).

Ira Berlin and Leslie Rowland, eds., *Families and Freedom: A Documentary History of African-American Kinship in the Civil War Era* (1997).

Robert F. Engs, *Freedom's First Generation: Black Hampton, Virginia, 1861–1890* (1979).

Jacqueline Jones, *Labor of Love, Labor of Sorrow: Black Women, Work, and the Family Since Slavery* (1985).

William S. McFeely, *Frederick Douglass* (1991).

Willie Lee Rose, *Rehearsal for Reconstruction: The Port Royal Experiment* (1964).

Battle Fronts and Home Fronts in 1863

Stephen V. Ash, *Middle Tennessee Society Transformed, 1860–1870: War and Peace in the Upper South* (1988).

Iver Bernstein, *The New York City Draft Riots: Their Significance for American Society and Politics in the Age of the Civil War* (1990).

Paul D. Escott, *Many Excellent People: Power and Privilege in North Carolina, 1850–1900* (1985).

Drew Gilpin Faust, *Mothers of Invention: Women of the Slaveholding South in the American Civil War* (1996).

J. Matthew Gallman, *The North Fights the War: The Home Front* (1994).

Frank Klement, *Dark Lanterns, Secret Political Societies, Conspiracies, and Treason in the Civil War* (1990).

Mark M. Smith, *Listening to Nineteenth-Century America* (2001).

The Prolonged Defeat of the Confederacy, 1864–1865

Michael B. Ballard, *A Long Shadow: Jefferson Davis and the Final Days of the Confederacy* (1997).

Richard Beringer et al., *Why the South Lost the Civil War* (1986).

Ernest Furgurson, *Ashes of Glory: Richmond at War* (1996).

Joseph Glatthaar, *The March to the Sea and Beyond: Sherman's Troops in the Savannah and Carolina Campaigns* (1985).

Mark Grimsley, *The Hard Hand of War: Union Military Policy Toward Southern Civilians, 1861–1865* (1995).

James M. McPherson, *For Cause and Comrades: Why Men Fought in the Civil War* (1997).

J. Tracy Power, *Lee's Miserables: Life in the Army of Northern Virginia from the Wilderness to Appomattox* (1998).

Online Practice Test

Test your understanding of this chapter with interactive review quizzes at

www.ablongman.com/jonescreatedequal/chapter14

Additional Photo Credits

Page 463: Chicago Historical Society, ICHi—22172

Page 465: The Museum of the Confederacy, Richmond, Virginia (CT #495b). Photograph by Katherine Wetzel

Page 475: University of Oklahoma, Western History Collections, Phillips Collection (#1459)

Page 478: Collection of The New-York Historical Society, Acc. #41526

Page 481: (Top) Confederate Memorial Hall, New Orleans, photo by John R. Miller; (bottom) New York Division of Military & Naval Affairs

Page 482: Courtesy, The Museum of the Confederacy, Richmond Virginia

Page 485: Library of Congress

Page 497: The National Park Service

In the Wake of War: Consolidating a Triumphant Union, 1865–1877

Edward Lamson Henry, *Kept In*, 1889. Fenimore Art Museum, Cooperstown, New York (N-309.61).
Photo by Richard Walker

■ The artist Edward L. Henry titled this 1888 painting *Kept In*. A pupil endures her punishment
while her classmates frolic outside during recess. Former slaves of all ages eagerly embraced the
opportunity to learn to read and write, and many African American communities established their own
schools after the war. Some Northerners, mostly young white women, traveled south to teach
the freedpeople.

I N SAVANNAH, GEORGIA, IN MID-DECEMBER 1864, AFRICAN AMERICAN MEN, WOMEN, AND children rejoiced when the troops of Union General William Tecumseh Sherman liberated the city: the day of jubilee had come at last! The city's black community immediately formed its own school system under the sponsorship of a new group, the Savannah Education Association (SEA). The association owed its creation to the desire of freedpeople of all ages to learn to read and write. A committee of nine black clergy began by hiring 15 black teachers and acquiring buildings (including the Old Bryan Slave Mart) for use as schools. By January 1, 1865, Savannah blacks had raised $800 to pay teachers' salaries, enabling several hundred black children to attend classes free of charge.

Following hard on the heels of the Union army, a group of northern white missionaries arrived in Savannah to seek black converts for two Protestant denominations, the Presbyterians and the Congregationalists. On the first day of school, in January 1865, these northern newcomers watched a grand procession of children wend its way through the streets of Savannah. The missionaries expressed amazement that the SEA was an entirely black-run organization; these whites had believed the former slaves incapable of creating such an impressive educational system.

Charleston, South Carolina, after Sherman's 1865 siege.

In March 1865, the federal government, under the auspices of the newly formed Bureau of Refugees, Freedmen, and Abandoned Lands (Freedmen's Bureau), agreed to work with missionaries in opening schools for black children throughout the former Confederate states. In Georgia, missionaries and government officials soon became alarmed that black leaders were willing to accept financial aid from them but not willing to relinquish control of SEA schools to the whites in return. The Northerners were also distressed by the militancy of certain local black leaders. One of these leaders was Aaron Bradley, who, armed with a pistol and bowie knife, was urging other black men to vote as a bloc in all elections.

In an effort to wrest control of the SEA from Savannah blacks, northern missionaries and agents of the Freedmen's Bureau decided to withhold funds from the association. By March 1866, these efforts had paid off: The city's black community, swollen by a refugee population, was no longer able to support its own schools. Northern whites took over SEA operations, and the association ceased to exist.

Postwar political interest in the South unleashed a major conflict between supporters of African American rights and supportors of southern privilege. Republican congressmen hoped to *reconstruct* the South by enabling African Americans to own their own land and to become full citizens. Southern freedpeople sought to free themselves from white employers, landlords, and clergy and to establish control over their own workplaces, families, and churches. In contrast, President Andrew Johnson appeared bent on *restoring* the antebellum

■ The Boston wing of the American Tract Society, an abolitionist group, published a series of reading primers for the newly freed slaves. The primers provided moral lessons as well as reading lessons for the pupils. This page from *The Freedman's Third Reader* focuses on the work of John W. Alvord, the Freedmen's Bureau general superintendent of education. The authors suggest (wrongly) that Alvord played a major role in organizing the Savannah Education Association in Savannah, Georgia, in early 1865.

power relations that made southern black people field laborers dependent on white landowners. For their part, many southern whites were determined to prevent black people from becoming truly free. Most former rebels remained embittered about the outcome of the war and vengeful toward the freedpeople.

The Civil War hardened the positions of the two major political parties. The Republicans remained in favor of a strong national government, one that promoted economic growth. The Democrats tended to support states' efforts to manage their own affairs, which included regulating relations between employers and employees, whites and blacks.

After the war, western economic development presented new challenges for men who had fought for the Union. In order to open the West to European American miners and homesteaders, the U.S. army clashed repeatedly with Native Americans. On the Plains and in the Northwest, Indians resisted white efforts to force them to abandon their nomadic way of life and take up sedentary farming. William Tecumseh Sherman, Philip H. Sheridan, and George Custer were among the U.S. military officers who had commanded troops in the Civil War and now attempted to subdue the Plains Indians and further white settlement. Sherman declared, "We must act with vindictive earnestness against the Sioux, even to their extermination, men, women and children." The former head of the Freedmen's Bureau, General Oliver O. Howard, oversaw the expulsion of Chief Joseph and his people, the Nez Perce, from their homeland in Washington's Walla Walla Valley in 1877.

U.S. soldiers also contributed to the building of the transcontinental railroad. A former Union military officer, Grenville Dodge, served as chief civil engineer for the Union Pacific Railroad, supervising huge workforces of immigrant laborers. The railroad industry was a potent symbol of postwar U.S. nationalism. It also represented a robust, Republican-sponsored partnership between private enterprise and the federal government. Between 1862 and 1872, the government gave the industry subsidies that included millions of dollars in cash and more than 100 million acres of land. On the Plains, U.S. soldiers protected Union Pacific Railroad land surveyors against the retaliatory raids conducted by Indians who were enraged by this incursion into their territory and by the government's failure to abide by its treaties.

The Civil War, and the economic growth unleashed after the conflict, transformed the physical landscape of the nation. In the South the scars of war were everywhere, in the form of ruined crop fields, pillaged forests, and smoldering cities. Pursuing a strategy of "total war" in the final months of the war, Sherman's troops had destroyed many of the towns and farms that lay in their path on their famous march from Atlanta to Savannah and then north into South Carolina. New train trestles, wharfs, and warehouses stood as monuments to the recent efforts of both rebel and Union forces to move and supply their troops. In the West, construction of new towns and railroad tracks demanded tremendous amounts of lumber. Some observers warned of an impending timber famine, spurring interest in the conservation of natural resources of all kinds.

The Republicans' triumph prompted dissent from people who feared that the victorious Union would serve the interests of specific groups such as men, employers, and white property owners. Some women's rights activists, for example, felt betrayed by the suggestion that this was "the hour of the Negro [man]." These women were not willing to wait indefinitely for their own voting rights. At the same time, in the bustling workshops of the nation's cities, many workers realized that they remained at the mercy of employers bent on using cheap labor. The founding of the National Labor Union in 1866 revealed that members of the laboring classes had a national vision of their own, one that valued the efforts of working people to earn a decent living for their families.

At great cost of human life, the Civil War decisively settled several immediate and long-standing political conflicts. The southern secessionists were defeated, and slavery as a legal institution was destroyed. Nevertheless, the relationship between federal power and group rights remained unresolved, leading to continued bloodshed between whites and Indians on the High Plains, as well as in the former Confederate states between Union supporters and diehard rebels. During the postwar period, federal government officials attempted to complete the political process that the military defeat of the South had only begun: the consolidation of the Union, North and South, East and West. This process encompassed the nation as a whole.

The Struggle over the South

The Civil War had a devastating impact on the South in physical, social, and economic terms. The region had lost an estimated $2 billion in investments in slaves; modest homesteads and grand plantations alike lay in ruins; and gardens, orchards, and cotton fields were barren. Along the seacoast and riverways, fish stocks were depleted. More than three million former slaves eagerly embraced freedom, but the vast majority lacked the land, cash, and credit necessary to build family homesteads for themselves. At the same time, landowning whites considered black people primarily as a source of agricultural labor; these whites resisted the idea that the freedpeople should be granted citizenship rights. This conflict—between blacks as family members determined to control their own lives and whites as landowners determined to reassert authority over blacks—assumed immense proportions.

In the North, Republican lawmakers disagreed among themselves how best to punish the defeated but defiant rebels. President Abraham Lincoln had indicated early that after the war the government should bring the South back into the Union quickly and painlessly. However, his successor wanted to see members of the southern planter elite humiliated, but resisted the notion that freedpeople should become independent of white landowners. In Congress, moderate and radical Republicans argued about how far the government should go in ensuring the former slaves' freedom.

Southern and northern blacks, staunch defenders of the Republican party, hoped to achieve social and economic self-determination. After the war, southern whites condemned what they called the freedpeople's "noxious liberty": their tendency to move around. In fact, all over the South, African American men and women had set out to claim what they believed was rightfully theirs. They traveled great distances, usually on foot, in efforts to locate loved ones and reunite families that had been separated during slavery. They also went to great lengths to resist attempts by white employers to bind them out as apprentices, a new form of bondage. Freed parents turned their energies toward providing for their families, cultivating food crops for their own consumption, and trying to buy land whenever possible. Just as black people had proved to be a military and political force during the war, so they became major actors in the reconstruction of the postwar South.

Wartime Preludes to Postwar Policies

The political and social complications of a northern victory became apparent long before the Confederates laid down their arms at Appomattox Courthouse. Wartime experiments with African American free labor in Union-occupied areas foreshadowed bitter postwar debates. As early as November 1861, Union forces had occupied the Sea Islands off Port Royal Sound in South Carolina. In response, wealthy cotton planters fled to the mainland. As many as 10,000 slaves stayed behind on the islands to fish and to cultivate corn for themselves.

Over the next few months, three groups of northern civilians landed on the Sea Islands with the intention of guiding blacks in the transition from slave to free labor. Teachers arrived intent on creating schools, and missionaries hoped to start churches. A third group, representing Boston investors, had also settled on the Sea Islands to assess economic opportunities; by early 1862, they decided to institute a system of wage labor that would reestablish a staple crop economy and funnel cotton directly into northern textile mills. The freed slaves gave a cautious welcome to the teachers and missionaries, but they resisted growing cotton for the wartime market. They preferred to grow crops for their families to eat rather than cotton to sell, relying on a system of barter and trade among networks of extended families. Their goal was to break free of white landlords, suppliers, and cotton merchants.

Not all Union military men relished the prospect of forcing blacks to work on the plantations where they had been enslaved.

Meanwhile, in southern Louisiana, the Union capture of New Orleans in the spring of 1862 enabled northern military officials to implement their own free (that is, nonslave) labor system. General Nathaniel Banks, the Union officer in charge of occupied New Orleans, outlined the plan. Many blacks had fled from their former owners when the Union army occupied the area. Banks proclaimed that U.S. troops should forcibly relocate blacks to plantations "where they belong"; there they would continue to work for their former owners in the sugar and cotton fields, but now for wages supposedly negotiated annually. The Union army would compel blacks to work if they resisted doing so. Furthermore, said Banks, black men, women, and children must "work diligently and faithfully for one year, respectful of their employers." In defiance of these orders, however, some blacks went on strike for higher wages, and others refused to work at all. Moreover, not all Union military men relished the prospect of forcing blacks to work on the plantations where they had been enslaved. Thus, federal policies returning blacks to plantations remained contested even within the ranks of the army itself. These disputes—between blacks and planters, and among Union officials—would continue throughout the postwar period.

The Port Royal and southern Louisiana precursors to Reconstruction offered variations on two themes: the Republicans' insistence on preserving the southern plantation economy and the former slaves' efforts to achieve freedom from white control.

The Lincoln administration had no hard-and-fast Reconstruction policy to guide congressional lawmakers looking toward the postwar period. In December 1863 the president outlined his Ten Percent Plan. This plan would allow former Confederate states to form new state governments once 10 percent of the men who had voted in the 1860 presidential election had pledged allegiance to the Union and renounced slavery. Congress never acted on Lincoln's plan because many Republicans felt the need for harsher measures.

Instead, at the end of their 1864 session, legislators passed the Wade-Davis Bill, which would have required a majority of southern voters in any state to take a loyalty oath affirming their allegiance to the United States. By refusing to sign the bill before Congress adjourned, Lincoln vetoed the measure (the so-called pocket veto). However, the president approved the creation of the Freedmen's Bureau in March 1865. The Bureau was responsible for coordinating relief efforts on behalf of blacks and poor whites loyal to the Union, for sponsoring schools, and for implementing a labor contract system on southern plantations. Congress also created the Freedman's Savings and Trust Bank in the hope that the former slaves would save a part of their earnings. At the time of his assassination, Lincoln seemed to be leaning toward giving the right to vote the southern black men.

Bettmann/CORBIS

■ Freedmen's Bureau agents distributed rations to former slaves and southern whites who had remained loyal to the Union. Agents also sponsored schools, legalized marriages formed under slavery, arbitrated domestic disputes, and oversaw labor contracts between workers and landowners. This photo shows the bureau office in Petersburg, Virginia.

Presidential Reconstruction, 1865–1867

When Andrew Johnson, the seventeenth president of the United States, assumed office in April 1865, he brought his own agenda for the defeated South. Throughout his political career, Johnson had seen himself as a champion of poor white farmers in opposition to the wealthy planter class. A man of modest background, he had been elected U.S. senator from Tennessee in 1857. He alone among southern senators remained in Congress and loyal to the Union after 1861. Lincoln first appointed Johnson military governor of Tennessee when that state was captured by the Union in 1862 and then tapped him as his running mate for the election of 1864.

Soon after he assumed the presidency, Johnson disappointed congressional Republicans who hoped that he would serve as a champion of the freedpeople. He welcomed back into the Union those states reorganized under Lincoln's 10 percent plan. On May 29, 1865, Johnson announced his own plan for Reconstruction. He advocated denying the vote to wealthy Confederates, though he would allow individuals to come to the White House to beg the president for special pardons. Johnson also outlined a fairly lenient plan for readmitting the other rebel states into the Union. Poor whites would have the right to vote, but they must convene special state conventions that would renounce secession and accept the Thirteenth Amendment abolishing slavery. Further, they must repudiate all Confederate debts—that is, they must default on any loans made by banks or private individuals to finance the southern war effort. The president opposed granting the vote to the former slaves; he believed that they should continue to toil as field workers for white landowners.

Johnson failed to anticipate the speed and vigor with which former Confederate leaders would move to reassert their political authority. In addition, he did not gauge accurately the resentment of congressional Republicans, who thought his policies toward the defeated South were too forgiving. A warning came in December 1865, when Carl Schurz, a German immigrant and former Union brigadier general, issued his "Report on the Condition of the South." In it, he warned that the Freedmen's Bureau was "very unpopular" among white Southerners, who would no doubt fill a power vacuum left by federal weakness and indecision.

By January 1865, both houses of Congress had approved the Thirteenth Amendment to the Constitution, abolishing slavery.

Several developments quickly proved Schurz right. The southern states that took advantage of Johnson's reunification policies passed so-called Black Codes. These state laws were an ill-disguised attempt to institute a system of near-slavery. They aimed to penalize "vagrant" blacks, defined as those who did not work in the fields for whites, and to deny blacks the right to vote, serve on juries, or in some cases even own land. The Black Code of Mississippi barred blacks from marrying whites and from owning land "except in incorporated towns or cities" and restricted the rights of a freedperson to "keep or carry fire-arms," ammunition, and knives and to "quit the service of his or her employer before the expiration of his or her term of service without good cause." The vagueness of this last provision threatened any blacks who happened not to be working under the supervision of whites at any given moment. People arrested under the Black Codes faced imprisonment or forced labor.

At the end of the war, congressional Republicans were divided into two camps. Radicals wanted to use strong federal measures to advance black people's civil rights and economic independence. In contrast, moderates were more concerned with the free market and private property rights; they took a hands-off approach regarding former slaves, arguing that blacks should fend for themselves and avoid dependence on federal aid. But members of both groups reacted with outrage to the Black Codes. Moreover, when the legislators returned to the Capitol in December 1865, they were in for a shock: among their new colleagues were four former Confederate generals, five colonels, and other high-ranking members of the Confederate elite, including former Vice President Alexander Stephens, now under indictment for treason. All of these rebels were duly elected senators and representatives from southern states. In a special session called for December 4, a joint committee of 15 lawmakers (6 senators and 9 members of the House) voted to bar these men from Congress.

By January 1865, both houses of Congress had approved the Thirteenth Amendment to the Constitution, abolishing slavery. The necessary three-fourths of the states ratified the measure by the end of the year. Unlike the Emancipation Proclamation (1863), which freed only slaves in Confederate territory, the Thirteenth Amendment abolished slavery wherever it existed. The federal government now guaranteed freedom for all black people.

However, President Johnson was becoming more openly defiant of his congressional foes who favored aggressive federal protection of black civil rights. He vetoed two crucial pieces of legislation: an extension and expansion of the Freedmen's Bureau and the Civil Rights Bill of 1866. This latter measure, a precursor to the Fourteenth Amendment, was an unprecedented piece of legislation. It called on the federal government—for the first time in history—to protect individual rights against the willful indifference of the states (as manifested, for example, in the Black Codes). Congress managed to override both vetoes by the summer of 1866.

In June of that year, Congress passed the Fourteenth Amendment. This amendment guaranteed the former slaves citizenship rights, punished states that denied citizens the right to vote, declared the former rebels ineligible for federal and state office, and voided Confederate debts. This amendment was the first to use gender-specific language, guarding against denying the vote "to any of the male inhabitants" of any state. The amendment, also, for the first time legally defined the rights of American citizenship and empowered the federal government to protect those rights.

Even before the war ended, Northerners had moved south; and the flow increased in 1865. Black and white teachers volunteered to teach the former slaves to read and write. Some white Northerners journeyed south to invest in land and become planters in the staple crop economy. White southern critics called all these migrants carpetbaggers. This derisive term suggested that the Northerners hastily packed their belongings in rough bags made of carpet scraps and then rushed south to take advantage of the region's devastation and confusion.

Former Confederates were not the only people suspicious of the newcomers. In 1865 a black abolitionist Union officer, Martin R. Delany, condemned the northern white people recently arrived in South Carolina. These Northerners, Delany told a group of freedpeople, had "come down here to drive you as much as ever. It's slavery again: northern, universal U.S. slavery." To many freedpeople, whether they worked for a white Northerner or Southerner, laboring in the cotton fields was but a continuation of slavery.

Freedmen and white Southerners sometimes differed within their own camps about political and economic aims. For example, southern blacks united in their demands for land and the vote but disagreed among themselves over the necessity of political cooperation with whites in general. Some former southern (white) Whigs, who had been reluctant secessionists, now found common ground with northern Republicans who supported government subsidies for railroads, banking institutions, and public improvements. This group consisted of some members of the humbled planter class as well as men of more modest means. Southern Democrats, who sneered at any alliances with the North, scornfully labeled these whites "scalawags" (the term referred to a scrawny, useless type of horse on the Scottish island of Scalloway).

Soon after the war's end, southern white vigilantes launched a campaign of violence and intimidation against freedpeople who dared to resist the demands of white planters and other employers. In 1866 former Confederate General Nathan Bedford Forrest, who had led the massacre of African American soldiers at Fort Pillow, founded a social club composed of Tennessee war veterans. Calling itself the Ku Klux Klan, this group soon became a white supremacist terrorist organization and spread to other states. In May 1866 violence initiated by white terrorists against blacks in Memphis, Tennessee, left 46 freedpeople and 2 whites dead, and in July, a riot in New Orleans claimed the lives of 34 blacks and 3 of their white allies. These bloody encounters demonstrated the lengths to which ex-Confederates would go to reassert their authority and defy the federal government.

Back in Washington, Johnson was not content to veto Republican legislation. In the summer of 1866, he also began to lobby against the Fourteenth Amendment, traveling around the country and urging the states not to ratify it. He argued that policies related to black suffrage should be decided by the states. The time had come for reconciliation between the North and South, maintained the president. (The amendment would not be adopted until 1868.)

Congressional Republicans fought back. In the election of November 1866, they won a two-thirds majority in both houses of Congress. These numbers allowed them to claim a mandate from their constituents and to override any future vetoes by the president. Taking heart from their newfound legislative successes, moderates and radicals together prepared to bypass Johnson to shape their own Reconstruction policies.

The Southern Postwar Labor Problem

Throughout the South, black people aspired to labor for themselves and gain independence from white overseers and landowners. Yet white landowners persisted in regarding blacks as field hands who must be coerced into working. With the creation of the Freedmen's Bureau in 1865, Congress intended to form an agency that would mediate between these two groups. Bureau agents encouraged workers and employers to sign annual labor contracts designed to eliminate the last vestiges of the slave system. All over the South, freed men, women, and children would contract with an employer on January 1 of each year. They would agree to work for either a monthly wage, an annual share of the crop, or some combination of the two.

The Bureau established elementary schools and distributed rations to southerners who had remained loyal to the Union, blacks and whites alike. Agents also conducted wedding ceremonies for the former slaves, who had been denied the right to legalize their unions as marriages. Yet the agency's most formidable challenge was its effort to usher in a new economic order in the South—one that relied on nonslave labor but also returned the region to prewar productivity levels in terms of planting and harvesting cotton.

In April 1866, a white planter in Thomson, Georgia, wrote to a local Freedmen's Bureau official and complained that the black wives and mothers living on his land had refused to sign labor contracts. The planter explained, "Their husbands are at work, while they are nearly idle as it is possible for them to be, pretending to spin—knit or something that really amounts to nothing." These "idle" women posed a threat to plantation order, the white man asserted.

Women who stayed home to care for their families were hardly idle. Yet Freedmen's Bureau agents and white planters alike tended to define productive labor (among blacks) as work carried out under the supervision of a white man in the fields or a white woman in the kitchen. During the postwar period, a struggle ensued. Who should toil in the fields of the South? And under what conditions should they labor?

The physical devastation wrought by the war gave these questions heightened urgency. Most freedpeople understood they must find a way to provide for themselves first and foremost. They thought of freedom in terms of welfare for their family rather than just for themselves as individuals. Men and women embraced the opportunity to live and work together as a unit. For many couples, their first act as free people was to legalize their marriage vows. Black women shunned the advice of Freedmen's Bureau agents and planters that they continue to pick cotton. These women withdrew from field labor whenever they could afford to do so. Enslaved women had been deprived of the opportunity to attend to family life. Now freedwomen sought to devote themselves to caring for their families.

The Freedmen's Bureau's functions in the areas of labor and education represented a new and significant federal role in the realm of social welfare. Yet the agency did not have the staff or money necessary to effect meaningful change.

According to the Northerners, the benefits of this system were clear. Employers would have an incentive to treat their workers fairly—to offer a decent wage and refrain from physical punishment. Disgruntled workers could leave at the end of the year to work for a more reasonable landowner. In the postbellum South, however, labor relations were shaped not by federal decree but by a process of negotiation that pitted white landowners against blacks who possessed little but their own labor.

For instance, blacks along the Georgia and South Carolina coast were determined to cultivate the land on which their forebears had lived and died. They urged General Sherman to confiscate the land owned by rebels in the area. In response, in early 1865, Sherman issued Field Order Number 15, mandating that the Sea Islands and the coastal region south of Charleston be divided into parcels of 40 acres for individual freed families. He also decreed that the army might lend mules to these families to help them begin planting. Given the provisions of this order, many freed families came to expect that the federal government would grant them "40 acres and a mule."

As a result of Sherman's order, 20,000 former slaves proceeded to cultivate the property once owned by Confederates. Within a few months of the war's end, however, the War Department bowed to pressure from the white landowners and revoked the order. The War Department also provided military protection for whites to return and occupy their former lands. In response, a group of black men calling themselves Commissioners from Edisto Island (one of the Sea Islands)

H.P. Moore/Collection of The New-York Historical Society, Neg. #37497

■ Residents of Edisto Island, off the coast of South Carolina, pose with a U.S. government mule cart immediately after the Civil War. U.S. troops captured the island in November 1861. The following March, the government began to distribute to blacks the lands abandoned by their former masters. In October 1865 President Andrew Johnson halted the program. A group of angry and disappointed blacks appealed to the president, claiming, "This is our home, we have made these lands what they are." After meeting with the group, General Oliver O. Howard noted, "I am convinced that something must be done to give these people and others the prospect of homesteads."

met in committee to protest to the Freedmen's Bureau what they considered a betrayal. Writing from the area in January 1866, one Freedmen's Bureau official noted that the new policy must be upheld but regretted that it had brought the freedpeople in "collision" with "U.S. forces."

During its brief life (1865 to 1868), the Freedmen's Bureau compiled a mixed record. The individual agents represented a broad range of backgrounds, temperaments, and political ideas. Some were former abolitionists who considered northern-style free labor to be "the noblest principle on earth." These men tried to ensure safe and fair working arrangements for black men, women, and children. In contrast, some agents had little patience with the freedpeople's drive for self-sufficiency. Some bureau offices became havens for blacks seeking redress against abusive or fraudulent labor practices, but other offices had little impact on the postwar political and economic landscape. For agents without means of transportation (a reliable horse),

A Southern Labor Contract

After the Civil War, many southern agricultural workers signed labor contracts. These contracts sought to control not only the output of laborers but also their lives outside the workplace.

On January 1, 1868, the planter John D. Williams assembled his workers for the coming year and presented them with a contract to sign. Williams owned a plantation in the Lower Piedmont county of Laurens, South Carolina. He agreed to furnish "the said negroes" (that is, the three black men and two black women whose names were listed on the document) with mules and horses to be used for cultivating the land. The workers could receive their food, clothing, and medical care on credit. They were allowed to keep one-third of all the corn, sweet potatoes, wheat, cotton, oats, and molasses they produced. Presumably, they would pay their debts to Williams using proceeds from their share of the crop.

According to the contract, Williams's workers promised to

bind them Selves to be steady & attentive to there work at all times and to work at keeping in repair all the fences on Said plantation and assist in cuting & taking care of—all the grain crops on Said plantation and work by the direction of me [Williams] or my Agent. . . .

And should any of them depart from the farm or from any services at any time with out our approval they shall forfeit one dollar per day, for the first time and for the second time without good cause they shall forfeit all of their interest in the crop their to me the enjured person—they shall not be allowed to keep firearms or deadly wapons or ardent Spirits and they shall obey all lawful orders from me

or my Agent and shall be honest—truthful—sober—civel—diligent in their business & for all wilful Disobedience of any lawful orders from me or my Agent drunkenness moral or legal misconduct want of respects or civility to me or my Agent or to my Family or any elce, I am permitted to discharge them forfeiting any claims upon me for any part of the crop. . . .

Moses Nathan	1 full hand
Jake Chappal	" "
Milly Williams	½ " "
Easter Williams	" "
Mack Williams	" "

At the end of the contract is this addition:

We the white labores now employed by John D. Williams on his white plains plantation have lisened and heard read the foregoing Contract on this sheet of paper assign equal for the black laborers employed by him on said place and we are perfectly Satisfied with it and heare by bind our selves to abide & be Governed & Controwed by it

Wm Wyatte	1 full hand
John Wyatte	1 full hand
Packingham Wyatte	½ " "
Franklin Wyatte	½ " "
R M Hughes	1 full hand
B G Pollard	1 full hand
George Washington Pollard	1 full hand

To sign the contract, all of the blacks and two of the whites "made their marks"; that is, they signed with an "X" because they were illiterate. ■

Source: Rosser H. Taylor, "Postbellum Southern Rental Contracts" [from Furman University library, Greenville, South Carolina], *Agricultural History* 17 (1943):122–123.

After the Civil War, many rural southern blacks, such as those shown here, continued to toil in cotton fields owned by whites.

Library of Congress

plantations scattered throughout the vast rural South remained outside their control. Because white landowners crafted the wording and specific provisions of labor contracts, the bureau agents who enforced such agreements often served the interests of employers rather than laborers.

In fact, for the most part, postwar freed people pressed for their labor rights independently of the federal government. In the cotton regions of the South, freedpeople resisted the near-slavery system of gang labor that planters tried to enforce right after the war. Instead, extended families came together in groups called squads to negotiate collectively with landowners. Gradually, squads gave way to sharecropping families.

The outlines of sharecropping, a system that defined southern cotton production until well into the twentieth century, were visible just a few years after the Civil War. Poor families, black and white, contracted annually with landlords, who advanced them supplies, such as crop seed, mules, plows, food, and clothing. Fathers directed the labor of their children in the fields. At the end of the year, many families remained indebted to their employer and, thus, entitled to nothing and obliged to work another year in the hope of repaying the debt. If a sharecropper's demeanor or work habits displeased the landlord, the family faced eviction.

Single women with small children were especially vulnerable to the whims of landlords in the postbellum period. Near Greensboro, North Carolina, for example, planter Presley George, Sr., settled accounts with his field worker Polly at the end of 1865. For her year's expenses, Polly was charged a total $69.00 for corn, cloth, thread, and board for a child who did not work. By George's calculations, Polly had earned exactly $69.00 for the labor she and her three children (two sons and a daughter) performed in the course of the year, leaving her no cash of her own. Under these harsh conditions, freedpeople looked to each other for support and strength.

Building Free Communities

Soon after the war's end, southern blacks set about organizing themselves as an effective political force and as free communities devoted to the social and educational welfare of their own people. As early as summer 1865, groups of freedpeople met in convention to press for their rights as U.S. citizens. A group calling itself Colored Citizens of Norfolk, Virginia, issued an address to the people of the United States, warning that the Emancipation Proclamation was insufficient to check the power of diehard rebels. Mass arrests of blacks had been authorized by "the rebel Mayor." Former slaveholders were bent on keeping the blacks "in a state of serfdom," charged the Norfolk petitioners.

Differences among blacks based on income, jobs, culture, and skin color at times inhibited institution-building. Some black communities found themselves divided by class, with blacks who had been free before the war (including many literate and skilled light-skinned men) assuming leadership over illiterate field hands. In New Orleans, a combination of factors contributed to class divisions among people of African heritage. During the antebellum period, light-skinned free people of color, many of whom spoke French, were much more likely to possess property and a formal education compared to enslaved people, who were dark-skinned English speakers. After the Civil War, the more privileged group pressed for public accommodations laws, which would open the city's theaters, opera, and expensive restaurants to all blacks for the first time. However, black churches and social organizations remained segregated according to class. Yet, citywide black conventions held in 1864 and 1867 brought together all groups of African descent in common cause, defined as "the actual liberation from social and political bondage."

For the most part, postbellum black communities united around the principle that freedom from slavery should also mean full citizenship rights: the ability to vote, own land, and educate their children. These rights must be enforced by federal firepower: "a military occupation will be absolutely necessary," declared the blacks of Norfolk, "to protect the white Union men of the South, as well as ourselves." Freedpeople in some states allied themselves with white

TABLE 15-1

Comparison of Black and White Household Structure in 27 Cotton-Belt Counties, 1870, 1880, 1900

1870 (N = 534)

Single Person %	Nuclear %	Ext. %	Aug. %	Ext./Aug. %	Adults %	Total	
3.1	80.7	14.4	1.4	.3	.3	290	Black
2.1	71.3	7.4	17.6	1.2	.4	244	White
2.6	76.4	11.0	8.8	.7	.4	534	

1880 (N = 679)

Single Person %	Nuclear %	Ext. %	Aug. %	Ext./Aug. %	Adults %	Total	
3.7	74.2	13.6	5.9	1.7	.8	353	Black
3.1	62.7	13.5	15.7	5.0	.0	319	White
3.4	68.8	13.5	10.6	3.3	.4	672	

1900 (N = 644)

Single Person %	Nuclear %	Ext. %	Aug. %	Ext./Aug. %	Adults %	Total	
5.7	64.9	22.9	4.0	1.7	.8	353	Black
3.4	65.2	19.0	.7	1.7	.0	290	White
4.7	65.0	21.2	7.0	1.7	.5	643	

Single person: one person living alone.
Nuclear: father, mother, and children.
Ext.: extended family consisting of parents, children, and kin.
Aug.: augmented household consisting of family and nonfamily members (boarders, servants, hired hands).
Ext./aug.: combination of extended and augmented.
Unrelated adults: more than one unrelated adult living together.

Source: Based on information from a sample of households (located in selected cotton staple counties in Alabama, Florida, Georgia, Louisiana, Mississippi, North Carolina, South Carolina, and Texas) listed in the 1870, 1880, and 1900 federal population manuscript censuses.

yeomen who had long resented the political power of the great planters and now saw an opportunity to use state governments as agents of democratization and economic reform.

Networks of freedpeople formed self-help organizations. Like the sponsors of the Savannah Education Association, blacks throughout the South formed committees to raise funds and hire teachers for neighborhood schools. Small Georgia towns, such as Cuthbert, Albany, Cave Spring, and Thomasville, with populations no greater than a few hundred, raised up to $70 per month and contributed as much as $350 each for the construction of school buildings. Funds came from the proceeds of fairs, bazaars, and bake sales; subscriptions raised by local school boards; and tuition fees. In the cash-starved postbellum South, these amounts represented a great personal and group sacrifice for the cause of education.

Black families sought to care for people who could not care for themselves. Freedmen's Bureau agents scoffed at blacks who took in "improvident" and "lazy" elderly kin: how could

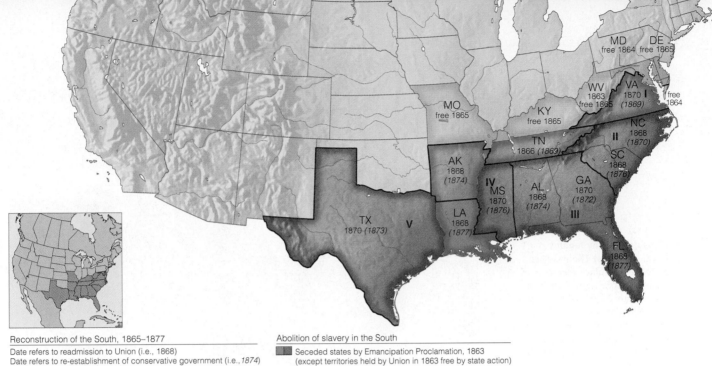

Reconstruction of the South, 1865–1877

Date refers to readmission to Union (i.e., 1868)
Date refers to re-establishment of conservative government (i.e., *1874*)

■ Reconstruction government set up under Lincoln

■ Reconstruction government set up under Johnson

□ Five military districts by Reconstruction Act, 1867

Abolition of slavery in the South

■ Seceded states by Emancipation Proclamation, 1863
(except territories held by Union in 1863 free by state action)

■ Delaware and Kentucky by Thirteenth Amendment, 1865;
Maryland, Missouri, and West Virginia by state action

■ **MAP 15.1**

RADICAL RECONSTRUCTION   Four of the former Confederate states, Louisiana, Arkansas, Tennessee, and Virginia, were reorganized under President Lincoln's 10 Percent Plan in 1864. Neither this plan nor the proposals of Lincoln's successor, Andrew Johnson, provided for the enfranchisement of the former slaves. In 1867 Congress established five military districts in the South and demanded that newly reconstituted state governments implement universal manhood suffrage. By 1870 all of the former Confederate states had rejoined the Union, and by 1877 all of those states had installed conservative (i.e., Democratic) governments.

the former slaves hope to advance their own interests if they had to support such unproductive people? All over the South, black families charted their own course. They elected to take in orphans, to pool resources with neighbors, and to arrange for mothers to stay home with their children. These choices challenged the power of former slaveholders and the influence of Freedmen's Bureau agents and northern missionaries and teachers. At the same time, in seeking to attend to their families and to provide for themselves, southern blacks resembled members of other mid-nineteenth-century laboring classes who valued family ties over the demands of employers and landlords.

Tangible signs of the new emerging black communities infuriated southern whites. A schoolhouse run by blacks proved threatening in a society where most white children had little opportunity to receive an education. Black communities were also quick to form their own churches, rather than continue to occupy an inferior place in white churches. Other sights proved equally unsettling: on a main street in Charleston, an armed black soldier marching proudly or a black woman wearing a fashionable hat and veil, the kind favored by white women of the planter class. These developments help to account for the speed with which whites organized themselves in the Klan and various other vigilante groups, such as Young Men's Democratic Clubs, White Brotherhood, and Knights of the White Camellia. Members of this last group took an initiation oath that stated, "Our main and fundamental object is the maintenance of the supremacy of the white race in this Republic."

Congressional Reconstruction: The Radicals' Plan

The rise of armed white supremacist groups in the South helped spur congressional Republicans to action. On March 2, 1867, Congress seized the initiative. A coalition led by two

■ This drawing by famous political cartoonist Thomas Nast depicts the first black members of Congress. Left to right, front row: Senator Hiram Revels of Mississippi (the first African American to serve in the U.S. Senate), Representatives Benjamin S. Turner of Alabama, Josiah T. Walls of Florida, Joseph H. Rainey of South Carolina, Robert B. Elliott of South Carolina. Back row: Representatives Robert G. DeLarge of South Carolina, Jefferson Long of Georgia.

THE FIRST COLORED SENATOR AND REPRESENTATIVES.
In the 41ˢᵗ and 42ⁿᵈ Congress of the United States.

radicals, Senator Charles Sumner of Massachusetts and Congressman Thaddeus Stevens of Pennsylvania, prodded Congress to pass the Reconstruction Act of 1867. The purpose of this measure was to purge the South of disloyalty once and for all. The act stripped thousands of former Confederates of voting rights. The former Confederate states would not be readmitted to the Union until they had ratified the Fourteenth Amendment and written new constitutions that guaranteed black men the right to vote. The South (with the exception of Tennessee, which had ratified the Fourteenth Amendment in 1866) was divided into five military districts. Federal troops were stationed throughout the region. These troops were charged with protecting Union personnel and supporters in the South and with restoring order in the midst of regional political and economic upheaval.

Congress passed two additional acts specifically intended to secure congressional power over the president. The intent of the Tenure of Office Act was to prevent the president from dismissing Secretary of War Edwin Stanton, a supporter of the radicals. The other measure, the Command of the Army Act, required the president to seek approval for all military orders from General Ulysses S. Grant, the army's senior officer. Grant also was a supporter of the Republicans. Both of these acts probably violated the separation of powers doctrine as put forth in the Constitution. Together, they would soon precipitate a national crisis.

The radicals' call for the redistribution of land from former slaveholders to freedpeople won few supporters among moderates in Congress. In contrast, both Republican factions threw their support behind an emerging southern Republican party, a move that had a significant impact on postwar politics. Alert to the designs of the "irritated, revengeful South," Thaddeus Stevens, the leading House radical, urged Republicans, black and white, to assume control of the South; otherwise, "all our blood and treasure will have been spent in vain." Giving the vote to black men spurred the growth of southern Republican party organizations, called Union Leagues, that provided a political forum for a host of black leaders.

During Reconstruction, approximately 2000 black men served as local elected officials, sheriffs, justices of the peace, tax collectors, and city councilors. Many of these leaders were of mixed ancestry, and many had been free before the war. They came in disproportionate numbers from the ranks of literate men, such as clergy, teachers, and skilled artisans. In Alabama, Florida, Louisiana, Mississippi, and South Carolina, black men constituted a majority of the voting public. Throughout the South, 600 black men won election to state legislatures. However, nowhere did blacks control a state government, although they did predominate in South Carolina's lower House. Sixteen black Southerners were elected to Congress during Reconstruction. Most of those elected to Congress in the years immediately after the war were freeborn. However, among the nine men elected for the first time after 1872, six were former slaves. All of these politicians exemplified the desire among southern blacks to become active, engaged citizens.

Among this group of black leaders was war hero Robert Smalls of South Carolina, who early in the war had seized a Confederate gunboat and escaped from Charleston Harbor. Other prominent leaders included Tunis G. Campbell, a native of New Jersey who served as a Georgia state senator and justice of the peace; and the Reverend Henry M. Turner of Georgia, who warned against political divisions between dark- and light-skinned blacks. In Mississippi, in February 1870, Hiram Revels became the first black man to serve in the U.S. Senate. Another Mississippi politician, Blanche K. Bruce, dominated the political scene in Bolivar County, where he served as sheriff, tax collector, and superintendent of education all at the same time. In 1875 Bruce was elected to the U.S. Senate.

Newly reconstructed southern state legislatures provided for public school systems, fairer taxation methods, bargaining rights of plantation laborers, racially integrated public transportation and accommodations, and public works projects, especially railroads. Nevertheless, the legislative coalitions forged between Northerners and Southerners, blacks and whites, were uneasy and, in many cases, less than productive. Southern Democrats (and later, historians sympathetic to them) claimed that Reconstruction governments were uniquely corrupt, with some carpetbaggers, scalawags, and freedpeople vying for kickbacks from railroad and construction magnates. In fact, whenever state legislatures sought to promote business interests, they opened the door to the bribery of public officials. In this respect, northern as well as southern politicians were vulnerable to charges of corruption. In the long run, southern Democrats cared less about charges of legislative corruption and more about the growing political power of local black Republican party organizations.

In Washington in early 1868 President Johnson forced a final showdown with Congress. He replaced several high military officials with more conservative men. He also fired Secretary of War Stanton, in apparent violation of the Tenure of Office Act. Shortly thereafter, in February, a newly composed House Reconstruction Committee impeached Johnson for ignoring the act, and the Senate began his trial on March 30. The president and Congress were locked in an extraordinary battle for political power.

During the House debate and the Senate trial, political rhetoric verged on the melodramatic. Representative Stevens condemned Johnson as "the nightmare that crouched on the heaving breast of the nation." Nevertheless, the president managed to avoid conviction. The final vote was 35 senators against Johnson, one vote short of the necessary two-thirds of all senators' votes needed for conviction. Nineteen senators voted to acquit Johnson of the charges. The president celebrated his victory by sharing a round of whiskey with his lawyers. Nevertheless, to win acquittal, he had had to promise moderates that he would not stand in the way of congressional plans for Reconstruction. Johnson essentially withdrew from policymaking in the spring of 1868.

TABLE 15-2			
The Election of 1868			
Candidate	Political Party	Popular Vote	Electoral Vote
Ulysses S. Grant	Republican	3,013,421	214
Horatio Seymour	Democratic	2,706,829	80

That November, Republicans urged Northerners to "vote as you shot" (that is, to cast ballots against the former Confederates) and elected Ulysses S. Grant to the presidency. Grant defeated the Democratic nominee, Horatio Seymour, a former governor of New York. An estimated half a million former slaves cast their ballots for Grant, whom they hailed as a liberator.

Two Presidents Impeached

The president, a Democrat, had humble roots in the South. He was raised by a hard-working single mother. His tenure as a state governor ill prepared him for the hostility he encountered as chief executive in Washington, where people persisted in gossiping about his personal life. The Republicans, firmly in control of Congress, despised him and managed to impeach him. At the same time, many observers questioned whether his misdeeds rose to the level of "high crimes and misdemeanors." With the aid of skillful lawyers, members of his own party, and a core of Republican moderates, he avoided conviction in the Senate. Nevertheless, the political battle diminished his capacity to lead forcefully for the rest of his term in office.

Andrew Johnson in 1868 or Bill Clinton 130 years later? The answer, of course, is both. Yet these superficial similarities in the careers of the two men mask dramatic differences between them. Andrew Johnson was charged with violating the Tenure of Office Act, a law that probably was unconstitutional in any case. His impeachment took place against the backdrop of a national debate over the course of Reconstruction, a debate that was intensely ideological.

In contrast, Bill Clinton was charged with lying and obstructing justice, charges that stemmed from an

President Andrew Johnson (1865–1868).

Library of Congress

President Bill Clinton (1992–2000).

White House Historical Association

extramarital affair the president had conducted with a young White House intern, Monica Lewinsky. His impeachment reflected the bitter partisanship and personal animosity between Democrats and Republicans in the 1990s. (See Chapter 29.)

Andrew Johnson was born in Raleigh, North Carolina, in 1808. At age 13, he was apprenticed to a tailor. As a young man, he moved to Tennessee. There he came to identify with the state's yeoman farmers and artisans in opposition to the great planters. Although he served as governor of Tennessee and later U.S. senator, he had little formal education; his wife, the daughter of a Scottish shoemaker, taught him how to write and do arithmetic.

In contrast, Bill Clinton attended Georgetown University and went on to graduate from Yale Law School. Clinton

also appreciated the help and support of his wife, but Hillary Rodham Clinton was a unique First Lady. She possessed impressive skills as a political campaigner and maintained a keen interest in policy issues. In 2000, just as her husband was leaving office, she was elected U.S. senator from the state of New York.

Generations of historians have disagreed about Johnson's case. In the early twentieth century, pro-South scholars sympathized with Lincoln's successor. Yet many scholars later in the century looked more favorably on the radical Republicans; influenced by the Civil Rights movement, these historians focused on Johnson's anti–civil rights stance. Therefore, it is difficult to predict how history will judge Bill Clinton and his battle with congressional Republicans. Historians themselves are an unpredictable lot. ■

The general had proved himself a brilliant strategist during the war, but he lacked political experience, a shortcoming that soon became abundantly clear.

Political reunion was an uneven process, but one that gradually eroded the newly won rights of former slaves in many southern states. By the end of 1868, Arkansas, North Carolina, South Carolina, Louisiana, Tennessee, Alabama, and Florida had met congressional conditions for readmission to the Union, and two years later, Mississippi, Virginia, Georgia, and Texas followed. The Fifteenth Amendment, passed by Congress in 1869 and ratified by the necessary number of states a year later, granted all black men the right to vote.

The National Archives

■ At Promontory Point near Ogden, Utah, workers joined the tracks linking the Central Pacific (its wood-burning locomotive, Jupiter, is on the left) with the Union Pacific's coal-burning engine No. 119. This photo was taken during the May 10, 1869, celebration marking the completion of the transcontinental railroad. According to one eyewitness, the crowd included Indians, Chinese and Irish immigrants, European Americans, and Mexicans "grouped in picturesque confusion." Yet this official photo shows little evidence of the Chinese workers who helped to engineer and build the Central Pacific line.

However, in some states, such as Louisiana, reunification gave Democrats license to engage in wholesale election fraud and violence toward freed men and women. In 1870–1871, a congressional inquiry into the Klan exposed pervasive and grisly assaults on Republican schoolteachers, preachers, and prospective voters, black and white. The Klan also targeted men and women who refused to work like slaves in the fields. In April 1871, Congress passed the Ku Klux Klan Act, which punished conspiracies intended to deny rights to citizens. But Klan violence and intimidation had already taken their toll. Republican voting strength began to decline in rural areas where blacks were the majority population and freedmen had attempted to assert their citizenship rights.

Claiming Territory for the Union

In 1871 poet Walt Whitman wrote an essay titled "Democratic Vistas." In it he celebrated the "manly and courageous instincts" that propelled a brave, adventurous people west. Whitman hailed the march across the prairies and over the mountains as a cavalcade of progress. He and other Americans believed that the postbellum migration fulfilled a mission of national regeneration begun by the Civil War. Kansas's population grew by 240 percent in the 1860s, Nebraska's by 355 percent.

To unite the entire country together as a single economic and political unit was the Republican ideal. Achieving this ideal entailed both technological and military means. The railroads in particular served as vehicles of national integration. When the Central Pacific and Union Pacific Railroads met at Promontory Point, Utah, in 1869, the hammering of the spike that joined the two roads produced a telegraphic signal received simultaneously on both coasts, setting off a national celebration. In Philadelphia, the Liberty Bell tolled.

Meanwhile, regular units of United States cavalry, including two regiments of blacks, were launching attacks on Indians on the Plains, in the Northwest, and in the Southwest. Between

■ With this 1870 photograph, the Kansas Pacific Railroad advertised the opportunity for western travelers to shoot buffalo from the comfort and safety of their railroad car. The company's official taxidermist shows off his handiwork. Railroad expansion facilitated the exploitation of natural resources while promoting tourism.

1865 and 1890, U.S. military forces conducted a dozen separate campaigns against western Indian peoples and met Indian warriors in battle or attacked Indian settlements in more than 1000 engagements. The war for the West pitted agents of American nationalism against Indian groups that battled to maintain their distinctive way of life in a rapidly changing world. In contrast to African Americans, who adamantly demanded their rights as American citizens, defiant western Indians battled a government to which they owed no allegiance.

Federal Military Campaigns Against Western Indians

In 1871 the U.S. government renounced the practice of seeking treaties with various Indian groups. This change in policy opened the way for a more aggressive effort to subdue native populations. It also hastened the expansion of the reservation system, an effort begun in the antebellum period to confine specific Indian groups to specific territories.

In the Southwest, clashes between Indians and U.S. soldiers persisted after the Civil War. In 1867 at Medicine Lodge Creek in southern Kansas the United States signed a treaty with an alliance of Comanche, Kiowa, Cheyenne, Arapaho, and Plains Apache. This treaty could not long withstand the provocation posed by the railroad. The year before, the Seventh U. S. Cavalry, under the command of Lieutenant Colonel George Custer, had been formed to ward off native attacks on the Union Pacific, snaking its way across the central Plains westward from Kansas. In November 1868 Custer destroyed a Cheyenne settlement on the Washita River, in present-day Oklahoma. The settlement's leader was Black Kettle, who had brought his people to reservation territory after the Sand Creek Massacre in Colorado in 1864. Custer's men murdered women and children, burned tepees, and destroyed 800 horses. Sickened by the scene, one army officer later wrote sarcastically of the "daring dash" on the part of "heroes of a bloody day." The soldiers left piles of corpses scattered among the smoldering ruins of the village.

A series of peace delegations to Washington, several led by Red Cloud of the Sioux, produced much curiosity among whites but no end to the slaughter of people or animals in the West.

■ **MAP 15.2**

PLAINS INDIAN WARS, 1865–1900   This map reveals that between 1865 and 1890, many of the conflicts between Indians and U.S. troops occurred along either railroad lines or trails used by European American settlers. For example, the Sioux, Cheyenne, and Arapaho fiercely resisted travelers along the Bozeman Trail running from Colorado to Montana.

Indians continued to attack the surveyors, supply caravans, and military escorts that preceded the railroad work crews. Lamenting the loss of his people's hunting grounds to the railroad, Red Cloud said, "The white children have surrounded me and have left me nothing but an island."

The Apache Indians managed to elude General George Crook until 1875. Crook employed some of these Apaches to track down the war chief Geronimo of the Chiricahuas. Like many other Indian leaders, Geronimo offered both religious and military guidance to his people. He believed that a spirit would protect him from the white man's bullets and from the arrows of Indians in league with government troops. Yet Geronimo was tricked into a momentary surrender in 1877. Sorrowfully, he agreed to bring his followers into the San Carlos reservation in eastern Arizona. There he was held in irons for several months before gaining his release and challenging authorities for another nine years.

In 1874 Custer took the Seventh into the Black Hills of the Dakotas, so-called unceded Indian territory. Supposedly, the 1868 Treaty of Fort Laramie had rendered this land off-limits to whites. Custer's mission was to offer protection for the surveyors of the Northern Pacific Railroad and to force Indians onto reservations as stipulated in the 1868 treaty. However, the officer lost no time trumpeting the fact that Indian lands were filled with gold. This report prompted a rush to the Black Hills, lands sacred to the Sioux. Within two years, 15,000 gold

■ During the morning of June 25, 1876, General George Custer and his force of 264 soldiers attacked a Sun Dance gathering of 2500 Sioux and Cheyenne on the banks of the Little Big Horn River in Montana. This European American version of the battle illustrated a book celebrating the life of Custer. The book was published soon after the battle, which took place in June 1876. At the time, the country was in the midst of a celebration marking the centennial of the nation's birth. The engraving portrays Custer and his men making a courageous "last stand."

miners had illegally descended on Indian lands to seek their fortunes. The federal government proposed to buy the land, but leaders of the Sioux, including Red Cloud, Spotted Tail, and Sitting Bull, spurned the offer. "The Black Hills belong to me," declared Sitting Bull. "If the whites try to take them, I will fight."

Indians throughout the West maintained their distinctive ways of life during these turbulent times. Horse holdings, so crucial for hunting, trading, and fighting, varied from group to group, with the Crow wealthy in relation to their Central Plains neighbors the Oglala and the Arikara. Plains and Plateau peoples engaged in a lively trading system. They exchanged horses and their trappings (bridles and blankets) for eastern goods such as kettles, guns, and ammunition. Despite their differences in economy, these groups held similar religious beliefs about an all-powerful life force that governed the natural world. People, plants, and animals were all part of the same order.

Even in the midst of brutal repression, Indian cultural traditions survived and in some cases flourished. On the West Central Plains and the Plateau, among the Crow, Shoshone, Nez Perce and other tribes, women developed a new, distinctive style of seed beadwork characterized by variations of triangular patterns. These designs, made of beads selected for their quality and consistency, adorned leggings, gauntlets, and belt pouches. In these ways, the decorative arts were endowed with great symbolic meaning. When wives embellished moccasins with patterns signifying their husband's military achievements, handicrafts assumed political as well as artistic significance.

The Postwar Western Labor Problem

In the eyes of many European Americans, the West offered vast challenges and opportunities. To construct a railroad across the plains and mountains, to extract rich reserves of timber and minerals, to harvest immense crops of wheat—all of these tasks demanded large numbers of willing workers. But such workers were in short supply. Moreover, available workers wanted employers to pay and treat them fairly.

In 1865 the owners of the Central Pacific Railroad seemed poised for one of the great engineering feats of the nineteenth century. In the race eastward from California, they would construct trestles spanning vast chasms and roadbeds traversing mountains and deserts. Government officials in Washington were eager to subsidize the railroad. What the owners lacked was a dependable labor force. The Irish workers who began the line in California struck for higher wages in compensation for brutal, dangerous work. These immigrants dropped their shovels and hammers at the first word of a gold strike nearby—or far away. As a result, in 1866 the Central Pacific had decided to tap into a vast labor source by importing thousands of Chinese men from their native Guandong province.

The Chinese toiled to extend the railroad tracks eastward from Sacramento, California, up to ten miles a day in the desert, only a few feet a day in the rugged Sierra Nevada Mountains. They alternately loaded and dumped millions of tons of earth and rocks to clear the land and construct the roadbed. In nerve-wracking feats of skill, they lowered themselves in woven baskets to implant nitroglycerine explosives in canyon walls. Chinese

Kicking Bear, *Battle of Little Big Horn*, c.1890. Southwest Museum, Los Angeles

■ Custer foolishly launched his attack without adequate backup, and he and his men were easily overwhelmed and killed by Indian warriors, led by the Oglala Sioux Crazy Horse and others. Reacting to this defeat, U.S. military officials reduced the Lakotas and Cheyennes to wardship status, ending their autonomy. Sioux artist Kicking Bear commemorated the Battle of Little Big Horn with this painting, completed in the 1890s. The figure in yellow buckskin at the left is Custer and the ghostlike figures behind the line of dead soldiers in the upper left are the spirits of the dead. At the center of the painting, Kicking Bear placed the figures of Sitting Bull, Rain-in-the-Face, Crazy Horse, and himself.

laborers toiled through snowstorms and blistering heat to blast tunnels and cut passes through granite mountains. Journalists marveled at the ability of a squad of Chinese to unload 200 tons of iron and 10 tons of spikes from railroad cars in just ten minutes. These reporters also commented on the strange sight of men in their native dress and traditional broad straw hats, taking afternoon tea breaks.

Charles Crocker, the general superintendent of the Central Pacific, observed of the Chinese, "Wherever we put them, we found them good." Paid $1 a day (less than the wage paid to whites), the Chinese had little leverage with which to press for higher compensation. In the spring of 1867, 5000 (out of a workforce of 12,000) walked off the job. They demanded $1.50 a day and an eight-hour day. Crocker responded by withholding rations, and the laborers were forced to return to work within a week. With the final linking of the railroad in Utah in 1869, many Chinese returned to California.

Signed in 1868, the Burlingame Treaty, named for Anson Burlingame, an American envoy to China, had supposedly guaranteed government protection for Chinese immigrants as visitors, traders, or permanent residents. Most immigrants were men. (Six out of ten California Chinese women were listed in the 1870 census as prostitutes, most the victims of their compatriots.) Yet the treaty did not inhibit U.S. employers, landlords, and government officials from discriminating against the Chinese.

By 1870, 40,000 Chinese lived in California and represented fully one-quarter of the state's wage earners. They found work in the cigar, woolen-goods, and boot and shoe factories of San Francisco; in the gold mining towns, now as laundry operators rather than as miners as

■ Chinese construction workers labor on the Central Pacific Railroad, c. 1868. Many Chinese immigrants toiled as indentured laborers, indebted to Chinese merchant creditors who paid for their passage to California. Isolated in all-male work camps, crews of railroad workers retained their traditional dress, language, and diet. After the completion of the transcontinental railroad in 1869, some immigrants returned to China, and others dispersed to small towns and cities throughout the West.

Carleton Watkins/Union Pacific Historical Collection

they had before the Civil War; and in the fields as agricultural laborers. White workers began to cry unfair competition against this Asian group that was becoming increasingly integrated into the region's economy.

As a group, Chinese men differed from California Indians, who remained trapped in the traditional agricultural economy of unskilled labor. Whites appropriated Indian land and forced many men, women, and children to work as wage earners for large landowners. Deprived of their familiar hunting and gathering lands, and wracked by disease and starvation, California Indians had suffered a drastic decline in their numbers by 1870, from 100,000 to 30,000 in 20 years.

By the early 1870s western manufacturers were faltering under the pressure of cheaper goods imported from the East by rail. At the same time, the growth of fledgling gigantic agricultural businesses opened new avenues of trade and commerce. Located in an arc surrounding the San Francisco Bay, large ("bonanza") wheat farmers grew huge crops and exported the grain to the East Coast and to England. These enterprises stimulated the building of wharves and railroad trunk lines and encouraged technological innovation in threshing and harvesting. Western enterprises showed a growing demand for labor whatever its skin color or nationality.

Land Use in an Expanding Nation

The end of the Civil War prompted new conflicts and deepened long-standing ones over the use of the land in a rich, sprawling country. In the South, staple crop planters began to share political power with an emerging elite, men who owned railroads and textile mills. Despairing of ever achieving antebellum levels of labor efficiency, some landowners turned to mining the earth and the forests for saleable commodities. These products, obtained through extraction, included phosphate (used in producing fertilizer), timber, coal, and turpentine. Labor in extractive industries complemented labor in the plantation economy. Sharecroppers alternated between tilling cotton fields in the spring and harvesting the crop in the fall, while seeking employment in sawmills and coal mines in the winter and summer.

As European Americans settled in the West and Southwest, they displaced natives who had been living there for generations. For example, the U.S. court system determined who could legally claim property. Western courts also decided whether natural resources such as water, land, timber, and fish and game constituted property that could be owned by private interests. In the Southwest, European American settlers, including army soldiers who had come to fight Indians and then stayed, continued to place Hispanic land titles at risk. Citing prewar precedents, American courts favored the claims of recent squatters over those of long-standing residents. In 1869 with the death of her husband (who had served as a general in the Union army), Maria Amparo Ruiz de Burton saw the large ranch they had worked together near San Diego slip out of her control. The first Spanish-speaking woman to be published in English in the United States, de Burton was a member of the Hispanic elite. Nevertheless, she had little political power. California judges backed the squatters who occupied the ranch.

As they controlled more land and assumed public office, some European Americans in the Southwest exploited their political connections and economic power. In the process they managed to wield great influence over people and vast amounts of natural resources. In the 1870s the so-called Santa Fe Ring wrested more than 80 percent of the original Spanish grants of land from Hispanic landholders in New Mexico. An alliance of European American lawyers, businesspeople, and politicians, the Santa Fe Ring defrauded families and kin groups of their land titles and speculated in property to make a profit. Whereas many ordinary Hispanic settlers saw land—with its crops, pasture, fuel, building materials, and game—as a source of livelihood, groups, such as the Santa Fe Ring, saw land primarily as a commodity to be bought and sold.

Seemingly overnight, boom towns sprang up wherever minerals or timber beckoned: southern Arizona and the Rocky Mountains west of Denver, Virginia City in western Nevada, the Idaho–Montana region, and the Black Hills of South Dakota. In all these places, increasing numbers of workers operated sophisticated kinds of machinery, such as rock crushers, and labored for wages. When the vein was exhausted or the forests depleted, the towns went bust.

Railroads facilitated not only the mining of minerals but also the growth of the cattle-ranching industry. By 1869 a quarter of a million cattle were grazing in Colorado Territory. Rail connections between the Midwest and East made it profitable for Texas ranchers to pay cowboys to drive their herds of long-horned steers to Abilene, Ellsworth, Wichita, or Dodge City, Kansas, for shipment to stockyards in Chicago or St. Louis. Large meatpackers, such as Swift and Armour, prepared the carcasses for the eastern market.

Cattle drives were huge; an estimated 10 million animals were herded north from Texas alone between 1865 and 1890. They offered employment to all kinds of men with sufficient skills and endurance. Among the cowhands were African American horsebreakers and gunmen and Mexicans skilled in the use of the *reata* (lasso). Blacks made up about 25 percent and Hispanics about 15 percent of all cowboy outfits. Tracing the evolution of the Chisholm Trail, which

TABLE 15-3

Estimates of Railroad Crossties Used and Acres of Forest Cleared, 1870–1910

Year	Miles of Track	Ties Renewed Annually (millions)	Ties Used on New Construction (millions)	Total Ties Annually (millions)	Acres of Forest Cleared (thousands)
1870	60,000	21	18	39	195
1880	107,000	37	21	58	290
1890	200,000	70	19	89	445
1900	259,000			91	455
1910	357,000			124	620

Source: Michael Williams, *Americans and Their Forests* (1989), 352.

linked southern Texas to Abilene, from Indian path to commercial route, one observer wrote in 1874, "So many cattle have been driven over the trail in the last few years that a broad highway is tread out, looking much like a national highway." Yet this new "national highway" traversed Indian Territory (present-day Oklahoma), lands supposedly promised to Indians forever.

In knitting regional economies together, federal land policies were crucial to the Republican vision of a developing nation. Yet a series of land use acts had a mixed legacy. The Mineral Act of 1866 granted title to millions of acres of mineral-rich land to mining companies, a gift from the federal government to private interests. In 1866 Congress passed the Southern Homestead Act to help blacks acquire land, but the measure accomplished little and was repealed in 1876. The Timber Culture Act of 1873 allotted 160 acres to individuals in selected western states if they agreed to plant one-fourth of the acreage with trees. Four years later, the Desert Land Act provided cheap land if buyers irrigated at least part of their parcels.

The exploitation of western resources raised many legal questions: Must ranchers pay for the prairies their cattle grazed on and the trails they followed to market? How could one "own" a stampeding buffalo herd or a flowing river? What was the point of holding title to a piece of property if only the timber, oil, water, or minerals on and in it (but not the soil) were of value?

The Apex Mining Act of 1872 sought to address at least some of these issues. This law legalized traditional mining practices in the West by validating titles approved by local courts. According to the law, a person who could locate the apex of a vein (its point closest to the surface) could lay claim to the entire vein beneath the surface. The measure contributed to the wholesale destruction of certain parts of the western landscape as mining companies blasted their way through mountains and left piles of rocks in their wake. It also spurred thousands of lawsuits as claimants argued over what constituted an apex or a vein.

It was during this period that a young Scottish-born naturalist named John Muir began to explore the magnificent canyons and mountains of California. Viewing nature as a means for regenerating the human spirit, Muir emphasized a deep appreciation of the natural world. He contrasted nature's majesty with the artificial landscape created by and for humans. In the wilderness, there is nothing "truly dead or dull, or any trace of

Colorado Historical Society (CHS.J 2067)

■ Chicago photographer Thomas J. Hine titled this stereograph "Old Faithful in Action, Fire Hole Basin." It is the first photograph of the eruption of the famous Yellowstone geyser. Costing 15–25 cents each, stereographs were a popular form of entertainment in middle-class households beginning in the 1860s. The stereoscope merged two identical photos to form a single three-dimensional image. Widely distributed stereographs of scenic natural wonders boosted western tourism.

what in manufactories is called rubbish or waste," he wrote; "everything is perfectly clean and pure and full of divine lessons." Muir believed that the need to protect breathtaking vistas and magnificent stands of giant redwoods compelled the federal government to act as land policy regulator.

Muir was gratified by the creation of the National Park system during the postwar period. By this time, pressure had been building on the federal government to protect vast tracts of undeveloped lands. Painters and geologists were among the first Easterners to appreciate the spectacular vistas of the western landscape. In 1864 Congress set aside a small area within California's Yosemite Valley for public recreation and enjoyment. Soon after the war, railroad promoters forged an alliance with government officials in an effort to block commercial development of particularly beautiful pockets of land. In the late 1860s the invention of the Pullman sleeping car—a luxurious hotel room on wheels—helped spur the drive to protect these areas from farming, lumbering, stock raising, and mining. Northern Pacific railroad financier Jay Cooke lobbied hard for the government to create a two-million-acre park in what is today the northwest corner of Wyoming. As a result, in March 1872, Congress created Yellowstone National Park. Tourism would continue to serve as a key component of the western economy.

Muir and others portrayed the Yosemite and Yellowstone Valleys as wildernesses, empty of human activity. In fact, both areas had long provided hunting and foraging grounds for native peoples. Yellowstone had been occupied by the people now called the Shoshone since the fifteenth century. This group, together with the Bannock, Crow, and Blackfeet, tried to retain access to Yellowstone's meadows, rivers, and forests after it became a national park. However, U.S. policymakers and military officials persisted in their efforts to mark off territory for specific purposes, while Indians were confined to reservations.

Buying Territory for the Union

Before the war, Republicans had opposed any federal expansionist schemes that they feared might benefit slaveholders. However, after 1865 and the outlawing of slavery, some Republican lawmakers and administration officials advocated the acquisition of additional territory. Secretary of State William Seward led the way in 1867 by purchasing Alaska from Russia and trying unsuccessfully to buy the Danish West Indies.

The purchase of Alaska immeasurably enriched the nation's natural resources. For $7.2 million (about 2 cents an acre), the United States gained 591,004 square miles of land. Within the territory were diverse indigenous groups—Eskimos, Aleuts, Tlingit, Tsimshian, Athabaskan, and Haida—and a small number of native Russians. Though derided at the time as "Seward's icebox," Alaska yielded enough fish, timber, minerals, and water power in the years to come to prove that the original purchase price was a tremendous bargain.

The impulse that prompted administration support for the Alaska purchase also spawned other plans for territorial acquisitions. In 1870 some Republicans joined with Democrats in calling for the annexation of the Dominican Republic. These congressmen argued that the tiny Caribbean country would make a fine naval base, provide investment opportunities for American businesspeople, and offer a refuge for southern freedpeople. Frederick Douglass, who had visited the country, claimed that annexing the Dominican Republic would "transplant within her tropical borders the glorious institutions" of the United States.

However, Charles Sumner, chairman of the Senate Foreign Relations Committee, opposed ratification of the annexation treaty. He warned against a takeover without considering the will of the Dominican people, who were currently involved in their own civil war. Some congressmen, in a prelude to foreign policy debates of the 1890s, suggested that the dark-skinned Dominican people were incapable of appreciating the blessings of American citizenship. In 1871 the treaty failed to win Senate approval. A firm supporter of annexation, President Grant felt personally betrayed by the Republicans who opposed him on this issue.

The Republican Vision and Its Limits

After the Civil War, victorious Republicans envisioned a nation united in the pursuit of prosperity. All citizens would be free to follow their individual economic self-interest and to enjoy the fruits of honest toil. In contrast, some increasingly vocal and well-organized groups saw the expansion of legal rights, and giving black men the right to vote in particular, as only initial, tentative steps on the path to an all-inclusive citizenship. Women, industrial workers, farmers, and African Americans made up overlapping constituencies pressing for equal political rights and economic opportunity. Together they challenged the mainstream Republican view that defeat of the rebels and destruction of slavery were sufficient to guarantee all people prosperity.

Government–business partnerships also produced unanticipated consequences for Republicans committed to what they believed was the collective good. Some politicians and business leaders saw these partnerships as opportunities for private gain. Consequently, private greed and public corruption accompanied postwar economic growth. Thus, Republican leaders faced challenges from two very different sources: people agitating for civil rights and people hoping to reap personal gain from political activities.

Postbellum Origins of the Women's Suffrage Movement

After the Civil War, the nation's middle class, which had its origins in the antebellum period, continued to grow. Dedicated to self-improvement and filled with a sense of moral authority, many middle-class Americans (especially Protestants) felt a deep cultural connection to their counterparts in England. Indeed, the United States produced its own "Victorians," so called for the self-conscious middle class that emerged in the England of Queen Victoria during her reign from 1837 to 1901.

At the heart of the Victorian sensibility was the ideal of domesticity: a harmonious family living in a well-appointed home, guided by a pious mother and supported by a father successful in business. Famous Protestant clergyman Henry Ward Beecher and his wife were outspoken proponents of this domestic ideal. According to Eunice Beecher, women had no "higher, nobler, more divine mission than in the conscientious endeavor to create a *true home*." Her husband added, "The laborer ought to be ashamed of himself who in 20 years does not own the ground on which his house stands . . . who has not in that house provided carpets for the rooms, who has not his China plates, who has not his chromos [decorative photographs], who has not some books nestling on the shelf."

Yet the traumatic events of the Civil War only intensified the desire among a growing group of American women to participate fully in the nation's political life. They wanted to extend their moral influence outside the narrow and exclusive sphere of the home. In countless everyday, unsung ways, Union women had supported the Union cause. They had managed farms, raised money for the U.S. Sanitary Commission, and sponsored patriotic rallies. Many women believed that they deserved the vote and that the time was right to demand it.

In 1866 veteran reformers Elizabeth Cady Stanton, Susan B. Anthony, and Lucy Stone founded the Equal Rights Association to link the rights of white women and African Americans. Nevertheless, in 1867, Kansas voters defeated a referendum proposing suffrage for both blacks and white women. This disappointment convinced some former abolitionists that the two causes should be separated—that women should wait patiently until the rights of African American men were firmly secured. Frederick Douglass declined an invitation to a women's suffrage convention in Washington, D.C., in 1868. He explained, "I am now devoting myself to a cause [if] not more sacred, certainly more urgent, because it is one of life and death to the long enslaved people of this country, and that is: negro suffrage."

Douglass left African American women out of his call for "negro suffrage." He implied that the chief advocates of women's suffrage were white and middle class. As a result, Douglass failed to gauge the way in which the issue of universal suffrage connected all black people with all women. African American activist and former slave Sojourner Truth warned white women not to presume to speak for all women, and she also urged black men not to speak for themselves only. At a meeting of the newly formed Equal Rights Association, Truth pointed out, "There is a great stir about colored men getting their rights, but not a word about the colored women; and if colored men get their rights, and not colored women get theirs, there will be a bad time about it."

In 1869 two factions of women parted ways and formed separate organizations devoted to women's rights. The more radical wing, including Cady Stanton and Anthony, bitterly denounced the Fifteenth Amendment because it gave the vote to black men only. In 1868 the two leaders had attempted to organize a Working Women's Party, which they hoped would appeal to female wage earners and serve as the foundation of a new political party dedicated to broad-based reform.

The following year they helped to found the National Woman Suffrage Association (NWSA). Members of NWSA argued for a renewed commitment to the original Declaration of Sentiments passed in Seneca Falls, New York two decades earlier. They favored married women's property rights, liberalization of divorce laws, opening colleges and trade schools to women, a new federal amendment to allow women to vote. In 1869, women's rights proponents Lucy Stone and her husband, Henry Blackwell, founded the rival American Woman Suffrage Association (AWSA). This group downplayed the larger struggle for women's rights and focused on the suffrage question exclusively. Its members supported the Fifteenth Amendment and retained ties to the Republican party. The AWSA focused on state-by-state campaigns for women's suffrage.

Library of Congress

■ New York City newspaper *The Daily Graphic* carried this caricature of Susan B. Anthony on its June 5, 1873, cover. The artist suggests that the drive for women's suffrage has resulted in a reversal of gender roles. Titled "The Woman Who Dared," the cartoon portrays Anthony as a masculine figure. One of her male supporters, on the right, holds a baby, while women activists march and give speeches. On the left, a female police officer keeps watch over the scene.

In 1871 the NWSA welcomed the daring, flamboyant Victoria Woodhull as a vocal supporter, only to renounce her a few years later. Woodhull's political agenda ranged from free love and dietary reform to legalized prostitution, working men's rights, and women's suffrage. (In the nineteenth century, free love advocates denounced what they called a sexual double standard, one that glorified female chastity while tolerating male promiscuity.) Woodhull's speeches gained her a great deal of publicity; in one political cartoon she was labeled "Mrs. Satan." This was hardly the kind of publicity the NWSA craved. At the group's 1871 convention Woodhull startled many of the old guard with her declaration, "We mean treason! We mean secession. . . . We are plotting Revolution! We will overthrow this bogus republic and plant a government of righteousness in its stead."

In 1872 one of Woodhull's critics successfully challenged her. Woodhull spent a month in jail as a result of the zealous prosecution by vice reformer Anthony Comstock, a clergyman who objected to her public discussions and writings on sexuality. Comstock assumed the role of an outspoken crusader against vice. A federal law passed in 1873, and named after him, equated information related to birth control with pornography, banning this and other "obscene material" from the mails.

Also in 1872, Woodhull formed what she called the Equal Rights Party. This new party nominated its founder for the U.S. presidency. However, Woodhull's proposed vice presidential running mate, Frederick Douglass, declined the honor. He announced that he planned to vote for Grant again.

For her part, Susan B. Anthony used the 1872 presidential election as a test case for women's suffrage. She attempted to vote and was arrested, tried, and convicted as a result. By this time, most women suffragists, and most members of the NWSA for that matter, had become convinced that they should focus on the vote exclusively; they therefore accepted the AWSA's policy on this issue. In the coming years, they would avoid other causes with which they might have allied themselves, including black civil rights and labor reform.

Workers' Organizations

Many Americans benefited from economic changes of the postwar era. Railroading, mining, and heavy industry helped fuel the national economy and in the process boosted the growth of the urban managerial class. In the Midwest, many landowning farmers prospered when they responded to an expanding demand for grain and other staple crops. In Wisconsin, wheat farmers cleared forests, drained swamps, diverted rivers, and profited from the booming world market in grain. Yet the economic developments that allowed factory managers and owners of large wheat farms to make a comfortable living for themselves did not necessarily benefit agricultural and manufacturing workers.

Several organizations offered laborers an alternative vision to the Republicans' brand of individualism and nationalism.

Indeed, during this period growing numbers of working people, in the countryside and in the cities, became caught up in a cycle of indebtedness. In the upcountry South (above the fall line, or Piedmont), formerly self-sufficient family farmers sought loans from banks to repair their war-damaged homesteads. To qualify for these loans, the farmer had to plant cotton as a staple crop, to the neglect of corn and other foodstuffs. Many sharecroppers, black and white, received payment in the form of credit only; for these families, the end-of-the-year reckoning yielded little more than rapidly accumulating debts. Midwestern farmers increasingly relied on expensive threshing and harvesting machinery and on bank loans to purchase the machinery. In cities all over the country, the mass production of shoes and textiles meant that members of the laboring classes depended more than ever on cash to buy such necessities, yet depressed wages and irregular employment put families at risk.

Several organizations founded within five years of the war's end offered laborers an alternative vision to the Republicans' brand of individualism and nationalism. In 1867 Oliver H. Kelly, a former Minnesota farmer now working in a Washington office, organized the National Grange of the Patrons of Husbandry, popularly known as the Grange. This movement sought to address a new, complex marketplace increasingly dominated by railroads, banks, and grain elevator operators. The Grange encouraged farmers to form cooperatives that would market their crops and to challenge discriminatory railroad rates that favored big business.

Founded in Baltimore in 1866, the National Labor Union (NLU) consisted of a collection of craft unions and claimed as many as 600,000 members at its peak in the early 1870s. The group welcomed farmers as well as factory workers and promoted a general program of social reform. The group also favored legislation for an eight-hour workday and the arbitration of industrial disputes.

William Sylvis, a leader of the Iron Molders' International Union in Philadelphia and the second president of the NLU, sounded twin themes that would mark national labor

State Historical Society of Wisconsin, WHi (D32) 821

■ A Norwegian immigrant extended family in the town of Norway Grove, Wisconsin, poses in front of their imposing home and up-to-date carriage in this photograph taken in the mid-1870s. Linking their fortunes to the world wheat market, these newcomers to the United States prospered. Wrote one woman to her brother back home in Norway, "We all have cattle, driving oxen, and wagons. We also have children in abundance."

union organizing efforts for generations to come. He called for an alliance of black and white workers. Yet at the same time, Sylvis defended the practice of excluding blacks from positions of leadership on the job and in the union. Impatient with such pronouncements, Isaac Myers, a black ship caulker from Baltimore, helped found the short-lived Colored National Labor Union in Washington, D.C., in 1868. (This association remained small and disbanded within three years.) Myers offered a view of citizenship that differed from white Republicans' exclusive emphasis on the franchise: "If citizenship means anything at all," the black labor leader declared, "it means the freedom of labor, as broad and as universal as freedom of the ballot."

In 1873 a nationwide depression threw thousands out of work and worsened the plight of debtors. Businesspeople in agriculture, mining, the railroad industry, and manufacturing had overexpanded their operations. The free-wheeling loan practices of major banks had

TABLE 15-4

**National and International Union Members of the
National Labor Union (with dates of each union's founding)**

National Typographical Union (printers and typesetters) (1850)
Iron Molders' I.U. (1859)
Machinists' and Blacksmiths' I.U. (1859)
American Miners' Association (1861)
  Miners' National Association (1873)
Sons of Vulcan (steel workers) (1862)
National Telegraphic Union (1863)
  Telegraphers' Protective League (1868)
Brotherhood of Locomotive Engineers (1863)
Ship Carpenters' and Caulkers' I.U. (1864)
Cigar Makers' I.U. (1864)
N.U. of Journeyman Curriers (tanners) (1864)
Plasterers' N.U. (1864, again 1871)
Iron and Steel Heaters' I.U. (1865, again 1872)
Coachmakers' I.U. (1865)
Dry Goods Clerks' Early Closing Ass'n. (1865)
Tailors I.U. (1865)
Carpenters' and Joiners' I.U. (1865)
Bricklayers' I.U. (1865)
Journeyman Painters' I.U. (1865, again 1871)
Stationary Engineers' N.U. (1866?)
Mule Spinners' I.U. (textile workers) (1866)
Knights of St. Crispin (shoemakers) (1867)
Conductors' Brotherhood (1868)
Workingmen's Benevolent Association (1868)
Wool Hat Finishers' N.U. (1869)
Daughters of St. Crispin (shoemakers) (1869)
Coopers' I.U. (barrel makers) (1870)
Morocco Dressers' N.U. (hide processors) (1870)
American Bricklayers' N.U. (1871)
N.U. of Woodworking Mechanics (1872)
Sons of Adam (cloth cutters) (1872)
Brotherhood of Locomotive Firemen (1873)
Boilers', Roughers', Catchers', and Hookers', N.U. (1873)

Note: I.U.= International Union; N.U. = National Union.

contributed to this situation. The inability of these businesspeople to repay their loans led to the failure of major banks. With the contraction of credit, thousands of small businesses went bankrupt. The NLU did not survive the crisis.

However, by this time, a new organization had appeared to champion the cause of the laboring classes in opposition to lords of finance. Founded in 1869 by Uriah Stephens and other Philadelphia tailors, the Knights of Labor began as a secret fraternal society. Extending their reach, the Knights aimed to unite industrial and rural workers, the self-employed and the wage earner, blacks and whites, and men and women. The Knights were committed to private property and to the independence of the farmer, the entrepreneur, and the industrial worker. The group banned from its ranks "nonproducers," such as liquor sellers, bankers, professional gamblers, stockbrokers, and lawyers. Both the Knights and the Farmers' Grange would enjoy their greatest successes in the 1880s.

This period of depression also laid the foundation for the Greenback Labor Party, organized in 1878. Debtors feared that government policies were leading to a contraction of the money supply. Within three years after the end of the Civil War, the Treasury had withdrawn from circulation $100 million in wartime, paper currency ("greenbacks"). With less money in circulation, debtors found it more difficult to repay their loans. The government also ceased coining silver dollars in 1873, despite the discovery of rich silver lodes in the West. "Cheap-money men" protested what they called the "Crime of '73." To add insult to injury, the Resumption Act (1875) called for the government to continue to withdraw paper "greenbacks." Thus, hard money became dearer, and debtors became more desperate. In 1878 the new Greenback Labor Party managed to win one million votes and elect 14 candidates to Congress. The party laid the foundation for the Populist Party that emerged in the 1890s.

Federal money policies had a great impact on diverse groups of workers, whether they toiled in the fields, the factory, or the workshop. However, several factors made coalition building among these groups difficult. One was the nation's increasingly multicultural workforce. Unions, such as the typographers, were notorious for excluding women and African Americans, a fact publicized by both Frederick Douglass and Susan B. Anthony, to no avail. In 1869 shoe factory workers (members of the Knights of St. Crispin) went on strike in North Adams, Massachusetts. They were soon shocked to see 75 Chinese strikebreakers arrive by train from California. Their employer praised the new arrivals for their "rare industry." The shoemakers' strike collapsed quickly after the appearance of what the workers called this "Mongolian battery." Employers would continue to manipulate and divide the laboring classes through the use of ethnic, religious, and racial prejudices.

Political Corruption and the Decline of Republican Idealism

Out of the new partnership between politics and business emerged an extensive system of bribes and kickbacks. Greedy politicians of both parties challenged the Republicans' high-minded idealism.

News related to the corrupt intertwining of government power and private economic interests burst upon the headlines in the early 1870s. In New York City, the *New York Times* exposed the schemes of William M. "Boss" Tweed. Tweed headed Tammany Hall, a political organization that courted labor unions and contributed liberally to Catholic schools and charities. Tammany Hall politicians routinely used bribery and extortion to fix elections and bilk taxpayers of millions of dollars. One plasterer employed on a city project received $138,000 in "payment" for two days' work. Political cartoonist Thomas Nast portrayed Tweed with a bulging stomach and a sneering face, taunting the public, "As long as I count the votes, what are you going to do about it?" After the *Times* exposé, Tweed was prosecuted and convicted. His downfall attested to the growing influence of newspaper reporters.

Another piece of investigative journalism rocked the political world in 1872. In 1867 major stockholders of the Union Pacific Railroad had formed a new corporation, called the Crédit Mobilier, to build railroads. Heads of powerful congressional committees received shares of stock in the new company. These gifts of stock were bribes to secure the legislators' support for public land grants favorable to the new corporation. The *New York Sun* exposed a number of the chief beneficiaries in the fall of 1872, findings confirmed by congressional investigation. Among the disgraced politicians was Grant's vice president Schuyler Colfax, who had lied under oath to a Congessional Committee investigating the scandal. Colfax denied accepting Crédit Mobilier stock, although bank records show he had deposited $1200 in cash from one of the finance company's supporters.

The 1872 presidential election pitted incumbent Grant against the Democratic challenger, *New York Tribune* editor Horace Greeley. Republicans, disillusioned with congressional corruption and eager to press forward with civil service reform, endorsed the Democratic candidate. Greeley and his Republican allies decried the patronage (or "spoils")

Harper's Weekly, September 16, 1871

■ In 1871 Thomas Nast drew a series of cartoons exposing the corruption of New York City Democratic boss William M. Tweed and his political organization, Tammany Hall. In this drawing, published in *Harper's Weekly* in 1871, Nast depicts Tweed and his cronies engaging in a "wholesale" looting of the New York City treasury with the assistance of compliant police officers. Those same officers stand ready to crack down on the impoverished father who robs a bakery to feed his family. By portraying Tweed as an enemy of the poor, Nast ignored the fact that the political boss gained a large following among immigrant voters.

TABLE 15-5

The Election of 1872

Candidate	Political Party	Popular Vote	Electoral Vote
Ulysses S. Grant	Republican	3,596,745	286
Horace Greeley	Democratic Liberal Republican	2,843,446	66

system by which politicians rewarded their supporters with government jobs. Nevertheless, Grant won the election.

In an 1872 article titled "The State of the South," a writer for the *Nation* magazine decried northern whites' apparent indifference toward the stalled process of Reconstruction. After four bloody years of war and seven squandered years of postwar opportunity, the federal government seemed prepared to hand the South back to unrepentant rebels. Together, the southern states readmitted to the Union would demonstrate little regard for black people as citizens or as workers. In 1874 the Freedman's Savings Bank failed, taking with it the dreams of many depositors who had saved, on average, $25 out of their hard-won earnings. Neither Congress nor the president attempted to save the bank or reimburse the depositors. Meanwhile, the North showed what one House Republican called "a general apathy among the people concerning the war and the negro." The Civil Rights Act of 1875 guaranteed blacks equal access to public accommodations and transportation. Yet this act represented the final, half-hearted gesture of radical Republicanism. The measure was never enforced, and the Supreme Court declared it unconstitutional in 1883 on the grounds that the government could protect only political and not social rights. White Southerners reasserted their control over the region's political economy.

Grant remained preoccupied by political problems plaguing his administration. In 1875 the so-called Whiskey Ring further tarnished his presidency. The St. Louis–based association consisted of the manufacturers of distilled liquors. Aided by Treasury Department officials and Grant's own private secretary, General Orville E. Babcock, these manufacturers avoided paying sales taxes. With influential friends, members of the ring had eluded detection for years.

The presidential election of 1876 intensified public cynicism about deal making in high places. A dispute over election returns led to what came to be known as the Compromise of 1877. The Republican nominee, Rutherford B. Hayes, a former three-term governor of Ohio, ran against Democrat Samuel J. Tilden. In the popular vote, Tilden outpolled Hayes. However, when the electoral votes were counted, the Democrat had only 184, one short of the necessary number. Nineteen of the 20 votes in dispute came from Louisiana, South Carolina, and Florida, and these three states submitted two new sets of returns, one from each of the two main parties. A specially appointed congressional electoral commission, the Committee of Fifteen, was charged with resolving the dispute. It divided along partisan lines. The eight Republicans outvoted the seven Democrats to accept the Republican set of returns from Florida.

TABLE 15-6

The Election of 1876

Candidate	Political Party	Popular Vote	Electoral Vote
Rutherford B. Hayes	Republican	4,036,572	185
Samuel J. Tilden	Democrat	4,284,020	184

To break the logjam, the Democrats agreed that Hayes could assume office in return for the withdrawal of all remaining federal troops from the South. The Republicans tacitly agreed that their work there was finished and that blacks in the region should fend for themselves. Hayes declined to enforce the Civil Rights Act of 1875. White Southerners were free to uphold the principle of states' rights that had been traditionally invoked to deny blacks their rights in the region.

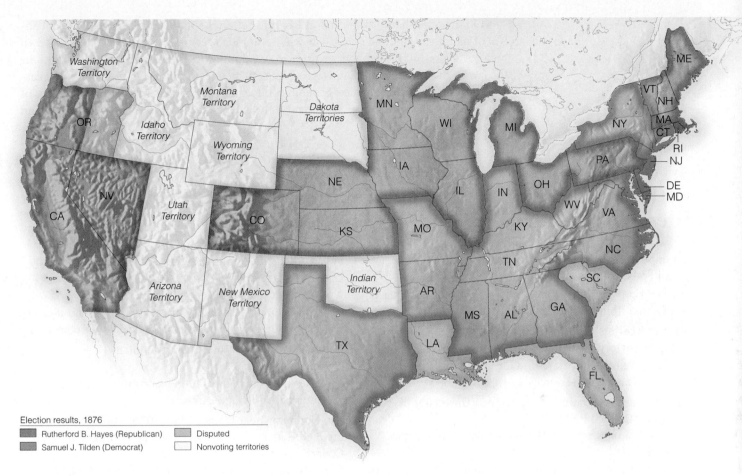

Election results, 1876

- ■ Rutherford B. Hayes (Republican)
- ■ Samuel J. Tilden (Democrat)
- ▢ Disputed
- ▢ Nonvoting territories

■ **MAP 15.3**

THE COMPROMISE OF 1877 During the presidential election of 1876, returns from South Carolina, Florida, and Louisiana (the only states that remained under Republican control) were disputed. Under a compromise reached by Republicans and Democrats in Congress, Republican Rutherford B. Hayes became president, and Congress removed all federal troops from the South. As a result, in many areas of the South, the Republican party all but disappeared.

Conclusion

During the dozen or so years after the Civil War, both northern Republicans and southern Democrats registered a series of spectacular wins and crushing losses. Though humiliated by the Union victory, southern white supremacists eventually won for themselves the freedom to control their own local and state governments. As landlords, sheriffs, and merchants, these men defied the postwar federal amendments to the Constitution and deprived African Americans of basic citizenship rights. By the end of Reconstruction, northern Republicans had conceded local power to their former enemies. Apparently, even an aggressive nationalism could accept traditional southern hierarchies: white over nonwhite, rich over poor.

On the other hand, at the end of Reconstruction, Republicans remained in firm control of national economic policy. The white South had secured its right to conduct its own political affairs, but the Republican vision of economic growth and development had become the law of the land. This vision was a guiding principle of historic national and, increasingly, international significance. Economic innovation in particular proved to be a force of great unifying power, stronger even than all the federal military forces deployed during and after the Civil War.

Sites to Visit

The Impeachment of Andrew Johnson
www.impeach-andrewjohnson.com/

This HarpWeek site about the impeachment includes images and text from the Reconstruction period.

Diary and Letters of Rutherford B. Hayes
www.ohiohistory.org/onlinedoc/hayes/index.cfm

The Rutherford B. Hayes Presidential Center in Fremont, Ohio, maintains the searchable database of his writings.

Freedmen and Southern Society Project (University of Maryland, College Park)
www.inform.umd.edu/ARHU/Depts/History/Freedman/home.html

This site contains a chronology and sample documents from several collections or primary sources about emancipation and freedom in the 1860s.

History of the Suffrage Movement
www.rochester.edu/SBA

This site includes a chronology, important texts relating to women's suffrage, and bibliographical information about Susan B. Anthony and Elizabeth Cady Stanton.

Indian Affairs: Laws and Treaties, compiled and edited by Charles J. Kappler (1904)
www.library.okstate.edu/kappler

This digitized text at Oklahoma State University includes pre-removal treaties with the five Civilized Tribes and other tribes.

National Museum of the American Indian
www.si.edu/nmai

The Smithsonian Institution maintains this site, providing information about the museum.

The Northern Great Plains, 1880–1920: Photographs from the Fred Hulstrand and F. A. Pazandak Photograph Collections
www.memory.loc.gov.ammem/award97/ndfahtml/ngphome.html

This American Memory site from the Library of Congress contains two collections from the Institute for Regional Studies at North Dakota State University with 900 photographs of rural and small-town life at the turn of the century. Included are images of sod homes and the people who built them, farms and the machinery that made them prosper, and one-room schools and the children who were educated in them.

For Further Reading

General Works

Ellen Carol DuBois, *Feminism and Suffrage: The Emergence of an Independent Women's Movement in America, 1848–1869* (1978).

Eric Foner, *Reconstruction: America's Unfinished Revolution, 1863–1877* (1988).

David Montgomery, *Beyond Equality: Labor and the Radical Republicans, 1862–1872* (1967).

Amy Dru Stanley, *From Bondage to Contract: Wage Labor, Marriage, and the Market in the Age of Slave Emancipation* (1998).

Ronald Takaki, *A Different Mirror: A History of Multicultural America* (1993).

Robert M. Utley, *The Indian Frontier of the American West, 1846–1890* (1984).

Richard White, *"It's Your Misfortune and None of My Own": A History of the American West* (1991).

The Struggle over the South

Peter Bardaglio, *Reconstructing the Household: Families, Sex and the Law in the Nineteenth-Century South* (1995).

Ira Berlin and Leslie S. Rowland, eds., *Families and Freedom: A Documentary History of African-American Kinship in the Civil War Era* (1997).

Dwight B. Billings, *Planters and the Making of a "New South": Class, Politics, and Development in North Carolina, 1865–1900* (1979).

Lucy M. Cohen, *Chinese in the Post–Civil War South: A People Without a History* (1984).

Frederick Cooper, Thomas C. Holt, and Rebecca J. Scott, eds., *Beyond Slavery: Explorations of Race, Labor, and Citizenship in Post-Emancipation Societies* (2000).

Michael W. Fitzgerald, *The Union League Movement in the Deep South: Politics and Agricultural Change During Reconstruction* (1989).

Michael Golay, *A Ruined Land: The End of the Civil War* (1999).

Thomas C. Holt, *Black over White: Negro Political Leadership in South Carolina During Reconstruction* (1977).

Jacqueline Jones, *Soldiers of Light and Love: Northern Teachers and Georgia Blacks, 1865–1873* (1980).

Leslie Schwalm, *"A Hard Fight for We": Women's Transition from Slavery to Freedom in South Carolina* (1997).

Claiming Territory for the Union

Stephen E. Ambrose, *Nothing Like It in the World: The Men Who Built the Transcontinental Railroad, 1863–1869* (2000).

Orin G. Libby, ed., *The Arikara Narrative of the Campaign Against the Hostile Dakotas, June, 1876* (1998).

Ruth B. Moynihan, Susan Armitage, and Christiane Fischer Dichamp, eds., *So Much to Be Done: Women Settlers on the Mining and Ranching Frontier* (1990).

Richard West Sellars, *Preserving Nature in the National Parks: A History* (1997).

Larry Sklenar, *To Hell with Honor: Custer and the Little Bighorn* (2000).

Robert Wooster, *The Military and United States Indian Policy, 1865–1903* (1988).

Judy Yung, *Unbound Feet: A Social History of Chinese Women in San Francisco* (1995).

The Republican Vision and Its Limits

Leon Fink, *Workingmen's Democracy: The Knights of Labor and American Politics* (1983).

Barbara Goldsmith, *Other Powers: The Age of Suffrage, Spiritualism, and the Scandalous Victoria Woodhull* (1998).

Lyde Cullen Sizer, *The Political Work of Northern Women Writers and the Civil War* (2000).

Irwin Unger, *The Greenback Era: A Social and Political History of American Finance, 1865–1879* (1964).

C. Vann Woodward, *Reunion and Reaction: The Compromise of 1877 and the End of Reconstruction* (1956).

Online Practice Test

Test your understanding of this chapter with interactive review quizzes at

www.ablongman.com/jonescreatedequal/chapter15

Additional Photo Credits

Page 501: Library of Congress
Page 507: Antique Textile Resource, Bethesda MD
Page 517: William T. Garrell Foundry, San Francisco, *The Golden Spike*. The Iris & B. Gerald Cantor Center for Visual Arts at Stanford University (1998.115). Gift of David Hewes

Appendix

The Declaration of Independence

The Articles of Confederation

The Constitution of the United States
of America

Amendments to the Constitution

Presidential Elections

Present Day United States

Present Day World

For additional reference material, go to
www.ablongman.com/jonescreatedequal/appendix
The online appendix includes the following:

The Declaration of Independence
The Articles of Confederation
The Constitution of the United States of America
Amendments to the Constitution
Presidential Elections
Vice Presidents and Cabinet Members by Administration
Supreme Court Justices
Presidents, Congresses, and Chief Justices, 1789–2001
Territorial Expansion of the United States (map)
Admission of States of the Union
U.S. Population, 1790–2000

Ten Largest Cities by Population, 1700–1900
Birthrate, 1820–2000 (chart)
Death Rate, 1900–2000 (chart)
Life Expectancy, 1900–2000 (chart)
Urban/Rural Population, 1750–1900 (chart)
Women in the Labor Force, 1890–1990 (chart)
United States Physical Features (map)
United States Native Vegetation (map)
Ancient Native American Communities (map)
Native American Peoples, c. 1500 (map)
Present Day United States (map)

The Declaration of Independence

In Congress, July 4, 1776

The Unanimous Declaration of the Thirteen United States of America

When, in the course of human events, it becomes necessary for one people to dissolve the political bonds which have connected them with another, and to assume, among the powers of the earth, the separate and equal station to which the laws of nature and of nature's God entitle them, a decent respect to the opinions of mankind requires that they should declare the causes which impel them to the separation.

We hold these truths to be self-evident: That all men are created equal; that they are endowed by their Creator with certain unalienable rights; that among these are life, liberty, and the pursuit of happiness; that, to secure these rights, governments are instituted among men, deriving their just powers from the consent of the governed; that whenever any form of government becomes destructive of these ends, it is the right of the people to alter or to abolish it, and to institute new government, laying its foundation on such principles, and organizing its powers in such form, as to them shall seem most likely to effect their safety and happiness. Prudence, indeed, will dictate that governments long established should not be changed for light and transient causes; and accordingly all experience hath shown that mankind are more disposed to suffer, while evils are sufferable, than to right themselves by abolishing the forms to which they are accustomed. But when a long train of abuses and usurpations, pursuing invariably the same object, evinces a design to reduce them under absolute despotism, it is their right, it is their duty, to throw off such government, and to provide new guards for their future security. Such has been the patient sufferance of these colonies; and such is now the necessity which constrains them to alter their former systems of government. The history of the present King of Great Britain is a history of repeated injuries and usurpations, all having in direct object the establishment of an absolute tyranny over these states. To prove this, let facts be submitted to a candid world.

He has refused his assent to laws, the most wholesome and necessary for the public good.

He has forbidden his governors to pass laws of immediate and pressing importance, unless suspended in their operation till his assent should be obtained; and, when so suspended, he has utterly neglected to attend to them.

He has refused to pass other laws for the accommodation of large districts of people, unless those people would relinquish the right of representation in the legislature, a right inestimable to them, and formidable to tyrants only.

He has called together legislative bodies at places unusual, uncomfortable, and distant from the depository of their public records, for the sole purpose of fatiguing them into compliance with his measures.

He has dissolved representative houses repeatedly, for opposing, with manly firmness, his invasions on the rights of the people.

He has refused for a long time, after such dissolutions, to cause others to be elected; whereby the legislative powers, incapable of annihilation, have returned to the people at large for their exercise; the state remaining, in the mean time, exposed to all the dangers of invasions from without and convulsions within.

He has endeavored to prevent the population of these states; for that purpose obstructing the laws for naturalization of foreigners; refusing to pass others to encourage their migration hither, and raising the conditions of new appropriations of lands.

He has obstructed the administration of justice, by refusing his assent to laws for establishing judiciary powers.

He has made judges dependent on his will alone, for the tenure of their offices, and the amount and payment of their salaries.

He has erected a multitude of new offices, and sent hither swarms of officers to harass our people and eat out their substance.

He has kept among us, in times of peace, standing armies, without the consent of our legislatures.

He has affected to render the military independent of, and superior to, the civil power.

He has combined with others to subject us to a jurisdiction foreign to our constitution, and unacknowledged by our laws, giving his assent to their acts of pretended legislation:

For quartering large bodies of armed troops among us;

For protecting them, by a mock trial, from punishment for any murder which they should commit on the inhabitants of these states;

For cutting off our trade with all parts of the world;

For imposing taxes on us without our consent;

For depriving us, in many cases, of the benefits of trial by jury;

For transporting us beyond seas, to be tried for pretended offenses;

For abolishing the free system of English laws in a neighboring province, establishing therein an arbitrary government, and enlarging its boundaries, so as to render it at once an example and fit instrument for introducing the same absolute rule into these colonies;

For taking away our charters, abolishing our most valuable laws, and altering fundamentally the forms of our governments;

For suspending our own legislatures, and declaring themselves invested with power to legislate for us in all cases whatsoever.

He has abdicated government here, by declaring us out of his protection and waging war against us.

He has plundered our seas, ravaged our coasts, burned our towns, and destroyed the lives of our people.

He is at this time transporting large armies of foreign mercenaries to complete the works of death, desolation, and tyranny already begun with circumstances of cruelty and perfidy scarcely paralleled in the most barbarous ages, and totally unworthy the head of a civilized nation.

He has constrained our fellow-citizens, taken captive on the high seas, to bear arms against their country, to become the executioners of their friends and brethren, or to fall themselves by their hands.

He has excited domestic insurrection among us, and has endeavored to bring on the inhabitants of our frontiers the merciless Indian savages, whose known rule of warfare is an undistinguished destruction of all ages, sexes, and conditions.

In every stage of these oppressions we have petitioned for redress in the most humble terms; our repeated petitions have been answered only by repeated injury. A prince, whose character is thus marked by every act which may define a tyrant, is unfit to be the ruler of a free people.

Nor have we been wanting in our attentions to our British brethren. We have warned them, from time to time, of attempts by their legislature to extend an unwarrantable jurisdiction over us. We have reminded them of the circumstances of our emigration and settlement here. We have appealed to their native justice and magnanimity; and we have conjured them, by the ties of our common kindred, to disavow these usurpations, which would inevitably interrupt our connections and correspondence. They,

too, have been deaf to the voice of justice and of consanguinity. We must, therefore, acquiesce in the necessity which denounces our separation, and hold them, as we hold the rest of mankind, enemies in war, in peace friends.

We, therefore, the representatives of the United States of America, in General Congress assembled, appealing to the Supreme Judge of the world for the rectitude of our intentions, do, in the name and by the authority of the good people of these colonies, solemnly publish and declare, that these United Colonies are, and of right ought to be, FREE AND INDEPENDENT STATES; that they are absolved from all allegiance to the British crown, and that all political connection between them and the state of Great Britain is, and ought to be, totally dissolved; and that, as free and independent states, they have full power to levy war, conclude peace, contract alliances, establish commerce, and do all other acts and things which independent states may of right do. And for the support of this declaration, with a firm reliance on the protection of Divine Providence, we mutually pledge to each other our lives, our fortunes, and our sacred honor.

JOHN HANCOCK

New Hampshire
Josiah Bartlett
William Whipple
Matthew Thornton

Massachusetts
John Adams
Samuel Adams
Robert Treat Paine
Elbridge Gerry

New York
William Floyd
Philip Livingston
Francis Lewis
Lewis Morris

Rhode Island
Stephen Hopkins
William Ellery

New Jersey
Richard Stockton
John Witherspoon
Francis Hopkinson
John Hart
Abraham Clark

Pennsylvania
Robert Morris
Benjamin Rush
Benjamin Franklin
John Morton
George Clymer
James Smith
George Taylor
James Wilson
George Ross

Delaware
Caeser Rodney
George Read
Thomas McKean

Maryland
Samuel Chase
William Paca
Thomas Stone
Charles Carroll of Carrollton

North Carolina
William Hooper
Joseph Hewes
John Penn

Virginia
George Wythe
Richard Henry Lee
Thomas Jefferson
Benjamin Harrison
Thomas Nelson, Jr.
Francis Lightfoot Lee
Carter Braxton

South Carolina
Edward Rutledge
Thomas Heyward, Jr.
Thomas Lynch, Jr.
Arthur Middleton

Connecticut
Roger Sherman
Samuel Huntington
William Williams
Oliver Wolcott

Georgia
Button Gwinnett
Lyman Hall
George Walton

The Articles of Confederation

Between the States of New Hampshire, Massachusetts Bay, Rhode Island and Providence Plantations, Connecticut, New York, New Jersey, Pennsylvania, Delaware, Maryland, Virginia, North Carolina, South Carolina, Georgia

Article 1

The stile of this confederacy shall be "The United States of America."

Article 2

Each State retains its sovereignty, freedom and independence, and every power, jurisdiction, and right, which is not by this confederation expressly delegated to the United States, in Congress assembled.

Article 3

The said states hereby severally enter into a firm league of friendship with each other for their common defence, the security of their liberties and their mutual and general welfare; binding themselves to assist each other against all force offered to, or attacks made upon them, or any of them, on account of religion, sovereignty, trade, or any other pretence whatever.

Article 4

The better to secure and perpetuate mutual friendship and intercourse among the people of the different states in this union, the free inhabitants of each of these states, paupers, vagabonds, and fugitives from justice excepted, shall be entitled to all privileges and immunities of free citizens in the several states; and the people of each State shall have free ingress and regress to and from any other State, and shall enjoy therein all the privileges of trade and commerce, subject to the same duties, impositions, and restrictions, as the inhabitants thereof respectively; provided, that such restrictions shall not extend so far as to prevent the removal of property, imported into any State, to any other State of which the owner is an inhabitant; provided also, that no imposition, duties, or restriction, shall be laid by any State on the property of the United States, or either of them.

If any person guilty of, or charged with treason, felony, or other high misdemeanor in any State, shall flee from justice and be found in any of the United States, he shall, upon demand of the governor or executive power of the State from which he fled, be delivered up and removed to the State having jurisdiction of his offence.

Full faith and credit shall be given in each of these states to the records, acts, and judicial proceedings of the courts and magistrates of every other State.

Article 5

For the more convenient management of the general interests of the United States, delegates shall be annually appointed, in such manner as the legislature of each State shall direct, to meet in Congress, on the 1st Monday in November in every year, with a power reserved to each State to recall its delegates, or any of them, at any time within the year, and to send others in their stead for the remainder of the year.

No State shall be represented in Congress by less than two, nor by more than seven members; and no person shall be capable of being a delegate for more than three years in any term of six years; nor shall any person, being a delegate, be capable of holding any office under the United States, for which he, or any other for his benefit, receives any salary, fees, or emolument of any kind.

Each State shall maintain its own delegates in a meeting of the states, and while they act as members of the committee of the states.

In determining questions in the United States, in Congress assembled, each State shall have one vote.

Freedom of speech and debate in Congress shall not be impeached or questioned in any court or place out of Congress: and the members of Congress shall be protected in their persons from arrests and imprisonments, during the time of their going to and from, and attendance on Congress, except for treason, felony or breach of the peace.

Article 6

No State, without the consent of the United States, in Congress assembled, shall send any embassy to, or receive any embassy from, or enter into any conference, agreement, alliance, or treaty with any king, prince, or state; nor shall any person, holding any office of profit or trust under the United States, or any of them, accept of any present, emolument, office or title, of any kind whatever, from any king, prince, or foreign state; nor shall the United States, in Congress assembled, or any of them, grant any title of nobility.

No two or more states shall enter into any treaty, confederation, or alliance, whatever, between them, without the consent of the United States, in Congress assembled, specifying accurately the purposes for which the same is to be entered into, and how long it shall continue.

No State shall lay any imposts or duties which may interfere with any stipulations in treaties entered into by the United States, in Congress assembled, with any king, prince, or state, in pursuance of any treaties already proposed by Congress to the courts of France and Spain.

No vessels of war shall be kept up in time of peace by any State, except such number only as shall be deemed necessary by the United States, in Congress assembled, for the defence of such State or its trade; nor shall any body of forces be kept up by any State, in time of peace, except such number only as, in the judgment of the United States, in Congress assembled, shall be deemed requisite to garrison the forts necessary for the defence of such State; but every State shall always keep up a well regulated and disciplined militia, sufficiently armed and accoutred, and shall provide, and constantly have ready for use, in public stores, a due number of field pieces and tents, and a proper quantity of arms, ammunition and camp equipage.

No State shall engage in any war without the consent of the United States, in Congress assembled, unless such State be actually invaded by enemies, or shall have received certain advice of a resolution being formed by some nation of Indians to invade such State, and the danger is so imminent as not to admit of a delay till the United States, in Congress assembled, can be consulted; nor shall any State grant commissions to any ships or vessels of war, nor letters of marque or reprisal, except it be after a declaration of war by the United States, in Congress assembled, and then only against the kingdom or state, and the subjects thereof, against which war has been so declared, and under such regulations as shall be established by the United States, in Congress assembled, unless such States be infested by pirates, in which case vessels of war may be fitted out for that occasion, and kept so long as the danger shall continue, or until the United States, in Congress assembled, shall determine otherwise.

Article 7

When land forces are raised by any State for the common defence, all officers of or under the rank of colonel, shall be appointed by the legislature of each State respectively, by whom such forces shall be raised, or in such manner as such State shall direct; and all vacancies shall be filled up by the State which first made the appointment.

Article 8

All charges of war and all other expences, that shall be incurred for the common defence or general welfare, and allowed by the United States, in Congress assembled, shall be defrayed out of a common treasury, which shall be supplied by the several states, in proportion to the value of all land within each State, granted to or surveyed for any person, as such land and the buildings and improvements thereon shall be estimated according to such mode as the United States, in Congress assembled, shall, from time to time, direct and appoint.

The taxes for paying that proportion shall be laid and levied by the authority and direction of the legislatures of the several states, within the time agreed upon by the United States, in Congress assembled.

Article 9

The United States, in Congress assembled, shall have the sole and exclusive right and power of determining on peace and war, except in the cases mentioned in the 6th article; of sending and receiving ambassadors; entering into treaties and alliances, provided that no treaty of commerce shall be made, whereby the legislative power of the respective states shall be restrained from imposing such imposts and duties on foreigners as their own people are subjected to, or from prohibiting the exportation or importation of any species of goods or commodities whatsoever; of establishing rules for deciding, in all cases, what captures on land or water shall be legal, and in what manner prizes, taken by land or naval forces in the service of the United States, shall be divided or appropriated; of granting letters of marque and reprisal in times of peace; appointing courts for the trial of piracies and felonies committed on the high seas, and establishing courts for receiving and determining, finally, appeals in all cases of captures; provided, that no member of Congress shall be appointed a judge of any of the said courts.

The United States, in Congress assembled, shall also be the last resort on appeal in all disputes and differences now subsisting, or that hereafter may arise between two or more states concerning boundary, jurisdiction or any other cause whatever; which authority shall always be exercised in the manner following: whenever the legislative or executive authority, or lawful agent of any State, in controversy with another, shall present a petition to Congress, stating the matter in question, and praying for a hearing, notice thereof shall be given, by order of Congress, to the legislative or executive authority of the other State in controversy, and a day assigned for the appearance of the parties by their lawful agents, who shall then be directed to appoint, by joint consent, commissioners or judges to constitute a court for hearing and determining the matter in question; but, if they cannot agree, Congress shall name three persons out of each of the United States, and from the list of such persons each party shall alternately strike out one, in the petitioners beginning, until the number shall be reduced to thirteen; and from that number not less than seven, nor more than nine names, as Congress shall direct, shall, in the presence of Congress, be drawn out by lot; and the persons whose names shall be drawn, or any five of them, shall be commissioners or judges to hear and finally determine the controversy, so always as a major part of the judges who shall hear the cause shall agree in the determination; and if either party shall neglect to attend at the day appointed, without shewing reasons which Congress shall judge sufficient, or, being present, shall refuse to strike, the Congress shall proceed to nominate three persons out of each State, and the secretary of Congress shall strike in behalf of such party absent or refusing; and the judgment and sentence of the court to be appointed, in the manner before prescribed, shall be final and conclusive; and if any of the parties shall refuse to submit to the authority of such court, or to appear or defend their claim or cause, the court shall nevertheless proceed to pronounce sentence or judgment, which shall, in like manner, be final and decisive, the judgment or sentence and other proceedings being, in either case, transmitted to Congress, and lodged among the acts of Congress for the security of the parties concerned: provided, that every commissioner, before he sits in judgment, shall take an oath, to be administered by one of the judges of the supreme or superior court of the State where the cause shall be tried, "well and truly to hear and determine the matter in question, according to the best of his judgment, without favour, affection, or hope of reward": provided, also, that no State shall be deprived of territory for the benefit of the United States.

All controversies concerning the private right of soil, claimed under different grants of two or more states, whose jurisdictions, as they may respect such lands and the states which passed such grants, are adjusted, the said grants, or either of them, being at the same time claimed to have originated antecedent to such settlement of jurisdiction, shall, on the petition of either party to the Congress of the United States, be finally determined, as near as may be, in the same manner as is before prescribed for deciding disputes respecting territorial jurisdiction between different states.

The United States, in Congress assembled, shall also have the sole and exclusive right and power of regulating the alloy and value of coin struck by their own authority, or by that of the respective states; fixing the standard of weights and measures throughout the United States; regulating the trade and managing all affairs with the Indians not members of any of the states; provided that the legislative right of any State within its own limits be not infringed or violated; establishing and regulating post offices from one State to another throughout all the United States, and exacting such postage on the papers passing through the same as may be requisite to defray the expences of the said office; appointing all officers of the land forces in the service of the United States, excepting regimental officers; appointing all the officers of the naval forces, and commissioning all officers whatever in the service of the United States; making rules for the government and regulation of the said land and naval forces, and directing their operations.

The United States, in Congress assembled, shall have authority to appoint a committee to sit in the recess of Congress, to be denominated "a Committee of the States," and to consist of one delegate from each State, and to appoint such other committees and civil officers as may be necessary for managing the general affairs of the United States, under their direction; to appoint one of their number to preside; provided that no person be allowed to serve in the office of president more than one year in any term of three years; to ascertain the necessary sums of money to be raised for the service of the United States, and to appropriate and apply the same for defraying the public expences; to borrow money or emit bills on the credit of the United States, transmitting, every half year, to the respective states, an account of the sums of money so borrowed or emitted; to build and equip a navy; to agree upon the number of land forces, and to make requisitions from each State for its quota, in proportion to the number of white inhabitants in such State; which requisitions shall be binding; and, thereupon, the legislature of each State shall appoint the regimental officers, raise the men, and cloathe, arm, and equip them in a soldier-like manner, at the expence of the United States; and the officers and men so cloathed, armed, and equipped, shall march to the place appointed and within the time agreed on by the United States, in Congress assembled; but if the United States, in Congress assembled, shall, on consideration of circumstances, judge proper that any State should not raise men, or should raise a smaller number than its quota, and that any other State should raise a greater number of men than the quota thereof, such extra number shall be raised, officered, cloathed, armed, and equipped in the same manner as the quota of such State, unless the legislature of such State shall judge that such extra number cannot be safely spared out of the same, in which case they shall raise, officer, cloathe, arm, and equip as many of such extra number as they judge can be safely spared. And the officers and men so cloathed, armed, and equipped, shall march to the place appointed and within the time agreed on by the United States, in Congress assembled.

The United States, in Congress assembled, shall never engage in a war, nor grant letters of marque and reprisal in time of peace, nor enter into any treaties or alliances, nor coin money, nor regulate the value thereof, nor ascertain the sums and expences necessary for the defence and welfare of the United States, or any of them: nor emit bills, nor borrow money on the credit of the United States, nor appropriate money, nor agree upon the number of vessels of war to be built or purchased, or the number of land or sea forces to be raised, nor appoint a commander in chief of the army or navy, unless nine states assent to the same; nor shall a question on any other point, except for adjourning from day to day, be determined, unless by the votes of a majority of the United States, in Congress assembled.

The Congress of the United States shall have power to adjourn to any time within the year, and to any place within the United States, so that no period of adjournment be for a longer duration than the space of six months, and shall publish the journal of their proceedings monthly, except such parts thereof, relating to treaties, alliances or military operations, as, in their judgment, require secrecy; and the yeas and nays of the delegates of each State on any question shall be entered on the journal, when it is desired by any delegate; and the delegates of a State, or any of them, at his, or their request, shall be furnished with a transcript of the said journal, except such parts as are above excepted, to lay before the legislatures of the several states.

Article 10

The committee of the states, or any nine of them, shall be authorized to execute, in the recess of Congress, such of the powers of Congress as the United States, in Congress assembled, by the consent of nine states, shall, from time to time, think expedient to vest them with; provided, that no power be delegated to the said committee for the exercise of which, by the articles of confederation, the voice of nine states, in the Congress of the United States assembled, is requisite.

Article 11

Canada acceding to this confederation, and joining in the measures of the United States, shall be admitted into and entitled to all the advantages of this union; but no other colony shall be admitted into the same, unless such admission be agreed to by nine states.

Article 12

All bills of credit emitted, monies borrowed and debts contracted by, or under the authority of Congress before the assembling of the United States, in pursuance of the present confederation, shall be deemed and considered as a charge against the United States, for payment and satisfaction whereof the said United States and the public faith are hereby solemnly pledged.

Article 13

Every State shall abide by the determinations of the United States, in Congress assembled, on all questions which, by this confederation, are submitted to them. And the articles of this confederation shall be inviolably observed by every State, and the union shall be perpetual; nor shall any alteration at any time hereafter be made in any of them, unless such alteration be agreed to in a Congress of the United States, and be afterwards confirmed by the legislatures of every State.

These articles shall be proposed to the legislatures of all the United States, to be considered, and if approved of by them, they are advised to authorize their delegates to ratify the same in the Congress of the United States; which being done, the same shall become conclusive.

The Constitution of the United States of America

Preamble

We the People of the United States, in Order to form a more perfect Union, establish Justice, insure domestic Tranquility, provide for the common defence, promote the general Welfare, and secure the Blessings of Liberty to ourselves and our Posterity, do ordain and establish this Constitution for the United States of America.

Article I

Section 1

All legislative Powers herein granted shall be vested in a Congress of the United States, which shall consist of a Senate and House of Representatives.

Section 2

The House of Representatives shall be composed of Members chosen every second Year by the People of the several States, and the Electors in each State shall have the Qualifications requisite for Electors of the most numerous Branch of the State Legislature.

No Person shall be a Representative who shall not have attained to the Age of twenty five Years, and been seven Years a Citizen of the United States, and who shall not, when elected, be an inhabitant of that State in which he shall be chosen.

Representatives and direct Taxes shall be apportioned among the several States which may be included within this Union, according to their respective Numbers, *which shall be determined by adding to the whole Number of free Persons, including those bound to Service for a Term of Years, and excluding Indians not taxed, three fifths of all other Persons.** The actual Enumeration shall be made within three Years after the first Meeting of the Congress of the United States, and within every subsequent Term of ten Years, in such Manner as they shall by Law direct. The Number of Representatives shall not exceed one for every thirty Thousand, but each State shall have at Least one Representative; *and until such enumeration shall be made, the State of New Hampshire shall be entitled to chuse three, Massachusetts eight, Rhode-Island and Providence Plantations one, Connecticut five, New York six, New Jersey four, Pennsylvania eight, Delaware one, Maryland six, Virginia ten, North Carolina five, South Carolina five, and Georgia three.*

When vacancies happen in the Representation from any State, the Executive Authority thereof shall issue Writs of Election to fill such Vacancies.

The House of Representatives shall chuse their Speaker and other Officers; and shall have the sole Power of Impeachment.

---

*Passages no longer in effect are printed in italic type.

Section 3

The Senate of the United States shall be composed of two Senators from each State, *chosen by the Legislature thereof,* for six Years; and each Senator shall have one Vote.

Immediately after they shall be assembled in Consequence of the first Election, they shall be divided as equally as may be into three Classes. The Seats of the Senators of the first Class shall be vacated at the Expiration of the second Year, of the second Class at the Expiration of the fourth Year, and of the third Class at the Expiration of the sixth Year so that one third may be chosen every second Year; and if Vacancies happen by Resignation, or otherwise, during the Recess of the Legislature of any state, the Executive thereof may make temporary Appointments until the next Meeting of the Legislature, which shall then fill such Vacancies.

No Person shall be a Senator who shall not have attained to the Age of thirty Years, and been nine Years a Citizen of the United States, and who shall not, when elected, be an Inhabitant of that State for which he shall be chosen.

The Vice President of the United States shall be President of the Senate, but shall have no Vote, unless they be equally divided.

The Senate shall chuse their other Officers, and also a President *pro tempore,* in the Absence of the Vice President, or when he shall exercise the Office of President of the United States.

The Senate shall have the sole Power to try all Impeachments. When sitting for that Purpose, they shall be on Oath or Affirmation. When the President of the United States is tried the Chief Justice shall preside: And no Person shall be convicted without the Concurrence of two thirds of the Members present.

Judgment in Cases of Impeachment shall not extend further than to removal from Office, and disqualification to hold and enjoy any Office of honor, Trust or Profit under the United States: but the Party convicted shall nevertheless be liable and subject to Indictment, Trial, Judgment and Punishment, according to Law.

Section 4

The Times, Places and Manner of holding Elections for Senators and Representatives, shall be prescribed in each State by the Legislature thereof; but the Congress may at any time by Law make or alter such Regulations, except as to the Places of chusing Senators.

The Congress shall assemble at least once in every Year, *and such Meeting shall be on the first Monday in December, unless they shall by Law appoint a different Day.*

Section 5

Each House shall be the Judge of the Elections, Returns and Qualifications of its own Members, and a Majority of each shall constitute a Quorum to do Business; but a smaller Number may adjourn from day to day, and may be authorized to compel the Attendance of absent Members, in such Manner, and under such Penalties as each House may provide.

Each House may determine the Rules of its Proceedings, punish its Members for disorderly Behaviour, and, with the Concurrence of two thirds, expel a Member.

Each House shall keep a Journal of its Proceedings, and from time to time publish the same, excepting such Parts as may in their Judgment require Secrecy; and the Yeas and Nays of the Members of either House on any question shall, at the Desire of one fifth of those Present, be entered on the Journal.

Neither House, during the Session of Congress, shall, without the Consent of the other, adjourn for more than three days, nor to any other Place than that in which the two Houses shall be sitting.

Section 6

The Senators and Representatives shall receive a Compensation for their Services, to be ascertained by Law, and paid out of the Treasury of the United States. They shall in all Cases, except Treason, Felony and Breach of the Peace, be privileged from Arrest during their Attendance at the Session of their respective Houses, and in going to and returning from the same; and for any Speech or Debate in either House, they shall not be questioned in any other Place.

No Senator or Representative shall, during the Time for which he was elected, be appointed to any civil Office under the Authority of the United States, which shall have been created, or the Emoluments whereof shall have been encreased during such time, and no Person holding any Office under the United States, shall be a Member of either House during his Continuance in Office.

Section 7

All Bills for raising Revenue shall originate in the House of Representatives; but the Senate may propose or concur with Amendments as on other Bills.

Every Bill which shall have passed the House of Representatives and the Senate, shall, before it become a Law, be presented to the President of the United States; If he approve he shall sign it, but if not he shall return it, with his Objections to the House in which it shall have originated, who shall enter the Objections at large on their Journal, and proceed to reconsider it. If after such Reconsideration two thirds of that House shall agree to pass the Bill, it shall be sent, together with the Objections, to the other House, by which it shall likewise be reconsidered, and if approved by two thirds of that House, it shall become a Law. But in all such Cases the Votes of both Houses shall be determined by yeas and Nays, and the Names of the Persons voting for and against the Bill shall be entered on the Journal of each House respectively. If any Bill shall not be returned by the President within ten Days (Sundays excepted) after it shall have been presented to him, the Same shall be a Law, in like Manner as if he had signed it, unless the Congress by their Adjournment prevent its Return, in which Case it shall not be a Law.

Every Order, Resolution, or Vote to which the Concurrence of the Senate and House of Representatives may be necessary (except on a question of Adjournment) shall be presented to the President of the United States; and before the Same shall take Effect, shall be approved by him, or being disapproved by him, shall be repassed by two thirds of the Senate and House of Representatives, according to the Rules and Limitations prescribed in the Case of a Bill.

Section 8

The Congress shall have Power To lay and collect Taxes, Duties, Imposts and Excises, to pay the Debts and provide for the common Defence and general Welfare of the United States; but all Duties, Imposts and Excises shall be uniform throughout the United States;

To borrow Money on the credit of the United States;

To regulate Commerce with foreign Nations, and among the several States, and with the Indian Tribes;

To establish an uniform Rule of Naturalization, and uniform Laws on the subject of Bankruptcies throughout the United States;

To coin Money, regulate the Value thereof, and of foreign Coin, and fix the Standard of Weights and Measures;

To provide for the Punishment of counterfeiting the Securities and current Coin of the United States;

To establish Post Offices and post Roads;

To promote the Progress of Science and useful Arts, by securing for limited Times to Authors and Inventors the exclusive Right to their respective Writings and Discoveries;

To constitute Tribunals inferior to the supreme Court;

To define and punish Piracies and Felonies committed on the high Seas, and Offences against the Law of Nations;

To declare War, grant Letters of Marque and Reprisal, and make Rules concerning Captures on Land and Water;

To raise and support Armies, but no Appropriation of Money to that Use shall be for a longer Term than two Years;

To provide and maintain a Navy;

To make Rules for the Government and Regulation of the land and naval Forces;

To provide for calling forth the Militia to execute the Laws of the Union, suppress Insurrections and repel Invasions;

To provide for organizing, arming, and disciplining, the Militia, and for governing such Part of them as may be employed in the Service of the United States, reserving to the States respectively, the Appointment of the Officers, and the Authority of training the Militia according to the discipline prescribed by Congress;

To exercise exclusive Legislation in all Cases whatsoever, over such District (not exceeding ten Miles square) as may, by Cession of particular States, and the Acceptance of Congress, become the Seat of the Government of the United States, and to exercise like Authority over all Places purchased by the Consent of the Legislature of the State in which the Same shall be, for the Erection of Forts, Magazines, Arsenals, dock-Yards, and other needful Buildings;—And

To make all Laws which shall be necessary and proper for carrying into Execution the foregoing Powers, and all other Powers vested by this Constitution in the Government of the United States, or in any Department of Officer thereof.

Section 9

The Migration or Importation of such Persons as any of the States now existing shall think proper to admit, shall not be prohibited by the Congress prior to the Year one thousand eight hundred and

eight, but a Tax or duty may be imposed on such Importation, not exceeding ten dollars for each Person.

The Privilege of the Writ of Habeas Corpus shall not be suspended, unless when in Cases of Rebellion or Invasion the public Safety may require it.

No Bill of Attainder or ex post facto Law shall be passed.

No Capitation, or other direct, Tax shall be laid, unless in Proportion to the Census or Enumeration herein before directed to be taken.

No Tax or Duty shall be laid on Articles exported from any State.

No Preference shall be given by any Regulation of Commerce or Revenue to the Ports of one State over those of another: nor shall Vessels bound to, or from, one State, be obliged to enter, clear, or pay Duties in another.

No Money shall be drawn from the Treasury, but in Consequence of Appropriations made by Law; and a regular Statement and Account of the Receipts and Expenditures of all public Money shall be published from time to time.

No Title of Nobility shall be granted by the United States: And no Person holding any Office of Profit or Trust under them, shall, without the Consent of the Congress, accept of any present, Emolument, Office, or Title, of any kind whatever, from any King, Prince, or foreign State.

Section 10

No State shall enter into any Treaty, Alliance, or Confederation; grant Letters of Marque and Reprisal; coin Money; emit Bills of Credit; make any Thing but gold and silver Coin a Tender in Payment of Debts; pass any Bill of Attainder, ex post facto Law, or Law impairing the obligation of Contracts, or grant any Title of Nobility.

No State shall, without the Consent of the Congress, lay any Imposts or Duties on Imports or Exports, except what may be absolutely necessary for executing its inspection Laws: and the net Produce of all Duties and Imposts, laid by any State on Imports or Exports, shall be for the Use of the Treasury of the United States; and all such Laws shall be subject to the Revision and Controul of the Congress.

No State shall, without the Consent of Congress, lay any Duty of Tonnage, keep Troops, or Ships of War in time of Peace, enter into any Agreement or Compact with another State, or with a foreign Power, or engage in War, unless actually invaded, or in such imminent Danger as will not admit of delay.

Article II

Section 1

The executive Power shall be vested in a President of the United States of America. He shall hold his Office during the Term of four Years, and, together with the Vice President, chosen for the same Term, be elected, as follows:

Each State shall appoint, in such Manner as the Legislature thereof may direct, a Number of Electors, equal to the whole Number of Senators and Representatives to which the State may be entitled in the Congress: but no Senator or Representative, or Person holding an Office of Trust or Profit under the United States, shall be appointed an Elector.

The Electors shall meet in their respective States, and vote by Ballot for two Persons, of whom one at least shall not be an Inhabitant of the same State with themselves. And they shall make a List of all the Persons voted for, and of the Number of Votes for each; which List they shall sign and certify, and transmit sealed to the Seat of the Government of the United States, directed to the President of the Senate. The President of the Senate shall, in the Presence of the Senate and House of Representatives, open all the Certificates, and the Votes shall then be counted. The Person having the greatest Number of Votes shall be the President, if such Number be a Majority of the whole number of Electors appointed; and if there be more than one who have such Majority, and have an equal Number of Votes, then the House of Representatives shall immediately chuse by Ballot one of them for President; and if no Person have a Majority, then from the five highest on the List the said House shall in like Manner chuse the President. But in chusing the President, the Votes shall be taken by States, the Representation from each State having one Vote; A quorum for this Purpose shall consist of a Member or Members from two thirds of the States, and a Majority of all the States shall be necessary to a Choice. In every Case, after the Choice of the President, the Person having the greatest Number of Votes of the Electors shall be the Vice President. But if there should remain two or more who have equal Votes, the Senate shall chuse from them by Ballot the Vice President.

The Congress may determine the time of chusing the Electors, and the Day on which they shall give their Votes; which Day shall be the same throughout the United States.

No person except a natural born Citizen, *or a Citizen of the United States, at the time of the Adoption of this Constitution,* shall be eligible to the Office of President; neither shall any Person be eligible to that Office who shall not have attained to the Age of thirty five Years, and been fourteen Years a Resident within the United States.

In Case of the Removal of the President from Office, or of his Death, Resignation, or Inability to discharge the Powers and Duties of the said Office, the Same shall devolve on the Vice President, and the Congress may by Law provide for the Case of Removal, Death, Resignation or Inability, both of the President and Vice President, declaring what Officer shall then act as President, and such Officer shall act accordingly, until the Disability be removed, or a President shall be elected.

The President shall, at stated Times, receive for his Services, a Compensation, which shall neither be increased nor diminished during the Period for which he shall have been elected, and he shall not receive within that period any other Emolument from the United States, or any of them.

Before he enter on the Execution of his Office, he shall take the following Oath or Affirmation:—"I do solemnly swear (or affirm) that I will faithfully execute the Office of President of the United States, and will to the best of my Ability, preserve, protect and defend the Constitution of the United States."

Section 2

The President shall be Commander in Chief of the Army and Navy of the United States, and of the Militia of the several States, when called into the actual Service of the United States; he may require the Opinion, in writing, of the principal Officer in each of the executive Departments, upon any Subject relating to the Duties of their respective Offices, and he shall have

Power to grant Reprieves and Pardons for Offences against the United States, except in Cases of Impeachment.

He shall have Power, by and with the Advice and Consent of the Senate, to make Treaties, provided two thirds of the Senators present concur; and he shall nominate, and by and with the Advice and Consent of the Senate, shall appoint Ambassadors, other public Ministers and Consuls, Judges of the supreme Court, and all other Officers of the United States, whose Appointments are not herein otherwise provided for, and which shall be established by Law: but the Congress may by Law vest the Appointment of such inferior Officers, as they think proper in the President alone, in the Courts of Law, or in the Heads of Departments.

The President shall have Power to fill up all Vacancies that may happen during the Recess of the Senate, by granting Commissions which shall expire at the End of their next Session.

Section 3

He shall from time to time give to the Congress Information of the State of the Union, and recommend to their Consideration such Measures as he shall judge necessary and expedient; he may, on extraordinary Occasions, convene both Houses, or either of them, and in Case of disagreement between them, with Respect to the Time of Adjournment, he may adjourn them to such Time as he shall think proper; he shall receive Ambassadors and other public Ministers; he shall take Care that the Laws be faithfully executed, and shall Commission all the officers of the United States.

Section 4

The President, Vice President and all civil Officers of the United States, shall be removed from Office on Impeachment for, and Conviction of, Treason, Bribery or other high Crimes and Misdemeanors.

Article III

Section 1

The judicial Power of the United States, shall be vested in one supreme Court, and in such inferior Courts as the Congress may from time to time ordain and establish. The Judges, both of the supreme and inferior Courts, shall hold their offices during good Behaviour, and shall, at stated Times, receive for their Services, a Compensation, which shall not be diminished during their Continuance in Office.

Section 2

The judicial Power shall extend to all Cases, in Law and Equity, arising under this Constitution, the Laws of the United States, and Treaties made, or which shall be made, under their Authority;—to all Cases affecting Ambassadors, other public Ministers and Consuls;—to all Cases of admiralty and maritime Jurisdiction;—to Controversies to which the United States shall be a Party;—to Controversies between two or more States;— *between a State and Citizens of another State;*—between Citizens of different States;—between Citizens of the same State claiming Lands under Grants of different States, and between a State, or the Citizens thereof, and foreign States, Citizens or Subjects.

In all Cases affecting Ambassadors, other public Ministers and Consuls, and those in which a State shall be Party, the supreme Court shall have original Jurisdiction. In all the other Cases before mentioned, the supreme Court shall have appellate Jurisdiction, both as to Law and Fact, with such Exceptions, and under such Regulations as the Congress shall make.

The Trial of all Crimes, except in Cases of Impeachment, shall be by Jury; and such Trial shall be held in the State where the said Crimes shall have been committed, but when not committed within any State, the Trial shall be at such Place or Places as the Congress may by Law have directed.

Section 3

Treason against the United States, shall consist only in levying War against them, or in adhering to their Enemies, giving them Aid and Comfort. No person shall be convicted of Treason unless on the Testimony of two Witnesses to the same overt Act, or on Confession in open Court.

The Congress shall have Power to declare the Punishment of Treason, but no Attainder of Treason shall work Corruption of Blood, or Forfeiture except during the Life of the Person attainted.

Article IV

Section 1

Full Faith and Credit shall be given in each State to the public Acts, Records, and judicial Proceedings of every other State. And the Congress may by general Laws prescribe the Manner in which such Acts, Records and Proceedings shall be proved, and the Effect thereof.

Section 2

The Citizens of each State shall be entitled to all Privileges and Immunities of Citizens in the several States.

A Person charged in any State with Treason, Felony, or other Crime, who shall flee from Justice, and be found in another State, shall on Demand of the executive Authority of the State from which he fled, be delivered up, to be removed to the State having Jurisdiction of the Crime.

No Person held to Service or Labour in one State, under the Laws thereof, escaping into another, shall, in Consequence of any Law or Regulation therein, be discharged from such Service or Labour, but shall be delivered up on Claim of the Party to whom such Service or Labour may be due.

Section 3

New States may be admitted by the Congress into this Union; but no new State shall be formed or erected within the Jurisdiction of any other State; nor any State be formed by the Junction of two or more States, or Parts of States, without the Consent of the Legislatures of the States concerned as well as of the Congress.

The Congress shall have Power to dispose of and make all needful Rules and Regulations respecting the Territory or other Property belonging to the United States; and nothing in this Constitution shall be so construed as to Prejudice any Claims of the United States, or of any particular States.

Section 4

The United States shall guarantee to every State in this Union a Republican Form of Government, and shall protect each of them against Invasion; and on Application of the Legislature, or of the Executive (when the Legislature cannot be convened) against domestic violence.

Article V

The Congress, whenever two thirds of both Houses shall deem it necessary, shall propose Amendments to this Constitution, or, on the Application of the Legislatures of two thirds of the several States, shall call a Convention for proposing Amendments, which, in either Case, shall be valid to all Intents and Purposes, as Part of this Constitution, when ratified by the Legislatures of three fourths of the several States, or by Conventions in three fourths thereof, as the one or the other Mode of Ratification may be proposed by the Congress; Provided *that no Amendment which may be made prior to the Year One thousand eight hundred and eight shall in any Manner affect the first and fourth Clauses in the Ninth Section of the first Article;* and that no State, without its Consent, shall be deprived of its equal Suffrage in the Senate.

Article VI

All Debts contracted and Engagements entered into, before the Adoption of this Constitution, shall be as valid against the United States under this Constitution, as under the Confederation.

This Constitution, and Laws of the United States which shall be made in Pursuance thereof; and all Treaties made, or which shall be made, under the Authority of the United States, shall be the supreme Law of the Land; and the Judges in every State shall be bound thereby, any Thing in the Constitution or Laws of any State to the Contrary notwithstanding.

The Senators and Representatives before mentioned, and the Members of the several State Legislatures, and all executive and Judicial Officers, both of the United States and of the several States, shall be bound by Oath or Affirmation, to support this Constitution; but no religious Test shall ever be required as a Qualification to any Office of public Trust under the United States.

Article VII

The Ratification of the Conventions of nine States, shall be sufficient for the Establishment of this Constitution between the States so ratifying the Same.

Done in Convention by the Unanimous Consent of the States present the Seventeenth Day of September in the Year of our Lord one thousand seven hundred and Eighty seven and of the Independence of the United States of America the Twelfth* IN WITNESS whereof We have hereunto subscribed our Names,

George Washington
President and Deputy from Virginia

Delaware	*South Carolina*	*New York*
George Read	John Rutledge	Alexander Hamilton
Gunning Bedford, Jr.	Charles Cotesworth Pinckney	
John Dickinson	Charles Pinckney	*New Jersey*
Richard Bassett	Pierce Butler	William Livingston
Jacob Broom		David Brearley
	Georgia	William Paterson
Maryland	William Few	Jonathan Dayton
James McHenry	Abraham Baldwin	
Daniel of St. Thomas Jenifer		*Pennsylvania*
Daniel Carroll	*New Hampshire*	Benjamin Franklin
	John Langdon	Thomas Mifflin
Virginia	Nicholas Gilman	Robert Morris
John Blair		George Clymer
James Madison, Jr.	*Massachusetts*	Thomas FitzSimons
	Nathaniel Gorham	Jared Ingersoll
North Carolina	Rufus King	James Wilson
William Blount		Gouverneur Morris
Richard Dobbs Spraight	*Connecticut*	
Hugh Williamson	William Samuel Johnson	
	Roger Sherman	

*The Constitution was submitted on September 17, 1787, by the Constitutional Convention, was ratified by conventions of the several states at various dates up to May 29, 1790, and became effective on March 4, 1789.

Amendments to the Constitution

Amendment I

Congress shall make no law respecting an establishment of religion, or prohibiting the free exercise thereof; or abridging the freedom of speech, or of the press; or the right of the people peaceably to assemble, and to petition the Government for a redress of grievances.

Amendment II

A well regulated Militia being necessary to the security of a free State, the right of the people to keep and bear Arms, shall not be infringed.

Amendment III

No Soldier shall, in time of peace be quartered in any house, without the consent of the Owner, nor in time of war, but in a manner to be prescribed by law.

Amendment IV

The right of the people to be secure in their persons, houses, papers, and effects, against unreasonable searches and seizures, shall not be violated, and no Warrants shall issue, but upon probable cause, supported by Oath or affirmation, and particularly describing the place to be searched, and the persons or things to be seized.

Amendment V

No person shall be held to answer for a capital, or otherwise infamous crime, unless on a presentment or indictment of a Grand Jury, except in cases arising in the land or naval forces, or in the Militia, when in actual service in time of War or public danger; nor shall any person be subject for the same offense to be twice put in jeopardy of life or limb; nor shall be compelled in any criminal case to be a witness against himself, nor be deprived of life, liberty, or property, without due process of law; nor shall private property be taken for public use, without just compensation.

Amendment VI

In all criminal prosecutions, the accused shall enjoy the right to a speedy and public trial, by an impartial jury of the State and district wherein the crime shall have been committed, which district shall have been previously ascertained by law, and to be informed of the nature and cause of the accusation; to be confronted with the witnesses against him; to have compulsory process for obtaining witnesses in his favor, and to have the Assistance of Counsel for his defence.

Amendment VII

In Suits at common law, where the value in controversy shall exceed twenty dollars, the right of trial by jury shall be preserved, and no fact tried by a jury, shall be otherwise re-examined in any Court of the United States, than according to the rules of the common law.

Amendment VIII

Excessive bail shall not be required, nor excessive fines imposed, nor cruel and unusual punishments inflicted.

Amendment IX

The enumeration in the Constitution, of certain rights, shall not be construed to deny or disparage others retained by the people.

Amendment X*

The powers not delegated to the United States by the Constitution, nor prohibited by it to the States, are reserved to the States respectively, or to the people.

Amendment XI
[Adopted 1798]

The Judicial power of the United States shall not be construed to extend to any suit in law or equity, commenced or prosecuted against one of the United States by Citizens of another State, or by Citizens or Subjects of any Foreign State.

Amendment XII
[Adopted 1804]

The Electors shall meet in their respective states, and vote by ballot for President and Vice President, one of whom, at least, shall not be an inhabitant of the same state with themselves; they shall name in their ballots the person voted for as President, and in distinct ballots the person voted for as Vice President, and they shall make distinct lists of all persons voted for as President, and of all persons voted for as Vice President, and of the number of votes for each, which lists they shall sign and certify, and transmit sealed to the seat of the government of the United States, directed to the President of the Senate;—The President of the Senate shall, in the presence of the Senate and House of Representatives, open all the certificates and the votes shall then be counted;—The person having the greatest number of votes for President, shall be the President, if such number be a majority of the whole number of Electors appointed; and if no person have such majority, then from the persons having the highest numbers not exceeding three on the list of those voted for as President, the House of Representatives shall choose immediately, by ballot, the President. But in choosing the President, the votes shall be taken by states, the representation from each state having one vote; a quorum for this purpose shall consist of a

---

*The first ten amendments (the Bill of Rights) were ratified and their adoption was certified on December 15, 1791.

member or members from two-thirds of the states, and a majority of all the states shall be necessary to a choice. And if the House of Representatives shall not choose a President whenever the right of choice shall devolve upon them, before *the fourth day of March* next following, then the Vice President shall act as President, as in the case of the death or other constitutional disability of the President.—The person having the greatest number of votes as Vice President, shall be the Vice President, if such number be a majority of the whole number of Electors appointed, and if no person have a majority, then from the two highest numbers on the list, the Senate shall choose the Vice President; a quorum for the purpose shall consist of two-thirds of the whole number of Senators, and a majority of the whole number shall be necessary to a choice. But no person constitutionally ineligible to the office of President shall be eligible to that of Vice President of the United States.

Amendment XIII
[Adopted 1865]

Section 1

Neither slavery nor involuntary servitude, except as a punishment for crime whereof the party shall have been duly convicted, shall exist within the United States, or any place subject to their jurisdiction.

Section 2

Congress shall have power to enforce this article by appropriate legislation.

Amendment XIV
[Adopted 1868]

Section 1

All persons born or naturalized in the United States, and subject to the jurisdiction thereof, are citizens of the United States and of the State wherein they reside. No State shall make or enforce any law which shall abridge the privileges or immunities of citizens of the United States; nor shall any State deprive any person of life, liberty, or property, without due process of law; nor deny to any person within its jurisdiction the equal protection of the laws.

Section 2

Representatives shall be apportioned among the several States according to their respective numbers, counting the whole number of persons in each State, excluding Indians not taxed. But when the right to vote at any election for the choice of electors for President and Vice President of the United States, Representatives in Congress, the Executive and Judicial officers of a State, or the members of the Legislature thereof, is denied to any of the male inhabitants of such State, being twenty-one years of age, and citizens of the United States, or in any way abridged, except for participation in rebellion, or other crime, the basis of representation therein shall be reduced in the proportion which the number of such male citizens shall bear to the whole number of male citizens twenty-one years of age in such State.

Section 3

No person shall be a Senator or Representative in Congress, or elector of President and Vice President, or hold any office, civil or military, under the United States, or under any State, who, having previously taken an oath, as a member of Congress, or as an officer of the United States, or as a member of any State legislature, or as an executive or judicial officer of any State, to support the Constitution of the United States, shall have engaged in insurrection or rebellion against the same, or given aid or comfort to the enemies thereof. But Congress may by a vote of two-thirds of each House, remove such disability.

Section 4

The validity of the public debt of the United States, authorized by law, including debts incurred for payment of pensions and bounties for services in suppressing insurrection or rebellion, shall not be questioned. But neither the United States nor any State shall assume or pay any debt or obligation incurred in aid of insurrection or rebellion against the United States, or any claim for the loss or emancipation of any slave; but all such debts, obligations and claims shall be held illegal and void.

Section 5

The Congress shall have power to enforce, by appropriate legislation, the provisions of this article.

Amendment XV
[Adopted 1870]

Section 1

The right of citizens of the United States to vote shall not be denied or abridged by the United States or by any State on account of race, color, or previous condition of servitude.

Section 2

The Congress shall have power to enforce this article by appropriate legislation.

Amendment XVI
[Adopted 1913]

The Congress shall have power to lay and collect taxes on incomes, from whatever source derived, without apportionment among the several States, and without regard to any census or enumeration.

Amendment XVII
[Adopted 1913]

The Senate of the United States shall be composed of two Senators from each State, elected by the people thereof, for six years; and each Senator shall have one vote. The electors in each State shall have the qualifications requisite for electors of the most numerous branch of the State legislatures.

When vacancies happen in the representation of any State in the Senate, the executive authority of such State shall issue writs of election to fill such vacancies: *Provided,* That the legislature of any State may empower the executive thereof to make temporary appointments until the people fill the vacancies by election as the legislature may direct.

This amendment shall not be so construed as to affect the election or term of any Senator chosen before it becomes valid as part of the Constitution.

Amendment XVIII
[Adopted 1919, repealed 1933]

Section 1

After one year from the ratification of this article the manufacture, sale, or transportation of intoxicating liquors within, the importation thereof into, or the exportation thereof from the United States and all territory subject to the jurisdiction thereof for beverage purposes is hereby prohibited.

Section 2

The Congress and the several States shall have concurrent power to enforce this article by appropriate legislation.

Section 3

This article shall be inoperative unless it shall have been ratified as an amendment to the Constitution by the legislatures of the several States, as provided in the Constitution, within seven years from the date of the submission hereof to the States by the Congress.

Amendment XIX
[Adopted 1920]

The right of citizens of the United States to vote shall not be denied or abridged by the United States or by any State on account of sex.

Congress shall have power to enforce this article by appropriate legislation.

Amendment XX
[Adopted 1933]

Section 1

The terms of the President and Vice President shall end at noon on the 20th day of January, and the terms of Senators and Representatives at noon on the 3d day of January, of the years in which such terms would have ended if this article had not been ratified and the terms of their successors shall then begin.

Section 2

The Congress shall assemble at least once in every year, and such meeting shall begin at noon on the 3d day of January, unless they shall by law appoint a different day.

Section 3

If, at the time fixed for the beginning of the term of the President, the President elect shall have died, the Vice President elect shall become President. If a President shall not have been chosen before the time fixed for the beginning of his term, or if the President elect shall have failed to qualify, then the Vice President elect shall act as President until a President shall have qualified; and the Congress may by law provide for the case wherein neither a President elect nor a Vice President elect shall have qualified, declaring who shall then act as President, or the manner in which one who is to act shall be selected, and such person shall act accordingly until a President or Vice President shall have qualified.

Section 4

The Congress may by law provide for the case of the death of any of the persons from whom the House of Representatives may choose a President whenever the right of choice shall have devolved upon them, and for the case of the death of any of the persons from whom the Senate may choose a Vice President whenever the right of choice shall have devolved upon them.

Section 5

Sections 1 and 2 shall take effect on the 15th day of October following the ratification of this article.

Section 6

This article shall be inoperative unless it shall have been ratified as an amendment to the Constitution by the legislatures of three fourths of the several States within seven years from the date of its submission.

Amendment XXI
[Adopted 1933]

Section 1

The eighteenth article of amendment to the Constitution of the United States is hereby repealed.

Section 2

The transportation or importation into any State, Territory, or possession of the United States for delivery or use therein of intoxicating liquors in violation of the laws thereof, is hereby prohibited.

Section 3

This article shall be inoperative unless it shall have been ratified as an amendment to the Constitution by conventions in the several States, as provided in the Constitution, within seven years from the date of the submission hereof to the States by the Congress.

Amendment XXII
[Adopted 1951]

Section 1

No person shall be elected to the office of the President more than twice, and no person who has held the office of President, or acted as President, for more than two years of a term to which some other person was elected President shall be elected to the office of the President more than once. But this Article shall not apply to any person holding the office of President when this Article was proposed by the Congress, and shall not prevent any person who may be holding the office of President, or acting as President, during the term within which this Article becomes operative from holding the office of President or acting as President during the remainder of such term.

Section 2

This article shall be inoperative unless it shall have been ratified as an amendment to the Constitution by the legislatures of three-fourths of the several States within seven years from the date of its submission to the States by the Congress.

Amendment XXIII
[Adopted 1961]

Section 1

The District constituting the seat of Government of the United States shall appoint in such manner as the Congress shall direct:

A number of electors of President and Vice President equal to the whole number of Senators and Representatives in Congress to which the District would be entitled if it were a State, but in no event more than the least populous State; they shall be in addition to those appointed by the States, but they shall be considered, for the purposes of the election of President and Vice President, to be electors appointed by a State; and they shall meet in the District and perform such duties as provided by the twelfth article of amendment.

Section 2

The Congress shall have power to enforce this article by appropriate legislation.

Amendment XXIV
[Adopted 1964]

Section 1

The right of citizens of the United States to vote in any primary or other election for President or Vice President, for electors for President or Vice President, or for Senator or Representative in Congress, shall not be denied or abridged by the United States or any state by reason of failure to pay any poll tax or other tax.

Section 2

The Congress shall have the power to enforce this article by appropriate legislation.

Amendment XXV
[Adopted 1967]

Section 1

In case of the removal of the President from office or his death or resignation, the Vice President shall become President.

Section 2

Whenever there is a vacancy in the office of the Vice President, the President shall nominate a Vice President who shall take the office upon confirmation by a majority vote of both houses of Congress.

Section 3

Whenever the President transmits to the President pro tempore of the Senate and the Speaker of the House of Representatives his written declaration that he is unable to discharge the powers and duties of his office, and until he transmits to them a written declaration to the contrary, such powers and duties shall be discharged by the Vice President as Acting President.

Section 4

Whenever the Vice President and a majority of either the principal officers of the executive departments or of such other body as Congress may by law provide, transmit to the President pro tempore of the Senate and the Speaker of the House of Representatives their written declaration that the President is unable to discharge the powers and duties of his office, the Vice President shall immediately assume the powers and duties of the office as Acting President.

Thereafter, when the President transmits to the President pro tempore of the Senate and the Speaker of the House of Representatives his written declaration that no inability exists, he shall resume the powers and duties of his office unless the Vice President and a majority of either the principal officers of the executive department or of such other body as Congress may by law provide, transmit within four days to the President pro tempore of the Senate and the Speaker of the House of Representatives their written declaration that the President is unable to discharge the powers and duties of his office. Thereupon Congress shall decide the issue, assembling within 48 hours for that purpose if not in session. If the Congress, within 21 days after receipt of the latter written declaration, or, if Congress is not in session, within 21 days after Congress is required to assemble, determines by two-thirds vote of both houses that the President is unable to discharge the powers and duties of his office, the Vice President shall continue to discharge the same as Acting President; otherwise, the President shall resume the powers and duties of his office.

Amendment XXVI
[Adopted 1971]

Section 1

The right of citizens of the United States, who are 18 years of age or older, to vote shall not be denied or abridged by the United States or any state on account of age.

Section 2

The Congress shall have the power to enforce this article by appropriate legislation.

Amendment XXVII
[Adopted 1992]

No law, varying the compensation for the services of the Senators and Representatives shall take effect, until an election of Representatives shall have intervened.

Presidential Elections

Year	Candidates	Parties	Popular Vote	Electoral Vote	Voter Participation
1789	**George Washington**		*	69	
	John Adams			34	
	Others			35	
1792	**George Washington**		*	132	
	John Adams			77	
	George Clinton			50	
	Others			5	
1796	**John Adams**	Federalist	*	71	
	Thomas Jefferson	Democratic-Republican		68	
	Thomas Pinckney	Federalist		59	
	Aaron Burr	Dem.-Rep.		30	
	Others			48	
1800	**Thomas Jefferson**	Dem.-Rep.	*	73	
	Aaron Burr	Dem.-Rep.		73	
	John Adams	Federalist		65	
	C. C. Pinckney	Federalist		64	
	John Jay	Federalist		1	
1804	**Thomas Jefferson**	Dem.-Rep.	*	162	
	C. C. Pinckney	Federalist		14	
1808	**James Madison**	Dem.-Rep.	*	122	
	C. C. Pinckney	Federalist		47	
	George Clinton	Dem.-Rep.		6	
1812	**James Madison**	Dem.-Rep.	*	128	
	De Witt Clinton	Federalist		89	
1816	**James Monroe**	Dem.-Rep.	*	183	
	Rufus King	Federalist		34	
1820	**James Monroe**	Dem.-Rep.	*	231	
	John Quincy Adams	Dem.-Rep.		1	
1824	**John Quincy Adams**	Dem.-Rep.	108,740 (30.5%)	84	26.9%
	Andrew Jackson	Dem.-Rep.	153,544 (43.1%)	99	
	William H. Crawford	Dem.-Rep.	46,618 (13.1%)	41	
	Henry Clay	Dem.-Rep.	47,136 (13.2%)	37	
1828	**Andrew Jackson**	Democratic	647,286 (56.0%)	178	57.6%
	John Quincy Adams	National Republican	508,064 (44.0%)	83	
1832	**Andrew Jackson**	Democratic	687,502 (55.0%)	219	55.4%
	Henry Clay	National Republican	530,189 (42.4%)	49	
	John Floyd	Independent		11	
	William Wirt	Anti-Mason	33,108 (2.6%)	7	
1836	**Martin Van Buren**	Democratic	765,483 (50.9%)	170	57.8%
	William Henry Harrison	Whig		73	
	Hugh L. White	Whig	739,795 (49.1%)	26	
	Daniel Webster	Whig		14	
	W. P. Magnum	Independent		11	
1840	**William Henry Harrison**	Whig	1,274,624 (53.1%)	234	80.2%
	Martin Van Buren	Democratic	1,127,781 (46.9%)	60	
	J. G. Birney	Liberty	7069	—	

*Electors selected by state legislatures.

Year	Candidates	Parties	Popular Vote	Electoral Vote	Voter Participation
1844	**James K. Polk**	Democratic	1,338,464 (49.6%)	170	78.9%
	Henry Clay	Whig	1,300,097 (48.1%)	105	
	J. G. Birney	Liberty	62,300 (2.3%)	—	
1848	**Zachary Taylor**	Whig	1,360,967 (47.4%)	163	72.7%
	Lewis Cass	Democratic	1,222,342 (42.5%)	127	
	Martin Van Buren	Free-Soil	291,263 (10.1%)	—	
1852	**Franklin Pierce**	Democratic	1,601,117 (50.9%)	254	69.6%
	Winfield Scott	Whig	1,385,453 (44.1%)	42	
	John P. Hale	Free-Soil	155,825 (5.0%)	—	
1856	**James Buchanan**	Democratic	1,832,955 (45.3%)	174	78.9%
	John C. Frémont	Republican	1,339,932 (33.1%)	114	
	Millard Fillmore	American	871,731 (21.6%)	8	
1860	**Abraham Lincoln**	Republican	1,865,593 (39.8%)	180	81.2%
	Stephen A. Douglas	Democratic	1,382,713 (29.5%)	12	
	John C. Breckinridge	Democratic	848,356 (18.1%)	72	
	John Bell	Union	592,906 (12.6%)	39	
1864	**Abraham Lincoln**	Republican	2,213,655 (55.0%)	212[*]	73.8%
	George B. McClellan	Democratic	1,805,237 (45.0%)	21	
1868	**Ulysses S. Grant**	Republican	3,012,833 (52.7%)	214	78.1%
	Horatio Seymour	Democratic	2,703,249 (47.3%)	80	
1872	**Ulysses S. Grant**	Republican	3,597,132 (55.6%)	286	71.3%
	Horace Greeley	Dem.; Liberal Republican	2,834,125 (43.9%)	66[†]	
1876	**Rutherford B. Hayes** ‡	Republican	4,036,298 (48.0%)	185	81.8%
	Samuel J. Tilden	Democratic	4,300,590 (51.0%)	184	
1880	**James A. Garfield**	Republican	4,454,416 (48.5%)	214	79.4%
	Winfield S. Hancock	Democratic	4,444,952 (48.1%)	155	
1884	**Grover Cleveland**	Democratic	4,874,986 (48.5%)	219	77.5%
	James G. Blaine	Republican	4,851,981 (48.2%)	182	
1888	**Benjamin Harrison**	Republican	5,439,853 (47.9%)	233	79.3%
	Grover Cleveland	Democratic	5,540,309 (48.6%)	168	
1892	**Grover Cleveland**	Democratic	5,556,918 (46.1%)	277	74.7%
	Benjamin Harrison	Republican	5,176,108 (43.0%)	145	
	James B. Weaver	People's	1,041,028 (8.5%)	22	
1896	**William McKinley**	Republican	7,104,779 (51.1%)	271	79.3%
	William Jennings Bryan	Democratic People's	6,502,925 (47.7%)	176	
1900	**William McKinley**	Republican	7,207,923 (51.7%)	292	73.2%
	William Jennings Bryan	Dem.-Populist	6,358,133 (45.5%)	155	
1904	**Theodore Roosevelt**	Republican	7,623,486 (57.9%)	336	65.2%
	Alton B. Parker	Democratic	5,077,911 (37.6%)	140	
	Eugene V. Debs	Socialist	402,283 (3.0%)	—	
1908	**William H. Taft**	Republican	7,678,908 (51.6%)	321	65.4%
	William Jennings Bryan	Democratic	6,409,104 (43.1%)	162	
	Eugene V. Debs	Socialist	420,793 (2.8%)	—	
1912	**Woodrow Wilson**	Democratic	6,293,454 (41.9%)	435	58.8%
	Theodore Roosevelt	Progressive	4,119,538 (27.4%)	88	
	William H. Taft	Republican	3,484,980 (23.2%)	8	
	Eugene V. Debs	Socialist	900,672 (6.0%)	—	
1916	**Woodrow Wilson**	Democratic	9,129,606 (49.4%)	277	61.6%
	Charles E. Hughes	Republican	8,538,221 (46.2%)	254	
	A. L. Benson	Socialist	585,113 (3.2%)	—	
1920	**Warren G. Harding**	Republican	16,152,200 (60.4%)	404	49.2%
	James M. Cox	Democratic	9,147,353 (34.2%)	127	
	Eugene V. Debs	Socialist	919,799 (3.4%)	—	

[*]Eleven secessionist states did not participate.
[†]Greeley died before the electoral college met. His electoral votes were divided among the four minor candidates.
[‡]Contested result settled by special election.

Year	Candidates	Parties	Popular Vote	Electoral Vote	Voter Participation
1924	**Calvin Coolidge**	Republican	15,725,016 (54.0%)	382	48.9%
	John W. Davis	Democratic	8,386,503 (28.8%)	136	
	Robert M. La Follette	Progressive	4,822,856 (16.6%)	13	
1928	**Herbert Hoover**	Republican	21,391,381 (58.2%)	444	56.9%
	Alfred E. Smith	Democratic	15,016,443 (40.9%)	87	
	Norman Thomas	Socialist	267,835 (0.7%)	—	
1932	**Franklin D. Roosevelt**	Democratic	22,821,857 (57.4%)	472	56.9%
	Herbert Hoover	Republican	15,761,841 (39.7%)	59	
	Norman Thomas	Socialist	881,951 (2.2%)	—	
1936	**Franklin D. Roosevelt**	Democratic	27,751,597 (60.8%)	523	61.0%
	Alfred M. Landon	Republican	16,679,583 (36.5%)	8	
	William Lemke	Union	882,479 (1.9%)	—	
1940	**Franklin D. Roosevelt**	Democratic	27,244,160 (54.8%)	449	62.5%
	Wendell L. Willkie	Republican	22,305,198 (44.8%)	82	
1944	**Franklin D. Roosevelt**	Democratic	25,602,504 (53.5%)	432	55.9%
	Thomas E. Dewey	Republican	22,006,285 (46.0%)	99	
1948	**Harry S Truman**	Democratic	24,105,695 (49.5%)	304	53.0%
	Thomas E. Dewey	Republican	21,969,170 (45.1%)	189	
	J. Strom Thurmond	State-Rights Democratic	1,169,021 (2.4%)	38	
	Henry A. Wallace	Progressive	1,156,103 (2.4%)	—	
1952	**Dwight D. Eisenhower**	Republican	33,936,252 (55.1%)	442	63.3%
	Adlai E. Stevenson	Democratic	27,314,992 (44.4%)	89	
1956	**Dwight D. Eisenhower**	Republican	35,575,420 (57.6%)	457	60.6%
	Adlai E. Stevenson	Democratic	26,033,066 (42.1%)	73	
	Other	—	—	1	
1960	**John F. Kennedy**	Democratic	34,227,096 (49.9%)	303	62.8%
	Richard M. Nixon	Republican	34,108,546 (49.6%)	219	
	Other	—	—	15	
1964	**Lyndon B. Johnson**	Democratic	43,126,506 (61.1%)	486	61.7%
	Barry M. Goldwater	Republican	27,176,799 (38.5%)	52	
1968	**Richard M. Nixon**	Republican	31,770,237 (43.4%)	301	60.6%
	Hubert H. Humphrey	Democratic	31,270,533 (42.7%)	191	
	George Wallace	American Indep.	9,906,141 (13.5%)	46	
1972	**Richard M. Nixon**	Republican	47,169,911 (60.7%)	520	55.2%
	George S. McGovern	Democratic	29,170,383 (37.5%)	17	
	Other	—	—	1	
1976	**Jimmy Carter**	Democratic	40,828,587 (50.0%)	297	53.5%
	Gerald R. Ford	Republican	39,147,613 (47.9%)	241	
	Other	—	1,575,459 (2.1%)	—	
1980	**Ronald Reagan**	Republican	43,901,812 (50.7%)	489	52.6%
	Jimmy Carter	Democratic	35,483,820 (41.0%)	49	
	John B. Anderson	Independent	5,719,722 (6.6%)	—	
	Ed Clark	Libertarian	921,188 (1.1%)	—	
1984	**Ronald Reagan**	Republican	54,455,075 (59.0%)	525	53.3%
	Walter Mondale	Democratic	37,577,185 (41.0%)	13	
1988	**George H. W. Bush**	Republican	48,886,000 (53.4%)	426	57.4%
	Michael S. Dukakis	Democratic	41,809,000 (45.6%)	111	
1992	**William J. Clinton**	Democratic	43,728,375 (43%)	370	55.0%
	George H. W. Bush	Republican	38,167,416 (38%)	168	
	H. Ross Perot	Independent	19,237,247 (19%)	—	
1996	**William J. Clinton**	Democratic	45,590,703 (50%)	379	48.8%
	Robert Dole	Republican	37,816,307 (41%)	159	
	H. Ross Perot	Reform	7,866,284		
2000	**George W. Bush**	Republican	50,456,167 (47.88%)	271	51.2%
	Al Gore	Democratic	50,996,064 (48.39%)	266*	
	Ralph Nader	Green	2,864,810 (2.72%)	—	
	Other		834,774 (< 1%)	—	

*One District of Columbia Gore elector abstained.

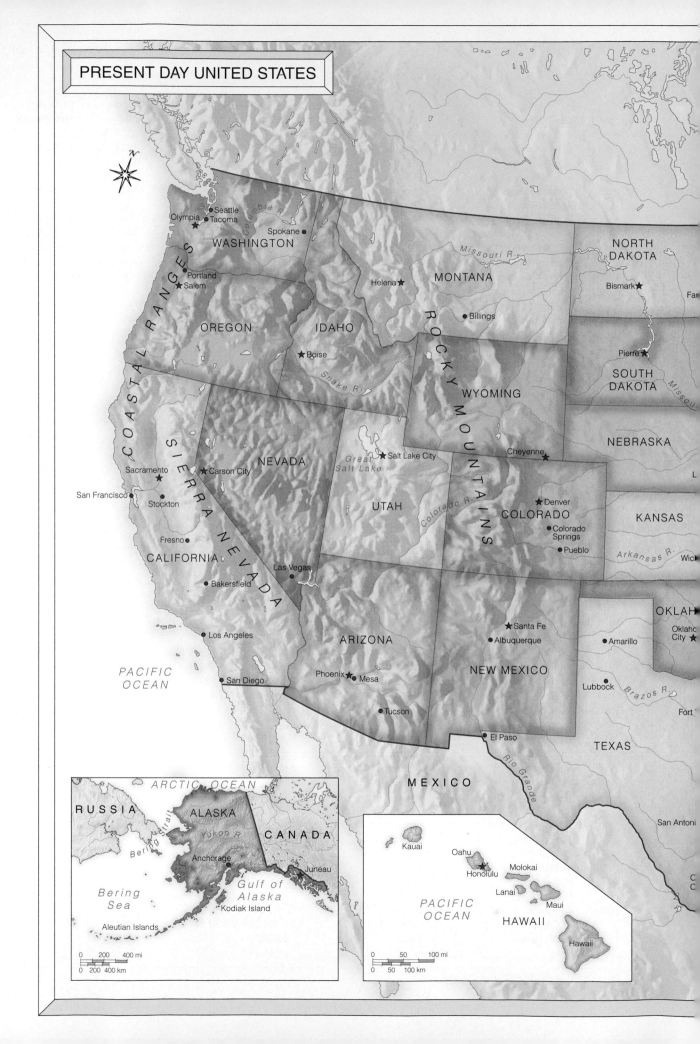

PRESENT DAY UNITED STATES

Seattle
Olympia ★ Tacoma
Spokane ●

WASHINGTON

Columbia R.

MONTANA

Missouri R.

Helena ★

NORTH
DAKOTA

Bismark ★

Far

Portland
Salem ★

OREGON

IDAHO

● Billings

R
O
C
K
Y

Boise ★

Snake R.

WYOMING

Pierre ★

SOUTH
DAKOTA

Missou

COASTAL RANGES

SIERRA NEVADA

NEVADA

*Great
Salt Lake*

★ Salt Lake City

M
O
U
N
T
A
I
N
S

Cheyenne ★

NEBRASKA

Sacramento ★

Carson City ★

San Francisco ●

● Stockton

UTAH

Colorado R.

COLORADO

Denver ★

● Colorado
Springs

● Pueblo

KANSAS

Arkansas R.

Wich

Fresno ●

CALIFORNIA

Las Vegas ●

Bakersfield ●

Los Angeles ●

ARIZONA

Santa Fe ★

● Albuquerque

Amarillo ●

OKLAH

Oklaho
City ★

PACIFIC
OCEAN

San Diego ●

Phoenix ★ ● Mesa

● Tucson

NEW MEXICO

Lubbock ●

Brazos R.

Fort

El Paso ●

Rio Grande

TEXAS

MEXICO

ARCTIC OCEAN

RUSSIA

ALASKA

Yukon R.

CANADA

San Antoni

Bering Strait

Anchorage ●

Juneau ●

Kauai

Oahu

Molokai

Honolulu ★

Bering
Sea

Gulf
of
Alaska

Lanai

Maui

Kodiak Island

PACIFIC
OCEAN

HAWAII

Aleutian Islands

Hawaii

0   200   400 mi

0   200 400 km

0   50   100 mi

0   50   100 km

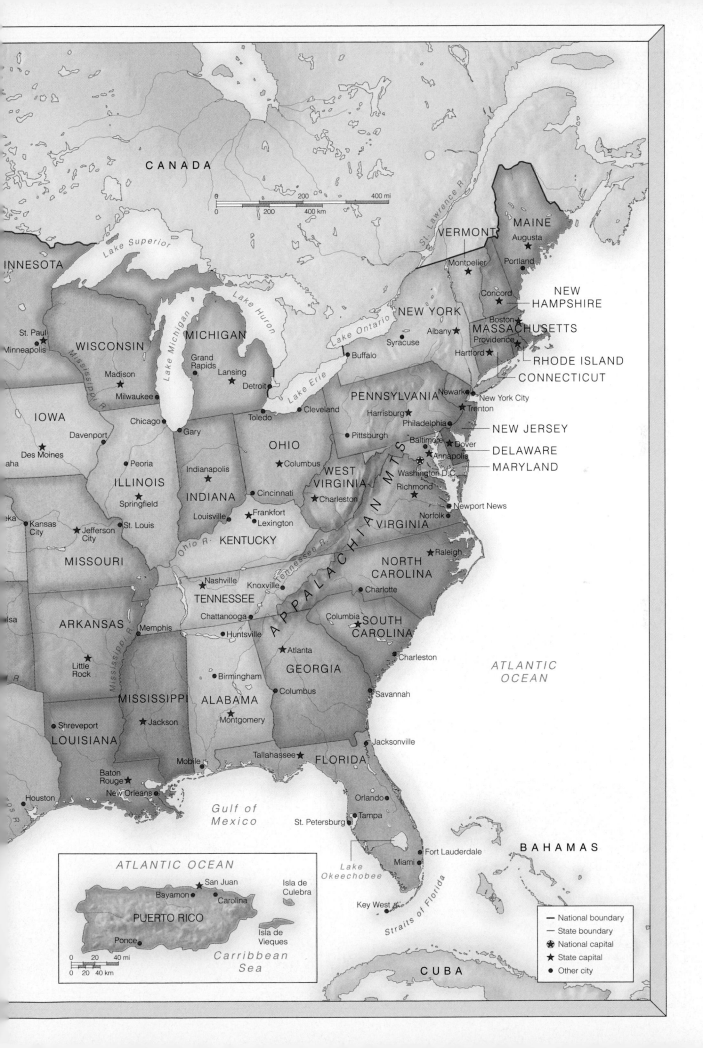

CANADA

Lake Superior

Lake Huron

Lake Michigan

Lake Ontario

Lake Erie

St. Lawrence R.

MINNESOTA

St. Paul
Minneapolis

WISCONSIN

MICHIGAN

Madison
Milwaukee

Grand
Rapids

Lansing

Detroit

IOWA

Davenport

Des Moines

aha

Chicago

Gary

Toledo

Cleveland

Peoria

ILLINOIS

Springfield

Indianapolis

INDIANA

OHIO

Columbus

Cincinnati

Louisville

Frankfort
Lexington

topeka

Kansas
City

Jefferson
City

St. Louis

KENTUCKY

Ohio R.

MISSOURI

lsa

ARKANSAS

Memphis

Nashville

Knoxville

Chattanooga

Huntsville

TENNESSEE

Tennessee R.

Little
Rock

R.

MISSISSIPPI

Jackson

Birmingham

ALABAMA

Columbus

GEORGIA

Atlanta

Montgomery

Shreveport

LOUISIANA

Baton
Rouge

New Orleans

Mobile

Tallahassee

FLORIDA

Jacksonville

Houston

Gulf of
Mexico

Orlando

Tampa

St. Petersburg

Lake
Okeechobee

Fort Lauderdale

Miami

Key West

Straits of Florida

VERMONT

Montpelier

MAINE

Augusta

Portland

NEW YORK

Concord

NEW
HAMPSHIRE

Albany

Syracuse

Buffalo

Boston

MASSACHUSETTS

Providence

Hartford

RHODE ISLAND

CONNECTICUT

PENNSYLVANIA

Harrisburg

Pittsburgh

Newark

New York City

Trenton

Philadelphia

NEW JERSEY

Baltimore

Dover

DELAWARE

Annapolis

Washington D.C.

MARYLAND

WEST
VIRGINIA

Charleston

Richmond

Newport News

Norfolk

VIRGINIA

APPALACHIAN MTS.

Raleigh

NORTH
CAROLINA

Charlotte

Columbia

SOUTH
CAROLINA

Charleston

Savannah

ATLANTIC
OCEAN

BAHAMAS

CUBA

ATLANTIC OCEAN

San Juan

Bayamon

Carolina

Isla de
Culebra

PUERTO RICO

Ponce

Isla de
Vieques

Carribean
Sea

0   20   40 mi

0   20   40 km

— National boundary
— State boundary
⍟ National capital
★ State capital
● Other city

0   200   400 mi
0   200   400 km

A-21

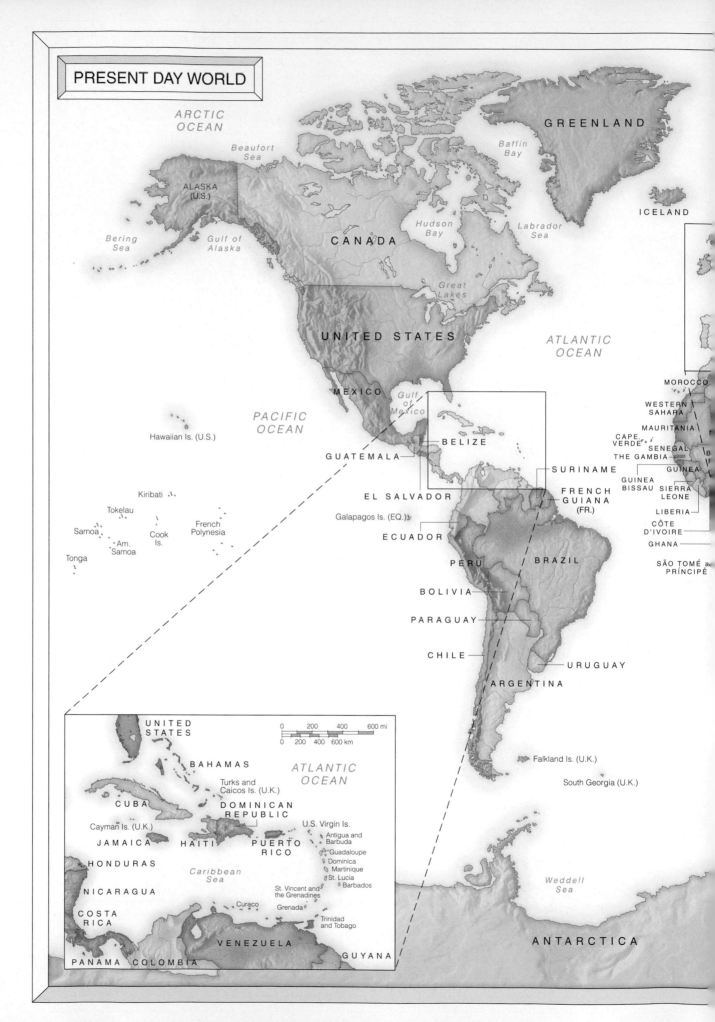

ARCTIC
OCEAN

GREENLAND

Beaufort
Sea

Baffin
Bay

ALASKA
(U.S.)

ICELAND

Bering
Sea

Gulf of
Alaska

Hudson
Bay

Labrador
Sea

CANADA

UNITED STATES

ATLANTIC
OCEAN

MOROCCO

MEXICO

Gulf
of
Mexico

WESTERN
SAHARA

PACIFIC
OCEAN

MAURITANIA

Hawaiian Is. (U.S.)

BELIZE

CAPE
VERDE

SENEGAL

GUATEMALA

THE GAMBIA

GUINEA

Kiribati

SURINAME

GUINEA
BISSAU

SIERRA
LEONE

Tokelau

EL SALVADOR

FRENCH
GUIANA
(FR.)

LIBERIA

French
Polynesia

Galapagos Is. (EQ.)

CÔTE
D'IVOIRE

Samoa

Cook
Is.

ECUADOR

GHANA

Am.
Samoa

Tonga

SÃO TOMÉ a
PRÍNCIPE

PERU

BRAZIL

BOLIVIA

PARAGUAY

CHILE

URUGUAY

ARGENTINA

Falkland Is. (U.K.)

South Georgia (U.K.)

UNITED
STATES

0   200   400   600 mi

0   200   400 600 km

BAHAMAS

ATLANTIC
OCEAN

Turks and
Caicos Is. (U.K.)

CUBA

DOMINICAN
REPUBLIC

Cayman Is. (U.K.)

U.S. Virgin Is.

Antigua and
Barbuda

JAMAICA

HAITI

PUERTO
RICO

Guadaloupe

Dominica

HONDURAS

Caribbean
Sea

Martinique

St. Lucia

Barbados

NICARAGUA

St. Vincent and
the Grenadines

Curaco

Grenada

ANTARCTICA

COSTA
RICA

Trinidad
and Tobago

Weddell
Sea

VENEZUELA

PANAMA COLOMBIA

GUYANA

Svalbard Is. (NOR.)

Novaya
Zemlya

*Barents
Sea*

*Kara
Sea*

*Laptev
Sea*

New Siberian Is.

*ARCTIC
OCEAN*

*East
Siberian
Sea*

RUSSIA

KAZAKHSTAN

*Lake
Baikal*

*Sea
of
Okhotsk*

Sakhalin

MONGOLIA

*Aral
Sea*

*Lake
Balkhash*

N. KOREA

JAPAN

PEOPLE'S
REPUBLIC
OF CHINA

S. KOREA

*East
China
Sea*

*PACIFIC
OCEAN*

JNISIA
LIBYA

ISRAEL
EGYPT

IRAQ
JORDAN
BAHRAIN
QATAR
SAUDI
ARABIA

IRAN

AFGHAN.
PAKISTAN

NEPAL

BHUTAN

BANG.

TAIWAN

U.A.E.
OMAN

INDIA

BURMA
(MYANMAR)

MACAO
LAOS
VIETNAM

*Philippine
Sea*

Northern
Mariana
Is.

R
A
CHAD

ERITREA
SUDAN

CENT.
AFRICAN REP.
MEROON

YEMEN

*Arabian
Sea*

*Bay of
Bengal*

THAILAND

PHILIPPINES

*South
China
Sea*

Marshall
Is.

DJIBOUTI
SOMALIA

ETHIOPIA

CAMBODIA

SRI
LANKA

EQUA.
GUINEA

UGANDA
KENYA

RWANDA

MALAYSIA

BRUNEI

PAPUA
NEW GUINEA

. Nauru

ON

DEM. REP.
OF
CONGO

SINGAPORE

INDONESIA

Solomon Is.

. Tuvalu

BURUNDI
TANZANIA

ANGOLA
ZAMBIA

MALAWI

*INDIAN
OCEAN*

*Coral
Sea*

Vanuatu

. Fiji

AMBIA

ZIMB.

MADAGASCAR

BOTSWANA

MAURITIUS

New Caledonia (FR.)

AUSTRALIA

MOZAMBIQUE

SOUTH
AFRICA

SWAZILAND

LESOTHO

*Tasman
Sea*

NEW
ZEALAND

NORWAY

FINLAND

SWEDEN

*North
Sea*

ESTONIA

IRELAND

DENMARK

LATVIA

*Baltic
Sea*

LITHUANIA

RUSSIA

UNITED
KINGDOM

*ATLANTIC
OCEAN*

NETHERLANDS
GERMANY
BELGIUM

POLAND

BELARUS

LUX.

CZECH
REPUBLIC

UKRAINE

FRANCE

LIECHT.

SLOVAKIA

MOLDOVA

SWITZ.

AUSTRIA

HUNGARY

SLOVENIA

ROMANIA

PORTUGAL

SPAIN

CROATIA
BOSNIA
HERZ.

SERBIA

BULGARIA

GEORGIA

*Caspian
Sea*

Black Sea

ARMENIA

ITALY

MACEDONIA

AZERBAIJAN

ALBANIA

TURKEY

Adriatic Sea

GREECE

*Mediterranean
Sea*

*Aegean
Sea*

CYPRUS

SYRIA

IRAQ

LEBANON

Credits

Part One Timeline

Page 1: (Top) Lee Boltin Picture Library; (middle) The Ohio Historical Society; (bottom) Museum of the History of Science, Oxford, Oxfordshire, UK/Bridgeman Art Library.

Page 2: (Top) Nettie Lee Benson Latin American Collection, University of Texas, Austin; (bottom) The Granger Collection, New York.

Chapter 1

Page 22 (Map 1.3): From *Columbus* by Bjorn Landstrom. Copyright © 1966 by Bjorn Landstrom. Copyright © 1967 by Bokforlaget Forum AB. Reprinted with the permission of Simon & Schuster, Inc.

Pages 26–27 (Figure 1.1): Adapted from "The Columbian Exchange" by Jeff Glick with Celeste Schaefer from *U.S. News and World Report,* July 8, 1991.

Page 31: From *Colonial Spanish America: A Documentary History* by Kenneth Mills and William B. Taylor. Wilmington, DE: Scholarly Resources, 1998.

Chapter 2

Page 66 (Figure 2.1): From *Founding of Massachusetts* by Edmund S. Morgan, © 1964. Reprinted by permission of Pearson Education, Inc., Upper Saddle River, NJ.

Page 69: From "Verses upon the Burning of Our House," July 18th, 1666 by Anne Bradstreet.

Part Two Timeline

Page 112: (Top) Chicago Historical Society, ICHi-x.1354; (middle) The Historical Society of Pennsylvania; (bottom) Courtesy, Reading Public Museum, Reading, Pennsylvania (44-132-1).

Page 113: (Top) Peabody Essex Museum. Photograph by Mark Sexton. (Bottom) Library of Congress.

Chapter 4

Page 136 (Figure 4.2): From *Blacks Who Stole Themselves: Advertisements for Runaways in The* Pennsylvania Gazette, *1728–1790* by Billy G. Smith and Richard Wojtowicz.

Page 139: From "Releese us out of this Cruell Bondegg: An Appeal from Virginia in 1723."

Chapter 5

Page 158 (Figure 5.1): Adapted from "Gender and Age Structure of Population: British Mainland Colonies, 1760s" and "Gender and Age Structure of Population: United States, 1980s" in *Mapping America's Past: A Historical Reference Book* by Mark C. Carnes and John A. Garraty with Patrick Williams, © 1996 by Arcadia Editions Limited. Reprinted by permission of Henry Holt and Company, LLC.

Chapter 6

Page 204: From a petition signed by thirty North Carolina Regulators, October 4, 1768.

Part Three Timeline

Page 216: (Top) The Bostonian Society; (bottom) Courtesy, Janice L and David Frent

Page 217: (Top) Abby Aldrich Rockefeller Folk Art Center, Williamsburg, VA; (bottom) The National Archives

Chapter 7

Pages 224–225: From a declaration signed by 15 grand jury members in South Carolina, May 1776.

Page 236 (Figure 7.1): From *British Historical Statistics,* Mitchell, 579.

Chapter 8

Page 259: From narratives by Joseph Plumb Martin, 1830.

Chapter 9

Page 312 (Figure 9.3): From Robert J. Dinkin, *Voting in Revolutionary America: A Study of Elections in the Original Thirteen States, 1776–1789* (1982), 36–39.

Pages 314–315: From *Means for the Preservation of Public Liberty* by Georges James Warner (New York, 1797).

Page 321 (Figure 9.4): From *Distribution of Wealth and Income in the United States,* 1798 by Lee Soltow (1989).

Part Four Timeline

Page 326: (Top) Courtesy, Missouri Historical Society; (bottom) The American Numismatic Society, New York.

Page 327: (Top) Massachusetts Historical Society, MHS image #0031; (bottom) Samuel J. Miller, *Frederick Douglass,* 1847–52. Major Acquisitions Centennial Endowment, 1996.433. ©The Art Institute of Chicago. All Rights Reserved

Chapter 10

Page 343: From Cherokee Women to Cherokee Council, May 2, 1817, series 1, Andrew Jackson Presidential Papers, Library of Congress Manuscripts Division, Washington, D.C.

Page 348 (Figure 10.1): From *Transatlantic Industrial Revolution: The Diffusion of Textile Technologies Between Britain and America,* 1790–1830s by David J. Jeremy. Copyright © 1981 by The MIT Press. Reprinted by permission of MIT Press.

Chapter 11

Pages 366 (Map 11.4) and 373 (Map 11.5): Adapted from *The Mexican Frontier 1821–1846: The American Southwest Under Mexico* by David J. Weber.

Page 372 (Figure 11.1): Table "Cherokee Nation Intercensus Changes, 1809–24" from *Cherokee Removal Before and After* edited by William L. Anderson. Reprinted by permission of The University of Georgia Press.

Page 375: From "Jose Agustin de Escudero Describes New Mexico as a Land of Opportunity, 1827" in H. Bailey Carroll and J. Villasana Haggard, trans. and ed., *Three New Mexico Chronicles* (Albuquerque, 1942)

Chapter 12

Page 395 (Map 12.2): Adapted from *Mapping America's Past: A Historical Reference Book* by Mark C. Carnes and John A. Garraty with Patrick Williams, © 1996 by Arcadia Editions Limited. Reprinted by permission of Henry Holt and Company, LLC.

Page 397 (Map 12.3): "The Grand Migration" from *The Penguin Atlas of Diasporas* by Gerard Chaliand and Jean-Pierre Rageau. New York: Viking Press, 1995.

Page 399 (Map 12.4): Adapted from "Expansion of the Cotton Belt" in *Mapping America's Past: A Historical Reference Book* by Mark C. Carnes and John A. Garraty with Patrick Williams, © 1996 by Arcadia Editions Limited. Reprinted by permission of Henry Holt and Company, LLC.

Page 402 (Map 12.5): Adapted from "Indian Removal from the Old Southeast" in *Mapping America's Past: A Historical Reference Book* by Mark C. Carnes and John A. Garraty with Patrick Williams, © 1996 by Arcadia Editions Limited. Reprinted by permission of Henry Holt and Company, LLC.

Page 403 (Table 12-1): From *Women and Men on the Overland Trail* by John Mack Faragher. Copyright 1979 by Yale University Press. Reprinted by permission.

Pages 424–425: From a speech by Senator John C. Calhoun, January 1848.

Part Five Timeline

Page 428: (Top) Michael Freeman/CORBIS; (middle) Harriet Beecher Stowe Center, Hartford, CT; (bottom) The Ohio Historical Society

Page 429: (Top) Antique Textile Resource, Bethesda MD; (bottom) William T. Garrell Foundry, San Francisco, *The Golden Spike.* The Iris & B. Gerald Cantor Center for Visual Arts at Stanford University (1998.115). Gift of David Hewes

Chapter 13

Pages 442–443: From *The Endowments, Position and Education of Woman. An Address Delivered Before the Hemans and Sigourney Societies of the Female High School at Limestone Springs,* July 23, 1850 (Columbia, SC: I.C. Morgan, 1850.)

Chapter 14

Page 468 (Figure 14.1): From "Alabama Secession Convention Occupations" and "Alabama Convention Property Holding" in Ralph Wooster, *The Secession Conventions of the South.* Copyright © 1962 by Princeton University Press. Reprinted by permission of Princeton University Press.

Pages 472–473: From a letter by John B. Spiece to the Confederate Attorney General, December 4, 1861.

Pages 475 (Figure 14.2) and 492 (Figure 14.3): From *Battle Cry of Freedom* by James McPherson. Oxford University Press, 1988.

Page 480 (Map 14.3): Adapted from Confederates Battle Southwestern Indians, Central New Mexico, 1861 by Jerry Thompson from *New Mexico Historical Review,* April 1998.

Page 489 (Map 14.4): From *Battle Cry of Freedom* by James McPherson. Oxford University Press, 1988.

Page 493 (Map 14.5): Adapted from Major African American Battle Sites in *The Atlas of African-American History and Politics: From the Slave Trade to Modern Times* by Arwin D. Smallwood with Jeffrey M. Elliot. McGraw Hill, 1998.

Page 496 (Map 14.6): Adapted from *The Atlas of African-American History and Politics: From the Slave Trade to Modern Times* by Arwin D. Smallwood with Jeffrey M. Elliot. McGraw-Hill, 1998.

Chapter 15

Page 510: From "Post-Bellum Southern Rental Contracts" by Rosser H. Taylor from *Agricultural History,* Volume 17, Number 2, April 1943. Published by The Agricultural History Society.

Page 523 (Table 15-3): From *Americans and Their Forests: A Historical Review* by Michael Williams. Copyright © 1989 by Cambridge University Press. Reprinted by permission of Cambridge University Press.

Page 530 (Table 15-4): From *Beyond Equality: Labor and the Radical Republicans, 1862–1872* by David Montgomery. New York: Alfred Knopf, 1967.

Index